CONTENTS

KT-117-104

PART II
CONTEMPORARY SOCIAL THEORISTS   259

SOCIAL THEORY

$£23.99

ESSENTIAL READINGS

SECOND EDITION

EDITED BY

GORDON BAILEY & NOGA GAYLE

OXFORD
UNIVERSITY PRESS

OXFORD
UNIVERSITY PRESS

70 Wynford Drive, Don Mills, Ontario M3C 1J9
www.oup.com/ca

Oxford University Press is a department of the University of Oxford.
It furthers the University's objective of excellence in research, scholarship,
and education by publishing worldwide in

Oxford New York
Auckland Bangkok Buenos Aires Cape Town Chennai
Dar es Salaam Delhi Hong Kong Istanbul Karachi Kolkata
Kuala Lumpur Madrid Melbourne Mexico City Mumbai Nairobi
São Paulo Shanghai Taipei Tokyo Toronto

Oxford is a trade mark of Oxford University Press
in the UK and in certain other countries

Published in Canada
by Oxford University Press

Copyright © Oxford University Press Canada 2003

The moral rights of the authors have been asserted

Database right Oxford University Press (maker)

First published 2003

Since this page cannot accommodate all the copyright notices,
pages 495–6 constitute an extension of the copyright page.

National Library of Canada Cataloguing in Publication

Social Theory: essential readings/edited by
Gordon Bailey and Noga Gayle. -- 2nd ed. Includes index.
Previous ed. published under title: Sociology: an introduction:
from the classics to contemporary feminism.

ISBN 0-19-541814-X

1. Sociology. I. Bailey, Gordon, 1946- II. Gayle, Noga Agnus

HM51.S6636 2003   301   C2003-900041-9

Cover & text design: Brett J. Miller

1 2 3 4 - 06 05 04 03

This book is printed on permanent (acid-free) paper ∞.
Printed in Canada

PREFACE
TO THE SECOND EDITION

It has been 10 years since this book first appeared under the title, *Sociology: An Introduction From the Classics to Contemporary Feminists*. We have changed the title, hopefully to better reflect the breadth of the undertaking within sociological theory. We have also added new theorists: Harriet Martineau, Edward Said, Jürgen Habermas, and Mike Featherstone. These additions take us both back and forward in terms of contemporary sociological theorizing and meaningfully expand the possibilities to reach wider global issues. A major work of Weber's, *Class, Status and Party*, has also been added. We have made other changes and additions to the book, maximizing its utility for students by adding an index, upgrading the Glossary, and extending the Further Readings. We have removed a few short readings to meet the demands of expansion.

In addition, the book is organized into two sections, Part I, Classical Social Theorists, and Part II, Contemporary Social Theorists, with part introductions that discuss the dramatic dynamics of these two different eras.

The power of sociological theory to stir the imagination of students, at whatever level of study, continues to amaze us. In a world that has often been characterized as anti-intellectual, we find it quite reassuring that young people continue to be compelled by the depth and breadth of sociological analysis. It is our hope that this edition will serve and inspire readers with this excitement in the same way that the first edition apparently did.

There are many people we would like to thank for bringing the two editions of this book to publication. Among them, Megan Mueller at Oxford has enthusiastically pursued the development of this new edition. Phyllis Wilson at Oxford has assisted us on both editions, for which we are grateful. We would like to thank Olive Koyama for her editorial work on the first edition and Richard Tallman for all his efforts on the second. Finally, we would like to extend a feeling of gratitude to Brian Henderson for supporting the initial project.

Gordon Bailey and Noga Gayle
Vancouver, 2003

Again, for our families
GB and NG

INTRODUCTION

In so far as an economy is so arranged that slumps occur, the problem of unemployment becomes incapable of personal solution. In so far as war is inherent in the nation-state system and in the uneven industrialization of the world, the ordinary individual in his [her] restricted milieu will be powerless—with or without psychiatric aid—to solve the troubles this system or lack of system imposes upon him [her]. In so far as the family as an institution turns women into darling little slaves and men into their chief providers and unweaned dependents, the problem of satisfactory marriage remains incapable of purely private solution. In so far as the overdeveloped megalopolis and the overdeveloped automobile are built-in features of the overdeveloped society, the issues of urban living will not be solved by personal ingenuity and private wealth.

—*C. Wright Mills*[1]

Only beings who can reflect upon the fact that they are determined are capable of freeing themselves. Their reflectiveness results not just in a vague and uncommitted awareness, but in the exercise of a profoundly transforming action upon the determining reality. *Consciousness of* and *action upon* reality are, therefore, inseparable constituents of the transforming act. . . .

—*Paulo Freire*[2]

There is always a past. But also, there is always a way of bringing it into being.

—*Dorothy Smith*[3]

An interest in society and how it works may be so embedded in the depths of consciousness that, for many of us, our perceptions of society may be characterized as a kind of glazed stare. To move from being a 'people watcher' to being a 'student of society' can be an arduous and challenging path. To further move to the study of the origins of sociology demands that we trace the works of the thinkers who have attempted to explain society in a disciplined manner. Once we begin to read the classics, we realize that the journey 'there to here' raises questions and alerts perceptions that do not always fit our contemporary and often superficial pictures of society. The classical thinkers' way of introducing us to the discipline of sociology is simple, yet profound. The complexities that arise from their perceptions sometimes overwhelm us, because the simple is often the most difficult to recognize and accept.

It has been said that sociology often reveals the obvious. Some of the works gathered here inform us that what is obvious today was ground-breaking fifty or a hundred years ago; it is those very works that have made the 'obvious', obvious. The selections we present here are intended as an introduction to sociology. The classic writings of the nineteenth century and of today are influential for many reasons. Some of the readings document the beginnings of the work of sociology; they raise questions that seem to penetrate to the core of society today as much as when they were first posed—for example, Marx's theory of social class, or Weber's conceptualization of authority. Some of them signal a shift in how social theorists needed to look at society, a shift in level of analysis or a shift in perspective significant enough to change the direction of research or theory—for instance, G.H. Mead's explorations of the symbolic interactions of human beings in small group contexts. Some of them demand that our investigations adopt a new set of perceptual lenses in order to disclose domains previously obscured—witness bell hooks's feminist approach to theory. Other works in this collection have initiated wide debate, even though the original text is now considered either in error or locked into another period.

To introduce both the theoretical and methodological questions of sociology, we have found the most meaningful starting point to be the macrotheoretical level of social analysis; we need first to explore the 'big picture'. We also need to gain access to the various *sites* and *patterns* of human interaction, the various *structures* of social life that seem to be inalienably 'there'. By recognizing that what is 'there' is much more than just the visible, that it is much deeper or more deeply experienced than just as sensation, we begin the search for conceptual analysis and adventure—a process both precipitated and guided by the works of the classics. Moreover, sociology reveals that the big picture of society always has *us* enclosed within it, as observers and participants; we are *located*. We therefore begin with a *sense of place*. If we begin the other way around—in the micro-theoretical domain—we may be able to see ourselves, but we won't be so precisely located. As sociologists we do not begin by finding our propensities in individual manifestations; we start our analysis rightfully with the social.

As students of society the classical writers explore the obvious not only to provide insight of lasting importance but also to examine those dimensions of our lives that are most taken for granted. The signal of the depth of the classic is its demand or challenge to this view. It not only describes the social world in an insightful or compelling manner, it intimately discloses the relationship that we, as individuals, have with our taken-for-granted social realities; it shakes our perceptions and should strengthen our resolve to better understand.

To explore the array of sociological thinkers presented here the reader should look for patterns or thematic continuities between and among writers. Traditionally, sociology explored the dynamic of the macro/micro split or judged theorists as 'consensus'- or 'conflict'-oriented. Some early theorists, would not today accept the whole rubric of sociology itself without concern. Overall, our perception is that commentaries on these writers apply such a wealth of labels, designations, and categories that we prefer to let the beginning reader start at the beginning. These works serve to introduce the reader to the power of these writers but they also demand recognition of the historical and intellectual context from which the work emerges. As Gertrud Lenzer notes,

> reestablishment of the relation with the past is necessary if individual self-consciousness is to attain a critical dimension of self-reflection, a dimension

that would necessarily include a critical awareness of the various sciences and their interdependence with the historical development of modern society. In this way there may be a possibility, if one exists at all, for the conscious and active self-creation of an individual who is overtly involved in the shaping of knowledge and therefore history, rather than being passively or merely reactively guided by it.[4]

These works let students comprehend not only the language of sociology but also the relationship of thought, language, and action (i.e. praxis) to historical time and place.

When you open this book we assume that your purpose is to come to a deeper understanding of the writer through his or her works, unencumbered by detours. Hence we have organized the writings collected here in chronological order with minimal biographic detail. Biographical material may be found in a number of easily accessible sources. We have also left the detail of study questions to the reader. Real reading is, in our view, both a writing- and a question-generating activity.

Who to include, who to exclude? There are those who are never excluded. They are part of the substance of sociology; in the true sense of the classic, they are timeless. Our choice of other writers was determined by their participation in challenges, in their questioning of social assumptions. Many of these writers are feminists. Their particular works, we feel, continue the tradition of intellectual challenge created in the classics of Europe and the United States. In a profoundly critical way they take us through, not back to, earlier sociological traditions.

It is our observation that contemporary feminists theorists are not simply building a new sociological tradition; they are very carefully, as Dorothy Smith points out, 'reinventing' the society. One of sociology's greatest contributions has been to reveal systematically the injustices and inequities characterizing most societies. Contemporary feminism, building upon the early classical sociological thinkers, has begun to indicate the direction to be travelled in order to overcome social injustices and inequalities.

For example, it is relatively modest work to research, quantify, and even theoretically explain that

> while women represent fifty per cent of the world population, they perform nearly two-thirds of all working hours, receive only one-tenth of world income, and own less than one per cent of world property.[5]

But the movement to overcome these inequities in our society is anything but modest. Indeed, those who know this fact have internalized it as taken-for-granted knowledge about how the world 'naturally works'. Feminist theory demands that theory not only be intimately tied to data, but that it constantly be tied to experience. In essence, the work of feminist sociology is not merely to describe or explain, but to present a new perspective, a new and more adequate understanding for action.

To redress the shortcomings of past sociological theory first demands adequate knowledge of that theory. It is therefore fundamental that the theoretical work activated by social observation and experience keeps moving toward social transformation.

Feminist theory begins the necessary work of changing our way of perceiving and experiencing the social world.

The major theoretical works at any point in history help us comprehend the complexities of society; they must also help us see the transformations necessary to move society to new possibilities—transformations that will hopefully alert us to, and move us towards, greater possibilities for social justice. Some of the works presented here arise from a conservative tradition; others are more progressive or even radical in nature. Our hope is that social transformations will be precipitated by understanding the structures, relationships, and dynamics in both historical and contemporary moments.

NOTES

1. *The Sociological Imagination* (New York: Oxford University Press, 1959): 10.
2. *Cultural Action for Freedom*, Harvard Educational Review (Cambridge, 1970): 28.
3. Lecture, Simon Fraser University, summer 1992.
4. *August Comte and Positivism: The Essential Writings*, ed. Gertrud Lenzer (New York: Harper & Row, 1975): xxii–xxiii.
5. D. Taylor, *Women: A World Report* (New York: Oxford University Press, 1985): 82.

PART 1

CLASSICAL
SOCIAL THEORISTS

The primary task of a useful teacher is to teach his students to recognize 'inconvenient' facts—I mean facts that are inconvenient for their party opinions.[1]

In the first part of the book the classical social theorists make their debut. But perhaps more importantly, the discipline of sociology makes its debut. As is noted in our introduction to Auguste Comte's work, he originally wanted to use the term 'social physics', but it had already been used by someone else. So he chose 'sociology'. As we will become aware in Part II, Foucault recognizes the double entendre or double edge to the term 'discipline'—both a form of control and a specific domain of study. He argues that the separation of these may be a falsification, in need of closer inspection. Interestingly, Comte begins our entry into this *discipline* of sociology recognizing its power to study and to control social worlds.

Part I also sets out the tendency towards grand and evolutionary theory-building that is inherent to sociology and, more generally, to the social sciences. From Comte through to Weber we are met with broad, overarching theoretical constructs intended to take into account society-wide behaviours and belief systems. Indeed, in their attempts to be all-inclusive we will recognize how exclusive these early theorists really were, for example, in their exclusion of women's perspective. It is noteworthy that the discipline emerged in Europe against the background of women's involvement in social protests and writings on the struggle for women's rights. Harriet Martineau's 'The Political Non-existence of Women' in her *Society in America* (1837) was well known, yet this work and others were never meaningfully incorporated into the sociological theorizing of the time. Also, with grand or macro-theoretical perspective comes the evolutionary dynamic—that the social world is progressing or going somewhere. As we move to Part II we see not only a denial of this potentiality but a continued resistance to grand theory in general (Foucault, for example) or a recognition of how blinded much of grand theory has been in its expression of a Eurocentric, patriarchal perspective.

Given these thoughts, let us not lose sight of the beginnings as beginnings. All of these early writers were struggling with building a discipline and were confronted by historically charged political, social, and economic realities. Some of the material explored by Karl Marx, for example, has become so fundamental to social scientific theorizing and perspective, yet many would like to dissociate themselves from it—in our view prematurely. Their hope is to discard the Marxist tradition while availing themselves of its insightful explanatory power. The social sciences as we know them today have emerged from the work of these early theorists. The scars that build and end relationships are not always apparent.

Marx's colleague and friend, Friedrich Engels, takes us into territory that is considered groundbreaking in terms of its power to situate the place of women in social analysis. Grounded in an economic (materialist) perspective, Engels in *The Origin of the Family, Private Property and the State* explores the historical roots of gender oppression and states that the 'overthrow of the mother right was the world historical defeat of the female sex.' This position was a shift from the dominant nineteenth-century notion that women's subordination was linked to their biology. This text has thus played a significant role in twentieth-century feminist thought.

The contemporary worldwide political context, regardless of variations in political intent or ideological perspective, demands recognition of the work of Herbert Spencer. Spencer's ideology of 'social Darwinism'—'the survival of the fittest'—is understood by most within the context of their everyday lives. The potential for sexism, racism, and classism (three central categories of sociological analysis) emerges from his work today in ways that were not part of the collective consciousness, particularly after World War II.

It is often noted that the three 'big' sociological theorists are Marx, Durkheim, and Weber, that they set the stage for social analysis and entertained the timeless questions that arise out of both social conflict and social order. Emile Durkheim, with his anthropological perspective and background, is seen as a consensus theorist, one who asks such questions as: 'What is the social glue that holds society together?' The counterpoint, of course, is forwarded by conflict-oriented theorists such as Karl Marx and Max Weber. Weber's contribution regarding the 'rationalization of the world' (later taken up by Habermas and by the popular work of George Ritzer, *The McDonaldization of Society*) and his analysis of bureaucracy, religion, and various forms of authority strengthen our understanding of an increasingly complex world.

The classical questions that emerge from the work of these early theorists really do seem timeless, at some level obvious, and therefore in need of recognition. Weber, particularly, as he moves methodologically to terms such as *verstehen* (understanding from the actors' point of view) takes us into the micro-theoretical world—he leads us and sends us there. Yet, as we explore the 'Big Picture' discussions of these early thinkers, we can see the beginnings of questions that by necessity must surface if we are to get as complete as possible an account of the human experience.

Thus, the 'symbolic interactionist' perspective, 'a barbaric neologism' coined by Herbert Blumer to describe the work of Cooley and Mead, begins recognition of very important terrain within sociology—the domain of micro theory. Cooley and Mead, exploring the 'genesis of the self', set the necessary ground for understanding the full spectrum of the sociological discussion—the elaborate tension between the individual and the societal. How does one gain a sense of identity and within what social, political, economic context does this process take place? The unity of the macro/micro analysis is both a place of departure and one of return to the authenticity of social description and analysis.

As we shall see, the theorists of the earlier era in the history of sociology place before us questions of classical, timeless depth. Both the adequacy and inadequacy of their analyses are profound. To name only a few of the central concepts and concerns, we begin to

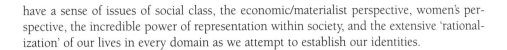

have a sense of issues of social class, the economic/materialist perspective, women's perspective, the incredible power of representation within society, and the extensive 'rationalization' of our lives in every domain as we attempt to establish our identities.

Notes

1. Max Weber, 'Science as a vocation', in H.H. Gerth and C. Wright Mills, eds, *From Max Weber: Essays in Sociology* (New York: Oxford University Press, 1946), 147.

Auguste Comte

1798–1857
FRANCE

Major Works

1842 Cours de Philosophie Positive
1851 Systeme de Politique Positive

> From Science comes Prevision; from Prevision comes Action. (Savoir pour prevoir et prevoir pour pouvoir.)[1]

> . . . it is only by knowing the laws of phenomena, and thus being able to foresee them, that we can, in active life, set them to modify one another to our advantage.[2]
>
> —*Auguste Comte*

Auguste Comte coined the term 'sociology'. For this he is endlessly congratulated. Seldom are his other major contributions noted; still more seldom his work read, although Isaiah Berlin states that 'Comte's views have affected the categories of our thought more deeply than is commonly supposed.'[3] His search for a 'positive science' that would use the methods of the natural sciences in the study of human societies began a bridging of the two domains that remains a point of argument even today. When Comte found that the term 'social physics' had been borrowed from someone else, he coined the term 'sociology'. But 'social physics' perhaps more aptly expresses his desire for a scientific study of society.

Comte's evolutionary theory—the Law of Three Stages—was an attempt to understand the successive stages of societal development and to elaborate a theoretical analysis to accompany his view of human 'progress'. He portrayed this evolutionary approach to societal change in the following manner:

> Each of our leading conceptions—each branch of our knowledge, passes successively through three different theoretical conditions: the Theological or fictitious; the Metaphysical or abstract; and the Scientific or positive. . . . In the theological state, the human mind, seeking the essential nature of beings, the first and final causes (the origin and purpose) of all effects . . . supposes all phenomena to be produced by the immediate action of supernatural beings. In the meta-

physical state . . . the mind supposes . . . abstract forces, veritable entities (that is, personified abstractions) . . . capable of producing all phenomena. . . . In the final, the positive state, the mind has given over the vain search after Absolute notions, the origin and destination of the universe, and the causes of phenomena, and applies itself to the study of their laws—that is, their invariable relations of succession and resemblance.[4]

This progression from the theological through the metaphysical to the scientific is paralleled in terms of moral attachments by a progression from the family to the state to wider humanity. Comte always considered the family to be the fundamental unit of social order. He suggested that society in general moved from a militaristic form to a legalistic form to an industrial form, the nineteenth-century birth of which he witnessed. Overall, Comte saw this motion as a progression of the mind or the ideas of humanity. His evolutionary perspective has been prescient in some ways, fundamentally inaccurate in others.

Comte's conservatism is best expressed through his conceptualizations of social statics (i.e., social order) and social dynamics (i.e., social change) in a search for the perfection of the social order. In the tension between social order and social change, he argued for the subordination of change or social dynamics to the need for social statics and order. Writing about the general tenor of his times, Gertrud Lenzer notes:

> The brief period brought forth a multitude of systems, schemes, and blueprints for the reorganization of knowledge, power, property, and feelings; they were put forward in the cause of restoring an old order or of instituting a new one, and vied with one another for adherents. Out of all this Comte and Marx emerged as the major synthesizers and the most distinctly representative social philosophers of the nineteenth century: in them the two major antagonistic forces found intellectual form.[5]

Where Marx saw the antagonism between the bourgeoisie and the proletariat as class struggle and necessitating revolution, Comte saw it as exemplifying poor management or organizational arrangements, a disruption of social order.

Comte's attempt to found a sociology—a 'social physics'—was really based in methodological notions of prediction and modification. By abandoning the search for first principles or esoteric abstractions, and relying on research into social realities through empirical observation, Comte hoped to move society away from moral anarchy towards a more orderly form. Through direct observation, observation by experiment, and observation by comparison, he hoped to combine reason with observed phenomena to develop fundamental social laws.

The impact of his 'positivism'—or positive science—on the social sciences

needs continual reiteration if we are to understand contemporary methodological debates in the social sciences.

Notes

1. Auguste Comte, *Cours de Philosophie Positive*, trans. Harriet Martineau (London: Bell, 1856), 20–1.
2. Gertud Lenzer, ed., *Auguste Comte and Positivism* (New York: Harper & Row, 1975), 88.
3. Isaiah Berlin, 'Historical Inevitability' (1953) in *Four Essays on Liberty* (Oxford: Oxford University Press, 1969), 41.
4. Auguste Comte, *Système de Politique Positive*, 4th edn, vol. 4 (Paris: Grès, 1912), 1–2.
5. Lenzer, ed., *Auguste Comte*, xxvii–xxviii.

THE SPIRIT OF POSITIVE SCIENCE

The scientific principle of the relation between the political and the social condition is simply this: that there must always be a spontaneous harmony between the whole and the parts of the social system, the elements of which must inevitably be, sooner or later, combined in a mode entirely conformable to their nature. It is evident not only that political institutions and social manners, on the one hand, and manners and ideas on the other, must be always mutually connected but, further, that this consolidated whole must be always connected, by its nature, with the corresponding state of the integral development of humanity, considered in all its aspects, of intellectual, moral, and physical activity; and the only object of any political system whatever, temporal or spiritual, is to regulate the spontaneous expansion so as best to direct it towards its determinate end. Even during revolutionary periods, when the harmony appears furthest from being duly realized, it still exists, for without it there would be a total dissolution of the social organism. During those exceptional seasons, the political regime is still, in the long run, in conformity with the corresponding state of civilization, as the disturbances that are manifest in the one proceed from equivalent derangements in the other. It is observable that when the popular theory attributes to the legislator the permanent power of infringing the harmony we are speaking of, it supposes him to be armed with a sufficient authority. But every social power, whether called authority or anything else, is constituted by a corresponding assent, spontaneous or deliberate, explicit or implicit, of various individual wills, resolved, from certain preparatory convictions, to concur in a common action, of which this power is first the organ, and then the regulator. Thus, authority is derived from concurrence, and not concurrence from authority (setting aside the necessary reaction), so that no great power can arise otherwise than from the strongly prevalent disposition of the society in which it exists; and when there is no strong preponderance, such powers as exist are weak accordingly, and the more extensive the society, the more irresistible is the correspondence. On the other hand, there is no denying the influence that, by a necessary reaction, the political system, as a whole, exercises over the general system of civilization, and that is so often exhibited in the action, fortunate or disastrous, of institutions, measures, or purely political events, even upon the course of the sciences and arts, in all ages of society, and especially the earliest. We need not dwell on this, for no one denies it. The common error, indeed, is to exaggerate it, so as to place the reaction before the primary action. It is evident, considering their scientific relation to each other, that both concur in creating that fundamental agreement of the social organism that I propose to set forth in a brief manner, as the philosophical principle of static sociology. We shall have to advert repeatedly to the subject of the general correspondence between the political regime and the contemporary state of civilization, in connection with the question of the necessary limits of political action, and in the chapter that I must devote to social statics; but I did not think fit to wait for these explanations before pointing out that the political system ought always to be regarded as relative. . . .

There are two principal considerations that induce me to insist on this elementary idea of the radical consensus proper to the social organism: first, the extreme philosophical importance of this master thought of social statics, which must, from its nature, constitute the rational basis of any new political philosophy; and, second, in an accessory way, that dynamic considerations of sociology must prevail throughout the rest of this work, as being at present more interesting and therefore better understood; and it is, on that account, the more necessary to characterize now the general spirit of social statics, which will henceforth be treated only in an indirect and implicit way. As all artificial and voluntary order is simply a prolongation of the natural and involuntary order to which all human society tends, every rational political institution must rest upon an exact preparatory analysis of corresponding spontaneous tendencies, which alone can furnish a sufficiently solid basis. In brief, it is our business to contemplate order, that we may perfect it, and not to create it, which would be impossible. In a scientific view, this master thought of universal social interconnection becomes the consequence and complement of a fundamental idea established, in our view of biology, as eminently proper to the study of living bodies. Not that this idea of interconnection is peculiar to that study: it is necessarily common to all phenomena, but amidst immense differences in intensity and variety, and therefore in philosophical importance. It is, in fact, true that wherever there is any system whatever, a certain interconnection must exist. The purely mechanical phenomena of astronomy offer the first suggestion of it; for the perturbations of one planet may sensibly affect another, through a modified gravitation. But the relation becomes closer and more marked in proportion to the complexity and diminished generality of the phenomena, and thus it is in organic systems that we must look for the fullest mutual connection. Hitherto, it had been merely an accessory idea; but then it becomes the basis of positive conceptions, and it becomes more marked, the more compound are the organisms, and the more complex the phenomena in question—the animal interconnection being more complete than the vegetable, and the human more than the brute, the nervous system being the chief seat of the biological interconnection. The idea must therefore be scientifically preponderant in social physics, even more than in biology, where it is so decisively recognized by the best order of students. But the existing political philosophy supposes the absence of any such inteconnection among the aspects of society: and it is this that has rendered it necessary for me now to establish the point, leaving the illustration of it to a future portion of the volume. Its consideration is, in fact, as indispensable in assigning its encyclopedic rank to social science as we before saw it to be in instituting social physics a science at all.

It follows from this attribute that there can be no scientific study of society, either in its conditions or its movements, if it is separated into portions, and its divisions are studied apart. . . . Materials may be furnished by the observation of different departments, and such observation may be necessary for that object; but it cannot be called science. The methodical division of studies that takes place in the simple inorganic sciences is thoroughly irrational in the recent and complex science of society, and can produce no results. The day may come when some sort of subdivision may be practicable and desirable; but it is impossible for us now to anticipate what the principle of distribution may be, for the principle itself must arise from the development of the science, and that development can take place no other way than by our formation of the science as a whole. The complete body will indicate for itself, at the right season, the particular points that need investigation, and then will be the time for such special study as may be required. By any other method of proceeding, we shall only find ourselves encumbered with special discussions, badly instituted, worse pursued, and accomplishing no other purpose than that of impeding the formation of real science. It is no easy matter to study social phenomena in the only right way—viewing each element in the light of the whole system. It is no easy matter to exercise such vigilance as that no one of the number of contemporary aspects shall be lost sight of. But it is the right and the only way. . . .

Before we go on to the subject of social dynamics, I will just remark that the prominent interconnection we have been considering prescribes a procedure in organic studies different from that which suits inorganic. The metaphysicians announce as an aphorism that we should always, in every kind of study, proceed from the simple to the compound, whereas it appears most rational to suppose that we should follow that or the reverse method, as may best suit our subject. There can be no absolute merit in the method enjoined, apart from its suitableness. The rule should rather be (and there probably was a time when the two rules were one) that we must proceed from the more known to the less. Now, in the inorganic sciences, the elements are much better known to us than the whole that they constitute, so that in that case we must proceed from the simple to the compound. But the reverse method is necessary in the study of man and of society, man and society as a whole being better known to us, and more accessible subjects of study, than the parts that constitute them. In exploring the universe, it is as a whole that it is inaccessible to us, whereas, in investigating man or society, our difficulty is in penetrating the details. . . .

Passing on from static to dynamic sociology, we will contemplate the philosophical conception that should govern our study of the movement of society. Part of this subject is already dispatched, from the explanations made in connection with statics having simplified the chief difficulties of the case. . . .

Though the static view of society is the basis of sociology, the dynamic view is not only the more interesting of the two, but the more marked in its philosophical character, from its being more distinguished from biology by the master thought of continuous progress or, rather, of the gradual development of humanity. If I were writing a methodical treatise on political philosophy, it would be necessary to offer a preliminary analysis of the individual impulsions that make up the progressive force of the human race, by referring them to that instinct that results from the concurrence of all our natural tendencies, and that urges man to develop the whole of his life, physical, moral, and intellectual, as far as his circumstances allow. But this view is admitted by all enlightened philosophers, so that I may proceed at once to consider the continuous succession of human development, regarded in the whole race, as if humanity were one. For clearness, we may take advantage of Condorcet's device of supposing a single nation to which we may refer all the consecutive social modifications actually witnessed among distinct peoples. This rational fiction is nearer the reality than we are accustomed to suppose, for, in a political view, the true successors of such a people are certainly those who, taking up and carrying out their primitive endeavours, have prolonged their social progress, whatever may be the soil that they inhabit, or even the race from which they spring. In brief, it is political continuity that regulates sociological succession, though having a common country must usually affect this continuity in a high degree. As a scientific artifice merely, however, I shall employ this hypothesis, and on the ground of its manifest utility.

The true general spirit of social dynamics, then, consists in conceiving of each of these consecutive social states as the necessary result of the proceeding, and the indispensable mover of the following, according to the axiom of Leibnitz: *the present is big with the future.* In this view, the object of science is to discover the laws that govern this continuity, and the aggregate of which determines the course of human development. In short, social dynamics studies the laws of succession, while social statics inquires into those of coexistence; so that the use of the first is to furnish the true theory of progress to political practice, while the second performs the same service in regard to order, and this suitability to the needs of modern society is a strong confirmation of the philosophical character of such a combination.

If the existence of sociological laws has been established in the more difficult and uncertain case of the static condition, we may assume that they will not be questioned in the dynamic province. In all times and places, the ordinary course of even our brief individual life has disclosed certain remarkable modifications that have occurred, in various ways, in the social state; and all the most ancient representations of human life bear unconscious and most interesting testimony to this, apart from all systematic estimate of the fact. Now it is the slow, continuous accumulation of these successive changes that gradually constitutes the social movement, whose steps are ordinarily marked by generations, as the most appreciable elementary variations are wrought by the constant renewal of adults. At a time when the average rapidity of this progression seems to all eyes to be remarkably accelerated, the reality of the movement cannot be disputed, even by those who most abhor it. The only question is about the constant subjection of these great dynamic phenomena to invariable natural laws, a proposition about which there is no question to anyone who takes his stand on positive philosophy. It is easy, however, to establish, from any point of view, that the successive modifications of society have always taken place in a determinate order, the rational explanation of which is already possible in so many cases that we may confidently hope to recognize it ultimately in all the rest. . . . Since, then, the existence of the social movement is unquestionable, on the one hand, and, on the other, the succession of social states is never arbitrary, we cannot but regard this continuous phenomenon as subject to natural laws as positive as those that govern all other phenomena, though more complex. There is in fact no intellectual alternative, and thus it is evident that it is on the ground of social science that the great conflict must soon terminate that has gone on for three centuries between the positive and the theologico-metaphysical spirit. . . .

As social physics assumes a place in the hierarchy of sciences after all the rest, and therefore dependent on them, its means of investigation must be of two kinds: those that are peculiar to itself, and that may be called direct, and those that arise from the connection of sociology with the other sciences; and these last, though indirect, are as indispensable as the first. I shall review, first, the direct resources of the science.

Here, as in all the other cases, there are three methods of proceeding: by observation, experiment, and comparison.

Very imperfect and even vicious notions prevail at present as to what observation can be and can effect in social science. The chaotic state of doctrine of the last century has extended to method, and amidst our intellectual disorganization, difficulties have been magnified. Precautionary methods, experimental and rational, have been broken up, and even the possibility of obtaining social knowledge by observation has been dogmatically denied; but if the sophisms put forth on this subject were true, they would destroy the certainty, not only of social science, but of all the simpler and more perfect ones that have gone before. The ground of doubt assigned is the uncertainty of human testimony; but all the sciences, up to the most simple, require proofs of testimony: that is, in the elaboration of the most positive theories, we have to admit observations that could not be directly made, or even repeated, by those who use them, and the reality of which rests only on the faithful testimony of the original investigators—there being nothing in this to prevent the use of such proofs, in concurrence with immediate observations. In astronomy, such a method is obviously necessary; it is equally though less obviously necessary even in mathematics—and, of course, much more evidently in the case of the more complex sciences. How could any science emerge from the nascent state—how could there be any organization of intellectual labour, even if research were restricted to the utmost, if everyone rejected all observations but his own? The stoutest advocates of historical scepticism do not go so far as to advocate this. It is only in the case of social phenomena that the paradox is proposed, and it is made use of there because it is one of the weapons of the philosophical arsenal that the revolutionary metaphysical doctrine constructed for the intellectual overthrow of the ancient political system. The next great hindrance to the use of observation is the empiricism that is introduced into it by those who, in the name of impartiality, would interdict the use of any theory whatever. No logical dogma could be more thoroughly irreconcilable with the spirit of the positive philosophy, or with its special character in regard to the study of social phenomena, than this. No real observation of any kind of phenomena is possible, except insofar as it is first directed, and finally interpreted, by some theory; and it was this logical need that, in the infancy of human reason, occasioned the rise of theological philosophy, as we shall see in the course of our historical survey. The positive philosophy does not dissolve this obligation but, on the contrary, extends and fulfils it more and more, the further the relations of phenomena are multiplied and perfected by it. Hence it is clear that, scientifically speaking, all isolated, empirical observation is idle and even radically uncertain; that science can use only those observations that are connected, at least hypothetically, with some law; that it is such a connection that makes the chief difference between scientific and popular observation, embracing the same facts but contemplating them from different points of view; and that observations empirically conducted can at most supply provisional materials, which must usually undergo an ulterior revision. The rational method of observation becomes more necessary in proportion to the complexity of the phenomena, amidst which the observer would not know what he ought to look at in the facts before his eyes, but for the guidance of a preparatory theory; and thus it is that by the connection of foregoing facts we learn to see the facts that follow. This is undisputed with regard to astronomical, physical, and chemical research, and in every branch of biological study, in which good observation of its highly complex phenomena is still very rare, precisely because its positive theories are very imperfect. Carrying on the analogy, it is evident that in corresponding divisions, static and dynamic, of social science, there is more need than anywhere else of theories that shall scientifically connect the facts that are happening with those that have happened; and the more we reflect, the more distinctly we shall see that in proportion as known facts are mutually connected we shall be better able not only to estimate but to perceive those that are yet unexplored. I am not blind to the vast difficulty that this requisition imposes on the institution of positive sociology—obliging us to create at once, so to speak, observations and laws, on account of their indispensable connection, placing us in a sort of vicious circle, from which we can issue only by employing in the first instance materials that are badly elaborated and doctrines that are ill conceived. How I may succeed in a task so difficult and delicate, we shall see at its close; but, however that may be, it is clear that it is the absence of any positive theory that at present renders social observations so vague and incoherent. There can never be any lack of facts, for in this case even more than in others, it is the commonest sort of facts that are most important, whatever the collectors of secret anecdotes may think; but, though we are steeped to the lips in them, we can make no use of them, or even be aware of them, for want of speculative guidance in examining them. The static observation of a crowd of phenomena cannot take place without some notion, however elementary, of the laws of social interconnection, and dynamic facts could have no fixed direction if they were not attached, at least by a provisional hypothesis, to the laws of social development. The positive philosophy is very far from discouraging historical or any other erudition; but the precious night watchings, now so lost in the laborious acquisition of a conscientious but barren learning, may be made available by it for the constitution of true social science and the increased honour of the earnest minds that are devoted to it. The new philosophy will supply fresh and nobler subjects, unhoped-for insight, a loftier aim, and therefore a higher scientific dignity. It will discard none but aimless labours, without principle and without character; as in physics, there is no room for compilations of empirical observations; and at the same time, philosophy will render justice to the zeal of students of a past generation, who, destitute of the favourable guidance that we, of this day, enjoy, followed up their laborious histori-cal researches with an instinctive perseverance, and in spite of the superficial disdain of the philosophers of the time. No doubt the same danger attends research here as else-where—the danger that, from the continuous use of scientific theories, the observer may sometimes pervert facts, by erroneously supposing them to verify some ill-grounded spec-ulative prejudices of his own. But we have the same guard here as elsewhere—in the fur-ther extension of the science—and the case would not be improved by a recurrence to empirical methods, which would be merely leaving theories that may be misapplied but can always be rectified, for imaginary notions that cannot be substantiated at all. Our fee-ble reason may often fail in the application of positive theories, but at least they transfer us from the domain of imagination to that of reality, and expose us infinitely less than any other kind of doctrine to the danger of seeing in facts that which is not.

It is now clear that social science requires, more than any other, the subordination of observation to the static and dynamic laws of phenomena. No social fact can have any sci-entific meaning till it is connected with some other social fact—without which connection it remains a mere anecdote, involving no rational utility. This condition so far increases the immediate difficulty that good observers will be rare at first, though more abundant than ever as the science expands. And here we meet with another confirmation of what I said at the outset of this volume, that the formation of social theories should be confided only to the best-organized minds, prepared by the most rational training. Explored by such minds, according to rational views of coexistence and succession, social phenomena no doubt admit of much more varied and extensive means of investigation than phenom-ena of less complexity. In this view, it is not only the immediate inspection or direct description of events that affords useful means of positive exploration, but the considera-tion of apparently insignificant customs, the appreciation of various kinds of monuments, the analysis and comparison of languages, and a multitude of other resources. In short, a mind suitably trained becomes able to exercise to convert almost all impressions from the events of life into sociological indications, when once the connection of all indications with the leading ideas of the science is understood. This is a facility afforded by the mutu-al relation of the various aspects of society, which may partly compensate for the difficul-ty caused by that mutual connection: if it renders observation more difficult, it affords more means for its prosecution.

It might be supposed beforehand that the second method of investigation, experi-ment, must be wholly inapplicable in social science; but we shall find that the science is not entirely deprived of this resource, though it must be one of inferior value. We must remember (what was before explained) that there are two kinds of experimentation—the direct and the indirect—and that it is not necessary to the philosophical character of this method that the circumstances of the phenomenon in question should be, as is vulgarly supposed in the learned world, artificially instituted. Whether the case be natural or fac-titious, experimentation takes place whenever the regular course of the phenomenon is interfered with in any determinate manner. The spontaneous nature of the alteration has no effect on the scientific value of the case, if the elements are known. It is in this sense that experimentation is possible in sociology. If direct experimentation had become too difficult amidst the complexities of biology, it may well be considered impossible in social science. Any artificial disturbance of any social element must affect all the rest, according to the laws of both coexistence and succession; and the experiment would therefore, if it could be instituted at all, be deprived of all scientific value, through the impossibility of isolating either the conditions or the results of the phenomenon. But we saw, in our survey of biology, that pathological cases are the true scientific equivalent of pure experimentation, and why. The same reasons apply, with even more force, to sociological researches. In them, pathological analysis consists in the examination of cases, unhappily too common, in which the natural laws, either of harmony or of succession, are disturbed by any causes, special or general, accidental or transient—as in revolutionary times especially and, above all, in our own. These disturbances are, in the social body, exactly analogous to diseases in the individual organism, and I have no doubt whatever that the analogy will be more evident (allowance being made for the unequal complexity of the organisms) the deeper the investigation goes. In both cases it is, as I said once before, a noble use to make of our reason, to disclose the real laws of our nature, individual or social, by the analysis of its sufferings. . . . The great natural laws exist and act in all conditions of the organism; for, as we saw in the case of biology, it is an error to suppose that they are violated or suspended in the case of disease, and we are therefore justified in drawing our conclusions, with due caution, from the scientific analysis of disturbance to the positive theory of normal existence. This is the nature and character of the indirect experimentation that discloses the real economy of the social body in a more marked manner than simple observation could do. It is applicable to all orders of sociological research, whether relating to existence or to movement, and regarded under any aspect whatever, physical, intellectual, moral, or political; and to all degrees of the social evolution, from which unhappily, disturbances have never been absent. As for its present extension, no one can venture to offer any statement of it because it has never been duly applied in any investigation in political philosophy, and it can become customary only by the institution of the new science that I am endeavouring to establish. But I could not omit this notice of it as one of the means of investigation proper to social science.

As for the third of those methods, comparison, the reader must bear in mind the explanations offered, in our survey of biological philosophy, of the reasons why the comparative method must prevail in all studies of which the living organism is the subject—and the more remarkably in proportion to the rank of the organism. The same considerations apply in the present case, in a more conspicuous degree, and I may leave it to the reader to make the application, merely pointing out the chief differences that distinguish the use of the comparative method of sociological inquiries.

It is a very irrational disdain that makes us object to all comparison between human society and the social state of the lower animals. This unphilosophical pride arose out of the protracted influence of the theologico-metaphysical philosophy; and it will be corrected by the positive philosophy, when we better understand and can estimate the social state of the higher orders of mammals, for instance. We have seen how important is the study of individual life, in regard to intellectual and moral phenomena—of which social phenomena are the natural result and complement. There was once the same blindness to the importance of the procedure in this case as now in the other; and, as it has given way in the one case, so it will in the other. The chief defect in the kind of sociological comparison that we want is that it is limited to static considerations, whereas the dynamic are, at the present time, the preponderant and direct subject of science. The restriction results from the social state of animals' being, though not so stationary as we are apt to suppose, susceptible only of extremely small variations, in no way comparable to the continued progression of humanity in its feeblest days. But there is no doubt of the scientific utility of such a comparison, in the static province, where it characterizes the elementary laws of social interconnection, by exhibiting their action in the most imperfect state of society, so as even to suggest useful inductions in regard to human society. There cannot be a stronger evidence of the natural character of the chief social relations, which some people fancy that they can transform at pleasure. Such sophists will cease to regard the great ties of the human family as factitious and arbitrary when they find them existing, with the same essential characteristics, among the animals, and more conspicuously, the nearer the organisms approach to the human type. In brief, in all that part of sociology that is almost one with intellectual and moral biology, or with the natural history of man; in all that relates to the first germs of the social relations, and the first institutions that were founded by the unity of the family or the tribe, there is not only great scientific advantage, but real philosophical necessity for employing the rational comparison of human with other animal societies. Perhaps it might even be desirable not to confine the comparison to societies that present a character of voluntary co-operation, in analogy to the human. They must always rank first in importance. But the scientific spirit, extending the process to its final logical term, might find some advantage in examining those strange associations, proper to the inferior animals, in which an involuntary co-operation results from an indissoluble organic union, either by simple adhesion or real continuity. If the science gained nothing by this extension, the method would. And there is nothing that can compare with such a habitual scientific comparison for the great service of casting out the absolute spirit that is the chief vice of political philosophy. It appears to me, moreover, that, in a practical view, the insolent pride that induces some ranks of society to suppose themselves as, in a manner, of another species than the rest of mankind is in close affinity with the irrational disdain that repudiates all comparison between human and other animal natures. . . .

HARRIET MARTINEAU

1802–1876
BRITAIN

Major Works

1832   *Illustrations of Political Economy*
1837   *Society in America*
1838   *How to Observe Morals and Manners*
1836   *Essays on the Art of Thinking*
1845   *Letters on Mesmerism*
1849   *History of the Thirty Years' Peace*
1853   *The Positive Philosophy of Auguste Comte*
1877   *An Autobiography*

> The question has been asked, from time to time, in more countries than one, how obedience to the laws can be required of women, when no woman has, either actually or virtually, given any assent to any law. No plausible answer has, as far as I can discover, been offered; for the good reason, that no plausible answer can be devised.[1]

> Politics are morals, all the world over; that is, politics universally implicate the duty and happiness of man. Every branch of morals is, and ought to be considered, a universal concern.[2]
>
> —*Harriet Martineau*

Harriet Martineau was a strong supporter of women's rights and an advocate for the abolition of slavery. Although she wrote on social issues before Auguste Comte coined the term 'sociology', it is he who is credited as the 'founding father' of the discipline. Even today, she is rarely listed among the early sociologists. Noting the disappearance from the record of such thinkers as Harriet Martineau, Clothilde de Vaux, Gertrud Simmel, and Marianne Weber, Ritzer writes:

> the invisibility of these women is due to conscious acts of exclusion by male sociologists who, over a hundred-year period, worked to create a male-dominated discipline and then to produce an account of that discipline which made the centrality of men within it appear to be the result of natural rather than political processes.[3]

Dorothy Smith's essay in this volume, 'A Peculiar Eclipsing: Women's Exclusion from Man's Culture', may help in situating Martineau's invisibility. Martineau grappled with the political, social, and philosophical issues of her time and, besides her books and articles, wrote pamphlets in a style accessible to the British working class. She was a journalist and novelist as well, receiving approval from such established women writers as George Eliot, Elizabeth Barrett Browning, and Charlotte Brontë.[4]

Fluent in French and Latin, Martineau is best known for her English translation and later publication of an abridged version of Auguste Comte's *Cours de Philosophie Positive*. Her most important work, *Society in America*, published in 1837 and excerpted here, is the result of her trip to the United States to observe and document the workings of America's social structure. It was not unusual, during this period, for foreigners to travel to the United States to observe its functioning. Alexis de Tocqueville and others had gone before, but as expressed by Lipset, 'methodological self-consciousness . . . characterized the work of Harriet Martineau.'[5]

She used a comparative approach in her studies and analysis of such topics as the government, the economy, slavery, morality, religious expression, and the condition of 'coloured' people, white women, and new immigrants. She interviewed prisoners, and also, in Philadelphia and Boston, spoke with inmates in a mental asylum and in an asylum for the blind, comparing the management of the two in terms of the 'spirit' of the inmates. She also visited an asylum for the deaf and dumb. Bearing in mind the condition of the inmates in these asylums, she writes:

> It may be worth suggesting here that while some of the thinkers of America, like many of the same classes in England, are mourning over the low state of the Philosophy of Mind in their country, society is neglecting a most important means of obtaining the knowledge requisite for the acquisition of such philosophy. Scholars are embracing alternately the systems of Kant, of Fichte, of Spurzheim, of the Scotch school; or abusing or eulogising Locke, asking who Hartley was, or weaving a rainbow arch of transcendentalism, which is to comprehend the whole that lies within human vision, but sadly liable to be puffed away in dark vapour with the first breeze of reality; scholars are thus labouring at a system of mental philosophy on any but the experimental method, while the materials for experiment lie all around and within them.[6]

Her writings reflect a sensitivity to the issues, particularly those dealing with the treatment of people of 'colour' and white women. Throughout her study she was interested in how the dominant American values were reflected in institutional structures. A recurring question was how the disfranchisement of certain groups could be reconciled with one of the fundamental principles of the Declaration of Independence, that governments derive their just powers from the consent of the governed.

She did not offer a formal conclusion to her study, stating it was too soon to theorize or to speak of conclusions. She did state, however, that even with their shortcomings, Americans have accomplished many things for which the rest of the civilized world was still struggling.

Notes

1. Harriet Martineau, *Society in America* (New York: Anchor Books, 1962), 125.
2. Ibid., 59.
3. George Ritzer, *Sociological Theory*, 3rd edn (New York: McGraw-Hill, 1992), 455.
4. Lynn McDonald, *The Women Founders of the Social Sciences* (Ottawa: Carleton University Press, 1994), 166.
5. Seymour Martin Lipset, 'Introduction', in Martineau, *Society in America*, 7.
6. Martineau, *Society in America*, 318–19.

SOCIETY IN AMERICA

IV. Morals of Politics

'Tis he whose law is reason; who depends
Upon that law as on the best of friends;
Whence, in a state where men are tempted still
To evil for a guard against worse ill,
And what in quality or act is best,
Doth seldom on a right foundation rest,
He fixes good on good alone, and owes
To virtue every triumph that he knows.

—*Wordsworth*

Under a pure despotism, the morals of politics would make but a very short chapter. Mercy in the ruler; obedience in his officers, with, perhaps, an occasional stroke of remonstrance; and taxpaying in the people, would comprehend the whole. Among a self-governing people, who profess to take human equality for their great common principle, and the golden rule for their political vow, a long chapter of many sections is required.

The morals of politics are not too familiar anywhere. The clergy are apt to leave out its topics from their list of subjects for the pulpit. Writers on morals make that chapter as brief as if they lived under the pure despotism, supposed above. An honest newspaper,

here and there, or a newspaper honest for some particular occasion, and therefore unin-
fluential in its temporary honesty, are the only speakers on the morals of politics. The only
speakers; but not the only exhibitors. Scattered here and there, through a vast reach of
ages, and expanse of communities, there may be found, to bless his race, an honest statesman. Statesmen, free from the gross vices of peculation, sordid, selfish ambition, cruelty
and tergiversation, are not uncommon. But the last degree of honesty has always been,
and is still, considered incompatible with statesmanship. To hunger and thirst after righteousness has been naturally, as it were, supposed a disqualification for affairs; and a man,
living for truth, and in a spirit of love, 'pure in the last recesses of the mind', who should
propose to seek truth through political action, and exercise love in the use of political
influence, and refine his purity by disinfecting the political atmosphere of its corruptions,
would hear it reported on every hand that he had a demon. The hour is come when
dwellers in the old world should require integrity of their rulers; and dwellers in the new
world, each in his turn a servant of society, should require it of each other and of themselves. The people of the United States are seeking after this, feebly and dimly. They have
retained one wise saying of the fathers to whom they owe so much; that the letter of laws
and constitutions is a mere instrument; with no vitality; no power to protect and bless;
and that the spirit is all in all. They have been far from acting upon this with such steadi-
ness as to show that they understand and believe it. But the saying is in their minds; and,
like every other true thing that lies there, it will in time exhibit itself in the appointed
mode—the will of the majority.

Office

I was told that holding office is the ruin of moral independence. The case is not, however, nearly so bad as this. There is a kind of public life which does seem to injure the morals
of all who enter it; but very few are affected by this. Office in a man's own neighbourhood,
where his character and opinions are known, and where the honour and emolument are
small, is not very seductive; and these are the offices filled by the greater number of citizens who serve society. The temptation to propitiate opinion becomes powerful when a
citizen desires to enter the legislature, or to be the chief magistrate of the State. The peril
increases when he becomes a candidate for Congress; and there seems to be no expectation whatever that a candidate for the presidentship, or his partizans, should retain any
simplicity of speech, or regard to equity in the distribution of places and promises. All this
is dreadfully wrong. It originates in a grand mistake, which cannot be rectified but by
much suffering. It is obvious that there must be mistake; for it can never be an arrangement of Providence that men cannot serve each other in their political relations without
being corrupted.

The primary mistake is in supposing that men cannot bear to hear the truth. It has
become the established method of seeking office, not only to declare a coincidence of
opinion with the supposed majority, on the great topics on which the candidate will have
to speak and act while in office, but to deny, or conceal, or assert anything else which it
is supposed will please the same majority. The consequence is, that the best men are not
in office. The morally inferior who succeed, use their power for selfish purposes, to a suf-

ficient extent to corrupt their constituents, in their turn. I scarcely knew, at first, how to understand the political conversations which I heard in travelling. If a citizen told another that A. had voted in a particular manner, the other invariably began to account for the vote. A. had voted thus to please B., because B.'s influence was wanted for the benefit of C., who had promised so and so to A.'s brother, or son, or nephew, or leading section of constituents. Those who would find the highest integrity had better not begin their observations on office-holders, much less on office-seekers, as a class. The office-holder finds, too often, that it may be easier to get into office than to have power to discharge its duties when there: and then the temptation to subservience, to dishonest silence, is well nigh too strong for mortal man. The office-seeker stands committed as desiring something for which he is ready to sacrifice his business or profession, his ease, his leisure, and the quietness of his reputation. He stands forth as either an adventurer, a man of ambition, or of self-sacrificing patriotism. Being once thus committed, failure is mortifying, and the allurement to compromise, in order to succeed, is powerful. Once in public life, the politician is committed forever, whether he immediately perceives this, or not. Almost every public man of my acquaintance owned to me the difficulty of retiring,—in mind, if not in presence,—after the possession of a public trust. This painful hankering is part of the price to be paid for the honours of public service: and I am disposed to think that it is almost universal; that scarcely any man knows quiet and content, from the moment of the success of his first election. The most modest men shrink from thus committing themselves. The most learned men, generally speaking, devote themselves, in preference, to professions. The most conscientious men, generally speaking, shun the snares which fatally beset public life, at present, in the United States.

A gentleman of the latter class, whose talents and character would procure him extensive and hearty support, if he desired it, told me, that he would never serve in office, because he believes it to be the destruction of moral independence: he pointed out to me three friends of his, men of remarkable talent, all in public life. 'Look at them,' said he, 'and see what they might have been! Yet A. is a slave, B. is a slave, and C. is a worm in the dust.' Too true.

Here is a grievous misfortune to the republic! My friend ascribes it to the want of protection from his neighbours, to which a man is exposed from the want of caste.

Scarcely anything that I observed in the United States caused me so much sorrow as the contemptuous estimate of the people entertained by those who were bowing the knee to be permitted to serve them. Nothing can be more disgusting than the contrast between the drawing-room gentleman, at ease among friends, and the same person courting the people, on a public occasion. The only comfort was a strong internal persuasion that the people do not like to be courted thus.

I attended a Lyceum lecture in Massachusetts. An agent of the Colonisation Society lectured; and, when he had done, introduced a clergyman of colour, who had just returned from Liberia, and could give an account of the colony in its then present state. As soon as this gentleman came forward, a party among the audience rose, and went out, with much ostentation of noise. Mr Wilson broke off till he could be again heard, and then observed in a low voice, 'that would not have been done in Africa'; upon which, there was an uproar of applause, prolonged and renewed. All the evidence on the subject that I could collect, went to prove that the people can bear, and do prefer to hear, the truth. It is a crime to withhold it from them; and a double crime to substitute flattery.

The tone of the orations was the sole, but great drawback from the enjoyment of the popular festivals I witnessed. I missed the celebration of the 4th of July,—both years; being, the first year, among the Virginia mountains, (where the only signs of festivity which I saw, were some slaves dressing up a marquee, in which their masters were to feast, after having read, from the Declaration of Independence, that all men are created free and equal, and that rulers derive their just powers from the consent of the governed;) and the second year on the lakes, arriving at Mackinaw too late in the evening of the great day for any celebration that might have taken place. But I was at two remarkable festivals, and heard two very remarkable orations. They were represented to me as fair or favourable specimens of that kind of address; and, to judge by the general sum of those which I read and heard, they were so.

One of the then candidates for the highest office in the State, [Massachusetts] is renowned for his oratory. He is one of the most accomplished scholars and gentlemen that the country possesses. It was thought, 'by his friends', that his interest wanted strengthening in the western part of the State. The commemoration of an Indian catastrophe was thought of as an occasion capable of being turned to good electioneering purposes. I was not aware of this till I sometime after heard it, on indisputable authority. I should have enjoyed it much less than I did, if I had known that the whole thing was got up, or its time and manner chosen, for electioneering objects; that advantage was taken of the best feelings of the people for the political interest of one.

The platform from which the orator was to address the assemblage was erected under a rather shabby walnut tree, which was rendered less picturesque by its lower branches being lopped off, for the sake of convenience. Long and deep ranges of benches were provided; and on these, with carriage cushions and warm cloaks, we found ourselves perfectly well accommodated. Nothing could be better. It was a pretty sight. The wind rustled fitfully in the old walnut-tree. The audience gathered around it were sober, quiet; some would have said dull. The girls appeared to me to be all pretty, after the fashion of American girls. Every body was well-dressed; and such a thing as ill-behaviour in any village assemblage in New England, is, I believe, unheard of.

The band arrived, leading the procession of gentlemen, and were soon called into action by the first hymn. They did their best; and, if no one of their instruments could reach the second note of the German Hymn, (the second note of three lines out of four,) it was not for want of trying.

The oration followed. I strove, as I always did, not to allow difference of taste, whether in oratory, or in anything else, to render me insensible to the merit, in its kind, of what was presented to me: but, upon this occasion, all my sympathies were baffled, and I was deeply disgusted. It mattered little what the oration was in itself, if it had only belonged in character to the speaker. If a Greenfield farmer or mechanic had spoken as he believed orators to speak, and if the failure had been complete, I might have been sorry or amused, or disappointed; but not disgusted. But here was one of the most learned and accomplished gentlemen in the country, a candidate for the highest office in the State, grimacing like a mountebank before the assemblage whose votes he desired to have, and delivering an address, which he supposed level to their taste and capacity. He spoke of the 'stately tree', (the poor walnut,) and the 'mighty assemblage', (a little flock in the middle of an orchard,) and offered them shreds of tawdry sentiment, without the intermixture of one sound thought, or simple and natural feeling, simply and naturally expressed. It was equally an under estimate of his hearers, and a degradation of himself.

The effect was very plain. Many, I know, were not interested, but were unwilling to say so of so renowned an orator. All were dull; and it was easy to see that none of the proper results of public speaking followed. These very people are highly imaginative. Speak to them of what interests them, and they are moved with a word.

All this would be of little importance, if these orations consisted of narrative,—or of any mere matter of fact. The grievance lies in the prostitution of moral sentiment, the clap-trap of praise and pathos, which is thus criminally adventured. This is one great evil. Another, as great, both to orators and listeners, is the mis-estimate of the people. No insolence and meanness can surpass those of the man of sense and taste who talks beneath himself to the people, because he thinks it suits them.

The other festival, to which I have alluded, was the celebration of Forefathers' Day;—of the landing of the Pilgrims on Plymouth Rock.

The oration was by an ex-senator of the United States. It consisted wholly of an elaboration of the transcendent virtues of the people of New England. His manner was more quiet than that of any other orator I heard; and I really believe that there was less of art than of weakness and bad taste in his choice of his mode of address. Nothing could be imagined worse,—more discordant with the fitting temper of the occasion,—more dangerous to the ignorant, if such there were,—more disgusting to the wise, (as I know, on the testimony of such,)—more unworthy of one to whom the ear of the people was open. He told his hearers of the superiority of their physical, intellectual, and moral constitution to that of their brethren of the middle and southern States, to that of Europeans, and all other dwellers in the earth; a superiority which forbade their being ever understood and appreciated by any but themselves. He spoke especially of the intensity of the New England character, as being a hidden mystery from all but natives. He contrasted the worst circumstances of European society, (now in course of correction,) with the best of New England arrangements, and drew the obvious inferences. He excused the bigotry of the Pilgrim Fathers, their cruel persecution of the Quakers, and other such deeds, on the ground that they had come over to have the colony to themselves, and did not want interlopers. He extenuated the recent mobbing practices in New England, on the ground of their rarity and small consequences, and declared it impossible that the sons of the pilgrims should trust to violence for the maintenance of opinion. This last sentiment, the only sound one that I perceived in the oration, was loudly cheered. The whole of the rest, I rejoice to say, fell dead.

The orator was unworthy of his hearers. No man of common sense could be made to believe that any community of mortal men has ever been what the orator described the inhabitants of New England to have attained. I am aware,—I had but too much occasion to observe,—how this practice of flattering the people from the rostrum is accounted for, and, as a matter of fact, smiled at by citizens of the United States. It is considered as a mode, inseparable from the philosophy of politics there.

I was frequently reminded by friends of what is undoubtedly very true, the great perils of office in the United States, as an excuse for the want of honesty in officials. It is perfectly true that it is ruin to a professional man without fortune, to enter public life for a time, and then be driven back into private life. I knew a senator of the United States who had served for nearly his twice six years, and who then had to begin life again, as regarded his profession. I knew a representative of the United States, a wealthy man, with a large family, who is doubting still, as he has been for a few years past, whether he shall give up commerce or public life, or go on trying to hold them both. He is rich enough to devote himself to public life; but at the very next election after he has relinquished his commercial affairs, he may be thrown out of politics. I see what temptations arise in such cases, to strain a few points, in order to remain in the public eye.

But the part for honest men to take is to expose the peril, to the end that the majority may find a remedy; and not to sanction it by yielding to it. Let the attention of the people be drawn towards the salaries of office, that they may discover whether they are too low; which is best, that adventurers of bad character should now and then get into office, because they have not reputation enough to obtain a living by other means, or that honest and intelligent men should be kept out, because the prizes of office are engrossed by more highly educated men; and whether the rewards of office are kept low by the democratic party, for the sake of putting in what their opponents call 'adventurers', or by the aristocratic, with the hope of offices being engrossed by the men of private fortune. Let the true state of the case, according to each official's view of it, be presented to the people, rather than any countenance be given to the present dreadful practice of wheedling and flattery; and the perils of office will be, by some means, lessened.

The popular scandal against the people of the United States, that they boast intolerably of their national institutions and character, appears to me untrue: but I see how it has arisen. Foreigners, especially the English, are partly to blame for this. They enter the United States with an idea that a republic is a vulgar thing: and some take no pains to conceal their thought. To an American, nothing is more venerable than a republic. The native and the stranger set out on a misunderstanding. The English attacks, the American defends, and, perhaps, boasts. But the vain-glorious flattery of their public orators is the more abundant source of this reproach. For my own part, I remember no single instance of patriotic boasting, from man, woman, or child, except from the rostrum; but from thence there was poured enough to spoil the auditory for life, if they had been simple enough to believe what they were told. But they were not.

Newspapers

Side by side with the sinners of the rostrum, stand the sinners of the newspaper press. The case is clear, and needs little remark or illustration. The profligacy of newspapers, wherever they exist, is a universal complaint; and, of all newspaper presses, I never heard any one deny that the American is the worst. Of course, this depravity being so general throughout the country, it must be occasioned by some overpowering force of circumstances. The causes are various; and it is a testimony to the strength and purity of the democratic sentiment in the country, that the republic has not been overthrown by its newspapers.

While the population is so scattered as it now is, throughout the greater part of the Union, nothing is easier than to make the people know only one side of a question; few things are easier than to keep from them altogether the knowledge of any particular affair; and, worse than all, on them may easily be practised the discovery that lies may work their intended effect, before the truth can overtake them.

It is hard to tell which is worse; the wide diffusion of things that are not true, or the suppression of things that are true. It is no secret that some able personage at Washington writes letters on the politics and politicians of the general government, and sends them to the remotest corners of the Union, to appear in their newspapers; after which, they are collected in the administration newspaper at Washington, as testimonies of public opinion in the respective districts where they appear. It is no secret that the newspapers of the south keep out of their columns all information which might enlighten their readers, near and afar, as to the real state of society at home. I can testify to the *remarkable events* which occur in the southern States, unnoticed by any press, and transpiring only through accident. Two men were burned alive, without trial by the gentlemen of Mobile, just before my arrival there; and no newspaper even alluded to the circumstance, till, many months after, a brief and obscure paragraph, in a northern journal, treated it as a matter of hearsay.

It is no secret that the systematic abuse with which the newspapers of one side assail every candidate coming forward on the other, is the cause of many honourable men, who have a regard to their reputation, being deterred from entering public life; and of the people being thus deprived of some better servants than any they have. A public man in New England gave me the history of an editor of a newspaper, who began his professional course by making an avowed distinction between telling lies in conversation and in a newspaper, where every body looks for them. Of course, he has sunk deeper and deeper in falsehood; but retribution has not yet overtaken him. My informant told me, that this editor has made some thousands of dollars by his abuse of one man; and jocosely proposed, that persons who are systematically railed at by any newspaper, should lay claim to a proportion of the profits arising out of the use of their names and characters.

The worst of it is, that the few exceptions to this depravity,—the few newspapers conducted by men of truth and superior intelligence, are not yet encouraged in proportion to their merits. It is easy to see how a youth, going into the wilds, to set up a newspaper for the neighbouring villages, should meet with support, however vicious or crude his production may be; but it is discouraging to perceive how little preference is given, in the Atlantic cities, to the best journals over the worst.

There will be no great improvement in the literary character of the American newspapers till the literature of the country has improved. Their moral character depends upon the moral taste of the people. This looks like a very severe censure. If it be so, the same censure applies elsewhere, and English morals must be held accountable for the slanders and captiousness displayed in the leading articles of British journals, and for the disgustingly jocose tone of their police reports, where crimes are treated as entertainments, and misery as a jest.

Some months before I left the United States, a man of colour was burned alive, without trial, at St Louis, in Missouri; a large assemblage of the 'respectable' inhabitants of the city being present. No one supposed that anybody out of the State of Missouri was any further implicated with this deed, than as men have an interest in every outrage done to man. The interest which residents in other States had in this deed, was like that which an Englishman has in a man being racked in the Spanish Inquisition; or a Frenchman, in a Turk being bastinadoed at Constantinople. He is not answerable for it, or implicated in it, as a fellow citizen; and he speaks his humane reprobation as a fellowman. Certain American citizens, out of Missouri, contrived, however, to implicate themselves in the responsibility for this awful outrage, which, one would have thought, any man would have been thankful to avoid. The majority of newspaper editors made themselves parties to the act, by refusing, from fear, to reprobate it. The state of the case was this, as described to me by some inhabitants of St Louis. The gentlemen of the press in that city dared not reprobate the outrage, for fear of the consequences from the murderers. They merely announced the deed, as a thing to be regretted, and recommended that the veil of oblivion should be drawn over the affair. Their hope was widely different from their recommendation. They hoped that the newspapers throughout the Union would raise such a chorus of execration as would annihilate the power of the executioners. But the newspapers of the Union were afraid to comment upon the affair, because they saw that the St Louis editors were afraid. The really respectable inhabitants of that disgraced city were thrown almost into despair by this dastardly silence, and believed all security of life and property in their State to be at an end. A few journals were honest enough to thunder the truth in the ears of the people; and the people awoke to perceive how their editors had involved themselves in this crime, by a virtual acquiescence,—like the unfaithful mastiff, if such a creature there be, which slinks away from its master's door, to allow a passage to a menacing thief. The influence of the will of the awakening people is already seen in the improved vigour in the tone of the newspapers against outrage. On occasion of the more recent riots at Cincinnati, the editorial silence has been broken by many voices.

There is a spirited newspaper at Louisville which has done its duty well, on occasions when it required some courage to do it; informing the Cincinnati people of the meanness of their conduct in repressing the expression of opinion, lest it should injure the commerce between Ohio and Kentucky; and also, justifying Judge Shaw of Massachusetts, against the outcries of the South, for a judgment he lately gave in favour of the release of a slave, voluntarily carried into a free State. Two New York papers, the New York American and the Evening Post, have gained themselves honour by intrepidity of the same kind, and by the comparative moderation and friendliness of their spirit. I hope that there may be many more, and that their number may be perpetually on the increase.

Apathy in Citizenship

In England the idea of an American citizen is of one who is always talking politics, canvassing, bustling about to make proselytes abroad, buried in newspapers at home, and hurrying to vote on election days.

There is another side to the object. A learned professor of a western college told me abundance of English news, but declared himself ignorant of everything that had passed in the home portion of the political world. He never took any interest in politics. What would be the use of his disturbing himself? How far does one man's vote go? He does more good by showing himself above such affairs.

A clergyman in the north was anxious to assure me that elections are merely personal matters, and do not affect the happiness of the people. It matters not to him, for instance, who is in office, and what party in politics is uppermost: life goes on the same to him. This gentleman had probably never heard of the old lady who said that she did not care what revolutions happened, as long as she had her roast chicken, and her little game at cards. But that old lady did not live in a republic, or perhaps even she might have perceived that there would have been no security for roast chickens and cards, if all were to neglect political action but those who want political power and profit. In a democracy, every man is supposed to be his own security for life and property: and, if a man devolves his political charge upon others, he must lay his accounts for not being so well taken care of as he might be.

A member of Congress gave me instances of what would have been the modifications of certain public affairs, but for the apathy of the minority about the use of their suffrage. If citizens regulate their exertions by the probabilities of immediate success, instead of by their faith in their own convictions, it is indeed no wonder if the minority leave everything to their adversaries; but this is not the way for men to show themselves worthy of the possession of political rights. A public man told me that it would be a great point gained, if every citizen could be induced to vote, at least once a year. So far is it from being true that all Americans are the bustling politicians the English have been apt to suppose. If such political bustle should be absurd, the actual apathy is something worse.

There is another cause for the reluctance to vote which is complained of by the best friends of the people; but it is almost too humbling and painful to be discussed. Some are afraid to vote!

There is not, in the United States, as with us, a system of intimidation exercised by the rich over the poor. In the country, there are no landlords and tenants at will. In the towns, the tradesmen do not stand in need of the patronage of the rich. Though they vote by ballot, and any man who chooses it may vote secretly, (and many do upon occasion,) there is rarely any need of such protection. If the educated and principled men of the community, as they are esteemed, fall back into idleness and silence, when the time comes for a struggle for principles, and there is a danger of disappointing expectations, and hurting feelings, their country has little to thank them for. They are the men from whom the open discharge of duty is looked for; they are the men who should show that political obligation is above private regards.

The fear of opinion sometimes takes the form of an almost insane dread of responsibility. There are occasions when public men, unable to judge for themselves of particular classes of circumstances, are obliged to ask advice of their friends and supporters. Happy he who obtains a full and true answer from any one! The chances against this are in proportion to the importance of the case. The illustrative details which might be given,—showing the general uniformity, with particular diversity, of the conduct of the advisers,—would be amusing if they were not too sad.

It is felt, and understood, in the United States, that their near future in politics is indiscernible. Odd, unexpected circumstances, determining the present, are perpetually turning up. Almost every man has his convictions as to what the state of affairs will be, in the gross, a century hence. Scarcely any man will venture a conjecture as to what will have happened next spring. This is the very condition, if the people could but see it, for the exercise of faith in principles.

Allegiance to Law

It is notorious that there is a remarkable failure in this department of political morals among certain parties in the United States. The mobbing events of the last few years are celebrated; the abolition riots in New York and Boston; the burning of the Charleston Convent; the bank riots at Baltimore; the burning of the mails at Charleston; the hangings by Lynch-law at Vickesburgh; the burning alive of a man of colour at St Louis; the subsequent proceedings there towards the students of Marion College; and the abolition riots at Cincinnati. Here is a fearful list!

The first question that arises is, who has done these things? Whose hands have lighted green fagots round a living man? and strung up a dozen or twenty citizens on the same gallows? and fired and razed houses; and sent a company of trembling nuns flying for their lives at midnight? Here is evidence enough of ignorance,—of desperate, brutal ignorance. Whose ignorance?

In Europe, the instantaneous and natural persuasion of men who hear the tidings is, that the lowest classes in America have risen against the higher. In Europe, desperate, brutal ignorance is the deepest curse in the cursed life of the pauper and the serf. In Europe, mobbing is usually the outbreak of exasperated misery against laws which oppress, and an aristocracy which insults humanity. Europeans, therefore, naturally assume that the gentry of the United States are the sinned against, and the poor the sinners, in their social disturbances. They draw conclusions against popular government, and suppose it proved that universal suffrage dissolves society into chaos. They picture to themselves a rabble of ragged, desperate workmen, with torches in their hands; while the gentry look on in dismay, or tremble within their houses.

It is not so. I was informed, twenty times over, by gentlemen, that the Boston mob of last year was wholly composed of gentlemen. The only working man in it was the truckman who saved the victim. They were the gentlemen of St Louis who burned the black man, and banished the students of Marion College. They were the gentlemen of Cincinnati who denounced the abolitionists, and raised the persecution against them. They were the magistrates and gentry of Vickesburgh who hanged way-farers, gamblers, and slaves in a long row. They were the gentlemen of Charleston who broke open the Post Office, and violated its sacred function, to the insult and injury of the whole country.

One complete narrative of a riot, for the fidelity of which I can vouch, will expose the truth of the case better than a list of deeds of horror which happened beyond my sight. It is least revolting, too, to treat of a case whose terror lies in its existence, more than in its consequences. The actors in the riot, which it was my fortune to understand, were scarcely less guilty than if they had bathed their hands in blood; but it is easier to examine, undisturbed by passion, the case of those whose hands are, to the outward eye, clean.

A very few years ago, certain citizens in New England began to discover that the planters of the south were making white slaves in the north, nearly as successfully as they were propagating black slavery in the territories of the south and west. Charleston and Boston were affectionate friends in old times, and are so still, notwithstanding the hard words that passed between them in nullification days: that is, the merchants and professional men of Boston are fond of Charleston, on account of their commercial relations. This attachment has been carried to such an extreme as to be almost fatal to the liberties of some of the best citizens of the northern city. They found their brothers dismissed from their pastoral charges, their sons expelled from colleges, their friends excluded from professorships, and themselves debarred from literary and social privileges, if they happened to entertain and express opinions unfavourable to the peculiar domestic institution by which Charleston declares it to be her intention to abide. Such is the plea of those citizens of Boston who have formed associations for the purpose of opposing, by moral influence, an institution which they feel to be inconsistent with the first principles of morals and politics. For a considerable time before my visit to that part of the country, they had encountered petty persecutions of almost every conceivable kind. There is no law in Massachusetts by which the free expression of opinion on moral subjects is punishable. I heard many regret the absence of such law. Everything was done that could be done to make up for its absence. Books on any subject, written by persons who avow by association their bad opinion of slavery, are not purchased: clergymen are no longer invited to preach: the proprietors of public rooms will not let them to members of such associations; and the churches are shut against them. Their notices of public meetings are torn in the pulpits, while all notices of other public meetings are read. The newspapers pour contempt and wrath upon them in one continued stream. Bad practices are imputed to them, and their denial is drowned in clamour. As a single instance of this last; I was told so universally in the south and west that the abolitionists of Boston and New York were in the habit of sending incendiary tracts among the slaves, that it never occurred to me to doubt the fact; though I was struck with surprise at never being able to find any one who had seen any one who had actually seen one of these tracts. Nor did it occur to me that as slaves cannot read, verbal messages would be more to the purpose of all parties, as being more effectual and more prudent. Mr Madison made the charge, so did Mr Clay, so did Mr Calhoun, so did every slave-holder and merchant with whom I conversed. I chose afterwards to hear the other side of the whole question; and I found, to my amazement, that this charge was wholly groundless. No Abolition Society of New York or Massachusetts has ever sent any anti-slavery paper south of Washington, except the circulars, addressed to public officers in the States, which were burnt at Charleston. The abolitionists of Boston have been denying this charge ever since it was first made, and offering evidence of its groundlessness; yet the calumny is persisted in, and, no doubt, honestly believed, to this hour, throughout the south, whither the voice of the condemned, stifled by their fellow-citizens, cannot reach.

Only mortal things, however, can be really suffocated; and there has never yet been an instance of a murder of opinion. There seemed, in 1835, so much danger of the abolitionists making themselves heard, that an emphatic contradiction was got up, it was hoped in good time.

The abolitionists had been, they believe illegally, denied by the city authority the use of Faneuil Hall; (called, in memory of revolutionary days, the 'Cradle of Liberty'). Certain merchants and lawyers of Boston held a meeting there, in August, 1835, for the purpose of reprobating the meetings of the abolitionists, and denouncing their measures, while approving of their principles. The less that is said of this meeting,—the deepest of all the disgraces of Boston,—the better. It bears its character in its face. Its avowed object was to put down the expression of opinion by opprobrium, in the absence of gag laws. Of the fifteen hundred who signed the requisition for this meeting, there are many, especially among the younger and more thoughtless, who have long repented of the deed. Some signed in anger; some in fear; many in mistake; and of each of these there are some who would fain, if it were possible, efface their signatures with their blood.

It is an invariable fact, and recognized as such, that meetings held to supply the deficiency of gag laws are the prelude to the violence which supplies the deficiency of executioners under such laws. Every meeting held to denounce opinion is followed by a mob. This was so well understood in the present case that the abolitionists were warned that if they met again publicly, they would be answerable for the disorders that might ensue. The abolitionists pleaded that this was like making the rich man answerable for the crime of the thief who robbed him, on the ground that if the honest man had not been rich, the thief would not have been tempted to rob him. The abolitionists also perceived how liberty of opinion and of speech depended on their conduct in this crisis; and they resolved to yield to no threats of illegal violence; but to hold their legal meeting, pursuant to advertisement, for the despatch of their usual business. One remarkable feature of the case was that this heavy responsibility rested upon women. It was a ladies' meeting that was in question. Upon consultation, the ladies agreed that they should never have sought the perilous duty of defending liberty of opinion and speech at the last crisis; but, as such a service seemed manifestly appointed to them, the women were ready.

On the 21st of October, they met, pursuant to advertisement, at the office of their association, No. 46, Washington Street. Twenty-five reached their room, by going three-quarters of an hour before the appointed time. Five more made their way up with difficulty through the crowd. A hundred more were turned back by the mob.

They knew that a hand-bill had been circulated on the Exchange, and posted on the City Hall, and throughout the city, the day before, which declared that Thompson, the abolitionist, was to address them; and invited the citizens, under promise of pecuniary reward, to 'snake Thompson out, and bring him to the tar-kettle before dark.' The ladies had been warned that they would be killed, 'as sure as fate', if they showed themselves on their own premises that day. They therefore informed the mayor that they expected to be attacked. The reply of the city marshal was, 'You give us a great deal of trouble.'

The committee-room was surrounded, and gazed into by a howling, shrieking mob of gentlemen, while the twenty-five ladies sat perfectly still, awaiting the striking of the clock. When it struck, they opened their meeting. They were questioned as to whether Thompson was there in disguise; to which they made no reply.

They began, as usual, with prayer; the mob shouting 'Hurra! here comes Judge Lynch!' Before they had done, the partition gave way, and the gentlemen hurled missiles at the lady who was presiding. The secretary having risen, and begun to read her report, rendered inaudible by the uproar, the mayor entered, and insisted upon their going home, to save their lives. The purpose of their meeting was answered: they had asserted their principle; and they now passed out, two and two, amidst the execration of some thousands of gentlemen;—persons who had silver shrines to protect. The ladies, to the number of fifty, walked to the house of one of their members, and were presently struck to the heart by the news that Garrison was in the hands of the mob. Garrison is the chief apostle of abolition in the United States. He had escorted his wife to the meeting; and, after offering to address the ladies, and being refused, out of regard to his safety, had left the room, and, as they supposed, the premises. He was, however, in the house when the ladies left it. He was hunted for by the mob; dragged from behind some planks where he had taken refuge, and conveyed into the street. Here his hat was trampled under-foot, and brick-bats were aimed at his bare head; a rope was tied round him, and thus he was dragged through the streets. His young wife saw all this. Her exclamation was, 'I think my husband will be true to his principles. I am sure my husband will not deny his principles.' Her confidence was just. Garrison never denies his principles.

He was saved by a stout truckman, who, with his bludgeon, made his way into the crowd, as if to attack the victim. He protected the bare head, and pushed on towards a station house, whence the mayor's officers issued, and pulled in Garrison, who was afterwards put into a coach. The mob tried to upset the coach, and throw down the horses; but the driver laid about him with his whip, and the constables with their staves, and Garrison was safely lodged in jail: for protection; for he had committed no offence.

Before the mayor ascended the stairs to dismiss the ladies, he had done a very remarkable deed;—he had given permission to two gentlemen to pull down and destroy the anti-slavery sign, bearing the inscription, 'Anti-Slavery Office',—which had hung for two years, as signs do hang before public offices in Boston. The plea of the mayor is, that he hoped the rage of the mob would thus be appeased: that is, he gave them leave to break the laws in one way, lest they should in another. The citizens followed up this deed of the mayor with one no less remarkable. They elected these two rioters members of the State legislature, by a large majority, within ten days.

I passed through the mob some time after it had begun to assemble. I asked my fellow-passengers in the stage what it meant. They supposed it was a busy foreign-post day, and that this occasioned an assemblage of gentlemen about the post-office. They pointed out to me that there were none but gentlemen. We were passing through from Salem, fifteen miles north of Boston, to Providence, Rhode Island; and were therefore uninformed of the events and expectations of the day. On the morrow, a visitor who arrived at Providence from Boston told us the story; and I had thenceforth an excellent opportunity of hearing all the remarks that could be made by persons of all ways of thinking and feeling, on this affair.

It excited much less attention than it deserved; less than would be believed possible by those at a distance who think more seriously of persecution for opinion, and less tenderly of slavery than a great many of the citizens of Boston. To many in the city of Boston the story I have told would be news and to yet more in the country, who know that some trouble was caused by abolition meetings in the city, but who are not aware that their own will, embodied in the laws, was overborne to gratify the mercenary interests of a few, and the political fears of a few more.

The first person with whom I conversed about this riot was the president of a university. We were perfectly agreed as to the causes and character of the outrage. This gentleman went over to Boston for a day or two; and when he returned, I saw him again. He said he was happy to tell me that we have been needlessly making ourselves uneasy about the affair: that there had been no mob, the persons assembled having been all gentlemen.

An eminent lawyer at Boston was one of the next to speak upon it. 'O, there was no mob,' said he. 'I was there myself, and saw they were all gentlemen. They were all in fine broad-cloth.'

'Not the less a mob for that,' said I.

'Why, they protected Garrison. He received no harm. They protected Garrison.'

'From whom, or what?'

'O, they would not really hurt him. They only wanted to show that they would not have such a person live among them.'

'Why should not he live among them? Is he guilty under any law?'

'He is an insufferable person to them.'

'So may you be to-morrow. If you can catch Garrison breaking the laws, punish him under the laws. If you cannot, he has as much right to live where he pleases as you.'

Two law pupils of this gentleman presently entered. One approved of all that had been done, and praised the spirit of the gentlemen of Boston. I asked whether they had not broken the law. Yes. I asked him if he knew what the law was. Yes; but it could not be always kept. If a man was caught in a house setting it on fire, the owner might shoot him; and Garrison was such an incendiary. I asked him for proof. He had nothing but hearsay to give. The case, as I told him, came to this. A. says Garrison is an incendiary. B. says he is not. A. proceeds on his own opinion to break the law, lest Garrison should do so.

The other pupil told me of the sorrow of heart with which he saw the law, the life of the republic, set at naught by those who should best understand its nature and value. He saw that the time was come for the true men of the republic to oppose a bold front to the insolence of the rich and the powerful, who were bearing down the liberties of the people for a matter of opinion. The young men, he saw, must brace themselves up against the tyranny of the monied mob, and defend the law; or the liberties of the country were gone. I afterwards found many such among the young men of the wealthier classes. If they keep their convictions, they and their city are safe.

No prosecutions followed. I asked a lawyer, an abolitionist, why. He said there would be difficulty in getting a verdict; and, if it was obtained, the punishment would be merely a fine, which would be paid on the spot, and the triumph would remain with the aggressors. This seemed to me no good reason.

I asked an eminent judge the same question; and whether there was not a public prosecutor who might prosecute for breach of the peace, if the abolitionists would not, for the assault on Garrison. He said it might be done; but he had given his advice against it. Why? The feeling was so strong against the abolitionists,—the rioters were so respectable in the city,—it was better to let the whole affair pass over without notice.

Of others, some knew nothing of it, because it was about such a low set of people; some could not take any interest in what they were tired of hearing about; some had not heard anything of the matter; some thought the abolitionists were served quite right; some were sure the gentlemen of Boston would not do anything improper; and some owned that there was such bad taste and meddlesomeness in the abolitionists, that people of taste kept out of the way of hearing anything about them.

Notwithstanding all this, the body of the people are sound. Many of the young lawyers are resolved to keep on the watch, to maintain the rights of the abolitionists in the legislature, and in the streets of the city. Many hundreds of the working men agreed to leave their work on the first rumour of riot, get sworn in as special constables, and keep the peace against the gentry; acting vigorously against the mob ringleaders, if such should be the magistrates of Boston themselves. I visited many of the villages in Massachusetts; and there everything seemed right. The country people are abolitionists, by nature and education, and they see the iniquity of mob-law. A sagacious gentleman told me that it did him good to hear, in New York, of this mob, because it proved the rest of Massachusetts to be in a sound state. It is always 'Boston *versus* Massachusetts'; and when the city, or the aristocracy there, who think themselves the city, are very vehemently wrong, it is a plain proof that the country people are eminently right. This may, for the humour of the thing, be strongly put; but there is much truth in it.

The philosophy of the case is very easy to understand; and supremely important to be understood.

The law, in a republic, is the embodiment of the will of the people. As long as the republic is in a natural and healthy state, containing no anomaly, and exhibiting no gross vices, the function of the law works easily, and is understood and reverenced. Its punishments bear only upon individuals, who have the opposition of society to contend with for violating its will, and who are helpless against the righteous visitations of the law.

If there be any anomaly among the institutions of a republic, the function of the law is certain to be disturbed, sooner or later: and that disturbance is usually the symptom by the exhibition of which the anomaly is first detected, and then cured. It was so with free-masonry. It will be so with slavery; and with every institution inconsistent with the fundamental principles of democracy. The process is easily traceable. The worldly interests of the minority,—of perhaps a single class,—are bound up with the anomaly:—of the minority, because, if the majority had been interested in any anti-republican institution, the republic would not have existed. The minority may go on for a length of time in apparent harmony with the expressed will of the many,—the law. But the time comes when their anomaly clashes with the law. For instance, the merchants of the north trade in products which are, as they believe, created out of a denial that all men are born free and equal, and that the just powers of rulers are derived from the consent of the governed; while the contrary principles are the root which produces the law. Which is to be given up, when both cannot be held? If the pecuniary interest of merchants is incompatible with freedom of speech in fellow-citizens, which is to suffer?—The will of the majority, the lawmaker, is to decide. But it takes some time to awaken the will of the majority; and till it awakes, the interest of the faction is active, and overbears the law. The retribution is certain; the result is safe. But the evils meanwhile are so tremendous, that no exertion should be spared to open the eyes of the majority to the insults offered to its will.

One compound fallacy is allowed daily to pass unexposed and unstigmatized. 'You make no allowance,' said a friend who was strangely bewildered by it,—'you make no allowance for the great number of excellent people who view the anomaly and the law as you do, but who keep quiet, because they sincerely believe that by speaking and acting they should endanger the Union.' This explains the conduct of a crowd of 'excellent people', neither merchants, nor the friends of slave-holders, nor approving slavery, or mobbing, or persecution for opinion; but who revile or satirize the abolitionists, and, for the rest, hold their tongues. But is it possible that such do not see that if slavery be wrong, and if it be indeed bound up with the Union, the Union must fall? Every day which passes over the unredressed wrongs of any class which a republic holds in her bosom; every day which brings persecution on those who act out the principles which all profess; every day which adds a sanction to brute force, and impairs the sacredness of law; every day which prolongs impunity to the oppressor and discouragement to the oppressed, is a more evil day than that which should usher in the work of renovation.

But the dictum is not true. This bitter satire upon the constitution, and upon all who have complacently lived under it, is not true. The Union is not incompatible with freedom of speech. The Union does not forbid men to act according to their convictions. The Union has never depended for its existence on hypocrisy, insult, and injury; and it never will.

Let citizens but take heed individually to respect the law, and see that others do,-that no neighbour transgresses it, that no statesman despises it unrebuked, that no child grows up ignorant or careless of it; and the Union is as secure as the ground they tread upon. If this be not done, everything is in peril, for the season; not only the Union, but property, home, life and integrity.

Sectional Prejudice

It is the practice at Washington to pay the Members of Congress, not only a per diem allowance, but their travelling expenses; at so much per twenty miles. Two Members of Congress from Missouri made charges widely different in amount. Complaints were made that the Members were not confined to a mail route, and that the country had to pay for any digressions the honourable gentlemen might be in the humour to make. Upon this, a Member observed that, so far from wishing to confine the congressional travellers to a mail route, he would, if possible, prescribe the condition that they should travel, both in coming and going, through every State of the Union. Any money thus expended, would be, he considered, a cheap price to pay for the conquest of prejudices and dispersion of unfriendly feelings, which would be the consequence of the rambles he proposed.

The southern members love to boast of the increase of colleges, so that every State will soon be educating its own youth. The northern men miss the sweet sounds of acknowledgment which used to meet their ears, as often as past days were referred to-the grateful mention of the New England retreats where the years of preparation for active life were spent. The southern men are mortified at the supposition that everything intellectual must come out of New England. When they boast that Virginia has produced almost all their Presidents, they are met by the boast that New England has furnished almost all the school-masters, professors, and clergy of the country. While the north is still fostering a reverence for the Union, the south loses no opportunity of enlarging lovingly on the virtue of passionate attachment to one's native state.

There is much nature and much reason in all this. It is true that there is advantage in the youth of the whole country being brought together within college walls, at the age when warm friendships are formed. They can hardly quarrel very desperately in Congress, after having striven, and loved, and learned together, in their bright early days. The cadets at West Point spoke warmly to me of this. They told me that when a youth is coming from afar, the youths who have arrived from an opposite point of the compass prepare to look cold upon him and quiz him, and receive him frigidly enough; but the second Sunday seldom comes round before they wonder at him and themselves, and acknowledge that he might almost have been born in their own State. On the other hand, it is true that it would be an absurdity and a hardship to the dwellers in the south and west to have no means of educating their youth at home; but to be obliged to send them a thousand miles in pursuit of necessary learning. It is also true that medical colleges should abound; that peculiar diseases, incident to climate and locality, may be studied on the spot. In this, as in many other cases, some good must be sacrificed for the attainment of a greater good.

The question is, need sectional prejudices increase under the new arrangements? Are there no means of counteracting this great evil, except the ancient methods? Is West Point the last spot whereon common interests may rally, and whence state jealousies may be excluded?

I should be sorry if the answer were unfavourable; for this Sectional Prejudice, carried beyond the point of due political vigilance, is folly,—childish folly. Events prove it to be so.

Yet 'hatred' is not too strong a term for this sectional prejudice. Many a time in America have I been conscious of that pang and shudder which are felt only in the presence of hatred. I question whether the enmity between the British and the Americans, at the most exasperating crisis of the war, could ever have been more intense than some that I have seen flashing in the eyes, and heard from the lips, of Americans against fellow-citizens in distant sections of their country. I have scarcely known whether to laugh or to mourn when I have been told that the New England people are all pedlars or canting priests; that the people of the south are all heathens; and those of the west all barbarians.

The most mortifying instance that I witnessed of this sectional prejudice was at Cincinnati. It was the most mortifying, on two accounts; because it did not give way before intercourse; and because its consequences are likely to be very serious to the city and, if it spreads, to the whole west.

Less than fifty years ago, it contained fewer than a hundred whites; and buffalo lodged in a cane brake where the city now stands; while the State at present contains upwards of a million of inhabitants, the city between thirty and forty thousand; and Cincinnati has four daily, and five or six weekly, newspapers, besides a variety of other periodicals.

The most remarkable circumstance, and the most favourable, with regard to the peopling of Cincinnati is, that its population contains contributions of almost every element that goes to constitute society; and each in its utmost vigour. There are here few of the arbitrary associations which exist among the members of other societies. Young men come with their wives, in all directions, from afar; with no parents, cousins, sects, or parties about them. Here is an assemblage from almost every nation under heaven,—a contribution from the resources of almost every country; and all unburdened, and ready for natural association and vigorous action. Like takes to like, and friendships are formed from congeniality, and not from accident or worldly design. But here it is that sectional prejudice interferes, to set up arbitrary associations where, of all places, they should be shunned. There are many New Englanders among the clergy, lawyers, and merchants; and this portion of society will not freely mix with the westerners. When I was one day expressing my admiration, and saying that it was a place for people of ambition, worldly or philanthropic, to live in, one of its noblest citizens said, 'Yes, we have a new creation going on here; won't you come and dabble in the mud?' If the merchants of Genoa were princes, the citizens of Cincinnati, as of every first city of a new region, are princes and prophets at once. They can foresee the future, if they please; and shape it, if they will: and petty personal regards are unworthy of such a destiny. It is melancholy to see how the crusading chiefs quarrelled for precedence on the soil of the Holy Land: it would be more so to see the leaders of this new enterprise desecrating their higher mission by a like contention.

Citizenship of People of Colour

Before I entered New England, while I was ascending the Mississippi, I was told by a Boston gentleman that the people of colour in the New England States were perfectly well-treated; that the children were educated in schools provided for them; and that their fathers freely exercised the franchise. This gentleman certainly believed he was telling me the truth. That he, a busy citizen of Boston, should know no better, is now as striking an exemplification of the state of the case to me as a correct representation of the facts would have been. There are two causes for his mistake. He was not aware that the schools for the coloured children in New England are, unless they escape by their insignificance, shut up, or pulled down, or the school-house wheeled away upon rollers over the frontier of a pious State, which will not endure that its coloured citizens should be educated. He was not aware of a gentleman of colour, and his family, being locked out of their own hired pew in a church, because their white brethren will not worship by their side. But I will not proceed with an enumeration of injuries, too familiar to Americans to excite any feeling but that of weariness; and too disgusting to all others to be endured. The other cause of this gentleman's mistake was, that he did not, from long custom, feel some things to be injuries, which he would call anything but good treatment, if he had to bear them himself. Would he think it good treatment to be forbidden to eat with fellow-citizens; to be assigned to a particular gallery in his church; to be excluded from college, from municipal office, from professions, from scientific and literary associations? If he felt himself excluded from every department of society, but its humiliations and its drudgery, would he declare himself to be 'perfectly well-treated in Boston'? Not a word more of statement is needed.

    The coloured race are citizens. They stand, as such, in the law, and in the acknowledgment of every one who knows the law. They are citizens, yet their houses and schools are pulled down, and they can obtain no remedy at law. They are thrust out of offices, and excluded from the most honourable employments, and stripped of all the best benefits of society by fellow-citizens who, once a year, solemnly lay their hands on their hearts, and declare that all men are born free and equal, and that rulers derive their just powers from the consent of the governed.

This system of injury is not wearing out. Lafayette, on his last visit to the United States, expressed his astonishment at the increase of the prejudice against colour. He remembered, he said, how the black soldiers used to mess with the whites in the revolutionary war. It should ever be remembered that America is the country of the best friends the coloured race has ever had. The more truth there is in the assertions of the oppressors of the blacks, the more heroism there is in their friends. The greater the excuse for the pharisees of the community, the more divine is the equity of the redeemers of the coloured race. If it be granted that the coloured race are naturally inferior, naturally depraved, disgusting, cursed,—it must be granted that it is a heavenly charity which descends among them to give such solace as it can to their incomprehensible existence. As long as the excuses of the one party go to enhance the merit of the other, the society is not to be despaired of, even with this poisonous anomaly at its heart.

Happily, however, the coloured race is not cursed by God, as it is by some factions of his children. The less clear-sighted of them are pardonable for so believing. Circumstances, for which no living man is answerable, have generated an erroneous conviction in the feeble mind of man, which sees not beyond the actual and immediate. No remedy could ever have been applied, unless stronger minds than ordinary had been brought into the case. But it so happens, wherever there is an anomaly, giant minds rise up to overthrow it: minds gigantic, not in understanding, but in faith. While the mass of common men and women are despising, and disliking, and fearing, and keeping down the coloured race, blinking the fact that they are citizens, the few of Nature's aristocracy are putting forth a strong hand to lift up this degraded race out of oppression, and their country from the reproach of it. If they were but one or two, trembling and toiling in solitary energy, the world afar would be confident of their success. But they number hundreds and thousands; and if ever they feel a passing doubt of their progress, it is only because they are pressed upon by the meaner multitude. Over the sea, no one doubts of their victory. It is as certain as that the risen sun will reach the meridian. Already have people of colour crossed the thresholds of many whites, as guests, not as drudges or beggars. Already are they admitted to worship, and to exercise charity, among the whites.

The world has heard and seen enough of the reproach incurred by America, on account of her coloured population. It is now time to look for the fairer side. Already is the world beyond the sea beginning to think of America, less as the country of the double-faced pretender to the name of Liberty, than as the home of the single-hearted, clear-eyed Presence which, under the name of Abolitionism, is majestically passing through the land which is soon to be her throne.

Political Non-Existence of Women

One of the fundamental principles announced in the Declaration of Independence is, that governments derive their just powers from the consent of the governed. How can the political condition of women be reconciled with this?

Governments in the United States have power to tax women who hold property; to divorce them from their husbands; to fine, imprison, and execute them for certain offences. Whence do these governments derive their powers? They are not just, as they are not derived from the consent of the women thus governed.

Governments in the United States have power to enslave certain women; and also to punish other women for inhuman treatment of such slaves. Neither of these powers are just; not being derived from the consent of the governed.

Governments decree to women in some States half their husbands' property; in others one-third. In some, a woman, on her marriage, is made to yield all her property to her husband; in others, to retain a portion, or the whole, in her own hands. Whence do governments derive the unjust power of thus disposing of property without the consent of the governed?

The democratic principle condemns all this as wrong; and requires the equal political representation of all rational beings. Children, idiots, and criminals, during the season of sequestration, are the only fair exceptions.

The case is so plain that I might close it here; but it is interesting to inquire how so obvious a decision has been so evaded as to leave to women no political rights whatever. The question has been asked, from time to time, in more countries than one, how obedience to the laws can be required of women, when no woman has, either actually or virtually, given any assent to any law. No plausible answer has, as far as I can discover, been offered; for the good reason, that no plausible answer can be devised. The most principled democratic writers on government have on this subject sunk into fallacies, as disgraceful as any advocate of despotism has adduced. In fact, they have thus sunk from being, for the moment, advocates of despotism. Jefferson in America, and James Mill at home, subside, for the occasion, to the level of the author of the Emperor of Russia's Catechism for the young Poles.

Jefferson says,[1] 'Were our State a pure democracy, in which all the inhabitants should meet together to transact all their business, there would yet be excluded from their deliberations,

'1. Infants, until arrived at years of discretion;

'2. Women, who, to prevent depravation of morals, and ambiguity of issue, could not mix promiscuously in the public meetings of men;

'3. Slaves, from whom the unfortunate state of things with us takes away the rights of will and of property.'

If the slave disqualification, here assigned, were shifted up under the head of Women, their case would be nearer the truth than as it now stands. Woman's lack of will and of property, is more like the true cause of her exclusion from the representation, than that which is actually set down against her. As if there could be no means of conducting public affairs but by promiscuous meetings! As if there would be more danger in promiscuous meetings for political business than in such meetings for worship, for oratory, for music, for dramatic entertainments,—for any of the thousand transactions of civilized life! The plea is not worth another word.

Mill says, with regard to representation, in his Essay on Government, 'One thing is pretty clear; that all those individuals, whose interests are involved in those of other individuals, may be struck off without inconvenience. . . . In this light, women may be regarded, the interest of almost all of whom is involved, either in that of their fathers or in that of their husbands.'

The true democratic principle is, that no person's interests can be, or can be ascertained to be, identical with those of any other person. This allows the exclusion of none but incapables.

The interests of women who have fathers and husbands can never be identical with theirs, while there is a necessity for laws to protect women against their husbands and fathers. This statement is not worth another word.

Some who desire that there should be an equality of property between men and women, oppose representation, on the ground that political duties would be incompatible with the other duties which women have to discharge. The reply to this is, that women are the best judges here. God has given time and power for the discharge of all duties; and, if he had not, it would be for women to decide which they would take, and which they would leave. But their guardians follow the ancient fashion of deciding what is best for their wards. The Emperor of Russia discovers when a coat of arms and title do not agree with a subject prince. The King of France early perceives that the air of Paris does not agree with a free-thinking foreigner. The English Tories feel the hardship that it would be to impose the franchise on every artizan, busy as he is in getting his bread. The Georgian planter perceives the hardship that freedom would be to his slaves. And the best friends of half the human race peremptorily decide for them as to their rights, their duties, their feelings, their powers. In all these cases, the persons thus cared for feel that the abstract decision rests with themselves; that, though they may be compelled to submit, they need not acquiesce.

I cannot enter upon the commonest order of pleas of all;—those which relate to the virtual influence of woman; her swaying the judgment and will of man through the heart; and so forth. One might as well try to dissect the morning mist. I knew a gentleman in America who told me how much rather he had be a woman than the man he is;—a professional man, a father, a citizen. He would give up all this for a woman's influence. I thought he was mated too soon. He should have married a lady, also of my acquaintance, who would not at all object to being a slave, if ever the blacks should have the upper hand; 'it is so right that the one race should be subservient to the other!' Or rather,—I thought it a pity that the one could not be a woman, and the other a slave; so that an injured individual of each class might be exalted into their places, to fulfil and enjoy the duties and privileges which they despise, and, in despising, disgrace.

That woman has power to represent her own interests, no one can deny till she has been tried. The modes need not be discussed here: they must vary with circumstances. The fearful and absurd images which are perpetually called up to perplex the question,— images of women on woolsacks in England, and under canopies in America, have nothing to do with the matter. The principle being once established, the methods will follow, easily, naturally, and under a remarkable transmutation of the ludicrous into the sublime. The kings of Europe would have laughed mightily, two centuries ago, at the idea of a commoner, without robes, crown, or sceptre, stepping into the throne of a strong nation. Yet who dared to laugh when Washington's super-royal voice greeted the New World from the presidential chair, and the old world stood still to catch the echo?

The principle of the equal rights of both halves of the human race is all we have to do with here. It is the true democratic principle which can never be seriously controverted, and only for a short time evaded. Governments can derive their just powers only from the consent of the governed.

NOTES

1. Correspondence vol. iv. p. 295.

KARL MARX

1818–1883
GERMANY

Major Works

1844   *The Economic and Philosophic Manuscripts of l844*
1845–6 *The German Ideology*
1847   *The Poverty of Philosophy*
1848   *The Communist Manifesto*
1857–8 *The Grundrisse: Foundations of the Critique of Political Economy*
1859   *A Contribution to the Critique of Political Economy*
1862–3 *Capital: A Critique of Political Economy*, vol. I
1869   *The 18th Brumaire of Louis Bonaparte*

> In the social production of their life, [men] enter into definite relations that are indispensable and independent of their will, relations of production which correspond to a definite stage of development of their material productive forces. The sum total of these relations of production constitutes the economic structure of society, the real foundations, on which rises a legal and political superstructure and to which correspond definite forms of consciousness. The mode of production in material life conditions the social, political and intellectual life processes in general. It is not the consciousness of men that determines their being, but on the contrary, their social being that determines their consciousness.[1]

> The ideas of the ruling class are in every epoch the ruling ideas, i.e., the class which is the ruling *material* force of society is at the same time its ruling *intellectual* force. The class which has the means of material production at its disposal, has control at the same time over the means of mental production, so that thereby, generally speaking, the ideas of those who lack the means of the mental production are subject to it.[2]
>
> —*Karl Marx*

Whenever one posits Marx among the major sociological theorists, one must ultimately justify the reason for doing so. Marx was a complex social thinker whose ideas have transformed many political regimes and have also been appropriated by a variety of academic disciplines. He is often classified as a philosopher, a term not unusual for several other classical sociologists. He is also considered to be an economist and a political scientist. Each academic discipline chooses the sphere of Marx's work appropriate to its particular focus of study.

In placing Marx within the domain of sociology, we emphasize Marx the dialectician. His dialectical mode of analysis, although derived from Hegel's dialectics of ideas, differed in that Marx situated his dialectics within the social relations of the material world: materialism. Marx's conscious move away from Hegel's philosophical idealism enabled him to explore the nature of the labour process in capitalist society. He saw it as economically exploitive, denying individuals the right to fulfill their creative potentials. His analyses focus on the social relationships that develop among people during the process of production, relationships between those who own and control the means of production and those who do not. For Marx, when an individual labours merely for subsistence, such labour is somehow forced and hence alienated. Under such conditions, individuals are alienated not only from what they produce, given the nature of the productive process, but also from themselves and from others. This alienation would end, he argues, with the abolition of private property and the class relationships that emerge from the ownership and non-ownership of property. In essence, there would then be no class struggle.

The distinctive feature of his analysis is that it identifies economic factors as those that shape the social structure. He argues that those in the same economic position tend to share a common interest and come together to protect that interest. This concentration of common interests is more apparent among the powerful in society. Among the less powerful it is more or less non-existent, for the ideology of the dominant class hinders among the less powerful the development of the class consciousness necessary for them to recognize their class identity and take social action. In capitalist societies the process is hampered by the entire state apparatus—political, economic, and social. In modern societies, the means of mental production (i.e., systems of mass communication) play a dominant role.

The work of Marx was informed by a historical analysis that he saw as crucial to an understanding of social change. He has argued that human beings will have to intervene in history to bring about change. 'Men make their own history, but they do not make it just as they please; they do not make it under circumstances chosen by themselves, but under circumstances directly encountered from the past.'[3]

Marx's specific contribution to sociology is his analysis of power, domination, ideological legitimation, alienation, and class consciousness in capitalist societies. His methodological approach to these specific problems is instructive.

Notes

1. Karl Marx, Preface to *A Critique of Political Economy*, in David McLellan, ed., *Karl Marx: Selected Writings* (New York: Oxford University Press, 1977), 389.

2. Karl Marx and Friedrich Engels, *The German Ideology* (New York: International Publishers, 1970), 64.
3. Karl Marx, *The 18th Brumaire of Louis Bonaparte*, in McLellan, ed., *Karl Marx: Selected Writings*, 300.

THE MATERIALIST CONCEPTION OF HISTORY

Preface to A Contribution to the Critique of Political Economy

I examine the system of bourgeois economics in the following order: *capital, landed property, wage labour; state, foreign trade, world market*. Under the first three headings, I investigate the economic conditions of life of the three great classes into which modern bourgeois society is divided; the interconnection of the three other headings is obvious at a glance. The first section of the first book, which deals with capital, consists of the following chapters: 1. Commodities; 2. Money, or simple circulation; 3. Capital in general. The first two chapters form the contents of the present part. The total material lies before me in the form of monographs, which were written at widely separated periods, for self-clarification, not for publication, and whose coherent elaboration according to the plan indicated will be dependent on external circumstances.

I am omitting a general introduction which I had jotted down because on closer reflection any anticipation of results still to be proved appears to me to be disturbing, and the reader who on the whole desires to follow me must be resolved to ascend from the particular to the general. A few indications concerning the course of my own politico-economic study may, on the other hand, appear in place here.

I was taking up law, which discipline, however, I only pursued as a subordinate subject along with philosophy and history. In the year 1842–43, as editor of the *Rheinische Zeitung*, I experienced for the first time the embarrassment of having to take part in discussions on so-called material interests. The proceedings of the Rhenish Landtag on thefts of wood and parcelling of landed property, the official polemic which Herr von Schaper, the *Oberpräsident* of the Rhine Province, opened against the *Rheinische Zeitung* on the conditions of the Moselle peasantry, and finally debates on free trade and protective tariffs provided the first occasions for occupying myself with economic questions. On the other hand, at that time when the good will 'to go further' greatly outweighed knowledge of the subject, a philosophically weakly tinged echo of French socialism and communism made itself audible in the *Rheinische Zeitung*. I declared myself against this amateurism, but frankly confessed at the same time in a controversy with the *Allgemeine Augsburger Zeitung*, that my previous studies did not permit me even to venture any judgement on the content of the French tendencies. Instead, I eagerly seized on the illusion of the managers of the *Rheinische Zeitung*, who thought that by a weaker attitude on the part of the paper they could secure a remission of the death sentence passed upon it, to withdraw from the public stage into the study.

The first work which I undertook for a solution of the doubts which assailed me was a critical review of the Hegelian philosophy of right,[1] a work the introduction[2] to which appeared in 1844 in the *Deutsch-Französische Jahrbücher*, published in Paris. My investigation led to the result that the legal relations as well as forms of state are to be grasped neither from themselves nor from the so-called general development of the human mind, but rather have their roots in the material conditions of life, the sum total of which Hegel, following the example of the Englishmen and Frenchmen of the eighteenth century, combines under the name of 'civil society', that, however, the anatomy of civil society is to be sought in political economy. The investigation of the latter, which I began in Paris, I continued in Brussels, whither I had emigrated in consequence of an expulsion order of M. Guizot. The general result at which I arrived and which, once won, served as a guiding thread for my studies, can be briefly formulated as follows: In the social production of their life, men enter into definite relations that are indispensable and independent of their will, relations of production which correspond to a definite stage of development of their material productive forces. The sum total of these relations of production constitutes the economic structure of society, the real foundation, on which rises a legal and political superstructure and to which correspond definite forms of social consciousness. The mode of production of material life conditions the social, political and intellectual life process in general. It is not the consciousness of men that determines their being, but, on the contrary, their social being that determines their consciousness. At a certain stage of their development, the material productive forces of society come in conflict with the existing relations of production, or—what is but a legal expression for the same thing—with the property relations within which they have been at work hitherto. From forms of development of the productive forces these relations turn into their fetters. Then begins an epoch of social revolution. With the change of the economic foundation the entire immense superstructure is more or less rapidly transformed. In considering such transformations a distinction should always be made between the material transformation of the economic conditions of production, which can be determined with the precision of natural science, and the legal, political, religious, aesthetic or philosophic—in short, ideological forms in which men become conscious of this conflict and fight it out. Just as our opinion of an individual is not based on what he thinks of himself, so can we not judge of such a period of transformation by its own consciousness; on the contrary, this consciousness must be explained rather from the contradictions of material life, from the existing conflict between the social productive forces and the relations of production. No social order ever perishes before all the productive forces for which there is room in it have developed; and new, higher relations of production never appear before the material conditions of their existence have matured in the womb of the old society itself. Therefore mankind always sets itself only such tasks as it can solve; since, looking at the matter more closely, it will always be found that the task itself arises only when the material conditions for its solution already exist or are at least in the process of formation. In broad outlines Asiatic, ancient, feudal, and modern bourgeois modes of production can be designated as progressive epochs in the economic formation of society. The bourgeois relations of production are the last antagonistic form of the social process of production—antagonistic not in the sense of individual antagonism, but of one arising from the social conditions of life of the individuals; at the same time the productive forces developing in the womb of bourgeois society create the material conditions for the solution of that antagonism. This social formation brings, therefore, the prehistory of human society to a close.

Friedrich Engels, with whom, since the appearance of his brilliant sketch on the criticism of the economic categories[3] (in the *Deutsch-Französische Jahrbücher*), I maintained a constant exchange of ideas by correspondence, had by another road (compare his *The Condition of the Working Class in England in 1844*) arrived at the same result as I, and when in the spring of 1845; he also settled in Brussels, we resolved to work out in common the opposition of our view to the ideological view of German philosophy, in fact, to settle accounts with our erstwhile philosophical conscience. The resolve was carried out in the form of a criticism of post-Hegelian philosophy.[4] The manuscript, two large octavo volumes, had long reached its place of publication in Westphalia when we received the news that altered circumstances did not allow of its being printed. We abandoned the manuscript to the gnawing criticism of the mice all the more willingly as we had achieved our main purpose—self-clarification. Of the scattered works in which we put our views before the public at that time, now from one aspect, now from another, I will mention only the *Manifesto of the Communist Party*,[5] jointly written by Engels and myself, and *Discours sur le libre échange* published by me. The decisive points of our view were first scientifically, although only polemically, indicated in my work published in 1847 and directed against Proudhon: *Misère de la Philosophie*, etc. A dissertation written in German on *Wage Labour*,[6] in which I put together my lectures on this subject delivered in the Brussels German Workers' Society, was interrupted, while being printed, by the February Revolution and my consequent forcible removal from Belgium.

The editing of the *Neue Rheinische Zeitung* in 1848 and 1849, and the subsequent events, interrupted my economic studies which could only be resumed in the year 1850 in London. The enormous material for the history of political economy which is accumulated in the British Museum, the favourable vantage point afforded by London for the observation of bourgeois society, and finally the new stage of development upon which the latter appeared to have entered with the discovery of gold in California and Australia, determined me to begin afresh from the very beginning and to work through the new material critically. These studies led partly of themselves into apparently quite remote subjects on which I had to dwell for a shorter or longer period. Especially, however, was the time at my disposal curtailed by the imperative necessity of earning my living. My contributions, during eight years now, to the first English-American newspaper, the *New York Tribune*, compelled an extraordinary scattering of my studies, since I occupy myself with newspaper correspondence proper only in exceptional cases. However, articles on striking economic events in England and on the Continent constituted so considerable a part of my contributions that I was compelled to make myself familiar with practical details which lie outside the sphere of the actual science of political economy.

The sketch of the course of my studies in the sphere of political economy is intended only to show that my views, however they may be judged and however little they coincide with the interested prejudices of the ruling classes, are the result of conscientious investigation lasting many years. But at the entrance to science, as at the entrance to hell, the demand must be posted:

Que si convien lasciare ogni sospetto;
Ogni viltà convien che qui sia morta.[7]

   Karl Marx

London, January 1859   Printed according to the text
First published in the book   of the book
Zur Kritik der politischen   translated from the German
Oekonomie von Karl Marx.
Erstes Heft, Berlin, 1859

NOTES

1. K. Marx, *Contribution to the Critique of Hegel's Philosophy of Right.* —*Ed.*[David McLellan]
2. K. Marx, *Contribution to the Critique of Hegel's Philosophy of Right. Introduction* (see Marx and Engels, *On Religion*, Moscow, 1962, pp. 41–58).— *Ed.*
3. F. Engels, *Outlines of a Critique of Political Economy* (see K. Marx, *Economic and Philosophic Manuscripts of 1844*, Moscow, 1959, pp. 175–309).—*Ed.*
4. Marx and Engels, *The German Ideology.*—*Ed.*
5. See pp. 65–73 of this volume.—*Ed.*
6. K. Marx, *Wage Labour and Capital* (see pp. 00–00 of this volume).—*Ed.*
7. Here all mistrust must be abandoned
    And here must perish every craven thought.
    [Dante, *The Divine Comedy*.].—*Ed.*

THESES ON FEUERBACH

I

The chief defect of all hitherto existing materialism—that of Feuerbach included—is that the thing [*Gegenstand*], reality, sensuousness, is conceived only in the form of the *object* [*Objekt*] or of *contemplation* [*Anshanung*], but not as *human sensuous activity, practice*, not subjectively. Hence it happened that the active side, in contradistinction to materialism, was developed by idealism—but only abstractly, since, of course, idealism does not know real, sensuous activity as such. Feuerbach wants sensuous objects, really differentiated from the thought objects, but he does not conceive human activity itself as *objective* [*gegen-ständliche*] activity. Hence, in the *Essence of Christianity*, he regards the theoretical attitude as the only genuinely human attitude, while practice is conceived and fixed only in its dirty-judaical form of appearance. Hence he does not grasp the significance of 'revolutionary', of 'practical-critical', activity.

II

The question whether objective [*gegenständliche*] truth can be attributed to human thinking is not a question of theory but is a *practical* question. In practice man must prove the truth, that is, the reality and power, the this-sidedness [*Diesseitigkeit*] of his thinking. The dispute over the reality or non-reality of thinking which is isolated from practice is a purely *scholastic* question.

III

The materialist doctrine that men are products of circumstances and upbringing, and that, therefore, changed men are products of other circumstances and changed upbringing, forgets that it is men that change circumstances and that the educator himself needs educating. Hence, this doctrine necessarily arrives at dividing society into two parts, of which one is superior to society (in Robert Owen, for example).

The coincidence of the changing of circumstances and of human activity can be conceived and rationally understood only as revolutionizing practice.

IV

Feuerbach starts out from the fact of religious self-alienation, the duplication of the world into a religious, imaginary world and a real one. His work consists in the dissolution of the religious world into its secular basis. He overlooks the fact that after completing this work, the chief thing still remains to be done. For the fact that the secular foundation detaches itself from itself and establishes itself in the clouds as an independent realm is really only to be explained by the self-cleavage and self-contradictoriness of this secular basis. The latter must itself, therefore, first be understood in its contradiction and then, by the removal of the contradiction, revolutionized in practice. Thus, for instance, once the earthly family is discovered to be the secret of the holy family, the former must then itself be criticized in theory and revolutionized in practice.

V

Feuerbach, not satisfied with *abstract thinking*, appeals to *sensuous contemplation*; but he does not conceive sensuousness as *practical*, human-sensuous activity.

VI

Feuerbach resolves the religious essence into the *human* essence. But the human essence is no abstraction inherent in each single individual. In its reality it is the ensemble of the social relations.

Feuerbach, who does not enter upon a criticism of this real essence, is consequently compelled:

1. To abstract from the historical process and to fix the religious sentiment [*Gemüt*] as something by itself and to presuppose an abstract isolated—human individual.

2. The human essence, therefore, can with him be comprehended only as a 'genus', as an internal, dumb generality which merely naturally unites the many individuals.

VII

Feuerbach, consequently, does not see that the 'religious sentiment' is itself a *social product*, and that the abstract individual whom he analyses belongs in reality to a particular form of society.

VIII

Social life is essentially *practical*. All mysteries which mislead theory to mysticism find their rational solution in human practice and in the comprehension of this practice.

IX

The highest point attained by *contemplative* materialism, that is, materialism which does not understand sensuousness as practical activity, is the contemplation of single individuals in 'civil society'.

X

The standpoint of the old materialism is '*civil*' society; the standpoint of the new is *human* society, or socialized humanity.

XI

The philosophers have only *interpreted* the world, in various ways; the point, however, is to *change* it.

Written by Marx in the spring of 1845
Originally published by Engels in
1888 in the Appendix to the separate
edition of his *Ludwig Feuerbach
and the end of Classical German
Philosophy*

Printed according to the text of the
separate 1888 edition and checked
with the ms. of Karl Marx
Translated from the German

ALIENATED LABOUR

First Manuscript

(XXII) We have begun from the presuppositions of political economy. We have accepted its terminology and its laws. We presupposed private property, the separation of labour, capital and land, as also of wages, profit and rent, the division of labour, competition, the concept of exchange value, etc. From political economy itself, in its own words, we have shown that the worker sinks to the level of a commodity, and to a most miserable commodity, that the misery of the worker increases with the power and volume of his production; that the necessary result of competition is the accumulation of capital in a few hands, and thus a restoration of monopoly in a more terrible form; and finally that the distinction between capitalist and landlord, and between agricultural labourer and industrial worker, must disappear and the whole of society divide into the two classes of property *owners* and propertyless *workers*.

Political economy begins with the fact of private property; it does not explain it. It conceives the *material process* of private property, as this occurs in reality, in general and abstract formulas which then serve it as laws. It does not *comprehend* these laws; that is, it does not show how they arise out of the nature of private property. Political economy provides no explanation of the basis of the distinction of labour from capital, of capital from land. When, for example, the relation of wages to profits is defined, this is explained in terms of the interests of capitalists; in other words, what should be explained is assumed. Similarly, competition is referred to at every point and is explained in terms of external conditions. Political economy tells us nothing about the extent to which these external and apparently accidental conditions are simply the expression of a necessary development. We have seen how exchange itself seems an accidental fact. The only moving forces which political economy recognizes are *avarice* and the *war between the avaricious, competition*.

Just because political economy fails to understand the interconnections within this movement it was possible to oppose the doctrine of competition to that of monopoly, the doctrine of freedom of the crafts to that of the guilds, the doctrine of the division of landed property to that of the great estates; for competition, freedom of crafts, and the division of landed property were conceived only as accidental consequences brought about by will and force, rather than as necessary, inevitable and natural consequences of monopoly, the guild system and feudal property.

Thus we have now to grasp the real connection between this whole system of alienation—private property, acquisitiveness, the separation of labour, capital, and land, exchange and competition, value and the devaluation of man, monopoly and competition and the system of *money*.

Let us not begin our explanation, as does the economist, from a legendary primordial condition. Such a primordial condition does not explain anything; it merely removes the question into a grey and nebulous distance. It asserts as a fact or event what it should deduce, namely, the necessary relation between two things; for example, between the division of labour and exchange. In the same way theology explains the origin of evil by the fall of man; that is, it asserts as a historical fact what it should explain.

We shall begin from a *contemporary* economic fact. The worker becomes poorer the more wealth he produces and the more his production increases in power and extent. The worker becomes an ever cheaper commodity the more goods he creates. The *devaluation* of the human world decreases in direct relation with the *increase in value* of the world of things. Labour does not only create goods; it also produces itself and the worker as a *commodity*, and indeed in the same proportion as it produces goods.

This fact simply implies that the object produced by labour, its product, now stands opposed to it as an *alien being*, as a *power independent* of the producer. The product of labour is labour which has been embodied in an object and turned into a physical thing: this product is an *objectification* of labour. The performance of work is at the same time its objectification. The performance of work appears in the sphere of political economy as a *vitiation* of the worker, objectification as a *loss* and as *servitude to the object*, and appropriation as *alienation*.

So much does the performance of work appear as vitiation that the worker is vitiated to the point of starvation. So much does objectification appear as loss of the object that the worker is deprived of the most essential things not only of life but also of work. Labour itself becomes an object which he can acquire only by the greatest effort and with unpredictable interruptions. So much does the appropriation of the object appear as alienation that the more objects the worker produces the fewer he can possess and the more he falls under the domination of his product, of capital.

All these consequences follow from the fact that the worker is related to the *product of his labour* as to an *alien* object. For it is clear on this presupposition that the more the worker expends himself in work the more powerful becomes the world of objects which he creates in face of himself, the poorer he becomes in his inner life, and the less he belongs to himself. It is just the same as in religion. The more of himself man attributes to God the less he has left in himself. The worker puts his life into the object, and his life then belongs no longer to himself but to the object. The greater his activity, therefore, the less he possesses. What is embodied in the product of his labour is no longer his own. The greater this product is, therefore, the more he is diminished. The *alienation* of the worker in his product means not only that his labour becomes an object, assumes an *external* existence, but that it exists independently, *outside himself*, and alien to him, and that it stands opposed to him as an autonomous power. The life which he has given to the object sets itself against him as an alien and hostile force.

(XXIII) Let us now examine more closely the phenomenon of *objectification*, the worker's production and the *alienation* and *loss* of the object it produces, which is involved in it. The worker can create nothing without *nature*, without the *sensuous external world*. The latter is the material in which his labour is realized, in which it is active, out of which and through which it produces things.

But just as nature affords the *means of existence* of labour in the sense that labour cannot *live* without objects upon which it can be exercised, so also it provides the *means of existence* in a narrower sense; namely the means of physical existence for the *worker* himself. Thus, the more the worker *appropriates* the external world of sensuous nature by his labour the more he deprives himself of *means of existence*, in two respects: first, that the sensuous external world becomes progressively less an object belonging to his labour or a means of existence of his labour, and secondly, that it becomes progressively less a means of existence in the direct sense, a means for the physical subsistence of the worker.

In both respects, therefore, the worker becomes a slave of the object; first, in that he receives an *object of work*, i.e., receives *work*, and secondly that he receives *means of subsistence*. Thus the object enables him to exist, first as a *worker* and secondly, as a *physical subject*. The culmination of this enslavement is that he can only maintain himself as a *physical subject* so far as he is a *worker*, and that it is only as a *physical subject* that he is a worker.

(The alienation of the worker in his object is expressed as follows in the laws of political economy: the more the worker produces the less he has to consume; the more value he creates the more worthless he becomes; the more refined his product the more crude and misshapen the worker; the more civilized the product the more barbarous the worker; the more powerful the work the more feeble the worker; the more the work manifests intelligence the more the worker declines in intelligence and becomes a slave of nature.)

Political economy conceals the alienation in the nature of labour insofar as it does not examine the direct relationship between the worker (work) and production. Labour certainly produces marvels for the rich but it produces privation for the worker. It produces palaces, but hovels for the worker. It produces beauty, but deformity for the worker. It replaces labour by machinery, but it casts some of the workers back into a barbarous kind of work and turns the others into machines. It produces intelligence, but also stupidity and cretinism for the workers.

The direct relationship of labour to its products is the relationship of the worker to the objects of his production. The relationship of property owners to the objects of production and to production itself is merely a *consequence* of this first relationship and confirms it. We shall consider this second aspect later.

Thus, when we ask what is the important relationship of labour, we are concerned with the relationship of the *worker* to production.

So far we have considered the alienation of the worker only from one aspect; namely, *his relationship with the products of his labour*. However, alienation appears not only in the result, but also in the *process*, of *production*, within *productive activity* itself. How could the worker stand in an alien relationship to the product of his activity if he did not alienate himself in the act of production itself? The product is indeed only the *résumé* of activity, of production. Consequently, if the product of labour is alienation, production itself must be active alienation—the alienation of activity and the activity of alienation. The alienation of the object of labour merely summarizes the alienation in the work activity itself.

What constitutes the alienation of labour? First, that the work is *external* to the worker, that it is not part of his nature; and that, consequently, he does not fulfil himself in his work but denies himself, has a feeling of misery rather than well being, does not develop freely his mental and physical energies but is physically exhausted and mentally debased.

The worker therefore feels himself at home only during his leisure time, whereas at work he feels homeless. His work is not voluntary but imposed, *forced labour*. It is not the satisfaction of a need, but only a *means* for satisfying other needs. Its alien character is clearly shown by the fact that as soon as there is no physical or other compulsion it is avoided like the plague. External labour, labour in which man alienates himself, is a labour of self-sacrifice, or mortification. Finally, the external character of work for the worker is shown by the fact that it is not his own work but work for someone else, that in work he does not belong to himself but to another person.

Just as in religion the spontaneous activity of human fantasy, of the human brain and heart, reacts independently as an alien activity of gods or devils upon the individual, so the activity of the worker is not his own spontaneous activity. It is another's activity and a loss of his own spontaneity.

We arrive at the result that man (the worker) feels himself to be freely active only in his animal functions—eating, drinking, and procreating, or at most also in his dwelling and in personal adornment—while in his human functions he is reduced to an animal. The animal becomes human and the human becomes animal.

Eating, drinking, and procreating are of course also genuine human functions. But abstractly considered, apart from the environment of other human activities, and turned into final and sole ends, they are animal functions.

We have now considered the act of alienation of practical human activity, labour, from two aspects: (1) the relationship of the worker to the *product of labour* as an alien object which dominates him. This relationship is at the same time the relationship to the sensuous external world, to natural objects, as an alien and hostile world; (2) the relationship of labour to the *act of production* within *labour*. This is the relationship of the worker to his own activity as something alien and not belonging to him, activity as suffering (passivity), strength as powerlessness, creation as emasculation, the *personal* physical and mental energy of the worker, his personal life (for what is life but activity?) as an activity which is directed against himself, independent of him and not belonging to him. This is *self-alienation* as against the above-mentioned alienation of the *thing*.

(XXIV) We have now to infer a third characteristic of *alienated labour* from the two we have considered.

Man is a species-being[1] not only in the sense that he makes the community (his own as well as those of other things) his object both practically and theoretically, but also (and this is simply another expression for the same thing) in the sense that he treats himself as the present, living species, as a *universal* and consequently free being.

Species-life, for man as for animals, has its physical basis in the fact that man (like animals) lives from inorganic nature, and since man is more universal than an animal so the range of inorganic nature from which he lives is more universal. Plants, animals, minerals, air, light, etc. constitute, from the theoretical aspect, a part of human consciousness as objects of natural science and art; they are man's spiritual inorganic nature, his intellectual means of life, which he must first prepare for enjoyment and perpetuation. So also, from the practical aspect they form a part of human life and activity. In practice man lives only from these natural products, whether in the form of food, heating, clothing, housing, etc. The universality of man appears in practice in the universality which makes the whole of nature into his inorganic body: (1) as a direct means of life; and equally (2) as the material object and instrument of his life activity. Nature is the *inorganic body* of man; that is to say, nature excluding the human body itself. To say that man *lives* from nature means that nature is his *body* with which he must remain in a continuous interchange in order not to die. The statement that the physical and mental life of man, and nature, are interdependent means simply that nature is interdependent with itself, for man is a part of nature.

Since alienated labour (1) alienates nature from man; and (2) alienates man from himself, from his own active function, his life activity; so it alienates him from the species. It makes *species-life* into a means of individual life. In the first place it alienates *species-life* and individual life, and secondly, it turns the latter, as an abstraction, into the purpose of the former, also in its abstract and alienated form.

For labour, *life activity*, *productive life*, now appear to man only as *means* for the satisfaction of a need, the need to maintain his physical existence. Productive life is, however, species-life. It is life creating life. In the type of life activity resides the whole character of a species, its species-character; and free, conscious activity is the species-character of human beings. Life itself appears only as a *means of life*.

The animal is one with its life activity. It does not distinguish the activity from itself. It is *its activity*. But man makes his life activity itself an object of his will and consciousness. He has a conscious life activity. It is not a determination with which he is completely identified. Conscious life activity distinguishes man from the life activity of animals. Only for this reason is he a species-being. Or rather, he is only a self-conscious being, i.e. his own life is an object for him, because he is a species-being. Only for this reason is his activity free activity. Alienated labour reverses the relationship, in that man because he is a self-conscious being makes his life activity, his *being*, only a means for his *existence*.

The practical construction of an *objective world*, the *manipulation* of inorganic nature, is the confirmation of man as a conscious species-being, i.e. a being who treats the species as his own being or himself as a species-being. Of course, animals also produce. They construct nests, dwellings, as in the case of bees, beavers, ants, etc. But they only produce what is strictly necessary for themselves or their young. They produce only in a single direction, while man produces universally. They produce only under the compulsion of direct physical need, while man produces when he is free from physical need and only truly produces in freedom from such need. Animals produce only themselves, while man reproduces the whole of nature. The products of animal production belong directly to their physical bodies, while man is free in face of his product. Animals construct only in accordance with the standards and needs of the species to which they belong, while man knows how to produce in accordance with the standards of every species and knows how to apply the appropriate standard to the object. Thus man constructs also in accordance with the laws of beauty.

It is just in his work upon the objective world that man really proves himself as a *species-being*. This production is his active species life. By means of it nature appears as *his* work and his reality. The object of labour is, therefore, the *objectification of man's species life*; for he no longer reproduces himself merely intellectually, as in consciousness, but actively and in a real sense, and he sees his own reflection in a world which he has constructed. While, therefore, alienated labour takes away the object of production from man, it also takes away his *species life*, his real objectivity as a species-being, and changes his advantage over animals into a disadvantage insofar as his inorganic body, nature, is taken from him.

Just as alienated labour transforms free and self-directed activity into a means, so it transforms the species life of man into a means of physical existence.

Consciousness, which man has from his species, is transformed through alienation so that species life becomes only a means for him.

(3) Thus alienated labour turns the *species life of man*, and also nature as his mental species-property, into an *alien* being and into a *means* for his *individual existence*. It alienates from man his own body, external nature, his mental life and his *human* life.

(4) A direct consequence of the alienation of man from the product of his labour, from his life activity and from his species life is that *man is alienated* from other *men*. When man confronts himself he also confronts *other* men. What is true of man's relationship to his work, to the product of his work and to himself, is also true of his relationship to other men, to their labour and to the objects of their labour.

In general, the statement that man is alienated from his species life means that each man is alienated from others, and that each of the others is likewise alienated from human life.

Human alienation, and above all the relation of man to himself, is first realized and expressed in the relationship between each man and other men. Thus in the relationship of alienated labour every man regards other men according to the standards and relationships in which he finds himself placed as a worker.

(XXV) We began with an economic fact, the alienation of the worker and his production. We have expressed this fact in conceptual terms as *alienated labour*, and in analysing the concept we have merely analysed an economic fact.

Let us now examine further how this concept of alienated labour must express and reveal itself in reality. If the product of labour is alien to me and confronts me as an alien power, to whom does it belong? If my own activity does not belong to me but is an alien, forced activity, to whom does it belong? To a being *other* than myself. And who is this being? The *gods*? It is apparent in the earliest stages of advanced production, e.g., temple building, etc. in Egypt, India, Mexico, and in the service rendered to gods, that the product belonged to the gods. But the gods alone were never the lords of labour. And no more was *nature*. What a contradiction it would be if the more man subjugates nature by his labour, and the more the marvels of the gods are rendered superfluous by the marvels of industry, he should abstain from his joy in producing and his enjoyment of the product for love of these powers.

The *alien* being to whom labour and the product of labour belong, to whose service labour is devoted, and to whose enjoyment the product of labour goes, can only be *man* himself. If the product of labour does not belong to the worker, but confronts him as an alien power, this can only be because it belongs to *a man other than the worker*. If his activity is a torment to him it must be a source of enjoyment and pleasure to another. Not the gods, nor nature, but only man himself can be this alien power over men.

Consider the earliest statement that the relation of man to himself is first realized, objectified, through his relation to other men. If therefore he is related to the product of his labour, his objectified labour, as to an *alien*, hostile, powerful, and independent object, he is related in such a way that another alien, hostile, powerful, and independent man is the lord of this object. If he is related to his own activity as to unfree activity, then he is related to it as activity in the service, and under the domination, coercion, and yoke of another man.

Every self-alienation of man, from himself and from nature, appears in the relation which he postulates between other men and himself and nature. Thus religious self-alienation is necessarily exemplified in the relation between laity and priest, or, since it is here a question of the spiritual world, between the laity and a mediator. In the real world of practice this self-alienation can only be expressed in the real, practical relation of man to his fellow-men. The medium through which alienation occurs is itself a *practical* one. Through alienated labour, therefore, man not only produces his relation to the object and to the process of production as to alien and hostile men; he also produces the relation of other men to his production and his product, and the relation between himself and other men. Just as he creates his own production as a vitiation, a punishment, and his own product as a loss, as a product which does not belong to him, so he creates the domination of the non-producer over production and its product. As he alienates his own activity, so he bestows upon the stranger an activity which is not his own.

We have so far considered this relation only from the side of the worker, and later on we shall consider it also from the side of the non-worker.

Thus, through alienated labour the worker creates the relation of another man, who does not work and is outside the work process, to this labour. The relation of the worker to work also produces the relation of the capitalist (or whatever one likes to call the lord of labour) to work. *Private property* is therefore the product, the necessary result, of *alienated labour*, of the external relation of the worker to nature and to himself.

Private property is thus derived from the analysis of the concept of *alienated labour*; that is, alienated man, alienated labour, alienated life, and estranged man.

We have, of course, derived the concept of *alienated labour* (*alienated life*) from political economy, from an analysis of the *movement of private property*. But the analysis of this concept shows that although private property appears to be the basis and cause of alienated labour, it is rather a consequence of the latter, just as the gods are *fundamentally* not the cause but the product of confusions of human reason. At a later stage, however, there is a reciprocal influence.

Only in the final stage of the development of private property is its secret revealed, namely, that it is on one hand the *product* of alienated labour, and on the other hand the *means* by which labour is alienated, the *realization of this alienation*.

This elucidation throws light upon several unresolved controversies:

(1) Political economy begins with labour as the real soul of production and then goes on to attribute nothing to labour and everything to private property. Proudhon, faced by this contradiction, has decided in favour of labour against private property. We perceive, however, that this apparent contradiction is the contradiction of *alienated labour* with itself and that political economy has merely formulated the laws of alienated labour.

We also observe, therefore, that *wages* and *private property* are identical, for wages, like the product or object of labour, labour itself remunerated, are only a necessary consequence of the alienation of labour. In the wage system labour appears not as an end in itself but as the servant of wages. We shall develop this point later on and here only bring out some of the (XXVI) consequences.

An enforced *increase in wages* (disregarding the other difficulties, and especially that such an anomaly could only be maintained by force) would be nothing more than a *better remuneration of slaves*, and would not restore, either to the worker or to the work, their human significance and worth.

Even the *equality of incomes* which Proudhon demands would only change the relation of the present day worker to his work into a relation of all men to work. Society would then be conceived as an abstract capitalist.

(2) From the relation of alienated labour to private property it also follows that the emancipation of society from private property, from servitude, takes the political form of the *emancipation of the workers*; not in the sense that only the latter's emancipation is involved, but because this emancipation includes the emancipation of humanity as a whole. For all human servitude is involved in the relation of the worker to production, and all the types of servitude are only modifications or consequences of this relation.

As we have discovered the concept of *private property* by an *analysis* of the concept of *alienated labour*, so with the aid of these two factors we can evolve all the categories of political economy, and in every category, e.g., trade, competition, capital, money, we shall discover only a particular and developed expression of these fundamental elements.

However, before considering this structure let us attempt to solve two problems.

(1) To determine the general nature of *private property* as it has resulted from alienated labour, in its relation to *genuine human and social property*.

(2) We have taken as a fact and analyzed the *alienation of labour*. How does it happen, we may ask, that *man alienates his labour*? How is this alienation founded in the nature of human development? We have already done much to solve the problem in so far as we have *transformed* the question concerning the *origin of private property* into a question about the relation between *alienated labour* and the process of development of mankind. For in speaking of private property one believes oneself to be dealing with something external to mankind. But in speaking of labour one deals directly with mankind itself. This new formulation of the problem already contains its solution.

ad (1) *The general nature of private property and its relation to genuine human property.*

We have resolved alienated labour into two parts, which mutually determine each other, or rather constitute two different expressions of one and the same relation. *Appropriation* appears as *alienation* and *alienation as appropriation*, alienation as genuine acceptance in the community.

We have considered one aspect, *alienated* labour, in its bearing upon the *worker* himself, i.e., *the relation of alienated labour to itself*. And we have found as the necessary consequence of this relation the *property relation* of the *nonworker* to the *worker* and to *labour*. *Private property* as the material summarized expression of alienated labour includes both relations: *the relation of the worker to labour, to the product of his labour and to the non-worker*, and the relation of the *non-worker to the worker and to the product of the latter's labour*.

We have already seen that in relation to the worker, who *appropriates* nature by his labour, appropriation appears as alienation, self-activity as activity for another and of another, living as the sacrifice of life, and production of the object as loss of the object to an alien power, an alien man. Let us now consider the relation of this *alien* man to the worker, to labour, and to the object of labour.

It should be noted first that everything which appears to the worker as an *activity of alienation*, appears to the non-worker as a *condition of alienation*. Secondly, the *real, practical* attitude of the worker in production and to the product (as a state of mind) appears to the non-worker who confronts him as a *theoretical* attitude.

(XXVII) Thirdly, the non-worker does everything against the worker which the latter does against himself, but he does not do against himself what he does against the worker. Let us examine these three relationships more closely.[2]

NOTES

1. The term 'species-being' is taken from Feuerbach's *Das Wesen des Christentums* (The Essence of Christianity). Feuerbach used the notion in making a distinction between consciousness in man and in animals. Man is conscious not merely of himself as an individual but of the human species or 'human essence'.—*Tr. Note*
2. The manuscript breaks off unfinished at this point.—*Tr. Note*

THE GERMAN IDEOLOGY

As we hear from German ideologists, Germany has in the last few years gone through an unparalleled revolution. The decomposition of the Hegelian philosophy, which began with Strauss, has developed into a universal ferment into which all the 'powers of the past' are swept. In the general chaos mighty empires have arisen only to meet with immediate doom, heroes have emerged momentarily only to be hurled back into obscurity by bolder and stronger rivals. It was a revolution beside which the French Revolution was child's play, a world struggle beside which the struggles of the Diadochi [successors of Alexander the Great] appear insignificant. Principles ousted one another, heroes of the mind overthrew each other with unheard-of rapidity, and in the three years 1842-45 more of the past was swept away in Germany than at other times in three centuries.

All this is supposed to have taken place in the realm of pure thought.

Certainly it is an interesting event we are dealing with: the putrescence of the absolute spirit. When the last spark of its life had failed, the various components of this *caput mortuum* began to decompose, entered into new combinations and formed new substances. The industrialists of philosophy, who till then had lived on the exploitation of the absolute spirit, now seized upon the new combinations. Each with all possible zeal set about retailing his apportioned share. This naturally gave rise to competition, which, to start with, was carried on in moderately staid bourgeois fashion. Later when the German market was glutted, and the commodity in spite of all efforts found no response in the world market, the business was spoiled in the usual German manner by fabricated and fictitious production, deterioration in quality, adulteration of the raw materials, falsification of labels, fictitious purchases, bill-jobbing and a credit system devoid of any real basis. The competition turned into a bitter struggle, which is now being extolled and interpreted to us as a revolution of world significance, the begetter of the most prodigious results and achievements.

If we wish to rate at its true value this philosophic charlatanry, which awakens even in the breast of the honest German citizen a glow of national pride, if we wish to bring out clearly the pettiness, the parochial narrowness of this whole Young-Hegelian movement and in particular the tragicomic contrast between the illusions of these heroes about their achievements and the actual achievements themselves, we must look at the whole spectacle from a standpoint beyond the frontiers of Germany.

German criticism has, right up to its latest efforts, never quitted the realm of philosophy. Far from examining its general philosophic premises, the whole body of its inquiries has actually sprung from the soil of a definite philosophical system, that of Hegel. Not only in their answers but in their very questions there was a mystification. This dependence on Hegel is the reason why not one of these modern critics has even attempted a comprehensive criticism of the Hegelian system, however much each professes to have advanced beyond Hegel. Their polemics against Hegel and against one another are confined to this—each extracts one side of the Hegelian system and turns this against the whole system as well as against the sides extracted by the others. To begin with they extracted pure unfalsified Hegelian categories such as 'substance' and 'self-consciousness', later they desecrated these categories with more secular names such as 'species', 'the Unique', 'Man', etc.

The entire body of German philosophical criticism from Strauss to Stirner is confined to criticism of *religious* conceptions. The critics started from real religion and actual theology. What religious consciousness and a religious conception really meant was determined variously as they went along. Their advance consisted in subsuming the allegedly dominant metaphysical, political, juridical, moral and other conceptions under the class of religious or theological conceptions; and similarly in pronouncing political, juridical, moral consciousness as religious or theological, and the political, juridical, moral man—'*man*' in the last resort—as religious. The dominance of religion was taken for granted. Gradually every dominant relationship was pronounced a religious relationship and transformed into a cult, a cult of law, a cult of the State, etc. On all sides it was only a question of dogmas and belief in dogmas. The world sanctified to an ever-increasing extent till at last our venerable Saint Max was able to canonize it *en bloc* and thus dispose of it once for all.

The Old Hegelians had *comprehended* everything as soon as it was reduced to an Hegelian logical category. The Young Hegelians *criticized* everything by attributing to it religious conceptions or by pronouncing it a theological matter. The Young Hegelians are in agreement with the Old Hegelians in their belief in the rule of religion, of concepts, of a universal principle in the existing world. Only, the one party attacks this dominion as usurpation, while the other extols it as legitimate.

Since the Young Hegelians consider conceptions, thoughts, ideas, in fact all the products of consciousness, to which they attribute an independent existence, as the real chains of men (just as the Old Hegelians declared them the true bonds of human society) it is evident that the Young Hegelians have to fight only against these illusions of consciousness. Since, according to their fantasy, the relationships of men, all their doings, their chains and their limitations are products of their consciousness, the Young Hegelians logically put to men the moral postulate of exchanging their present consciousness for human, critical or egoistic consciousness, and thus of removing their limitations. This demand to change consciousness amounts to a demand to interpret reality in another way, i.e. to recognize it by means of another interpretation. The Young-Hegelian ideologists, in spite of their allegedly 'world-shattering' statements, are the staunchest conservatives. The most recent of them have found the correct expression for their activity when they declare they are only fighting against *'phrases'*. They forget, however, that to these phrases they themselves are only opposing other phrases, and that they are in no way combating the real existing world when they are merely combating the phrases of this world. The only results which this philosophic criticism could achieve were a few (and at that thoroughly one-sided) elucidations of Christianity from the point of view of religious history; all the rest of their assertions are only further embellishments of their claim to have furnished, in these unimportant elucidations, discoveries of universal importance.

It has not occurred to any of these philosophers to inquire into the connection of German philosophy with German reality, the relation of their criticism to their own material surroundings.

First Premises of Materialist Method

The premises from which we begin are not arbitrary ones, not dogmas, but real premises from which abstraction can only be made in the imagination. They are the real individuals, their activity and the material conditions under which they live, both those which they find already existing and those produced by their activity. These premises can thus be verified in a purely empirical way.

The first premise of all human history is, of course, the existence of living human individuals. Thus the first fact to be established is the physical organization of these individuals and their consequent relation to the rest of nature. Of course, we cannot here go either into the actual physical nature of man, or into the natural conditions in which man finds himself—geological, oreohydrographical, climatic and so on. The writing of history must always set out from these natural bases and their modification in the course of history through the action of men.

Men can be distinguished from animals by consciousness, by religion or by anything else you like. They themselves begin to distinguish themselves from animals as soon as they begin to *produce* their means of subsistence, a step which is conditioned by their physical organization. By producing their means of subsistence men are indirectly producing their actual material life.

The way in which men produce their means of subsistence depends first of all on the nature of the actual means of subsistence they find in existence and have to reproduce.

This mode of production must not be considered simply as being the production of the physical existence of the individuals. Rather it is a definite form of activity of these individuals, a definite form of expressing their life, a definite *mode of life* on their part. As individuals express their life, so they are. What they are, therefore, coincides with their production, both with *what* they produce and with *how* they produce. The nature of individuals thus depends on the material conditions determining their production.

This production only makes its appearance with the *increase of population*. In its turn this presupposes the *intercourse* [*Verkehr*][1] of individuals with one another. The form of this intercourse is again determined by production.

The relations of different nations among themselves depend upon the extent to which each has developed its productive forces, the division of labour and internal intercourse. This statement is generally recognized. But not only the relation of one nation to others, but also the whole internal structure of the nation itself depends on the stage of development reached by its production and its internal and external intercourse. How far the productive forces of a nation are developed is shown most manifestly by the degree to which the division of labour has been carried. Each new productive force, insofar as it is not merely a quantitative extension of productive forces already known (for instance the bringing into cultivation of fresh land), causes a further development of the division of labour.

The division of labour inside a nation leads at first to the separation of industrial and commercial from agricultural labour, and hence to the separation of *town* and *country* and to the conflict of their interests. Its further development leads to the separation of commercial from industrial labour. At the same time through the division of labour inside these various branches there develop various divisions among the individuals co-operating in definite kinds of labour. The relative position of these individual groups is determined by the methods employed in agriculture, industry, and commerce (patriarchalism, slavery, estates, classes). These same conditions are to be seen (given a more developed intercourse) in the relations of different nations to one another.

The various stages of development in the division of labour are just so many different forms of ownership, i.e. the existing stage in the division of labour determines also the relations of individuals to one another with reference to the material, instrument, and product of labour.

The first form of ownership is tribal [*Stammeigentum*][2] ownership. It corresponds to the undeveloped stage of production, at which a people lives by hunting and fishing, by the rearing of beasts or, in the highest stage, agriculture. In the latter case it presupposes a great mass of uncultivated stretches of land. The division of labour is at this stage still very elementary and is confined to a further extension of the natural division of labour existing in the family. The social structure is, therefore, limited to an extension of the family; patriarchal family chieftains, below them the members of the tribe, finally slaves. The slavery latent in the family only develops gradually with the increase of population, the growth of wants, and with the extension of external relations, both of war and of barter.

The second form is the ancient communal and State ownership which proceeds especially from the union of several tribes into a *city* by agreement or by conquest, and which is still accompanied by slavery. Beside communal ownership we already find movable, and later also immovable, private property developing, but as an abnormal form subordinate to communal ownership. The citizens hold power over their labouring slaves only in their community, and on this account alone, therefore, they are bound to the form of communal ownership. It is the communal private property which compels the active citizens to remain in this spontaneously derived form of association over against their slaves. For this reason the whole structure of society based on this communal ownership, and with it the power of the people, decays in the same measure as, in particular, immovable private property evolves. The division of labour is already more developed. We already find the antagonism of town and country; later the antagonism between those states which represent town interests and those which represent country interests, and inside the towns themselves the antagonism between industry and maritime commerce. The class relation between citizens and slaves is now completely developed.

With the development of private property, we find here for the first time the same conditions which we shall find again, only on a more extensive scale, with modern private property. On the one hand, the centralization of private property, which began very early in Rome (as the Licinian agrarian law proves[3]) and proceeded very rapidly from the time of the civil wars and especially under the Emperors; on the other hand, coupled with this, the transformation of the plebeian small peasantry into a proletariat, which, however, owing to its intermediate position between propertied citizens and slaves, never achieved an independent development.

The third form of ownership is feudal or estate property. If antiquity started out from the *town* and its little territory, the Middle Ages started out from the *country*. This different starting-point was determined by the sparseness of the population at that time, which was scattered over a large area and which received no large increase from the conquerors. In contrast to Greece and Rome, feudal development at the outset, therefore, extends over a much wider territory, prepared by the Roman conquests and the spread of agriculture at first associated with it. The last centuries of the declining Roman Empire and its conquest by the barbarians destroyed a number of productive forces; agriculture had declined, industry had decayed for want of a market, trade had died out or been violently suspended, the rural and urban population had decreased. From these conditions and the mode of organization of the conquest determined by them, feudal property developed under the influence of the Germanic military constitution. Like tribal and communal ownership, it is based again on a community; but the directly producing class standing over against it is not, as in the case of the ancient community, the slaves, but the enserfed small peasantry. As soon as feudalism is fully developed, there also arises antagonism to the towns. The hierarchical structure of landownership, and the armed bodies of retainers associated with it, gave the nobility power over the serfs. This feudal organization was, just as much as the ancient communal ownership, an association against a subjected producing class; but the form of association and the relation to the direct producers were different because of the different conditions of production.

This feudal system of landownership had its counterpart in the *towns* in the shape of corporative property, the feudal organization of trades. Here property consisted chiefly in the labour of each individual person. The necessity for association against the organized robber-nobility, the need for communal covered markets in an age when the industrialist was at the same time a merchant, the growing competition of the escaped serfs swarming into the rising towns, the feudal structure of the whole country: these combined to bring about the *guilds*. The gradually accumulated small capital of individual craftsmen and their stable numbers, as against the growing population, evolved the relation of journeyman and apprentice, which brought into being in the towns a hierarchy similar to that in the country.

Thus the chief form of property during the feudal epoch consisted on the one hand of landed property with serf labour chained to it, and on the other of the labour of the individual with small capital commanding the labour of journeymen. The organization of both was determined by the restricted conditions of production—the small-scale and primitive cultivation of the land, and the craft type of industry. There was little division of labour in the heyday of feudalism. Each country bore in itself the antithesis of town and country; the division of estates was certainly strongly marked; but apart from the differentiation of princes, nobility, clergy, and peasants in the country, and masters, journeymen, apprentices, and soon also the rabble of casual labourers in the towns, no division of importance took place. In agriculture it was rendered difficult by the strip-system, beside which the cottage industry of the peasants themselves emerged. In industry there was no division of labour at all in the individual trades themselves, and very little between them. The separation of industry and commerce was found already in existence in older towns; in the newer it only developed later, when the towns entered into mutual relations.

The grouping of larger territories into feudal kingdoms was a necessity for the landed nobility as for the towns. The organization of the ruling class, the nobility, had, therefore, everywhere a monarch at its head.

The fact is, therefore, that definite individuals who are productively active in a definite way enter into these definite social and political relations. Empirical observation must in each separate instance bring out empirically, and without any mystification and speculation, the connection of the social and political structure with production. The social structure and the State are continually evolving out of the life-process of definite individuals, but of individuals, not as they may appear in their own or other people's imagination, but as they *really* are; i.e. as they operate, produce materially, and hence as they work under definite material limits, presuppositions and conditions independent of their will.

The production of ideas, of conceptions, of consciousness, is at first directly interwoven with the material activity and the material intercourse of men, the language of real life. Conceiving, thinking, the mental intercourse of men, appear at this stage as a direct efflux of their material behaviour. The same applies to mental production as expressed in the language of politics, laws, morality, religion, metaphysics, etc. of a people. Men are the producers of their conceptions, ideas, etc.—real, active men, as they are conditioned by a definite development of their productive forces and of the intercourse corresponding to these, up to its furthest forms. Consciousness can never be anything else than conscious existence, and the existence of men is their actual life-process. If in all ideology men and their circumstances appear upside-down as in a *camera obscura*, this phenomenon arises just as much from their historical life-process as the inversion of objects on the retina does from their physical life-process.

In direct contrasts to German philosophy which descends from heaven to earth, here we ascend from earth to heaven. That is to say, we do not set out from what men say, imagine, conceive, nor from men as narrated, thought of, imagined, conceived, in order to arrive at men in the flesh. We set out from real, active men, and on the basis of their real life-process we demonstrate the development of the ideological reflexes and echoes of this life-process. The phantoms formed in the human brain are also, necessarily, sublimates of their material life-process, which is empirically verifiable and bound to material premises. Morality, religion, metaphysics, all the rest of ideology and their corresponding forms of consciousness, thus no longer retain the semblance of independence. They have no history, no development; but men, developing their material production and their material intercourse, alter along with this their real existence, their thinking, and the products of their thinking. Life is not determined by consciousness, but consciousness by life. In the first method of approach the starting-point is consciousness taken as the living individual; in the second method, which conforms to real life, it is the real living individuals themselves, and consciousness is considered solely as *their* consciousness.

This method of approach is not devoid of premises. It starts out from the real premises and does not abandon them for a moment. Its premises are men, not in any fantastic isolation and rigidity, but in their actual, empirically perceptible process of development under definite conditions. As soon as this active life-process is described, history ceases to be a collection of dead facts as it is with the empiricists (themselves still abstract), or an imagined activity of imagined subjects, as with the idealists.

Where speculation ends—in real life—there real, positive science begins: the representation of the practical activity, of the practical process of development of men. Empty talk about consciousness ceases, and real knowledge has to take its place. When reality is depicted, philosophy as an independent branch of knowledge loses its medium of existence. At the best its place can only be taken by a summing-up of the most general results, abstractions which arise from the observation of the historical development of men. Viewed apart from real history, these abstractions have in themselves no value whatsoever. They can only serve to facilitate the arrangement of historical material, to indicate the sequence of its separate strata. But they by no means afford a recipe or schema, as does philosophy, for neatly trimming the epochs of history. On the contrary, our difficulties begin only when we set about the observation and the arrangement—the real depiction—of our historical material, whether of a past epoch or of the present. The removal of these difficulties is governed by premises which it is quite impossible to state here, but which only the study of the actual life-process and the activity of the individuals of each epoch will make evident ...

NOTES

1. In *The German Ideology* the word *Verkehr* is used in a very wide sense, encompassing the material and spiritual intercourse of separate individuals, social groups and entire countries. Marx and Engels argue that material intercourse, and above all the intercourse of men with each other in the production process, is the basis of every other form of intercourse.

The terms *Verkehrsform* (form of intercourse), *Verkehrsweise* (mode of intercourse) and *Verkehrsverhaltnisse* (relations, or conditions, of intercourse) which we encounter in *The German Ideology* are used by Marx and Engels to express the concept 'relations of production' which during that period was taking shape in their minds.

The ordinary dictionary meanings of *Verkehr* are traffic, intercourse, commerce. In this translation the word *Verkehr* has been mostly rendered as 'intercourse' and occasionally as 'association' or 'commerce'.—Ed.

2. The term *Stamm*—rendered in the present volume by the word 'tribe'—played a considerably greater part in historical works written during the forties of the nineteenth century than it does at present. It was used to denote a community of people descended from a common ancestor, and comprised the modern concepts of 'gens' and 'tribe'. The first to define and differentiate these concepts was Lewis Henry Morgan in his work *Ancient Society; or, Researches in the Lines of Human Progress from Savagery Through Barbarism to Civilisation*, London, 1877. This outstanding American ethnographer and historian showed for the first time the significance of the gens as the nucleus of the primitive communal system and thereby laid the scientific foundations for the history of primitive society as a whole. Engels drew the general conclusions from Morgan's discoveries and made a comprehensive analysis of the meaning of the concepts 'gens' and 'tribe' in his work *The Origin of the Family, Private Property and the State* (1884).—Ed.

3. The *Licinian agrarian law*—the agrarian law of Licinius and Sextius, Roman tribunes of the people, passed in 367 B.C. as a result of the struggle which the plebeians waged against the patricians. According to this law a Roman citizen could not hold more than 500 Yugera (approximately 309 acres) of common land (*ager publicus*).—Ed.

4. [Marginal note by Marx:] Universality corresponds to (1) the class versus the estate, (2) the competition, world-wide intercourse, etc., (3) the great numerical strength of the ruling class, (4) the illusion of the *common* interests (in the beginning this illusion is true), (5) the delusion of the ideologists and the division of labour.

THE CLASS STRUGGLE

Ruling Class and Ruling Ideas

The ideas of the ruling class are in every epoch the ruling ideas, i.e. the class which is the *ruling* material force of society, is at the same time its ruling *intellectual* force. The class which has the means of material production at its disposal, has control at the same time over the means of mental production, so that thereby, generally speaking, the ideas of those who lack the means of mental production are subject to it. The ruling ideas are nothing more than the ideal expression of the dominant material relationships, the dominant material relationships grasped as ideas; hence of the relationship which make the one class the ruling one, therefore, the ideas of its dominance. The individuals composing the ruling class possess among other things consciousness, and therefore think. Insofar, therefore, as they rule as a class and determine the extent and compass of an epoch, it is self-evident that they do this in its whole range, hence among other things rule also as thinkers, as producers of ideas, and regulate the production and distribution of the ideas of their age: thus their ideas are the ruling ideas of the epoch. For instance, in an age and in a country where royal power, aristocracy, and bourgeoisie are contending for mastery and where, therefore, mastery is shared, the doctrine of the separation of powers proves to be the dominant idea and is expressed as an 'eternal law'.

The division of labour, . . . one of the chief forces of history up till now, manifests itself also in the ruling class as the division of mental and material labour, so that inside this class one part appears as the thinkers of the class (its active, conceptive ideologists, who make the perfecting of the illusion of the class about itself their chief source of livelihood), while the others' attitude to these ideas and illusions is more passive and receptive, because they are in reality the active members of this class and have less time to make up illusions and ideas about themselves. Within this class this cleavage can even develop into a certain opposition and hostility between the two parts, which, however, in the case of a practical collision, in which the class itself is endangered, automatically comes to nothing, in which case there also vanishes the semblance that the ruling ideas were not the ideas of the ruling class and had a power distinct from the power of this class. The existence of revolutionary ideas in a particular period presupposes the existence of a revolutionary class; about the premises for the latter sufficient has already been said above.

If now in considering the course of history we detach the ideas of the ruling class from the ruling class itself and attribute to them an independent existence, if we confine ourselves to saying that these or those ideas were dominant at a given time, without bothering ourselves about the conditions of production and the producers of these ideas, if we thus ignore the individuals and world conditions which are the source of the ideas, we can say, for instance, that during the time that the aristocracy was dominant, the concepts honour, loyalty, etc. were dominant, during the dominance of the bourgeoisie the concepts freedom, equality, etc. The ruling class itself on the whole imagines this to be so. This conception of history, which is common to all historians, particularly since the eighteenth century, will necessarily come up against the phenomenon that increasingly abstract ideas hold sway, i.e., ideas which increasingly take on the form of universality. For each new class which puts itself in the place of one ruling before it, is compelled, merely in order to carry through its aim, to represent its interest as the common interest of all the members of society, that is, expressed in ideal form: it has to give its ideas the form of universality, and represent them as the only rational, universally valid ones. The class making a revolution appears from the very start, if only because it is opposed to a *class*, not as a class but as the representative of the whole of society; it appears as the whole mass of society confronting the one ruling class.[1] It can do this because, to start with, its interest really is more connected with the common interest of all other non-ruling classes, because under the pressure of hitherto existing conditions its interest has not yet been able to develop as the particular interest of a particular class. Its victory, therefore, benefits also many individuals of the other classes which are not winning a dominant position, but only insofar as it now puts these individuals in a position to raise themselves into the ruling class. When the French bourgeoisie overthrew the power of the aristocracy, it thereby made it possible for many proletarians to raise themselves above the proletariat, but only insofar as they become bourgeois. Every new class, therefore, achieves its hegemony only on a broader basis than that of the class ruling previously, whereas the opposition of the non-ruling class against the new ruling class later develops all the more sharply and profoundly. Both these things determine the fact that the struggle to be waged against this new ruling class, in its turn, aims at a more decided and radical negation of the previous conditions of society than could all previous classes which sought to rule.

This whole semblance, that the rule of a certain class is only the rule of certain ideas, comes to a natural end, of course, as soon as class rule in general ceases to be the form in which society is organized, that is to say, as soon as it is no longer necessary to represent a particular interest as general or the 'general interest' as ruling.

Once the ruling ideas have been separated from the ruling individuals and, above all, from the relationships which result from a given stage of the mode of production, and in this way the conclusion has been reached that history is always under the sway of ideas, it is very easy to abstract from these various ideas '*the* idea', the notion, etc. as the dominant force in history, and thus to understand all these separate ideas and concepts as 'forms of self-determination' on the part of *the* concept developing in history. It follows then naturally, too, that all the relationships of men can be derived from the concept of man, man as conceived, the essence of man, *Man*. This has been done by the speculative philosophers. Hegel himself confesses at the end of the *Geschichtsphilosophie* that he 'has considered the progress of the *concept* only' and has represented in history the 'true *theodicy*'. Now one can go back again to the producers of the 'concept', to the theorists, ideologists and philosophers, and one comes then to the conclusion that the philosophers, the thinkers as such, have at all times been dominant in history: a conclusion, as we see, already expressed by Hegel. The whole trick of proving the hegemony of the spirit in history (hierarchy Stirner calls it) is thus confined to the following three efforts.

No. 1. One must separate the ideas of those ruling for empirical reasons, under empirical conditions and as empirical individuals, from these actual rulers, and thus recognize the rule of ideas or illusions in history.

No. 2. One must bring an order into this rule of ideas, prove a mystical connection among the successive ruling ideas, which is managed by understanding them as 'acts of self-determination on the part of the concept' (this is possible because by virtue of their empirical basis these ideas are really connected with one another and because, conceived as *mere* ideas, they become self-distinctions, distinctions made by thought).

No. 3. To remove the mystical appearance of this 'self-determining concept' it is changed into a person—'Self-Consciousness'—or, to appear thoroughly materialistic, into a series of persons, who represent the 'concept' in history, into the 'thinkers', the 'philosophers', the ideologists, who again are understood as the manufacturers of history, as the 'council of guardians', as the rulers. Thus the whole body of materialistic elements has been removed from history and now full rein can be given to the speculative steed.

Whilst in ordinary life every shopkeeper is very well able to distinguish between what somebody professes to be and what he really is, our historians have not yet won even this trivial insight. They take every epoch at its word and believe that everything it says and imagines about life is true.

This historical method which reigned in Germany, and especially the reason why, must be understood from its connection with the illusion of ideologists in general, e.g. the illusions of the jurist, politicians (of the practical statesmen among them, too), from the dogmatic dreamings and distortions of these fellows; this is explained perfectly easily from their practical position in life, their job, and the division of labour.

NOTE

1. [Marginal note by Marx:] Universality corresponds to (1) the class versus the estate, (2) the competition, world-wide intercourse, etc., (3) the great numerical strength of the ruling class, (4) the illusion of the *common* interests (in the beginning this illusion is true), (5) the delusion of the ideologists and the division of labour.

MANIFESTO OF THE COMMUNIST PARTY

A spectre is haunting Europe—the spectre of Communism. All the Powers of old Europe have entered into a holy alliance to exorcise this spectre: Pope and Czar, Metternich and Guizot, French Radicals and German police-spies.

Where is the party in opposition that has not been decried as Communistic by its opponents in power? Where the Opposition that has not hurled back the branding reproach of Communism, against the more advanced opposition parties, as well as against its reactionary adversaries?

Two things result from this fact.

I. Communism is already acknowledged by all European Powers to be itself a Power.

II. It is high time that Communists should openly, in the face of the whole world, publish their views, their aims, their tendencies, and meet this nursery tale of the Spectre of Communism with a Manifesto of the party itself.

To this end, Communists of various nationalities have assembled in London, and sketched the following Manifesto, to be published in the English, French, German, Italian, Flemish, and Danish languages.

Bourgeois and Proletarians[1]

The history of all hitherto existing society[2] is the history of class struggles.

Freeman and slave, patrician and plebeian, lord and serf, guildmaster[3] and journeyman, in a word, oppressor and oppressed, stood in constant opposition to one another, carried on an uninterrupted, now hidden, now open fight, a fight that each time ended, either in a revolutionary re-constitution of society at large, or in the common ruin of the contending classes.

In the earlier epochs of history, we find almost everywhere a complicated arrange-ment of society into various orders, a manifold gradation of social rank. In ancient Rome we have patricians, knights, plebeians, slaves; in the Middle Ages, feudal lords, vassals, guild-masters, journeymen, apprentices, serfs; in almost all of these classes, again, sub-ordinate gradations.

The modern bourgeois society that has sprouted from the ruins of feudal society has not done away with class antagonisms. It has but established new classes, new conditions of oppression, new forms of struggle in place of the old ones.

Our epoch, the epoch of the bourgeoisie, possesses, however, this distinctive feature: it has simplified the class antagonisms. Society as a whole is more and more splitting up into two great hostile camps, into two great classes directly facing each other: Bourgeoisie and Proletariat.

From the serfs of the Middle Ages sprang the chartered burghers of the earliest towns. From these burgesses the first elements of the bourgeoisie were developed.

The discovery of America, the rounding of the Cape, opened up fresh ground for the rising bourgeoisie. The East-Indian and Chinese markets, the colonization of America, trade with the colonies, the increase in the means of exchange and in commodities gen-erally, gave to commerce, to navigation, to industry, an impulse never before known, and thereby, to the revolutionary element in the tottering feudal society, a rapid development.

The feudal system of industry, under which industrial production was monopolized by closed guilds, now no longer sufficed for the growing wants of the new markets. The manufacturing system took its place. The guild-masters were pushed on one side by the manufacturing middle class; division of labour between the different corporate guilds vanished in the face of division of labour in each single workshop.

Meantime the markets kept ever growing, the demand ever rising. Even manufacture no longer sufficed. Thereupon, steam and machinery revolutionized industrial produc-tion. The place of manufacture was taken by the giant, Modern Industry, the place of the industrial middle class by industrial millionaires, the leaders of whole industrial armies, the modern bourgeois.

Modern industry has established the world-market, for which the discovery of America paved the way. This market has given an immense development to commerce, to navigation, to communication by land. This development has, in its turn, reacted on the extension of industry; and in proportion as industry, commerce, navigation, railways extended, in the same proportion the bourgeoisie developed, increased its capital, and pushed into the background every class handed down from the Middle Ages.

We see, therefore, how the modern bourgeoisie is itself the product of a long course of development, of a series of revolutions in the modes of production and of exchange.

Each step in the development of the bourgeoisie was accompanied by a correspon-ding political advance of that class. An oppressed class under the sway of the feudal nobility, an armed and self-governing association in the mediaeval commune[*]; here inde-pendent urban republic (as in Italy and Germany), there taxable 'third estate' of the monarchy (as in France), afterwards, in the period of manufacture proper, serving either the semi-feudal or the absolute monarchy as a counterpoise against the nobility, and, in fact, corner-stone of the great monarchies in general, the bourgeoisie has at last, since the establishment of Modern Industry and of the world-market, conquered for itself, in the modern representative State, exclusive political sway. The executive of the modern State is but a committee for managing the common affairs of the whole bourgeoisie.

The bourgeoisie, historically, has played a most revolutionary part.

The bourgeoisie, wherever it has got the upper hand, has put an end to all feudal, patriarchal, idyllic relations. It has pitilessly torn asunder the motley feudal ties that bound man to his 'natural superiors', and has left remaining no other nexus between man and man than naked self-interest, than callous 'cash payment'. It has drowned the most heavenly ecstasies of religious fervour, of chivalrous enthusiasm, of philistine sentimentalism, in the icy water of egotistical calculation. It has resolved personal worth into exchange value, and in place of the numberless indefeasible chartered freedoms, has set up that single, unconscionable freedom—Free Trade. In one word, for exploitation, veiled by religious and political illusions, it has substituted naked, shameless, direct, brutal exploitation.

The bourgeoisie has stripped of its halo every occupation hitherto honoured and looked up to with reverent awe. It has converted the physician, the lawyer, the priest, the poet, the man of science, into its paid wage-labourers.

The bourgeoisie has torn away from the family its sentimental veil, and has reduced the family relation to a mere money relation.

The bourgeoisie has disclosed how it came to pass that the brutal display of vigour in the Middle Ages, which Reactionists so much admire, found its fitting complement in the most slothful indolence. It has been the first to show what man's activity can bring about. It has accomplished wonders far surpassing Egyptian pyramids, Roman aqueducts, and Gothic cathedrals; it has conducted expeditions that put in the shade all former Exoduses of nations and crusades.

The bourgeoisie cannot exist without constantly revolutionizing the instruments of production, and thereby the relations of production, and with them the whole relations of society. Conservation of the old modes of production in unaltered form, was, on the contrary, the first condition of existence for all earlier industrial classes. Constant revolutionizing of production, uninterrupted disturbance of all social conditions, everlasting uncertainty and agitation distinguish the bourgeois epoch from all earlier ones. All fixed, fast frozen relations, with their train of ancient and venerable prejudices and opinions, are swept away, all new-formed ones become antiquated before they can ossify. All that is solid melts into air, all that is holy is profaned, and man is at last compelled to face with sober senses, his real conditions of life, and his relations with his kind.

The need of a constantly expanding market for its products chases the bourgeoisie over the whole surface of the globe. It must nestle everywhere, settle everywhere, establish connexions everywhere.

The bourgeoisie has through its exploitation of the world-market given a cosmopolitan character to production and consumption in every country. To the great chagrin of Reactionists, it has drawn from under the feet of industry the national ground on which it stood. All old-established national industries have been destroyed or are daily being destroyed. They are dislodged by new industries, whose introduction becomes a life and death question for all civilized nations, by industries that no longer work up indigenous raw material, but raw material drawn from the remotest zones; industries whose products are consumed, not only at home, but in every quarter of the globe. In place of the old wants, satisfied by the productions of the country, we find new wants, requiring for their satisfaction the products of distant lands and climes. In place of the old local and national seclusion and self-sufficiency, we have intercourse in every direction, universal inter-dependence of nations. And as in material, so also in intellectual production. The intellectual creations of individual nations become common property. National one-sidedness and narrow-mindedness become more and more impossible, and from the numerous national and local literatures, there arises a world literature.

The bourgeoisie, by the rapid improvement of all instruments of production, by the immensely facilitated means of communication, draws all, even the most barbarian, nations into civilization. The cheap prices of its commodities are the heavy artillery with which it batters down all Chinese walls, with which it forces the barbarians' intensely obstinate hatred of foreigners to capitulate. It compels all nations, on pain of extinction, to adopt the bourgeois mode of production; it compels them to introduce what it calls civilization into their midst, i.e., to become bourgeois themselves. In one word, it creates a world after its own image.

The bourgeoisie has subjected the country to the rule of the towns. It has created enormous cities, has greatly increased the urban population as compared with the rural, and has thus rescued a considerable part of the population from the idiocy of rural life. Just as it has made the country dependent on the towns, so it has made barbarian and semi-barbarian countries dependent on the civilized ones, nations of peasants on nations of bourgeois, the East on the West.

The bourgeoisie keeps more and more doing away with the scattered state of the population, of the means of production, and of property. It has agglomerated population, centralized means of production, and has concentrated property in a few hands. The necessary consequence of this was political centralization. Independent or but loosely connected provinces, with separate interests, laws, governments and systems of taxation, became lumped together into one nation, with one government, one code of laws, one national class-interest, one frontier and one customs-tariff.

The bourgeoisie, during its rule of scarce one hundred years, has created more massive and more colossal productive forces than have all preceding generations together. Subjection of Nature's forces to man, machinery, application of chemistry to industry and agriculture, steam-navigation, railways, electric telegraphs, clearing of whole continents for cultivation, canalization of rivers, whole populations conjured out of the ground—what earlier century had even a presentiment that such productive forces slumbered in the lap of social labour?

We see then: the means of production and of exchange, on whose foundation the bourgeoisie built itself up, were generated in feudal society. At a certain stage in the development of these means of production and of exchange, the conditions under which feudal society produced and exchanged, the feudal organization of agriculture and manufacturing industry, in one word, the feudal relations of property became no longer compatible with the already developed productive forces; they became so many fetters. They had to be burst asunder; they were burst asunder.

Into their place stepped free competition, accompanied by a social and political constitution adapted to it, and by the economical and political sway of the bourgeois class.

A similar movement is going on before our own eyes. Modern bourgeois society with its relations of production, of exchange and of property, a society that has conjured up such gigantic means of production and exchange, is like the sorcerer, who is no longer able to control the powers of the nether world whom he has called up by his spells. For many a decade past the history of industry and commerce is but the history of the revolt of modern productive forces against modern conditions of production, against the property relations that are the conditions for the existence of the bourgeoisie and of its rule. It is enough to mention the commercial crises that are by their periodical return put on its trial, each time more threateningly, the existence of the entire bourgeois society. In these crises a great part not only of the existing products, but also of the previously created productive forces, are periodically destroyed. In these crises there breaks out an epidemic that, in all earlier epochs, would have seemed an absurdity—the epidemic of overproduction. Society suddenly finds itself put back into a state of momentary barbarism; it appears as if a famine, a universal war of devastation had cut off the supply of every means of subsistence; industry and commerce seem to be destroyed; and why? Because there is too much civilization, too much means of subsistence, too much industry, too much commerce. The productive forces at the disposal of society no longer tend to further the development of the conditions of bourgeois property; on the contrary, they have become too powerful for these conditions, by which they are fettered, and so soon as they overcome these fetters, they bring disorder into the whole bourgeois society, endanger the existence of bourgeois property. The conditions of bourgeois society are too narrow to comprise the wealth created by them. And how does the bourgeoisie get over these crises? On the one hand by enforced destruction of a mass of productive forces; on the other, by the conquest of new markets, and by the more thorough exploitation of the old ones. That is to say, by paving the way for more extensive and more destructive crises, and by diminishing the means whereby crises are prevented.

The weapons with which the bourgeoisie felled feudalism to the ground are now turned against the bourgeoisie itself.

But not only has the bourgeoisie forged the weapons that bring death to itself; it has also called into existence the men who are to wield those weapons—the modern working class—the proletarians.

In proportion as the bourgeoisie, i.e., capital, is developed, in the same proportion is the proletariat, the modern working class, developed—a class of labourers, who live only so long as they find work, and who find work only so long as their labour increases capital. These labourers, who must sell themselves piecemeal, are a commodity, like every other article of commerce, and are consequently exposed to all the vicissitudes of competition, to all the fluctuations of the market.

Owing to the extensive use of machinery and to division of labour, the work of the proletarians has lost all individual character, and, consequently, all charm for the workman. He becomes an appendage of the machine, and it is only the most simple, most monotonous, and most easily acquired knack, that is required of him. Hence, the cost of production of a workman is restricted, almost entirely, to the means of subsistence that he requires for his maintenance, and for the propagation of his race. But the price of a commodity, and therefore also of labour, is equal to its cost of production. In proportion, therefore, as the repulsiveness of the work increases, the wage decreases. Nay more, in proportion as the use of machinery and division of labour increases, in the same proportion the burden of toil also increases, whether by prolongation of the working hours, by increase of the work exacted in a given time or by increased speed of the machinery, etc.

Modern industry has converted the little workshop of the patriarchal master into the great factory of the industrial capitalist. Masses of labourers, crowded into the factory, are organized like soldiers. As privates of the industrial army they are placed under the command of a perfect hierarchy of officers and sergeants. Not only are they slaves of the bourgeois class, and of the bourgeois State; they are daily and hourly enslaved by the machine, by the overlooker, and, above all, by the individual bourgeois manufacturer himself. The more openly this despotism proclaims gain to be its end and aim, the more petty, the more hateful and the more embittering it is.

The less the skill and exertion of strength implied in manual labour, in other words, the more modern industry becomes developed, the more is the labour of men superseded by that of women. Differences of age and sex have no longer any distinctive social validity for working class. All are instruments of labour, more or less expensive to use, according to their age and sex.

No sooner is the exploitation of the labourer by the manufacturer, so far, at an end, and he receives his wages in cash, than he is set upon by the other portions of the bourgeoisie, the landlord, the shopkeeper, the pawnbroker, etc.

The lower strata of the middle class—the small tradespeople, shopkeepers, and retired tradesmen generally, the handicraftsmen and peasants—all these sink gradually into the proletariat, partly because their diminutive capital does not suffice for the scale on which Modern Industry is carried on, and is swamped in the competition with the large capitalists, partly because their specialized skill is rendered worthless by new methods of production. Thus the proletariat is recruited from all classes of the population.

The proletariat goes through various stages of development. With its birth begins its struggle with the bourgeoisie. At first the contest is carried on by individual labourers, then by the workpeople of a factory, then by the operatives of one trade, in one locality, against the individual bourgeois who directly exploits them. They direct their attacks not against the bourgeois conditions of production, but against the instruments of production themselves; they destroy imported wares that compete with their labour, they smash to pieces machinery, they set factories ablaze, they seek to restore by force the vanished status of the workman of the Middle Ages.

At this stage the labourers still form an incoherent mass scattered over the whole country, and broken up by their mutual competition. If anywhere they unite to form more compact bodies, this is not yet the consequence of their own active union, but of the union of the bourgeoisie, which class, in order to attain its own political ends, is compelled to set the whole proletariat in motion, and is moreover yet, for a time, able to do so. At this stage, therefore, the proletarians do not fight their enemies, but the enemies of their enemies, the remnants of absolute monarchy, the landowners, the non-industrial bourgeois, the petty bourgeoisie. Thus the whole historical movement is concentrated in the hands of the bourgeoisie; every victory so obtained is a victory for the bourgeoisie.

But with the development of industry the proletariat not only increases in number; it becomes concentrated in greater masses, its strength grows, and it feels that strength more. The various interests and conditions of life within the ranks of the proletariat are more and more equalized, in proportion as machinery obliterates all distinctions of labour, and nearly everywhere reduces wages to the same low level. The growing competition among the bourgeois, and the resulting commercial crises, make the wages of the workers ever more fluctuating. The unceasing improvement of machinery, ever more rapidly developing, makes their livelihood more and more precarious; the collisions between individual workmen and individual bourgeois take more and more the character of collisions between two classes. Thereupon the workers begin to form combinations (Trades' Unions) against the bourgeois; they club together in order to keep up the rate of wages; they found permanent associations in order to make provisions beforehand for these occasional revolts. Here and there the contest breaks out into riots.

Now and then the workers are victorious, but only for a time. The real fruit of their battles lies, not in the immediate result, but in the ever-expanding union of the workers. This union is helped on by the improved means of communication that are created by modern industry and that place the workers of different localities in contact with one another. It was just this contact that was needed to centralize the numerous local struggles, all of the same character, into one national struggle between classes. But every class struggle is a political struggle. And that union, to attain which the burghers of the Middle Ages, with their miserable highways, required centuries, the modern proletarians, thanks to railways, achieve in a few years.

This organization of the proletarians into a class, and consequently into a political party, is continually being upset again by the competition between the workers themselves. But it ever rises up again, stronger, firmer, mightier. It compels legislative recognition of particular interests of the workers, by taking advantage of the divisions among the bourgeoisie itself. Thus the ten-hours' bill in England was carried.

Altogether collisions between the classes of the old society further, in many ways, the course of development of the proletariat. The bourgeoisie finds itself involved in a constant battle. At first with the aristocracy; later on, with those portions of the bourgeoisie itself, whose interests have become antagonistic to the progress of industry; at all times, with the bourgeoisie of foreign countries. In all these battles it sees itself compelled to appeal to the proletariat, to ask for its help, and thus, to drag it into the political arena. The bourgeoisie itself, therefore, supplies the proletariat with its own elements of political and general education, in other words, it furnishes the proletariat with weapons for fighting the bourgeoisie.

Further, as we have already seen, entire sections of the ruling classes are, by the advance of industry, precipitated into the proletariat, or are at least threatened in their conditions of existence. These also supply the proletariat with fresh elements of enlightenment and progress.

Finally, in times when the class struggle nears the decisive hour, the process of dissolution going on within the ruling class, in fact within the whole range of old society, assumes such a violent, glaring character, that a small section of the ruling class cuts itself adrift, and joins the revolutionary class, the class that holds the future in its hands. Just as, therefore, at an earlier period, a section of the nobility went over to the bourgeoisie, so now a portion of the bourgeoisie goes over to the proletariat, and in particular, a portion of the bourgeois ideologists, who have raised themselves to the level of comprehending theoretically the historical movement as a whole.

Of all the classes that stand face to face with the bourgeoisie today, the proletariat alone is a really revolutionary class. The other classes decay and finally disappear in the face of Modern Industry; the proletariat is its special and essential product.

The lower middle class, the small manufacturer, the shopkeeper, the artisan, the peasant, all these fight against the bourgeoisie, to save from extinction their existence as fractions of the middle class. They are therefore not revolutionary, but conservative. Nay more, they are reactionary, for they try to roll back the wheel of history. If by chance they are revolutionary, they are so only in view of their impending transfer into the proletariat, they thus defend not their present, but their future interests, they desert their own standpoint to place themselves at that of the proletariat.

The 'dangerous class', the social scum, that passively rotting mass thrown off by the lowest layers of old society, may, here and there, be swept into the movement by a proletarian revolution; its conditions of life, however, prepare it far more for the part of a bribed tool of reactionary intrigue.

In the conditions of the proletariat, those of old society at large are already virtually swamped. The proletarian is without property; his relation to his wife and children has no longer anything in common with the bourgeois family-relations; modern industrial labour, modern subjection to capital, the same in England as in France, in America as in Germany, has stripped him of every trace of national character. Law, morality, religion, are to him so many bourgeois prejudices, behind which lurk in ambush just as many bourgeois interests.

All the preceding classes that got the upper hand, sought to fortify their already acquired status by subjecting society at large to their conditions of appropriation. The proletarians cannot become masters of the productive forces of society, except by abolishing their own previous mode of appropriation, and thereby also every other previous mode of appropriation. They have nothing of their own to secure and to fortify; their mission is to destroy all previous securities for, and insurances of, individual property.

All previous historical movements were movements of minorities, or in the interests of minorities. The proletarian movement is the self-conscious, independent movement of the immense majority, in the interests of the immense majority. The proletariat, the lowest stratum of our present society, cannot stir, cannot raise itself up, without the whole superincumbent strata of official society being sprung into the air.

Though not in substance, yet in form, the struggle of the proletariat with the bourgeoisie is at first a national struggle. The proletariat of each country must, of course, first of all settle the matters with its own bourgeoisie.

In depicting the most general phases of the development of the proletariat, we traced the more or less veiled civil war, raging within existing society, up to the point where that war breaks out into open revolution, and where the violent overthrow of the bourgeoisie lays the foundation for the sway of the proletariat.

Hitherto, every form of society has been based, as we have already seen, on the antagonism of oppressing and oppressed classes. But in order to oppose a class, certain conditions must be assured to it under which it can, at least, continue its slavish existence. The serf, in the period of serfdom, raised himself to membership in the commune, just as the petty bourgeois, under the yoke of feudal absolutism, managed to develop into a bourgeois. The modern labourer, on the contrary, instead of rising with the progress of industry, sinks deeper and deeper below the conditions of existence of his own class. He becomes the pauper, and pauperism develops more rapidly than population and wealth. And here it becomes evident, that the bourgeoisie is unfit any longer to be the ruling class in society, and to impose its conditions of existence upon society as an over-riding law. It is unfit to rule because it is incompetent to assure an existence to its slave within his slavery, because it cannot help letting him sink into such a state, that it has to feed him, instead of being fed by him. Society can no longer live under this bourgeoisie, in other words, its existence is no longer compatible with society.

The essential condition for the existence, and for the sway of the bourgeois class, is the formation and augmentation of capital; the condition for capital is wage-labour. Wage-labour rests exclusively on competition between the labourers. The advance of industry, whose involuntary promoter is the bourgeoisie, replaces the isolation of the labourers, due to competition, by their revolutionary combination, due to association. The development of Modern Industry, therefore, cuts from under its feet the very foundation on which the bourgeoisie produces and appropriates products. What the bourgeoisie, therefore, produces, above all, is its own grave-diggers. Its fall and the victory of the proletariat are equally inevitable.

F. Engels

London, May 1, 1890
Written by Engels for the German
edition which appeared in London in
1890

Printed according to the
1890 edition
Translated from the German

NOTES

1. By bourgeoisie is meant the class of modern Capitalists, owners of the means of social production and employers of wage-labour. By proletariat, the class of modern wage-labourers who, having no means of production of their own, are reduced to selling their labour-power in order to live. [*Note by Engels to the English edition of 1888.*]

2. That is, all *written* history. In 1847, the pre-history of society, the social organization existing previous to recorded history, was all but unknown. Since then, Haxthausen discovered common ownership of land in Russia, Maurer proved it to be the social foundation from which all Teutonic races started in history, and by and by village communities were found to be, or to have been the primitive form of society everywhere from India to Ireland. The inner organization of this primitive Communistic society was laid bare, in its typical form, by Morgan's crowning discovery of the true nature of the *gens* and its relation to the *tribe*. With the dissolution of these

primeval communities society begins to be differentiated into separate and finally antagonistic classes. I have attempted to retrace this process of dissolution in: 'Der Ursprung der Familie, des Privateigentums und des Staats' [*The Origin of the Family, Private Property and the State*, 2nd ed., Stuttgart 1886. [*Note by Engels to the English edition of 1888.*]

3. Guild-master, that is, a full member of a guild, a master within, not a head of a guild. [*Note by Engels to the English edition of 1888.*]

4. 'Commune' was the name taken, in France, by the nascent towns even before they had conquered from their feudal lords and masters local self-government and political rights as the 'Third Estate'. Generally speaking, for the economical development of the bourgeoisie, England is here taken as the typical country; for its political development, France. [*Note by Engels to the English edition of 1888.*]

    This was the name given their urban communities by the townsmen of Italy and France, after they had purchased or wrested their initial rights of self-government from their feudal lords. [*Note by Engels to the German edition, 1890.*]

FRIEDRICH ENGELS

1820–1895
GERMANY

Major Works

1844	*The Condition of the Working Class in England*
1845	*The German Ideology*
1848	*The Communist Manifesto*
1878	*Anti-Duhring*
1884	*The Origin of the Family, Private Property and the State*
1885	Completion of Vol. II of *Capital* from Marx's sketchy notes
1895	Completion of Vol III of *Capital*

> The overthrow of the mother right was the world historical defeat of the female sex.[1]

> With the transfer of the means of production into common ownership, the single family ceases to be the economic unit of society. Private housekeeping is transformed into a social industry. The care and education of the children becomes [*sic*] a public affair; society looks after all children alike, whether they are legitimate or not.[2]
>
> —*Friedrich Engels*

Friedrich Engels, a close collaborator of Karl Marx, was a powerful force behind the development of the social and economic ideas of Marxist philosophy. Most of these ideas were expressed in co-authorship with Marx, particularly in *The German Ideology* and *The Communist Manifesto*. Engels also contributed to a variety of journals, focusing on his interests in history, anthropology, and science. His 1878 publication, *Anti-Duhring*, was a refutation of the views of Eugen Duhring, a socialist intellectual who attacked Marx's ideas as not being clearly materialist. Engels's refutation, a systematic interpretation of the world informed by a Marxist philosophy, was later to become a guide for those interested in Marxism.

    Engels has often been portrayed as intellectually subordinate to Marx, a portrait he himself modestly endorsed to the extent that it has become widely accepted. It is ironic that subordination is the theme of the work for which he is most famous: *The Origin of the Family, Private Property and the State*. In this work he proffers an explanation of women's subordination, utilizing a materialist approach. He explores the link between the ownership of private property and the subordinate position of women. Examining society from the period of primitive communalism, when no distinct classes existed, to a period when private property became a reality, he finds that the emergence of a surplus of goods controlled by particular men made structured family relationships an imperative. Sheila Ruth points out:

> As the importance of private property developed, the matter of inheritance altered the significance of children, and women's reproductive labour was appropriated by men just as their productive labour had been. Hence (as many feminists today also theorize), the imperatives of virginity, chastity, and monogamy developed for women as the patterns of inheritance persuaded men to insure their paternity.[3]

With the emergence of the second wave of feminism in North America and Europe in the 1960s, there has been a revival of Marxist discourse on the much ignored 'woman question'. Such a discourse was important not only to the issue within the parameters of the socialist agenda (which occurred after Marx's death) but presented the only viable discourse on sexual inequality to be found within the Marxist tradition (see MacKinnon, this volume).

In contemporary times, Engels's views on the origin of women's subordination have come under severe criticism from different theoretical perspectives.[4] Most of the criticisms have pointed out the inadequacies of the explanation, while others have emphasized the importance of his positive contributions to the ongoing debate. Much of his argument focuses on the institutionalization of monogamy as a means of protecting the legitimacy of heirs. This, he argues, was at the expense of women's sexual freedom, culminating in 'the world historical defeat of the female sex'. For Engels, monogamy with all its constraints on women will disappear only with the dissolution of private property and class divisions. In this event, marriage and sex will then be based on choice, which will ultimately bring about the restoration of women's sexual freedom.

For most feminist theorists, this approach is inadequate, as it does not demonstrate how such a dissolution is to take place. What, then, is the decisive role of class struggle in the origin and maintenance of women's subordination? What is the extent of the link, if any, between capitalism and patriarchy? Is such a link inextricable, or do these concepts represent parallel processes?

Notes

1. Engels, *The Origin of the Family, Private Property and the State* (New York: International Publishers, 1942), 50.
2. Ibid., 67.
3. Sheila Ruth, *Issues in Feminism: An Introduction to Women's Studies*, 2nd edn

(Mountain View, Calif.: Mayfield Publishing Co., 1990), 179.
4. See Janet Sayers et al., *Engels Revisited: New Feminist Essays* (London and New York: Tavistock, 1987).

THE OVERTHROW OF THE MOTHER-RIGHT AND MONOGAMOUS MARRIAGE

The Pairing Family

A certain pairing for longer or shorter periods took place already under group marriage, or even earlier. Among his numerous wives, the man had a principal wife (one can scarcely yet call her his favourite wife) and he was her principal husband, among the others. This situation contributed in no small degree to the confusion among the missionaries, who see in group marriage, now promiscuous community of wives, now wanton adultery. Such habitual pairing, however, necessarily became more and more established as the gens developed and as the numbers of classes of 'brothers' and 'sisters' between which marriage was now impossibly increased. The impetus given by the gens to prevent marriage between blood relatives drives things still further. Thus we find that among the Iroquois and most other Indian tribes in the lower stage of barbarism, marriage is prohibited between *all* relatives recognized by their system, and these are of several hundred kinds. This growing complexity of marriage prohibitions rendered group marriages more and more impossible; they were supplanted by the *pairing family*. At this stage one man lives with one woman, yet in such manner that polygamy and occasional infidelity remain men's privileges, even though the former is seldom practised for economic reasons; at the same time, the strictest fidelity is demanded of the woman during the period of cohabitation, adultery on her part being cruelly punished. The marriage tie can, however, be easily dissolved by either side, and the children belong solely to the mother, as previously.

In this ever widening exclusion of blood relatives from marriage, natural selection also continues to have its effect. In Morgan's words,

> marriage between non-consanguineous gentes 'tended to create a more vigorous stock physically and mentally. When two advancing tribes are blended into one people ... the new skull and brain would widen and lengthen to the sum of the capabilities of both'.

Tribes constituted according to gentes were bound, therefore, to gain the upper hand over the more backward ones, or carry them along by force of their example.

Thus, the evolution of the family in prehistoric times consisted in the continual narrowing of the circle—originally embracing the whole tribe—within which marital community between the two sexes prevailed. By the successive exclusion, first of closer, then of ever remoter relatives, and finally even of those merely related by marriage every kind of group marriage was ultimately rendered practically impossible; and in the end there remained only the one, for the moment still loosely united, couple, the molecule, with the dissolution of which marriage itself completely ceases. The fact alone shows how little individual sex love, in the modern sense of the word, had to do with the origin of monogamy. The practice of all peoples in this stage affords still further proof of this. Whereas under previous forms of the family men were never in want of women but, on the contrary, had a surfeit of them, women now became scarce and were sought after. Consequently, with pairing marriage begins the abduction and purchase of women—widespread *symptoms*, but nothing more, of a much more deeply-rooted change that had set in. These symptoms, mere methods of obtaining women, McLennan, the pedantic Scot, nevertheless metamorphosed into special classes of families which he called 'marriage by abduction' and 'marriage by purchase'. Moreover, among the American Indians, and also among other tribes (at the same stage), the arrangement of a marriage is not the affair of the two parties to the same, who, indeed, are often not even consulted, but of their respective mothers. Two complete strangers are thus often betrothed and only learn of the conclusion of the deal when the marriage day approaches. Prior to the marriage, presents are made by the bridegroom to the gentile relatives of the bride (that is, to her relatives on her mother's side, not to the father and his relatives), these presents serving as purchase gifts for the ceded girl. The marriage may be dissolved at the pleasure of either of the two spouses. Nevertheless, among many tribes, for example, the Iroquois, public sentiment gradually developed against such separations. When conflicts arise, the gentile relatives of both parties intervene and attempt a reconciliation, and separation takes place only after such efforts prove fruitless, the children remaining with the mother and each party being free to marry again.

The pairing family, itself too weak and unstable to make an independent household necessary, or even desirable, did not by any means dissolve the communistic household transmitted from earlier times. But the communistic household implies the supremacy of women in the house, just as the exclusive recognition of a natural mother, because of the impossibility of determining the natural father with certainty, signifies high self esteem for the women, that is, for the mothers. That woman was the slave of man at the commencement of society is one of the most absurd notions that have come down to us from the period of Enlightenment of the eighteenth century. Women occupied not only a free but also a highly respected position among all savages and all barbarians of the lower and middle stages and partly even of the upper stage. Let Ashur Wright, missionary for many years among the Seneca Iroquois, testify what her place still was in the pairing family:

> As to their family system, when occupying the old long houses [communistic households embracing several families] . . . it is probable that some one clan [gens] predominated, the women taking in husbands from other clans [gentes] . . . Usually the female portion ruled the house; the stores were in common; but woe to the luckless husband or lover who was too shiftless to do his share of the providing. No matter how many children or whatever goods he might have in the house, he might at any time be ordered to pack up his blanket and budge; and after such orders it would not be healthful for him to attempt to disobey. The house would be too hot for him;

and he had to retreat to his own clan [gens]; or, as was often done, go and start a new matrimonial alliance in some other. The women were the great power among the clans [gentes], as everywhere else. They did not hesitate, when occasion required, to knock off the horns, as it was technically called, from the head of the chief and send him back to the ranks of the warriors.

The communistic household, in which most of the women or even all the women belong to one and the same gens, while the men come from various other gentes, is the material foundation of that predominance of women which generally obtained in primitive times; and Bachofen's discovery of this constitutes the third great service he has rendered. I may add, furthermore, that the reports of travellers and missionaries about women among savages and barbarians being burdened with excessive toil in no way conflict with what has been said above. The division of labour between the two sexes is determined by causes entirely different from those that determine the status of women in society. Peoples whose women have to work much harder than we would consider proper often have far more real respect for women than our Europeans have for theirs. The social status of the lady of civilization, surrounded by sham homage and estranged from all real work, is socially infinitely lower than that of the hard-working woman of barbarism, who was regarded among her people as a real lady (lady, *frowa*, *Frau* - mistress [*Herrin*]) and was such by the nature of her position.

Whether or not the pairing family has totally supplanted group marriage in America today must be decided by closer investigation among the North-Western and particularly among the South American peoples who are still in the higher stage of savagery. So very many instances of sexual freedom are reported with regard to these latter that the complete suppression of the old group marriage can scarcely be assumed. At any rate, not all traces of it have as yet disappeared. Among at least forty North American tribes, the man who marries the eldest sister in a family is entitled to all her sisters as wives as soon as they reach the requisite age—a survival of the community of husbands for a whole group of sisters. And Bancroft relates that the tribes of the Californian peninsula (in the upper stage of savagery) have certain festivities, during which several 'tribes' congregate for the purpose of indiscriminate sexual intercourse. These are manifestly gentes for whom these festivities represent dim memories of the times when the women of one gens had all the men of another for their common husbands, and *vice versa*. The same custom still prevails in Australia. Among a few peoples it happens that the older men, the chiefs and sorcerer-priests, exploit the community of wives for their own ends and monopolize most of the women for themselves; but they, in their turn, have to allow the old common possession to be restored during certain feasts and great popular gatherings and permit their wives to enjoy themselves with the young men. Westermarck (pp. 28, 29) adduces a whole series of examples of such periodical Saturnalian feasts during which the old free sexual intercourse comes into force again for a short period, as, for example, among the Hos, the Santais, the Panjas and Kotars of India, among some African peoples, etc. Curiously enough, Westermarck concludes from this that they are relics, not of group marriage, which he rejects, but—of the mating season common alike to primitive man and the other animals.

We now come to Bachofen's fourth great discovery, that of the widespread form of transition from group marriage to pairing. What Bachofen construes as a penance for infringing the ancient commandments of the gods, the penance with which the woman buys her right to chastity, is in fact nothing more than a mystical expression for the penance by means of which the woman purchases her redemption from the ancient community of husbands and acquires the right to give herself to *one* man only. This penance takes the form of limited surrender: the Babylonian women had to surrender themselves once a year in the temple of Mylitta. Other Middle Eastern peoples sent their girls for years to the Temple of Anaitis, where they had to practise free love with favourites of their own choice before they were allowed to marry. Similar customs bearing religious guise are common to nearly all Asiatic peoples between the Mediterranean and the Ganges. The propitiatory sacrifice for the purpose of redemption becomes gradually lighter in the course of time, as Bachofen notes:

> The annually repeated offering yields place to the single performance; the hetaerism of the matrons is succeeded by that of the maidens, its practice during marriage by practice before marriage, the indiscriminate surrender to all by surrender to certain persons. (Mother Right: XIX)

Among other peoples, the religious guise is absent; among some—the Thracians, Celts, etc., of antiquity, and many aboriginal inhabitants of India, the Malay peoples, South Sea Islanders and many American Indians even to this day—the girls enjoy the greatest sexual freedom until their marriage. Particularly is this the case throughout almost the whole of South America, as anybody who has penetrated a little into the interior can testify. Thus, Agassiz (*A Journey in Brazil*, Boston and New York, 1886: 266) relates the following about a rich family of Indian descent. When he was introduced to the daughter and enquired after her father, who, he supposed, was the mother's husband, an officer on active service in the war against Paraguay, the mother answered smilingly: '*naõ tem pai, é filha da fortuna*'—she has no father, she is the daughter of chance.

> It is the way the Indian or half-breed women here always speak of their illegitimate children, unconscious of any wrong or shame. So far is this from being an unusual case that the opposite seems the exception. Children [often] know [only] about their mother, for all the care and responsibility falls upon her; but they have no knowledge of their father, nor does it seem to occur to the woman that she or her children have any claim upon him.

What here appears to be so strange to the civilized man is simply the rule according to mother right and in group marriage.

Among still other peoples, the bridegroom's friends and relatives, or the wedding guests, exercise their old traditional right to the bride at the wedding itself, and the bridegroom has his turn last of all; for instance, on the Balearic Islands and among the African Augilas of antiquity, and among the Bareas of Abyssinia even now. In the case of still other peoples, again, an official person—the chief of the tribe or of the gens, the cacique, shaman, priest, prince or whatever his title—represents the community and exercises the right of first night with the bride. Despite all neoromantic whitewashing, this *jus primae noctis* [right on the first night] persists to this day as a relic of group marriage among most of the natives of the Alaska territory (Bancroft, *Native Races*, I: 81), among the Tahus in North Mexico (*ibid.*: 584) and among other peoples: and it existed throughout the Middle Ages at least in the originally Celtic countries, where it was directly transmitted from group marriage; for instance, in Aragon. While the peasant in Castile was never a serf, in Aragon the most ignominious serfdom prevailed until abolished by the decree issued by Ferdinand the Catholic in 1486. This public act states:

> We pass judgement and declare that the aforementioned lords (señors, barons) ... also shall not sleep the first night with the woman taken in wedlock by a peasant, nor on the wedding night, after she has gone to bed, stride over it and over the woman as a sign of their authority; nor shall the aforementioned lords avail themselves of the services of the sons or daughters of the peasant, with or without payment, against their will. (Quoted in the Catalonian original by Sugenheim, Serfdom, Petersburg 1861: 355.)

Bachofen is again absolutely right when he contends throughout that the transition from what he terms 'hetaerism' or *Sumpfzeugung* to monogamy was brought about essentially by the women. The more the old traditional sexual relations lost their naive, primitive jungle character, as a result of the development of the economic conditions of life, that is, with the undermining of the old communism and the growing density of the population, the more degrading and oppressive must they have appeared to the women; the more fervently must they have longed for the right to chastity, to temporary or permanent marriage with one man only, as a deliverance. This advance could not have originated from the men, if only for the reason that they have never—not even to the present day—dreamed of renouncing the pleasures of actual group marriage. Only after the transition to pairing marriage had been effected by the women could the men introduce strict monogamy—for the women only, of course.

The pairing family arose on the border line between savagery and barbarism, mainly at the upper stage of savagery, and here and there only at the lower stage of barbarism. It is the form of the family characteristic of barbarism, in the same way as group marriage is characteristic of savagery and monogamy of civilization. For its further development to stable monogamy, causes different from those we have hitherto found operating were required. In the pairing family, the group was already reduced to its last unit, its two-atom molecule—to one man and one woman. Natural selection had completed its work by constantly reducing the circle of community marriage; there was nothing more left for it to do in this direction. If no new, *social* driving forces had come into operation, there would have been no reason why a new form of the family should arise out of the pairing family. But these driving forces did commence to operate.

We now leave America, the classical soil of the pairing family. There is no evidence to enable us to conclude that a higher form of the family developed there, or that strict monogamy existed in any part of it at any time before its discovery and conquest. It was otherwise in the Old World.

Here the domestication of animals and the breeding of herds had developed a hitherto unsuspected source of wealth and created entirely new social relationships. Until the lower stage of barbarism, fixed wealth consisted almost entirely of the house, clothing, crude ornaments, and the implements for procuring and preparing food: boats, weapons and household utensils of the simplest kind. Food had to be won anew day by day. Now, with herds of horses, camels, donkeys, oxen, sheep, goats and pigs, the advancing pastoral peoples—the Aryans in the Indian land of the five rivers and the Ganges area, as well as in the then much more richly watered steppes of the Oxus and the Jaxartes, and the Semites on the Euphrates and the Tigris—acquired possessions demanding merely supervision and most elementary care in order to propagate in ever-increasing numbers and to yield the richest nutriment in milk and meat. All previous means of procuring food now sank into the background. Hunting, once a necessity, now became a luxury.

But to whom did this new wealth belong? Originally, undoubtedly, to the gens. But private property in herds must have developed at a very early stage. It is hard to say whether Father Abraham appeared to the author of the so-called First Book of Moses as the owner of his herds and flocks in his own right as head of a family community or by virtue of his status as actual hereditary chief of a gens. One thing, however, is certain, and that is that we must not regard him as a property owner in the modern sense of the term. Equally certain is it that on the threshold of authenticated history we find that everywhere the herds are already the separate property of the family chiefs, in exactly the same way as were the artistic products of barbarism, metal utensils, articles of luxury and, finally, human cattle—the slaves.

For now slavery also was invented. The slave was useless to the barbarian of the lower stage. It was for this reason that the American Indians treated their vanquished foes quite differently from the way they were treated in the upper stage. The men were either killed or adopted as brothers by the tribe of the victors. The women were either taken in marriage or likewise just adopted along with their surviving children. Human labour power at this stage yielded no noticeable surplus as yet over the cost of its maintenance. With the introduction of cattle breeding, of the working up of metals, of weaving and, finally, of field cultivation, this changed. Just as the once so easily obtainable wives had now acquired an exchange value and were bought, so it happened with labour power, especially after the herds had finally been converted into family possessions. The family did not increase as rapidly as the cattle. More people were required to tend them; the captives taken in war were useful for just this purpose, and, furthermore, they could be bred like the cattle itself.

Such riches, once they had passed into the private possession of families and there rapidly multiplied, struck a powerful blow at a society founded on pairing marriage and mother-right gens. Pairing marriage had introduced a new element into the family. By the side of the natural mother it had placed the authenticated natural father—who was probably better authenticated than many a 'father' of the present day. According to the division of labour then prevailing in the family, the procuring of food and the implements necessary thereto, and therefore, also, the ownership of the latter, fell to the man; he took them with him in case of separation, just as the woman retained the household goods. Thus, according to the custom of society at that time, the man was also the owner of the new sources of foodstuffs—the cattle—and later, of the new instrument of labour—the slaves. According to the custom of the same society, however, his children could not inherit from him, for the position in this respect was as follows:

According to mother right, that is, as long as descent was reckoned solely through the female line, and according to the original custom of inheritance in the gens, it was the gentile relatives that at first inherited from a deceased member of the gens. The property had to remain within the gens. At first, in view of the insignificance of the chattels in question, it may, in practice, have passed to the nearest gentile relatives—that is, to the blood relatives on the mother's side. The children of the deceased, however, belonged not to his gens, but to that of their mother. In the beginning, they inherited from their mother, along with the rest of their mother's blood relatives, and later, perhaps, had first claim upon her property; but they could not inherit from their father, because they did not belong to his gens, and his property had to remain in the latter. On the death of the herd owner, therefore, his herds passed, first of all, to his brothers and sisters and to his sisters' children or the descendants of his mother's sisters. His own children, however, were disinherited.

Thus, as wealth increased, it, on the one hand, gave the man a more important status in the family than the woman, and, on the other hand, created a stimulus to utilize this strengthened position in order to overthrow the traditional order of inheritance in favour of his children. But this was impossible as long as descent according to mother right prevailed. This had, therefore, to be overthrown, and it was overthrown; and it was not so difficult to do this as it appears to us now. For this revolution—one of the most decisive ever experienced by mankind—need not have disturbed one single living member of a gens. All the members could remain what they were previously. The simple decision sufficed that in future the descendants of the male members should remain in the gens, but that those of females were to be excluded from the gens and transferred to that of their father. The reckoning of descent through the female line and the right of inheritance through the mother were hereby overthrown and male lineage and right of inheritance from the father instituted. We know nothing as to how and when this revolution was effected among the civilized peoples. It falls entirely within prehistoric times. That it was actually *effected* is more than proved by the abundant traces of mother right which have been collected, especially by Bachofen. How easily it is accomplished can be seen from a whole number of Indian tribes, among whom it has only recently taken place and is still proceeding, partly under the influence of increasing wealth and changed methods of life (transplantation from the forests to the prairies), and partly under the moral influence of civilization and the missionaries. Of eight Missouri tribes, six have male and two still retain the female lineage and female inheritance line. Among the Shawnees, Miamis and Delawares it has become the custom to transfer the children to the father's gens by giving them one of the gentile names obtaining therein, in order that they may inherit from him. 'Innate human casuistry to seek to change things by changing their names! And to find loopholes for breaking through tradition within tradition itself, wherever a direct interest provided a sufficient motive!' (Marx) As a consequence, hopeless confusion arose; and matters could only be straightened out, and partly were straightened out, by the transition to father right. 'This appears altogether to be the most natural transition.' (Marx) As for what the experts on comparative law have to tell us regarding the ways and means by which this transition was effected among the civilized peoples of the Old World—almost mere hypotheses, of course—see M. Kovalevsky, *Outline of the Origin and Evolution of the Family and Property*, Stockholm 1890.

The overthrow of mother right was the *world-historic defeat of the female sex*. The man seized the reins in the house also, the woman was degraded, enthralled, the slave of the man's lust, a mere instrument for breeding children. This lowered position of women, especially manifest among the Greeks of the Heroic and still more of the Classical Age, has become gradually embellished and dissembled and, in part, clothed in a milder form, but by no means abolished.

The first effect of the sole rule of the men that was now established is shown in the intermediate form of the family which now emerges, the patriarchal family. Its chief attribute is not polygamy—of which more anon—but

> the organization of a number of persons, bond and free, into a family, under the paternal power of the head of the family. In the Semitic form, this family chief lives in polygamy, the bondsman has a wife and children, and the purpose of the whole organization is the care of flocks and herds over a limited area.

The essential features are the incorporation of bondsmen and the paternal power; the Roman family, accordingly, constitutes the perfected type of this form of family. The word *familia* did not originally signify the ideal of our modern Philistine, which is a compound of sentimentality and domestic discord. Among the Romans, in the beginning, it did not even refer to the married couple and their children, but to the slaves alone. *Famulus* means a household slave and *familia* signifies the totality of slaves belonging to one individual. Even in the time of Gaius the *familia, id est patrimonium* (that is, the inheritance) was bequeathed by will. The expression was invented by the Romans to describe a new social organism, the head of which had under him wife and children and a number of slaves, under Roman paternal power, with power of life and death over them all.

> The term, therefore, is no older than the ironclad family system of the Latin tribes, which came in after field agriculture and after legalized servitude, as well as after the separation of the Greeks and (Aryan) Latins.

To which Marx adds: 'The modern family contains in embryo not only slavery (*servitus*) but serfdom also, since from the very beginning it is connected with agricultural services. It contains within itself *in miniature* all the antagonisms which later develop on a wide scale within society and its state.'

Such a form of the family shows the transition of the pairing family to monogamy. In order to guarantee the fidelity of the wife, that is, the paternity of the children, the woman is placed in the man's absolute power; if he kills her, he is but exercising his right.

With the patriarchal family we enter the field of written history and, therewith, a field in which the science of comparative law can render us important assistance. And in fact it has here procured us considerable progress. We are indebted to Maxim Kovalevsky

(*Outline of the Origin and Evolution of the Family and Property*: 60-100) for the proof that the patriarchal household community (*Hausgenossenschaft*), such as we still find it today among the Serbs and the Bulgars under the designations of *Zadruga* (meaning something like fraternity) or *Bratstvo* (brotherhood), and among the Oriental peoples in a modified form, constituted the transition stage between the mother-right family which evolved out of group marriage and the individual family known to the modern world. This appears to be proved at least as far as the civilized peoples of the Old World, the Aryans and Semites, are concerned.

The South-Slavic *Zadruga* provides the best existing example of such a family community. It embraces several generations of the descendants of one father and their wives, who all live together in one household, till their fields in common, feed and clothe themselves from the common store and communally own all surplus products. The community is under the supreme management of the master of the house (*domàcin*), who represents it in external affairs, may dispose of smaller objects, and manages the finances, being responsible for the latter as well as for the regular conduct of business. He is elected and does not by any means need to be the eldest. The women and their work are under the direction of the mistress of the house (*domàcica*), who is usually the *domàcin's* wife. In the choice of husbands for the girls she has an important, often the decisive voice. Supreme power, however, is vested in the Family Council, the assembly of all adult members, women as well as men. To this assembly the master of the house renders his account; it makes all the important decisions, administers justice among the members, decides on purchases and sales of any importance, especially of landed property, etc.

It was only about ten years ago that the existence of such large family communities in Russia also was proved; they are now generally recognized as being just as firmly rooted in the popular customs of the Russians as the *obscina*, or village community. They figure in the most ancient Russian law code—the *Pravda* of Yaroslav—under the same name (*verv*) as in the Dalmatian Laws, and references to them may be found also in Polish and Czech historical sources.

According to Heusler (*Institutes of German Right*) the economic unit among the Germans also was not originally the individual family in the modern sense, but the 'house community' [*Hausgenossenschaft*], consisting of several generations, or individual families, and more often than not including plenty of bondsmen. The Roman family, too, has been traced back to this type, and in consequence the absolute power of the head of the house, as also the lack of rights of the remaining members of the family in relation to him, has recently been strongly questioned. Similar family communities are likewise supposed to have existed among the Celts in Ireland; in France they continued to exist in Nivernais under the name of *parçonneries* right up to the French Revolution, while in Franche-Comté they are not quite extinct even today. In the district of Louhans (Saône et Loire) may be seen large peasant houses with a lofty communal central hall reaching up to the roof, surrounded by sleeping rooms, to which access is had by staircases of from six to eight steps, and in which dwell several generations in the same family.

In India, the household community with common tillage of the soil was already mentioned by Nearchus, in the time of Alexander the Great, and exists to this day in the same area, in the Punjab and the entire North-Western part of this country. Kovalevsky himself was able to testify to its existence in the Caucasus. It still exists in Algeria among the Kabyles. It is said to have existed even in America; attempts are being made to identify it with the *calpullis* in ancient Mexico, described by Zurita; Cunow, on the other hand, has proved fairly clearly (in *Ausland*, 1890, Nos. 42-4) that a kind of Mark constitution existed in Peru (where, peculiarly enough, the Mark was called *marca*) at the time of the Conquest, with periodical allotment of the cultivated land, that is, individual tillage.

At any rate, the patriarchal household community with common land ownership and common tillage now assumes quite another significance than hitherto. We can no longer doubt the important transitional role which it played among the civilized and many other peoples of the Old World between the mother-right family and the monogamian family. We shall return later on to the further conclusion drawn by Kovalevsky, namely, that it was likewise the transition stage out of which developed the village, or Mark, community with individual cultivation and at first periodical, then permanent allotment of arable and pasture lands.

As regards family life within these household communities, it should be noted that in Russia, at least, the head of the house is reputed to be strongly abusing his position as far as the younger women, particularly his daughters-in-law, are concerned, and to be very often converting them into a harem; these conditions are rather eloquently reflected in the Russian folk songs.

A few words more about polygamy and polyandry before we deal with monogamy, which developed rapidly following the overthrow of mother right. Both these marriage forms can only be exceptions, historical luxury products, so to speak, unless they appeared side by side in any country, which, as is well known, is not the case. As, therefore, the men, excluded from polygamy, could not console themselves with the women left over from polyandry, the numerical strength of men and women without regard to social institutions having been fairly equal hitherto, it is evident that neither the one nor the other form of marriage could rise to general prevalence. Actually, polygamy on the part of a man was clearly a product of slavery and limited to a few exceptional cases. In the Semitic patriarchal family, only the patriarch himself and, at most, a couple of his sons lived in polygamy; the others had to be content with one wife each. It remains the same today throughout the entire Orient. Polygamy is a privilege of the rich and the grandees, the wives being recruited chiefly by the purchase of female slaves; the mass of the people live in monogamy. Just such an exception is provided by polyandry in India and Tibet, the certainly not uninteresting origin of which from group marriage requires closer investigation. In its practice, at any rate, it appears to be much more tolerable than the jealous harem establishments of the Mohammedans. At least, among the Nairs in India, the men, in groups of three, four or more, have, to be sure, one wife in common; but each of them can simultaneously have a second wife in common with three or more other men, and, in the same way, a third wife, a fourth and so on. It is a wonder that McLennan did not discover a new class—that of *club marriage*—in these marriage clubs, membership of several of which at a time was open to the men, and which he himself described. This marriage club business, however, is by no means real polyandry: on the contrary, as has been noted by Giraud-Teulon, it is a specialized form of group marriage, the men living in polygamy, the women in polyandry.

The Monogamian Family

As already indicated, this arises out of the pairing family in the transition period from the middle to the upper stage of barbarism, its final victory being one of the signs of the beginning of civilization. It is based on the supremacy of the man; its express aim is the begetting of children of undisputed paternity, this paternity being required in order that these children may in due time inherit their father's wealth as his natural heirs. The monogamian family differs from pairing marriage in the far greater rigidity of the marriage tie, which can now no longer be dissolved at the pleasure of either party. Now, as a rule, only the man can dissolve it and cast off his wife. The right of conjugal infidelity remains his even now, sanctioned, at least, by custom (the *Code Napoléon* expressly concedes this right to the husband as long as he does not bring his concubine into the conjugal home), and is exercised more and more with the growing development of society. Should the wife recall the ancient sexual practice and desire to revive it, she is punished more severely than ever before.

We are confronted with this new form of the family in all its severity among the Greeks. While, as Marx observes, the position of the goddesses in mythology represents an earlier period, when women still occupied a freer and more respected place, in the Heroic Age we already find women degraded owing to the predominance of the man and the competition of female slaves. One may read in the *Odyssey* how Telemachus cuts his mother short and enjoins silence upon her. In Homer the young female captives become the objects of the sensual lust of the victors; the military chiefs, one after the other, according to rank, choose the most beautiful ones for themselves. The whole of the *Iliad*, as we know, revolves around the quarrel between Achilles and Agamemnon over such a female slave. In connection with each Homeric hero of importance mention is made of a captive maiden with whom he shares tent and bed. These maidens are taken back home, to the conjugal house, as was Cassandra by Agamemnon in Aeschylus. Sons born of these slaves receive a small share of their father's estate and are regarded as freemen. Teukros was such an illegitimate son of Telamon and was permitted to adopt his father's name. The wedded wife is expected to tolerate all this, but to maintain strict chastity and conjugal fidelity herself. True, in the Heroic Age the Greek wife is more respected than in the period of civilization; for the husband, however, she is, in reality, merely the mother of his legitimate heirs, his chief housekeeper, and the superintendent of the female slaves, whom he may make, and does make, his concubines at will. It is the existence of slavery side by side with monogamy, the existence of beautiful young slaves who belong to the *man* with all they have, that from the very beginning stamped on monogamy its specific character as monogamy *only for the woman*, but not for the man. And it retains this character to this day.

As regards the Greeks of later times, we must differentiate between the Dorians and the Ionians. The former, of whom Sparta was the classical example, had in many respects more ancient marriage relationships than even Homer indicates. In Sparta we find a form of pairing marriage—modified by the state in accordance with the conceptions there prevailing—which still retains many vestiges of group marriage. Childless marriages were dissolved: King Anaxandridas (about 650 B.C.) took another wife in addition to the first, childless one, and maintained two households; King Aristones of the same period added a third to two previous wives who were barren, one of whom he, however, let go. On the other hand, several brothers could have a wife in common. A person having a preference for his friend's wife could share her with him; and it was regarded as proper to place one's wife at the disposal of a lusty 'stallion', as Bismarck would say, even when this person was not a citizen. A passage in Plutarch, where a Spartan woman sends a lover who is pursuing her with his attentions to interview her husband, would indicate, according to Schömann, still greater sexual freedom. Real adultery, the infidelity of the wife behind the back of her husband, was thus unheard of. On the other hand, domestic slavery was unknown in Sparta, at least in its heyday; the Helot serfs lived segregated on the estates and thus there was less temptation for the Spartiates to have intercourse with their women. That in all these circumstances the women of Sparta enjoyed a very much more respected position than all other Greek women was quite natural. The Spartan women and the élite of the Athenian *hetaerae* are the only Greek women of whom the ancients speak with respect, and whose remarks they consider as being worthy of record.

Among the Ionians—of whom Athens is characteristic—things were quite different. Girls learned only spinning, weaving, and sewing, at best a little reading and writing. They were practically kept in seclusion and consorted only with other women. The women's quarter was a separate and distinct part of the house, on the upper floor, or in the rear building, not easily accessible to men, particularly strangers; to this the women retired when men visitors came. The women did not go out unless accompanied by a female slave; at home they were virtually kept under guard; Aristophanes speaks of Molossian hounds kept to frighten off adulterers, while in Asiatic towns, at least, eunuchs were maintained to keep guard over the women; they were manufactured for the trade in Chios as early as Herodotus' day, and according to Wachsmuth, not merely for the barbarians. In Euripides, the wife is described as *oikurema*, a thing for housekeeping (the word is in the neuter gender), and apart from the business of bearing children, she was nothing more to the Athenian than the chief housemaid. The husband had his gymnastic exercises, his public affairs, from which the wife was excluded; in addition he often had female slaves at his disposal and, in the heyday of Athens, extensive prostitution, which was viewed with favour by the state, to say the least. It was precisely on the basis of this prostitution that the sole outstanding Greek women developed, who by their *esprit* and artistic taste towered as much above the general level of ancient womanhood as the Spartiate women did by virtue of their character. That one had first to become a *hetaera* in order to become a woman is the strongest indictment of the Athenian family.

In the course of time, this Athenian family became the model of which not only the rest of the Ionians, but also all the Greeks of the mainland and of the colonies increasingly moulded their domestic relationships. But despite all seclusion and surveillance the Greek women found opportunities often enough for deceiving their husbands. The latter, who would have been ashamed to evince any love for their own wives, amused themselves with *hetaerae* in all kinds of amours. But the degradation of the women recoiled on the men themselves and degraded them too, until they sank into the perversion of boy-love, degrading both themselves and their gods by the myth of Ganymede.

This was the origin of monogamy, as far as we can trace it among the most civilized and highly developed people of antiquity. It was not in any way the fruit of individual sex love, with which it had absolutely nothing in common, for the marriages remained marriages of convenience, as before. It was the first form of the family based not on natural but on economic conditions, namely, on the victory of private property over original, naturally developed, common ownership. The rule of the man in the family, the procreation of children who could only be his, destined to be the heirs of his wealth—these alone were frankly avowed by the Greeks as the exclusive aims of monogamy. For the rest, it was a burden, a duty to the gods, to the state and to their ancestors, which just had to be fulfilled. In Athens the law made not only marriage compulsory, but also the fulfilment by the man of a minimum of the so-called conjugal duties.

Thus, monogamy does not by any means make its appearance in history as the reconciliation of man and woman, still less as the highest form of such a reconciliation. On the contrary, it appears as the subjection of one sex by the other, as the proclamation of a conflict between the sexes entirely unknown hitherto in prehistoric times. In an old unpublished manuscript, the work of Marx and myself in 1846, I find the following: 'The first division of labour is that between man and woman for child breeding.' And today I can add: The first class antagonism which appears in history coincides with the development of the antagonism between man and woman in monogamian marriage, and the first class oppression with that of the female sex by the male. Monogamy was a great historical advance, but at the same time it inaugurated, along with slavery and private wealth, that epoch, lasting until today, in which every advance is likewise a relative regression, in which the well-being and development of the one group are attained by the misery and repression of the other. It is the cellular form of civilized society, in which we can already study the nature of the antagonisms and contradictions which develop fully in the latter.

The old relative freedom of sexual intercourse by no means disappeared with the victory of the pairing family, or even of monogamy.

> The old conjugal system, now reduced to narrower limits by the gradual disappearance of the punaluan groups, still environed the advancing family, which it was to follow to the verge of civilization. . . . It finally disappeared in the new form of hetaerism, which still follows mankind in civilization as a dark shadow upon the family.

By hetaerism Morgan means that extramarital sexual intercourse between men and unmarried women which exists *alongside of monogamy*, and, as is well known, has flourished in the most diverse forms during the whole period of civilization and is steadily developing into open prostitution. This hetaerism is directly traceable to group marriage, to the sacrificial surrender of the women, whereby they purchased their right to chastity. The surrender for money was first a religious act, taking place in the temple of the Goddess of Love, and the money originally flowed into the coffers of the temple. The hierodules of Anaitis in Armenia, of Aphrodite in Corinth, as well as the religious dancing girls attached to the temples of India—the so-called bayaders (the word is a corruption of the Portuguese *bailadeira*, a female dancer)—were the first prostitutes. This sacrificial surrender, originally obligatory for all women, was later practised vicariously by these priestesses alone on behalf of all other women. Hetaerism among other peoples grows out of the sexual freedom permitted to girls before marriage—hence likewise a survival of group marriage, only transmitted to us by another route. With the rise of property differentiation—that is, as far back as the upper stage of barbarism—wage labour appears sporadically alongside of slave labour; and simultaneously, as its necessary correlate, the professional prostitution of free women appears side by side with the forced surrender of the female slave. Thus, the heritage bequeathed to civilization by group marriage is double-sided, just as everything engendered by civilization is double-sided, double-tongued, self-contradictory and antagonistic: on the one hand, monogamy, on the other, hetaerism, including its most extreme form, prostitution. Hetaerism is as much a social institution as any other; it is a continuation of the old sexual freedom—in favour of men. Although, in reality, it is not only tolerated but even practised with gusto, particularly by the ruling classes, it is condemned in words. In reality, however, this condemnation by no means hits the men who indulge in it, it hits only the women: they are ostracized and cast out in order to proclaim once again the absolute domination of the male over the female sex as the fundamental law of society.

A second contradiction, however, is hereby developed within monogamy itself. By the side of the husband, whose life is embellished by hetaerism, stands the neglected wife. And it is just as impossible to have one side of a contradiction without the other as it is to retain the whole of an apple in one's hand after half has been eaten. Nevertheless, the men appear to have thought differently, until their wives taught them to know better. Two permanent social figures, previously unknown, appear on the scene along with monogamy—the wife's paramour and the cuckold. The men had gained the victory over the women, but the act of crowning the victor was magnanimously undertaken by the vanquished. Adultery—proscribed, severely penalised, but irrepressible—became an unavoidable social institution alongside of monogamy and hetaerism. The assured paternity of children was now, as before, based, at best, on moral conviction; and in order to solve the insoluble contradiction, Article 312 of the *Code Napoléon* decreed:

> L'enfant conçu pendant le marriage a pour père le mari (a child conceived during marriage has for its father the husband).

This is the final outcome of three thousand years of monogamy.

Thus, in the monogamian family, in those cases that faithfully reflect its historical origin and that clearly bring out the sharp conflict between man and woman resulting from the exclusive domination of the male, we have a picture in miniature of the very antagonisms and contradictions in which society, split up into classes since the commencement of civilization, moves without being able to resolve and overcome them. Naturally, I refer here only to those cases of monogamy where matrimonial life really takes its course according to the rules governing the original character of the whole institution, but where the wife rebels against the domination of the husband. That this is not the case with all marriages no one knows better than the German Philistine, who is no more capable of ruling in the home than in the state, and whose wife, therefore, with full justification, wears the breeches of which he is unworthy. But in consolation he imagines himself to be far superior to his French companion in misfortune, who, more often than he, fares far worse.

The monogamian family, however, did not by any means appear everywhere and always in the classically harsh form which it assumed among the Greeks. Among the Romans, who as future world conquerors took a longer, if less refined, view than the Greeks, woman was more free and respected. The Roman believed the conjugal fidelity of his wife to be adequately safeguarded by his power of life and death over her. Besides, the wife, just as well as the husband, could dissolve the marriage voluntarily. But the greatest advance in the development of monogamy definitely occurred with the entry of the Germans into history, because, probably owing to their poverty, monogamy does not yet appear to have completely evolved among them out of the pairing marriage. This we can conclude from three circumstances mentioned by Tacitus: Firstly, despite their firm belief in the sanctity of marriage—'each man is contented with a single wife, and the women lived fenced around with chastity'—polygamy existed for men of rank and the tribal chiefs, a situation similar to that of the Americans among whom pairing marriage prevailed. Secondly, the transition from mother right to father right could only have been accomplished a short time previously, for the mother's brother—the closest male gentile relative according to mother right—was still regarded as being an almost closer relative than one's own father, which likewise corresponds to the standpoint of the American Indians, among whom Marx found the key to the understanding of our own prehistoric past, as he often used to say. And thirdly, women among the Germans were highly respected and were influential in public affairs also—which directly conflicts with the domination of the male characteristic of monogamy. Nearly all these are points on which the Germans are in accord with the Spartans, among whom, likewise, as we have already seen, pairing marriage had not completely disappeared. Thus, in the connection also, an entirely new element acquired world supremacy with the emergence of the Germans. The new monogamy which now developed out of the mingling of races on the ruins of the Roman world clothed the domination of the men in milder forms and permitted women to occupy, at least with regard to externals, a far freer and more respected position than classical antiquity had ever known. This, for the first time, created the possibility for the greatest moral advance which we derive from and owe to monogamy—a development taking place within it, parallel with it, or in opposition to it, as the case might be, namely, modern individual sex love, previously unknown to the whole world.

This advance, however, definitely arose out of the circumstance that the Germans still lived in the pairing family, and as far as possible, grafted the position of woman corresponding thereto on to monogamy. It by no means arose as a result of the legendary, wonderful moral purity of temperament of the Germans, which was limited to the fact that, in practice, the pairing family did not reveal the same glaring moral antagonisms as monogamy. On the contrary, the Germans, in their migrations, particularly South-East, to the nomads of the steppes on the Black Sea, suffered considerable moral degeneration and, apart from their horsemanship, acquired serious unnatural vices from them, as is attested to explicitly by Ammianus about the Taifali, and by Procopius about the Heruli.

Although monogamy was the only known form of the family out of which modern sex love could develop, it does not follow that this love developed within it exclusively, or even predominantly, as the mutual love of man and wife. The whole nature of strict monogamian marriage under male domination ruled this out. Among all historically active classes, that is, among all ruling classes, matrimony remained what it had been since pairing marriage—a matter of convenience arranged by the parents. And the first form of sex love that historically emerges as a passion, and as a passion in which any person (at least of the ruling classes) has the right to indulge, as the highest form of the sexual impulse—which is precisely its specific feature—this, its first form, the chivalrous love of the Middle Ages, was by no means conjugal love. On the contrary, in its classical form, among the Provençals, it steers under full sail towards adultery, the praises of which are sung by their poets. The *Albas*, in German *Tagelieder* [Songs of the Dawn], are the flower of Provençal love poetry. They describe in glowing colours how the knight lies with his love—the wife of another—while the watchman stands guard outside, calling him at the first faint streaks of dawn (*alba*) so that he may escape unobserved. The parting scene then constitutes the climax. The Northern French as well as the worthy Germans, likewise adopted this style of poetry, along with the manners of chivalrous love which corresponded to it; and on this same suggestive theme our own old Wolfram von Eschenbach has left us three exquisite Songs of the Dawn, which I prefer to his three long heroic poems.

Bourgeois marriage of our own times is of two kinds. In Catholic countries the parents, as heretofore, still provide a suitable wife for their young bourgeois son, and the consequence is naturally the fullest unfolding of the contradiction inherent in monogamy—flourishing hetaerism on the part of the husband, and flourishing adultery on the part of the wife. The Catholic Church doubtless abolished divorce only because it was convinced that for adultery, as for death, there is no cure whatsoever. In Protestant countries, on the other hand, it is the rule that the bourgeois son is allowed to seek a wife for himself from his own class, more or less freely. Consequently, marriage can be based on a certain degree of love which, for decency's sake, is always assumed, in accordance with Protestant hypocrisy. In this case, hetaerism on the part of the men is less actively pursued, and adultery on the woman's part is not so much the rule. Since, in every kind of marriage, however, people remain what they were before they married, and since the citizens of Protestant countries are mostly Philistines, this Protestant monogamy leads merely, if we take the average of the best cases, to a wedded life of leaden boredom, which is described as domestic bliss. The best mirror of these two ways of marriage is the novel; the French novel for the Catholic style, and the German novel for the Protestant. In both cases 'he gets it': in the German novel the young man gets the girl; in the French, the husband gets the cuckold's horns. Which of the two is in the worse plight is not always easy to make out. For the dullness of the German novel excites the same horror in the French bourgeois as the 'immorality' of the French novel excites in the German Philistine, although lately, since 'Berlin is becoming a metropolis,' the German novel has begun to deal a little less timidly with hetaerism and adultery, long known to exist there.

In both cases, however, marriage is determined by the class position of the participants, and to that extent always remains marriage of convenience. In both cases, this marriage of convenience often enough turns into the crassest prostitution—sometimes on both sides, but much more generally on the part of the wife, who differs from the ordinary courtesan only in that she does not hire out her body, like a wage-worker, on piecework, but sells it into slavery once for all. And Fourier's words hold good for all marriages of convenience:

> Just as in grammar two negatives make a positive, so in the morals of marriage, two prostitutions make one virtue.

Sex love in the relation of husband and wife is and can become the rule only among the oppressed classes, that is, at the present day, among the proletariat, no matter whether this relationship is officially sanctioned or not. But here all the foundations of classical monogamy are removed. Here, there is a complete absence of all property, for the safeguarding and inheritance of which monogamy and male domination were established. Therefore, there is no stimulus whatever here to assert male domination. What is more, the means, too, are absent; bourgeois law, which protects this domination, exists only for the propertied classes and their dealings with the proletarians. It costs money, and therefore, owing to the worker's poverty, has no validity in his attitude towards his wife. Personal and social relations of quite a different sort are the decisive factors here. Moreover, since large-scale industry has transferred the woman from the house to the labour market and the factory, and makes her, often enough, the bread-winner of the family, the last remnants of male domination in the proletarian home have lost all foundation—except, perhaps, for some of that brutality towards women which became firmly rooted with the establishment of monogamy. Thus, the proletarian family is no longer monogamian in the strict sense, even in cases of the most passionate love and strictest faithfulness of the two parties, and despite all spiritual and worldly benedictions which may have been received. The two eternal adjuncts of monogamy—hetaerism and adultery—therefore, play an almost negligible role here; the woman has regained, in fact, the right of separation, and when the man and woman cannot get along they prefer to part. In short, proletarian marriage is monogamian in the etymological sense of the word, but by no means in the historical sense.

Our jurists, to be sure, hold that the progress of legislation to an increasing degree removes all cause for complaint on the part of the woman. Modern civilized systems of law are recognizing more and more, first, that, in order to be effective, marriage must be an agreement voluntarily entered into by both parties; and secondly, that during marriage, too, both parties must be on an equal footing in respect to rights and obligations. If, however, these two demands were consistently carried into effect, women would have all that they could ask for.

This typical lawyer's reasoning is exactly the same as that with which the radical republican bourgeois dismisses the proletarian. The labour contract is supposed to be voluntarily entered into by both parties. But it is taken to be voluntarily entered into as soon as the law has put both parties on an equal footing *on paper*. The power given to one party by its different class position, the pressure it exercises on the other—the real economic position of both—all this is no concern of the law. And both parties, again, are supposed to have equal rights for the duration of the labour contract, unless one or the other of the parties expressly waived them. That the concrete economic situation compels the worker to forego even the slightest semblance of equal rights—this again is something the law cannot help.

As far as marriage is concerned, even the most progressive law is fully satisfied as soon as the parties formally register their voluntary desire to get married. What happens behind the legal curtains, where real life is enacted, how this voluntary agreement is arrived at—is no concern of the law and the jurist. And yet the simplest comparison of laws should serve to show the jurist what this voluntary agreement really amounts to. In countries where the children are legally assured of an obligatory share of their parents' property and thus cannot be disinherited—in Germany, in the countries under French law, etc.— the children must obtain their parents' consent in the question of marriage. In countries under English law, where parental consent to marriage is not legally requisite, the parents have full testatory freedom over their property and can, if they so desire, cut their children off with a shilling. It is clear, therefore, that despite this, or rather just because of this, among those classes which have something to inherit, freedom to marry is not one whit greater in England and America than in France or Germany.

The position is no better with regard to the juridical equality of man and woman in marriage. The inequality of the two before the law, which is a legacy of previous social conditions, is not the cause but the effect of the economic oppression of women. In the old communistic household, which embraced numerous couples and their children, the administration of the household, entrusted to the women, was just as much a public, a socially necessary industry as the providing of food by the men. This situation changed with the patriarchal family, and even more with the monogamian individual family. The administration of the household lost its public character. It was no longer the concern of society. It became a *private service*. The wife became the first domestic servant, pushed out of participation in social production. Only modern large-scale industry again threw open to her—and only to the proletarian woman at that—the avenue to social production; but in such a way that, when she fulfils her duties in the private service of her family, she remains excluded from public production and cannot earn anything; and when she wishes to take part in public industry and earn her living independently, she is not in a position to fulfil her family duties. What applies to the woman in the factory applies to her in all the professions, right up to medicine and law. The modern individual family is based on the open or disguised domestic enslavement of the woman; and modern society is a mass composed solely of individual families as its molecules. Today, in the great majority of cases, the man has to be the earner, the bread-winner of the family, at least among the propertied classes, and this gives him a dominating position which requires no special legal privileges. In the family, he is the bourgeois; the wife represents the proletariat. In the industrial world, however, the specific character of the economic oppression that weighs down the proletariat stands out in all its sharpness only after all the special privileges of the capitalist class have been set aside and the complete juridical equality of both classes is established. The democratic republic does not abolish the antagonism between the two classes; on the contrary, it provides the field on which it is fought out. And, similarly, the peculiar character of man's domination over woman in the modern family, and the necessity, as well as the manner, of establishing real social equality between the two, will be brought out into full relief only when both are completely equal before the law. It will then become evident that the first premise for the emancipation of women is the reintroduction of the entire female sex into public industry; and that this again demands that the quality possessed by the individual family of being the economic unit of society be abolished.

We have, then, three chief forms of marriage, which, by and large, conform to the three main stages of human development. For savagery—group marriage; for barbarism—pairing marriage; for civilization—monogamy, supplemented by adultery and prostitution. In the upper stage of barbarism, between pairing marriage and monogamy, there is wedged in the dominion exercised by men over female slaves, and polygamy.

As our whole exposition has shown, the advance to be noted in this sequence is linked with the peculiar fact that while women are more and more deprived of the sexual freedom of group marriage, the men are not. Actually, for men, group marriage exists to this day. What for a woman is a crime entailing dire legal and social consequences, is regarded in the case of a man as being honourable or, at most, as a slight moral stain that one bears with pleasure. The more the old traditional hetaerism is changed in our day by capitalist commodity production and adapted to it, and the more it is transformed into unconcealed prostitution, the more demoralizing are its effects. And it demoralizes the men far more than it does the women. Among women, prostitution degrades only those unfortunates who fall into its clutches; and even these are not degraded to the degree that is generally believed. On the other hand, it degrades the character of the entire male world. Thus, in nine cases out of ten, a long engagement is practically a preparatory school for conjugal infidelity.

We are now approaching a social revolution in which the hitherto existing economic foundations of monogamy will disappear just as certainly as will those of its supplement—prostitution. Monogamy arose out of the concentration of considerable wealth in the hands of one person—and that a man—and out of the desire to bequeath this wealth to this man's children and to no one else's. For this purpose monogamy was essential on the woman's part, but not on the man's; so that this monogamy of the woman in no way hindered the overt or covert polygamy of the man. The impending social revolution, however, by transforming at least the far greater part of permanent inheritable wealth—the means of production—into social property, will reduce all this anxiety about inheritance to a minimum. Since monogamy arose from economic causes, will it disappear when these causes disappear?

One might not unjustly answer: far from disappearing, it will only begin to be completely realized. For with the conversion of the means of production into social property, wage labour, the proletariat, also disappears, and therewith, also, the necessity for a certain—statistically calculable—number of women to surrender themselves for money. Prostitution disappears; monogamy, instead of declining, finally becomes a reality—for the men as well.

At all events, the position of the men thus undergoes considerable change. But that of the women, of *all* women, also undergoes important alteration. With the passage of the means of production into common property, the individual family ceases to be the economic unit of society. Private housekeeping is transformed into a social industry. The care and education of the children becomes [sic] a public matter. Society takes care of all children equally, irrespective of whether they are born in wedlock or not. Thus, the anxiety about the 'consequences', which is today the most important social factor—both moral and economic—that hinders a girl from giving herself freely to the man she loves, disappears. Will this not be cause enough for a gradual rise of more unrestrained sexual intercourse, and along with it, a more lenient public opinion regarding virginal honour and feminine shame? And finally, have we not seen that monogamy and prostitution in the modern world, although opposites, are nevertheless inseparable opposites, poles of the same social conditions? Can prostitution disappear without dragging monogamy with it into abyss?

Here a new factor comes into operation, a factor that, at most, existed in embryo at the time when monogamy developed, namely, individual sex love.

No such thing as individual sex love existed before the Middle Ages. That personal beauty, intimate association, similarity in inclinations, etc., aroused desire for sexual intercourse among people of opposite sexes, that men as well as women were not totally indifferent to the question of with whom they entered into this most intimate relation is obvious. But this is still a far cry from the sex love of our day. Throughout antiquity marriages were arranged by the parents; the parties quietly acquiesced. The little conjugal love that was known to antiquity was not in any way a subjective inclination, but an objective duty; not a reason for but a correlate of marriage. In antiquity, love affairs in the modern sense occur only outside official society. The shepherds, whose joys and sorrows in love are sung by Theocritus and Moschus, or by Longus's *Daphnis and Chloë*, are mere slaves, who have no share in the state, the sphere of the free citizen. Except among the slaves, however, we find love affairs only as disintegration products of the declining ancient world; and with women who are also beyond the pale of official society, with *hetaerae*, that is, with alien or freed women: in Athens beginning with the eve of its decline, in Rome at the time of the emperors. If love affairs really occurred between free male and female citizens, it was only in the form of adultery. And sex love in our sense of the term was so immaterial to that classical love poet of antiquity, old Anacreon, that even the sex of the beloved one was a matter of complete indifference to him.

Our sex love differs materially from the simple sexual desire, the *eros*, of the ancients. First, it presupposes reciprocal love on the part of the loved one; in this respect, the woman stands on a par with the man; whereas in the ancient *eros*, the woman was by no means always consulted. Secondly, sex love attains a degree of intensity and permanency where the two parties regard non-possession or separation as a great, if not the greatest, misfortune; in order to possess each other they take great hazards, even risking life itself—what in antiquity happened, at best, only in cases of adultery. And finally, a new moral standard arises for judging sexual intercourse. The question asked is not only whether such intercourse was legitimate or illicit, but also whether it arose from mutual love or not? It goes without saying that in feudal or bourgeois practice this new standard fares no better than all the other moral standards—it is simply ignored. But it fares no worse, either. It is recognized in theory, on paper, like all the rest. And more than this cannot be expected for the present.

Where antiquity broke off with its start toward sex love, the Middle Ages began, namely, with adultery. We have already described chivalrous love, which gave rise to the Songs of the Dawn. There is still a wide gulf between this kind of love, which aimed at breaking up matrimony, and the love destined to be its foundation, a gulf never completely bridged by the age of chivalry. Even when we pass from the frivolous Latins to the virtuous Germans, we find, in the *Nibelungenlied*, that Kriemhild—although secretly in love with Siegfried every whit as much as he is with her—nevertheless, in reply to

Gunther's intimation that he has plighted her to a knight whom he does not name, answers simply:

> You have no need to ask; as you command, so will I be for ever. He whom you, my lord, choose for my husband, to him I will gladly plight my troth.

It never even occurs to her that her love could possibly be considered in this matter. Gunther seeks the hand of Brunhild without ever having seen her, and Etzel does the same with Kriemhild. The same occurs in the *Gudrun*, where Sigebant of Ireland seeks the hand of Ute the Norwegian, Hettel of Hegelingen that of Hilde of Ireland; and lastly, Siegfried of Morland, Hartmut of Ormany and Herwing of Seeland seek the hand of Gudrun; and here for the first time it happens that Gudrun, of her own free will, decides in favour of the last named. As a rule, the bride of a young prince is selected by his parents; if these are no longer alive, he chooses her himself with the counsel of his highest vassal chiefs, whose word carries great weight in all cases. Nor can it be otherwise. For the knight, or baron, just as for the prince himself, marriage is a political act, an opportunity for the accession of power through new alliances; the interest of the *House* and not individual inclination are the decisive factor. How can love here hope to have the last word regarding marriage?

It was the same for the guildsman of the medieval towns. The very privileges which protected him—the guild charters with their special stipulations, the artificial lines of demarcation which legally separated him from other guilds, from his own fellow guildsmen and from his journeymen and apprentices—considerably restricted the circle in which he could hope to secure a suitable spouse. And the question as to who was the most suitable was definitely decided under this complicated system, not by individual inclination, but by family interest.

Up to the end of the Middle Ages, therefore, marriage, in the overwhelming majority of cases, remained what it had been from the commencement, an affair that was not decided by the two principal parties. In the beginning one came into the world married, married to a whole group of the opposite sex. A similar relation probably existed in the later forms of group marriage, only with an ever increasing narrowing of the group. In the pairing family it is the rule that the mothers arrange their children's marriages; and here also, considerations of new ties of relationship that are to strengthen the young couple's position in the gens and tribe are the decisive factor. And when, with the predominance of private property over common property, and with the interest of inheritance, father right and monogamy gain the ascendancy, marriage becomes more than ever dependent on economic considerations. The *form* of marriage by purchase disappears, the transaction itself is to an ever increasing degree carried out in such a way that not only the woman but the man also is appraised, not by his personal qualities but by his possessions. The idea that the mutual inclinations of the principal parties should be the overriding reason for matrimony had been unheard of in the practice of the ruling classes from the very beginning. Such things took place, at best, in romance only, or—among the oppressed classes, which did not count.

This was the situation found by capitalist production when, following the era of geographical discoveries, it set out to conquer the world through world trade and manufacture. One would think that this mode of matrimony should have suited it exceedingly, and such was actually the case. And yet—the irony of world history is unfathomable—it was capitalist production that had to make the decisive breach in it. By transforming all things into commodities, it dissolved all ancient traditional relations, and for inherited customs and historical rights it substituted purchase and sale, 'free' contract. And H.S. Maine, the English jurist, believed that he made a colossal discovery when he said that our entire progress in comparison with previous epochs consists in our having evolved from status to contract, from an inherited state of affairs to one voluntarily contracted—a statement which, in so far as it is correct, was contained long ago in the *Communist Manifesto*.

But the closing of contracts presupposes people who can freely dispose of their persons, actions and possessions, and who meet each other on equal terms. To create such 'free' and 'equal' people was precisely one of the chief tasks of capitalist production. Although in the beginning this took place only in a semiconscious manner, and in religious guise to boot, nevertheless, from the time of the Lutheran and Calvinistic Reformation it became a firm principle that a person was completely responsible for his actions only if he possessed full freedom of the will when performing them, and that it was an ethical duty to resist all compulsion to commit unethical acts. But how does this fit in with the previous practice of matrimony? According to bourgeois conceptions, matrimony was a contract, a legal affair, indeed the most important of all, since it disposed of the body and mind of two persons for life. True enough, formally the bargain was struck voluntarily; it was not done without the consent of the parties; but how this consent was obtained, and who really arranged the marriage was known only too well. But if real freedom to decide was demanded for all other contracts, why not for this one? Had not the two young people about to be paired the right freely to dispose of themselves, their bodies and organs? Did not sex love become the fashion as a consequence of chivalry, and was not the love of husband and wife its correct bourgeois form, as against the adulterous love of the knights? But if it was the duty of married people to love each other, was it not just as much the duty of lovers to marry each other and nobody else? And did not the right of these lovers stand higher than that of parents, relatives and other traditional marriage brokers and matchmakers? If the right of free personal investigation unceremoniously forced its way into church and religion, how could it halt at the intolerable claim of the older generation to dispose of body and soul, the property, the happiness and unhappiness of the younger generation?

These questions were bound to arise in a period which loosened all the old social ties and which shook the foundations of all traditional conceptions. At one stroke the size of the world had increased nearly tenfold. Instead of only a quadrant of a hemisphere the whole globe was now open to the gaze of the West Europeans who hastened to take possession of the other seven quadrants. And the thousand-year-old barriers set up by the medieval prescribed mode of thought vanished in the same way as did the old, narrow barriers of the homeland. An infinitely wider horizon opened up both to man's outer and inner eye. Of what avail were the good intentions of respectability, the honoured guild privileges handed down through the generations, to the young man who was allured by India's riches, by the gold and silver mines of Mexico and Potosi? It was the knight-errant period of the bourgeoisie; it had its romance also, and its love dreams, but on a bourgeois basis and in the last analysis, with bourgeois ends in view.

Thus it happened that the rising bourgeoisie, particularly in the Protestant countries, where the existing order was shaken up most of all, increasingly recognized freedom of contract for marriage also and carried it through in the manner described above. Marriage remained class marriage, but, within the confines of the class, the parties were accorded a certain degree of freedom of choice. And on paper, in moral theory as in poetic description, nothing was more unshakably established than that every marriage not based on mutual sex love and on the really free agreement of man and wife was immoral. In short, love marriage was proclaimed a human right; not only as man's right (*droit de l'homme*) but also, by way of exception, as woman's right (*droit de la femme*).

But in one respect this human right differed from all other so-called human rights. While, in practice, the latter remained limited to the ruling class, the bourgeoisie—the oppressed class, the proletariat, being directly or indirectly deprived of them—the irony of history asserts itself here once again. The ruling class continues to be dominated by the familiar economic influences and, therefore, only in exceptional cases can it show really voluntary marriages; whereas, as we have seen, these are the rule among the dominated class.

Thus, full freedom in marriage can become generally operative only when the abolition of capitalist production, and of the property relations created by it, has removed all those secondary economic considerations which still exert so powerful an influence on the choice of a partner. Then, no other motive remains than mutual affection.

Since sex love is by its very nature exclusive—although this exclusiveness is fully realized today only in the woman—then marriage based on sex love is by its very nature monogamy. We have seen how right Bachofen was when he regarded the advance from group marriage to individual marriage chiefly as the work of the women; only the advance from pairing marriage to monogamy can be placed to the men's account, and, historically, this consisted essentially in a worsening of the position of women and in facilitating infidelity on the part of the men. With the disappearance of the economic considerations which compelled women to tolerate the customary infidelity of the men—the anxiety about their own livelihood and even more about the future of their children—the equality of woman thus achieved will, judging from all previous experience, result far more effectively in the men becoming really monogamous than in the women becoming polyandrous.

What will most definitely disappear from monogamy, however, is all the characteristics stamped on it in consequence of its having arisen out of property relationships. These are, first, the dominance of the man, and secondly, the indissolubility of marriage. The predominance of the man in marriage is simply a consequence of his economic predominance and will vanish with it automatically. The indissolubility of marriage is partly the result of the economic conditions under which monogamy arose, and partly a tradition from the time when the connection between these economic conditions and monogamy was not yet correctly understood and was exaggerated by religion. Today it has been breached a thousandfold. If only marriages that are based on love are moral, then, also, only those are moral in which love continues. The duration of the urge of individual sex love differs very much according to the individual, particularly among men; and a definite cessation of affection, or its displacement by a new passionate love, makes separation a blessing for both parties as well as for society. People will only be spared the experience of wading through the useless mire of divorce proceedings.

Thus, what we can conjecture at present about the regulation of sex relationships after the impending effacement of capitalist production is, in the main, of a negative character, limited mostly to what will vanish. But what will be added? That will be settled after a new generation has grown up: a generation of men who never in all their lives have had occasion to purchase a woman's surrender either with money or with any other means of social power, and of women who have never been obliged to surrender to any man out of any consideration other than that of real love, or to refrain from giving themselves to their beloved for fear of the economic consequences. Once such people appear, they will not care a rap about what we today think they should do. They will establish their own practice and their own public opinion, conformable therewith, on the practice of each individual—and that's the end of it.

In the meantime, let us return to Morgan, from whom we have strayed quite considerably. The historical investigation of the social institutions which developed during the period of civilization lies outside the scope of his book. Consequently, he concerns himself only briefly with the fate of monogamy during this period. He, too, regards the development of the monogamian family as an advance, as an approximation to the complete equality of the sexes, without, however, considering that this goal has been reached. But, he says,

> when the fact is accepted that the family has passed through four successive forms, and is now in the fifth, the question arises at once whether this form can be permanent in the future. The only answer that can be given is that it must advance as society advances, and change as society changes, even as it has done in the past. It is the creation of the social system, and will reflect its culture. As the monogamian family has improved greatly since the commencement of civilization, and very sensibly in modern times, it is at least supposable that it is capable of still further improvement until the equality of the sexes is attained. Should the monogamian family in the distant future fail to answer the requirements of society it is impossible to predict the nature of its successor.

HERBERT SPENCER

1820–1903
BRITAIN

Major Works

1851   *Social Statics*
1854   *The Principles of Psychology*
1864   *The Principles of Biology*
1873   *The Study of Sociology*
1876   *The Principles of Sociology*
1904   *An Autobiography*

> What is Comte's professed aim? To give a coherent account of the progress of human conceptions. What is my aim? To give a coherent account of the progress of the external world. Comte proposes to describe the necessary, and the actual, filiation of ideas. I propose to describe the necessary, and the actual, filiation of things. Comte professes to interpret the genesis of our knowledge of nature. My aim is to interpret . . . the genesis of the phenomena which constitute nature. The one is subjective. The other is objective.[1]

> There can be no complete acceptance of sociology as a science, so long as the belief in a social order not conforming to natural law, survives.[2]
> —*Herbert Spencer*

Like that of Comte, Herbert Spencer's contribution to sociology and to social scientific inquiry in general has perhaps had more impact than many would either like to admit or perhaps suspect. His work continued that of Comte's organicist and evolutionary approach, even though Spencer apparently claimed no intellectual antecedents. The organicist perspective also prefigured a great deal of what Durkheim was to work out in relation to social solidarity.

Spencer developed a functionalist approach to social structure and social evolution, arguing that as society moved from simple to more complex forms it also moved from relative homogeneity to a greater division of labour, i.e., heterogeneity. He considered interrelated size, growth, function, and structure to be conceptual dimensions of social organization and differentiation leading always to some form of social integration. As societies became more complex the need for 'regulating systems' came to be of paramount importance. Spencer later perceived this aspect of social integration and organization as 'government intervention', a distortion of the natural processes of societal development.

One aspect of Spencer's thought—social Darwinism—has had profound impact in recent political ideology. A number of years before Darwin published his *Origin of Species,* Spencer coined the phrase, 'survival of the fittest':

> Fostering the good-for-nothing at the expense of the good, is an extreme cruelty. It is a deliberate storing-up of miseries for future generations. There is no greater curse to posterity than that of bequeathing them an increasing population of imbeciles and idlers and criminals. To aid the bad in multiplying, is, in effect, the same as maliciously providing for our descendants a multitude of enemies. It may be doubted whether the maudlin philanthrophy which, looking only at direct mitigations, persistently ignores indirect mischiefs, does not inflict a greater total of misery than the extremest selfishness inflicts.[3]

The use of this concept in relationship to social evolution, and as a guiding principle of individual human experience, has been criticized, but it has nevertheless become part of the ideological substratum of right-wing political thought. Spencer's individualism, his adoption of the notion of competitive struggle as the basis of social progress, clearly contradicts the fundamental work of Karl Marx and others.

Herbert Spencer's work, situated in late nineteenth-century England's rapid industrialization, seemed not only to describe but also to explain. It laid the groundwork for perspectives in sociological theory as well as political theory, for example, the ideology of 'blaming the victim'. Its contemporary impact needs to be thoroughly discussed and understood.

Notes

1. Herbert Spencer, *An Autobiography,* vol. 2 (New York: Appleton, 1904), 570.
2. Herbert Spencer, *The Study of Sociology* (Don Mills, Ont.: Longman, 1969), 395.
3. Ibid., 324.

SOCIETY AND 'SURVIVAL OF THE FITTEST'

The Study of Sociology

The study of Sociology [is] the study of Evolution in its most complex form. It is clear that to one who considers the facts societies exhibit as having had their origin in supernatural interpositions, or in the wills of individual ruling men, the study of these facts will have an aspect wholly unlike that which it has to one who contemplates them as generated by processes of growth and development continuing through centuries. Ignoring as the first view tacitly does, that conformity to law, in the scientific sense of the word, which the second view tacitly asserts, there can be but little community between the methods of inquiry proper to them respectively. Continuous causation, which in the one case there is little or no tendency to trace, becomes, in the other case, the chief object of attention; whence it follows that there must be formed wholly different ideas of the appropriate modes of investigation. A foregone conclusion respecting the nature of social phenomena, is thus inevitably implied in any suggestions for the study of them.

While, however, it must be admitted that throughout this work there runs the assumption that the facts, simultaneous and successive, which societies present, have a genesis no less natural than the genesis of facts of all other classes; it is not admitted that this assumption was made unawares, or without warrant. At the outset, the grounds for it were examined. The notion, widely accepted in name though not consistently acted upon, that social phenomena differ from phenomena of most other kinds as being under special providence, we found to be entirely discredited by its expositors; nor, when closely looked into, did the great-man-theory of social affairs prove to be more tenable. Besides finding that both these views, rooted as they are in the ways of thinking natural to primitive men, would not bear criticism, we found that even their defenders continually betrayed their beliefs in the production of social changes by natural causes—tacitly admitted that after certain antecedents certain consequents are to be expected—tacitly admitted, therefore, that some prevision is possible, and therefore some subject-matter for Science. From these negative justifications for the belief that Sociology is a science, we turned to the positive justifications. We found that every aggregate of units of any order, has certain traits necessarily determined by the properties of its units. Hence it was inferrable, *a priori*, that, given the natures of the men who are their units, and certain characters in the societies formed are pre-determined—other characters being determined by the co-operation of surrounding conditions. The current assertion that Sociology is not possible, implies a misconception of its nature. Using the analogy supplied by a human life, we saw that just as bodily development and structure and function furnish subject matter for biological science, though the events set forth by the biographer go beyond its range; so, social growth, and the rise of structures and functions accompanying it, furnish subject matter for a Science of Society, though the facts with which historians fill their pages mostly yield no material for Science. Thus conceiving the scope of the science, we saw, on comparing rudimentary societies with one another and with societies in different stages of progress, that they *do* present certain common traits of structure and of function, as well as certain common traits of development. Further comparisons similarly made opened large questions, such as that of the relation between social growth and organization, which form parts of this same science;—questions of transcendent importance compared with those occupying the minds of politicians and writers of history.

The difficulties of the Social Science next drew our attention. We saw that in this case, though in no other case, the facts to be observed and generalized by the student are exhibited by an aggregate of which he forms a part. In his capacity of inquirer he should have no inclination towards one or other conclusion respecting the phenomena to be generalized; but in his capacity of citizen, helped to live by the life of his society, imbedded in its structures, sharing in its activities, breathing its atmosphere of thought and sentiment, he is partially coerced into such views as favour harmonious co-operation with his fellow-citizens. Hence immense obstacles to the Social Science, unparalleled by those standing in the way of any other science.

From considering thus generally these causes of error, we turned to consider them specially. Under the head of objective difficulties, we glanced at those many ways in which evidence collected by the sociological inquirer is vitiated. That extreme untrustworthiness of witnesses which results from carelessness, or fanaticism, or self-interest, was illustrated; and we saw that, in addition to the perversions of statement hence arising, there are others which arise from the tendency there is for some kinds of evidence to draw attention, while evidence of opposite kinds, much larger in quantity, draws no attention. Further, it was shown that the nature of sociological facts, each of which is not observable in a single object or act, but is reached only through registration and comparison of many objects and acts, make the perception of them harder than that of other facts. It was pointed out that the wide distribution of social phenomena in Space greatly hinders true apprehensions of them; and it was also pointed out that another impediment, even still greater, is consequent on their distribution in Time—a distribution such that many of the facts to be dealt with, take centuries to unfold, and can be grasped only by combining in thought multitudinous changes that are slow, involved, and not easy to trace. Beyond these difficulties which we grouped as distinguishing the science itself, objectively considered, we saw that there are other difficulties, conveniently to be grouped as subjective, which are also great. For the interpretation of human conduct as socially displayed, every one is compelled to use, as a key, his own nature—ascribing to others thoughts and feelings like his own; and yet, while this automorphic interpretation is indispensable, it is necessarily more or less misleading. Very generally, too, a subjective difficulty arises from the lack of intellectual faculty complex enough to grasp these social phenomena, which are so extremely involved. And again, very few have by culture gained that plasticity of faculty requisite for conceiving and accepting those immensely varied actualities which societies in different times and places display, and those multitudinous possibilities to be inferred from them. Nor, of subjective difficulties, did these exhaust the list. From the emotional, as well as from the intellectual, part of the nature, we saw that there arise obstacles. The ways in which beliefs about social affairs are perverted by intense fears and excited hopes, were pointed out. We noted the feeling of impatience, as another common cause of misjudgement. A contrast was drawn showing, too, what perverse estimates of public events men are led to make by their sympathies and antipathies—how, where their hate has been aroused, they utter unqualified condemnations of ill-deeds for which there was much excuse, while, if their admiration is excited by vast successes, they condone inexcusable ill-deeds immeasurably greater in amount. And we also saw that among the distortions of judgement caused by the emotions, have to be included those immense ones generated by the sentiment of loyalty to a personal ruler, or to a ruling power otherwise embodied.

. . . Recognizing the truth that the preservation of a society is made possible only by a due amount of patriotic feeling in citizens, we saw that this feeling inevitably disturbs the judgement when comparisons between societies are made, and that the data required for Social Science are thus vitiated; and we saw that the effort to escape this bias, leading as it does to an opposite bias, is apt to vitiate the data in another way. While finding the class-bias to be no less essential, we found that it no less inevitably causes one-sidedness in the conceptions of social affairs. Noting how the various sub-classes have their specialties of prejudice corresponding to their class-interests, we noted, at greater length, how the more general prejudices of the larger and more widely distinguished classes prevent them from forming balanced judgements. That in politics the bias of party interferes with those calm examinations by which alone the conclusions of Social Science can be reached, scarcely needed pointing out. We observed, however, that beyond the political bias under its party-form, there is a more general political bias—the bias towards an exclusively political view of social affairs, and a corresponding faith in political instrumentalities. As affecting the study of Social Science, this bias was shown to be detrimental as directing the attention too much to the phenomena of social regulation, and excluding from thought the activities regulated, constituting an aggregate of phenomena far more important. . . .

Having thus contemplated, in general and in detail, the difficulties of the Social Science, we turned our attention to the preliminary discipline required. Of the conclusions reached so recently, the reader scarcely needs reminding. Study of the sciences in general having been pointed out as the proper means of generating fit habits of thought, it was shown that the sciences especially to be attended to are those treating of Life and of Mind. There can be no understanding of social actions without some knowledge of human nature; there can be no deep knowledge of human nature without some knowledge of the laws of Mind; there can be no adequate knowledge of the laws of Mind without knowledge of the laws of Life. And that knowledge of the Laws of Life, as exhibited in Man, may be properly grasped, attention must be given to the laws of Life in general.

. . . The implication throughout the argument has been that for every society, and for each stage in its evolution, there is an appropriate mode of feeling and thinking; and that no mode of feeling and thinking not adapted to its degree of evolution, and to its surroundings, can be permanently established. Though not exactly, still approximately, the average opinion in any age and country, is a function of the social structure in that age and country. There may be, as we see during times of revolution, a considerable incongruity between the ideas that become current and the social arrangements which exist, and are, in great measure, appropriate; though even then the incongruity does but mark the need for a re-adjustment of institutions to character. While, however, those successive compromises which, during social evolution, have to be made between the changed natures of citizens and the institutions evolved by ancestral citizens, imply disagreements, yet these are but partial and temporary—in those societies, at least, which are developing and not in course of dissolution. For a society to hold together, the institutions that are needed and the conceptions that are generally current must be in tolerable harmony. Hence, it is not to be expected that modes of thinking on social affairs are to be in any considerable degree changed by whatever may be said respecting the Social Science, its difficulties, and the required preparations for studying it.

The only reasonable hope is, that here and there one may be led, in calmer moments, to remember how largely his beliefs about public matters have been made for him by circumstances, and how probable it is that they are either untrue or but partially true. . . .

The illogicalities and the absurdities to be found so abundantly in current opinions and existing arrangements, are those which inevitably arise in the course of perpetual re-adjustments to circumstances perpetually changing. Ideas and institutions proper to a past social state, but incongruous with the new social state that has grown out of it, surviving into this new social state they have made possible, and disappearing only as this new social state establishes its own ideas and institutions, are necessarily, during their survival, in conflict with these new ideas and institutions—necessarily furnish elements of contradiction in men's thoughts and deeds. And yet as, for the carrying-on of social life, the old must continue so long as the new is not ready, this perpetual compromise is an indispensable accompaniment of a normal development. . . .

. . . From the doctrines set forth in this work, some have drawn the corollary that effort in furtherance of progress is superfluous. 'If', they argue, 'the evolution of a society conforms to general laws—if the changes which, in the slow course of things bring it about, are naturally determined; then what need is there of endeavours to aid it? The hypothesis implies that the transformation results from causes beyond individual wills; and, if so, the acts of individuals in fulfilment of their wills are not required to effect it. Hence we may occupy ourselves exclusively with personal concerns leaving social evolution to go its own way.'

This is a misapprehension naturally fallen into and not quite easy to escape from; for to get out of it the citizen must simultaneously conceive himself as one whose will is a factor in social evolution, and yet as one whose will is a product of all antecedent influences, social included.

. . . An analogy will best show how there may be reconciled the two propositions that social evolution is a process conforming to natural laws, and yet that it results from the voluntary efforts of citizens.

It is a truth statistically established, that in each community, while its conditions remain the same, there is a uniform rate of marriage: such variations in the numbers of marriages as accompany variations in the prices of food, serving to show that so long as the impediments to marriage do not vary, the frequency of marriages does not vary. Similarly, it is found that along with an average frequency of marriages there goes an average frequency of births. But though these averages show that the process of human multiplication presents uniformities, implying constancy in the action of general causes, it is not therefore inferred that the process of human multiplication is independent of people's wills. If anyone were to argue that marriages and births, considered in the aggregate, are social phenomena statistically proved to depend on influences which operate uniformly, and that therefore the maintenance of population does not depend on individual actions, his inference would be rejected as absurd. Daily experience proves that marrying and the rearing of children in each case result from the pursuit of exclusively private ends. It is only by fulfilling their individual wills in establishing and maintaining the domestic relations that citizens produce these aggregate results which exhibit uniformities apparently independent of individual wills. In this instance, then, it is obvious that social phenomena follow certain general courses; and yet that they can do this only on condition that social units voluntarily act out their natures. While everyone holds that, in the matter of marriage, his will is, in the ordinary sense of the word, free; yet he is obliged to recognize the fact that his will, and the wills of others, are so far determined by common elements of human nature, as to produce these average social results; and that no such social results could be produced did they not fulfil their wills . . . .[1]

Here let it once more be distinctly asserted that there exist no analogies between the body politic and a living body, save those necessitated by that mutual dependence of parts which they display in common. Though, in foregoing chapters, sundry comparisons of social structures and functions to structures and functions in the human body, have been made, they have been made only because structures and functions in the human body furnish familiar illustrations of structures and functions in general. The social organism, discrete instead of concrete, asymmetrical instead of symmetrical, sensitive in all its units instead of having a single sensitive centre, is not comparable to any particular type of individual organism, animal or vegetal. All kinds of creatures are alike insofar as each exhibits co-operation among its components for the benefit of the whole; and this trait, common to them, is a trait common also to societies. Further, among individual organisms, the degree of co-operation measures the degree of evolution; and this general truth, too, holds among social organisms. Once more, to effect increasing co-operation, creatures of every order show us increasingly complex appliances for transfer and mutual influence; and to this general characteristic, societies of every order furnish a corresponding characteristic. These, then are the analogies alleged: community in the fundamental principles of organization is the only community asserted.

But now let us drop this alleged parallelism between individual organizations and social organizations. I have used the analogies elaborated, but as a scaffolding to help in building up a coherent body of sociological inductions. Let us take away the scaffolding: the inductions will stand by themselves.

We saw that societies are aggregates which grow; that in the various types of them there are great varieties in the growths reached; that types of successively larger sizes result from the aggregation and reaggregation of those of smaller sizes; and that this increase by coalescence, joined with interstitial increase, is the process through which have been formed the vast civilized nations.

Along with increase of size in societies goes increase of structure. Primitive hordes are without established distinctions of parts. With growth of them into tribes habitually come some unlikenesses; both in the powers and occupations of their members. Unions of tribes are followed by more unlikenesses, governmental and industrial—social grades running through the whole mass, and contrasts between the differently-occupied parts in different localities. Such differentiations multiply as the compounding progresses. They proceed from the general to the special. First the broad division between ruling and ruled; then within the ruling part divisions into political, religious, military, and within the ruled part divisions into food-producing classes and handicraftsmen; then within each of these divisions minor ones, and so on.

Passing from the structural aspect to the functional aspect, we note that so long as all parts of a society have like natures and activities, there is hardly any mutual dependence, and the aggregate scarcely forms a vital whole. As its parts assume different functions they become dependent on one another, so that injury to one hurts others; until, in highly evolved societies, general perturbation is caused by derangement of any portion. This contrast between undeveloped and developed societies arises from the fact that with increasing specialization of functions comes increasing inability in each part to perform the functions of other parts.

The organization of every society begins with a contrast between the division which carries on relations, habitually hostile, with environing societies, and the division which is devoted to procuring necessaries of life; and during the earlier stages of development these two divisions constitute the whole. Eventually there arises an intermediate division serving to transfer products and influences from part to part. And in all subsequent stages, evolution of the two earlier systems of structures depends on evolution of this additional system.

While the society as a whole has the character of its sustaining system determined by the character of its environment, inorganic and organic, the respective parts of this system differentiate in adaptation to local circumstances; and, after primary industries have been thus localized and specialized, secondary industries dependent on them arise in conformity with the same principle. Further, as fast as societies become compounded and re-compounded, and the distributing system develops, the parts devoted to each kind of industry, originally scattered, aggregate in the most favourable localities; and the localized industrial structures, unlike the governmental structures, grow regardless of the original lines of division.

Increase of size, resulting from the massing of groups, necessitates means of communication, both for achieving combined offensive and defensive actions, and for exchange of products. Faint tracks, then paths, rude roads, finished roads, successively arise; and as fast as intercourse is thus facilitated, there is a transition from direct barter to trading carried on by a separate class; out of which evolves a complex mercantile agency of wholesale and retail distributors. The movement of commodities effected by this agency, beginning as a slow flux to and re-flux from certain places at long intervals, passes into rhythmical, regular, rapid currents; and materials for sustentation distributed hither and thither, from being few and crude become numerous and elaborated. Growing efficiency of transfer with greater variety of transferred products, increases the mutual dependence of parts at the same time that it enables each part to fulfil its function better.

Unlike the sustaining system, evolved by converse with the organic and inorganic environments, the regulating system is evolved by converse, offensive and defensive, with environing societies. In primitive headless groups temporary chieftainship results from temporary war; chronic hostilities generate permanent chieftainship; and gradually from the military control results the civil control. Habitual war, requiring prompt combination in the actions of parts, necessitates subordination. Societies in which there is little subordination disappear, and leave outstanding those in which subordination is great; and so there are produced societies in which the habit fostered by war and surviving in peace, brings about permanent submission to a government. The centralizing regulating system thus evolved is in early stages the sole regulating system. But in large societies which have become predominantly industrial, there is added a decentralized regulating system for the industrial structures; and this, at first subject in every way to the original system, acquires at length substantial independence. Finally there arises, for the distributing structures also, an independent controlling agency.

Societies fall firstly into the classes of simple, compound, doubly-compound, trebly-compound; and from the lowest the transition to the highest is through these stages. Otherwise, though less definitely, societies may be grouped as militant and industrial; of which the one type in its developed form is organized on the principle of compulsory co-operation, while the other in its developed form is organized on the principle of voluntary cooperation. The one is characterized not only by a despotic central power, but also by unlimited political control of personal conduct; while the other is characterized not only by a democratic or representative central power, but also by limitation of political control over personal conduct.

Lastly we noted the corollary that change in the predominant social activities brings metamorphosis. If, where the militant type has not elaborated into so rigid a form as to prevent change, a considerable industrial system arises, there come mitigations of the coercive restraints characterizing the militant type, and weakening of its structures. Conversely, where an industrial system largely developed has established freer social forms, resumption of offensive and defensive activities causes reversion towards the militant type.

And now, summing up the results of this general survey, let us observe the extent to which we are prepared by it for further inquiries.

The many facts contemplated unite in proving that social evolution forms a part of evolution at large. Like evolving aggregates in general, societies show *integration*, both by simple increase of mass and by coalescence and recoalescence of masses. The change from *homogeneity* to *heterogeneity* is multitudinously exemplified; up from the simple tribe, alike in all its parts, to the civilized nation, full of structural and functional unlikenesses. With progressing integration and heterogeneity goes increasing *coherence*. We see the wandering group dispersing, dividing, held together by no bonds; the tribe with parts made more coherent by subordination to a dominant man; the cluster of tribes united in a political plexus under a chief with sub-chiefs; and so on up to the civilized nation, consolidated enough to hold together for a thousand years or more. Simultaneously comes increasing *definiteness*. Social organization is at first vague; advance brings settled arrangements which grow slowly more precise; customs pass into laws which, while gaining fixity, also become more specific in their applications to varieties of actions; and all institutions, at first confusedly intermingled, slowly separate, at the same time that each within itself marks off more distinctly its component structures. Thus in all respects is fulfilled the formula of evolution. There is progress towards greater size, coherence, multiformity, and definiteness.

Besides these general truths, a number of special truths have been disclosed by our survey. Comparisons of societies in their ascending grades have made manifest certain cardinal facts respecting their growths, structures and functions—facts respecting the systems of structures, sustaining, distributing, regulating, of which they are composed; respecting the relations of these structures to the surrounding conditions and the dominant forms of social activities entailed; and respecting the metamorphoses of types caused by changes in the activities. The inductions arrived at, thus constituting in rude outline an Empirical Sociology, show that in social phenomena there is a general order of coexistence and sequence; and that therefore social phenomena form the subject-matter of a science reducible, in some measure at least, to the deductive form.[2]

. . . Like other kinds of progress, social progress is not linear but divergent and re-divergent. Each differentiated product gives origin to a new set of differentiated products. While spreading over the Earth mankind have found environments of various characters, and in each case the social life fallen into, partly determined by the social life previously led, has been partly determined by the influences of the new environment; so that the multiplying groups have tended ever to acquire differences, now major and now minor: there have arisen genera and species of societies.

. . . The cosmic process brings about retrogression as well as progression, where the conditions favour it. Only amid an infinity of modifications, adjusted to an infinity of changes of circumstances, do there now and then occur some which constitute an advance: other changes meanwhile caused in other organisms, usually not constituting forward steps in organization, and often constituting steps backwards. Evolution does not imply a latent tendency to improve, everywhere in operation. There is no uniform ascent from lower to higher, but only an occasional production of a form which, in virtue of greater fitness for more complex conditions, becomes capable of a longer life of a more varied kind. And while such higher type begins to dominate over lower types and to spread at their expense, the lower types survive in habitats or modes of life that are not usurped, or are thrust into inferior habitats or modes of life in which they retrogress.

What thus holds with organic types must hold also with types of societies. Social evolution throughout the future, like social evolution throughout the past, must, while producing step after step higher societies, leave outstanding many lower.

NOTES

1. The excerpt from *The Principles of Sociology*, vol. 1, starts here.
2. The excerpts from *The Principles of Sociology*, vol. 2, start here.

EMILE DURKHEIM

1858–1917
FRANCE

Major Works

1893   *The Division of Labour in Society*
1895   *The Rules of Sociological Method*
1897   *Suicide*
1912   *The Elementary Forms of Religious Life*
1928   *Socialism*

> Why does the individual, while becoming more autonomous, depend more upon society? How can he be at once more individual and more solidary? Certainly, these two movements, contradictory as they appear, develop in parallel fashion.[1]

> Everything which is a source of solidarity is moral, everything which forces man to take account of other men is moral, everything which forces him to regulate his conduct through something other than the striving of his ego is moral, and morality is as solid as these ties are numerous and strong.[2]

> —*Emile Durkheim*

Emile Durkheim's contribution to sociology is of major importance. His work elaborates crucial elements first explored by Auguste Comte and Herbert Spencer—especially the use of the term 'organism' or 'organistic' as metaphor for understanding and explaining society. Durkheim not only employed an organistic perspective in his theoretical treatises, but moved sociological understanding forward by integrating theory with methodological initiatives. In 1896, his founding of the journal *L'Année Sociologique* provided the discipline of sociology a new legitimacy within the academic world.

Division of Labour and Social Cohesion

Durkheim's advocacy of scientific knowledge as a basis for authority in society and his search for a recognizable moral authority—the fabric that holds the society together—are often understood as conservative, overly concerned with the maintenance of the social order. However, his pursuit of an understanding of social solidarity, first expressed in *The Division of Labour in Society*, reveals an underlying desire to comprehend social change.

Although Durkheim wrote explicitly about sociological method in *The Rules of Sociological Method*, the theme of all his works is the primacy of methodology. His discussion of the types of solidarity produced within societies by the division of labour attempts to explore the social forces that bind people to their society. He describes this force in part as the 'conscience collective' (often translated as either 'collective consciousness' or 'collective conscience', with obvious differences of meaning):

> The totality of beliefs and sentiments common to average citizens of the same society forms a determinate system which has its own life; one may call it the collective or common conscience . . . it is, by definition, diffuse in every reach of society.[3]

But in order to explore this 'diffuse' dimension of society Durkheim suggests that we need to observe such phenomena indirectly. In other words, we need some external expression of a quality that is essentially within or internalized by members of a given society. He therefore posits two types of law as indexes of the degree of social integration. *Penal* or repressive law, characteristic of societies expressing 'mechanical solidarity', represents a form of law that protects the collective consciousness or conscience of a society. Those who violate the common belief are punished or penalized. With greater division of labour and the greater differentiation and specialization characteristic of 'organic solidarity', *restitutive* law is conceived. This formation is the basis of modern contractual law: law concerned with adequate restitution or return to balance, in the case of wrongdoing, and concerned with social balance in the mutual recognition of contractual obligations.

In attempting to examine the ways in which individuals are normally integrated into the society, Durkheim also recognized the pathologies in society. His term, *anomie*, meaning normlessness or boundlessness, has become fundamental to sociological understanding. *The Division of Labour in Society* explores anomie in its general form in society as well as the anomic division of labour in work relationships.

Sociological Method

Throughout Durkheim's work the notion of social cohesion is paramount. What is it that holds society together? What is the place of the moral in this process? With greater division of labour, greater specialization and individualization characterizing modern societies, Durkheim felt compelled to document the expressions of these changes. *The Rules of Sociological Method* expresses the overriding intimacy of method and substance. While describing methodological questions, his conceptualization of social facts as 'things' that have impact on the individual—external to us and constraining on us—reveals once again the force of society. 'Individuals are born of society, not society born of individuals', a paraphrase of one of his elemental ideas, parallels the notion of social facts exhibiting both exteriority to and constraint upon individuals.

Suicide

Two years after his seminal work on method, Durkheim employed his methodological considerations in the classic study, *Suicide*. By examining rates of suicide in various European countries and correlating these data with variables related to marriage, religious affiliation, etc., he again explored the question of individuals' integration into society and the forces of regulation that acted upon them. He was emphatic that by working with the social facts that describe social life we transcend the individual manifestations that are the substance of psychological study. His study of suicide attests to sociological reality; the contradiction of relating what appears to be such an individual phenomenon with, in his view, such essentially social causes illuminates our understanding of how people are or are not integrated into social reality. Durkheim's statistical investigation of suicide prepared the ground for modern sociological study. An emerging theme in his work is the fundamental distinction between egoistic behaviour (i.e., unregulated individual behaviour) and the incipient individualism (i.e., creative individuality) possible in modern society.

This distinction helps us understand his placing of the occupational group (or what he called 'corporations') at the forefront of moral restitution within society. He suggests that religious, political, and domestic lives are either inadequate or too abstract and distant to reintegrate people into the fabric of society. He calls on the occupational group to fill this moral vacuum:

> Of course, nothing but a moral power can set a law for men; but this must also be sufficiently associated with affairs of this world to be able to estimate them at their true value. The occupational group has just this two-fold character. Being a group, it sufficiently dominates individuals to set limits to their greed; but sees too much of their life not to sympathize with their needs.[4]

Society and Religious Life

Having stated that religion as a social force may not correct the ills of modernity or stem the possible disintegration of social life, in his final major work, *The Elementary Forms of Religious Life*, Durkheim explores the origins of religious life. Looking at anthropological studies of totemism and other archaic religious forms, Durkheim once again posits the centrality of society in all human affairs. He sees religion as fundamentally a transfiguration of society, and challenges our understanding of its place in the society. He sees religion as a human creation— a celebration of the power of society.

> But from the moment when it is recognized that above the individual there is society, and that this is not a nominal being created by reason, but a system of active forces, a new manner of explaining men becomes possible. To conserve his distinctive traits it is no longer necessary to put them outside experience.[5]

Conceptualizing religion as a social force, Durkheim defines the sacred and the profane as essential social categories. This division is based on the social, humanly initiated and sustained: people invest or 'add on' the sacredness to objects of religious power. We are made aware of this most profoundly by the recognition that '*the images of totemic beings are more sacred than the beings themselves.*'[6] In essence, the social imputation is the source of the force.

> Howsoever complex the outward manifestations of the religious life may be, at bottom it is one and simple. It responds everywhere to one and the same need, and is everywhere derived from one and the same mental state. In all its forms, its object is to raise man above himself and to make him lead a life superior to that which he would lead, if he followed only his own individual whims: beliefs express this life in representations; rites organize it and regulate its working.[7]

Durkheim's aspiration to explain the nature of the society and its power to act on the individual, a power continually internalized by the individual, exhibits a desire to find the moral force to sustain society in view of the complexities facing modern human beings. His attention to substantial questions, as well as how to acquire elemental comprehension of them, has been central to sociology.

Notes

1. Emile Durkheim, *The Division of Labour in Society* (New York: Free Press, 1964), 37.
2. Ibid., 398.
3. Ibid., 79.
4. Emile Durkheim, *Suicide* (New York: Free Press, 1966), 384.
5. Emile Durkheim, *The Elementary Forms of Religious Life* (New York: Free Press, 1965), 495.
6. Ibid., 156; Durkheim's italics.
7. Ibid., 461.

DIVISION OF LABOUR IN SOCIETY

Mechanical and Organic Solidarity

The social relations to which the division of labour gives birth have often been considered only in terms of exchange, but this misinterprets what such exchange implies and what results from it. It suggests two beings mutually dependent because they are each incomplete, and translates this mutual dependence outwardly. It is, then, only the superficial expression of an internal and very deep state. Precisely because this state is constant, it calls up a whole mechanism of images which function with a continuity that exchange does not possess. The image of the one who completes us becomes inseparable from ours, not only because it is frequently associated with ours, but particularly because it is the natural complement of it. It thus becomes an integral and permanent part of our conscience, to such a point that we can no longer separate ourselves from it and seek to increase its force. That is why we enjoy the society of the one it represents, since the presence of the object that it expresses, by making us actually perceive it, sets it off more. On the other hand, we will suffer from all circumstances which, like absence or death, may have as effect the barring of its return or the diminishing of its vivacity.

As short as this analysis is, it suffices to show that this mechanism is not identical with that which serves as a basis for sentiments of sympathy whose source is resemblance. Surely there can be no solidarity between others and us unless the image of others unites itself with ours. But when the union results from the resemblance of two images, it consists in an agglutination. The two representations become solidary because, being indistinct, totally or in part, they confound each other, and become no more than one, and they are solidary only in the measure which they confound themselves. On the contrary, in the case of the division of labour, they are outside each other and are linked only because they are distinct. Neither the sentiments nor the social relations which derive from these sentiments are the same in the two cases.

We are thus led to ask if the division of labour would not play the same role in more extensive groups, if, in contemporary societies where it has developed as we know, it would not have as its function the integration of the social body to assure unity. It is quite legitimate to suppose that the facts which we have just observed reproduce themselves here, but with greater amplitude, that great political societies can maintain themselves in equilibrium only thanks to the specialization of tasks, that the division of labour is the source, if not unique, at least principal, of social solidarity. Comte took this point of view. Of all sociologists, to our knowledge, he is the first to have recognized in the division of labour something other than a purely economic phenomenon. He saw in it 'the most essential condition of social life', provided that one conceives it 'in all its rational extent; that is to say, that one applies it to the totality of all our diverse operations of whatever kind, instead of attributing it, as is ordinarily done, to simple material usages'. Considered in this light, he says, 'it leads immediately to regarding not only individuals and classes, but also, in many respects, different peoples, as at once participating, following a definite path in a special degree, exactly determined, in a work, immense and communal, whose inevitable gradual development links actual co-operators to their predecessors and even to their successors. It is thus the continuous repartition of different human endeavours which especially constitutes social solidarity and which becomes the elementary cause of the extension and growing complication of the social organism'.[1]

If this hypothesis were proved, the division of labour would play a role much more important than that which we ordinarily attribute to it. It would serve not only to raise societies to luxury, desirable perhaps, but superfluous; it would be a condition of their existence. Through it, or at least particularly through it, their cohesion would be assured; it would determine the essential traits of their constitution. Accordingly, although we may not yet be in position to resolve the question rigorously, we can, however, imply from it now that, if such is really the function of the division of labour, it must have a moral character, for the need of order, harmony, and social solidarity is generally considered moral.

But before seeing whether this common opinion is well founded, we must verify the hypothesis that we have just given forth concerning the role of the division of labour. Let us see if, in effect, in the societies in which we live, it is from this that social solidarity essentially derives.

But how shall we proceed to such verification?

We must not simply look to see if, in these types of society, there exists a social solidarity which comes from the division of labour. That is a self-evident truism, since in such societies the division of labour is highly developed and produces solidarity. Rather we must especially determine in what degree the solidarity that it produces contributes to the general integration of society, for it is only then that we shall know how far necessary it is, whether it is an essential factor of social cohesion, or whether, on the contrary, it is only an accessory and secondary condition. To reply to this question, we must compare this social link to others in order to measure how much credit is due to it in the total effect; and to that end, we must begin by classifying the different types of social solidarity.

But social solidarity is a completely moral phenomenon which, taken by itself, does not lend itself to exact observation nor indeed to measurement. To proceed to this classification and this comparison, we must substitute for this internal fact which escapes us an external index which symbolizes it and study the former in the light of the latter.

This visible symbol is law. In effect, despite its immaterial character, wherever social solidarity exists, it resides not in a state of pure potentiality, but manifests its presence by sensible indices. Where it is strong, it leads men strongly to one another, frequently puts them in contact, multiplies the occasions when they find themselves related. To speak correctly, considering the point our investigation has reached, it is not easy to say whether social solidarity produces these phenomena, or whether it is a result of them, whether men relate themselves because it is a driving force, or whether it is a driving force because they relate themselves. However, it is not, at the moment, necessary to decide this question; it suffices to state that the two orders of fact are linked and vary at the same time and in the same sense. The more solidary the members of a society are, the more they sustain diverse relations, one with another, or with the group taken collectively, for, if their meetings were rare, they would depend upon one another only at rare intervals, and then tenuously. Moreover, the number of these relations is necessarily proportional to that of the juridical rules which determine them. Indeed, social life, especially where it exists durably, tends inevitably to assume a definite form and to organize itself, and law is nothing else than this very organization in so far as it has greater stability and precision. The general life of society cannot extend its sway without juridical life extending its sway at the same time and in direct relation. We can thus be certain of finding reflected in law all the essential varieties of social solidarity.

The objection may be raised, it is true, that social relations can fix themselves without assuming a juridical form. Some of them do not attain this degree of consolidation and precision, but they do not remain undetermined on that account. Instead of being regulated by law, they are regulated by custom. Law, then, reflects only part of social life and furnishes us with incomplete data for the solution of the problem. Moreover, it often happens that custom is not in accord with law; we usually say that it tempers law's severity, that it corrects law's formalism, sometimes, indeed, that it is animated by a different spirit. Would it not then be true that custom manifests other sorts of solidarity than that expressed in positive law?

This opposition, however, crops up only in quite exceptional circumstances. This comes about when law no longer corresponds to the state of existing society, but maintains itself, without reason for so doing, by the force of habit. In such a case, new relations which establish themselves in spite of it are not bereft of organization, for they cannot endure without seeking consolidation. But since they are in conflict with the old existing law, they can attain only superficial organization. They do not pass beyond the stage of custom and do not enter into the juridical life proper. Thus conflict ensues. But it arises only in rare and pathological cases which cannot endure without danger. Normally, custom is not opposed to law, but is, on the contrary, its basis. It happens, in truth, that on such a basis nothing may rear its head. Social relations ensue which convey a diffuse regulation which comes from custom; but they lack importance and continuity, except in the abnormal cases of which we were just speaking. If, then, there are types of social solidarity which custom alone manifests, they are assuredly secondary; law produces those which are essential and they are the only ones we need to know.

. . .

Our method has now been fully outlined. Since law reproduces the principal forms of social solidarity, we have only to classify the different types of law to find therefrom the different types of social solidarity which correspond to it. It is now probable that there is a type which symbolizes this special solidarity of which the division of labour is the cause. That found, it will suffice, in order to measure the part of the division of labour, to compare the number of juridical rules which express it with the total volume of law.

For this task, we cannot use the distinctions utilized by the jurisconsults. Created for practical purposes, they can be very useful from this point of view, but science cannot content itself with these empirical classifications and approximations. The most accepted is that which divides law into public and private; the first is for the regulation of the relations of the individual to the State, the second, of individuals among themselves. But when we try to get closer to these terms, the line of demarcation which appeared so neat at the beginning fades away. All law is private in the sense that it is always about individuals who are present and acting; but so, too, all law is public, in the sense that it is a social function and that all individuals are, whatever their varying titles, functionaries of society. Marital functions, paternal, etc., are neither delimited nor organized in a manner different from ministerial and legislative functions, and it is not without reason that Roman law entitled tutelage *munus publicum*. What, moreover, is the State? Where does it begin and where does it end? We know how controversial the question is; it is not scientific to make a fundamental classification repose on a notion so obscure and so badly analysed.

To proceed scientifically, we must find some characteristic which, while being essential to juridical phenomena, varies as they vary. Every precept of law can be defined as a rule of sanctioned conduct. Moreover, it is evident that sanctions change with the gravity attributed to precepts, the place they hold in the public conscience, the role they play in society. It is right, then, to classify juridical rules according to the different sanctions which are attached to them.

They are of two kinds. Some consist essentially in suffering, or at least a loss, inflicted on the agent. They make demands on his fortune, or on his honour, or on his life, or on his liberty, and deprive him of something he enjoys. We call them repressive. They constitute penal law. It is true that those which are attached to rules which are purely moral have the same character, only they are distributed in a diffuse manner, by everybody indiscriminately, whereas those in penal law are applied through the intermediary of a definite organ; they are organized. As for the other type, it does not necessarily imply suffering for the agent, but consists only of *the return of things as they were*, in the reestablishment of troubled relations to their normal state, whether the incriminated act is restored by force to the type whence it deviated, or is annulled, that is, deprived of all social value. We must then separate juridical rules into two great classes, accordingly as they have organized repressive sanctions or only restitutive sanctions.[2] The first comprise all penal law; the second, civil law, commercial law, procedural law, administrative and constitutional law, after abstraction of the penal rules which may be found there.

[T]here exists a social solidarity which comes from a certain number of states of conscience which are common to all the members of the same society. This is what repressive law materially represents, at least in so far as it is essential. The part that it plays in the general integration of society evidently depends upon the greater or lesser extent of the social life which the common conscience embraces and regulates. The greater the diversity of relations wherein the latter makes its action felt, the more also it creates links which attach the individual to the group; the more, consequently, social cohesion derives completely from this source and bears its mark. But the number of these relations is itself proportional to that of the repressive rules. In determining what fraction of the juridical system penal law represents, we, at the same time, measure the relative importance of this solidarity. It is true that in such a procedure we do not take into account certain elements of the collective conscience which, because of their smaller power or their indeterminateness, remain foreign to repressive law while contributing to the assurance of social harmony. These are the ones protected by punishments which are merely diffuse. But the same is the case with other parts of law. There is not one of them which is not complemented by custom, and as there is no reason for supposing that the relation of law and custom is not the same in these different spheres, this elimination is not made at the risk of having to alter the results of our comparison.

Organic Solidarity Due to the Division of Labour

. . . To sum up: The relations governed by co-operative law with restitutive sanctions and the solidarity which they express, result from the division of social labour. We have explained, moreover, that, in general, co-operative relations do not convey other sanctions. In fact, it is in the nature of special tasks to escape the action of the collective conscience, for, in order for a thing to be the object of common sentiments, the first condition is that it be common, that is to say, that it be present in all consciences and that all can represent it in one and the same manner. To be sure, in so far as functions have a certain generality, everybody can have some idea of them. But the more specialized they are, the more circumscribed the number of those cognizant of each of them. Consequently, the more marginal they are to the common conscience. The rules which determine them cannot have the superior force, the transcendent authority which, when offended, demands expiation. It is also from opinion that their authority comes, as is the case with penal rules, but from an opinion localized in restricted regions of society.

Moreover, even in the special circles where they apply and where, consequently, they are represented in people, they do not correspond to very active sentiments, nor even very often to any type of emotional state. For, as they fix the manner in which the different functions ought to concur in diverse combinations of circumstances which can arise, the objects to which they relate themselves are not always present to consciences. We do not always have to administer guardianship, trusteeship,[3] or exercise the rights of creditor or buyer, etc., or even exercise them in such and such a condition. But the states of conscience are strong only in so far as they are permanent. The violation of these rules reaches neither the common soul of society in its living parts, nor even, at least not generally, that of special groups, and, consequently, it can determine only a very moderate reaction. All that is necessary is that the functions concur in a regular manner. If this regularity is disrupted, it behooves us to re-establish it. Assuredly, that is not to say that the development of the division of labour cannot be affective of penal law. There are as we already know, administrative and governmental functions in which certain relations are regulated by repressive law, because of the particular character which the organ of common conscience and everything that relates to it has. In still other cases, the links of solidarity which unite certain social functions can be such that from their break quite general repercussions result invoking a penal sanction. But, for the reason we have given, these counter-blows are exceptional.

This law definitely plays a role in society analogous to that played by the nervous system in the organism. The latter has as its task, in effect, the regulation of the different functions of the body in such a way as to make them harmonize. It thus very naturally expresses the state of concentration at which the organism has arrived, in accordance with the division of physiological labour. Thus, on different levels of the animal scale, we can measure the degree of this concentration according to the development of the nervous system. Which is to say that we can equally measure the degree of concentration at which a society has arrived in accordance with the division of social labour according to the development of co-operative law with restitutive sanctions. We can foresee the great services that this criterion will render us.

Since negative solidarity does not produce any integration by itself, and since, moreover, there is nothing specific about it, we shall recognize only two kinds of positive solidarity which are distinguishable by the following qualities:

1. The first binds the individual directly to society without any intermediary. In the second, he depends upon society, because he depends upon the parts of which it is composed.

2. Society is not seen in the same aspect in the two cases. In the first, what we call society is a more or less organized totality of beliefs and sentiments common to all the members of the group: this is the collective type. On the other hand, the society in which we are solidary in the second instance is a system of different, special functions which definite relations unite. These two societies really make up only one. They are two aspects of one and the same reality, but none the less they must be distinguished.

3. From this second difference there arises another which helps us to characterize and name the two kinds of solidarity.

The first can be strong only if the ideas and tendencies common to all the members of the society are greater in number and intensity than those which pertain personally to each member. It is as much stronger as the excess is more considerable. But what makes our personality is how much of our own individual qualities we have, what distinguishes us from others. This solidarity can grow only in inverse ratio to personality. There are in each of us, as we have said, two consciences: one which is common to our group in its entirety, which, consequently, is not ourself, but society living and acting within us; the other, on the contrary, represents that in us which is personal and distinct, that which makes us an individual.[4] Solidarity which comes from likenesses is at its maximum when the collective conscience completely envelops our whole conscience and coincides in all points with it. But, at that moment, our individuality is nil. It can be born only if the community takes smaller toll of us. There are, here, two contrary forces, one centripetal, the other centrifugal, which cannot flourish at the same time. We cannot, at one and the same time, develop ourselves in two opposite senses. If we have a lively desire to think and act for ourselves, we cannot be strongly inclined to think and act as others do. If our ideal is to present a singular and personal appearance, we do not want to resemble everybody else. Moreover, at the moment when this solidarity exercises its force, our personality vanishes, as our definition permits us to say, for we are no longer ourselves, but the collective life.

The social molecules which can be coherent in this way can act together only in the measure that they have no actions of their own, as the molecules of inorganic bodies. That is why we propose to call this type of solidarity mechanical. The term does not signify that it is produced by mechanical and artificial means. We call it that only by analogy to the cohesion which unites the elements of an inanimate body, as opposed to that which makes a unity out of the elements of a living body. What justifies this term is that the link which thus unites the individual to society is wholly analogous to that which attaches a thing to a person. The individual conscience, considered in this light, is a simple dependent upon the collective type and follows all of its movements, as the possessed object follows those of its owner. In societies where this type of solidarity is highly developed, the individual does not appear, as we shall see later. Individuality is something which the society possesses. Thus, in these social types, personal rights are not yet distinguished from real rights.

It is quite otherwise with the solidarity which the division of labour produces. Whereas the previous type implies that individuals resemble each other, this type presumes their difference. The first is possible only in so far as the individual personality is absorbed into the collective personality; the second is possible only if each one has a sphere of action which is peculiar to him; that is, a personality. It is necessary, then, that the collective conscience leave open a part of the individual conscience in order that special functions may be established there, functions which it cannot regulate. The more this region is extended, the stronger is the cohesion which results from this solidarity. In effect, on the one hand, each one depends as much more strictly on society as labour is more divided; and, on the other, the activity of each is as much more personal as it is more specialized. Doubtless, as circumscribed as it is, it is never completely original. Even in the exercise of our occupation, we conform to usages, to practices which are common to our whole professional brotherhood. But, even in this instance, the yoke that we submit to is much less heavy than when society completely controls us, and it leaves much more place open for the free play of our initiative. Here, then, the individuality of all grows at the same time as that of its parts. Society becomes more capable of collective movement, at the same time that each of its elements has more freedom of movement. This solidarity resembles that which we observe among the higher animals. Each organ, in effect, has its special physiognomy, its autonomy. And, moreover, the unity of the organism is as great as the individuation of the parts is more marked. Because of this analogy, we propose to call the solidarity which is due to the division of labour, organic.

At the same time, this chapter and the preceding furnish us with the means to calculate the part which remains to each of these two social links in the total common result which they concur in producing through their different media. We know under what external forms these two types of solidarity are symbolized, that is to say, what the body of juridical rules which corresponds to each of them is. Consequently, in order to recognize their respective importance in a given social type, it is enough to compare the respective extent of the two types of law which express them, since law always varies as the social relations which it governs.[5]

. . .

The Causes

Since this visible and measurable symbol reflects the variations of what we have called moral density,[6] we can substitute it for this latter in the formula we have proposed.

Moreover, we must repeat here what we said before. If society, in concentrating, deter-mines the development of the division of labour, the latter, in its turn, increases the con-centration of society. But no matter, for the division of labour remains the derived fact, and, consequently, the advances which it has made are due to parallel advances of social density, whatever may be the causes of the latter. That is all we wish to prove.

But this factor is not the only one.

If condensation of society produces this result, it is because it multiplies intra-social relations. But these will be still more numerous, if, in addition, the total number of mem-bers of society becomes more considerable. If it comprises more individuals at the same time as they are more intimately in contact, the effect will necessarily be re-enforced. Social volume, then, has the same influence as density upon the division of labour.

In fact, societies are generally as voluminous as they are more advanced, and conse-quently as labour is more divided. Societies, as living organisms, in Spencer's words, begin in the form of a bud, sprouting extremely tenuous bodies, compared to those they finally become. The greatest societies, as he says, have emerged from little wandering hordes, such as those of lower races. This is a conclusion which Spencer finds cannot be denied.[7] What we have said of the segmental constitution makes this an indisputable truth. We know, indeed, that societies are formed by a certain number of segments of unequal extent which mutually envelop one another. These moulds are not artificial cre-ations, especially in origin, and even when they have become conventional, they imitate and reproduce, as far as possible, the forms of the natural arrangement which has pre-ceded. There are a great many old societies maintained in this form. The most vast among these subdivisions, those comprising the others, correspond to the nearest inferior social type. Indeed, among the segments of which they are in turn composed, the most exten-sive are vestiges of the type which comes directly below the preceding, and so on. There are found traces of the most primitive social organization among the most advanced peo-ples.[8] Thus, the tribe is formed of an aggregate of hordes of clans. The nation (the Jewish nation, for example) and the city are formed of an aggregate of tribes; the city, in turn, with the villages subordinate to it, enters as an element of the most complex societies, etc. Thus, the social volume cannot fail to increase, since each species is constituted by a repetition of societies of the immediately anterior species.

There are exceptions, however. . . . China and Russia are a great deal more populous than the most civilized nations of Europe. With these people, consequently, the division of labour is not developed in proportion to the social volume. That is because the increase of volume is not necessarily a mark of superiority if the density does not increase at the same time and in the same relation, for a society can attain great dimensions because it comprises a very great number of segments, whatever may be the nature of the latter. If, then, even the most vast among them reproduce only societies of very inferior type, the segmental structure will remain very pronounced, and, consequently, social organization little elevated. Even an immense aggregate of clans is below the smallest organized society, since the latter has run through stages of evolution within which the other has remained. In the same way, if the number of social units has influence on the division of labour, it is not through itself and necessarily, but it is because the number of social relations generally increases with that of individuals. But, for this result to be attained, it is not enough that society take in a great many people, but they must be, in addition, intimately enough in contact to act and react on one another. If they are, on the contrary, separated by opaque milieux, they can only be bound by rare and weak relations, and it is as if they had small populations. The increase of social volume does not, then, always accelerate the advances of the division of labour, but only when the mass is contracted at the same time and to the same extent. Consequently, it is only an additional factor, but when it is joined to the first, it amplifies its effects by action peculiar to it, and therefore is to be distinguished from that.

We can then formulate the following proposition: *The division of labour varies in direct ratio with the volume and density of societies, and, if it progresses in a continuous manner in the course of social development, it is because societies become regularly denser and generally more voluminous.*

At all times, it is true, it has been well understood that there was a relation between these two orders of fact, for, in order that functions be more specialized, there must be more co-operators, and they must be related to co-operate. But, ordinarily, this state of societies is seen only as the means by which the division of labour develops, and not as the cause of its development. The latter is made to depend upon individual aspirations toward well being and happiness, which can be satisfied so much better as societies are more extensive and more condensed. The law we have just established is quite otherwise. We say, not that the growth and condensation of societies *permit*, but that they *necessitate* a greater division of labour. It is not an instrument by which the latter is realized; it is its determining cause.[9]

. . .

In fact, we may observe that labour becomes more continuous as it is more divided. Animals and savages work in a very capricious manner when they are forced by necessity to satisfy some immediate need. In societies which are exclusively agricultural and pastoral, labour is almost entirely suspended during the season of bad weather. In Rome, it was interrupted by a multitude of holidays and days of rest.[10] In the middle ages, cessation from work occurred even more often.[11] As we go forward, however, work becomes a permanent occupation, a habit, and indeed, if this habit is sufficiently strengthened, a need. But it would not have been set up and the corresponding need would not have arisen, if work had remained irregular and intermittent as heretofore.

We are thus led to the recognition of a new reason why the division of labour is a source of social cohesion. It makes individuals solidary, as we have said before, not only because it limits the activity of each, but also because it increases it. It adds to the unity of the organism, solely through adding to its life. At least, in its normal state, it does not produce one of these effects without the other.

. . .

The requirements of our subject have obliged us to classify moral rules and to review the principal types. We are thus in a better position than we were in the beginning to see, or at least to conjecture, not only upon the external sign, but also upon the internal character which is common to all of them and which can serve to define them. We have put them into two groups: rules with repressive sanctions, which may be diffuse or organized, and rules with restitutive sanctions. We have seen that the first of these express the conditions of the solidarity, *sui generis*, which comes from resemblances, and to which we have given the name mechanical; the second, the conditions of negative solidarity and organic solidarity. We can thus say that, in general, the characteristic of moral rules is that they enunciate the fundamental conditions of social solidarity. Law and morality are the totality of ties which bind each of us to society, which make a unitary, coherent aggregate of the mass of individuals. Everything which is a source of solidarity is moral, everything which forces man to take account of other men is moral, everything which forces him to regulate his conduct through something other than the striving of his ego is moral, and morality is as solid as these ties are numerous and strong. We can see how inexact it is to define it, as is often done, through liberty. It rather consists in a state of dependence. Far from serving to emancipate the individual, or disengaging him from the environment which surrounds him, it has, on the contrary, the function of making him an integral part of a whole, and, consequently, of depriving him of some liberty of movement. We sometimes, it is true, come across people not without nobility who find the idea of such dependence intolerable. But that is because they do not perceive the source from which their own morality flows, since these sources are very deep. Conscience is a bad judge of what goes on in the depths of a person, because it does not penetrate to them.

. . .

But how little a thing it is when one contemplates the ever-increasing extent of social life, and, consequently, of individual consciences! For, as they become more voluminous, as intelligence becomes richer, activity more varied, in order for morality to remain constant, that is to say, in order for the individual to remain attached to the group with a force equal to that of yesterday, the ties which bind him to it must become stronger and more numerous. If, then, he formed no others than those which come from resemblances, the effacement of the segmental type would be accompanied by a systematic debasement of morality. Man would no longer be sufficiently obligated; he would no longer feel about and above him this salutary pressure of society which moderates his egoism and makes him a moral being. This is what gives moral value to the division of labour. Through it, the individual becomes cognizant of his dependence upon society; from it come the forces which keep him in check and restrain him. In short, since the division of labour becomes the chief source of social solidarity, it becomes, at the same time, the foundation of the moral order.

NOTES

1. *Cours de philosophie positive* IV: 425. Analogous ideas are found in Schaeffle, *Bau und Leben des sozialen Koerpers* II, passim, and Clement, *Science Sociale* I: 235ff.
2. Translator's note: In the first edition the following footnote . . . is found at this point: 'If this division is combined with the definition that we have given of purely moral rules . . . the following table is obtained, based on a complete classification of all obligatory rules of conduct:

Obligatory rules of conduct

With repressive sanctions { Diffuse (common morality without juridical sanctions)

Organized (Penal Law)

With restitutive sanctions.

This table shows anew how difficult it is to separate the study of simple moral rules from the study of juridical rules.'

3. That is why the law which governs the relations of domestic functions is not penal, although these functions are very general.

4. However, these two consciences are not in regions geographically distinct from us, but penetrate from all sides.

5. To make these ideas precise, we develop in the following table the classification of juridical rules which is found implicit in this chapter and the preceding:

I.   *Rules With Organized Repressive Sanction (See note 2)*

II. *Rules With Restitutive Sanction Determining*

Negative or Abstentive Relations {

Of the thing with the person {
Law of property in its various forms (movable, immovable, etc.)
Various modalities of the law of property (servitudes, usufruct, etc.)

Of persons with persons {
Determined by the normal exercise of real rights
Determined by the violation of real rights

Positive Relations of Co-operation {

Between domestic functions

Between diffuse economic functions {
Contractual relations in general
Special contracts

Of administrative functions {
Between themselves
With governmental functions
With diffuse functions of society

Of governmental functions {
Between themselves
With administrative functions
With diffuse political functions

6. There are particular, exceptional cases, however, where material and moral density are perhaps not entirely in accord.

7. *Principles of Sociology* II: 23.

8. The village, which is originally only a fixed clan.

9. On this point, we can still rely on Comte as authority. 'I must,' he said, 'now indicate the pro-

gressive condensation of our species as a last general concurrent element in regulating the effective speed of the social movement. We can first easily recognize that this influence contributes a great deal, especially in origin, in determining a more special division of human labour, necessarily incompatible with a small number of co-operators. *Besides, by a most intimate and little known property, although still most important, such a condensation stimulates directly, in a very powerful manner, the most rapid development of social evolution,* either in driving individuals to new efforts to assure themselves by more refined means of an existence which otherwise would become more difficult, or by obliging society with more stubborn and better concentrated energy to fight more stiffly against the more powerful effort of particular divergences. With one and the other, we see that it is not a question here of the absolute increase of the number of individuals, but especially of their intense concourse in a given space.' *Cours* IV: 455.

10. Marquardt, *Romische Staatsverwaltung* III: 545ff.

11. See Levasseur, *Les classes ouvrières en France jusqu'à la Revolution* l: 474, 475.

SOCIOLOGICAL METHOD

What is a Social Fact

Before inquiring into the method suited to the study of social facts, it is important to know which facts are commonly called 'social'. This information is all the more necessary since the designation 'social' is used with little precision. It is currently employed for practically all phenomena generally diffused within society, however small their social interest. But on that basis, there are, as it were, no human events that may not be called social. Each individual drinks, sleeps, eats, reasons; and it is to society's interest that these functions be exercised in an orderly manner. If, then, all these facts are counted as 'social' facts, sociology would have no subject matter exclusively its own, and its domain would be confused with that of biology and psychology.

But in reality there is in every society a certain group of phenomena which may be differentiated from those studied by the other natural sciences. When I fulfil my obligations as brother, husband, or citizen, when I execute my contracts, I perform duties which are defined, externally to myself and my acts, in law and in custom. Even if they conform to my own sentiments and I feel their reality subjectively, such reality is still objective, for I did not create them; I merely inherited them through my education. How many times it happens, moreover, that we are ignorant of the details of the obligations incumbent upon us, and that in order to acquaint ourselves with them we must consult the law and its authorized interpreters! Similarly, the church-member finds the beliefs and practices of his religious life ready-made at birth; their existence prior to his own implies their existence outside of himself. The system of signs I use to express my thought, the system of currency I employ to pay my debts, the instruments of credit I utilize in my commercial relations, the practices followed in my profession, etc., function independently of my own use of them. And these statements can be repeated for each member of society. Here, then, are ways of acting, thinking, and feeling that present the noteworthy property of existing outside the individual consciousness.

These types of conduct or thought are not only external to the individual but are, moreover, endowed with coercive power, by virtue of which they impose themselves upon him, independent of his individual will. Of course, when I fully consent and conform to them, this constraint is felt only slightly, if at all, and is therefore unnecessary. But it is, nonetheless, an intrinsic characteristic of these facts, the proof thereof being that it asserts itself as soon as I attempt to resist it. If I attempt to violate the law, it reacts against me so as to prevent my act before its accomplishment, or to nullify my violation by restoring the damage, if it is accomplished and reparable, or to make me expiate it if it cannot be compensated for otherwise.

In the case of purely moral maxims; the public conscience exercises a check on every act which offends it by means of the surveillance it exercises over the conduct of citizens, and the appropriate penalties at its disposal. In many cases the constraint is less violent, but nevertheless it always exists. If I do not submit to the conventions of society, if in my dress I do not conform to the customs observed in my country and in my class, the ridicule I provoke, the social isolation in which I am kept, produce, although in an attenuated form, the same effects as a punishment in the strict sense of the word. The constraint is nonetheless efficacious for being indirect. I am not obliged to speak French with my fellow-countrymen nor to use the legal currency, but I cannot possibly do otherwise. If I tried to escape this necessity, my attempt would fail miserably. As an industrialist, I am free to apply my technical methods of former centuries; but by doing so, I should invite certain ruin. Even when I free myself from these rules and violate them successfully, I am always compelled to struggle with them. When finally overcome, they make their constraining power sufficiently felt by the resistance they offer. The enterprises of all innovators, including successful ones, come up against resistance of this kind.

Here, then, is a category of facts with very distinctive characteristics: it consists of ways of acting, thinking, and feeling, external to the individual, and endowed with a power of coercion, by reason of which they control him. These ways of thinking could not be confused with biological phenomena, since they consist of representations and of actions; nor with psychological phenomena, which exist only in the individual consciousness and through it. They constitute, thus, a new variety of phenomena; and it is to them exclusively that the term 'social' ought to be applied. And this term fits them quite well, for it is clear that, since their source is not in the individual, their substratum can be no other than society, either the political society as a whole or some one of the partial groups it includes, such as religious denominations, political, literary, and occupational associations, etc. On the other hand, this term 'social' applies to them exclusively, for it has a distinct meaning only if it designates exclusively the phenomena which are not included in any of the categories of facts that have already been established and classified. These ways of thinking and acting therefore constitute the proper domain of sociology. It is true that, when we define them with this word 'constraint', we risk shocking the zealous partisans of absolute individualism. For those who profess the complete autonomy of the individual, man's dignity is diminished whenever he is made to feel that he is not completely self-determinant. It is generally accepted today, however, that most of our ideas and our tendencies are not developed by ourselves but come to us from without. How can they become a part of us except by imposing themselves upon us? This is the whole meaning of our definition. And it is generally accepted, moreover, that social constraint is not necessarily incompatible with the individual personality.[1]

Since the examples that we have just cited (legal and moral regulations, religious faiths, financial systems, etc.) all consist of established beliefs and practices, one might be led to believe that social facts exist only where there is some social organization. But there are other facts without such crystallized form which have the same objectivity and the same ascendency over the individual. These are called 'social currents'. Thus the great movements of enthusiasm, indignation, and pity in a crowd do not originate in any one of the particular individual consciousnesses. They come to each one of us from without and can carry us away in spite of ourselves. Of course, it may happen that, in abandoning myself to them unreservedly, I do not feel the pressure they exert upon me. But it is revealed as soon as I try to resist them. Let an individual attempt to oppose one of these collective manifestations, and the emotions that he denies will turn against him. Now, if this power of external coercion asserts itself so clearly in cases of resistance, it must exist also in the first-mentioned cases, although we are unconscious of it. We are then victims of the illusion of having ourselves created that which actually forced itself from without. If the complacency with which we permit ourselves to be carried along conceals the pressure undergone, nevertheless it does not abolish it. Thus, air is no less heavy because we do not detect its weight. So, even if we ourselves have spontaneously contributed to the production of the common emotion, the impression we have received differs markedly from that which we would have experienced if we had been alone. Also, once the crowd has dispersed, that is, once these social influences have ceased to act upon us and we are alone again, the emotions which have passed through the mind appear strange to us, and we no longer recognize them as ours. We realize that these feelings have been impressed upon us to a much greater extent than they were created by us. It may even happen that they horrify us, so much were they contrary to our nature. Thus, a group of individuals, most of whom are perfectly inoffensive, may, when gathered in a crowd, be drawn into acts of atrocity. And what we say of these transitory outbursts applies similarly to those more permanent currents of opinion on religious, political, literature, or artistic matters which are constantly being formed around us, whether in society as a whole or in more limited circles.

To confirm this definition of the social fact by a characteristic illustration from common experience, one need only observe the manner in which children are brought up. Considering the facts as they have always been, it becomes immediately evident that all education is a continuous effort to impose on the child ways of seeing, feeling, and acting which he could not have arrived at spontaneously. From the very first hours of his life, we compel him to eat, drink, and sleep at regular hours; we constrain him to cleanliness, calmness, and obedience; later we exert pressure upon him in order that he may learn proper consideration for others, respect for customs and conventions, the need for work, etc. If, in time, this constraint ceases to be felt, it is because it gradually gives rise to habits and to internal tendencies that render constraint unnecessary; but nevertheless it is not abolished, for it is still the source from which these habits were derived. It is true that, according to Spencer, a rational education ought to reject such methods, allowing the child to act in complete liberty; but as this pedagogic theory has never been applied by any known people, it must be accepted only as an expression of personal opinion, not as a fact which can contradict the aforementioned observations. What makes these facts particularly instructive is that the aim of education is, precisely, the socialization of the human being; the process of education, therefore, gives us in a nutshell the historical fashion in which the social being is constituted. This unremitting pressure to which the child is subjected is the very pressure of the social milieu which tends to fashion him in its own image, and of which parents and teachers are merely the representatives and intermediaries.

It follows that sociological phenomena cannot be defined by their universality. A thought which we find in every individual consciousness, a movement repeated by all individuals, is not thereby a social fact. If sociologists have been satisfied with defining them by this characteristic, it is because they confused them with what one might call their reincarnation in the individual. It is, however, the collective aspects of the beliefs, tendencies, and practices of a group that characterize truly social phenomena. As for the forms that the collective states assume when refracted in the individual, these are things of another sort. This duality is clearly demonstrated by the fact that these two orders of phenomena are frequently found dissociated from one another. Indeed, certain of these social manners of acting and thinking acquire, by reason of their repetition, a certain rigidity which on its own account crystallizes them, so to speak, and isolates them from the particular events which reflect them. They thus acquire a body, a tangible form, and constitute a reality in their own right, quite distinct from the individual facts which produce it. Collective habits are inherent not only in the successive acts which they determine but, by a privilege of which we find no example in the biological realm, they are given permanent expression in a formula which is repeated from mouth to mouth, transmitted by education, and fixed even in writing. Such is the origin and nature of legal and moral rules, popular aphorisms and proverbs, articles of faith wherein religious or political groups condense their beliefs, standards of taste established by literary schools, etc. None of these can be found entirely reproduced in the applications made of them by individuals, since they can exist even without being actually applied.

No doubt, this dissociation does not always manifest itself with equal distinctness, but its obvious existence in the important and numerous cases just cited is sufficient to prove that the social fact is a thing distinct from its individual manifestations. Moreover, even when this dissociation is not immediately apparent, it may often be disclosed by certain devices of method. Such dissociation is indispensable if one wishes to separate social facts from their alloys in order to observe them in a state of purity. Currents of opinion, with an intensity varying according to the time and place, impel certain groups either to more marriages, for example, or to more suicides, or to a higher or lower birthrate, etc. These currents are plainly social facts. At first sight they seem inseparable from the forms they take in individual cases. But statistics furnish us with the means of isolating them. They are, in fact, represented with considerable exactness by the rates of births, marriages, and suicides, that is, by the number obtained by dividing the average annual total of marriages, births, suicides, by the number of persons whose ages lie within the range in which marriages, births and suicides occur.[2] Since each of these figures contains all the individual cases indiscriminately, the individual circumstances which may have had a share in production of the phenomenon are neutralized and, consequently, do not contribute to its determination. The average, then, expresses a certain state of the group mind (*l'âme collective*).

Such are social phenomena, when disentangled from all foreign matter. As for their individual manifestations, these are indeed, to a certain extent, social, since they partly reproduce a social model. Each of them also depends, and to a large extent, on the organopsychological constitution of the individual and on the particular circumstances in which he is placed. Thus they are not sociological phenomena in the strict sense of the word. They belong to two realms at once; one could call them sociopsychological. They interest the sociologist without constituting the immediate subject matter of sociology. There exist in the interior of organisms similar phenomena, compound in their nature, which form in their turn the subject matter of the 'hybrid sciences', such as physiological chemistry, for example.

The objection may be raised that a phenomenon is collective only if it is common to all members of society, or at least to most of them—in other words, if it is truly general. This may be true; but it is general because it is collective (that is, more or less obligatory), and certainly not collective because general. It is a group condition repeated in the individual because imposed on him. It is found in each part because it exists in the whole, rather than in the whole because it exists in the parts. This becomes conspicuously evident in those beliefs and practices which are transmitted to us ready-made by previous generations; we receive and adopt them because, being both collective and ancient, they are invested with a particular authority that education has taught us to recognize and respect. It is, of course, true that a vast portion of our social culture is transmitted to us in this way; but even when the social fact is due in part to our direct collaboration, its nature is not different. A collective emotion which bursts forth suddenly and violently in a crowd does not express merely what all the individual sentiments had in common; it is something entirely different, as we have shown. It results from their being together, a product of the actions and reactions which take place between individual consciousnesses; and if each individual consciousness echoes the collective sentiment, it is by virtue of the special energy resident in its collective origin. If all hearts beat in unison, this is not the result of a spontaneous and pre-established harmony but rather because an identical force propels them in the same direction. Each is carried along by all.

We thus arrive at the point where we can formulate and delimit in a precise way the domain of sociology. It comprises only a limited group of phenomena. A social fact is to be recognized by the power of external coercion which it exercises or is capable of exercising over individuals, and the presence of this power may be recognized in its turn either by the existence of some specific sanction or by the resistance offered against every individual effort that tends to violate it. One can, however, define it also by its diffusion within the group, provided that, in conformity with our previous remarks, one takes care to add as a second and essential characteristic that its own existence is independent of the individual forms it assumes in its diffusion. This last criterion is perhaps, in certain cases, easier to apply than the preceding one. In fact, the constraint is easy to ascertain when it expresses itself externally by some direct reaction of society, as is the case in law, morals, beliefs, customs, and even fashions. But when it is only indirect, like the constraint which an economic organization exercises, it cannot always be so easily detected. Generality combined with externality may, then, be easier to establish. Moreover, this second definition, is but another form of the first; for if a mode of behaviour whose existence is external to individual consciousnesses become general, this can only be brought about by its being imposed upon them.[3]

But these several phenomena present the same characteristic by which we defined the others. These 'ways of existing' are imposed on the individual precisely in the same fashion as the 'ways of acting' of which we have spoken. Indeed, when we wish to know how a society is divided politically, of what these divisions themselves are composed, and how complete is the fusion existing between them, we shall not achieve our purpose by physical inspection and by geographical observations; for these phenomena are social, even when they have some basis in physical nature. It is only by a study of public law that a comprehension of this organization is possible, for it is this law that determines the organization, as it equally determines our domestic and civil relations. This political organization is, then, no less obligatory than the social facts mentioned above. If the population crowds into our cities instead of scattering into the country, this is due to a trend of public opinion, a collective drive that imposes this concentration upon the individuals. We can no more choose the style of our houses than of our clothing—at least, both are equally obligatory. The channels of communication prescribe the direction of internal migrations and commerce, etc., and even their extent. Consequently, at the very most, it should be necessary to add to the list of phenomena which we have enumerated as presenting the distinctive criterion of a social fact only one additional category, 'ways of existing'; and, as this enumeration was not meant to be rigorously exhaustive, the addition would not be absolutely necessary.

Such an addition is perhaps not necessary, for these 'ways of existing' are only crystallized 'ways of acting'. The political structure of a society is merely the way in which its component segments have become accustomed to live with one another. If their relations are traditionally intimate, the segments tend to fuse with one another, or, in the contrary case, to retain their identity. The type of habitation imposed upon us is merely the way in which our contemporaries and our ancestors have been accustomed to construct their houses. The methods of communication are merely the channels which the regular currents of commerce and migrations have dug, by flowing in the same direction. To be sure, if the phenomena of a structural character alone presented the permanence, one might believe that they constituted a distinct species. A legal regulation is an arrangement no less permanent than a type of architecture, and yet the regulation is a 'physiological' fact. A simple moral maxim is assuredly somewhat more malleable, but it is much more rigid than a simple professional custom or a fashion. There is thus a whole series of degrees without a break in continuity between the facts of the most articulated structure and those free currents of social life which are not yet definitely moulded. The differences between them are, therefore, only differences in the degree of consolidation they present. Both are simply life, more or less crystallized. No doubt, it may be of some advantage to reserve the term 'morphological' for those social facts which concern the social substratum, but only on condition of not overlooking the fact that they are of the same nature as the others. Our definition will then include the whole relevant range of facts if we say: *A social fact is every way of acting, fixed or not, capable of exercising on the individual an external constraint; or again, every way of acting which is general throughout a given society, while at the same time existing in its own right independent of its individual manifestations.*[4]

. . .

[T]he experience of our predecessors has shown that, in order to assure the practical realization of the truth just enunciated, it is not enough to be thoroughly convinced one's self, or even to set forth a theoretical demonstration of it. The mind is so naturally inclined to underrate and disregard this particular truth that a relapse into the old errors will inevitably follow unless sociologists are willing to submit themselves to a rigorous discipline. We shall therefore formulate the principal rules for such a discipline, all of them corollaries of the foregoing theorem.

1. The first corollary is: *All preconceptions must be eradicated.* A special demonstration of this rule is unnecessary; it follows easily from all our previous statements. It is, moreover, the basis of all scientific method. The logical doubt of Descartes is, in its essence, only an application of it. If, at the moment of the foundation of science, Descartes resolves to question all ideas he had previously received, it is because he wishes to employ only scientifically developed concepts, that is, concepts constructed according to the method instituted by himself; all those having some other origin, then, must be rejected, at least provisionally. We have already seen that Bacon's theory of the 'idols' has the same meaning. The two great doctrines that have been so often opposed to one another thus agree on this essential point. The sociologist ought, therefore, whether at the moment of the determination of his research objectives or in the course of his demonstrations, to repudiate resolutely the use of concepts originating outside of science for totally unscientific needs. He must emancipate himself from the fallacious ideas that dominate the mind of the layman; he must throw off, once and for all, the yoke of these empirical categories, which from long continued habit have become tyrannical. At the very least, if at times he is obliged to resort to them, he ought to do so fully conscious of their trifling value, so that he will not assign to them a role out of proportion to their real importance.

The frequent interference of sentiment makes this emancipation from lay ideas particularly difficult in sociology. Indeed, our political and religious beliefs and our moral standards carry with them an emotional tone that is not characteristic of our attitude toward physical objects; consequently, this emotional character infects our manner of conceiving and explaining them. The ideas we form of things have a vital interest for us, just as the objects, themselves, and thus assume an authority which brooks no contradiction. Every opinion that disturbs them is treated with hostility. If a proposition is not in agreement, for example, with one's idea of patriotism or of individual dignity, it is denied, whatever its proofs may be. We cannot admit its truth; it is given no consideration at all; and our emotion, to justify our attitude, has no difficulty in suggesting reasons that are readily found convincing. These ideas may, indeed, have such prestige that they do not even tolerate scientific examination. The very fact of submitting them, as well as the phenomena they represent, to cold, dry analysis, is revolting to certain minds. Whoever undertakes the study of morality objectively, and as an external reality, seems to these sensitive creatures to be devoid of all moral sense, just as the vivisectionist seems to the layman devoid of common sensibility. Far from admitting that these sentiments should themselves be drawn under scientific scrutiny, it is to them that these writers feel they must appeal in order to treat scientifically the parallel social facts.

'Woe to the scholar,' writes an eloquent historian of religions, 'who approaches divine matters without having in the depths of his consciousness, in the innermost indestructible regions of his being, where the souls of his ancestors sleep, an unknown sanctuary from which rises now and then the aroma of incense, a line of a psalm, a sorrowful or triumphal cry that as a child he sent to heaven along with his brothers, and that creates immediate communion with the prophets of yore!'[5]

One cannot protest too strongly against this mystical doctrine, which, like all mysticism, is essentially a disguised empiricism, the negation of all science. Sentiments pertaining to social things enjoy no privilege not possessed by other sentiments, for their origin is the same. They, too, have been formed in the course of history; they are a product of human experience, which is, however, confused and unorganized. They are not due to some transcendental insight into reality but result from all sorts of impressions and emotions accumulated according to circumstances, without order and without methodical interpretation. Far from conveying insights superior to rational ones, these sentiments are simply strong but confused states of mind. To accord them a dominant role means giving supremacy to the inferior faculties of intelligence over the superior, condemning one's self to pure logomachy. Such a science can satisfy only those who prefer to think with their feelings and emotions rather than with their understanding, and who prefer the immediate and confused syntheses of first impression to the patient and luminous analyses of reason. Sentiment is a subject for scientific study, not the criterion of scientific truth. Moreover, every science encounters analogous resistances at the outset. There was a time when sentiments relating to the things of the physical world opposed with equal energy the establishment of the physical sciences, because they, too, had a religious or moral character. We believe, therefore, that this prejudice, pursued from one science to the next, will finally disappear also from its last retreat, sociology, leaving a free field for the true scientific endeavour.

2. As it happens, this first rule from sociology is entirely negative. It teaches the sociologist to escape the realm of lay ideas and to turn his attention toward facts, but it does not tell him how to take hold of the facts in order to study them objectively.

Every scientific investigation is directed toward a limited class of phenomena, included in the same definition. The first step of the sociologist, then, ought to be to define the things he treats, in order that his subject matter may be known. This is the first and most indispensable condition of all proofs and verifications. A theory, indeed, can be checked only if we know how to recognize the facts of which it is intended to give an account. Moreover, since this initial definition determines the very subject matter of science, this subject matter will or will not be a thing, depending on the nature of the definition.

In order to be objective, the definition must obviously deal with phenomena not as ideas but in terms of their inherent properties. It must characterize them by elements essential to their nature, not by their conformity to an intellectual ideal. Now, at the very beginning of research, when the facts have not yet been analysed, the only ascertainable characteristics are those external enough to be immediately perceived. Those that are less obvious may be perhaps more significant, and their explanatory value is more important; but they are unknown to science at this stage, and they can be anticipated only by substituting some hypothetical conception in the place of reality. It is imperative, then, that the material included under this fundamental definition be sought among the more external characteristics of sociological phenomena. On the other hand, this definition should include, without exception or distinction, all phenomena presenting to an equal extent these characteristics, for we have neither the reason nor the means for choosing among them. These characteristics are our only clue to reality; consequently, they must be given complete authority in our selection of facts. No other criterion could even partially justify any suspension of, or exception to, this rule. Whence our second corollary: *The subject matter of every sociological study should comprise a group of phenomena defined in advance by certain common external characteristics, and all phenomena so defined should be included within this group.*

For example, we note the existence of certain acts, all presenting the external characteristic that they evoke from society the particular reaction called punishment. We constitute them as a separate group, to which we give a common label; we call every punished act a crime, and crime thus defined becomes the object of a special science, criminology. Similarly, we observe within all known societies small groups whose special characteristic is that they are composed preponderantly of individuals who are blood-kin, united by legal bonds. We classify together the facts relating thereto, and give a particular name to the group of facts so created, 'domestic relations'. We call every aggregate of this kind a family, and this becomes the subject of a special investigation which has not yet received a specific name in sociological terminology. In passing from the family in general to the different family types, the same rule should be applied. For example, the study of the clan and the matriarchal or the patriarchal family should begin with a definition constructed according to the same method. The field of each problem, whether general or particular, must be similarly circumscribed.

By proceeding thus, the sociologist, from the very first, is firmly grounded in reality. Indeed, the pattern of such a classification does not depend on him or on the cast of his individual mind but on the nature of things. The criteria according to which they are placed in a particular category, can be recognized by everyone; and the concepts thus formed do not always, or even generally, tally with that of the layman. For example, manifestations of free thought or violations of etiquette, so regularly and severely penalized in many societies, are evidently considered crimes in the common-sense view even in these societies. Similarly, in the usual acceptance of the words a clan is not a family. But such discrepancies are not important, for it is not our aim simply to discover a method for identifying with sufficient accuracy the facts to which the words of ordinary language refer and the ideas they convey. We need, rather, to formulate entirely new concepts, appropriate to the requirements of science and expressed in an appropriate terminology. Of course, lay concepts are not entirely useless to the scholar; they serve as suggestions and guides. They inform us of the existence, somewhere, of an aggregation of phenomena which, bearing the same name, must, in consequence, probably have certain characteristics in common.

Since these concepts have always had some reference to phenomena, they even indicate to us at times, though roughly, where these phenomena are to be found. But, as they have been crudely formed, they quite naturally do not coincide exactly with the scientific concepts, which have been established for a set purpose.[6]

This rule, as obvious and important as it is, is seldom observed in sociology. Precisely because it treats everyday things, such as the family, property, crime, etc., the sociologist most often thinks it unnecessary to define them rigorously at the outset. We are so accustomed to use these terms, and they recur so constantly in our conversation, that it seems unnecessary to render their meaning precise. We simply refer to the common notion, but this common notion is very often ambiguous. As a result of this ambiguity, things that are very different in reality are given the same name and the same explanation, and this leads to boundless confusion.

For example, two sorts of monogamous unions exist: those monogamous in fact, and those monogamous by law. In the former, the husband has only one wife, although he is allowed by law to possess several; in the latter, polygamy is legally forbidden. In several animal species and in certain primitive societies monogamy 'in fact' is to be found, not sporadically, but with the same prevalence as if imposed by law. When a tribe is dispersed over a vast area, there is little social contact, and consequently the individuals live isolated from one another. In such a case each man naturally seeks only one wife, because in this state of isolation it is difficult from him to secure several. Compulsory monogamy, on the contrary, is observed only in the highest societies. These two types of conjugal unions have, then a very different significance; and yet the same word serves to designate them both. We commonly call certain animals 'monogamous', although they have nothing resembling legal control. Now Spencer, in his study of marriage, uses the word 'monogamy', in its ordinary equivocal meaning, without defining it. As a result the evolution of marriage seems to him to present an unaccountable anomaly, since he thinks he observes a higher form of the sexual union as early as the first phase of historical development, while it seems to disappear in the intermediate period, only to reappear later. He then concludes that there is no positive correlation between social progress in general and progress toward a perfect type of family life. A timely definition would have prevented this error.[7]

In other cases great care may be exercised in defining the objects of investigation; but instead of grouping under the same heading all phenomena having the same external properties, only a selected number of them are included. Thus, only certain ones are designated as a kind of 'élite', and these alone are regarded as coming within the category. As for the others, they are considered as having usurped these distinctive signs and are disregarded. It is easy to foresee that in this way only a subjective and incomplete picture can be attained. Such an omission can be made only by applying a preconceived idea, since, at the beginning of science, no research could possibly have already established the legitimacy of this usurpation, even if it were possible to have done so. The only possible reason for retaining the phenomena chosen was, then, that they conformed, more than the others, to a certain ideal conception concerning this sort of reality.

For example, M. Garofalo, at the beginning of his *Criminologie*, demonstrates very well that 'the sociological concept of crime' has to form the point of departure of this science. Only, in setting up his concept, he does not compare indiscriminately all acts which have been repressed by regular punishments in the different social types. He compares only certain ones among them, namely, those offending the most general and universal of the moral feelings. The moral sentiments which have disappeared in the course of evolution are not, to him, grounded in the nature of things, since they have not survived; consequently, the acts which have been deemed criminal because of their violation of these particular sentiments seem to him to have owed this designation only to accidental and more or less pathological circumstances. But it is by virtue of an entirely personal conception of morality that he makes this elimination. He starts from the idea that moral evolution, taken at its very fount or near its source, carries with it all sorts of dross and impurities, which it then progressively eliminates, and that it is only today that it has succeeded in freeing itself from all the adventitious elements which, in primitive times, troubled its course. But this principle is neither an evident axiom nor a demonstrated truth; it is only a hypothesis, and indeed one without justification. The variable aspects of the moral sense are not less grounded in the nature of things than are the immutable; the variations in standards of morality merely testify to the corresponding variations in life. In zoology, the forms peculiar to the lower species are not regarded as less natural than those occurring at the other points on the evolutionary scale. Similarly, these acts which were condemned as crimes by primitive societies and have since lost this designation are really criminal in relation to these societies, quite like those which we continue to repress today. The former correspond to the changing, the latter to the constant, conditions of social life; but the former are not any more artificial than those acts which are considered crimes today.

But, even if these acts had unduly assumed the criminal character, they ought not to be sharply separated from the others; for the pathological forms of a phenomenon are not different in nature from the normal forms, and it is therefore necessary to observe the former as well as the latter in order to determine this nature. Morbidity is not absolutely antithetical to health; these are two varieties of the same phenomenon, and each tends to explain the other. This is a rule long recognized and practised in biology and in psychology, and the sociologist is equally under an obligation to respect it. Unless one asserts that the same phenomenon can be due sometimes to one cause and sometimes to another, that is, unless one denies the principle of causality, the causes which impress on an act the mark of crime, in an abnormal manner, cannot differ qualitatively from those producing the same effect in a normal manner; they differ only in degree or they differ because they do not act in the same environment. The abnormal crime, then, is still a crime and ought, consequently, to be included in the definition of crime. What M. Garofalo actually does is to take as the genus that which is only a species or merely a simple variety. The facts to which his definition of criminality applies represent only an infinitesimal minority among those it should include for it applies neither to religious crimes, nor to violations of etiquette, ceremonial, tradition, etc. If these have disappeared from our modern codes, they make up, on the contrary, almost the entire penal law of former societies.

The same flaw in method causes certain observers to deny the existence of any species of morality among savages.[8] They start with the idea that our morality is *the* morality. It is evident, however, that our morality is either unknown or in a rudimentary state among primitive peoples and that this discrimination is clearly arbitrary. If we apply our second corollary in this case, everything changes. To decide whether a precept belongs to the moral order, we must determine whether or not it presents the external mark of morality; this mark is a widespread repressive sanction, that is, a condemnation by public opinion that punishes all violations of the precept. Whenever we are presented with a fact having this characteristic, we have no right to deny its moral character, for this characteristic proves that it has the same nature as other moral facts. Not only are social regulations of this kind met with in primitive societies, but they are even more numerous there than in civilized societies. A large number of acts which today are left to the free choice of individuals are obligatory among them. Thus we may realize the errors we commit by omitting definitions or by defining inadequately.

But, it will be said that, in defining phenomena by their apparent characteristics, we are allowing to certain superficial properties a significance greater than that of more fundamental attributes. Are we not, by a veritable inversion of logical order, beginning at the summit instead of the base? Thus, when we define crime in terms of punishment, one is almost inevitably exposed to the accusation of deriving crime from punishment, or, as a well-known quotation puts it, of considering the scaffold, and not the crime, as the source of ignominy. This reproach rests upon a confusion. Since the definition in question is placed at the beginnings of the science, it cannot possibly aim at a statement concerning the essence of reality; that must be attained subsequently. The sole function of the definition is to establish contact with things; and since the latter can be grasped by the mind only from its exteriors, the definition expresses them in terms of their external qualities. It does not explain these things thereby; it furnishes merely a just basis for further explanations. Certainly, punishment is not the essence of crime; but it does constitute a symptom thereof, and consequently, in order to understand crime, we must begin with punishment.

The aforementioned objection would be well founded only if these external characteristics were at the same time accidental, that is, if they were not bound up with the fundamental properties of things. Under these conditions indeed, after science had pointed them out, it could not possibly go farther; it could not penetrate the deeper layers of reality, since there would be no necessary connection between surface and essence. But, if the principle of causality is valid, when certain characteristics are found identically and without exceptions in all the phenomena of a certain order, one may be assured that they are closely connected with the nature of the latter and bound up with it. And if to a given group of acts there is attached also the peculiarity of a penal sanction, an intimate bond must exist between punishment and the intrinsic attributes of these acts. Consequently, however superficial they may be, these properties, provided that they have been systematically observed, clearly point out to the scientist the course which he must follow in order to penetrate more to the core of the things in question. They are the first and indispensable link in the sequence to be unfolded by science in the course of its explanations.

Since objects are perceived only through sense perception, we can conclude: Science, to be objective, ought to start, not with concepts formed independent to them, but with these same perceptions. It ought to borrow the materials for its initial definitions directly from perceptual data. And, as a matter of fact, one need only reflect on the real nature of scientific work to understand that it cannot proceed otherwise. It needs concepts that adequately express things as they actually are, and not as everyday life finds it useful to conceive them. Now those concepts formulated without the discipline of science do not fulfil this condition. Science, then, has to create new concepts; it must dismiss all lay notions and the terms expressing them, and return to sense perception, the primary and necessary substance underlying all concepts. From sensation all general ideas flow, whether they be true of false, scientific or impressionistic. The point of departure of science, or speculative knowledge, cannot be different from that of lay, or practical, knowledge. It is only beyond this point, namely, in the manner of elaboration of these common data, that divergences begin.

3. But sensation may easily be subjective. It is a rule in the natural sciences to discard those data of sensation that are too subjective, in order to retain exclusively those presenting a sufficient degree of objectivity. Thus the physicist substitutes, for the vague impressions of temperature and electricity, the visual registrations of the thermometer or the electrometer. The sociologist must take the same precautions. The external characteristics in terms of which he defines the objects of his researches should be as objective as possible.

We may lay down as a principle that social facts lend themselves more readily to objective representation in proportion as their separation from the individual facts expressing them is more complete. Indeed, the degree of objectivity of a sense perception is proportionate to the degree of stability of its object; for objectivity depends upon the existence of a constant and identical point of reference to which the representation can be referred and which permits the elimination of what is variable, and hence subjective, in it. But if the points of reference themselves are variable, if they are perpetually shifting in relation to each other, there is no common standard, and the scientist has no means of distinguishing between those impressions which are external and those that are subjective. So long as social life is not separated from the individual or particular events which comprise it, and has no separate existence, it will present this dilemma. As these events differ among themselves and change in time, and as we assume the life of society to be inseparable from them, they communicate their mutability to it. Social life consists, then, of free currents perpetually in the process of transformation and incapable of being mentally fixed by the observer, and the scholar cannot approach the study of social reality from this angle. But we know that it possesses the power of crystallization without ceasing to be itself. Thus, apart from the individual acts to which they give rise, collective habits find expression in definite forms: legal rules, moral regulations, popular proverbs, social conventions, etc. As these forms have a permanent existence and do not change with the diverse applications made of them, they constitute a fixed object, a constant standard within the observer's reach, exclusive of subjective impressions and purely personal observations. A legal regulation is what it is, and there are no two ways of looking at it. Since, on the other hand, these practices are merely social life consolidated, it is legitimate, except where otherwise stated,[9] to study the latter through the former.

When, then, the sociologist undertakes the investigation of some order of social facts, he must endeavour to consider them from an aspect that is independent of their individual manifestations. It is this principle that we have applied in studying the diverse forms of social solidarity and their evolution, through the medium of the legal structure which reflects them. On the other hand, an attempt to distinguish and classify the different family types on the basis of the literary description given us by travellers and historians is exposed to the danger of confusing the most diverse species and of bringing together the most dissimilar types. If the legal structure of the family and, more specifically, the right of succession are taken as the basis of classification, objective criteria are at hand which, while not infallible, will prevent many errors. In order to classify the different kinds of crimes, one has to try to reconstruct the ways of living and the occupational customs that are practiced in the different worlds of crime. One will then recognize as many criminological types as there are different forms of this organization. To achieve an understanding of customs and popular beliefs, one must investigate the proverbs and epigrams that express them. No doubt, in proceeding thus, we leave the concrete data of collective life temporarily outside the realm of science; and yet, however changeable and unstable it may be, its unintelligibility need not be assumed. In order to follow a methodical course, we must establish the foundations of science on solid ground and not on shifting sand. We must approach the social realm where it offers the easiest access to scientific investigation. Only subsequently will it be possible to push research further and, by successive approximations, to encompass, little by little, this fleeting reality, which the human mind will never, perhaps, be able to grasp completely.

NOTES

1. We do not intend to imply, however, that all constraint is normal. We shall return to this point later.

2. Suicides do not occur at every age, and they take place with varying intensity at the different ages in which they occur.

3. It will be seen how this definition of the social fact diverges from that which forms the basis of the ingenious system of M. Tarde. First of all, we wish to state that our researches have nowhere led us to observe that preponderant influence in the genesis of collective facts which M. Tarde attributes to imitation. Moreover, from the preceding definition, which is not a theory but simply a résumé of the immediate data of observation, it seems indeed to follow, not only that imitation does not always express the essential and characteristic features of the social fact, but even that it never expresses them. No doubt, every social fact is imitated; it has, as we have just shown, a tendency to become general, but that is because it is social, i.e., obligatory. Its power of expansion is not the cause but the consequence of its sociological character. If, further, only social facts produced this consequence, imitation could perhaps serve, if not to explain them, at least to define them. But an individual condition which produces a whole series of effects remains individual nevertheless. Moreover, one may ask whether the word 'imitation' is indeed fitted to designate an effect due to a coercive influence. Thus, by this single expression, very different phenomena, which ought to be distinguished, are confused.

4. This close connection between life and structure, organ and function, may easily be proved in sociology because between these two extreme terms there exists a whole series of immediately observable intermediate stages which show the bond between them. Biology is not in the same favourable position. But we may well believe that the inductions on this subject made by soci-

ology are applicable to biology and that, in organisms as well as in societies, only differences in degree exist between these two orders of facts.

5.   J. Darmesteter, *Les Prophètes d'Israël*: 9.

6.   In actual practice one always starts with the lay concept and the lay term. One inquires whether, among the things which this word confusedly connotes, there are some which present common external characteristics. If this is the case, and if the concept formed by the grouping of the facts thus brought together coincides, if not totally (which is rare), at least to a large extent, with the lay concept, it will be possible to continue to designate the former by the same term as the latter, that is, to retain in science the expression used in everyday language. But if the gap is too considerable, if the common notion confuses a plurality of distinct ideas, the creation of new and distinctive terms becomes necessary.

7.   The same absence of definition caused the occasional statements that democracy is realized both at the beginning and at the end of history. The truth is that primitive and modern democracy are very different from one another.

8.   See Lubbock, *Origin of Civilization*, ch. VIII: it is a still more widespread, and not less false, opinion that the ancient religions are amoral or immoral. The truth is that they have a morality of their own.

9.   It would be necessary, for example, in order to invalidate this substitution, to have reason to believe that, at a given moment, law no longer expresses the actual state of social relations.

EGOISTIC AND ANOMIC SUICIDE

The suicide-rate is . . . a factual order, unified and definite, as is shown by both its permanence and its variability. For this permanence would be inexplicable if it were not the result of a group of distinct characteristics, solidary one with another, and simultaneously effective in spite of different attendant circumstances; and this variability proves the concrete and individual quality of these same characteristics, since they vary with the individual character of society itself. In short, these statistical data express the suicidal tendency with which each society is collectively afflicted. We need not state the actual nature of this tendency, whether it is a state *sui generis* of the collective mind[1] with its own reality, or represents merely a sum of individual states. Although the preceding considerations are hard to reconcile with the second hypothesis, we reserve this problem for treatment in the course of this work.[2] Whatever one's opinion on this subject, such a tendency certainly exists under one heading or another. Each society is predisposed to contribute a definite quota of voluntary deaths. This predisposition may therefore be the subject of a special study belonging to sociology. This is the study we are going to undertake.

We do not accordingly intend to make as nearly complete an inventory as possible of all the conditions affecting the origin of individual suicides, but merely to examine those on which the definite fact that we have called the social suicide-rate depends. The two questions are obviously quite distinct, whatever relation may nevertheless exist between them. Certainly many of the individual conditions are not general enough to affect the relation between the total number of voluntary deaths and the population. They may perhaps cause this or that separate individual to kill himself, but not give society as a whole a greater or lesser tendency to suicide. As they do not depend on a certain state of social organization, they have no social repercussions. Thus they concern the psychologist, not the sociologist. The latter studies the causes capable of affecting not separate individuals but the group. Therefore among the factors of suicide the only ones which concern him are those whose action is felt by society as a whole. The suicide-rate is the product of these factors. This is why we must limit our attention to them.

. . .

Egoistic Suicide

We have thus successively set up the three following propositions:

> *Suicide varies inversely with the degree of integration of religious society.*
> *Suicide varies inversely with the degree of integration of domestic society.*
> *Suicide varies inversely with the degree of integration of political society.*

This grouping shows that whereas these different societies have a moderating influence upon suicide, this is due not to special characteristics of each but to a characteristic common to all. Religion does not owe its efficacy to the special nature of religious sentiments, since domestic and political societies both produce the same effects when strongly integrated. This, moreover, we have already proved when studying directly the manner of action of different religions upon suicide. Inversely, it is not the specific nature of the domestic or political tie which can explain the immunity they confer, since religious society has the same advantage. The cause can only be found in a single quality possessed by all these social groups, though perhaps to varying degrees. The only quality satisfying this condition is that they are all strongly integrated social groups. So we reach the general conclusion: suicide varies inversely with the degree of integration of the social groups of which the individual forms a part.

But society cannot disintegrate without the individual simultaneously detaching himself from social life, without his own goals becoming preponderant over those of the community, in a word without his personality tending to surmount the collective personality. The more weakened the groups to which he belongs, the less he depends on them, the more he consequently depends only on himself and recognizes no other rules of conduct than what are founded on his private interests. If we agree to call this state egoism, in which the individual ego asserts itself to excess in the face of the social ego and at its expense, we may call egoistic the special type of suicide springing from excessive individualism.

But how can suicide have such an origin?

First of all, it can be said that, as collective force is one of the obstacles best calculated to restrain suicide, its weakening involves a development of suicide. When society is strongly integrated, it holds individuals under its control, considers them at its service and thus forbids them to dispose wilfully of themselves. Accordingly it opposes their evading their duties to it through death. But how could society impose its supremacy upon them when they refuse to accept this subordination as legitimate? It no longer then possesses the requisite authority to retain them in their duty if they wish to desert; and conscious of its own weakness, it even recognizes their right to do freely what it can no longer prevent. So far as they are the admitted masters of their destinies, it is their privilege to end their lives. They, on their part, have no reason to endure life's sufferings patiently. For they cling to life more resolutely when belonging to a group they love, so as not to betray interests they put before their own. The bond that unites them with the common cause attaches them to life and the lofty goal they envisage prevents their feeling personal troubles so deeply. There is, in short, in a cohesive and animated society a constant interchange of ideas and feelings from all to each and each to all, something like a mutual moral support, which instead of throwing the individual on his own resources, leads him to share in the collective energy and supports his own when exhausted.

But these reasons are purely secondary. Excessive individualism not only results in favouring the action of suicidogenic causes, but it is itself such a cause. It not only frees man's inclination to do away with himself from a protective obstacle, but creates this inclination out of whole cloth and thus gives birth to a special suicide which bears its mark. This must be clearly understood for this is what constitutes the special character of the type of suicide just distinguished and justifies the name we have given it. What is there then in individualism that explains this result?

It has been sometimes said that because of his psychological constitution, man cannot live without attachment to some object which transcends and survives him, and that the reason for this necessity is a need we must have not to perish entirely. Life is said to be intolerable unless some reason for existing is involved, some purpose justifying life's trials. The individual alone is not a sufficient end for his activity. He is too little. He is not only hemmed in spatially; he is also strictly limited temporally. When, therefore, we have no other object than ourselves we cannot avoid the thought that our efforts will finally end in nothingness, since we ourselves disappear. But annihilation terrifies us. Under these conditions one would lose courage to live, that is, to act and struggle, since nothing will remain of our exertions. The state of egoism, in other words, is supposed to be contradictory to human nature and, consequently, too uncertain to have chances of permanence.

In this absolute formulation the proposition is vulnerable. If the thought of the end of our personality were really so hateful, we could consent to live only by blinding ourselves voluntarily as to life's value. For if we may in a measure avoid the prospect of annihilation we cannot extirpate it; it is inevitable, whatever we do. We may push back the frontier for some generations, force our name to endure for some years or centuries longer than our body; a moment, too soon for most men, always comes when it will be nothing. For the groups we join in order to prolong our existence by their means are themselves mortal; they too must dissolve, carrying with them all our deposit of ourselves. Those are few whose memories are closely enough bound to the very history of humanity to be assured of living until its death. So, if we really thus thirsted after immortality, no such brief perspectives could ever appease us. Besides, what of us is it that lives? A word, a sound, an imperceptible trace, most often anonymous,[3] therefore nothing comparable to the violence of our efforts or able to justify them to us. In actuality, though a child is naturally an egoist who feels not the slightest craving to survive himself, and the old man is very often a child in this and so many other respects, neither ceases to cling to life as much or more than the adult; indeed we have seen that suicide is very rare for the first fifteen years and tends to decrease at the other extreme of life. Such too is the case with animals, whose psychological constitution differs from that of men only in degree. It is therefore untrue that life is only possible by its possessing its rationale outside of itself.

Indeed, a whole range of functions concern only the individual; these are the ones indispensable for physical life. Since they are made for this purpose only, they are perfected by its attainment. In everything concerning them, therefore, man can act reasonably without thought of transcendental purposes. These functions serve by merely serving him. In so far as he has no other needs, he is therefore self-sufficient and can live happily with no other objective than living. This is not the case, however, with the civilized adult. He has many ideas, feelings and practices unrelated to organic needs. The roles of art, morality, religion, political faith, science itself are not to repair organic exhaustion nor to provide sound functioning of the organs. All this supra-physical life is built and expanded not because of the demands of the cosmic environment but because of the social environment. The influence of society is what has aroused in us the sentiments of sympathy and solidarity drawing us toward others; it is society which, fashioning us in its image, fills us with religious, political and moral beliefs that control our actions. To play our social role we have striven to extend our intelligence and it is still society that has supplied us with tools for this development by transmitting to us its trust fund of knowledge.

Through the very fact that these superior forms of human activity have a collective origin, they have a collective purpose. As they derive from society they have reference to it; rather they are society itself incarnated and individualized in each one of us. But for them to have a *raison d'être* in our eyes, the purpose they envisage must be one not indifferent to us. We can cling to these forms of human activity only to the degree that we cling to society itself. Contrariwise, in the same measure as we feel detached from society we become detached from that life whose source and aim is society. For what purpose do these rules of morality, these precepts of law binding us to all sorts of sacrifices, these restrictive dogmas exist, if there is no being outside us whom they serve and in whom we participate? What is the purpose of science itself? If its only use is to increase our chances for survival, it does not deserve the trouble it entails. Instinct acquits itself better of this role; animals prove this. Why substitute for it a more hesitant and uncertain reflection? What is the end of suffering, above all? If the value of things can only be estimated by their relation to this positive evil for the individual, it is without reward and incomprehensible. This problem does not exist for the believer firm in his faith or the man strongly bound by ties of domestic or political society. Instinctively and unreflectively they ascribe all that they are and to, the one to his Church or his God, the living symbol of the Church, the other to his family, the third to his country or party. Even in their sufferings they see only a means of glorifying the group to which they belong and thus do homage to it. So, the Christian ultimately desires and seeks suffering to testify more fully to his contempt for the flesh and more fully resemble his divine model. But the more the believer doubts, that is, the less he feels himself a real participant in the religious faith to which he belongs, and from which he is freeing himself; the more the family and community become foreign to the individual, so much the more does he become a mystery to himself, unable to escape the exasperating and agonizing question: to what purpose?

If, in other words, as has often been said, man is double, that is because social man superimposes himself upon physical man. Social man necessarily presupposes a society which he expresses and serves. If this dissolves, if we no longer feel it in existence and action about and above us, whatever is social in us is deprived of all objective foundation. All that remains is an artificial combination of illusory images, a phantasmagoria vanishing at the least reflection; that is, nothing which can be a goal for our action. Yet this social man is the essence of civilized man; he is the masterpiece of existence. Thus we are bereft of reasons for existence; for the only life to which we could cling no longer corresponds to anything actual; the only existence still based upon reality no longer meets our needs. Because we have been initiated into a higher existence, the one which satisfies an animal or a child can satisfy us no more and the other itself fades and leaves us helpless. So there is nothing more for our efforts to lay hold of, and we feel them lose themselves in emptiness. In this sense it is true to say that our activity needs an object transcending it. We do not need it to maintain ourselves in the illusion of an impossible immortality; it is implicit in our moral constitution and cannot be even partially lost without this losing its *raison d'être* in the same degree. No proof is needed that in such a state of confusion the least cause of discouragement may easily give birth to desperate resolutions. If life is not worth the trouble of being lived, everything becomes a pretext to rid ourselves of it.

But this is not all. This detachment occurs not only in single individuals. One of the constitutive elements of every national temperament consists of a certain way of estimating the value of existence. There is a collective as well as an individual humour inclining peoples to sadness or cheerfulness, making them see things in bright or sombre lights. In fact, only society can pass a collective opinion on the value of human life; for this the individual is incompetent. The latter knows nothing but himself and his own little horizon; thus his experience is too limited to serve as a basis for a general appraisal. He may indeed consider his own life to be aimless; he can say nothing applicable to others. On the contrary, without sophistry, society may generalize its own feeling as to itself, its state of health or lack of health. For individuals share too deeply in the life of society for it to be diseased without their suffering infection. What it suffers they necessarily suffer. Because it is the whole, its ills are communicated to its parts. Hence it cannot disintegrate without awareness that the regular conditions of general existence are equally disturbed. Because society is the end on which our better selves depend, it cannot feel us escaping it without a simultaneous realization that our activity is purposeless. Since we are its handiwork, society cannot be conscious of its own decadence without the feeling that henceforth this work is of no value. Thence are formed currents of depression and disillusionment emanating from no particular individual but expressing society's state of disintegration. They reflect the relaxation of social bonds, a sort of collective asthenia, or social malaise, just as individual sadness, when chronic, in its way reflects the poor organic state of the individual. Then metaphysical and religious systems spring up which, by reducing these obscure sentiments to formulae, attempt to prove to men the senselessness of life and that it is self-deception to believe that it has purpose. Then new moralities originate which, by elevating fact to ethics, commend suicide or at least tend in that direction by suggesting a minimal existence. On their appearance they seem to have been created out of whole cloth by their makers who are sometimes blamed for the pessimism of their doctrines. In reality they are an effect rather than a cause; they merely symbolize in abstract language and systematic form the physiological distress of the body social.[4] As these currents are collective, they have, by virtue of their origin, an authority which they impose upon the individual and they drive him more vigorously on the way to which he is already inclined by the state of moral distress directly aroused in him by the disintegration of society. Thus, at the very moment that, with excessive zeal, he frees himself from the social environment, he still submits to its influence. However individualized a man may be, there is always something collective remaining—the very depression and melancholy resulting from this same exaggerated individualism. He effects communion through sadness when he no longer has anything else with which to achieve it.

Hence this type of suicide well deserves the name we have given it. Egoism is not merely a contributing factor in it; it is its generating cause. In this case the bond attaching man to life relaxes because that attaching him to society is itself slack. The incidents of private life which seem the direct inspiration of suicide and are considered its determining causes are in reality only incidental causes. The individual yields to the slightest shock of circumstance because the state of society has made him a ready prey to suicide.

Several facts confirm this explanation. Suicide is known to be rare among children and to diminish among the aged at the last confines of life; physical man, in both, tends to become the whole of man. Society is still lacking in the former, for it has not had the time to form him in its image; it begins to retreat from the latter or, what amounts to the same thing, he retreats from it. Thus both are more self-sufficient. Feeling a lesser need for self-completion through something not themselves, they are also less exposed to feel the lack of what is necessary for living. The immunity of an animal has the same causes. We shall likewise see in the next chapter that, though lower societies practise a form of suicide of their own, the one we have just discussed is almost unknown to them. Since their social life is very simple, the social inclinations of individuals are simple also and thus they need little for satisfaction. They readily find external objectives to which they become attached. If he can carry with him his gods and his family, primitive man, everywhere that he goes, has all that his social nature demands.

This is also why women can endure life in isolation more easily than man. When a widow is seen to endure her condition much better than a widower and desires marriage less passionately, one is led to consider this ease in dispensing with the family a mark of superiority; it is said that woman's affective faculties, being very intense, are easily employed outside the domestic circle, while her devotion is indispensable to man to help him endure life. Actually, if this is her privilege it is because her sensibility is rudimentary rather than highly developed. As she lives outside of community existence more than man, she is less penetrated by it; society is less necessary to her because she is less impregnated with sociability. She has few needs in this direction and satisfies them easily. With a few devotional practices and some animals to care for, the old unmarried woman's life is full. If she remains faithfully attached to religious traditions and thus finds ready protection against suicide, it is because these very simple social forms satisfy all her needs. Man, on the contrary, is hard beset in this respect. As his thought and activity develop, they increasingly overflow these antiquated forms. But then he needs others. Because he is a more complex social being, he can maintain his equilibrium only by finding more points of support outside himself, and it is because his moral balance depends on a larger number of conditions that it is more easily disturbed.

. . .

Altruistic Suicide

. . . We thus confront a type of suicide differing by incisive qualities from the preceding one. Whereas the latter is due to excessive individuation, the former is caused by too rudimentary individuation. One occurs because society allows the individual to escape it, being insufficiently aggregated in some parts or even in the whole; the other, because society holds him in too strict tutelage. Having given the name of *egoism* to the state of the ego living its own life and obeying itself alone, that of *altruism* adequately expresses the opposite state, where the ego is not its own property, where it is blended with something not itself, where the goal of conduct is exterior to itself, that is, in one of the groups in which it participates. So we call the suicide caused by intense altruism *altruistic suicide*. But since it is also characteristically performed as a duty, the terminology adopted should express this fact. So we will call such a type *obligatory altruistic suicide*.

The combination of these two adjectives is required to define it; for not every altruistic suicide is necessarily obligatory. Some are not so expressly imposed by society, having a more optional character. In other words, altruistic suicide is a species with several varieties. We have just established one; let us now examine the others.

. . .

In Polynesia, a slight offence often decides a man to commit suicide. It is the same among the North American Indians; a conjugal quarrel or jealous impulse suffices to cause a man or woman to commit suicide. Among the Dacotas and Creeks the least disappointment often leads to desperate steps. The readiness of the Japanese to disembowel themselves for the slightest reason is well known.

. . .

In all such cases, a man kills himself without being explicitly forced to do so. Yet these suicides are of the same nature as obligatory suicide. Though public opinion does not formally require them, it is certainly favourable to them. Since here not clinging to life is a virtue, even of the highest rank, the man who renounces life on least provocation of circumstances or through simple vainglory is praiseworthy. A social prestige thus attaches to suicide, which receives encouragement from this fact, and the refusal of this reward has effects similar to actual punishment, although to a lesser degree. What is done in one case to escape the stigma of insult is done in the other to win esteem. When people are accustomed to set no value on life from childhood on, and to despise those who value it excessively, they inevitably renounce it on the least pretext. So valueless a sacrifice is easily assumed. Like obligatory suicide, therefore, these practices are associated with the most fundamental moral characteristics of lower societies. As they can only persist if the individual has no interests of his own, he must be trained to renunciation and an unquestioned abnegation; whence come such partially spontaneous suicides· Exactly like those more explicitly prescribed by society, they arise from this state of impersonality, or as we have called it, altruism, which may be regarded as a moral characteristic of primitive man. Therefore, we shall give them, also, the name altruistic, and if *optional* is added to make their special quality clearer, this word simply means that they are less expressly required by society than when strictly obligatory. Indeed, the two varieties are so closely related that it is impossible to distinguish where one begins and the other ends.

Anomic Suicide

But society is not only something attracting the sentiments and activities of individuals with unequal force. It is also a power controlling them. There is a relation between the way this regulative action is performed and the social suicide-rate.

I

It is a well-known fact that economic crises have an aggravating effect on the suicidal tendency.

In Vienna, in 1873 a financial crisis occurred which reached its height in 1874; the number of suicides immediately rose. From 141 in 1872, they rose to 153 in 1873 and 216 in 1874. The increase in 1874 is 53 per cent above 1872 and 41 per cent above 1873. What proves this catastrophe to have been the sole cause of the increase is the special prominence of the increase when the crisis was acute, or during the first four months of 1874. From January 1 to April 30 there had been 48 suicides in 1871, 44 in 1872, 43 in 1873; there were 73 in 1874. The increase is 70 per cent.[5] The same crisis occurring at the same time in Frankfurt-on-Main produced the same effects there. In the years before 1874, 22 suicides were committed annually on the average; in 1874 there were 32, or 45 per cent more.

The famous crash is unforgotten which took place on the Paris Bourse during the winter of 1882. Its consequences were felt not only in Paris but throughout France. From 1874 to 1886 the average annual increase was only 2 per cent; in 1882 it was 7 per cent. Moreover, it was unequally distributed among the different times of year, occurring principally during the first three months or at the very time of the crash. Within these three months alone 59 per cent of the total rise occurred. So distinctly is the rise the result of unusual circumstances that it not only is not encountered in 1881 but has disappeared in 1883, although on the whole the latter year had a few more suicides than the preceding one:

	1881	1882	1883
Annual total	6,741	7,213 (plus 7%)	7,267
First three months	1,589	1,770 (plus 11%)	1,604

This relation is found not only in some exceptional cases, but is the rule. The number of bankruptcies is a barometer of adequate sensitivity, reflecting the variations of economic life. When they increase abruptly from year to year, some serious disturbances have certainly occurred. From 1845 to 1869 there were sudden rises, symptomatic of crises, on three occasions. While the annual increase in the number of bankruptcies during this period is 3.2 per cent, it is 26 per cent in 1847, 37 per cent in 1854 and 20 per cent in 1861. At these three moments, there is also to be observed an unusually rapid rise in the number of suicides. While the average annual increase during these 24 years was only 2 per cent, it was 17 per cent in 1847, 8 per cent in 1854 and 9 per cent in 1861.

But to what do these crises owe their influence? Is it because they increase poverty by causing public wealth to fluctuate? Is life more readily renounced as it becomes more difficult? The explanation is seductively simple; and it agrees with the popular idea of suicide. But it is contradicted by facts.

. . .

So far is the increase in poverty from causing the increase in suicide that even fortunate crises, the effect of which is abruptly to enhance a country's prosperity, affect suicide like economic disasters.

The conquest of Rome by Victor-Emmanuel in 1870, by definitely forming the basis of Italian unity, was the starting point for the country of a process of growth which is making it one of the great powers of Europe. Trade and industry received a sharp stimulus from it and surprisingly rapid changes took place. Whereas in 1876, 4,459 steam boilers with a total of 54,000 horse-power were enough for industrial needs, the number of machines in 1887 was 9,983 and their horse-power of 167,000 was threefold more. Of course the amount of production rose proportionately during the same time. Trade followed the same rising course; not only did the merchant marine, communications and transportation develop, but the number of persons and things transported doubled. As this generally heightened activity caused an increase in salaries (an increase of 35 per cent is estimated to have taken place from 1873 to 1889), the material comfort of workers rose, especially since the price of bread was falling at the same time. Finally, according to calculations by Bodio, private wealth rose from 45 and a half billions on the average during the period 1875-80 to 51 billions during the years 1880-85 and 54 billions and a half in 1885-90.[6]

Now, an unusual increase in the number of suicides is observed parallel with this collective renaissance. From 1866 to 1870 they were roughly stable; from 1871 to 1877 they increased 36 per cent. There were in

1864–70	29 suicides per million	1874	37 suicides per million
1871	31 suicides per million	1875	34 suicides per million
1872	33 suicides per million	1876	36.5 suicides per million
1873	36 suicides per million	1877	40.6 suicides per million

And since then the movement has continued. The total figure, 1,139 in 1877, was 1,463 in 1889, a new increase of 28 per cent.

. . .

What proves still more conclusively that economic distress does not have the aggravating influence often attributed to it, is that it tends rather to produce the opposite effect. There is very little suicide in Ireland, where the peasantry leads so wretched a life. Poverty-stricken Calabria has almost no suicides; Spain has a tenth as many as France. Poverty may even be considered a protection. In the various French departments the more people there are who have independent means, the more numerous are suicides.

Departments Where, per 100,000 Inhabitants, Suicides Were Committed (1878–1887)		Average Number of Persons of Independent Means per 1,000 Inhabitants in Each Group of Departments (1886)
Suicides	Number of Departments	
From 48 to 43	5	127
From 38 to 3	6	73
From 30 to 24	6	69
From 23 to 18	15	59
From 17 to 13	18	49
From 12 to 8	26	49
From 7 to 3	10	42

If therefore industrial or financial crises increase suicides, this is not because they cause poverty, since crises of prosperity have the same result; it is because they are crises, that is, disturbances of the collective order.[7] Every disturbance of equilibrium, even though it achieves greater comfort and a heightening of general vitality, is an impulse to voluntary death. Whenever serious readjustments take place in the social order, whether or not due to a sudden growth or to an unexpected catastrophe, men are more inclined to self-destruction. How is this possible? How can something considered generally to improve existence serve to detach men from it?

For the answer, some preliminary considerations are required.

II

No living being can be happy or even exist unless his needs are sufficiently proportioned to his means. In other words, if his needs require more than can be granted, or even merely something of a different sort, they will be under continual friction and can only function painfully. Movements incapable of production without pain tend not to be reproduced. Unsatisfied tendencies atrophy, and as the impulse to live is merely the result of all the rest, it is bound to weaken as the others relax.

In the animal, at least in a normal condition, the equilibrium is established with automatic spontaneity because the animal depends on purely material conditions. All the organism needs is that the supplies of substance and energy constantly employed in the vital process should be periodically renewed by equivalent quantities; that replacement be equivalent to use. When the void created by existence in its own resources is filled, the animal, satisfied, asks nothing further. Its power of reflection is not sufficiently developed to imagine other ends than those implicit in its physical nature. On the other hand, as the work demanded of each organ itself depends on the general state of vital energy and the needs of organic equilibrium, use is regulated in turn by replacement and the balance is automatic. The limits of one are those of the other; both are fundamental to the constitution of the existence in question, which cannot exceed them.

This is not the case with man, because most of his needs are not dependent on his body or not to the same degree. Strictly speaking, we may consider that the quantity of material supplies necessary to the physical maintenance of a human life is subject to computation, though this be less exact than in the preceding case and a wider margin left for the free combinations of the will; for beyond the indispensable minimum which satisfies nature when instinctive, a more awakened reflection suggests better conditions, seemingly desirable ends craving fulfilment. Such appetites, however, admittedly sooner or later reach a limit which they cannot pass. But how determine the quantity of well-being, comfort or luxury legitimately to be craved by a human being? Nothing appears in man's organic nor in his psychological constitution which sets a limit to such tendencies. The functioning of individual life does not require them to cease at one point rather than at another; the proof being that they have constantly increased since the beginnings of history, receiving more and more complete satisfaction, yet with no weakening of average health. Above all, how establish their proper variation with different conditions of life, occupations, relative importance of services, etc.? In no society are they equally satisfied in the different stages of the social hierarchy. Yet human nature is substantially the same among all men, in its essential qualities. It is not human nature which can assign the variable limits necessary to our needs. They are thus unlimited so far as they depend on the individual alone. Irrespective of any external regulatory force, our capacity for feeling is in itself an insatiable and bottomless abyss.

But if nothing external can restrain this capacity, it can only be a source of torment to itself. Unlimited desires are insatiable by definition and insatiability is rightly considered a sign of morbidity. Being unlimited, they constantly and infinitely surpass the means at their command; they cannot be quenched. Inextinguishable thirst is constantly renewed torture. It has been claimed, indeed, that human activity naturally aspires beyond assignable limits and sets itself unattainable goals. But how can such an undetermined state be any more reconciled with the conditions of mental life than with the demands of physical life? All man's pleasure in acting, moving and exerting himself implies the sense that his efforts are not in vain and that by walking he has advanced. However, one does not advance when one walks toward no goal, or—which is the same thing—when his goal is infinity. Since the distance between us and it is always the same, whatever road we take, we might as well have made the motions without progress from the spot. Even our glances behind and our feeling of pride at the distance covered can cause only deceptive satisfaction, since the remaining distance is not proportionately reduced. To pursue a goal which is by definition unattainable is to condemn oneself to a state of perpetual unhappiness. Of course, man may hope contrary to all reason, and hope has its pleasures even when unreasonable. It may sustain him for a time; but it cannot survive the repeated disappointments of experience indefinitely. What more can the future offer him than the past, since he can never reach a tenable condition nor even approach the glimpsed ideal? Thus, the more one has, the more one wants, since satisfactions received only stimulate instead of filling needs. Shall action as such be considered agreeable? First, only on condition of blindness to its uselessness. Secondly, for this pleasure to be felt and to temper and half veil the accompanying painful unrest, such unending motion must at least always be easy and unhampered. If it is interfered with only restlessness is left, with the lack of ease which it, itself, entails. But it would be a miracle if no insurmountable obstacle were never encountered. Our thread of life on these conditions is pretty thin, breakable at any instant.

To achieve any other result, the passions first must be limited. Only then can they be harmonized with the faculties and satisfied. But since the individual has no way of limiting them, this must be done by some force exterior to him. A regulative force must play the same role for moral needs which the organism plays for physical needs. This means that the force can only be moral. The awakening of conscience interrupted the state of equilibrium of the animal's dormant existence; only conscience, therefore, can furnish the means to re-establish it. Physical restraint would be ineffective; hearts cannot be touched by physio-chemical forces. So far as the appetites are not automatically restrained by physiological mechanisms, they can be halted only by a limit that they recognize as just. Men would never consent to restrict their desires if they felt justified in passing the assigned limit. But, for reasons given above, they cannot assign themselves this law of justice. So they must receive it from an authority which they respect, to which they yield spontaneously. Either directly and as a whole, or through the agency of one of its organs, society alone can play this moderating role; for it is the only moral power superior to the individual, the authority of which he accepts. It alone has the power necessary to stipulate law and to set the point beyond which the passions must not go. Finally, it alone can estimate the reward to be prospectively offered to every class of human functionary, in the name of the common interest.

As a matter of fact, at every moment of history there is a dim perception, in the moral consciousness of societies, of the respective value of different social services, the relative reward due to each, and the consequent degree of comfort appropriate on the average to workers in each occupation. The different functions are graded in public opinion and a certain coefficient of well-being assigned to each, according to its place in the hierarchy. According to accepted ideas, for example, a certain way of living is considered the upper limit to which a workman may aspire in his efforts to improve his existence, and there is another limit below which he is not willingly permitted to fall unless he has seriously demeaned himself. Both differ for city and country workers, for the domestic servant and the day-labourer, for the business clerk and the official, etc. Likewise the man of wealth is reproved if he lives the life of a poor man, but also if he seeks the refinements of luxury overmuch. Economists may protest in vain; public feeling will always be scandalized if an individual spends too much wealth for wholly superfluous use, and it even seems that this severity relaxes only in times of moral disturbance.[8] A genuine regimen exists, therefore, although not always legally formulated, which fixes with relative precision the maximum degree of ease of living to which each social class may legitimately aspire. However, there is nothing immutable about such a scale. It changes with the increase or decrease of collective revenue and the changes occurring in the moral ideas of society. Thus what appears luxury to one period no longer does so to another; and the well-being which for long periods was granted to a class only by exception and supererogation, finally appears strictly necessary and equitable.

Under this pressure, each in his sphere vaguely realizes the extreme limit set to his ambitions and aspires to nothing beyond. At least if he respects regulations and is docile to collective authority, that is, has a wholesome moral constitution, he feels that it is not well to ask more. Thus, an end and goal are set to the passions. Truly, there is nothing rigid nor absolute about such determination. The economic ideal assigned each class of citizens is itself confined to certain limits, within which the desires have free range. But it is not infinite. This relative limitation and the moderation it involves make men contented with their lot while stimulating them moderately to improve it; and this average contentment causes the feeling of calm, active happiness, the pleasure in existing and living which characterizes health for societies as well as for individuals. Each person is then at least, generally speaking, in harmony with his condition, and desires only what he may legitimately hope for as the normal reward of his activity. Besides, this does not condemn man to a sort of immobility. He may seek to give beauty to his life; but his attempts in this direction may fail without causing him despair. For, loving what he has and not fixing his desire solely on what he lacks, his wishes and hopes may fail of what he has happened to aspire to, without his being wholly destitute. He has the essentials. The equilibrium of his happiness is secure because it is denied, and a few mishaps cannot disconnect him.

But it would be of little use for everyone to recognize the justice of the hierarchy of functions established by public opinion, if he did not also consider the distribution of these functions just. The workman is not in harmony with his social position if he is not convinced that he has his deserts. If he feels justified in occupying another, what he has would not satisfy him. So it is not enough for the average level of needs for each social condition to be regulated by public opinion, but another, more precise rule, must fix the way in which these conditions are open to individuals. There is no society in which such regulation does not exist. It varies with times and places. Once it regarded birth as the almost exclusive principle of social classification; today it recognizes no other inherent inequality than hereditary fortune and merit. But in all these various forms its object is unchanged. It is also only possible, everywhere, as the restriction upon individuals imposed by superior authority, that is, by collective authority. For it can be established only by requiring of one or another group of men, usually of all, sacrifices and concessions in the name of the public interest.

. . .

It is not true, then, that human activity can be released from all restraint. Nothing in the world can enjoy such a privilege. All existence being a part of the universe is relative to the remainder; its nature and method of manifestation accordingly depend not only on itself but on other beings, who consequently restrain and regulate it. Here there are only differences of degree and form between the mineral realm and the thinking person. Man's characteristic privilege is that the bond he accepts is not physical but moral; that is, social. He is governed not by a material environment brutally imposed on him, but by a conscience superior to his own, the superiority of which he feels. Because the greater, better part of his existence transcends the body, he escapes the body's yoke, but is subject to that of society.

But when society is disturbed by some painful crisis or by beneficent but abrupt transitions, it is momentarily incapable of exercising this influence; thence come the sudden rises in the curve of suicides which we have pointed out above.

In the case of economic disasters, indeed, something like a declassification occurs which suddenly casts certain individuals into a lower state than their previous one. Then they must reduce their requirements, restrain their needs, learn greater self-control. All the advantages of social influence are lost so far as they are concerned; their moral education has to be recommenced. But society cannot adjust them instantaneously to this new life and teach them to practise the increased self-repression to which they are unaccustomed. So they are not adjusted to the condition forced on them, and its very prospect is intolerable; hence the suffering which detaches them from a reduced existence even before they have made trial of it.

It is the same if the source of the crisis is an abrupt growth of power and wealth. Then, truly, as the conditions of life are changed, the standard according to which needs were regulated can no longer remain the same; for it varies with social resources, since it largely determines the share of each class of producers. The scale is upset; but a new scale cannot be immediately improvised. Time is required for the public conscience to reclassify men and things. So long as the social forces thus freed have not regained equilibrium, their respective values are unknown and so all regulation is lacking for a time. The limits are unknown between the possible and the impossible, what is just and what is unjust, legitimate claims and hopes and those which are immoderate. Consequently, there is no restraint upon aspirations. If the disturbance is profound, it affects even the principles controlling the distribution of men among various occupations. Since the relations between various parts of society are necessarily modified, the ideas expressing these relations must change. Some particular class especially favoured by the crisis is no longer resigned to its former lot, and, on the other hand, the example of its greater good fortune arouses all sorts of jealousy below and about it. Appetites, not being controlled by a public opinion, become disoriented, no longer recognize the limits proper to them. Besides, they are at the same time seized by a sort of natural erethism simply by the greater intensity of public life. With increased prosperity desires increase. At the very moment when traditional rules have lost their authority, the richer prize offered these appetites stimulates them and makes them more exigent and impatient of control. The state of deregulation or anomy is thus further heightened by passions being less disciplined, precisely when they need more disciplining.

But then their very demands make fulfilment impossible. Overweening ambition always exceeds the results obtained, great as they may be, since there is no warning to pause here. Nothing gives satisfaction and all this agitation is uninterruptedly maintained without appeasement. Above all, since this race for an unattainable goal can give no other pleasure but that of the race itself, if it is one, once it is interrupted the participants are left empty-handed, both from being less controlled and because competition is greater. All classes contend among themselves because no established classification any longer exists. Effort grows, just when it becomes less productive. How could the desire to live not be weakened under such conditions?

This explanation is confirmed by the remarkable immunity of poor countries. Poverty protects against suicide because it is a restraint in itself. No matter how one acts, desires have to depend upon resources to some extent; actual possessions are partly the criterion of those aspired to. So the less one has the less he is tempted to extend the range of his needs indefinitely. Lack of power, compelling moderation, accustoms men to it, while nothing excites envy if no one has superfluity. Wealth, on the other hand, by the power it bestows, deceives us into believing that we depend on ourselves only. Reducing the resistance we encounter from objects, it suggests the possibility of unlimited success against them. The less limited one feels, the more intolerable all limitation appears. Not without reason, therefore, have so many religions dwelt on the advantages and moral value of property. It is actually the best school for teaching self-restraint. Forcing us to constant self-discipline, it prepares us to accept collective discipline with equanimity, while wealth, exalting the individual, may always arouse the spirit of rebellion which is the very source of immorality. This, of course, is no reason why humanity should not improve its material condition. But though the moral danger involved in every growth of prosperity is not irremediable, it should not be forgotten.

III

If anomy never appeared except, as in the above instances, in intermittent spurts and acute crisis, it might cause the social suicide-rate to vary from time to time, but it would not be a regular, constant factor. In one sphere of social life, however—the sphere of trade and industry—it is actually in a chronic state.

. . .

Industrial and commercial functions are really among the occupations which furnish the greatest number of suicides (see Table 24). Almost on a level with the liberal professions, they sometimes surpass them; they are especially more afflicted that agriculture, where the old regulative forces still make their appearance felt most and where the fever of business has least penetrated. Here is best recalled what was once the general constitution of the economic order. And the divergence would be yet greater if, among the suicides of industry, employers were distinguished from workmen, for the former are probably most stricken by the state of anomy. The enormous rate of those with independent means (720 million) sufficiently shows that the possessors of most comfort suffer most. Everything that enforces subordination attenuates the effects of this state. At least the horizon of the lower classes is limited by those above them, and for this same reason their desires are most modest. Those who have only empty space above them are almost inevitably lost in it, if no force restrains them.

TABLE 24   Suicides per Million Persons of Different Occupations

	Trade	Transportation	Industry	Agriculture	Liberal[a] Professions
France (1878–87)[b]	440	...	340	240	300
Switzerland (1876)	664	1,514	577	304	558
Italy (1866–76)	277	152.6	80.4	26.7	618[c]
Prussia (1883–90)	754	...	456	315	832
Bavaria (1884–91)	465	...	369	153	454
Belgium (1886–90)	421	...	160	160	100
Wurttemberg (1873–78)	273	...	190	206	...
Saxony (1878)		341.59[d]		71.17	...

[a]When statistics distinguish several different sorts of liberal occupations, we show as a specimen the one in which the suicide-rate is highest.
[b]From 1826 to 1880 economic functions seem less affected (see *Compte-rendu* of 1880); but were occupational statistics very accurate?
[c]This figure is reached only by men of letters.
[d]Figure represents Trade, Transportation and Industry combined for Saxony. Ed.

Anomy, therefore, is a regular and specific factor in suicide in our modern societies; one of the springs from which the annual contingent feeds. So we have here a new type to distinguish from the others. It differs from them in its dependence, not on the way in which individuals are attached to society, but on how it regulates them. Egoistic suicide results from man's no longer finding a basis for existence in life; altruistic suicide, because this basis for existence appears to man situated beyond life itself. The third sort of suicide, the existence of which has just been shown, results from man's activity's lacking regulation and his consequent sufferings. By virtue of its origin we shall assign this last variety the name of *anomic suicide*.

Certainly, this and egoistic suicide have kindred ties. Both spring from society's insufficient presence in individuals. But the sphere of its absence is not the same in both cases. In egoistic suicide it is deficient in truly collective activity, thus depriving the latter of object and meaning. In anomic suicide, society's influence is lacking in the basically individual passions, thus leaving them without a check-rein. In spite of their relationship, therefore, the two types are independent of each other. We may offer society everything social in us, and still be unable to control our desires; one may live in an anomic state without being egoistic, and vice versa. These two sorts of suicide therefore do not draw their chief recruits from the same social environments; one has its principal field among intellectual careers, the world of thought—the other, the individual or commercial world.

IV

But economic anomy is not the only anomy which may give rise to suicide.

The suicides occurring at the crisis of widowhood . . . are really due to domestic anomy resulting from the death of husband or wife. A family catastrophe occurs which affects the survivor. He is not adapted to the new situation in which he finds himself and according-ly offers less resistance to suicide.

TABLE 25 Comparison of European States from the Point of View of Both Divorce and Suicide

	Annual Divorces per 1,000 Marriages	Suicide per Million Inhabitants
I. Countries Where Divorce and Separation are Rare		
Norway	0.54 (1875–80)	73
Russia	1.6 (1871–77)	30
England and Wales	1.3 (1871–79)	68
Scotland	2.1 (1871–81)	...
Italy	1.05 (1871–73)	31
Finland	3.9 (1875–79)	30.8
Averages	2.07	46.5
II. Countries Where Divorce and Separation are of Average Frequency		
Bavaria	1.0 (1881)	90.5
Belgium	1.1 (1871–80)	68.5
Holland	6.0 (1871–80)	35.5
Sweden	6.4 (1871–80)	81
Baden	6.5 (1874–79)	156.6
France	1.5 (1871–79)	150
Wurttemberg	8.4 (1876–78)	162.4
Prussia	...	133
Averages	6.4	109.6
III. Countries Where Divorce and Separation are Frequent		
Kingdom of Saxony	26.9 (1876–80)	299
Denmark	38 (1871–80)	258
Switzerland	47 (1876–80)	216
Averages	37.3	257

But another variety of anomic suicide should draw greater attention, both because it is more chronic and because it will serve to illustrate the nature and functions of marriage.

In the *Annales de demographie internationale* (September 1882), Bertillon published a remarkable study of divorce, in which he proved the following proposition: throughout Europe the number of suicides varies with that of divorces and separations.

If the different countries are compared from this twofold point of view, this paral-lelism is apparent (see Table 25). Not only is the relation between

TABLE 26 Comparison of Swiss Cantons from the Point of View of Divorce and Suicide

	Divorces and Separations per 1,000 Marriages	Suicides per Million		Divorces and Separations per 1,000 Marriages	Suicides per Million
			I. Catholic Cantons		
			French and Italian		
Tessino	7.6	57	Freiburg	15.9	119
Valais	4.0	47			
Averages	5.8	50	Averages	15.9	119
			German		
Uri	...	60	Solothurn	37.7	205
Upper Unterwalden	4.9	20	Inner Appenzell	18.9	158
Lower Unterwalden	5.2	1	Zug	14.8	87
Schwyz	5.6	70	Luzern	13.0	100
Averages	3.9	37.7	Averages	21.1	137.5
			II. Protestant Cantons		
			French		
Neufchâtel	42.4	560	Vaud	43.5	352
			German		
Bern	47.2	229	Schaffhausen	106.0	602
Basel (city)	34.5	323	Outer Appenzell	100.7	213
Basel (country)	33.0	288	Glaris	83.1	127
			Zurich	80.0	288
Averages	38.2	280	Averages	92.4	307
			III. Cantons Mixed As To Religion		
Argau	40.0	195	Geneva	70.5	360
Grisons	30.9	116	Saint Gall	57.6	179
Averages	36.9	155	Averages	64.0	269

the averages evident, but the single irregular detail of any importance is that of Holland, where suicides are not as frequent as divorces.

The law may be yet more vigorously verified if we compare not different countries but different provinces of a single country. Notably, in Switzerland the agreement between the two series of phenomena is striking (see Table 26). The Protestant cantons have the most divorces and also the most suicides. The mixed cantons follow, from both points of view, and only then come the Catholic cantons. Within each group the same agreements appear.

. . .

One must seek the cause of this remarkable relation, not in the organic predispositions of people but in the intrinsic nature of divorce. As our first proposition here we may assert: in all countries for which we have the necessary data, suicides of divorced people are immensely more numerous than those of other portions of the population.

	Suicides in a Million							
	Unmarried Above 15 Years		Married		Widowed		Divorced	
	Men	Women	Men	Women	Men	Women	Men	Women
Prussia (1887–1889)[a]	360	120	430	90	1,471	215	1,875	290
Prussia (1883–1890)[a]	388	129	498	100	1,552	194	1,952	328
Baden (1885–1893)	458	93	460	85	1,172	171	1,328	...
Saxony (1847–1858)	...	...	481	120	1,242	240	3,102	312
Saxony (1876)	555.18[b]		821	146	...	...	3,252	389
Wurttemberg (1846–1860)	...	...	226	52	530	97	1,298	281
Wurttemberg (1873–1892)	251	...	218[b]		405[b]		796[b]	

[a]There appears to be some error in the figures for Prussia here. — Ed.
[b]Men and women combined. — Ed.

Thus, divorced persons of both sexes kill themselves between three and four times more often as married persons, although younger (40 years in France as against 46 years), and considerably more often than widowed persons in spite of the aggravation resulting for the latter from their advanced age. What is the explanation?

There is no doubt that the change of moral and material regimen which is a consequence of divorce is of some account in this result. But it does not sufficiently explain the matter. Widowhood is indeed as complete a disturbance of existence as divorce; it usually even has much more unhappy results, since it was not desired by husband and wife, while divorce is usually a deliverance for both. Yet divorced persons who, considering their age, should commit suicide only one half as often as widowed persons, do so more often everywhere, even twice as often in certain countries. This aggravation, to be represented by a coefficient between 2.5 and 4, does not depend on their changed condition in any way.

Let us refer to one of the propositions established above to discover the causes of this fact. We saw that in a given society the tendency of widowed persons to suicide was a function of the corresponding tendency of married persons. While the latter are highly protected, the former enjoy an immunity less, to be sure, but still considerable, and the sex best protected by marriage is also that best protected in the state of widowhood. Briefly, when conjugal society is dissolved by the death of one of the couple, the effects which it had with reference to suicide continue to be felt in part by the survivor. Then, however, is it not to be supposed that the same thing takes place when the marriage is interrupted, not by death, but by a judicial act, and that the aggravation which afflicts divorced persons is a result not of the divorce but of the marriage ended by divorce? It must be connected with some quality of the matrimonial society, the influence of which the couple continue to experience even when separated. If they have so strong an inclination to suicide, it is because they were already strongly inclined to it while living together and by the very effect of their common life.

TABLE 27   Influence of Divorce on the Immunity of Married Persons

Country	Suicides per Million Persons		
	Unmarried Men Above 15 Years	Married Men	Coefficient of Preservation of Married with Reference to Unmarried Men
Where divorce does not exist			
Italy (1884–88)	145	88	1.64
France (1863–68)[a]	273	245.7	1.11
Where divorce is common			
Baden (1885–93)	458	460	0.99
Prussia (1883–90)	388	498	0.77
Prussia (1887–89)	364	431	0.83

Per one hundred suicides of every marital status.

Unmarried men   Married men

Where divorce is very frequent[b]			
	27.5	52.5	0.63
Saxony (1879–80)			

Per one hundred male inhabitants of every marital status.

Unmarried men   Married men

42.10   52.47

[a]We take this distant period because divorce did not exist at all at the time. The law of 1884 re-establishing it seems, however, up to the present, to have had no perceptible effects on the suicides of married men; their coefficient of preservation had not appreciably changed in 1888-92; an institution does not produce its effects in so short a time.

[b]For Saxony we have only the relative numbers given above and taken from Oettingen; they are enough for the purpose. In Legoyt (171) other data will be found likewise proving that in Saxony married persons have a higher rate than unmarried. Legoyt himself notes this with surprise.

Admitting so much, the correspondence between divorces and suicides becomes explicable. Actually, among the people where divorce is common, this peculiar effect of marriage in which divorce shares must necessarily be very widespread; for it is not confined to households predestined to legal separation. If it reaches its maximum intensity among them, it must also be found among the others, or the majority of the others, though to a lesser degree. For just as where there are many suicides, there are many attempted suicides, and just as mortality cannot grow without morbidity increasing simultaneously, so wherever there are many actual divorces there must be many households more or less close to divorce. The number of actual divorces cannot rise, accordingly, without the family condition predisposing to suicide also developing and becoming general in the same degree, and thus the two phenomena naturally vary in the same general direction.

Not only does this hypothesis agree with everything demonstrated above but it is susceptible of direct proof. Indeed, if it is well-founded, married persons in countries where divorces are numerous must have less immunity against suicide than where marriage is indissoluble. This is the net result of the facts, at least *so far as husbands are concerned* as appears from Table 27 above. Italy, a Catholic country in which divorce is unknown, is also the country with the highest coefficient of preservation for husbands; it is less in France, where separations have always been more frequent, and can be seen to diminish as we pass to countries where divorce is more widely practiced.[9]

TABLE 28 Influence of Divorce on the Immunity of Married Women[a]

	Suicides per Million		Coefficient of Preservation		How Many Times	How Many Times
	Unmarried Women Over 16 Years	Wives	Wives	Husbands	Husbands' Coefficient Above Wives'	Wives' Coefficient Above Husbands'
Italy	21	22	0.95	1.64	1.72	...
France	59	62.5	0.96	1.11	1.15	...
Baden	93	85	1.09	0.99	...	1.10
Prussia	129	100	1.29	0.77	...	1.67
Prussia (1887–89)	120	90	1.33	0.83	...	1.60

Per 100 suicides of every marital status.
    Unmarried
        Women   Wives
        35.3   42.6

Saxony
Per 100 inhabitants of every marital status.
    Unmarried
        Women   Wives
        37.9   49.74   1.19   0.63   ...   1.73

[a]The periods are the same as in Table 27.

. . .

This is one more proof that the large number of suicides in countries where divorce is widespread has no reference to any organic predisposition, especially to the number of unstable people. For if such were the real case, it would affect unmarried as well as married men. Now the latter are actually those most affected. The origin of the evil is therefore undoubtedly to be sought, as we have supposed, in some peculiarity either of marriage or of family life. It remains for us to choose between the last two hypotheses. Is the lesser immunity of husbands due to the condition of domestic society, or to that of matrimonial society? Is the family morale inferior or the conjugal bond not all that it should be?

A first fact which makes the former explanation improbable is that among peoples where divorce is most frequent the birth rate is very high and, consequently, the density of the domestic group is also very high. Now we know that where the family is dense, family spirit is usually strong. There is reason to believe, then, that the cause of the phenomenon is to be sought in the nature of marriage.

Actually, if it were imputable to the constitution of the family, wives should also be less protected from suicide in countries where divorce is current than in those where it is rare; for they are as much affected by the poor state of domestic relations as husbands. Exactly the reverse is the truth. The coefficient of preservation of married women rises proportionately to the fall of that of husbands, or in proportion as divorces are more frequent and vice versa. The more often and easily the conjugal bond is broken, the more the wife is favoured in comparison with the husband (see Table 28).

The inversion between the two series of coefficients is remarkable. In countries where there in no divorce, the wife is less protected than the husband; but her inferiority is greater in Italy than in France, where the matrimonial tie has always been more easily broken. On the contrary, wherever divorce is practised (Baden), the husband is less protected than the wife, and the latter's advantage increases regularly with the increase in the frequency of divorce.

. . .

Comparison of the Seine with other French departments confirms this law in a striking manner. In the provinces, where there is less divorce, the average coefficient of married women is only 1.49; it is therefore only half the average coefficient of husbands, which is 2.88. In the Seine the relation is reversed. The immunity of men is only 1.56 and even 1.44 if we omit the uncertain figures referring to the period of from 20 to 25 years; the immunity of women is 1.79. The woman's situation in relation to the husband's there is thus more than twice as good as in the departments.

The same result is obtained by comparing the various provinces of Prussia:

Provinces Containing, per 100,000 Married Persons

From 810 to 405 Divorced	Preservation of Wives	From 371 to 324 Divorced	Preservation of Wives	From 229 to 116 Divorced	Preservation of Wives
Berlin	1.72	Pomerania	1	Posen	1
Brandenburg	1.75	Silesia	1.18	Hesse	1.44
East Prussia	1.50	West Prussia	1	Hanover	0.90
Saxony	2.08	Schleswig	1.20	Rhineland	1.25
				Westphalia	0.80

All the coefficients of the first group are distinctly above those of the second, and the lowest are found in the third. The only anomaly is Hesse, where, for unknown reasons, married women have a considerable immunity although divorced persons are few in number.[10]

In spite of these concurrent proofs, let us seek a final verification of this law. Instead of comparing the immunity of husbands with that of wives, let us discover how different-ly marriage in different countries modifies the respective situations of the sexes with regard to suicide. This comparison forms the subject of Table 29. Here it appears that, in countries where divorce does not exist or has only recently been instituted, woman's share is greater in the suicides of married than of unmarried persons. This means that marriage here favours the husband rather than the wife, and the latter's unfavourable position is more pronounced in Italy than in France. The average excess of the proportional share of married over unmarried women is indeed twice as much in the former as in the latter of the two countries. Turning to peoples among whom the institution of divorce is wide-spread, the reverse is the case. Here woman gains by marriage and man loses; and her profit is greater in Prussia than in Baden, and greater in Saxony than in Prussia. Her prof-it is greatest in the country where divorces also are greatest.

TABLE 29   Proportional Share of Each Sex in Suicides of Each Category of Marital Status in Different Countries of Europe

	Per 100 Suicides of Unmarried		Per 100 Suicides of Married		Average Excess per Country on the Part of	
	Men	Women	Husbands	Wives	Wives Over Unmarried Women	Unmarried Women Over Women
Italy (1871)	87	13	79	21	6.2	
Italy (1872)	82	18	78	22		
Italy (1873)	86	14	79	21		
Italy (1884-88)	85	15	79	21		
France (1863–66)	84	16	78	22	3.6	
France (1867–71)	84	16	79	21		
France (1888–91)	81	19	81	19		
Baden (1869–73)	84	16	85	15		1
Baden (1885–93)	84	16	85	15		
Prussia (1873–75)	78	22	83	17		5
Prussia (1887–89)	77	23	83	17		
Saxony (1866–70)	77	23	84	16		7
Saxony (1879–90)	80	20	86	14		

Accordingly, the following law may be regarded as beyond dispute: *From the standpoint of suicide, marriage is more favourable to the wife the more widely practised divorce is; and vice versa.*

From this proposition, two consequences flow.

First, only husbands contribute to the rise in the suicide rate observable in societies where divorces are frequent, wives on the contrary committing suicide more rarely than elsewhere. If, then, divorce can only develop with the improvement of woman's moral situation, it cannot be connected with an unfavourable state of domestic society calculated to aggravate the tendency to suicide; for such an aggravation should occur in the case of the wife, as well as of the husband. A lowering of family morale cannot have such opposite effects on the two sexes: it cannot favour the mother and seriously afflict the father. Consequently, the cause of the phenomenon which we are studying is found in the state of marriage and not in the constitutions of the family. And indeed, marriage may very possibly act in an opposite way on husband and wife. For though they have the same objects as parents, as partners their interests are different and often hostile. In certain societies therefore, some peculiarity of the matrimonial institution may very well benefit one and harm the other. All of the above tends to show that this is precisely the case with divorce.

Secondly, for the same reason we have to reject the hypothesis that this unfortunate state of marriage, with which divorces and suicides are closely connected, is simply caused by more frequent domestic disputes; for no such case could increase the woman's immunity, any more than could the loosening of the family tie. If, where divorce is common, the number of suicides really depends on the number of conjugal disputes, the wife should suffer from them as much as the husband. There is nothing in this situation to afford her exceptional immunity. The hypothesis is the less tenable since divorce is usually asked for by the wife from the husband (in France, 60 per cent of divorces and 83 per cent of separations).[11] Accordingly, domestic troubles are most often attributable to the man. Then, however, it would not be clear why, in countries of frequent divorce, the husband kills himself with greater frequency because he causes his wife more suffering, and the wife kills herself less often because her husband makes her suffer more. Nor is it proven that the number of conjugal dissensions increases in the same measure with divorce.[12]

If we discard this hypothesis, only one other remains possible. The institution of divorce must itself cause suicide through its effect on marriage.

After all, what is marriage? A regulation of sexual relations, including not merely the physical instincts which this intercourse involves but the feelings of every sort gradually engrafted by civilization on the foundation of physical desire. For among us love is a far more mental than organic fact. A man looks to a woman, not merely to the satisfaction of the sexual impulse. Though this natural proclivity has been the germ of all sexual evolution, it has become increasingly complicated with aesthetic and moral feelings, numerous and varied, and today it is only the smallest element of the total complex process to which it has given birth. Under the influence of these intellectual elements it has itself been partially freed from its physical nature and assumed something like an intellectual one. Moral reasons as well as physical needs impel love. Hence, it no longer has the regular, automatic periodicity which it displays in animals. A psychological impulse may awaken it at any time: it is not seasonal. But just because these various inclinations, thus changed, do not directly depend upon organic necessities, social regulation becomes necessary. They must be restrained by society since the organism has no means of restraining them. This is the function of marriage. It completely regulates the life of passion, and monogamic marriage more strictly than any other. For by forcing a man to attach himself forever to the same woman it assigns a strictly definite object to the need from love, and closes the horizon.

This determination is what forms the state of moral equilibrium from which the husband benefits. Being unable to seek other satisfactions than those permitted, without transgressing his duty, he restricts his desires to them. The salutary discipline to which he is subjected makes it his duty to find his happiness in his lot, and by doing so supplies him with the means. Besides, if his passion is forbidden to stray, its fixed object is forbidden to fail him; the obligation is reciprocal. Though his enjoyment is restricted, it is assured and this certainty forms his mental foundation. The lot of the unmarried man is different. As he has the right to form attachment wherever inclination leads him, he aspires to everything and is satisfied with nothing. This morbid desire for the infinite which everywhere accompanies anomy may as readily assail this as any other part of our consciousness; it very often assumes a sexual form which was described by Musset.[13] When one is no longer checked, one becomes unable to check one's self. Beyond experienced pleasures one senses and desires others; if one happens almost to have exhausted the range of what is possible, one dreams of the impossible; one thirsts for the non-existent.[14] How can the feelings not be exacerbated by such unending pursuit? For them to reach that state, one need not even have intimately multiplied the experiences of love and lived the life of a Don Juan. The humdrum existence of the ordinary bachelor suffices. New hopes constantly awake, only to be deceived, leaving a trail of weariness and disillusionment behind them. How can desire, then, become fixed, being uncertain that it can retain what it attracts; for the anomy is twofold. Just as the person makes no definitive gift of himself, he has definitive title to nothing. The uncertainty of the future plus his own indeterminateness therefore condemns him to constant change. The result of it all is a state of disturbance, agitation and discontent which inevitably increases the possibilities of suicide.

Now divorce implies a weakening of matrimonial regulation. Where it exists, and especially where law and custom permit its excessive practice, marriage is nothing but a weakened simulacrum of itself; it is an inferior form of marriage. It cannot produce its useful effects to the same degree. Its restraint upon desire is weakened; since it is more easily disturbed and superseded, it controls passion less and passion tends to rebel. It consents less readily to its assigned limit. The moral calmness and tranquillity which were the husband's strength are less; they are replaced to some extent by an uneasiness which keeps a man from being satisfied with what he has. Besides, he is less inclined to become attached to his present state as his enjoyment of it is not completely sure: the future is less certain. One cannot be strongly restrained by a chain which may be broken on one side or the other at any moment. One cannot help looking beyond one's own position when the ground underfoot does not feel secure. Hence, in the countries where marriage is strongly tempered by divorce, the immunity of the married man is inevitably less. As he resembles the unmarried under his regime, he inevitably loses some of his own advantages. Consequently, the total number of suicides rises.[15]

But this consequence of divorce is peculiar to the man and does not affect the wife. Woman's sexual needs have less of a mental character because, generally speaking, her mental life is less developed. These needs are more closely related to the needs of the organism, following rather than leading them, and consequently find in them an efficient restraint. Being a more instinctive creature than man, woman has only to follow her instincts to find calmness and peace. She thus does not require so strict a social regulation as marriage, and particularly as monogamic marriage. Even when useful, such a discipline has its inconveniences. By fixing the conjugal state permanently, it prevents all retreat, regardless of consequences. By limiting the horizon, it closes all egress and forbids even legitimate hope. Man himself doubtless suffers from this immutability; but for him the evil is largely compensated by the advantages he gains in other respects. Custom, moreover, grants him certain privileges which allow him in some measure to lessen the strictness of the regime. There is no compensation or relief for the woman. Monogamy is strictly obligatory for her, with no qualification of any sort, and, on the other hand, marriage is not in the same degree useful to her for limiting her desires, which are naturally limited, and for teaching her to be contented with her lot; but it prevents her from changing it if it becomes intolerable. The regulation therefore is a restraint to her without any great advantages. Consequently, everything that makes it more flexible and lighter can only better the wife's situation. So divorce protects her and she has frequent recourse to it.

The state of conjugal anomy, produced by the institution of divorce, thus explains the parallel development of divorces and suicides. Accordingly, the suicides of husbands which increase the number of voluntary deaths in countries where there are many divorces, form a division of anomic suicide. They are not the result of the existence of more bad husbands or bad wives in these societies, that is, of more unhappy households. They result from a moral structure *sui generis*, itself caused by a weakening of matrimonial regulation. This structure, established by marriage, by surviving it produces the exceptional tendency to suicide shown by divorced men. But we do not mean that this enervation of the regulation is created out of whole cloth by the legal establishment of divorce. Divorce is never granted except out of respect for a pre-existing state of customs. If the public conscience had not gradually decided that the indissolubility of the conjugal bond is unreasonable, no legislator would ever have thought of making it easier to break up. Matrimonial anomy may therefore exist in public opinion even without being inscribed in law. On the other hand, only when it has assumed a legal form, can it produce all its consequences. So long as the marriage law is unmodified, it at least serves considerably to restrict the passions; above all, it opposes the increase of the taste for anomy merely by reproof. That is why anomy has pronounced and readily recognizable effects only where it has become a legal institution.

While this explanation accounts both for the observed parallelism between divorces and suicides[16] and the inverse variations shown by the immunity of husband and that of the wife, it is confirmed by several other facts:

1. Only where divorce applies, can there be real matrimonial instability; for it alone completely severs marriage, whereas separation merely partially suspends certain of its effects without giving the couple their liberty. If, then, this special anomy really increases the suicidal tendency, divorced people should have a far higher aptitude than those merely separated. This is in fact the gist of the only document on this matter known to us. According to a calculation by Legoyt, in Saxony, during the period 1847-56, there were, as an annual average, 1,400 suicides for a million divorced persons and only 176 for a million separated persons. This latter rate is even below that of husbands (318).

2. If the strong suicidal tendency of the unmarried is partially connected with the sexual anomy in which they chronically exist, the aggravation they suffer must be most perceptible just when sexual feelings are most aroused. And in fact, the suicide rate of the unmarried grows between 20 and 45 years much more rapidly than after that; it quadruples during this period, while from 45 to the maximum age (after 80 years) it only doubles. But no such acceleration appears among women; the rate of unmarried women does not even double from 20 to 45; years, but merely rises from 106 to 171. The sexual period therefore does not affect the increase of female suicides. This is just what we should expect if, as we have granted, woman is not very sensitive to this form of anomy.

3. Finally, several facts established in Chapter III of this very book are explained by the theory just set forth and consequently help to verify it.

We saw in that chapter that marriage in France, by itself and irrespective of family, gives man a coefficient of preservation of 1.5. We know now to what this coefficient corresponds. It represents the advantages obtained by a man from the regulative influence exerted upon him by marriage, from the moderation it imposes on his inclinations and from his consequent moral well-being. But at the same time we noted that in the same country the condition of a married woman was, on the contrary, made worse with respect to suicide unless the advent of children corrects the ill effects of marriage for her. We have just stated the reason. Not that man is naturally a wicked and egoistic being whose role in a household is to make his companion suffer. But in France where, until recently, marriage was not weakened by divorce, the inflexible rule it imposed on women was a very heavy, profitless yoke for them. Speaking generally, we now have the cause of that antagonism of the sexes which prevents marriage favouring them equally: their interests are contrary; one needs restraint and the other liberty.

Furthermore, it does seem that at a certain time of life man is affected by marriage in the same way as woman, though for different reasons. If, as we have shown, very young husbands kill themselves much more often than unmarried men of the same age, it is doubtless because their passions are too vehement at that period and too self-confident to be subjected to so severe a rule. Accordingly, this rule seems to them an unendurable obstacle against which their desire dashes and is broken. This is probably why marriage produces all its beneficent effects only when age, supervening, tempers man somewhat and makes him feel the need of discipline.[17]

Finally, in this same Chapter III we saw that where marriage favours the wife rather than the husband, the difference between that sexes is always less than when the reverse is true. This proves that, even in those societies where the status of matrimony is wholly in the woman's favour, it does her less service than it does man where it is he that profits more by it. Woman can suffer more from marriage if it is unfavourable to her than she can benefit by it if it conforms to her interest. This is because she has less need of it. This is the assumption of the theory just set forth. The results obtained previously and those arising from the present chapter therefore combine and check each other mutually.

Thus we reach a conclusion quite different from the current idea of marriage and its role. It is supposed to have been originated for the wife, to protect her weakness against masculine caprice. Monogamy, especially, is often represented as a sacrifice made by man of his polygamous instincts, to raise and improve woman's condition in marriage. Actually, whatever historical causes may have made him accept this restriction, he benefits more by it. The liberty he thus renounces could only be a source of torment to him. Woman did not have the same reasons to abandon it and, in this sense, we may say that by submitting to the same rule, it was she who made a sacrifice.[18]

NOTES

1. By the use of this expression we of course do not at all intend to hypostasize the collective conscience. We do not recognize any more substantial a soul in society than in the individual. But we shall revert to this point.
2. Bk. III Ch. 1.
3. We say nothing of the ideal protraction of life involved in the belief in immortality of the soul, for (1) this cannot explain why the family or attachment to political society preserves us from suicide; and (2) it is not even this belief which forms religion's prophylactic influence, as we have shown above.
4. This is why it is unjust to accuse these theorists of sadness of generalizing personal impressions. They are the echo of a general condition.
5. In 1874 over 1873.—Ed.
6. The increase is less during the period 1885–90 because of a financial crisis.
7. To prove that an increase in prosperity diminishes suicides, the attempt has been made to show that they become less when emigration, the escape-valve of poverty, is widely practised (see Legoyt: 257–9). But cases are numerous where parallelism instead of inverse proportions exist between the two. In Italy from 1876 to 1890 the number of emigrants rose from 76 per 100,000 inhabitants to 335, a figure itself exceeded between 1887 and 1889. At the same time suicides did not cease to grow in numbers.
8. Actually, this is a purely moral reprobation and can hardly be judicially implemented. We do not consider any reestablishment of sumptuary laws desirable or even possible.
9. If we compare only these few countries from this point of view, it is because statistics for the others combine the suicides of husbands with those of wives; and we shall see below how imperative it is to keep them separate.

    But one should not conclude from this table that in Prussia, Baden and Saxony husbands really kill themselves more than unmarried men. We must not forget that these coefficients were compiled independently of age and of its influence on suicide. Now, as men of the average age of the unmarried, or from 25 to 30 years, commit suicide about half as often as men of 40 to 45 years, the average age for husbands, the latter enjoy some immunity even in countries with frequent divorce; but it is less than elsewhere. For this to be considered negligible, the rate of married men without reference to age would have to be twice that of unmarried men; which is not the case. However, this omission had no bearing on our conclusion. For the average age of husbands varies little from one country to another, only two or three years, and moreover the law of the effect of age on suicide is everywhere the same. Consequently by disregarding the effect of this factor, we have indeed reduced the absolute value of the coefficients of preservation, but as we have reduced them in the same proportion everywhere, we have not altered what is of sole importance to us—their relative value. For we are not seeking to estimate the absolute value of the immunity of married men of every country, but to classify the different countries from the point of view of this immunity. As for our reasons for making this simplification, it was first to avoid complicating the problem unnecessarily, but also because we have not in all cases the necessary data for the exact calculation of the effect of age.

10. It has been necessary to classify these provinces by the number of divorced persons recorded, the number of annual divorces not having been available.

11. Levasseur, *Population française*, vol. II: 92. Cf. Bertillon, *Annales de Dem. Inter.*, 1880: 460. In Saxony, demands for divorce from men are almost as frequent as those from women.

12. Bertillon, *Annales*, etc., 1882: 275ff.

13. See *Rolla* and in *Namouna* the portrait of Don Juan.

14. See the monologne of Faust in Goethe's work.

15. It will be objected that where marriage is not tempered by divorce the rigid obligation of monogamy may result in disgust. This result will of course follow if the moral character of the obligation is no longer felt. What actually matters in fact is not only that the regulation should exist, but that it should be accepted by the conscience. Otherwise, since this regulation no longer has moral authority and continues only through the force of inertia, it can no longer play any useful role. It chafes without accomplishing much.

16. Since the wife's immunity is greater where the husband's is less, it may seem strange that there is no compensation. But as the wife's share in the total number of suicides is very slight, the decrease in female suicides is imperceptible in the whole and does not balance the increase of male suicides. Thus divorce is ultimately associated with a rise in the total number of suicides.

17. It is even probable that marriage in itself produces a prophylactic effect only later, after the age of thirty. Actually, until that age, childless married men commit as many suicides in absolute numbers as married men with children, 6.6 from 20 to 25 years, for both, and from 25 to 30 years, 33 for the former and 34 for the latter. Of course, however, marriages with children are much more common than infertile marriages at this period. The tendency of the husbands of the latter marriages to suicide must therefore be several times as strong as that of husbands with children; or very close in intensity to that of unmarried men. Unfortunately we can only form hypotheses on the subject; for, as the census does not give the population of husbands without children for each age, as distinct from husbands with children, we cannot calculate separately the rate of each for each period of life. We can give only the absolute numbers, as we have them from the Ministry of Justice for 1889–91.

18. The above considerations show that there is a type of suicide the opposite of anomic suicide, just as egoistic and altruistic suicides are opposites. It is the suicide deriving from excessive regulation, that of persons with futures pitilessly blocked and passions violently choked by oppressive discipline. It is the suicide of very young husbands, of the married woman who is childless. So, for completeness' sake, we should set up a fourth suicidal type. But it has so little contemporary importance and examples are so hard to find aside from the cases just mentioned that it seems useless to dwell upon it. However it might be said to have historical interest. Do not the suicides of slaves, said to be frequent under certain conditions (see Corre, *Le crime en pays creoles*: 48), belong to this type, or all suicides attributable to excessive physical or moral despotism? To bring out the ineluctible and inflexible nature of a rule against which there is no appeal, and in contrast with the expression 'anomy' which has just been used, we might call it *fatalistic suicide*.

RELIGION AS A COLLECTIVE FORCE

First of all, let us remark that in all these formulae it is the nature of religion as a whole that they seek to express. They proceed as if it were a sort of indivisible entity, while, as a matter of fact, it is made up of parts; it is a more or less complex system of myths, dogmas, rites and ceremonies. Now a whole cannot be defined except in relation to its parts. It will be more methodical, then, to try to characterize the various elementary phenomena of which all religions are made up, before we attack the system produced by their union. This method is imposed still more forcibly by the fact that there are religious phenomena which belong to no determined religion. Such are those phenomena which constitute the matter of folklore. In general, they are the debris of past religions, unorganized survivals; but there are some which have been formed spontaneously under the influence of local causes. In our European countries Christianity has forced itself to absorb and assimilate them; it has given them a Christian colouring. Nevertheless, there are many which have persisted up until a recent date, or which still exist with a relative autonomy: celebrations of May Day, the summer solstice or the carnival, beliefs relative to genii, local demons, etc., are cases in point. If the religious character of these facts is now diminishing, their religious importance is nevertheless so great that they have enabled Mannhardt and his school to revive the science of religions. A definition which did not take account of them would not cover all that is religious.

Religious phenomena are naturally arranged in two fundamental categories: beliefs and rites. The first are states of opinion, and consist in representation; the second are determined modes of action. Between these two classes of facts there is all the difference which separates thought from action.

The rites can be defined and distinguished from other human practices, moral practices, for example, only by the special nature of their object. A moral rule prescribes certain manners of acting to us, just as a rite does, but which are addressed to a different class of objects. So it is the object of the rite which must be characterized, if we are to characterize the rite itself. Now it is in the beliefs that the special nature of this object is expressed. It is possible to define the rite only after we have defined the belief.

All known religious beliefs, whether simple or complex, present one common characteristic: they presuppose a classification of all the things, real and ideal, of which men think, into two classes or opposed groups, generally designated by two distinct terms which are translated well enough by the words *profane* and *sacred* (*profane, sacré*). This division of the world into two domains, the one containing all that is sacred, the other all that is profane, is the distinctive trait of religious thought; the beliefs, myths, dogmas and legends are either representations or systems of representations which express the nature of sacred things, the virtues and powers which are attributed to them, or their relations with each other and with profane things. But by sacred things one must not understand simply those personal beings which are called gods or spirits; a rock, a tree, a spring, a pebble, a piece of wood, a house, in a word, anything can be sacred. A rite can have this character; in fact, the rite does not exist which does not have it to a certain degree. There are words, expressions and formulae which can be pronounced only by the mouths of consecrated persons; there are gestures and movements which everybody cannot perform. If the Vedic sacrifice has had such an efficacy that, according to mythology, it was the creator of the gods, and not merely a means of winning their favour, it is because it possessed a virtue comparable to that of the most sacred beings. The circle of sacred objects cannot be determined, then, once for all. Its extent varies infinitely, according to the different religions. That is how Buddhism is a religion: in default of gods, it admits the existence of sacred things, namely, the four noble truths and the practices derived from them.[1]

Up to the present we have confined ourselves to enumerating a certain number of sacred things as examples: we must now show by what general characteristics they are to be distinguished from profane things.

One might be tempted, first of all, to define them by the place they are generally assigned in the hierarchy of things. They are naturally considered superior in dignity and power to profane things, and particularly to man, when he is only a man and has nothing sacred about him. One thinks of himself as occupying an inferior and dependent position in relation to them; and surely this conception is not without some truth. Only there is nothing in it which is really characteristic of the sacred. It is not enough that one thing be subordinated to another for the second to be sacred in regard to the first. Slaves are inferior to their masters, subjects to their king, soldiers to their leaders, the miser to his gold, the man ambitious for power to the hands which keep it from him; but if it is sometimes said of a man that he makes a religion of those beings or things whose eminent value and superiority to himself he thus recognizes, it is clear that in any case the word is taken in a metaphorical sense, and that there is nothing in these relations which is really religious.[2]

On the other hand, it must not be lost to view that there are sacred things of every degree, and that there are some in relation to which man feels himself relatively at his ease. An amulet has a sacred character, yet the respect which it inspires is nothing exceptional. Even before his gods, a man is not always in such a marked state of inferiority; for it very frequently happens that he exercises a veritable physical constraint upon them to obtain what he desires. He beats the fetish with which he is not contented, but only to reconcile himself with it again, if in the end it shows itself more docile to the wishes of its adorer.[3] To have rain, he throws stones into the spring or sacred lake where the god of rain is thought to reside; he believes that by this means he forces him to come out and show himself.[4] Moreover, if it is true that man depends upon his gods, this dependence is reciprocal. The gods also have need of man; without offerings and sacrifices they would die. We shall even have occasion to show that this dependence of the gods upon their worshippers is maintained even in the most idealistic religions.

But if a purely hierarchic distinction is a criterion at once too general and too imprecise, there is nothing left with which to characterize the sacred in its relation to the profane except their heterogeneity. However, this heterogeneity is sufficient to characterize this classification of things and to distinguish it from all others, because it is very particular: *it is absolute*. In all the history of human thought there exists no other example of two categories of things so profoundly differentiated or so radically opposed to one another. The traditional opposition of good and bad is nothing beside this; for the good and the bad are only two opposed species of the same class, namely morals, just as sickness and health are two different aspects of the same order of facts, life, while the sacred and the profane have always and everywhere been conceived by the human mind as two distinct classes, as two worlds between which there is nothing in common. The forces which play in one are not simply those which are met with in the other, but a little stronger; they are of a different sort. In different religions, this opposition has been conceived in different ways. Here, to separate these two sorts of things, it has seemed sufficient to localize them in different parts of the physical universe; there, the first have been put into an ideal and transcendental world, while the material world is left in full possession of the others. But howsoever much of the forms of the contrast may vary,[5] the fact of the contrast is universal.

This is not equivalent to saying that a being can never pass from one of these worlds into the other: but the manner in which this passage is effected, when it does take place, puts into relief the essential duality of the two kingdoms. In fact, it implies a veritable metamorphosis. This is notably demonstrated by the initiation rites, such as they are prac-tised by a multitude of peoples. This initiation is a long series of ceremonies with the object of introducing the young man into the religious life: for the first time, he leaves the purely profane world where he passed his first infancy, and enters into the world of sacred things. Now this change of state is thought of, not as a simple and regular development of pre-existent germs, but as a transformation *totius substantiae*—of the whole being. It is said that at this moment the young man dies, that the person that he was ceases to exist, and that another is instantly substituted for it. He is re-born under a new form. Appropriate ceremonies are felt to bring about this death and re-birth, which are not understood in a merely symbolic sense, but are taken literally.[6] Does this not prove that between the profane being which he was and the religious being which he becomes, there is a break of continuity?

This heterogeneity is even so complete that it frequently degenerates into a veritable antagonism. The two worlds are not only conceived of as separate, but as even hostile and jealous rivals of each. Since men cannot fully belong to one except on condition of leav-ing the other completely, they are exhorted to withdraw themselves completely from the profane world, in order to lead an exclusively religious life. Hence comes the monasticism which is artificially organized outside of and apart from the natural environment in which the ordinary man leads the life of this world, in a different one, closed to the first, and nearly its contrary. Hence comes the mystic asceticism whose object is to root out from man all the attachment for the profane world that remains in him. From that come all the forms of religious suicide, the logical working-out of this asceticism; for the only manner of fully escaping the profane life is, after all, to forsake all life.

The opposition of these two classes manifests itself outwardly with a visible sign by which we can easily recognize this very special classification, wherever it exists. Since the idea of the sacred is always and everywhere separated from the idea of the profane in the thought of men, and since we picture a sort of logical chasm between the two, the mind irresistibly refuses to allow the two corresponding things to be confounded, or even to be merely put in contact with each other; for such a promiscuity, or even too direct a conti-guity, would contradict too violently the dissociation of these ideas in the mind. The sacred thing is *par excellence* that which the profane should not touch, and cannot touch with impunity. To be sure, this interdiction cannot go so far as to make all communication between the two worlds impossible; for if the profane could in no way enter into relations with the sacred, this latter could be good for nothing. But, in addition to the fact that this establishment of relations is always a delicate operation in itself, demanding great precautions and a more or less complicated initiation, it is quite impossible, unless the profane is to lose its specific characteristics and become sacred after a fashion and to a certain degree itself. The two classes cannot even approach each other and keep their own nature at the same time.

Thus we arrive at the first criterion of religious beliefs. Undoubtedly there are secondary species within these two fundamental classes which, in their turn, are more or less incompatible with each other. But the real characteristic of religious phenomena is that they always suppose a bipartite division of the whole universe, known and knowable, into two classes which embrace all that exists, but which radically exclude each other. Sacred things are those which the interdictions protect and isolate; profane things, those to which these interdictions are applied and which must remain at a distance from the first. Religious beliefs are the representations which express the nature of sacred things and the relations which they sustain, either with each other or with profane things. Finally, rites are the rules of conduct which prescribe how a man should comport himself in the presence of these sacred objects.

When a certain number of sacred things sustain relations of co-ordination or subordination with each other in such a way as to form a system having a certain unity, but which is not comprised within any other system of the same sort, the totality of these beliefs and their corresponding rites constitutes a religion. From this definition it is seen that a religion is not necessarily contained within one sole and single idea, and does not proceed from one unique principle which, though varying according to the circumstances under which it is applied, is nevertheless at bottom always the same: it is rather a whole made up of distinct and relatively individualized parts. Each homogeneous group of sacred things, or even each sacred thing of some importance, constitutes a centre of organization about which gravitate a group of beliefs and rites, or a particular cult; there is no religion, howsoever unified it may be, which does not recognize a plurality of sacred things. Even Christianity, at least in its Catholic form, admits, in addition to the divine personality which, incidentally, is triple as well as one, the Virgin, angels, saints, souls of the dead, etc. Thus a religion cannot be reduced to one single cult generally, but rather consists in a system of cults, each endowed with a certain autonomy. Also this autonomy is variable. Sometimes they are arranged in a hierarchy, and subordinated to some predominating cult, into which they are finally absorbed; but sometimes, also, they are merely rearranged and united. The religions which we are going to study will furnish us with an example of just this latter sort of organization.

At the same time we find the explanation of how there can be groups of religious phenomena which do not belong to any special religion; it is because they have not been, or are no longer, a part of any religious system. If, for some special reason, one of the cults of which we just spoke happens to be maintained while the group of which it was a part disappears, it survives only in a disintegrated condition. That is what has happened to many agrarian cults which have survived themselves as folk-lore. In certain cases, it is not even a cult, but a simple ceremony or particular rite which persists in this way.[7]

Although this definition is only preliminary, it permits us to see in what terms the problem which necessarily dominates the science of religions should be stated. When we believed that sacred beings could be distinguished from others merely by the greater intensity of the powers attributed to them, the question of how men came to imagine them was sufficiently simple: it was enough to demand which forces had, because of their exceptional energy, been able to strike the human imagination forcefully enough to inspire religious sentiments. But if, as we have sought to establish, sacred things differ in nature from profane things, if they have a wholly different essence, then the problem is more complex. For we must first of all ask what has been able to lead men to see in the world two heterogeneous and incompatible worlds, though nothing in sensible experience seems able to suggest the idea of so radical a duality to them.

. . .

The really religious beliefs are always common to a determined group, which makes profession of adhering to them and of practising the rites connected with them. They are not merely received individually by all the members of this group; they are something belonging to the group, and they make its unity. The individuals which compose it feel themselves united to each other by the simple fact that they have a common faith. A society whose members are united by the fact that they think in the same way in regard to the sacred world and its relations with the profane world, and by the fact that they translate these common ideas into common practices, is what is called a Church. In all history, we do not find a single religion without a Church. Sometimes the Church is strictly national, sometimes it passes the frontiers; sometimes it embraces an entire people (Rome, Athens, the Hebrews), sometimes it embraces only a part of them (the Christian societies since the advent of Protestantism); sometimes it is directed by a corps of priests, sometimes it is almost completely devoid of any official directing body.[8] But wherever we observe the religious life, we find that it has a definite group as its foundation. Even the so-called private cults, such as the domestic cult or the cult of a corporation, satisfy this condition; for they are always celebrated by a group, the family or the corporation. Moreover, even these particular religions are ordinarily only special forms of a more general religion which embraces all;[9] these restricted Churches are in reality only chapels of a vaster Church which, by reason of this very extent, merits this name still more.[10]

. . .

When a methodical analysis is made of the doctrines of any Church whatsoever, sooner or later we come upon those concerning private cults. So these are not two religions of different types, and turned in opposite directions; both are made up of the same ideas and the same principles, here applied to circumstances which are of interest to the group as a whole, there to the life of the individual. This solidarity is even so close that among certain peoples,[11] the ceremonies by which the faithful first enter into communication with their protecting geniuses are mixed with rites whose public character is incontestable, namely the rites of initiation.[12]

There still remain those contemporary aspirations towards a religion which would consist entirely in internal and subjective states, and which would be constructed freely by each of us. But howsoever real these aspirations may be, they cannot affect our definition, for this is to be applied only to facts already realized, and not to uncertain possibilities. One can define religions such as they are, or such as they have been, but not such as they more or less vaguely tend to become. It is possible that this religious individualism is destined to be realized in facts; but before we can say just how far this may be the case, we must first know what religion is, of what elements it is made up, from what causes it results, and what function it fulfils—all questions whose solution cannot be foreseen before the threshold of our study has been passed. It is only at the close of this study that we can attempt to anticipate the future.

Thus we arrive at the following definition: *A religion is a unified system of beliefs and practices relative to sacred things, that is to say, things set apart and forbidden—beliefs and practices which unite into one single moral community called a Church, all those who adhere to them.* The second element which thus finds a place in our definition is no less essential than the first; for by showing that the idea of religion is inseparable from that of the Church, it makes it clear that religion should be an eminently collective thing.[13]

Origin of the Idea of the Totemic Principle or Mana

The proposition established in the preceding chapter determines the terms in which the problem of the origins of totemism should be posed. Since totemism is everywhere dominated by the idea of a quasi-divine principle, imminent in certain categories of men and things and thought of under the form of an animal or vegetable, the explanation of this religion is essentially the explanation of this belief; to arrive at this, we must seek to learn how men have been led to construct this idea and out of what materials they have constructed it.

It is obviously not out of the sensations which the things serving as totems are able to arouse in the mind; we have shown that these things are frequently insignificant. The lizard, the caterpillar, the rat, the ant, the frog, the turkey, the beam-fish, the plum-tree, the cockatoo, etc., to cite only those names which appear frequently in the lists of Australian totems, are not of a nature to produce upon men these great and strong impressions which in a way resemble religious emotions and which impress a sacred character upon the objects they create. It is true that this is not the case with the stars and the great atmospheric phenomena, which have, on the contrary, all that is necessary to strike the imagination forcibly; but as a matter of fact, these serve only very exceptionally as totems. It is even probable that they were very slow in taking this office. So it is not the intrinsic nature of the thing whose name the clan bears that marked it out to become the object of a cult. Also, if the sentiments which it inspired were really the determining cause of the totemic rites and beliefs, it would be the pre-eminently sacred thing; the animals or plants employed as totems would play an eminent part in the religious life. But we know that the centre of the cult is actually elsewhere. It is the figurative representations of this plant or animal and the totemic emblems and symbols of every sort, which have the greatest sanctity; so it is in them that is found the source of that religious nature, of which the real objects represented by these emblems receive only a reflection.

Thus the totem is before all a symbol, a material expression of something else. But of what?

From the analysis to which we have been giving our attention, it is evident that it expresses and symbolizes two different sorts of things. In the first place, it is the outward and visible form of what we have called the totemic principle or god. But it is also the symbol of the determined society called the clan. It is its flag; it is the sign by which each clan distinguishes itself from the others, the visible mark of its personality, a mark borne by everything which is a part of the clan under any title whatsoever, men, beasts or things. So if it is at once the symbol of the god and of the society, is that not because the god and the society are only one? How could the emblem of the group have been able to become the figure of this quasi-divinity, if the group and the divinity were two distinct realities? The god of the clan, the totemic principle, can therefore be nothing else than the clan itself, personified and represented to the imagination under the visible form of the animal or vegetable which serves as totem.

. . .

Now the ways of action to which society is strongly enough attached to impose them upon its members, are, by that very fact, marked with a distinctive sign provocative of respect. Since they are elaborated in common, the vigour with which they have been thought of by each particular mind is retained in all the other minds, and reciprocally. The representations which express them within each of us have an intensity which no purely private states of consciousness could ever attain; for they have the strength of the innumerable individual representations which have served to form each of them. It is society who speaks through the mouths of those who affirm them in our presence; it is society whom we hear in hearing them; and the voice of all has an accent which that of one alone could never have. The very violence with which society reacts, by the way of blame or material suppression, against every attempted dissidence, contributes to strengthening its empire by manifesting the common conviction through this burst of ardour. In a word, when something is the object of such a state of opinion, the representation which each individual has of it gains a power of action from its origins and the conditions in which it was born, which even those feel who do not submit themselves to it. It tends to repel the representations which contradict it, and it keeps them at a distance; on the other hand, it commands those acts which will realize it, and it does so, not by a material coercion or by the perspective of something of this sort, but by the simple radiation of the mental energy which it contains. It has an efficacy coming solely from its psychical properties, and it is by just this sign that moral authority is recognized. So opinion, primarily a social thing, is a source of authority, and it might even be asked whether all authority is not the daughter of opinion.[14] It may be objected that science is often the antagonist of opinion, whose errors it combats and rectifies. But it cannot succeed in this task if it does not have sufficient authority, and it can obtain this authority only from opinion itself. If a people did not have faith in science, all the scientific demonstrations in the world would be without any influence whatsoever over their minds. Even to-day, if science happened to resist a very strong current of public opinion, it would risk losing its credit there.[15]

Since it is in spiritual ways that social pressure exercises itself, it could not fail to give men the idea that outside themselves there exist one or several powers, both moral and, at the same time, efficacious, upon which they depend. They must think of these powers, at least in part, as outside themselves, for these address them in a tone of command and sometimes even order them to do violence to their most natural inclinations. It is undoubtedly true that if they were able to see that these influences which they feel emanate from society, then the mythological system of interpretations would never be born. But social action follows ways that are too circuitous and obscure, and employs psychical mechanisms that are too complex to allow the ordinary observer to see when it comes. As long as scientific analysis does not come to teach it to them, men know well that they are acted upon, but they do not know by whom. So they must invent by themselves the idea of these powers with which they feel themselves in connection, and from that, we are able to catch a glimpse of the way by which they were led to represent them under forms that are really foreign to their nature and to transfigure them by thought.

But a god is not merely an authority upon whom we depend; it is a force upon which our strength relies. The man who has obeyed his god and who for this reason believes the god is with him, approaches the world with confidence and with the feeling of an increased energy. Likewise, social action does not confine itself to demanding sacrifices, privations and efforts from us. For the collective force is not entirely outside of us; it does not act upon us wholly from without; but rather, since society cannot exist except in and through individual consciousness,[16] this force must also penetrate us and organize itself within us; it thus becomes an integral part of our being and by that very fact this is elevated and magnified.

. . .

Since religious force is nothing other than the collective and anonymous force of the clan, and since this can be represented in the mind only in the form of the totem, the totemic emblem is like the visible body of the god. Therefore it is from it that those kindly and dreadful actions seem to emanate, which the cult seeks to provoke or prevent; consequently, it is to it that the cult is addressed. This is the explanation of why it holds the first place in the series of sacred things.

But the clan, like every other sort of society, can live only in and through the individual consciousnesses that compose it. So if religious force, in so far as it is conceived as incorporated in the totemic emblem, appears to be outside of the individuals and to be endowed with a sort of transcendence over them, it, like the clan of which it is the symbol, can be realized only in and through them; in this sense, it is imminent in them and they necessarily represent it as such. They feel it present and active within them, for it is this which raises them to a superior life. This is why men have believed that they contain within them a principle comparable to the one residing in the totem, and consequently, why they have attributed a sacred character to themselves, but one less marked than that of the emblem. It is because the emblem is the pre-eminent source of the religious life; the man participates in it only indirectly, as he is well aware; he takes into account the fact that the force that transports him into the world of sacred things is not inherent in him, but comes to him from the outside.

But for still another reason, the animals or vegetables of the totemic species should have the same character and even to a higher degree. If the totemic principle is nothing else than the clan, it is the clan thought of under the material form of the totemic emblem; now this form is also that of the concrete beings whose name the clan bears. Owing to this resemblance, they could not fail to evoke sentiments analogous to those aroused by the emblem itself. Since the latter is the object of a religious respect, they too should inspire respect of the same sort and appear to be sacred. Having external forms so nearly identical, it would be impossible for the native not to attribute to them forces of the same nature. It is therefore forbidden to kill or eat the totemic animal, since its flesh is believed to have the positive virtues resulting from the rites; it is because it resembles the emblem of the clan, that is to say, it is in its own image. And since the animal naturally resembles the emblem more than the man does, it is placed on a superior rank in the hierarchy of sacred things. Between these two beings there is undoubtedly a close relationship, for they both partake of the same essence: both incarnate something of the totemic principle. However, since the principle itself is conceived under an animal form, the animal seems to incarnate it more fully than the man. Therefore, if men consider it and treat it as a brother, it is at least as an elder brother.[17]

But even if the totemic principle has its preferred seat in a determined species of animal or vegetable, it cannot remain localized there. A sacred character is to a high degree contagious; it therefore spreads out from the totemic being to everything that is closely or remotely connected with it. The religious sentiments inspired by the animal are communicated to the substances upon which it is nourished and which serve to make or remake its flesh and blood, to the things that resemble it, and to the different beings with which it has constant relations. Thus, little by little, sub-totems are attached to the totems and from the cosmological systems expressed by the primitive classifications. At last, the whole world is divided up among the totemic principles of each tribe.

We are now able to explain the origin of the ambiguity of religious forces as they appear in history, and how they are physical as well as human, moral as well as material. They are moral powers because they are made up entirely of the impressions this moral being, the group, arouses in those other moral beings, its individual members; they do not translate the manner in which physical things affect our senses, but the way in which the collective consciousness acts upon individual consciousnesses. Their authority is only one form of the moral ascendancy of society over its members. But, on the other, since they are conceived of under material forms, they could not fail to be regarded as closely related to material things.[18] Therefore they dominate the two worlds. Their residence is in men, but at the same time they are the vital principles of things. They animate minds and discipline them, but it is also they who make plants grow and animals reproduce. It is this double nature which has enabled religion to be like the womb from which come all the leading germs of human civilization. Since it has been made to embrace all of reality, the physical world as well as the moral one, the forces that move bodies as well as those that move minds have been conceived in a religious form. That is how the most diverse methods and practices, both those that make possible the continuation of the moral life (law, morals, beaux-arts) and those serving the material life (the natural, technical and practical sciences), are either directly or indirectly derived from religion.[19]

. . .

But collective representations very frequently attribute to the things to which they are attached qualities which do not exist under any form or to any degree. Out of the commonest object, they can make a most powerful sacred being.

Yet the powers which are thus conferred, though purely ideal, act as though they were real; they determine the conduct of men with the same degree of necessity as physical forces. The Arunta who has been rubbed with his churinga feels himself stronger; he is stronger. If he has eaten the flesh of an animal which, though perfectly healthy, is forbidden to him, he will feel himself sick, and may die of it. Surely the soldier who falls while defending his flag does not believe that he sacrifices himself for a bit of cloth. This is all because social thought, owing to the imperative authority that is in it, has an efficacy that individual thought could never have; by the power which it has over our minds, it can make us see things in whatever light it pleases; it adds to reality or deducts from it according to the circumstances. Thus there is one division of nature where the formula of idealism is applicable almost to the letter: this is the social kingdom. Here more than anywhere else, the idea is the reality. Even in this case, of course, idealism is not true without modification. We can never escape the duality of our nature and free ourselves completely from physical necessities: in order to express our own ideas to ourselves, it is necessary, as has been shown above, that we fix them upon material things which symbolize them. But here the part of matter is reduced to a minimum. The object serving as support for the idea is not much in comparison with the ideal superstructure, beneath which it disappears, and also, it counts for nothing in the superstructure. This is what that pseudodelirium consists in, which we find at the bottom of so many collective representations: it is only a form of this essential idealism.[20] So it is not properly called a delirium, for the ideas thus objectified are well founded, not in the nature of the material things upon which they settle themselves, but in the nature of society.

We are now able to understand how the totemic principle, and in general, every religious force, comes to be outside of the object in which it resides. It is because the idea of it is in no way made up of the impressions directly produced by this thing upon our senses or minds. Religious force is only the sentiment inspired by the group in its members, but projected outside of the consciousnesses that experience them, and objectified. To be objectified, they are fixed upon some object which thus becomes sacred; but any object might fulfil this function. In principle, there are none whose nature predestines them to it to the exclusion of all others; but also there are none that are necessarily impossible.[21] Everything depends upon the circumstances which lead the sentiment creating religious ideas to establish itself here or there, upon this point or upon that one. Therefore, the sacred character assumed by an object is not implied in the intrinsic properties of this latter: *it is added to them*. The world of religious things is not one particular aspect of empirical nature; *it is superimposed upon it*.

This conception of the religious, finally, allows us to explain an important principle found at the bottom of a multitude of myths and rites, and which may be stated thus: when a sacred thing is subdivided, each of its parts remains equal to the thing itself. In other words, as far as religious thought is concerned, the part is equal to the whole; it has the same powers, the same efficacy. The debris of a relic has the same virtue as a relic in good condition. The smallest drop of blood contains the same active principle as the whole thing. The soul, as we shall see, may be broken up into nearly as many pieces as there are organs or tissues in the organism; each of these partial souls is worth a whole soul. This conception would be inexplicable if the sacredness of something were due to the constituent properties of the thing itself; for in that case, it should vary with this thing, increasing and decreasing with it. But if the virtues it is believed to possess are not intrinsic in it, and if they come from certain sentiments which it brings to mind and symbolizes, though these originate outside of it, then, since it has no need of determined dimensions to play this role of reminder, it will have the same value whether it is entire or not. Since the part makes us think of the whole, it evokes the same sentiments as the whole. A mere fragment of the flag represents the fatherland just as well as the flag itself: so it is sacred in the same way and to the same degree.[22]

. . .

It is religion that was the agent of this transfiguration; it is religious beliefs that have substituted for the world, as it is perceived by the senses, another different one. This is well shown by the case of totemism. The fundamental thing in this religion is that the men of the clan and the different beings who form the totemic emblems reproduce pass as being made of the same essence. Now when this belief was once admitted, the bridge between the different kingdoms was already built. The man was represented as a sort of animal or plant; the plants and animals were thought of as the relatives of men, or rather, all these beings, so different for the senses, were thought of as participating in a single nature. So this remarkable aptitude for confusing things that seem to be obviously distinct comes from the fact that the first forces with which the human intellect has peopled the world were elaborated by religion. Since these were made up of elements taken from the different kingdoms, men conceived a principle common to the most heterogeneous things, which thus became endowed with a sole and single essence.

But we also know that these religious conceptions are the result of determined social causes. Since the clan cannot exist without a name and an emblem, and since this emblem is always before the eyes of men, it is upon this, and the objects whose image it is, that the sentiments which society arouses in its members are fixed. Men were thus compelled to represent the collective force, whose action they felt, in the form of the thing serving as flag to the group. Therefore, in the idea of this force were mixed up the most different kingdoms; in one sense, it was essentially human, since it was made up of human ideas and sentiments; but at the same time, it could not fail to appear as closely related to the animate or inanimate beings who gave it its outward form. Moreover, the cause whose action we observe here is not peculiar to totemism; there is no society where it is not active. In a general way, a collective sentiment can become conscious of itself only by being fixed upon some material object; but by this very fact, it participates in the nature of this object, and reciprocally, the object participates in its nature. So it was social necessity which brought about the fusion of notions appearing distinct at first, and social life has facilitated this fusion by the great mental effervescences it determines.[23] This is one more proof that logical understanding is a function of society, for it takes the forms and attitudes that this latter presses upon it.

. . .

But this circle will appear still more natural to us, and we shall understand its meaning and the reason for its existence still better if, carrying our analysis still farther and substituting for the religious symbols the realities which they represent, we investigate how these behave in the rite. If, as we have attempted to establish, the sacred principle is nothing more nor less than society transfigured and personified, it should be possible to interpret the ritual in lay and social terms. And, as a matter of fact, social life, just like the ritual, moves in a circle. On the one hand, the individual gets from society the best part of himself, all that gives him a distinct character and a special place among other beings, his intellectual and moral culture. If we should withdraw from men their language, sciences, arts and moral beliefs, they would drop to the rank of animals. So the characteristic attributes of human nature come from society. But, on the other hand, society exists and lives only in and through individuals. If the idea of society were extinguished in individual minds and the beliefs, traditions and aspirations of the group were no longer felt and shared by the individuals, society would die. We can say of it what we just said of the divinity: it is real only in so far as it has a place in human consciousnesses, and this place is whatever one we may give it. We now see the real reason why the gods cannot do without their worshippers any more than these can do without their gods; it is because society, of which the gods are only a symbolic expression, cannot do without individuals any more than these can without society.

Here we touch the solid rock upon which all the cults are built and which has caused their persistence ever since human societies have existed. When we see what religious rites consist of and towards what they seem to tend, we demand with astonishment how men have been able to imagine them, and especially how they can remain so faithfully attached to them. Whence could the illusion have come that with a few grains of sand thrown to the wind, or a few drops of blood shed upon a rock or the stone of an altar, it is possible to maintain the life of an animal species or of a god? We have undoubtedly made a step in advance towards the solution of this problem when we have discovered, behind these outward and apparently unreasonable movements, a mental mechanism which gives them a meaning and a moral significance. But we are in no way assured that this mechanism itself does not consist in a simple play of hallucinatory images. We have pointed out the psychological process which leads the believers to imagine that the rite causes the spiritual forces of which they have need to be reborn about them; but it does not follow from the fact that this belief is psychologically explicable that it has any objective value. If we are to see in the efficacy attributed to the rites anything more than the product of a chronic delirium with which humanity has abused itself, we must show that the effect of the cult really is to recreate periodically a moral being upon which we depend as it depends on us. Now this being does exist: it is society.

. . .

In résumé, the two poles of the religious life correspond to the two opposed states through which all social life passes. Between the propitiously sacred and the unpropitiously sacred there is the same contrast as between the states of collective well-being and ill-being. But since both are equally collective, there is, between the mythological constructions symbolizing them, an intimate kinship of nature. The sentiments held in common vary from extreme dejection to extreme joy, from painful irritation to ecstatic enthusiasm; but, in any case, there is a communion of minds and a mutual comfort resulting from this communion. The fundamental process is always the same; only circumstances colour it differently. So, at bottom, it is the unity and the diversity of social life which make the simultaneous unity and the diversity of sacred beings and things.

This ambiguity, moreover, is not peculiar to the idea of sacredness alone; something of this characteristic has been found in all the rites which we have been studying. Of course it was essential to distinguish them; to confuse them would have been to misunderstand the multiple aspects of the religious life. But, on the other hand, howsoever different they may be, there is no break of continuity between them. Quite on the contrary, they overlap one another and may even replace each other mutually. We have already shown how the rites of oblation and communion, the imitative rites and the commemorative rites frequently fulfil the same function. One might imagine that the negative cult, at least, would be more sharply separated from the positive cult; yet we have seen that the former may produce positive effects, identical with those produced by the latter. The same results are obtained by fasts, abstinences and self-mutilations as by communions, oblations and commemorations. Inversely, offerings and sacrifices imply privations and renunciations of every sort. The continuity between ascetic and piacular rites is even more apparent: both are made up of sufferings, accepted or undergone, to which an analogous efficacy is attributed. Thus the practices, like the beliefs, are not arranged in two separate classes. Howsoever complex the outward manifestations of the religious life may be, at bottom it is one and simple. It responds everywhere to one and the same need, and is everywhere derived from one and the same mental state. In all its forms, its object is to raise man above himself and to make him lead a life superior to that which he would lead, if he followed only his own individual whims: beliefs express this life in representations; rites organize it and regulate its working.

NOTES

1. Not to mention the sage and the saint who practise these truths and for that reason are sacred.
2. This is not saying that these relations cannot take a religious character. But they do not do so necessarily.
3. Schultze, *Fetichismus*: 129.
4. Examples of these usages will be found in Frazer, *Golden Bough*, 2nd ed., 1: 81ff.
5. The conception according to which the profane is opposed to the sacred, just as the irrational is to the rational, or the intelligible to the mysterious, is only one of the forms under which this opposition is expressed. Science being once constituted, it has taken a profane character, especially in the eyes of the Christian religions; from that it appears as though it could not be applied to sacred things.
6. See Frazer, 'On Some Ceremonies of the Central Australian Tribes' in *Australian Association for the Advancement of Science*, 1901: 313ff. This conception is also of an extreme generality. In India, the simple participation in the sacrificial act has the same effect; the sacrificer, by the mere act of entering within the circle of sacred things, changes his personality. (See Hubert and Mauss,

'Essai sur le Sacrifice' in *Année Sociologique* II: 101.)

7. This is the case with certain marriage and funeral rites, for example.

8. Undoubtedly it is rare that a ceremony does not have some director at the moment when it is celebrated; even in the most crudely organized societies there are generally certain men whom the importance of their social position points out to exercise a directing influence over the religious life (for example, the chiefs of the local groups of certain Australian societies). But this attribution of functions is still very uncertain.

9. At Athens, the gods to whom the domestic cult was addressed were only specialized forms of the gods of the city. In the same way, in the Middle Ages, the patrons of the guilds were saints of the calendar.

10. For the name Church is ordinarily applied only to a group whose common beliefs refer to a circle of more special affairs.

11. Notably among numerous Indian tribes of North America.

12. This statement of fact does not touch the question whether exterior and public religion is not merely the development of an interior and personal religion which was the primitive fact, or whether, on the contrary, the second is not the projection of the first into individual consciences. . . . For the moment, we confine ourselves to remarking that the individual cult is presented to the observer as an element of, and something dependent upon, the collective cult.

13. It is by this that our present definition is connected to the one we have already proposed in the *Année Sociologique*. In this other work we defined religious beliefs exclusively by their obligatory character; but, as we shall show, this obligation evidently comes from the fact that these beliefs are the possession of a group which imposes them upon its members. The two definitions are thus in a large part the same. If we have thought it best to propose a new one, it is because the first was too formal, and neglected the contents of the religious representations too much. It will be seen, in the discussions which follow, how important it is to put this characteristic into evidence at once. Moreover, if their imperative character is really a distinctive trait of religious beliefs, it allows of an infinite number of degrees; consequently there are even cases where it is not easily perceptible. Hence come difficulties and embarrassments which are avoided by substituting for this criterion the one we now employ.

14. This is the case at least with all moral authority recognized as such by the group as a whole.

15. We hope that this analysis and those which follow will put an end to an inexact interpretation of our thought, from which more than one misunderstanding has resulted. Since we have made constraint the *outward sign* by which social facts can be the most easily recognized and distinguished from the facts of individual psychology, it has been assumed that according to our opinion, physical constraint is the essential thing for social life. As a matter of fact, we have never considered it more than the material and apparent expression of an interior and profound fact which is wholly ideal: this is *moral authority*. The problem of sociology—if we can speak of *a* sociological problem—consists in seeking, among the different forms of external constraint, the different sorts of moral authority corresponding to them and in discovering the causes which have determined these latter. The particular question which we are treating in this present work has as its principal object, the discovery of the form under which that particular variety of moral authority which is inherent in all that is religious has been born, and out of what elements it is made. It will be seen presently that even if we do make social pressure one of the distinctive characteristics of sociological phenomena, we do not mean to say that it is the only one. We shall

show another aspect of the collective life, nearly opposite to the preceding one, but none the less real.

16. Of course this does not mean to say that the collective consciousness does not have distinctive characteristics of its own (on this point, see 'Représentations individuelles et représentations collectives' in *Revue de Métaphysique et de Morale,* 1898: 273ff.).

17. Thus we see that this fraternity is the logical consequence of totemism, rather than its basis. Men have not imagined their duties toward the animals of the totemic species because they regarded them as kindred, but have imagined the kinship to explain the nature of the beliefs and rites of which they were the object. The animal was considered a relative of the man because it was a sacred being like the man, but it was not treated as a sacred being because it was regarded as a relative.

18. At the bottom of this conception there is a well-founded and persistent sentiment. Modern science also tends more and more to admit that the duality of man and nature does not exclude their unity, and that physical and moral forces, though distinct, are closely related. We undoubtedly have a different conception of this unity and relationship than the primitive, but beneath these different symbols, the truth affirmed by the two is the same.

19. We say that this derivation is sometimes indirect on account of the industrial methods which, in a large number of cases, seem to be derived from religion through the intermediacy of magic (see Hubert and Mauss, 'Théorie générale de la Magie', *Année Sociol.* VII: 144ff.); for, as we believe, magic forces are only a special form of religious forces. We shall have occasion to return to this point several times.

20. Thus we see how erroneous those theories are which, like the geographical materialism of Ratzel (see especially his *Politische Geographie*), seek to derive all social life from its material foundation (either economic or territorial). They commit an error precisely similar to the one committed by Maudsley in individual psychology. Just as this latter reduced all the psychical life of the individual to a mere epiphenomenon of his psysiological basis, they seek to reduce the whole psychical life of the group to its psysical basis. But they forget that ideas are realities and forces, and that collective representations are forces even more powerful than individual representations. On this point, see our 'Représentations individuelles et représentations collectives' in the *Revue de Métaphysique et de Morale',* May 1898.

21. Even the *excreta* have a religious character. See Preuss, *Der Ursprung der Religion und Kunst*, especially ch. ii, entitled 'Der Zauber der defàkation' (*Globus*, LXXXVI 325ff.).

22. This principle has passed from religion into magic; it is the *totem ex parte* of the alchemists.

23. Another cause has contributed much to this fusion; this is the extreme contagiousness of religious forces. They seize upon every object within their reach, whatever it may be. Thus a single religious force many animate the most diverse things which, by that very fact, become closely connected and classified within a single group.

MAX WEBER

1864–1920
GERMANY

Major Works

1904 *The Protestant Ethic and the Spirit of Capitalism*
1916 *The Sociology of Religion*
1922 *Economy and Society*
1924 *General Economic History*
1949 *The Methodology of the Social Sciences*

> Not ideas, but material and ideal interests, directly govern men's con-
> duct. Yet very frequently the 'world images' that have been created by
> 'ideas' have, like switchmen, determined the tracks along which action
> has been pushed by the dynamic of interest.[1]

> The increasing intellectualization and rationalization do *not*, therefore,
> indicate an increased and general knowledge of the conditions under
> which one lives.
>   It means something else, namely, the knowledge or belief that if
> one but wished one *could* learn it at any time. Hence, it means that
> principally there are no mysterious incalculable forces that come into
> play, but rather that one can, in principle, master all things by calcula-
> tion. This means that the world is disenchanted.[2]
>
> —*Max Weber*

It has been said that Max Weber spent a good deal of his intellectual life joust-
ing with the ghost of Marx. As the first of the quotations above indicates, there
is a certain challenge to Marx in Weber's work, but the work is nevertheless
independent and classically self-directed. As a theorist whose major works fall
into what is presently called macro theory, Weber prepares the ground for the
movement into micro-sociological investigation. He moves from the almost
philosophical conceptualization related to the 'rationalization of the world'
with insightful discussion of bureaucracy and forms of domination, to the lines
of social action experienced in interaction and the meanings that people bring
to these actions. His work initiates the development of interpretive theory that
has led sociology towards negotiated, interpretive understandings of micro situations in society.

Social Action, Meaning, and Sociological Method

One advantage of Weber's perspective in sociology is its weaving back and forth between social structure and the actions and meanings people bring to or give situations. A crucial element of his work is his notion of ideal types—analytical constructs for explanation of social phenomena. For example, in his work on social action he elaborates four main types: purposive-rational action (e.g., scientific), value-rational (e.g., religious), affective action (e.g., emotional), and traditional (e.g., habitual). Ideal typical forms of action fall into two categories that Weber describes as the morality of responsibility (i.e., instrumental action) and the morality of conviction or ultimate ends (i.e., expressive action).

In observing social action, Weber emphasizes the concept of *verstehen*—meaning or understanding. Actors in a situation give meaning to and make meaning in terms of their understanding; researchers need to take this into account in such situations. Perhaps one of the most contested areas of Weber's thought is the methodological notion of value-neutrality in social science. He suggests that the researcher must bring passion to the choice of field of study, but then become a detached observer using value-free methodological procedures. His definition of sociology encapsulates many of these methodological ideas:

> [Sociology is] a science which attempts the interpretive understanding of social action in order thereby to arrive at a causal explanation of its course and effects. In 'action' is included all human behaviour when and insofar as the acting individual attaches a subjective meaning to it.[3]

Domination, Legitimacy, Bureaucracy, and the Iron Cage

A major contribution to modern thought is Weber's study of power relationships, authority structures, and the general understanding of bureaucracy. We now take for granted many of the understandings that he brought to the fore. Power, 'the possibility of imposing one's own will upon the behaviour of other persons',[4] in Weber's conceptualization needs to be placed within a legitimizing framework; it implies the necessity of consent. This interpretation of the dynamics of authority structures is clearly illustrated by Reinhard Bendix's comment on the translation of *Herrschaft*:

> It is difficult to find an English equivalent for the German term *Herrschaft* which emphasizes equally the ruler's exercise of power and the follower's acceptance of that exercise as legitimate, a meaning which goes back to the relations between lord and vassal under feudalism. The English terms 'domination' and 'authority' are not equally apt, because the first emphasizes the power of command whether or not consent is present, while the second emphasizes the right of command

and hence implies the follower's acceptance almost to the exclusion of the ruler's very real power. Weber wished to emphasize that both power and consent are problematic, but as a realist in the analysis of power he would have been critical of any translation that tended to obscure the 'threat of force' present in all relations between superiors and subordinates. For these reasons, I prefer the term 'domination'.[5]

Bendix's useful articulation of this concept clarifies the structuring of power within organizations and social groups. The domination of people in organizations is not simply a process of intimidation or the threat of force; the establishment of consent recognizes the essential importance of legitimacy and legitimating structures within social interactions. Weber presents three grounds for authority or domination: rational-legal (e.g., contemporary bureaucracy), traditional (e.g., tribal chiefs), and charismatic (e.g., religious or political figures). Weber not only describes the essential structures of domination that accompany each type, he also specifies the apparatus necessary for their efficient functioning. Of course, these bureaucratic structures fetter human spontaneity and democratic action. Such structures give rise to the notion of the 'iron cage', the conformity of the individual in social institutions.

Sociology of Religion

Perhaps Max Weber is best known for his early work, *The Protestant Ethic and the Spirit of Capitalism*. But he studied and wrote extensively on the major religions of the world. Examining the origins of capitalism, Weber confronts Marx's economic determinism and argues the power of ideas or religious ideologies to provide the nurturing consciousness necessary to advance capitalism. Calvinism, in Weber's analysis, provided the ideologically fertile soil for the inculcation of the spirit of capitalism. Predestination, the concept of being destined for heaven or hell; prosperity as proof of having been chosen; the concept of a vocation or calling; inner-worldly asceticism or self-denial: all of these Calvinist tenets 'led to' the necessary productivity and capital accumulation for the integration of capitalist economics into society.

Weber's legacy to modern sociology is truly wide-ranging. His search for interpretive sociological understanding, through the recognition of the multiplicity of causes for social actions and events—causal pluralism—has broadened the scope of sociological investigation.

Notes

1. H.H. Gerth and C. Wright Mills, *From Max Weber: Essays in Sociology* (New York: Oxford University Press, 1946), 280.
2. Ibid., 139.

3. Max Weber, *The Theory of Social and Economic Organization*, ed. T. Parsons (London: Collier Macmillan, 1942), 88.
4. Max Weber, *Economy and Society*, eds Guenther Roth and Claus Witlich (Berkeley: University of California Press, 1972), 942.
5. Reinhard Bendix, *Max Weber: An Intellectual Portrait* (London: Methuen, 1960), 481–2.

CLASS, STATUS, PARTY

1: Economically Determined Power and the Social Order

Law exists when there is a probability that an order will be upheld by a specific staff of men who will use physical or psychical compulsion with the intention of obtaining conformity with the order, or of inflicting sanctions for infringement of it.[1] The structure of every legal order directly influences the distribution of power, economic or otherwise, within its respective community. This is true of all legal orders and not only that of the state. In general, we understand by 'power' the chance of a man or of a number of men to realize their own will in a communal action even against the resistance of others who are participating in the action.

'Economically conditioned' power is not, of course, identical with 'power' as such. On the contrary, the emergence of economic power may be the consequence of power existing on other grounds. Man does not strive for power only in order to enrich himself economically. Power, including economic power, may be valued 'for its own sake.' Very frequently the striving for power is also conditioned by the social 'honor' it entails. Not all power, however, entails social honor: The typical American Boss, as well as the typical big speculator, deliberately relinquishes social honor. Quite generally, 'mere economic' power, and especially 'naked' money power, is by no means a recognized basis of social honor. Nor is power the only basis of social honor. Indeed, social honor, or prestige, may even be the basis of political or economic power, and very frequently has been. Power, as well as honor, may be guaranteed by the legal order, but, at least normally, it is not their primary source. The legal order is rather an additional factor that enhances the chance to hold power or honor; but it cannot always secure them.

The way in which social honor is distributed in a community between typical groups participating in this distribution we may call the 'social order'. The social order and the economic order are, of course, similarly related to the 'legal order'. However, the social and the economic order are not identical. The economic order is for us merely the way in which economic goods and services are distributed and used. The social order is of course conditioned by the economic order to a high degree, and in its turn reacts upon it.

Now: 'classes', 'status groups', and 'parties' are phenomena of the distribution of power within a community.

2: Determination of Class-Situation by Market-Situation

In our terminology, 'classes' are not communities; they merely represent possible, and frequent, bases for communal action. We may speak of a 'class' when (1) a number of people have in common a specific causal component of their life chances, in so far as (2) this component is represented exclusively by economic interests in the possession of goods and opportunities for income, and (3) is represented under the conditions of the commodity or labor markets. [These points refer to 'class situation', which we may express more briefly as the typical chance for a supply of goods, external living conditions, and personal life experiences, in so far as this chance is determined by the amount and kind of power, or lack of such, to dispose of goods or skills for the sake of income in a given economic order. The term 'class' refers to any group of people that is found in the same class situation.]

It is the most elemental economic fact that the way in which the disposition over material property is distributed among a plurality of people, meeting competitively in the market for the purpose of exchange, in itself creates specific life chances. According to the law of marginal utility this mode of distribution excludes the non-owners from competing for highly valued goods; it favors the owners and, in fact, gives to them a monopoly to acquire such goods. Other things being equal, this mode of distribution monopolizes the opportunities for profitable deals for all those who, provided with goods, do not necessarily have to exchange them. It increases, at least generally, their power in price wars with those who, being propertyless, have nothing to offer but their services in native form or goods in a form constituted through their own labor, and who above all are compelled to get rid of these products in order barely to subsist. This mode of distribution gives to the propertied a monopoly on the possibility of transferring property from the sphere of use as a 'fortune', to the sphere of 'capital goods'; that is, it gives them the entrepreneurial function and all chances to share directly or indirectly in returns on capital. All this holds true within the area in which pure market conditions prevail. 'Property' and 'lack of property' are, therefore, the basic categories of all class situations. It does not matter whether these two categories become effective in price wars or in competitive struggles.

Within these categories, however, class situations are further differentiated: on the one hand, according to the kind of property that is usable for returns; and, on the other hand, according to the kind of services that can be offered in the market. Ownership of domestic buildings; productive establishments; warehouses; stores; agriculturally usable land, large and small holdings—quantitative differences with possibly qualitative consequences—; ownership of mines; cattle; men (slaves); disposition over mobile instruments of production, or capital goods of all sorts, especially money or objects that can be exchanged for money easily and at any time; disposition over products of one's own labor or of others' labor differing according to their various distances from consumability; disposition over transferable monopolies of any kind—all these distinctions differentiate the class situations of the propertied just as does the 'meaning' which they can and do give to the utilization of property, especially to property which has money equivalence. Accordingly, the propertied, for instance, may belong to the class of rentiers or to the class of entrepreneurs.

Those who have no property but who offer services are differentiated just as much according to their kinds of services as according to the way in which they make use of these services, in a continuous or discontinuous relation to a recipient. But always this is the generic connotation of the concept of class: that the kind of chance in the *market* is the decisive moment which presents a common condition for the individual's fate. 'Class situation' is, in this sense, ultimately 'market situation.' The effect of naked possession *per se*, which among cattle breeders gives the non-owning slave or serf into the power of the cattle owner, is only a forerunner of real 'class' formation. However, in the cattle loan and in the naked severity of the law of debts in such communities, for the first time mere 'possession' as such emerges as decisive for the fate of the individual. This is very much in contrast to the agricultural communities based on labor. The creditor-debtor relation becomes the basis of 'class situations' only in those cities where a 'credit market', however primitive, with rates of interest increasing according to the extent of dearth and a factual monopolization of credits, is developed by a plutocracy. Therewith 'class struggles' begin.

Those men whose fate is not determined by the chance of using goods or services for themselves on the market, e.g. slaves, are not, however, a 'class' in the technical sense of the term. They are, rather, a 'status group'.

3: Communal Action Flowing From Class Interest

According to our terminology, the factor that creates 'class' is unambiguously economic interest, and indeed, only those interests involved in the existence of the 'market'. Nevertheless, the concept of 'class-interest' is an ambiguous one: even as an empirical concept it is ambiguous as soon as one understands by it something other than the factual direction of interests following with a certain probability from the class situation for a certain 'average' of those people subjected to the class situation. The class situation and other circumstances remaining the same, the direction in which the individual worker, for instance, is likely to pursue his interests may vary widely, according to whether he is constitutionally qualified for the task at hand to a high, to an average, or to a low degree. In the same way, the direction of interests may vary according to whether or not a *communal* action of a larger or smaller portion of those commonly affected by the 'class situation', or even an association among them, e.g. a 'trade union', has grown out of the class situation from which the individual may or may not expect promising results. [Communal action refers to that action which is oriented to the feeling of the actors that they belong together. Societal action, on the other hand, is oriented to a rationally motivated adjustment of interests.] The rise of societal or even of communal action from a common class situation is by no means a universal phenomenon.

The class situation may be restricted in its effects to the generation of essentially *similar* reactions, that is to say, within our terminology, of 'mass actions'. However, it may not have even this result. Furthermore, often merely an amorphous communal action emerges. For example, the 'murmuring' of the workers known in ancient oriental ethics: the moral disapproval of the work-master's conduct, which in its practical significance was probably equivalent to an increasingly typical phenomenon of precisely the latest industrial development, namely, the 'slow down' (the deliberate limiting of work effort) of laborers by virtue of tacit agreement. The degree in which 'communal action' and possibly 'societal action', emerges from the 'mass actions' of the members of a class is linked to general cultural conditions, especially to those of an intellectual sort. It is also linked to the extent of the contrasts that have already evolved, and is especially linked to the *transparency* of the connections between the causes and the consequences of the 'class situation'. For however different life chances may be, this fact in itself, according to all experience, by no means gives birth to 'class action' (communal action by the members of a class). The fact of being conditioned and the results of the class situation must be distinctly recognizable. For only then the contrast of life chances can be felt not as an absolutely given fact to be accepted, but as a resultant from either (1) the given distribution of property, or (2) the structure of the concrete economic order. It is only then that people may react against the class structure not only through acts of an intermittent and irrational protest, but in the form of rational association. There have been 'class situations' of the first category (1), of a specifically naked and transparent sort, in the urban centers of Antiquity and during the Middle Ages; especially then, when great fortunes were accumulated by factually monopolized trading in industrial products of these localities or in foodstuffs. Furthermore, under certain circumstances, in the rural economy of the most diverse periods, when agriculture was increasingly exploited in a profit-making manner. The most important historical example of the second category (2) is the class situation of the modern 'proletariat'.

4: Types of 'Class Struggle'

Thus every class may be the carrier of any one of the possibly innumerable forms of 'class action', but this is not necessarily so. In any case, a class does not in itself constitute a community. To treat 'class' conceptually as having the same value as 'community' leads to distortion. That men in the same class situation regularly react in mass actions to such tangible situations as economic ones in the direction of those interests that are most adequate to their average number is an important and after all simple fact for the understanding of historical events. Above all, this fact must not lead to that kind of pseudo-scientific operation with the concepts of 'class' and 'class interests' so frequently found these days, and which has found its most classic expression in the statement of a talented author, that the individual may be in error concerning his interests but that the 'class' is 'infallible' about its interests. Yet, if classes as such are not communities, nevertheless class situations emerge only on the basis of communalization. The communal action that brings forth class situations, however, is not basically action between members of the identical class; it is an action between members of different classes. Communal actions that directly determine the class situation of the worker and the entrepreneur are: the labor market, the commodities market, and the capitalistic enterprise. But, in its turn, the existence of a capitalistic enterprise presupposes that a very specific communal action exists and that it is specifically structured to protect the possession of goods *per se*, and especially the power of individuals to dispose, in principle freely, over the means of production. The existence of a capitalistic enterprise is preconditioned by a specific kind of 'legal order'. Each kind of class situation, and above all when it rests upon the power of property *per se*, will become most clearly efficacious when all other determinants of reciprocal relations are, as far as possible, eliminated in their significance. It is in this way that the utilization of the power of property in the market obtains its most sovereign importance.

Now 'status groups' hinder the strict carrying through of the sheer market principle. In the present context they are of interest to us only from this one point of view. Before we briefly consider them, note that not much of a general nature can be said about the more specific kinds of antagonism between 'classes' (in our meaning of the term). The great shift, which has been going on continuously in the past, and up to our times, may be summarized, although at the cost of some precision: the struggle in which class situations are effective has progressively shifted from consumption credit toward, first, competitive struggles in the commodity market and, then, toward price wars on the labor market. The 'class struggles' of antiquity—to the extent that they were genuine class struggles and not struggles between status groups—were initially carried on by indebted peasants, and perhaps also by artisans threatened by debt bondage and struggling against urban creditors. For debt bondage is the normal result of the differentiation of wealth in commercial cities, especially in seaport cities. A similar situation has existed among cattle breeders. Debt relationships as such produced class action up to the time of Cataline. Along with this, and with an increase in provision of grain for the city by transporting it from the outside, the struggle over the means of sustenance emerged. It centered in the first place around the provision of bread and the determination of the price of bread. It lasted throughout antiquity and the entire Middle Ages. The propertyless as such flocked together against those who actually and supposedly were interested in the dearth of bread. This fight spread until it involved all those commodities essential to the way of life and to handicraft production. There were only incipient discussions of wage disputes in antiquity and in the Middle Ages. But they have been slowly increasing up into modern times. In the earlier periods they were completely secondary to slave rebellions as well as to fights in the commodity market.

The propertyless of antiquity and of the Middle Ages protested against monopolies, pre-emption, forestalling, and the withholding of goods from the market in order to raise prices. Today the central issue is the determination of the price of labor.

This transition is represented by the fight for access to the market and for the determination of the price of products. Such fights went on between merchants and workers in the putting-out system of domestic handicraft during the transition to modern times. Since it is quite a general phenomenon we must mention here that the class antagonisms that are conditioned through the market situation are usually most bitter between those who actually and directly participate as opponents in price wars. It is not the rentier, the share-holder, and the banker who suffer the ill will of the worker, but almost exclusively the manufacturer and the business executives who are the direct opponents of workers in price wars. This is so in spite of the fact that it is precisely the cash boxes of the rentier, the share-holder, and the banker into which the more or less 'unearned' gains flow, rather than into the pockets of the manufacturers or of the business executives. This simple state of affairs has very frequently been decisive for the role the class situation has played in the formation of political parties. For example, it has made possible the varieties of patriarchal socialism and the frequent attempts—formerly, at least—of threatened status groups to form alliances with the proletariat against the 'bourgeoisie'.

5: Status Honor

In contrast to classes, *status groups* are normally communities. They are, however, often of an amorphous kind. In contrast to the purely economically determined 'class situation' we wish to designate as 'status situation' every typical component of the life fate of men that is determined by a specific, positive or negative, social estimation of honor. This honor may be connected with any quality shared by a plurality, and, of course, it can be knit to a class situation: class distinctions are linked in the most varied ways with status distinctions. Property as such is not always recognized as a status qualification, but in the long run it is, and with extraordinary regularity. In the subsistence economy of the organized neighborhood, very often the richest man is simply the chieftain. However, this often means only an honorific preference. For example, in the so-called pure modern 'democracy', that is, one devoid of any expressly ordered status privileges for individuals, it may be that only the families coming under approximately the same tax class dance with one another. This example is reported of certain smaller Swiss cities. But status honor need not necessarily be linked with a 'class situation'. On the contrary, it normally stands in sharp opposition to the pretensions of sheer property.

Both propertied and propertyless people can belong to the same status group, and frequently they do with very tangible consequences. This 'equality' of social esteem may, however, in the long run become quite precarious. The 'equality' of status among the American 'gentlemen', for instance, is expressed by the fact that outside the subordination determined by the different functions of 'business', it would be considered strictly repugnant—wherever the old tradition still prevails—if even the richest 'chief', while playing billiards or cards in his club in the evening, would not treat his 'clerk' as in every sense fully his equal in birthright. It would be repugnant if the American 'chief' would bestow upon his 'clerk' the condescending 'benevolence' marking a distinction of 'position', which the German chief can never dissever from his attitude. This is one of the most important reasons why in America the German 'clubby-ness' has never been able to attain the attraction that the American clubs have.

6: Guarantees of Status Stratification

In content, status honor is normally expressed by the fact that above all else a specific *style of life* can be expected from all those who wish to belong to the circle. Linked with this expectation are restrictions on 'social' intercourse (that is, intercourse which is not subservient to economic or any other of business's 'functional' purposes). These restrictions may confine normal marriages to within the status circle and may lead to complete endogamous closure. As soon as there is not a mere individual and socially irrelevant imitation of another style of life, but an agreed-upon communal action of this closing character, the 'status' development is under way.

In its characteristic form, stratification by 'status groups' on the basis of conventional styles of life evolves at the present time in the United States out of the traditional democracy. For example, only the resident of a certain street ('the street') is considered as belonging to 'society', is qualified for social intercourse, and is visited and invited. Above all, this differentiation evolves in such a way as to make for strict submission to the fashion that is dominant at a given time in society. This submission to fashion also exists among men in America to a degree unknown in Germany. Such submission is considered to be an indication of the fact that a given man *pretends* to qualify as a gentleman. This submission decides, at least *prima facie*, that he will be treated as such. And this recognition becomes just as important for his employment chances in 'swank' establishments, and above all, for social intercourse and marriage with 'esteemed' families, as the qualification for dueling among Germans in the Kaiser's day. As for the rest: certain families resident for a long time, and, of course, correspondingly wealthy, e.g. 'F.F.V., i.e. First Families of Virginia,' or the actual or alleged descendants of the 'Indian Princess' Pocahontas, of the Pilgrim fathers, or of the Knickerbockers, the members of almost inaccessible sects and all sorts of circles setting themselves apart by means of any other characteristics and badges . . . all these elements usurp 'status' honor. The development of status is essentially a question of stratification resting upon usurpation. Such usurpation is the normal origin of almost all status honor. But the road from this purely conventional situation to legal privilege, positive or negative, is easily traveled as soon as a certain stratification of the social order has in fact been 'lived in' and has achieved stability by virtue of a stable distribution of economic power.

7: 'Ethnic' Segregation and 'Caste'

Where the consequences have been realized to their full extent, the status group evolves into a closed 'caste'. Status distinctions are then guaranteed not merely by conventions and laws, but also by rituals. This occurs in such a way that every physical contact with a member of any caste that is considered to be 'lower' by the members of a 'higher' caste is considered as making for a ritualistic impurity and to be a stigma which must be expiated by a religious act. Individual castes develop quite distinct cults and gods.

In general, however, the status structure reaches such extreme consequences only where there are underlying differences which are held to be 'ethnic'. The 'caste' is, indeed, the normal form in which ethnic communities usually live side by side in a 'societalized' manner. These ethnic communities believe in blood relationship and exclude exogamous marriage and social intercourse. Such a caste situation is part of the phenomenon of 'pariah' peoples and is found all over the world. These people form communities, acquire specific occupational traditions of handicrafts or of other arts, and cultivate a belief in their ethnic community. They live in a 'diaspora' strictly segregated from all personal intercourse, except that of an unavoidable sort, and their situation is legally precarious. Yet, by virtue of their economic indispensability, they are tolerated, indeed, frequently privileged, and they live in interspersed political communities. The Jews are the most impressive historical example.

A 'status' segregation grown into a 'caste' differs in its structure from a mere 'ethnic' segregation: the caste structure transforms the horizontal and unconnected coexistences of ethnically segregated groups into a vertical social system of super- and subordination. Correctly formulated: a comprehensive societalization integrates the ethnically divided communities into specific political and communal action. In their consequences they differ precisely in this way: ethnic coexistences condition a mutual repulsion and disdain but allow each ethnic community to consider its own honor as the highest one; the caste structure brings about a social subordination and an acknowledgment of 'more honor' in favor of the privileged caste and status groups. This is due to the fact that in the caste structure ethnic distinctions as such have become 'functional' distinctions within the political societalization (warriors, priests, artisans that are politically important for war and for building, and so on). But even pariah people who are most despised are usually apt to continue cultivating in some manner that which is equally peculiar to ethnic and to status communities: the belief in their own specific 'honor'. This is the case with the Jews.

Only with the negatively privileged status groups does the 'sense of dignity' take a specific deviation. A sense of dignity is the precipitation in individuals of social honor and of conventional demands which a positively privileged status group raises for the deportment of its members. The sense of dignity that characterizes positively privileged status groups is naturally related to their 'being' which does not transcend itself, that is, it is to their 'beauty and excellence' (καλο–κάγανια). Their kingdom is 'of this world'. They live for the present and by exploiting their great past. The sense of dignity of the negatively privileged strata naturally refers to a future lying beyond the present, whether it is of this life or of another. In other words, it must be nurtured by the belief in a providential 'mission' and by a belief in a specific honor before God. The 'chosen people's' dignity is nurtured by a belief either that in the beyond 'the last will be the first', or that in this life a Messiah will appear to bring forth into the light of the world which has cast them out the hidden honor of the pariah people. This simple state of affairs, and not the 'resentment' which is so strongly emphasized in Nietzsche's much admired construction in the *Genealogy of Morals*, is the source of the religiosity cultivated by pariah status groups. In passing, we may note that resentment may be accurately applied only to a limited extent; for one of Nietzsche's main examples, Buddhism, it is not at all applicable.

Incidentally, the development of status groups from ethnic segregations is by no means the normal phenomenon. On the contrary, since objective 'racial differences' are by no means basic to every subjective sentiment of an ethnic community, the ultimately racial foundation of status structure is rightly and absolutely a question of the concrete individual case. Very frequently a status group is instrumental in the production of a thoroughbred anthropological type. Certainly a status group is to a high degree effective in producing extreme types, for they select personally qualified individuals (e.g. the Knighthood selects those who are fit for warfare, physically and psychically). But selection is far from being the only, or the predominant, way in which status groups are formed: Political membership or class situation has at all times been at least as frequently decisive. And today the class situation is by far the predominant factor, for of course the possibility of a style of life expected for members of a status group is usually conditioned economically.

8: Status Privileges

For all practical purposes, stratification by status goes hand in hand with a monopolization of ideal and material goods or opportunities, in a manner we have come to know as typical. Besides the specific status honor, which always rests upon distance and exclusiveness, we find all sorts of material monopolies. Such honorific preferences may consist of the privilege of wearing special costumes, of eating special dishes taboo to others, of carrying arms—which is most obvious in its consequences—the right to pursue certain non-professional dilettante artistic practices, e.g. to play certain musical instruments. Of course, material monopolies provide the most effective motives for the exclusiveness of a status group; although, in themselves, they are rarely sufficient, almost always they come into play to some extent. Within a status circle there is the question of intermarriage: the interest of the families in the monopolization of potential bridegrooms is at least of equal importance and is parallel to the interest in the monopolization of daughters. The daughters of the circle must be provided for. With an increased inclosure of the status group, the conventional preferential opportunities for special employment grow into a legal monopoly of special offices for the members. Certain goods become objects for monopolization by status groups. In the typical fashion these include 'entailed estates' and frequently also the possessions of serfs or bondsmen and, finally, special trades. This monopolization occurs positively when the status group is exclusively entitled to own and to manage them; and negatively when, in order to maintain its specific way of life, the status group must not own and manage them.

The decisive role of a 'style of life' in status 'honor' means that status groups are the specific bearers of all 'conventions'. In whatever way it may be manifest, all 'stylization' of life either originates in status groups or is at least conserved by them. Even if the principles of status conventions differ greatly, they reveal certain typical traits, especially among those strata which are most privileged. Quite generally, among privileged status groups there is a status disqualification that operates against the performance of common physical labor. This disqualification is now 'setting in' in America against the old tradition of esteem for labor. Very frequently every rational economic pursuit, and especially 'entrepreneurial activity', is looked upon as a disqualification of status. Artistic and literary activity is also considered as degrading work as soon as it is exploited for income, or at least when it is connected with hard physical exertion. An example is the sculptor working like a mason in his dusty smock as over against the painter in his salon-like 'studio' and those forms of musical practice that are acceptable to the status group.

9: Economic Conditions and Effects of Status Stratification

The frequent disqualification of the gainfully employed as such is a direct result of the principle of status stratification peculiar to the social order, and of course, of this principle's opposition to a distribution of power which is regulated exclusively through the market. These two factors operate along with various individual ones, which will be touched upon below.

We have seen above that the market and its processes 'knows no personal distinctions': 'functional' interests dominate it. It knows nothing of 'honor'. The status order means precisely the reverse, viz.: stratification in terms of 'honor' and of styles of life peculiar to status groups as such. If mere economic acquisition and naked economic power still bearing the stigma of its extra-status origin could bestow upon anyone who has won it the same honor as those who are interested in status by virtue of style of life claim for themselves, the status order would be threatened at its very root. This is the more so as, given equality of status honor, property *per se* represents an addition even if it is not overtly acknowledged to be such. Yet if such economic acquisition and power gave the agent any honor at all, his wealth would result in his attaining more honor than those who successfully claim honor by virtue of style of life. Therefore all groups having interests in the status order react with special sharpness precisely against the pretensions of purely economic acquisition. In most cases they react the more vigorously the more they feel themselves threatened. Calderon's respectful treatment of the peasant, for instance, as opposed to Shakespeare's simultaneous and ostensible disdain of the *canaille* illustrates the different way in which a firmly structured status order reacts as compared with a status order that has become economically precarious. This is an example of a state of affairs that recurs everywhere. Precisely because of the rigorous reactions against the claims of property *per se*, the 'parvenu' is never accepted, personally and without reservation, by the privileged status groups, no matter how completely his style of life has been adjusted to theirs. They will only accept his descendants who have been educated in the conventions of their status group and who have never besmirched its honor by their own economic labor.

As to the general *effect* of the status order, only one consequence can be stated, but it is a very important one: the hindrance of the free development of the market occurs first for those goods which status groups directly withheld from free exchange by monopolization. This monopolization may be effected either legally or conventionally. For example, in many Hellenic cities during the epoch of status groups, and also originally in Rome, the inherited estate (as is shown by the old formula for indiction against spendthrifts) was monopolized just as were the estates of knights, peasants, priests, and especially the clientele of the craft and merchant guilds. The market is restricted, and the power of naked property *per se*, which gives its stamp to 'class formation', is pushed into the background. The results of this process can be most varied. Of course, they do not necessarily weaken the contrasts in the economic situation. Frequently they strengthen these contrasts, and in any case, where stratification by status permeates a community as strongly as was the case in all political communities of antiquity and of the Middle Ages, one can never speak of a genuinely free market competition as we understand it today. There are wider effects than this direct exclusion of special goods from the market. From the contrariety between the status order and the purely economic order mentioned above, it follows that in most instances the notion of honor peculiar to status absolutely abhors that which is essential to the market: higgling. Honor abhors higgling among peers and occasionally it taboos higgling for the members of a status group in general. Therefore, everywhere some status groups, and usually the most influential, consider almost any kind of overt participation in economic acquisition as absolutely stigmatizing.

With some over-simplification, one might thus say that 'classes' are stratified according to their relations to the production and acquisition of goods; whereas 'status groups' are stratified according to the principles of their *consumption* of goods as represented by special 'styles of life'.

An 'occupational group' is also a status group. For normally, it successfully claims social honor only by virtue of the special style of life which may be determined by it. The differences between classes and status groups frequently overlap. It is precisely those status communities most strictly segregated in terms of honor (viz. the Indian castes) who today show, although within very rigid limits, a relatively high degree of indifference to pecuniary income. However, the Brahmins seek such income in many different ways.

As to the general economic conditions making for the predominance of stratification by 'status', only very little can be said. When the bases of the acquisition and distribution of goods are relatively stable, stratification by status is favored. Every technological repercussion and economic transformation threatens stratification by status and pushes the class situation into the foreground. Epochs and countries in which the naked class situation is of predominant significance are regularly the periods of technical and economic transformations. And every slowing down of the shifting of economic stratifications leads, in due course, to the growth of status structures and makes for a resuscitation of the important role of social honor.

10: Parties

Whereas the genuine place of 'classes' is within the economic order, the place of 'status groups' is within the social order, that is, within the sphere of the distribution of 'honor'. From within these spheres, classes and status groups influence one another and they influence the legal order and are in turn influenced by it. But 'parties' live in a house of 'power'.

Their action is oriented toward the acquisition of social 'power', that is to say, toward influencing a communal action no matter what its content may be. In principle, parties may exist in a social 'club' as well as in a 'state'. As over against the actions of classes and status groups, for which this is not necessarily the case, the communal actions of 'parties' always mean a societalization. For party actions are always directed toward a goal which is striven for in planned manner. This goal may be a 'cause' (the party may aim at realizing a program for ideal or material purposes), or the goal may be 'personal' (sinecures, power, and from these, honor for the leader and the followers of the party). Usually the party action aims at all these simultaneously. Parties are, therefore, only possible within communities that are societalized, that is, which have some rational order and a staff of persons available who are ready to enforce it. For parties aim precisely at influencing this staff, and if possible, to recruit it from party followers.

In any individual case, parties may represent interests determined through 'class situation' or 'status situation,' and they may recruit their following respectively from one or the other. But they need be neither purely 'class' nor purely 'status' parties. In most cases they are partly class parties and partly status parties, but sometimes they are neither. They may represent ephemeral or enduring structures. Their means of attaining power may be quite varied, ranging from naked violence of any sort to canvassing for votes with coarse or subtle means: money, social influence, the force of speech, suggestion, clumsy hoax, and so on to the rougher or more artful tactics of obstruction in parliamentary bodies.

The sociological structure of parties differs in a basic way according to the kind of communal action which they struggle to influence. Parties also differ according to whether or not the community is stratified by status or by classes. Above all else, they vary according to the structure of domination within the community. For their leaders normally deal with the conquest of a community. They are, in the general concept which is maintained here, not only products of specially modern forms of domination. We shall also designate as parties the ancient and medieval 'parties', despite the fact that their structure differs basically from the structure of modern parties. By virtue of these structural differences of domination it is impossible to say anything about the structure of parties without discussing the structural forms of social domination *per se*. Parties, which are always structures struggling for domination, are very frequently organized in a very strict 'authoritarian' fashion. . .

Concerning 'classes', 'status groups', and 'parties', it must be said in general that they necessarily presuppose a comprehensive societalization, and especially a political framework of communal action, within which they operate. This does not mean that parties would be confined by the frontiers of any individual political community. On the contrary, at all times it has been the order of the day that the societalization (even when it aims at the use of military force in common) reaches beyond the frontiers of politics. This has been the case in the solidarity of interests among the Oligarchs and among the democrats in Hellas, among the Guelfs and among Ghibellines in the Middle Ages, and within the Calvinist party during the period of religious struggles. It has been the case up to the solidarity of the landlords (international congress of agrarian landlords), and has continued among princes (holy alliance, Karlsbad decrees), socialist workers, conservatives (the longing of Prussian conservatives for Russian intervention in 1850). But their aim is not necessarily the establishment of new international political, i.e. *territorial*, dominion. In the main they aim to influence the existing dominion.[2]

NOTES

One cross-reference footnote to a passage in *Wirtschaft und Gesellschaft*, p. 277, has been omitted, and one footnote has been placed in the text. A brief unfinished draft of a classification of status groups is appended to the German text; it has been omitted here.

1. *Wirtschaft und Gesellschaft*, part III, chap. 4, pp. 631–40. The first sentence in paragraph one and the several definitions in this chapter which are in brackets do not appear in the original text. They have been taken from other contexts of *Wirtschaft und Gesellschaft*.
2. The posthumously published text breaks off here. We omit an incomplete sketch of types of 'warrior estates'.

SOCIAL SCIENTIFIC METHOD

Science as a Vocation

Plato's passionate enthusiasm in *The Republic* must, in the last analysis, be explained by the fact that for the first time the *concept*, one of the great tools of all scientific knowledge, had been consciously discovered. Socrates had discovered it in its bearing. He was not the only man in the world to discover it. In India one finds the beginnings of a logic that is quite similar to that of Aristotle's. But nowhere else do we find this realization of the significance of the concept. In Greece, for the first time, appeared a handy means by which one could put the logical screws upon somebody so that he could not come out without admitting either that he knew nothing or that this and nothing else was truth, the *eternal* truth that never would vanish as the doings of the blind men vanish. That was the tremendous experience which dawned upon the disciples of Socrates. And from this it seemed to follow that if one only found the right concept of the beautiful, the good, or, for instance, of bravery, of the soul—or whatever—that then one could also grasp its true being. And this, in turn, seemed to open the way for knowing and for teaching how to act rightly in life and, above all, how to act as a citizen of the state; for this question was everything to the Hellenic man, whose thinking was political throughout. And for these reasons one engaged in science.

The second great tool of scientific work, the rational experiment, made its appearance at the side of this discovery of the Hellenic spirit during the Renaissance period. The experiment is a means of reliably controlling experience. Without it, present-day empirical science would be impossible. There were experiments earlier; for instance, in India physiological experiments were made in the service of ascetic yoga technique; in Hellenic antiquity, mathematical experiments were made for purposes of war technology; and in the Middle Ages, for purposes of mining. But to raise the experiment to a principle of research was the achievement of the Renaissance. They were the great innovators in *art*, who were the pioneers of experiment. Leonardo and his like and, above all, the sixteenth-century experimenters in music with their experimental pianos were characteristic. From these circles the experiment entered science, especially through Galileo, and it entered theory through Bacon; and then it was taken over by the various exact disciplines of the continental universities, first of all those of Italy and then those of the Netherlands.

What did science mean to these men who stood at the threshold of modern times? To artistic experimenters of the type of Leonardo and the musical innovators, science meant the path to *true* art, and that meant for them the path to true *nature*. Art was to be raised to the rank of science, and this meant at the same time and above all to raise the artist to the rank of the doctor, socially and with reference to the meaning of his life. This is the ambition on which, for instance, Leonardo's sketch book was based. And today? 'Science as the way to nature' would sound like blasphemy to youth. Today, youth proclaims the opposite: redemption from the intellectualism of science in order to return to one's own nature and therewith to nature in general. Science as a way to art? Here no criticism is even needed.

But during the period of the rise of the exact sciences one expected a great deal more. If you recall Swammerdam's statement, 'Here I bring you the proof of God's providence in the anatomy of a louse', you will see what the scientific worker, influenced (indirectly) by Protestantism and Puritanism, conceived to be his task: to show the path to God. People no longer found this path among the philosophers, with their concepts and deductions. All pietist theology of the time, above all Spencer, knew that God was not to be found along the road by which the Middle Ages had sought him. God is hidden, His ways are not our ways, His thoughts are not our thoughts. In the exact sciences, however, where one could physically grasp His works, one hoped to come upon the traces of what He planned for the world. And today? Who—aside from certain big children who are indeed found in the natural sciences—still believes that the findings of astronomy, biology, physics, or chemistry could teach us anything about the *meaning* of the world? If there is any such 'meaning', along what road could one come upon its tracks? If these natural sciences lead to anything in this way, they are apt to make the belief that there is such a thing as the 'meaning' of the universe die out at its very roots.

And finally, science as a way 'to God'? Science, this specifically irreligious power? That science today is irreligious no one will doubt in his innermost being, even if he will not admit it to himself. Redemption from the rationalism and intellectualism of science is the fundamental presupposition of living in union with the divine. This, or something similar in meaning, is one of the fundamental watchwords one hears among German youth, whose feelings are attuned to religion or who crave religious experiences. They crave not only religious experience but experience as such. The only thing that is strange is the method that is now followed: the spheres of the irrational, the only spheres that intellectualism has not yet touched, are now raised into consciousness and put under its lens. For in practice this is where the modern intellectualist form of romantic irrationalism leads. This method of emancipation from intellectualism may well bring about the very opposite of what those who take to it conceive as its goal.

After Nietzsche's devastating criticism of those 'last men' who 'invented happiness', I may leave aside altogether the naive optimism in which science—that is, the technique of mastering life which rests upon science—has been celebrated as the way to happiness. Who believes in this?—aside from a few big children in university chairs or editorial offices. Let us resume our argument.

Under these internal presuppositions, what is the meaning of science as a vocation, now after all these former illusions, the 'way to true being', the 'way to true art', the 'way to true nature', the 'way to true God', the 'way to true happiness', have been dispelled? Tolstoi has given the simplest answer, with the words: 'Science is meaningless because it gives no answer to our question, the only question important for us: "What shall we do and how shall we live?"' That science does not give an answer to this is indisputable. The only question that remains is the sense in which science gives 'no' answer, and whether or not science might yet be of some use to the one who puts the question correctly.

Today one usually speaks of science as 'free from presuppositions'. Is there such a thing? It depends upon what one understands thereby. All scientific work presupposes that the rules of logic and method are valid; these are the general foundations of our orientation in the world; and, at least for our special question, these presuppositions are the least problematic aspect of science. Science further presupposes that what is yielded by scientific work is important in the sense that it is 'worth being known'. In this, obviously, are contained all our problems. For this presupposition cannot be proved by scientific means. It can only be *interpreted* with reference to its ultimate meaning, which we must reject or accept according to our ultimate position towards life.

Furthermore, the nature of the relationship of scientific work and its presuppositions varies widely according to their structure. The natural sciences, for instance, physics, chemistry, and astronomy, presuppose as self-evident that it is worth while to know the ultimate laws of cosmic events as far as science can construe them. This is the case not only because with such knowledge one can attain technical results but for its own sake, if the quest for such knowledge is to be a 'vocation'. Yet this presupposition can by no means be proved. And still less can it be proved that the existence of the world which these sciences describe is worth, that it has any 'meaning', or that it makes sense to live in such a world. Science does not ask for the answers to such questions.

. . .

Consider the historical and cultural sciences. They teach us how to understand and interpret political, artistic, literary, and social phenomena in terms of their origins. But they give us no answer to the question, whether the existence of these cultural phenomena have been and are *worth while*. And they do not answer the further question, whether it is worth the effort required to know them. They presuppose that there is an interest in partaking, through this procedure, of the community of 'civilized men'. But they cannot prove 'scientifically' that this is the case; and that they presuppose this interest by no means proves that it goes without saying. In fact it is not at all self-evident.

Finally, let us consider the disciplines close to me: sociology, history, economics, political science, and those types of cultural philosophy that make it their task to interpret these sciences. It is said, and I agree, that politics is out of place in the lecture-room. It does not belong there on the part of the students. If, for instance, in the lecture-room of my former colleague Dietrich Schäfer in Berlin, pacifist students were to surround his desk and make an uproar, I should deplore it just as much as I should deplore the uproar which anti-pacifist students are said to have made against Professor Förster, whose views in many ways are as remote as could be from mine. Neither does politics, however, belong in the lecture-room on the part of the docents, and when the docent is scientifically concerned with politics, it belongs there least of all.

. . .

But the true teacher will beware of imposing from the platform any political position upon the student, whether it is expressed or suggested. 'To let the facts speak for themselves' is the most unfair way of putting over a political position to the student.

Why should we abstain from doing this? I state in advance that some highly esteemed colleagues are of the opinion that it is not possible to carry through this self-restraint and that, even if it were possible, it would be a whim to avoid declaring oneself. Now one cannot demonstrate scientifically what the duty of an academic teacher is. One can only demand of the teacher that he have the intellectual integrity to see that it is one thing to state facts, to determine mathematical or logical relations or the internal structure of cultural values, while it is another thing to answer questions of the *value* of culture and its individual contents and the question of how one should act in the cultural community and in political associations. These are quite heterogeneous problems. If he asks further why he should not deal with both types of problems in the lecture-room, the answer is: because the prophet and the demagogue do not belong on the academic platform.

· · ·

I am ready to prove from the works of our historians that whenever the man of science introduces his personal value judgement, a full understanding of the facts *ceases*. But this goes beyond tonight's topic and would require lengthy elucidation.

· · ·

The primary task of a useful teacher is to teach his students to recognize 'inconvenient' facts—I mean facts that are inconvenient for their party opinions. And for every party opinion there are facts that are extremely inconvenient, for my own opinion no less than for others. I believe the teacher accomplishes more than a mere intellectual task if he compels his audience to accustom itself to the existence of such facts. I would be so immodest as even to apply the expression 'moral achievement', though perhaps this may sound too grandiose for something that should go without saying.

· · ·

Finally, you will put the question: 'If this is so, what then does science actually and positively contribute to practical and personal "life"?' Therewith we are back again at the problem of science as a 'vocation'.

First, of course, science contributes to the technology of controlling life by calculating external objects as well as man's activities. Well, you will say, that, after all, amounts to no more than the greengrocer of the American boy. I fully agree.

Second, science can contribute something that the greengrocer cannot: methods of thinking, the tools and the training for thought. Perhaps you will say: well, that is no vegetable, but it amounts to no more than the means for procuring vegetables. Well and good, let us leave it at that for today.

Fortunately, however, the contribution of science does not reach its limits with this. We are in a position to help you to a third objective: to gain *clarity*. Of course, it is presupposed that we ourselves possess clarity. As far as this is the case, we can make clear to you the following:

In practice, you can take this or that position when concerned with a problem of value—for simplicity's sake, please think of social phenomena as examples. *If* you take such and such a stand, then according to scientific experience, you have to use such and such a *means* in order to carry out your conviction practically. Now, these means are perhaps such that you believe you must reject them. Then you simply must choose between the end and the inevitable means. Does the end 'justify' the means? Or does it not? The teacher can confront you with the necessity of this choice. He cannot do more, so long as he wishes to remain a teacher and not to become a demagogue. He can, of course, also tell you that if you want such and such an end, then you must take into the bargain the subsidiary consequences which according to all experience will occur. Again we find ourselves in the same situation as before. There are still problems that can also emerge for the technician, who in numerous instances has to make decisions according to the principle of the lesser evil or of the relatively best. Only to him one thing, the main thing, is usually given, namely, the end. But as soon as truly 'ultimate' problems are at stake for us this is not the case. With this, at long last, we come to the final service that science as such can render to the aim of clarity, and at the same time we come to the limits of science.

Besides we can and we should state: In terms of its meaning, such and such a practical stand can be derived with inner consistency, and hence integrity, from this or that ultimate *weltanschauliche* position. Perhaps it can only be derived from one such fundamental position, or maybe from several, but it cannot be derived from these or those other positions. Figuratively speaking, you serve this god and you offend the other god when you decide to adhere to this position. And if you remain faithful to yourself, you will necessarily come to certain final conclusions that subjectively make sense. This much, in principle at least, can be accomplished. Philosophy, as a special discipline, and the essentially philosophical discussions of principles in the other sciences attempt to achieve this. Thus, if we are competent in our pursuit (which must be presupposed here) we can force the individual, or at least we can help him, to give himself an *account of the ultimate meaning of his own conduct.* This appears to me as not so trifling a thing to do, even for one's own personal life. Again, I am tempted to say of a teacher who succeeds in this: he stands in the service of 'moral' forces; he fulfils the duty of bringing about self-clarification and a sense of responsibility. And I believe he will be the more able to accomplish this, the more conscientiously he avoids the desire personally to impose upon or suggest to his audience his own stand.

. . .

The fate of our times is characterized by rationalization and intellectualization and, above all, by the 'disenchantment of the world'. Precisely the ultimate and most sublime values have retreated from public life either into the transcendental realm of mystic life or into the brotherliness of direct and personal human relations. It is not accidental that our greatest art is intimate and not monumental, nor is it accidental that today only within the smallest and intimate circles, in personal human situations, in *pianissimo*, that something is pulsating that corresponds to the prophetic *pneuma*, which in former times swept through the great communities like a firebrand, welding them together. If we attempt to force and to 'invent' a monumental style in art, such miserable monstrosities are produced as the many monuments of the last twenty years. If one tries intellectually to construe new religions without a new and genuine prophecy, then, in an inner sense, something similar will result, but with still worse effects. And academic prophecy, finally, will create only fanatical sects but never a genuine community.

To the person who cannot bear the fate of the times like a man, one must say: may he rather return silently, without the usual publicity build-up of renegades, but simply and plainly. The arms of the old churches are opened widely and compassionately for him.

After all, they do not make it hard for him. One way or another he has to bring his 'intellectual sacrifice'—that is inevitable. If he can really do it, we shall not rebuke him. For such an intellectual sacrifice in favour of an unconditional religious devotion is ethically quite a different matter than the evasion of the plain duty of intellectual integrity, which sets in if one lacks the courage to clarify one's own ultimate standpoint and rather facilitates this duty by feeble relative judgements. In my eyes, such religious return stands higher than the academic prophecy, which does not clearly realize that in the lecture-rooms of the university no other virtue holds but plain intellectual integrity. Integrity, however, compels us to state that for the many who today tarry for new prophets and saviours, the situation is the same as resounds in the beautiful Edomite watchman's song of the period of exile that has been included among Isaiah's oracles:

> He calleth to me out of Seir, Watchman, what of the night? The watchman said, The morning cometh, and also the night: if ye will enquire, enquire ye: return, come.

The people to whom this was said has enquired and tarried for more than two millennia, and we are shaken when we realize its fate. From this we want to draw the lesson that nothing is gained by yearning and tarrying alone, and we shall act differently. We shall set to work and meet the 'demands of the day', in human relations as well as in our vocation. This, however, is plain and simple, if each finds and obeys the demon who holds the fibres of his very life.

THE DEFINITIONS OF SOCIOLOGY AND OF SOCIAL ACTION

Sociology (in the sense in which this highly ambiguous word is used here) is a science which attempts the interpretive understanding[1] of social action in order thereby to arrive at a causal explanation of its course and effects. In 'action' is included all human behaviour when and in so far as the acting individual attaches a subjective meaning to it. Action in this sense may be either overt or purely inward or subjective; it may consist of positive intervention in a situation, or of deliberately refraining from such intervention or passively acquiescing in the situation. Action is social in so far as, by virtue of the subjective meaning attached to it by the acting individual (or individuals), it takes account of the behaviour of others and is thereby oriented in its course.[2]

The Methodological Foundations of Sociology[3]

1. 'Meaning' may be of two kinds. The term may refer first to the actual existing meaning in the given concrete case of a particular actor, or to the average or approximate meaning attributable to a given plurality of actors; or secondly to the theoretically conceived *pure type*[4] of subjective meaning attributed to the hypothetical actor or actors in a given type of

action. In no case does it refer to an objectively 'correct' meaning or one which is 'true' in some metaphysical sense. It is this which distinguishes the empirical sciences of action, such as sociology and history, from the dogmatic disciplines in that area, such as jurisprudence, logic, ethics, and esthetics, which seek to ascertain the 'true' and 'valid' meanings associated with the objects of their investigation.

2. The line between meaningful action and merely reactive behaviour to which no subjective meaning is attached, cannot be sharply drawn empirically. A very considerable part of all sociologically relevant behaviour, especially purely traditional behaviour, is marginal between the two. In the case of many psychophysical processes, meaningful, i.e. subjectively understandable, action is not to be found at all; in others it is discernible only by the expert psychologist. Many mystical experiences which cannot be adequately communicated in words are, for a person who is not susceptible to such experiences, not fully understandable. At the same time the ability to imagine one's self performing a similar action is not a necessary prerequisite to understanding; 'one need not have been Caesar in order to understand Caesar'. For the verifiable accuracy[5] of interpretation of the meaning of a phenomenon, it is a great help to be able to put one's self imaginatively in the place of the actor and thus sympathetically to participate in his experiences, but this is not an essential condition of meaningful interpretation. Understandable and non-understandable components of a process are often intermingled and bound up together.

3. All interpretation of meaning, like all scientific observation, strives for clarity and verifiable accuracy of insight and comprehension (*Evidenz*). The basis for certainty in understanding can be either rational, which can be further subdivided into logical and mathematical, or it can be of an emotionally empathic or artistically appreciative quality. In the sphere of action things are rationally evident chiefly when we attain a completely clear intellectual grasp of the action-elements in their intended context of meaning. Empathic or appreciative accuracy is attained when, through sympathetic participation, we can adequately grasp the emotional context in which the action took place. The highest degree of rational understanding is attained in cases involving the meanings of logically or mathematically related propositions; their meaning may be immediately and unambiguously intelligible. We have a perfectly clear understanding of what it means when somebody employs the proposition 2 x 2 = 4 or the Pythagorean theorem in reasoning or argument, or when someone correctly carries out a logical train of reasoning according to our accepted modes of thinking. In the same way we also understand what a person is doing when he tries to achieve certain ends by choosing appropriate means on the basis of the facts of the situation as experience has accustomed us to interpret them. Such an interpretation of this type of rationally purposeful action possesses, for the understanding of the choice of means, the highest degree of verifiable certainty. With a lower degree of certainty, which is, however, adequate for most purposes of explanation, we are able to understand errors, including confusion of problems of the sort that we ourselves are liable to, or the origin of which we can detect by sympathetic self-analysis.

On the other hand, many ultimate ends or values toward which experience shows that human action may be oriented, often cannot be understood completely, though sometimes we are able to grasp them intellectually. The more radically they differ from our own ultimate values, however, the more difficult it is for us to make them understandable by imaginatively participating in them. Depending upon the circumstances of the particular case we must be content either with a purely intellectual understanding of such values or when even that fails, sometimes we must simply accept them as given data. Then we can try to understand the action motivated by them on the basis of whatever opportunities for approximate emotional and intellectual interpretation seem to be available at different points in its course. These difficulties apply, for instance, for people not susceptible to the relevant values, to many unusual acts of religious and charitable zeal; also certain kinds of extreme rationalistic fanaticism of the type involved in some forms of the ideology of the 'rights of man' are in a similar position for people who radically repudiate such points of view.

. . .

The Concept of Social Action

1. Social action, which includes both failure to act and passive acquiescence, may be oriented to the past, present, or expected future behaviour of others. Thus it may be motivated by revenge for a past attack, defence against present, or measures of defence against future aggression. The 'others' may be individual persons, and may be known to the action as such, or may constitute an indefinite plurality and may be entirely unknown as individuals. Thus 'money' is a means of exchange which the actor accepts in payment because he orients his action to the expectation that a large but unknown number of individuals he is personally unacquainted with will be ready to accept it in exchange on some future occasion.

2. Not every kind of action, even of overt action, is 'social' in the sense of the present discussion. Overt action is non-social if it is oriented solely to the behaviour of inanimate objects. Subjective attitudes constitute social action only so far as they are oriented to the behaviour of others. For example, religious behaviour is not social if it is simply a matter of contemplation or of solitary prayer. The economic activity of an individual is only social if, and then only in so far as, it takes account of the behaviour of someone else. Thus very generally in formal terms it becomes social in so far as the actor's actual control over economic goods is respected by others. Concretely it is social, for instance, if in relation to the actor's own consumption the future wants of others are taken into account and this becomes one consideration affecting the actor's own saving. Or, in another connexion, production may be oriented to the future wants of other people.

3. Not every type of contact of human beings has a social character; this is rather confined to cases where the actor's behaviour is meaningfully oriented to that of others. For example, a mere collision of two cyclists may be compared to a natural event. On the other hand, their attempt to avoid hitting each other, or whatever insults, blows, or friendly discussion might follow the collision, would constitute 'social action'.

4. Social action is not identical either with the similar actions of many persons or with action influenced by other persons. Thus, if at the beginning of a shower a number of people on the street put up their umbrellas at the same time, this would not ordinarily be a case of action mutually oriented to that of each other, but rather of all reacting in the same way to the like need of protection from the rain. It is well known that the actions of the individual are strongly influenced by the mere fact that he is a member of a crowd con-

fined within a limited space. Thus, the subject matter of studies of 'crowd psychology', such as those of Le Bon will be called 'action conditioned by crowds'. It is also possible for large numbers, though dispersed, to be influenced simultaneously or successively by a source of influence operating similarly on all the individuals, as by means of the press. Here also the behaviour of an individual is influenced by his membership in the crowd and by the fact that he is aware of being a member. Some types of reaction are only made possible by the mere fact that the individual acts as part of a crowd. Others become more difficult under these conditions. Hence it is possible that a particular event or mode of human behaviour can give rise to the most diverse kinds of feeling—gaiety, anger, enthusiasm, despair, and passions of all sorts—in a crowd situation which would not occur at all or not nearly so readily if the individual were alone. But for this to happen there need not, at least in many cases, be any meaningful relation between the behaviour of the individual and the fact that he is a member of a crowd. It is not proposed in the present sense to call action 'social' when it is merely a result of the effect on the individual of the existence of a crowd as such and the action is not oriented to that fact on the level of meaning. At the same time the borderline is naturally highly indefinite. In such cases as that of the influence of the demagogue, there may be a wide variation in the extent to which his mass clientele is affected by a meaningful reaction to the fact of its large numbers; and whatever this relation may be, it is open to varying interpretations.

But furthermore, mere 'imitation' of the action of others, such as that on which Tarde has rightly laid emphasis, will not be considered a case of specifically social action if it is purely reactive so that there is no meaningful orientation to the actor imitated. The borderline is, however, so indefinite that it is often hardly possible to discriminate. The mere fact that a person is found to employ some apparently useful procedure which he learned from someone else does not, however, constitute, in the present sense, social action. Action such as this is not oriented to the action of the other person, but the actor has, through observing the other, become acquainted with certain objective facts; and it is these to which his action is oriented. His action is then *causally* determined by the action of others, but not meaningfully. On the other hand, if the action of others is imitated because it is 'fashionable' or traditional or exemplary, or lends social distinction, or on similar grounds, it is meaningfully oriented either to the behaviour of the source of imitation or of third persons or of both. There are of course all manner of transitional cases between the two types of imitation. Both the phenomena discussed above, the behaviour of crowds and imitation, stand on the indefinite borderline of social action. The same is true, as will often appear, of traditionalism and charisma. The reason for the indefiniteness of the line in these and other cases lies in the fact that both the orientation to the behaviour of others and the meaning which can be imputed to the actor himself, are by no means always capable of clear determination and are often altogether unconscious and seldom fully self-conscious. Mere 'influence' and meaningful orientation cannot therefore always be clearly differentiated on the empirical level. But conceptually it is essential to distinguish them, even though merely 'reactive' imitation may well have a degree of sociological importance at least equal to that of the type which can be called social action in the strict sense. Sociology, it goes without saying, is by no means confined to the study of 'social action'; this is only, at least for the kind of sociology being developed here, its central subject matter, that which may be said to be decisive for its status as a science. But this does not imply any judgement on the comparative importance of this and other factors.

The Types of Social Action

Social action, like other forms of action, may be classified in the following four types according to its mode of orientation: (1) in terms of rational orientation to a system of discrete individual ends (*zweckrational*), that is, through expectations as to the behaviour of objects in the external situation and of other human individuals, making use of these expectations as 'conditions' or 'means' for the successful attainment of the actor's own rationally chosen ends; (2) in terms of rational orientation to an absolute value (*wertrational*); involving a conscious belief in the absolute value of some ethical, aesthetic, religious, or other form of behaviour, entirely for its own sake and independently of any prospects of external success; (3) in terms of affectual orientation, especially emotional, determined by the specific affects and states of feeling of the actor; (4) traditionally oriented, through the habituation of long practice.[6]

1. Strictly traditional behaviour, like the reactive type of imitation discussed above, lies very close to the borderline of what can justifiably be called meaningfully oriented action, and indeed often on the other side. For it is very often a matter of almost automatic reaction to habitual stimuli which guide behaviour in a course which has been repeatedly followed. The great bulk of all everyday action to which people have become habitually accustomed approaches this type. Hence, its place in a systematic classification is not merely that of a limiting case because, as will be shown later, attachment to habitual forms can be upheld with varying degrees of self-consciousness and in a variety of senses. In this case the type may shade over into number two (*Wertrationalität*).

2. Purely affectual behaviour also stands on the borderline of what can be considered 'meaningfully' oriented, and often it, too, goes over the line. It may, for instance, consist in an uncontrolled reaction to some exceptional stimulus. It is a case of sublimation when affectually determined action occurs in the form of conscious release of emotional tension. When this happens it is usually, though not always, well on the road to rationalization in one or the other or both of the above senses.

3. The orientation of action in terms of absolute value is distinguished from the affectual type by its clearly self-conscious formulation of the ultimate values governing the action and the consistently planned orientation of its detailed course to these values. At the same time the two types have a common element, namely that the meaning of the action does not lie in the achievement of a result ulterior to it, but in carrying out the specific type of action for its own sake. Examples of affectual action are the satisfaction of a direct impulse to revenge, to sensual gratification, to devote oneself to a person or ideal, to contemplative bliss, or, finally, toward the working off of emotional tensions. Such impulses belong in this category regardless of how sordid or sublime they may be.

Examples of pure rational orientation to absolute values would be the action of persons who, regardless of possible cost to themselves, act to put into practice their convictions of what seems to them to be required by duty, honour, the pursuit of beauty, a religious call, personal loyalty, or the importance of some 'cause' no matter in what it consists. For the purposes of this discussion, when action is oriented to absolute values, it always involves 'commands' or 'demands' to the fulfilment of which the actor feels obligated. It is only in cases where human action is motivated by the fulfilment of such unconditional demands that it will be described as oriented to absolute values. This is empirically the case in widely varying degrees, but for the most part only to a relatively slight extent. Nevertheless, it will be shown that the occurrence of this mode of action is important enough to justify its formulation as a distinct type; though it may be remarked that there is no intention here of attempting to formulate in any sense an exhaustive classification of types of action.

4. Action is rationally oriented to a system of discrete individual ends (*zweckrational*) when the end, the means, and the secondary results are all rationally taken into account and weighed. This involves rational consideration of alternative means to the end, of the relations of the end to other prospective results of employment of any given means, and finally of the relative importance of different possible ends. Determination of action, either in affectual or in traditional terms, is thus incompatible with this type. Choice between alternative and conflicting ends and results may well be determined by considerations of absolute value. In that case, action is rationally oriented to a system of discrete individual ends only in respect to the choice of means. On the other hand, the actor may, instead of deciding between alternative and conflicting ends in terms of a rational orientation to a system of values, simply take them as given subjective wants and arrange them in a scale of consciously assessed relative urgency. He may then orient his action to this scale in such a way that they are satisfied as far as possible in order of urgency, as formulated in the principle of 'marginal utility'. The orientation of action to absolute values may thus have various different modes of relation to the other type of rational action, in terms of a system of discrete individual ends. From the latter point of view, however, absolute values are always irrational. Indeed, the more the value to which action is oriented is elevated to the status of an absolute value, the more 'irrational' in this sense the corresponding action is. For, the more unconditionally the actor devotes himself to this value for its own sake, to pure sentiment or beauty, to absolute goodness or devotion to duty, the less is he influenced by considerations of the consequences of his action. The orientation of action wholly to the rational achievement of ends without relation to fundamental values is, to be sure, essentially only a limiting case.

5. It would be very unusual to find concrete cases of action, especially of social action, which were oriented *only* in one or another of these ways. Furthermore, this classification of the modes of orientation of action is in no sense meant to exhaust the possibilities of the field, but only to formulate in conceptually pure form certain sociologically important types, to which actual action is more or less closely approximated or, in much the more common case, which constitute the elements combining to make it up. The usefulness of the classification for the purposes of this investigation can only be judged in terms of its results.

The Concept of Social Relationship

The term 'social relationship' will be used to denote the behaviour of a plurality of actors in so far as, in its meaningful content, the action of each takes account of that of the others and is oriented in these terms. The social relationship thus *consists* entirely and exclusively in the existence of a *probability* that there will be, in some meaningfully understandable sense, a course of social action. For purposes of definition there is no attempt to specify the basis of this probability.

1. Thus, as a defining criterion, it is essential that there should be at least a minimum of mutual orientation of the action of each to that of the others. Its content may be of the most varied nature; conflict, hostility, sexual attraction, friendship, loyalty, or economic exchange. It may involve the fulfilment, the evasion, or the denunciation of the terms of an agreement; economic, erotic, or some other form of 'competition'; common membership in national or class groups or those sharing a common tradition of status. In the latter cases mere group membership may or may not extend to include social action; this will be discussed later. The definition, furthermore, does not specify whether the relation of the actors is 'solidary' or the opposite.

2. The 'meaning' relevant in this context is always a case of the meaning imputed to the parties in a given concrete case, on the average or in a theoretically formulated pure type—it is never a normatively 'correct' or a metaphysically 'true' meaning. Even in cases of such forms of social organization as a state, church, association, or marriage, the social relationship consists exclusively in the fact that there has existed, exists, or will exist a probability of action in some definite way appropriate to this meaning. It is vital to be continually clear about this in order to avoid the 'reification' of these concepts. A 'state', for example, ceases to exist in a sociologically relevant sense whenever there is no longer a probability that certain kinds of meaningfully oriented social action will take place. This probability may be very high or it may be negligibly low. But in any case it is only in the sense and degree in which it does exist or can be estimated that the corresponding social relationship exists. It is impossible to find any other clear meaning for the statement that, for instance, a given 'state' exists or has ceased to exist.

3. The subjective meaning need not necessarily be the same for all the parties who are mutually oriented in a given social relationship: there need not in this sense be 'reciprocity'. 'Friendship', 'love', 'loyalty', 'fidelity to contracts', 'patriotism', on one side, may well be faced with an entirely different attitude on the other. In such cases the parties associate different meanings with their actions and the social relationship is in so far objectively 'asymmetrical' from the points of view of the two parties. It may nevertheless be a case of mutual orientation in so far as, even though partly or wholly erroneously, one party presumes a particular attitude toward him on the part of the other and orients his action to this expectation. This can, and usually will, have consequences for the course of action and the form of the relationship. A relationship is objectively symmetrical only as, according the typical expectations of the parties, the meaning for one party is the same as that for the other. Thus the actual attitude of a child to its father may be at least approximately that which the father, in the individual case, on the average or typically, has come to expect. A social relationship in which the attitudes are completely and fully corresponding is in reality a limiting case. But the absence of reciprocity will, for terminological purposes, be held to exclude the existence of a social relationship only if it actually results in the absence of a mutual orientation of the action of the parties. Here as elsewhere all sorts of transitional cases are the rule rather than the exception.

4. A social relationship can be of a temporary character or of varying degrees of permanence. That is, it can be of such a kind that there is a probability of the repeated recurrence of the behaviour which corresponds to its subjective meaning, behaviour which is an understandable consequence of the meaning and hence is expected. In order to avoid fallacious impressions, let it be repeated and continually kept in mind, that it is *only* the existence of the probability that, corresponding to a given subjective meaning complex, a certain type of action will take place, which constitutes the 'existence' of the social relationship. Thus that a 'friendship' or a 'state' exists or has existed means this and only this: that we, the observers, judge that there is or has been a probability that on the basis of certain kinds of known subjective attitude of certain individuals there will result in the average sense a certain specific type of action. For the purpose of legal reasoning it is essential to be able to decide whether a rule of law does or does not carry legal authority, hence whether a legal relationship does or does not 'exist'. This type of question is not, however, relevant to sociological problems.

5. The subjective meaning of a social relationship may change, thus a political relationship, once based on solidarity, may develop into a conflict of interest. In that case it is only a matter of terminological convenience and of the degree of continuity of the change whether we say that a new relationship has come into existence or that the old one continues but has acquired a new meaning. It is also possible for the meaning to be partly constant, partly changing.

6. The meaningful content which remains relatively constant in a social relationship is capable of formulation in terms of maxims which the parties concerned expect to be adhered to by their partners, on the average and approximately. The more rational in relation to values or to given ends the action is, the more is this likely to be the case. There is far less possibility of a rational formulation of subjective meaning in the case of a relation of erotic attraction or of personal loyalty or any other affectual type than, for example, in the case of a business contract.

7. The meaning of a social relationship may be agreed upon by mutual consent. This implies that the parties make promises covering their future behaviour, whether toward each other or toward third persons. In such cases each party then normally counts, so far as he acts rationally, in some degree on the fact that the other will orient his action to the meaning of the agreement as he (the first actor) understands it. In part, they orient their action rationally to these expectations as given facts with, to be sure, varying degrees of subjectively 'loyal' intention of doing their part. But in part also they are motivated each by the value to him of his 'duty' to adhere to the agreement in the sense in which he understands it. This much may be anticipated.

Modes of Orientation of Social Action

It is possible in the field of social action to observe certain empirical uniformities. Certain types, that is, of action which corresponds to a typically appropriate subjective meaning attributable to the same actors, are found to be wide-spread, being frequently repeated by the same individual or simultaneously performed by many different ones. Sociological investigation is concerned with these typical modes of action. Thereby it differs from history, the subject of which is rather the causal explanation of important individual events; important, that is, in having an influence on human destiny.

An actually existent probability of a uniformity in the orientation of social action will be called 'usage' (*Brauch*), if and in so far as the probability of its maintenance among a group of persons is determined entirely by its actual practice. Usage will be called 'custom' (*Sitte*) if the actual performance rests on long familiarity. On the other hand, a uniformity of action may be said to be 'determined by the exploitation of the opportunities of his situation in the self-interest of the actor'. This type of uniformity exists in so far as the probability of its empirical performance is determined by the purely rational (*zweckrational*) orientation of the actors to similar ulterior expectations.[7]

1. Usage also includes 'fashion' (*Mode*). As distinguished from custom and in direct contrast to it, usage will be called fashion so far as the mere fact of the novelty of the corresponding behaviour is the basis of the orientation of action. Its place is closely related to that of 'convention',[8] since both of them usually spring from a desire for social prestige. It will not, however, be further discussed here.

2. As distinguished from both 'convention' and 'law', 'custom' refers to rules devoid of any external sanction. The actor conforms with them of his own free will, whether his motivation lies in the fact that he merely fails to think about it, that it is more comfortable to conform, or whatever else the reason may be. But always it is a justified expectation on the part of the members of the group that a customary rule will be adhered to. Thus custom is not 'valid'[9] in anything like the legal sense; conformity with it is not 'demanded' by anybody. Naturally, the transition from this to validly enforced convention and to law is gradual. Everywhere what has been traditionally handed down has been an important source of what has come to be enforced. To-day it is customary every morning to eat a breakfast which, within limits, conforms to a certain pattern. But there is no obligation to do so, except possibly for hotel guests ('American plan'), and it has not always been customary. On the other hand, the current mode of dress, even though it has partly originated in custom, is to-day very largely no longer customary alone, but conventional.[10]

3. Many of the especially notable uniformities in the course of social action are not determined by orientation to any sort of norm which is held to be valid, nor do they rest on custom, but entirely on the fact that the corresponding type of social action is in the nature of the case best adapted to the normal interests of the actors as they themselves are aware of them. This is above all true of economic action, for example, the uniformities of price determination in a 'free' market, but is by no means confined to such cases. The dealers in a market thus treat their own actions as means for obtaining the satisfaction of the ends defined by what they realize to be their own typical economic interests, and similarly treat as conditions the corresponding typical expectations as to the prospective behaviour of others. The more strictly rational their action is, the more will they tend to react similarly to the same situation. In this way there arise similarities, uniformities, and continuities in their attitudes and actions which are often far more stable than they would be if action were oriented to a system of norms and duties which were considered binding on the members of a group. This phenomenon—the fact that orientation to the situation in terms of the pure self-interest of the individual and of the others to whom he is

related can bring about results which are very similar to those which an authoritarian agency, very often in vain, has attempted to obtain by coercion—has aroused a lively interest, especially in economic affairs. Observation of this has, in fact, been one of the important sources of economics as a science. But it is true in all other spheres of action as well. This type, with its clarity of self-consciousness and freedom from subjective scruples, is the polar antithesis of every sort of unthinking acquiescence in customary ways, as well as, on the other hand, of devotion to norms consciously accepted as absolute values. One of the most important aspects of the process of 'rationalization' of action is the substitution for the unthinking acceptance of ancient custom, of deliberate adaptation to situations in terms of self-interest. To be sure, this process by no means exhausts the concept of rationalization of action. For in addition this can proceed in a variety of other directions; positively in that of a conscious rationalization of ultimate values; or negatively, at the expense not only of custom, but of emotional values; and, finally, in favour of a morally sceptical type of rationality, at the expense of any belief in absolute values. The many possible meanings of the concept of rationalization will often enter into the discussion.[11] Further remarks on the analytical problem will be found below.[12]

4. The stability of merely customary action rests essentially on the fact that the person who does not adapt himself to it is subjected to both petty and major inconveniences and annoyances as long as the majority of the people he comes in contact with continue to uphold the custom and conform with it.

Similarly, the stability of action in terms of self-interest rests on the fact that the person who does not orient his action to the interests of others, does not 'take account' of them, arouses their antagonism or may end up in a situation different from that which he had foreseen or wished to bring about. He thus runs the risk of damaging his own interest.

NOTES

1. Weber employs *Verstehen*. 'Understanding' has been most commonly used. Other expressions such as 'subjectively understandable', 'interpretation in subjective terms', 'comprehension', etc., have been used from time to time as the context seemed to demand.—Ed. [Talcott Parsons]

2. In this series of definitions Weber employs several important terms which need discussion. In addition to *Verstehen*, which has already been commented upon, there are four important ones: *Deuten, Sinn, Handeln*, and *Verhalten*. *Deuten* has generally been translated as 'interpret'. As used by Weber in this context it refers to the interpretation of subjective states of mind and the meanings which can be imputed as intended by an actor. Any other meaning of the word 'interpretation' is irrelevant to Weber's discussion. The term *Sinn* has generally been translated as 'meaning'; and its variations, particularly the corresponding adjectives, *sinnhaft, sinnvoll, sinnfremd*, have been dealt with by appropriately modifying the term meaning. The reference here again is always to features of the content of subjective states of mind or of symbolic systems which are ultimately referable to such states of mind.

The terms *Handeln* and *Verhalten* are directly related, *Verhalten* is the broader term referring to any mode of behaviour of human individuals, regardless of the frame of reference in terms of which it is analysed. 'Behaviour' has seemed to be the most appropriate English equivalent. *Handeln*, on the other hand, refers to the concrete phenomenon of human behaviour only in so far as it is capable of 'understanding', in Weber's technical sense, in terms of subjective categories. The most appropriate English equivalent has seemed to be 'action'. This corresponds to the editor's usage in *The Structure of Social Action* and would seem to be fairly well established. 'Conduct' is also closely similar and has sometimes been used. *Deuten*, *Verstehen*, and *Sinn* are thus applicable to human behaviour only in so far as it constitutes action or conduct in this specific sense.—Ed.

3. Weber's text is organized in a somewhat unusual manner. He lays down certain fundamental definitions and then proceeds to comment upon them. The definitions themselves are in the original printed in large type, the subsidiary comments in smaller type. For the purposes of this translation it has not seemed best to made a distinction in type form, but the reader should be aware that the numbered paragraphs which follow a definition or group of them are in the nature of comments, rather than the continuous development of a general line of argument. This fact accounts for what is sometimes a relatively fragmentary character of the development and for the abrupt transition from one subject to another. Weber apparently did not intend this material to be 'read' in the ordinary sense, but rather to serve as a reference work for the clarification and systematization of theoretical concepts and their implications. While the comments under most of the definitions are relatively brief, under the definitions of Sociology and of Social Action, Weber wrote what is essentially a methodological essay. This makes sec. 1 out of proportion to the other sections of this and the following chapters. It has, however, seemed best to retain Weber's own plan for the subdivision of the material—Ed.

4. Weber means by 'pure type' what he himself generally called and what has come to be known in the literature about his methodology as the 'ideal type'. The reader may be referred for general orientation to Weber's own Essay (to which he himself refers below), *Die Objektivität sozialwissenschaftlicher Erkenntnis*; to two works of Dr Alexander yon Schelting, 'Die logische Theorie der historschen Kulturwissenschaften von Max Weber' (*Archiv fuer Sozialwissenschaft*, vol. xlix), and *Max Webers Wissenschaftslehre*; and to the editor's *Structure of Social Action*, ch. xvi. A somewhat different interpretation is given in Theodore Abel, *Systematic Sociology in Germany*, ch. iv.—Ed.

5. This is an imperfect rendering of the German term *Evidenz*, for which, unfortunately, there is no good English equivalent. It has hence been rendered in a number of different ways, varying with the particular context in which it occurs. The primary meaning refers to the basis on which a scientist or thinker becomes satisfied of the certainty or acceptability of a proposition. As Weber himself points out, there are two primary aspects of this. On the one hand a conclusion can be 'seen' to follow from given premises by virtue of logical, mathematical, or possibly other modes of meaningful relation. In this sense one 'sees' the solution of an arithmetical problem or the correctness of the proof of a geometrical theorem. The other aspect is concerned with empirical observation. If an act of observation is competently performed, in a similar sense one 'sees' the truth of the relevant descriptive proposition. The term *Evidenz* does not refer to the process of observing, but to the quality of its result, by virtue of which the observer feels justified in affirming a given statement. Hence 'certainty' has seemed a suitable translation in some contexts, 'clarity' in others, 'accuracy' in still others. The term 'intuition' is not usable because it refers to the process rather than to the result.—Ed.

6. The two terms *zweckrational* and *wertrational* are of central significance to Weber's theory, but at the same time present one of the most difficult problems to the translator. Perhaps the keynote

of the distinction lies in the absoluteness with which the values involved in *Wertrationalität* are held. The sole important consideration to the actor becomes the realization of the value. In so far as it involves ends, rational consideration, such as those of efficiency, are involved in the choice of means. But there is no question either of rational weighing of this end against others, nor is there a question of 'counting the cost' in the sense of taking account of possible results other than the attainment of the absolute end. In the case of *Zweckrationalität*, on the other hand, Weber conceives action as motivated by a plurality of relatively independent ends, none of which is absolute. Hence, rationality involves on the one hand the weighing of the relative importance of their realization, on the other hand, consideration of whether undesirable consequences would outweigh the benefits to be derived from the projected course of action. It has not seemed possible to find English terms which would express this distinction succinctly. Hence the attempt has been made to express the ideas as clearly as possible without specific terms.

It should also be pointed out that, as Weber's analysis proceeds, there is a tendency of the meaning of these terms to shift, so that *Wertrationalität* comes to refer to a system of ultimate ends, regardless of the degree of their absoluteness, while *Zweckrationalität* refers primarily to considerations respecting the choice of means and ends which are in turn means to further ends, such as money. What seems to have happened is that Weber shifted from a classification of ideal types of action to one of elements in the structure of action. In the latter context 'expediency' is often an adequate rendering of *Zweckrationalität*. This process has been analysed in the editor's *Structure of Social Action*, ch. xvi.

The other two terms *affektuell* and *traditional* do not present any difficulty of translation. The term affectual has come into English psychological usage from the German largely through the influence of psychoanalysis.

7. In the above classification as well as in some of those which follow, the terminology is not standardized either in German or in English. Hence, just as there is a certain arbitrariness in Weber's definitions, the same is true of any corresponding set of definitions in English. It should be kept in mind that all of them are modes of orientation of action to patterns which contain a normative element. 'Usage' has seemed to be the most appropriate translation of *Brauch* since, according to Weber's own definition, the principal criterion is that 'it is done to conform with the pattern'. There would also seem to be good precedent for the translation of *Sitte* by 'custom'. The contrast with fashion, which Weber takes up in his first comment, is essentially the same in both languages. The term *Interessenlage* presents greater difficulty. It involves two components: the motivation in terms of self-interest and orientation to the opportunities presented by the situation. It has not seemed possible to use any single term to convey this meaning in English and hence, a more roundabout expression has had to be resorted to.—Ed.

8. The term 'convention' in Weber's usage is narrower than *Brauch*. The difference consists in the fact that a normative pattern to which action is oriented is conventional only in so far as it is regarded as part of a legitimate order, whereas the question of moral obligation to conformity which legitimacy implies is not involved in 'usage'. The distinction is closely related to that of W.G. Sumner between 'mores' and 'folkways'. It has seemed best to retain the English term closest to Weber's own.—Ed.

9. The German term which has been translated as 'validity' is *Geltung*. The primary use of this term is in a legal context and hence the validity in question is not empirical or logical validity, but legal. A legal rule is 'valid' in so far as it is judged binding upon those who recognize the legiti-

macy of the legal order.—Ed.

10. On the concepts of usage and custom, the relevant parts of vol. ii of Ihering's *Zweck im Recht* are still worth reading. Compare also, K. Oertmann, *Rechtesregelung und Verkehrssitte* (1914); and more recently, E. Weigelin, *Sitte, Recht und Moral*, 1919, which agrees with the author's position as opposed to that of Stammler.

11. It is, in a sense, the empirical reference of this statement which constitutes the central theme of Weber's series of studies in the Sociology of Religion. In so far as he finds it possible to attribute importance to 'ideas' in the determination of action, the most important difference between systems of ideas are not so much those in the degree of rationalization as in the direction which the process of rationalization in each case has taken. This series of studies was left uncompleted at his death, but all the material which was in a condition fit for publication has been assembled in the three volumes of the *Gesammelte Aufsätze zur Religionssoziologie.*—Ed.

12. It has not been possible to identify this reference of Weber's. It refers most probably to a projected conclusion of the whole work which was never written.—Ed.

LEGITIMATE DOMINATION

The Basis of Legitimacy

Domination and Legitimacy

Domination was defined above (ch. 1) as the probability that certain specific commands (or all commands) will be obeyed by a given group of persons. It thus does not include every mode of exercising 'power' or 'influence' over other persons. Domination ('authority')[1] in this sense may be based on the most diverse motives of compliance: all the way from simple habituation to the most purely rational calculation of advantage. Hence every genuine form of domination implies a minimum of voluntary compliance, that is, an *interest* (based on ulterior motives or genuine acceptance) in obedience.

Not every case of domination makes use of economic means; still less does it always have economic objectives. However, normally the rule over a considerable number of persons requires a staff, that is, a *special* group which can normally be trusted to execute the general policy as well as the specific commands. The members of the administrative staff may be bound to obedience to their superior (or superiors) by custom, by affectual ties, by a purely material complex of interests, or by ideal (*wertrationale*) motives. The quality of these motives largely determines the type of domination. *Purely* material interests and calculations of advantages as the basis of solidarity between the chief and his administrative staff result, in this as in other connexions, in a relatively unstable situation. Normally other elements, affectual and ideal, supplement such interests. In certain exceptional cases the former alone may be decisive. In everyday life these relationships, like others, are governed by custom and material calculation of advantage. But custom, personal advantage, purely affectual or ideal motives of solidarity, do not form a sufficiently reliable basis for a given domination. In addition there is normally a further element, the belief in *legitimacy*.

Experience shows that in no instance does domination voluntarily limit itself to the appeal to material or affectual or ideal motives as a basis for its continuance. In addition every such system attempts to establish and to cultivate the belief in its legitimacy. But according to the kind of legitimacy which is claimed, the type of obedience, the kind of administrative staff developed to guarantee it, and the mode of exercising authority, will all differ fundamentally. Equally fundamental is the variation in effect. Hence, it is useful to classify the types of domination according to the kind of claim to legitimacy typically made by each. In doing this, it is best to start from modern and therefore more familiar examples.

1. The choice of this rather than some other basis of classification can only be justified by its results. The fact that certain other typical criteria of variation are thereby neglected for the time being and can only be introduced at a later stage is not a decisive difficulty. The legitimacy of a system of control has far more than a merely 'ideal' significance, if only because it has very definite relations to the legitimacy of property.

2. Not every claim which is protected by custom or law should be spoken of as involving a relation of authority. Otherwise the worker, in his claim for fulfilment of the wage contract, would be exercising authority over his employer because his claim can, on occasion, be enforced by order of a court. Actually his formal status is that of party to a contractual relationship with his employer, in which he has certain 'rights' to receive payments. At the same time the concept of an authority relationship (*Herrschaftsverhältnis*) naturally does not exclude the possibility that it has originated in a formally free contract. This is true of the *authority* of the employer over the worker as manifested in the former's rules and instructions regarding the work process; and also of the *authority* of a feudal lord over a vassal who has freely entered into the relation of fealty. That subjection to military discipline is formally 'involuntary' while that to the discipline of the factory is voluntary does not alter the fact that the latter is also a case of subjection to *authority*. The position of a bureaucratic official is also entered into by contract and can be freely resigned, and even the status of 'subject' can often be freely entered into and (in certain circumstances) freely repudiated. Only in the limiting case of the slave is formal subjection to authority absolutely involuntary.

On the other hand, we shall not speak of formal domination if a monopolistic position permits a person to exert economic power, that is, to dictate the terms of exchange to contractual partners. Taken by itself, this does not constitute authority any more than any other kind of influence which is derived from some kind of superiority, as by virtue of erotic attractiveness, skill in sport or in discussion. Even if a big bank is in a position to force other banks into a cartel arrangement, this will not alone be sufficient to justify calling it an authority. But if there is an immediate relation of command and obedience such that the management of the first bank can give orders to the others with the claim that they shall, and the probability that they will, be obeyed regardless of particular content, and if their carrying out is supervised, it is another matter. Naturally, here as everywhere the transitions are gradual; there are all sorts of intermediate steps between mere indebtedness and debt slavery. Even the position of a 'salon' can come very close to the borderline of authoritarian domination and yet not necessarily constitute 'authority'.

Sharp differentiation in concrete fact is often impossible, but this makes clarity in the analytical distinctions all the more important.

3. Naturally, the legitimacy of a system of domination may be treated sociologically only as the probability that to a relevant degree the appropriate attitudes will exist, and the corresponding practical conduct ensue. It is by no means true that every case of submissiveness to persons in positions of power is primarily (or even at all) oriented to this belief. Loyalty may be hypocritically simulated by individuals or by whole groups on purely opportunistic grounds, or carried out in practice for reasons of material self-interest. Or people may submit from individual weakness and helplessness because there is no acceptable alternative. But these considerations are not decisive for the classification of types of domination. What is important is the fact that in a given case the particular claim to legitimacy is to a significant degree and according to its type treated as 'valid'; that this fact confirms the position of the persons claiming authority and that it helps to determine the choice of means of its exercise.

Furthermore, a system of domination may—as often occurs in practice—be so completely protected, on the one hand by the obvious community of interests between the chief and his administrative staff (bodyguards, Pretorians, 'red' or 'white' guards) as opposed to the subjects, on the other hand by the helplessness of the latter, that it can afford to drop even the pretense of a claim to legitimacy. But even then the mode of legitimation of the relation between chief and his staff may vary widely according to the type of basis of the relation of the authority between them, and, as will be shown, this variation is highly significant for the structure of domination.

4. 'Obedience' will be taken to mean that the action of the person obeying follows in essentials such a course that the content of the command may be taken to have become the basis of action of its own sake. Furthermore, the fact that it is so taken is referable only to the formal obligation, without regard to the actor's own attitude to the value or lack of value of the content of the command as such.

5. Subjectively, the causal sequence may vary, especially as between 'intuition' and 'sympathetic agreement'. This distinction is not, however, significant for the present classification of types of authority.

6. The scope of determination of social relationships and cultural phenomena by virtue of domination is considerably broader than appears at first sight. For instance, the authority exercised in the schools has much to do with the determination of the forms of speech and of written language which are regarded as orthodox. Dialects used as the 'chancellery language' of autocephalous political units, hence of their rulers, have often become orthodox forms of speech and writing and have even led to the formation of separate 'nations' (for instance, the separation of Holland from Germany). The rule by parents and the school, however, extends far beyond the determination of such cultural patterns, which are perhaps only apparently formal, to the formation of the young, and hence of human beings generally.

7. The fact that the chief and his administrative staff often appear formally as servants or agents of those they rule, naturally does nothing whatever to disprove the quality of dominance. There will be occasion later to speak of the substantive features of so-called 'democracy'. But a certain minimum of assured power to issue commands, thus of domi-

nation, must be provided for in nearly every conceivable case.

The Three Pure Types of Authority

There are three pure types of legitimate domination. The validity of the claims to legitimacy may be based on:

1. Rational grounds—resting on a belief in the legality of enacted rules and the right of those elevated to authority under such rules to issue commands (legal authority).

2. Traditional grounds—resting on an established belief in the sanctity of immemorial traditions and the legitimacy of those exercising authority under them (traditional authority); or finally,

3. Charismatic grounds—resting on devotion to the exceptional sanctity, heroism or exemplary character of an individual person, and of the normative patterns or order revealed or ordained by him (charismatic authority).

In the case of legal authority, obedience is owed to the legally established impersonal order. It extends to the persons exercising the authority of office under it by virtue of the formal legality of their commands and only within the scope of authority of the office. In the case of traditional authority, obedience is owed to the *person* of the chief who occupies the traditionally sanctioned position of authority and who is (within its sphere) bound by tradition. But here the obligation of obedience is a matter of personal loyalty within the area of accustomed obligations. In the case of charismatic authority, it is the charismatically qualified leader as such who is obeyed by virtue of personal trust in his revelation, his heroism or his exemplary qualities so far as they fall within the scope of the individual's belief in his charisma.

1. The usefulness of the above classification can only be judged by its results in promoting systematic analysis. The concept of 'charisma' ('the gift of grace') is taken from the vocabulary of early Christianity. For the Christian hierocracy Rudolf Sohm, in his *Kirchenrecht*, was the first to clarify the substance of the concept, even though he did not use the same terminology. Others (for instance, Holl in *Enthusiasmus und Bussgewalt*) have clarified certain important consequences of it. It is thus nothing new.

2. The fact that none of these three ideal types, the elucidation of which will occupy the following pages, is usually to be found in historical cases in 'pure' form, is naturally not a valid objection to attempting their conceptual formulation in the sharpest possible form. In this respect the present case is no different from many others. Later on the transformation of pure charisma by the process of routinization will be discussed and thereby the relevance of the concept to the understanding of empirical systems of authority considerably increased. But even so it may be said of every historical phenomenon of authority that it is not likely to be 'as an open book'. Analysis in terms of sociological types has, after all, as compared with purely empirical historical investigation, certain advantages which should not be minimized. That is, it can in the particular case of a concrete form of authority determine what conforms to or approximates such types as 'charisma', 'hereditary charisma', 'the charisma of office', 'patriarchy', 'bureaucracy', the authority of status groups, and in doing so it can work with relatively unambiguous concepts. But the idea that the whole of concrete historical reality can be exhausted in the conceptual scheme about to be developed is as far from the author's thoughts as anything could be.

Legal Authority with a Bureaucratic Administrative Staff

Note: The specifically modern type of administration has intentionally been taken as a point of departure in order to make it possible later to contrast the others with it.

Legal Authority: The Pure Type

Legal authority rests on the acceptance of the validity of the following mutually interdependent ideas.

1. That any given legal norm may be established by agreement or by imposition on grounds of expediency or value-rationality or both, with a claim to obedience at least on the part of the members of the organization. This is, however, usually extended to include all persons within the sphere of power in question—which in the case of territorial bodies is the territorial area—who stand in certain social relationships or carry out forms of social action which in the order governing the organization have been declared to be relevant.

2. That every body of law consists essentially in a consistent system of abstract rules which have normally been intentionally established. Furthermore, administration of law is held to consist in the application of these rules to particular cases; the administrative process in the rational pursuit of the interests which are specified in the order governing the organization within the limits laid down by legal precepts and following principles which are capable of generalized formulation and are approved in the order governing the group, or at least not disapproved in it.

3. That thus the typical person in authority, the 'superior', is himself subject to an impersonal order by orienting his actions to it in his own dispositions and commands. (This is true not only for persons exercising legal authority who are in the usual sense 'officials', but, for instance, for the elected president of a state.)

4. That the person who obeys authority does so, as it is usually stated, only in his capacity as a 'member' of the organization and what he obeys is only 'the law'. (He may in this connection be the member of an association, of a community, of a church, or a citizen of a state.)

5. In conformity with point 3, it is held that the members of the organization, insofar as they obey a person in authority, do not owe this obedience to him as an individual, but to the impersonal order. Hence, it follows that there is an obligation to obedience only within the sphere of the rationally delimited jurisdiction which, in terms of the order, has been given to him.

. . .

Legal Authority: The Pure Type (continued)

The purest type of exercise of legal authority is that which employs a bureaucratic administrative staff. Only the supreme chief of the organization occupies his position of dominance (*Herrenstellung*) by virtue of appropriation, of election, or of having been designated for the succession. But even *his* authority consists in a sphere of legal 'competence'. The whole administrative staff under the supreme authority then consists, in the purest type, of individual officials (constituting a 'monocracy' as opposed to the 'collegial' type, which will be discussed below) who are appointed and function according to the following criteria:

(1) They are personally free and subject to authority only with respect to their impersonal official obligations.

(2) They are organized in a clearly defined hierarchy of offices.

(3) Each office has a clearly defined sphere of competence in the legal sense.

(4) The office is filled by a free contractual relationship. Thus, in principle, there is free selection.

(5) Candidates are selected on the basis of technical qualifications. In the most rational case, this is tested by examination or guaranteed by diplomas certifying technical training, or both. They are *appointed*, not elected.

(6) They are remunerated by fixed salaries in money, for the most part with a right to pensions. Only under certain circumstances does the employing authority, especially in private organizations, have a right to terminate the appointment, but the official is always free to resign. The salary scale is graded according to rank in the hierarchy; but in addition to this criterion, the responsibility of the position and the requirements of the incumbent's social status may be taken into account.

(7) The office is treated as the sole, or at least the primary, occupation of the incumbent.

(8) It constitutes a career. There is a system of 'promotion' according to seniority or to achievement, or both. Promotion is dependent on the judgement of superiors.

(9) The official works entirely separated from ownership of the means of administration and without appropriation of his position.

(10) He is subject to strict and systematic discipline and control in the conduct of the office.

. . .

Bureaucratic administration means fundamentally domination through knowledge. This is the feature of it which makes it specifically rational. This consists on the one hand in technical knowledge which, by itself, is sufficient to ensure it a position of extraordinary power. But in addition to this, bureaucratic organizations, or the holders of power who make use of them, have the tendency to increase their power still further by the knowledge growing out of experience in the service. For they acquire through the conduct of office a special knowledge of facts and have available a store of documentary material peculiar to themselves. While not peculiar to bureaucratic organizations, the concept of 'official secrets' is certainly typical of them. It stands in relation to technical knowledge in somewhat the same position as commercial secrets do to technological training. It is a product of the striving for power.

. . .

Traditional Authority

The Pure Type

Authority will be called traditional if legitimacy is claimed for it and believed in by virtue of the sanctity of age-old rules and powers. The masters are designated according to traditional rules and are obeyed because of their traditional status (*Eigenwürde*). This type of organized rule is, in the simplest case, primarily based on personal loyalty which results from common upbringing. The person exercising authority is not a 'superior' but a personal master, his administrative staff does not consist mainly of officials but of personal retainers, and the ruled are not 'members' of an association but are either his traditional 'comrades' or his 'subjects'. Personal loyalty, not the official's impersonal duty, determines the relations of the administrative staff to the master.

Obedience is owed not to enacted rules but to the person who occupies a position of authority by tradition or who has been chosen for it by the traditional master. The commands of such a person are legitimized in one of two ways:

a) partly in terms of traditions which themselves directly determine the content of the command and are believed to be valid within certain limits that cannot be overstepped without endangering the master's traditional status;

b) partly in terms of the master's discretion in that sphere which tradition leaves open to him; this traditional prerogative rests primarily on the fact that the obligations of personal obedience tend to be essentially unlimited.

Thus there is a double sphere:

a) that of action which is bound to specific traditions;

b) that of action which is free of specific rules.

In the latter sphere, the master is free to do good turns on the basis of his personal pleasure and likes, particularly in return for gifts—the historical sources of dues (*Gebühren*). So far as his action follows principles at all, these are governed by considerations of ethical common sense, of equity or of utilitarian expediency. They are not formal principles, as in the case of legal authority. The exercise of power is oriented toward the consideration of how far master and staff can go in view of the subjects' traditional compliance without arousing their resistance. When resistance occurs, it is directed against the master or his servant personally, the accusation being that he failed to observe the traditional limits of his power. Opposition is not directed against the system as such—it is a case of 'traditionalist revolution'.

In the pure type of traditional authority it is impossible for law or administrative rule to be deliberately created by legislation. Rules which in fact are innovations can be legitimized only by the claim that they have been 'valid of yore', but have only now been recognized by means of 'Wisdom' [the *Weistum* of ancient Germanic law]. Legal decisions as 'finding of the law' (*Rechtsfindung*) can refer only to documents of tradition, namely to precedents and earlier decisions.

. . .

Charismatic Authority

Charismatic Authority and Charismatic Community

The term 'charisma' will be applied to a certain quality of an individual personality by virtue of which he is considered extraordinary and treated as endowed with supernatural, superhuman, or at least specifically exceptional powers or qualities. These are such as are not accessible to the ordinary person, but are regarded as of divine origin or as exemplary, and on the basis of them the individual concerned is treated as a 'leader'. In primitive circumstances this peculiar kind of quality is thought of as resting on magical powers, whether of prophets, persons with a reputation for therapeutic or legal wisdom, leaders in the hunt, or heroes in war. How the quality in question would be ultimately judged from any ethical, aesthetic, or other such point of view is naturally entirely indifferent for purposes of definition. What is alone important is how the individual is actually regarded by those subject to charismatic authority, by his 'followers' or 'disciples'.

For present purposes it will be necessary to treat a variety of different types as being endowed with charisma in this sense. It includes the state of a 'berserk' whose spells of maniac passion have, apparently wrongly, sometimes been attributed to the use of drugs. In medieval Byzantium a group of these men endowed with the charisma of fighting frenzy was maintained as a kind of weapon. It includes the 'shaman', the magician who in the pure type has to be subject to epileptoid seizures as a means of falling into trances. Another type is represented by Joseph Smith, the founder of Mormonism, who may have been a very sophisticated swindler (although this cannot be definitely established). Finally it includes the type of *littérateur*, such as Kurt Eisner,[2] who is overwhelmed by his own demagogic success. Value-free sociological analysis will treat all these on the same level as it does the charisma of men who are the 'greatest' heroes, prophets, and saviours according to conventional judgements.

1. It is recognition on the part of those subject to authority which is decisive for the validity of charisma. This recognition is freely given and guaranteed by what is held to be a proof, originally always a miracle, and consists in devotion to the corresponding revelation, hero worship, or absolute trust in the leader. But where charisma is genuine, it is not this which is the basis of the claim to legitimacy. This basis lies rather in the conception that it is the duty of those subject to charismatic authority to recognize its genuineness and to act accordingly. Psychologically this recognition is a matter of complete personal devotion to the possessor of the quality, arising out of enthusiasm, or of despair and hope.

No prophet has ever regarded his quality as dependent on the attitudes of the masses toward him. No elective king or military leader has ever treated those who have resisted him or tried to ignore him otherwise than as a delinquent in duty. Failure to take part in a military expedition under such leader, even though the recruitment is formally voluntary, has universally met with disdain.

2. If proof and success elude the leader for long, if he appears deserted by his god or his magical or heroic powers, above all, if his leadership fails to benefit his followers, it is likely that his charismatic authority will disappear. This is the genuine meaning of the divine right of kings (*Gottesgnadentum*).

Even the old Germanic kings were sometimes rejected with scorn. Similar phenomena are very common among so-called primitive peoples.

In China the charismatic quality of the monarch, which was transmitted unchanged by heredity, was upheld so rigidly that any misfortune whatever, not only defeats in war, but drought, floods, or astronomical phenomena which were considered unlucky, forced him to do public penance and might even force his abdication. If such things occurred, it was a sign that he did not possess the requisite charismatic virtue and was thus not a legitimate 'Son of Heaven'.

3. An organized group subject to charismatic authority will be called a charismatic community (*Gemeinde*). It is based on an emotional form of communal relationship (*Vergemeinschaftung*). The administrative staff of a charismatic leader does not consist of 'officials'; least of all are its members technically trained. It is not chosen on the basis of social privilege nor from the point of view of domestic or personal dependency. It is rather chosen in terms of the charismatic qualities of its members. The prophet has his disciples; the warlord his bodyguard; the leader, generally, his agents (*Vertrauensmänner*). There is no such thing as appointment or dismissal, no career, no promotion. There is only a call at the instance of the leader on the basis of the charismatic qualification of those he summons. There is no hierarchy; the leader merely intervenes in general or in individual cases when he considers the members of his staff lacking in charismatic qualification for a given task. There is no such thing as a bailiwick or definite sphere of competence, and no appropriation of official powers on the basis of social privileges. There may, however, be territorial or functional limits to charismatic powers and to the individual's mission. There is no such thing as a salary or a benefice.

Disciples or followers tend to live primarily in a communistic relationship with their leader on means which have been provided by voluntary gift. There are no established administrative organs. In their place are agents who have been provided with charismatic authority by their chief or who possess charisma of their own. There is no system of formal rules, of abstract legal principles, and hence no process of rational judicial decision oriented to them. But equally there is no legal wisdom oriented to judicial precedent. Formally concrete judgements are newly created from case to case and are originally regarded as divine judgements and revelations. From a substantive point of view, every charismatic authority would have to subscribe to the proposition, 'It is written . . . but I say unto you . . .'. The genuine prophet, like the genuine military leader and every true leader in this sense, preaches, creates, or demands *new* obligations—most typically, by virtue of revelation, oracle, inspiration, or of his own will, which are recognized by the members of the religious, military, or party group because they come from such a source. Recognition is a duty. When such an authority comes into conflict with the competing authority of another who also claims charismatic sanction, the only recourse is to some kind of a contest, by magical means or an actual physical battle of the leaders. In principle, only one side can be right in such a conflict; the other must be guilty of a wrong which has to be expiated.

Since it is 'extra-ordinary', charismatic authority is sharply opposed to rational, and particularly bureaucratic, authority, and to traditional authority, whether in its patriarchal, patrimonial, or estate variants, all of which are everyday forms of domination; while the charismatic type is the direct antitheses of this. Bureaucratic authority is specifically rational in the sense of being bound to intellectually analysable rules; while charismatic authority is specifically irrational in the sense of being foreign to all rules. Traditional authority is bound to the precedents handed down from the past and to this extent is also oriented to rules. Within the sphere of its claims, charismatic authority repudiates the past, and is in this sense a specifically revolutionary force. It recognizes no appropriation of positions of power by virtue of the possession of property, either on the part of a chief or of socially privileged groups. The only basis of legitimacy for it is personal charisma so long as it is proved; that is, as long as it receives recognition and as long as the followers and disciples prove their usefulness charismatically.

. . .

The Routinization of Charisma

The Rise of the Charismatic Community and the Problem of Succession

In its pure form charismatic authority has a character specifically foreign to everyday routine structures. The social relationships directly involved are strictly personal, based on the validity and practice of charismatic personal qualities. If this is not to remain a purely transitory phenomenon, but to take on the character of a permanent relationship, a 'community' of disciples or followers or a party organization or any sort of political or hierocratic organization, it is necessary for the character of charismatic authority to become radically changed. Indeed, in its pure form charismatic authority may be said to exist only *in statu nascendi*. It cannot remain stable, but becomes either traditionalized or rationalized, or a combination of both.

NOTES

1. Weber put *Autorität* in quotation marks and parentheses behind *Herrschaft*, referring to an alternative colloquial term, but the sentence makes it clear that this does not yet specify the basis of compliance. However, the chapter is devoted to a typology of legitimate domination, which will alternatively be translated as authority.

2. Kurt Eisner, a brilliant Social Democratic (not Communist) intellectual, proclaimed the Bavarian Republic in Nov. 1918. He was murdered on Feb. 21, 1919. When the death sentence of the murderer, Count Arco, was commuted to a life sentence in Jan. 1920, Weber announced at the beginning of one of his lectures that he favoured Arco's execution on substantive and pragmatic grounds. In the next lecture this resulted in a packed audience and noisy right-wing demonstration, which prevented Weber from lecturing. See now the account of two eyewitnesses in René König and Johannes Winckelmann, eds, *Max Weber zum Gedächtnis*. Special issue 7 of the *Kölner Zeitschrift für Soziologie*, 1963: 24–9.

BUREAUCRACY

Characteristics of Bureaucracy

Modern officialdom functions in the following specific manner:

I. There is the principle of fixed and official jurisdictional areas, which are generally ordered by rules, that is, by laws or administrative regulations.

1. The regular activities required for the purposes of the bureaucratically governed structure are distributed in a fixed way as official duties.

2. The authority to give the commands required for the discharge of these duties is distributed in a stable way and is strictly delimited by rules concerning the coercive means, physical, sacerdotal, or otherwise, which may be placed at the disposal of officials.

3. Methodical provision is made for the regular and continuous fulfilment of these duties and for the execution of the corresponding rights; only persons who have the generally regulated qualifications to serve are employed.

In public and lawful government these three elements constitute 'bureaucratic authority'. In private economic domination, they constitute bureaucratic 'management'. Bureaucracy, thus understood, is fully developed in political and ecclesiastical communities only in the modern state, and, in the private economy, only in the most advanced institutions of capitalism. Permanent and public office authority, with fixed jurisdiction, is not the historical rule but rather the exception. This is so even in large political structures such as those of the ancient Orient, the Germanic and Mongolian empires of conquest, or of many feudal structures of state. In all these cases, the ruler executes the most important measures through personal trustees, table-companions, or court-servants. Their commissions and authority are not precisely delimited and are temporarily called into being for each case.

II. The principles of the office hierarchy and of levels of graded authority mean a firmly ordered system of super- and subordination in which there is a supervision of the lower offices by the higher one. Such a system offers the governed the possibility of appealing the decision of a lower office to its higher authority, in a definitely regulated manner. With the full development of the bureaucratic type, the office hierarchy is monocratically organized. The principle of hierarchical office authority is found in all bureaucratic structures: in state and ecclesiastical structures as well as large party organizations and private enterprises. It does not matter for the character of bureaucracy whether its authority is called 'private' or 'public'.

When the principle of jurisdictional 'competency' is fully carried through, hierarchical subordination—at least in public office—does not mean that the 'higher' authority is simply authorized to take over the business of the 'lower'. Indeed, the opposite is the rule. Once established and having fulfilled its task, an office tends to continue in existence and be held by another incumbent.

III. The management of the modern office is based upon written documents ('the files'), which are preserved in their original or draught form. There is, therefore, a staff of subaltern officials and scribes of all sorts. The body of officials actively engaged in a 'public' office, along with the respective apparatus of material implements and the files, make up a 'bureau'. In private enterprise, 'the bureau' is often called 'the office'.

In principle, the modern organization of the civil service separates the bureau from the private domicile of the official, and, in general, bureaucracy segregates official activity as something distinct from the sphere of private life. Public monies and equipment are divorced from the private property of the official. This condition is everywhere the product of a long development. Nowadays, it is found in public as well as in private enterprises; in the latter, the principle extends even to the leading entrepreneur. In principle, the executive office is separated from the household, business from private correspondence, and business assets from private fortunes. The more consistently the modern type of business management has been carried through the more are these separations the case. The beginnings of this process are to be found as early as the Middle Ages.

It is the peculiarity of the modern entrepreneur that he conducts himself as the 'first official' of his enterprise, in the very same way in which the ruler [Frederick II of Prussia] of a specifically modern bureaucratic state spoke of himself as 'the first servant' of the state. The idea that the bureau activities of the state are intrinsically different in character from the management of private economic offices is a continental European notion and, by way of contrast, is totally foreign to the American way.

IV. Office management, at least all specialized office management—and such management is distinctly modern—usually presupposes thorough and expert training. This increasingly holds for the modern executive and employee of private enterprises, in the same manner as it holds for the state official.

V. When the office is fully developed, official activity demands the full working capacity of the official, irrespective of the fact that his obligatory time in the bureau may be firmly delimited. In the normal case, this is only the product of a long development, in the public as well as in the private office. Formerly, in all cases, the normal state of affairs was reversed: official business was discharged as a secondary activity.

VI. The management of the office follows general rules, which are more or less stable, more or less exhaustive, and which can be learned. Knowledge of these rules represents a special technical learning which the officials possess. It involved jurisprudence, or administrative or business management.

The reduction of modern office management to rules is deeply embedded in its very nature. The theory of modern public administration, for instance, assumes that the authority to order certain matters by decree—which has been legally granted to public authorities—does not entitle the bureau to regulate the matter by commands given for each case, but only to regulate the matter abstractly. This stands in extreme contrast to the regulation of all relationships through individual privileges and bestowals of favour, which is absolutely dominant in patrimonialism, at least in so far as such relationships are not fixed by sacred tradition.

THE PROTESTANT ETHIC
AND THE SPIRIT OF CAPITALISM

Religious Affiliation and Social Stratification

A glance at the occupational statistics of any country of mixed religious composition brings to light with remarkable frequency a situation which has several times provoked discussion in the Catholic press and literature, and in Catholic congresses in Germany, namely, the fact that business leaders and owners of capital, as well as the higher grades of skilled labour, and even more the higher technically and commercially trained personnel of modern enterprises, are overwhelmingly Protestant. This is true not only in cases where the difference in religion coincides with one of nationality, and thus of cultural development, as in Eastern Germany between Germans and Poles. The same thing is shown in the figures of religious affiliation almost wherever capitalism, at the time of its great expansion, has had a free hand to alter the social distribution of the population in accordance with its needs, and to determine its occupational structure. The more freedom it has had, the more clearly is the effect shown. It is true that the greater relative participation of Protestants in the ownership of capital, in management, and the upper ranks of labour in great modern industrial and commercial enterprises, may in part be explained in terms of historical circumstances which extend far back into the past, and in which religious affiliation is not a cause of the economic conditions, but to a certain extent appears to be a result of them. Participation in the above economic functions usually involves some previous ownership of capital, and generally an expensive education; often both. These are today largely dependent on the possession of inherited wealth, or at least on a certain degree of material well-being. A number of those sections of the old Empire which were most highly developed economically and most favoured by natural resources and situation, in particular a majority of the wealthy towns, went over to Protestantism in the sixteenth century. The results of that circumstance favour the Protestants even today in the struggle for economic existence. There arises thus the historical question: why were the districts of highest economical development at the same time particularly favourable to a revolution in the Church? The answer is by no means so simple as one might think.

. . .

The Spirit of Capitalism

In the title of this study is used the somewhat pretentious phrase, the *spirit* of capitalism. What is to be understood by it? The attempt to give anything like a definition of it brings out certain difficulties which are in the very nature of this type of investigation.

If any object can be found to which this term can be applied with any understandable meaning, it can only be an historical individual, i.e. a complex of elements associated in historical reality which we unite into a conceptual whole from the standpoint of their cultural significance.

Such an historical concept, however, since it refers in its content to a phenomenon significant for its unique individuality, cannot be defined according to the formula *genus proximum, differentia specifica*, but it must be gradually put together out of the individual parts which are taken from historical reality to make it up. Thus the final and definitive concept cannot stand at the beginning of the investigation, but must come at the end. We must, in other words, work out in the course of the discussion, as its most important result, the best conceptual formulation of what we here understand by the spirit of capitalism, that is the best from the point of view which interests us here. This point of view (the one of which we shall speak later) is, further, by no means the only possible one from which the historical phenomena we are investigating can be analysed. Other standpoints would, for this as for every historical phenomenon, yield other characteristics as the essential ones. The result is that it is by no means necessary to understand by the spirit of capitalism only what it will come to mean to *us* for the purposes of our analysis. This is a necessary result of the nature of historical concepts which attempt for their methodological purposes not to grasp historical reality in abstract general formulae, but in concrete genetic sets of relations which are inevitably of a specifically unique and individual character.

Thus, if we try to determine the object, the analysis and historical explanation of which we are attempting, it cannot be in the form of a conceptual definition, but at least in the beginning only a provisional description of what is here meant by the spirit of capitalism. Such a description is, however, indispensable in order clearly to understand the object of the investigation. For this purpose we turn to a document of that spirit which contains what we are looking for in almost classical purity, and at the same time has the advantage of being free from all direct relationship to religion, being thus, for our purposes, free of preconceptions.

'Remember, that *time* is money. He that can earn ten shillings a day by his labour, and goes abroad, or sits idle, one half of that day, though he spends but sixpence during his diversion or idleness, ought not to reckon *that* the only expense; he has really spent, or rather thrown away, five shillings besides.

'Remember, that *credit* is money. If a man lets his money lie in my hands after it is due, he gives me the interest, or so much as I can make of it during that time. This amounts to a considerable sum where a man has good and large credit, and makes good use of it.

'Remember, that money is of the prolific, generating nature. Money can beget money, and its offspring can beget more, and so on. Five shillings turned is six, turned again it is seven and threepence, and so on, till it becomes a hundred pounds. The more there is of it the more it produces every turning, so that the profits rise quicker and quicker. He that kills a breeding sow, destroys all her offspring to the thousandth generation. He that murders a crown, destroys all that it might have produced, even scores of pounds.'

'Remember this saying, *The good paymaster is lord of another man's purse*. He that is known to pay punctually and exactly to the time he promises, may at any time, and on any occasion, raise all the money his friends can spare. This is sometimes of great use. After industry and frugality, nothing contributes more to the raising of a young man in the world than punctuality and justice in all his dealings; therefore never keep borrowed money an hour beyond the time you promised, lest a disappointment shut up your friend's purse for ever.

'The most trifling actions that affect a man's credit are to be regarded. The sound of your hammer at five in the morning, or eight at night, heard by a creditor, makes him easy six months longer; but if he sees you at a billiard-table, or hears your voice at a tavern, when you should be at work, he sends for his money the next day; demands it, before he can receive it, in a lump.

'It shows, besides, that you are mindful of what you owe; it makes you appear a careful as well as an honest man, and that still increases your credit.

'Beware of thinking all your own that you possess, and of living accordingly. It is a mistake that many people who have credit fall into. To prevent this, keep an exact account for some time both of your expenses and your income. If you take the pains at first to mention particulars, it will have this good effect: you will discover how wonderfully small, trifling expenses mount up to large sums, and will discern what might have been, and may for the future be saved, without occasioning any great inconvenience.'

'For six pounds a year you may have the use of one hundred pounds, provided you are a man of known prudence and honesty.

'He that spends a groat a day idly, spends idly above six pounds a year, which is the price for the use of one hundred pounds.

'He that wastes idly a groat's worth of his time per day, one day with another, wastes the privilege of using one hundred pounds each day.

'He that idly loses five shillings' worth of time, loses five shillings, and might as prudently throw five shillings into the sea.

'He that loses five shillings, not only loses that sum, but all the advantage that might be made by turning it in dealing, which by the time that a young man becomes old, will amount to a considerable sum of money.'

It is Benjamin Franklin who preaches to us in these sentences, the same which Ferdinand Kürnberger satirizes in his clever and malicious *Picture of American Culture* as the supposed confession of faith of the Yankee. That it is the spirit of capitalism which here speaks in characteristic fashion, no one will doubt, however little we may wish to claim that everything which could be understood as pertaining to that spirit is contained in it. Let us pause a moment to consider this passage, the philosophy of which Kürnberger sums up in the words, 'They make tallow out of cattle and money out of men'. The peculiarity of this philosophy of avarice appears to be the ideal of the honest man of recognized credit, and above all the idea of a duty of the individual toward the increase of his capital, which is assumed as an end in itself. Truly what is here preached is not simply a means of making one's way in the world, but a peculiar ethic. The infraction of its rules is treated not as foolishness but as forgetfulness of duty. That is the essence of the matter. It is not mere business astuteness, that sort of thing is common enough, it is an ethos. *This* is the quality which interests us.

When Jacob Fugger, in speaking to a business associate who had retired and who wanted to persuade him to do the same, since he had made enough money and should let others have a chance, rejected that as pusillanimity and answered that 'he (Fugger) thought otherwise, he wanted to make money as long as he could', the spirit of his statement is evidently quite different from that of Franklin. What in the former case was an expression of commercial daring and a personal inclination morally neutral, in the latter takes on the character of an ethically coloured maxim for the conduct of life. The concept spirit of capitalism is here used in this specific sense, it is the spirit of modern capitalism. For that we are here dealing only with Western European and American capitalism is obvious from the way in which the problem was stated. Capitalism existed in China, India, Babylon, in the classic world, and in the Middle Ages. But in all these cases, as we shall see, this particular ethos was lacking.

Now, all Franklin's moral attitudes are coloured with utilitarianism. Honesty is useful, because it assures credit; so are punctuality, industry, frugality, and that is the reason they are virtues. A logical deduction from this would be that where, for instance, the appearance of honesty serves the same purpose, that would suffice, and an unnecessary surplus of this virtue would evidently appear to Franklin's eyes as unproductive waste. And as a matter of fact, the story in his autobiography of his conversion to those virtues, or the discussion of the value of a strict maintenance of the appearance of modesty, the assiduous belittlement of one's own deserts in order to gain general recognition later, confirms this impression. According to Franklin, those virtues, like all others, are only in so far virtues as they are actually useful to the individual, and the surrogate of mere appearance is always sufficient when it accomplishes the end in view. It is a conclusion which is inevitable for strict utilitarianism. The impression of many Germans that the virtues professed by Americanism are pure hypocrisy seems to have been confirmed by this striking case. But in fact the matter is not by any means so simple. Benjamin Franklin's own character, as it appears in the really unusual candidness of his autobiography, belies that suspicion. The circumstance that he ascribes his recognition of the utility of virtue to a divine revelation which was intended to lead him in the path of righteousness, shows that something more than mere garnishing for purely egocentric motives is involved.

In fact, the *summum bonum* of this ethic, the earning of more and more money, combined with the strict avoidance of all spontaneous enjoyment of life, is above all completely devoid of any eudaemonistic, not to say hedonistic, admixture. It is thought of so purely as an end in itself, that from the point of view of the happiness of, or utility to, the single individual, it appears entirely transcendental and absolutely irrational. Man is dominated by the making of money, by acquisition as the ultimate purpose of his life. Economic acquisition is no longer subordinated to man as the means for the satisfaction of his material needs. This reversal of what we should call the natural relationship, so irrational from a naive point of view, is evidently as definitely a leading principle of capitalism as it is foreign to all peoples not under capitalistic influence. At the same time it expresses a type of feeling which is closely connected with certain religious ideas. If we thus ask, *why* should 'money be made out of men', Benjamin Franklin himself, although he was a colourless deist, answers in his autobiography with a quotation from the Bible, which his strict Calvinistic father drummed into him again and again in his youth: 'Seest thou a man diligent in his business? He shall stand before kings' (Prov. xxii. 29). The earning of money within the modern economic order is, so long as it is done legally, the result and the expression of virtue and proficiency in a calling; and this virtue and proficiency are, as it is now not difficult to see, the real Alpha and Omega of Franklin's ethic, as expressed in the passages we have quoted, as well as in all his works without exception.

And in truth this peculiar idea, so familiar to us today, but in reality so little a matter of course, of one's duty in a calling, is what is most characteristic of the social ethic of capitalistic culture, and is in a sense the fundamental basis of it. It is an obligation which the individual is supposed to feel and does feel towards the content of his professional activity, no matter in what it consists, in particular no matter whether it appears on the surface as a utilization of his personal powers, or only of his material possessions (as capital).

Of course, this conception has not appeared only under capitalistic conditions. On the contrary, we shall later trace its origins back to a time previous to the advent of capitalism. Still less, naturally, do we maintain that a conscious acceptance of these ethical maxims on the part of individuals, entrepreneurs or labourers, in modern capitalistic enterprises, is a condition of the further existence of present-day capitalism. The capitalistic economy of the present day is an immense cosmos into which the individual is born, and which presents itself to him, at least as an individual, as an unalterable order of things in which he must live. It forces the individual, in so far as he is involved in the system of market relationships, to conform to capitalistic rules of action. The manufacturer who in the long run acts counter to these norms, will just as inevitably be eliminated from the economic scene as the worker who cannot or will not adapt himself to them will be thrown into the streets without a job.

Thus the capitalism of today, which has come to dominate economic life, educates and selects the economical subjects which it needs through a process of economical survival of the fittest. But here one can easily see the limits of the concept of selection as a means of historical explanation. In order that a manner of life so well adapted to the peculiarities of capitalism could be selected at all, i.e. should come to dominate others, it had to originate somewhere, and not in isolated individuals alone, but as a way of life common to whole groups of men. This origin is what really needs explanation. Concerning the doctrine of the more naive historical materialism, that such ideas originate as a reflection or superstructure of economic situations, we shall speak more in detail below. At this point it will suffice for our purpose to call attention to the fact that without doubt, in the country of Benjamin Franklin's birth (Massachusetts), the spirit of capitalism (in the sense we have attached to it) was present before the capitalistic order. There were complaints of a peculiarly calculating sort of profit-seeking in New England, as distinguished from other parts of America, as early as 1632. It is further undoubted the capitalism remained far less developed in some of the neighbouring colonies, the later Southern States of the United States of America, in spite of the fact that these latter were founded by large capitalists for business motives, while the New England colonies were founded by preachers and seminary graduates with the help of small bourgeois, craftsmen and yeomen, for religious reasons. In this case the causal relation is certainly the reverse of that suggested by the materialistic standpoint.

Calvinism

Now Calvinism was the faith over which the great political and cultural struggles of the sixteenth and seventeenth centuries were fought in the most highly developed countries, the Netherlands, England, and France. To it we shall hence turn first. At that time, and in general even today, the doctrine of predestination was considered its most characteristic dogma. It is true that there has been controversy as to whether it is the most essential dogma of the Reformed Church or only an appendage. Judgements of the importance of a historical phenomenon may be judgements of value or faith, namely, when they refer to what is alone interesting, or alone in the long run valuable in it. Or, on the other hand, they may refer to its influence on the other historical processes as a causal factor. Then we are concerned with judgements of historical imputation. If now we start, as we must do here, from the latter standpoint and inquire into the significance which is to be attributed to that dogma by virtue of its cultural and historical consequences, it must certainly be rated very highly. The movement which Oldenbarneveld led was shattered by it. The schism in the English Church became irrevocable under James I after the Crown and the Puritans came to differ dogmatically over just this doctrine. Again and again it was looked upon as the real element of political danger in Calvinism and attacked as such by those in authority. The great synods of the seventeenth century, above all those of Dordrecht and Westminster, besides numerous smaller ones, made its elevation to canonical authority the central purpose of their work. It served as a rallying-point to countless heroes of the Church militant, and in both the eighteenth and the nineteenth centuries it caused schisms in the Church and formed the battle cry of great new awakenings. We cannot pass it by, and since today it can no longer be assumed as known to all educated men, we can best learn its content from the authoritative words of the Westminster Confession of 1647, which in this regard is simply repeated by both Independent and Baptist creeds.

'Chapter IX (of Free Will), No. 3. Man, by his fall into a state of sin, hath wholly lost all ability of will to any spiritual good accompanying salvation. So that a natural man, being altogether averse from that Good, and dead in sin, is not able, by his own strength, to convert himself, or to prepare himself thereunto.

'Chapter III (of God's Eternal Decree), No. 3. By the decree of God, for the manifestation of His glory, some men and angels are predestined unto everlasting life, and others foreordained to everlasting death.

'No. 5. Those of mankind that are predestined unto life, God before the foundation of the world was laid, according to His eternal and immutable purpose, and the secret counsel and good pleasure of His will, hath chosen in Christ unto everlasting glory, out of His mere free grace and love, without any foresight of faith or good works, or perseverance in either of them, or any other thing in the creature as conditions, or causes moving Him thereunto, and all to the praise of His glorious grace.

'No. 7. The rest of mankind God was pleased, according to the unsearchable counsel of His own will, whereby He extendeth, or withholdeth mercy, as He pleaseth, for the glory of His sovereign power over His creatures, to pass by, and to ordain them to dishonour and wrath for their sin, to the praise of His glorious justice.

'Chapter X (of Effectual Calling), No. 1. All those whom God hath predestinated unto life, and those only, He is pleased in His appointed and accepted time effectually to call, by His word and spirit (out of that state of sin and death, in which they are by nature) . . . taking away their heart of stone, and giving unto them an heart of flesh; renewing their wills, and by His almighty power determining them to that which is good . . . .

' Chapter V (of Providence), No. 6. As for those wicked and ungodly men, whom God as a righteous judge, for former sins doth blind and harden, from them He not only withholdeth His grace, whereby they might have been enlightened in their understandings and wrought upon in their hearts, but sometimes also withdraweth the gifts which they had and exposeth them to such objects as their corruption makes occasion of sin: and withal, gives them over to their own lusts, the temptations of the world, and the power of Satan: whereby it comes to pass that they harden themselves, even under those means, which God useth for the softening of others.'

'Though I may be sent to Hell for it, such a God will never command my respect', was Milton's well-known opinion of the doctrine. But we are here concerned not with the evaluation, but the historical significance of the dogma. We can only briefly sketch the question of how the doctrine originated and how it fitted into the framework of Calvinistic theology.

Two paths leading to it were possible. The phenomenon of the religious sense of grace is combined, in the most active and passionate of those great worshippers which Christianity has produced again and again since Augustine, with the feeling of certainty that that grace is the sole product of an objective power, and not in the least to be attributed to personal worth. The powerful feeling of light-hearted assurance, in which the tremendous pressure of their sense of sin is released, apparently breaks over them with elemental force and destroys every possibility of the belief that this over-powering gift of grace could owe anything to their own co-operation or could be connected with achievements or qualities of their own faith and will. At the time of Luther's greatest religious creativeness, when he was capable of writing his *Freiheit eines Christenmenschen*, God's secret decree was also to him most definitely the sole and ultimate source of his state of religious grace. Even later he did not formally abandon it. But not only did the idea not assume a central position for him, but it receded more and more into the background, the more his position as responsible head of his Church forced him into practical politics. Melancthon quite deliberately avoided adopting the dark and dangerous teaching in the Augsburg Confession, and for the Church fathers of Lutheranism it was an article of faith that grace was revocable (*amissibilis*), and could be won again by penitent humility and faithful trust in the word of God and in the sacraments.

With Calvin the process was just the opposite; the significance of the doctrine for him increased, perceptibly in the course of his polemical controversies with theological opponents. It is not fully developed until the third edition of his *Institutes*, and only gained its position of central prominence after his death in the great struggles which the Synods of Dordrecht and Westminster sought to put an end to. With Calvin the *decretum horrible* is derived not, as with Luther, from religious experience, but from the logical necessity of his thought; therefore its importance increases with every increase in the logical consistency of that religious thought. The interest of it is solely in God, not in man; God does not exist for men, but men for the sake of God. All creation, including of course the fact, as it undoubtedly was for Calvin, that only a small proportion of men are chosen for eternal grace, can have any meaning only as means to the glory and majesty of God. To apply earthly standards of justice to His sovereign decrees is meaningless and an insult to His Majesty, since He and He alone is free, i.e., is subject to no law. His decrees can only be understood by or even known to us in so far as it has been His pleasure to reveal them. We can only hold to these fragments of eternal truth. Everything else, including the meaning of our individual destiny, is hidden in dark mystery which it would be both impossible to pierce and presumptuous to question.

For the damned to complain of their lot would be much the same as for animals to bemoan the fact they were not born as men. For everything of the flesh is separated from God by an unbridgeable gulf and deserves of Him only eternal death, in so far as He has not decreed otherwise for the glorification of His Majesty. We know only that a part of humanity is saved, the rest damned. To assume that human merit or guilt play a part in determining this destiny would be to think of God's absolutely free decrees, which have been settled from eternity, as subject to change by human influence, an impossible contradiction. The Father in heaven of the New Testament, so human and understanding, who rejoices over the repentance of a sinner as a woman over the lost piece of silver she has found, is gone. His place has been taken by a transcendental being, beyond the reach of human understanding, who with His quite incomprehensible decrees has decided the fate of every individual and regulated the tiniest details of the cosmos from eternity. God's grace is, since His decrees cannot change, as impossible for those to whom He has granted it to lose as it is unattainable for those to whom He has denied it.

In its extreme inhumanity this doctrine must above all have had one consequence for the life of a generation which surrendered to its magnificent consistency. That was a feeling of unprecedented inner loneliness of the single individual. In what was for the man of the age of the Reformation the most important thing in life, his eternal salvation, he was forced to follow his path alone to meet a destiny which had been decreed for him from eternity. No one could help him. No priest, for the chosen one can understand the word of God only in his own heart. No sacraments, for though the sacraments had been ordained by God for the increase of His glory, and must hence be scrupulously observed, they are not a means to the attainment of grace, but only the subjective *externa subsidia* of faith. No Church, for though it was held that *extra ecclesiam nulla salus* in the sense that whoever kept away from the true Church could never belong to God's chosen band, nevertheless the membership of the external Church included the doomed. They should belong to it and be subjected to its discipline, not in order thus to attain salvation, that is impossible, but because, for the glory of God, they too must be forced to obey His commandments. Finally, even no God. For even Christ had died only for the elect, for whose benefit God had decreed His martyrdom from eternity. This the complete elimination of salvation through the Church and the sacraments (which was in Lutheranism by no means developed to its final conclusions), was what formed the absolutely decisive difference from Catholicism.

That great historic process in the development of religions, the elimination of magic from the world which had begun with the old Hebrew prophets and, in conjunction with

Hellenistic scientific thought, had repudiated all magical means to salvation as superstition and sin, came here to its logical conclusion. The genuine Puritan even rejected all signs of religious ceremony at the grave and buried his nearest and dearest without song or ritual in order that no superstition, no trust in the effects of magical and sacramental forces on salvation, should creep in.

There was not only no magical means of attaining the grace of God for those to whom God had decided to deny it, but no means whatever. Combined with the harsh doctrines of the absolute transcendentality of God and the corruption of everything pertaining to the flesh, this inner isolation of the individual contains, on the one hand, the reason for the entirely negative attitude of Puritanism to all the sensuous and emotional elements in culture and in religion, because they are of no use toward salvation and promote sentimental illusions and idolatrous superstitions. Thus it provides a basis for a fundamental antagonism to sensuous culture of all kinds. On the other hand, it forms one of the roots of that disillusioned and pessimistically inclined individualism which can even today be identified in the national characters and the institutions of the peoples with a Puritan past, in such a striking contrast to the quite different spectacles through which the Enlightenment later looked upon men.

. . .

One of the fundamental elements of the spirit of modern capitalism, and not only of that but of all modern culture: rational conduct on the basis of the ideas of the calling, was born—that is what this discussion has sought to demonstrate—from the spirit of Christian asceticism. One has only to reread the passage from Franklin, quoted at the beginning of this essay, in order to see that the essential elements of the attitude which was there called the spirit of capitalism are the same as what we have just shown to be the content of the Puritan worldly asceticism, only without the religious basis, which by Franklin's time had died away. The idea that modern labour has an ascetic character is of course not new. Limitation to specialized work, with a renunciation of the Faustian universality of man which it involves, is a condition of any valuable work in the modern world; hence deeds and renunciation inevitably condition each other today. This fundamentally ascetic trait of middle-class life, if it attempts to be a way of life at all, and not simply the absence of any, was what Goethe wanted to teach, at the height of his wisdom, in the *Wanderjahren*, and in the end which he gave to the life of his *Faust*. For him the realization meant a renunciation, a departure from an age of full and beautiful humanity, which can no more be repeated in the course of our cultural development than can the flower of the Athenian culture of antiquity.

The Puritan wanted to work in a calling; we are forced to do so. For when asceticism was carried out of monastic cells into everyday life, and began to dominate worldly morality, it did its part in building the tremendous cosmos of the modern economic order. This order is now bound to the technical and economic conditions of machine production which today determine the lives of all the individuals who are born into this mechanism, not only those directly concerned with economic acquisition, with irresistible force. Perhaps it will so determine them until the last ton of fossilized coal is burnt. In Baxter's view the care for external goods should only lie on the shoulders of the 'saint like a light cloak, which can be thrown aside at any moment'. But fate decreed that the cloak should become an iron cage.

Since asceticism undertook to remodel the world and to work out its ideals in the world, material goods have gained an increasing and finally inexorable power over the lives of men as at no previous period in history. Today the spirit of religious asceticism—whether finally, who knows?—has escaped from the cage. But victorious capitalism, since it rests on mechanical foundations, needs its support no longer. The rosy blush of its laughing heir, the Enlightenment, seems also to be irretrievably fading, and the ideas of duty in one's calling prowls about in our lives like the ghost of dead religious beliefs. Where the fulfilment of the calling cannot directly be related to the highest spiritual and cultural values, or when, on the other hand, it need not be felt simply as economic compulsion, the individual generally abandons the attempt to justify it at all. In the field of its highest development, in the United States, the pursuit of wealth, stripped of its religious and ethical meaning, tends to become associated with purely mundane passions, which often actually give it the character of sport.

No one knows who will live in this cage in the future, or whether at the end of this tremendous development entirely new prophets will arise, or there will be a great rebirth of old ideas and ideals, or, if neither, mechanized petrification, embellished with a sort of convulsive self-importance. For of the last stage of this cultural development, it might well be truly said: 'Specialists without spirit, sensualists without heart; this nullity imagines that it has attained a level of civilization never before achieved.'

But this brings us to the world of judgements of value and of faith, with which this purely historical discussion need not be burdened. The next task would be rather to show the significance of ascetic rationalism, which has only been touched in the foregoing sketch, for the content of practical social ethics, thus for the types of organization and the functions of social groups from the conventicle to the State. Then its relations to humanistic rationalism, its ideals of life and cultural influence; further to the development of philosophical and scientific empiricism, to technical development and to spiritual ideals would have to be analysed. Then its historical development from the medieval beginnings of worldly asceticism to its dissolution into pure utilitarianism would have to be traced out through all the areas of ascetic religion. Only then could the quantitative cultural significance of ascetic Protestantism in its relation to the other plastic elements of modern culture be estimated.

Here we have only attempted to trace the fact and the direction of its influence to their motives in one, though a very important point. But it would also further be necessary to investigate how Protestant Asceticism was in turn influenced in its development and its character by the totality of social conditions, especially economic. The modern man is in general, even with the best will, unable to give religious ideas a significance for culture and national character which they deserve. But it is, of course, not my aim to substitute for a one-sided materialistic an equally one-sided spiritualistic causal interpretation of culture and of history. Each is equally possible, but each, if it does not serve as the preparation, but as the conclusion of an investigation, accomplishes equally little in the interest of historical truth.

CHARLES HORTON COOLEY

1864–1929
UNITED STATES

Major Works

1902   *Human Nature and the Social Order*
1909   *Social Organization*
1918   *Social Process*
1927   *Life and the Student*
1930   *Sociological Theory and Social Research*

Self and society are twin born.[1]

Society is an interweaving and interworking of mental selves.[2]
—*Charles Horton Cooley*

Charles Horton Cooley's work began a shift of emphasis in sociological theory. Along with Weber's interpretive theory acknowledging the meanings that actors bring to situations and, later, George Herbert Mead's understandings of the genesis of the self, Cooley brings us to a dialectical comprehension of self in society. Durkheim and Marx recognized the power of the society in the creation of self or personality; Cooley and the symbolic interactionists (a term later bestowed on Cooley and Mead by Herbert Blumer) emphasize social-psychological analyses.

Cooley's looking-glass self theory that the individual or the self grows out of the relationships and interactions with others in social contexts is his most important contribution to our understanding of the individual in society. He explained that the conscious representations or images that we have of ourselves and others are of social origin and that this interactive process is a 'reciprocal activity'. Today the themes that Cooley articulated with regard to the looking-glass self may seem so obvious that we may feel no need to investigate them further. But if we are to recognize the power of the relationship between self and society, what appears self-evident needs comprehensive examination within changing social contexts and organizations. The challenge of the looking-glass self theory is not only its power of description of human behaviour but its demand for analysis and action that moves beyond such 'reflections' of self.

Cooley's organic view of society held that competition and conflicts within social groups can be beneficial and productive. His conceptualization of the primary group has also enriched sociology:

By primary groups I mean those characterized by intimate face-to-face association and cooperation. They are primary in several senses but chiefly in that they are fundamental in forming the social nature and ideals of individuals. The result of intimate association, psychologically, is a certain fusion of individualities in a common whole, so that one's self, for many purposes at least, is the common life and purpose of the group. Perhaps the simplest way of describing this wholeness is by saying that it is a 'we'.[3]

Cooley's presentation of both the looking-glass self and the primary group initiates a search for a whole new terrain in sociology—the micro-interactionist domain of persons in society. His work has made us aware of the unity of self and society and has in some respects transcended the Cartesian tradition of separation of mind and society.

Notes

1. Charles Horton Cooley, *Social Organization* (New York: Schocken, 1962), 5.
2. Charles Horton Cooley, *Life and the Student* (New York: Alfred A. Knopf, 1927), 200–1.
3. Cooley, *Social Organization*, 23.

THE SOCIAL SELF

On the Meanings of 'I'

It is well to say at the outset that by the word 'self' in this discussion is meant simply that which is designated in common speech by the pronouns of the first person singular, 'I', 'me', 'mine', and 'myself'. 'Self' and 'ego' are used by metaphysicians and moralists in many other senses, more or less remote from the 'I' of daily speech and thought, and with these I wish to have as little to do as possible. What is here discussed is what psychologists call the empirical self, the self that can be apprehended or verified by ordinary observation. I qualify it by the word social not as implying the existence of a self that is not social—for I think that the 'I' of common language always has more or less distinct reference to other people as well as the speaker—but because I wish to emphasize and dwell upon the social aspect of it.

The distinctive thing in the idea for which the pronouns of the first person are names is apparently a characteristic kind of feeling which may be called the my-feeling or sense of appropriation. Almost any sort of ideas may be associated with this feeling, and so come to be named 'I' or 'mine', but the feeling, and that alone it would seem, is the determining factor in the matter. As Professor James says in his admirable discussion of the self, the words 'me' and 'self' designate 'all the things which have the power to produce in a stream of consciousness excitement of a certain peculiar sort'.

I do not mean that the feeling aspect of the self is necessarily more important than any other, but that it is the immediate and decisive sign and proof of what 'I' is; there is no appeal from it; if we go behind it it must be to study its history and conditions, not to question its authority. But, of course, this study of history and conditions may be quite as profitable as the direct contemplation of self-feeling. What I would wish to do is to present each aspect in its proper light.

The emotion or feeling of self may be regarded as an instinct doubtless evolved in connection with its important function in stimulating and unifying the special activities of individuals. . . .

. . . Meantime the feeling itself does not remain unaltered, but undergoes differentiation and refinement just as does any other sort of crude innate feeling. Thus, while retaining under every phase its characteristic tone or flavour, it breaks up into innumerable self-sentiments. And concrete self-feeling, as it exists in mature persons, is a whole made up of these various sentiments, along with a good deal of primitive emotion not thus broken up. It partakes fully of the general development of the mind, but never loses that peculiar gusto of appropriation that causes us to name a thought with a first-personal pronoun.

Since 'I' is known to our experience primarily as a feeling, or as a feeling-ingredient in our ideas, it cannot be described or defined without suggesting that feeling. We are sometimes likely to fall into a formal and empty way of talking regarding questions of emotion, by attempting to define that which is in its nature primary and indefinable. A formal definition of self-feeling, or indeed of any sort of feeling, must be as hollow as a formal definition of the taste of salt, or the colour red; we can expect to know what it is only by experiencing it. There can be no final test of the self except the way we feel; it is that toward which we have the 'my' attitude. But as this feeling is quite as familiar to us and as easy to recall as the taste of salt or the colour red, there should be no difficulty in understanding what is meant by it. One need only imagine some attack on his 'me', say ridicule of his dress or an attempt to take away his property or his child, or his good name by slander, and self-feeling immediately appears. Indeed, he need only pronounce, with strong emphasis, one of the self-words, like 'I' or 'my', and self-feeling will be recalled by association.

As many people have the impression that the verifiable self, the object that we name with 'I', is usually the material body, it may be well to say that this impression is an illusion, easily dispelled by anyone who will undertake a simple examination of facts. It is true that when we philosophize a little about 'I' and look around for a tangible object to which to attach it, we soon fix upon the material body as the most available locus; but when we use the word naïvely, as in ordinary speech, it is not very common to think of the body in connection with it; not nearly so common as it is to think of other things. There is no difficulty in testing this statement, since the word 'I' is one of the commonest in conversation and literature, so that nothing is more practicable than to study its meaning at any length that may be desired. One need only listen to ordinary speech until the word has occurred, say, a hundred times, noting its connections, or observe its use in a similar number of cases by the characters in a novel. Ordinarily it will be found that in not more than ten cases in a hundred does 'I' have reference to the body of the person speaking. It refers chiefly to opinions, purposes, desires, claims, and the like, concerning matters that involve no thought of the body. *I* think or feel so and so; *I* wish or intend so and so; *I* want this or that; are typical uses, the self-feeling being associated with the view, purpose, or object mentioned. It should also be remembered that 'my' and 'mine' are as much the names of the self as 'I' and these, of course, commonly refer to miscellaneous possessions.

As already suggested, instinctive self-feeling is doubtless connected in evolution with its important function in stimulating and unifying the special activities of individuals. It appears to be associated chiefly with ideas of the exercise of power, of being a cause, ideas that emphasize the antithesis between the mind and the rest of the world. The first definite thoughts that a child associates with self-feeling are probably those of his earliest endeavours to control visible objects—his limbs, his playthings, his bottle, and the like. Then he attempts to control the actions of the persons about him, and so his circle of power and self-feeling widens without interruption to the most complex objects of mature ambition. Although he does not say 'I' or 'my' during the first year or two, yet he expresses so clearly by his actions the feeling that adults associate with these words that we cannot deny him a self even in the first weeks.

The correlation of self-feeling with purposeful activity is easily seen by observing the course of any productive enterprise. If a boy sets about making a boat, and has any success, his interest in the matter waxes, he gloats over it, the keel and stem are dear to his heart, and its ribs are more to him than those of his own frame. He is eager to call in his friends and acquaintances, saying to them, 'See what I am doing! Is it not remarkable?', feeling elated when it is praised, and resentful or humiliated when fault is found with it. But as soon as he finishes it and turns to something else, his self-feeling begins to fade away from it, and in a few weeks at most he will have become comparatively indifferent. We all know that much the same course of feeling accompanies the achievements of adults. It is impossible to produce a picture, a poem, an essay, a difficult bit of masonry, or any other work of art or craft, without having self-feeling regarding it, amounting usually to considerable excitement and desire for some sort of appreciation; but this rapidly diminishes with the activity itself, and often lapses into indifference after it ceases.

It may perhaps be objected that the sense of self, instead of being limited to times of activity and definite purpose, is often most conspicuous when the mind is unoccupied or undecided, and that the idle and ineffectual are commonly the most sensitive in their self-esteem. This, however, may be regarded as an instance of the principle that all instincts are likely to assume troublesome forms when denied wholesome expression. The need to exert power, when thwarted in the open fields of life, is the more likely to assert itself in trifles.

The social self is simply any idea, or system of ideas, drawn from the communicative life, that the mind cherishes as its own. Self-feeling has its chief scope *within* the general life, not outside of it, the special endeavour or tendency of which it is the emotional aspect finding its principal field in the mind by a world of personal impressions.

As connected with the thought of other persons it is always a consciousness of the peculiar or differentiated aspect of one's life, because that is the aspect that has to be sustained by purpose or endeavour, and its more aggressive forms tend to attach themselves to whatever one finds to be at once congenial to one's own tendencies and at variance with those of others with whom one is in mental contact. It is here that they are most needed to serve their function of stimulating characteristic activity, of fostering those personal variations which the general plan of life seems to require. Heaven, says Shakespeare, doth divide

> The state of man in divers functions,
> Setting endeavour in continual motion,

and self-feeling is one of the means by which this diversity is achieved.

Agreeably to this view we find that the aggressive self manifests itself most conspicuously in an appropriativeness of objects to secure his own peculiar development, and to the danger of opposition from others who also need them. And this extends from material objects to lay hold, in the same spirit, of the attentions and affections of other people, of all sorts of plans and ambitions, including the noblest special purposes the mind can entertain, and indeed of any conceivable idea which may come to seem a part of one's life and in need of assertion against someone else.

That the 'I' of common speech has a meaning which includes some sort of reference to other persons is involved in the very fact that the word and the ideas it stands for are phenomena of language and the communicative life. It is doubtful whether it is possible to use language at all without thinking more or less distinctly of someone else, and certainly the things to which we give names and which have a large place in reflective thought are almost always those which are impressed upon us by our contact with other people. Where there is no communication there can be no nomenclature and no developed thought. What we call 'me', 'mine', or 'myself' is, then, not something separate from the general life, but the most interesting part of it, a part whose interest arises from the very fact that it is both general and individual. That is, we care for it just because it is that phase of the mind that is living and striving in the common life, trying to impress itself upon the minds of others. 'I' is a militant social tendency, working to hold and enlarge its place in the general current of tendencies. So far as it can it waxes, as all life does. To think of it as apart from society is a palpable absurdity of which no one could be guilty who really *saw* it as a fact of life.

> Der Mensch erkennt sich nur im Menschen, nur
> Das Leben lehret jedem was er sei.[1]

If a thing has no relation to others of which one is conscious he is unlikely to think of it at all, and if he does think of it he cannot, it seems to me, regard it as emphatically *his*. The appropriative sense is always the shadow, as it were, of the common life, and when we have it we have a sense of the latter in connection with it. Thus, if we think of a secluded part of the woods as 'ours', it is because we think, also, that others do not go there. As regards the body I doubt if we have a vivid my-feeling about any part of it which is not thought of, however vaguely, as having some actual or possible reference to someone else. Intense self-consciousness regarding it arises along with instincts or experiences which connect it with the thought of others. Internal organs, like the liver, are not thought of as peculiarly ours unless we are trying to communicate something regarding them, as, for instance, when they are giving us trouble and we are trying to get sympathy.

'I', then, is not all of the mind, but a peculiarly central, vigorous, and well-knit portion of it, not separate from the rest but gradually merging into it, and yet having a certain practical distinctness, so that a man generally shows clearly enough by his language and behaviour what his 'I' is as distinguished from thoughts he does not appropriate. It may be thought of, as already suggested, under the analogy of a central coloured area on a lighted wall. It might also, and perhaps more justly, be compared to the nucleus of a living cell, not altogether separate from the surrounding matter, out of which indeed it is formed, but more active and definitely organized.

The reference to other persons involved in the sense of self may be distinct and particular, as when a boy is ashamed to have his mother catch him at something she has forbidden, or it may be vague and general, as when one is ashamed to do something which only his conscience, expressing his sense of social responsibility, detects and disapproves; but it is always there. There is no sense of 'I', as in pride or shame, without its correlative sense of you, or he, or they.

In a very large and interesting class of cases the social reference takes the form of a somewhat definite imagination of how one's self—that is any idea he appropriates—appears in a particular mind, and the kind of self-feeling one has is determined by the attitude toward this attributed to that other mind. A social self of this sort might be called the reflected or looking-glass self:

> Each to each a looking-glass
> Reflects the other that doth pass.

As we see our face, figure, and dress in the glass, and are interested in them because they are ours, and pleased or otherwise with them according as they do or do not answer to what we should like them to be; so in imagination we perceive in another's mind some thought of our appearance, manners, aims, deeds, character, friends, and so on, and are variously affected by it.

A self-idea of this sort seems to have three principal elements: the imagination of our appearance to the other person; the imagination of his judgement of that appearance; and some sort of self-feeling, such as pride or mortification. The comparison with a looking-glass hardly suggests the second element, the imagined judgement, which is quite essential. The thing that moves us to pride or shame is not the mere mechanical reflection of ourselves, but an imputed sentiment, the imagined effect of this reflection upon another's mind. This is evident from the fact that the character and weight of that other, in whose mind we see ourselves, makes all the difference with our feeling. We are ashamed to seem evasive in the presence of a straightforward man, cowardly in the presence of a brave one, gross in the eyes of a refined one, and so on. We always imagine, and in imagining share, the judgements of the other mind. A man will boast to one person of an action—say some sharp transaction in trade—which he would be ashamed to own to another.

It should be evident that the ideas that are associated with self-feeling and form the intellectual content of the self cannot be covered by any simple description, as by saying that the body has such a part in it, friends such a part, plans so much, etc., but will vary indefinitely with particular temperaments and environments. The tendency of the self, like every aspect of personality, is expressive of far-reaching hereditary and social factors, and is not to be understood or predicted except in connection with the general life. Although special, it is in no way separate—specialty and separateness are not only different but contradictory, since the former implies connection with a whole. The object of self-feeling is affected by the general course of history, by the particular development of nations, classes, and professions, and other conditions of this sort.

Habit and familiarity are not of themselves sufficient to cause an idea to be appropriated into the self. Many habits and familiar objects that have been forced upon us by circumstances rather than chosen for their congeniality remain external and possibly repulsive to the self; and, on the other hand, a novel but very congenial element in experience, like the idea of a new toy, or, if you please, Romeo's idea of Juliet, is often appropriated almost immediately, and becomes, for the time at least, the very heart of the self. Habit has the same fixing and consolidating action in the growth of the self that it has elsewhere, but is not its distinctive characteristic.

As suggested [above], self-feeling may be regarded as in a sense the antithesis, or better perhaps, the complement, of that disinterested and contemplative love that tends to obliterate the sense of divergent individuality. Love of this sort has no sense of bounds, but is what we feel when we are expanding and assimilating new and indeterminate experience, while self-feeling accompanies the appropriating, delimiting, and defending of a certain part of experience; the one impels us to receive life, the other to individuate it. The self, from this point of view, might be regarded as a sort of citadel of the mind, fortified without and containing selected treasures within, while love is an undivided share in the rest of the universe. In a healthy mind each contributes to the growth of the other: what we love intensely or for a long time we are likely to bring within the citadel, and to assert as part of ourself. On the other hand, it is only on the basis of a substantial self that a person is capable of progressive sympathy or love.

The sickness of either is to lack the support of the other. There is no health in a mind except as it keeps expanding, taking in fresh life, feeling love and enthusiasm; and so long as it does this its self-feeling is likely to be modest and generous; since these sentiments accompany that sense of the large and the superior which love implies. But if love closes, the self contracts and hardens: the mind having nothing else to occupy its attention and give it that change and renewal it requires, busies itself more and more with self-feeling, which takes on narrow and disgusting forms, like avarice, arrogance, and fatuity. It is necessary that we should have self-feeling about a matter during its conception and execution; but when it is accomplished or has failed the self ought to break loose and escape, renewing its skin like the snake, as Thoreau says. No matter what a man does, he is not fully sane or human unless there is a spirit of freedom in him, a soul unconfined by purpose and larger than the practicable world. And this is really what those mean who inculcate the suppression of the self; they mean that its rigidity must be broken up by growth and renewal, that it must be more or less decisively 'born again'. A healthy self must be both vigorous and plastic, a nucleus of solid, well-knit private purpose and feeling, guided and nourished by sympathy.

NOTE

1. Only in man does man know himself; life alone teaches each one what he is.'—Goethe, *Tasso*, Act 2, Scene 3.

GEORGE HERBERT MEAD

1863–1931
UNITED STATES

Major Works[1]

1932   *The Philosophy of the Present*
1934   *Mind, Self and Society*
1936   *Movements of Thought in the Nineteenth Century*
1938   *The Philosophy of the Act*
1964   *Selected Writings*

> It is just because the individual finds himself taking the attitudes of the others who are involved in his conduct that he becomes an object for himself.[2]

> The term gesture I am using to refer to that part of the act or attitude of one indvidual engaged in a social act which serves as the stimulus to another individual to carry out his part of the whole act.[3]
>
> —*George Herbert Mead*

The works of George Herbert Mead and C.H. Cooley established the field of what has become known as symbolic interactionism. One of Mead's major contributions to sociology has been his understanding of socialization theory. In exploring how an individual becomes a member of society he elaborated a dialectical concept of self and society. Mead considered himself a 'social behaviourist' in that his interest in human consciousness, its power of imagination and interpretation, moved him away from the more mechanical stimulus-response behaviourism of J.B. Watson and others. His understanding of consciousness explored the dynamic of self-reflexivity, i.e., that the individual could become an object to him or herself. Action in the social world not only defines one's relationship between self and environment, but also allows the self to be an object of reflection within social actions. In Mead's work language is the most profound gesture, fundamental to the communication process. In his view, consciousness is not a given, but emerges through our relationships externally and internally.

> Our thinking is an inner conversation in which we may be taking the roles of specific acquaintances over against ourselves, but usually it is with what I have termed the 'generalized other' that we converse, and

so attain to the levels of abstract thinking, and that impersonality, that so-called objectivity that we cherish.[4]

Mead's conception of the 'genesis of the self' as part of the socialization process demands 'taking the role of the other'. In the early stages of socialization the significant others are those intimate and immediate to the child, and he or she will take on their definitions of social situations. Later, the generalized other—the attitudes and values of the community—becomes part of the consciousness of the socialized individual. Mead's classic expression of this process is explored in his distinction between play and games: as 'rules' come into a play situation, play becomes games involving the attitudes, values, and structures of the social group.

Perhaps one of the more important aspects of Mead's work is recognition of what Anselm Strauss calls the 'negotiated order'. Mead's dialectical view of the individual's relationship with society and the genesis of self within social structures and institutions acknowledges the negotiated nature of social realities. The profound power for micro-interactionist theory of such a dynamic has given new direction to our understandings of the individual and society, especially within the 'social constructionist' perspective.

Notes

1. Mead published no books during his life. Many of his works were published by his students after his death.
2. George Herbert Mead, 'The Genesis of the Self and Social Control', *International Journal of Ethics* 35, 3 (Apr. 1925): 268.
3. Ibid., 270.
4. Ibid., 272.

THE SIGNIFICANT OTHER AND THE GENERALIZED OTHER

Thought as Internalized Conversation

We can distinguish very definitely between the self and the body. The body can be there and can operate in a very intelligent fashion without there being a self involved in the experience. The self has the characteristic that it is an object to itself, and that characteristic distinguishes it from other objects and from the body. It is perfectly true that the eye can see the foot, but it does not see the body as a whole. We cannot see our backs; we can feel certain portions of them, if we are agile, but we cannot get an experience of our whole body. There are, of course, experiences which are somewhat vague and difficult of location, but the bodily experiences are for us organized about a self. The foot and hand belong to the self. We can see our feet, especially if we look at them from the wrong end of an opera glass, as strange things which we have difficulty recognizing as our own. The parts of the body are quite distinguishable from the self. The mere ability to experience different parts of the body is not different from the experience of a table. The table presents a different feel from what the hand does when one hand feels another, but it is an experience of something with which we come definitely into contact. The body does not experience itself as a whole, in the sense in which the self in some way enters into the experiences of the self.

It is the characteristic of the self as an object to itself that I want to bring out. This characteristic is represented in the word 'self', which is a reflexive, and indicates that which can be both subject and object. This type of object is essentially different from other objects, and in the past it has been distinguished as conscious, a term which indicates an experience with, an experience of, one's self. It was assumed that consciousness in some way carried this capacity of being an object to itself. In giving a behaviouristic statement of consciousness we have to look for some sort of experience in which the physical organism can become an object to itself.[1]

When one is running to get away from someone who is chasing him, he is entirely occupied in this action, and his experience may be swallowed up in the objects about him, so that he has, at the time being, no consciousness of self at all. We must be, of course, very completely occupied to have that take place, but we can, I think, recognize that sort of a possible experience in which the self does not enter. . . . In such instances there is a contrast between an experience that is absolutely wound up in outside activity in which the self as an object does not enter, and an activity of memory and imagination in which the self is the principal object. The self is then entirely distinguishable from an organism that is surrounded by things and acts with reference to things, including parts of its own body. These latter may be objects like other objects, but they are just objects out there in the field, and they do not involve a self that is an object to the organism. This is, I think, frequently overlooked. It is that fact which makes anthropomorphic reconstructions of animal life so fallacious. How can an individual get outside himself (experientially) in such a way as to become an object to himself? This is the essential psychological problem of selfhood or self-consciousness; and its solution is to be found by referring to the process of social conduct or activity in which the given person or individual is implicated. The apparatus of reason would not be complete unless it swept itself into its own analysis of the field of experience; or unless the individual brought himself into the same experiential field as that of the other individual selves in relation to whom he acts in any given social situation. Reason cannot become impersonal unless it takes an objective, non-affective attitude toward itself; otherwise we have just consciousness, not *self*-consciousness. And it is necessary to rational conduct that the individual should thus take an objective, impersonal attitude toward himself, that he should become an object to himself. For the individual organism is obviously an essential and important fact or constituent element of the empirical situation in which it acts; and without taking objective account of itself as such, it cannot act intelligently, or rationally.

The individual experiences himself as such, not directly, but only indirectly, from the particular standpoints of other individual members of the same social group, or from the generalized standpoint of the social group as a whole to which he belongs. For he enters his own experience as a self or individual, not directly or immediately, not by becoming a subject to himself, but only in so far as he first becomes an object to himself just as other individuals are objects to him or in his experience; and he becomes an object to himself only by taking the attitudes of other individuals towards himself within a social environment or context of experiences and behaviour in which both he and they are involved.

The importance of what we term 'communication' lies in the fact that it provides a form of behaviour in which the organism or the individual may become an object to himself. It is that sort of communication which we have been discussing—not communication in the sense of the cluck of the hen to the chickens, or the bark of a wolf to the pack, or the lowing of a cow, but communication in the sense of significant symbols, communication which is directed not only to others but also to the individual himself. So far as that type of communication is a part of behaviour it at least introduces a self. Of course, one may hear without listening; one may see things that he does not realize; do things that he is not really aware of. But it is where one does respond to that which he addresses to another and where that response of his own becomes a part of his conduct, where he not only hears himself but responds to himself, talks and replies to himself as truly as the other person replies to him, that we have behaviour in which the individuals become objects to themselves.

The self, as that which can be an object to itself, is essentially a social structure, and it arises in social experience. After a self has arisen, it in a certain sense provides for itself its social experiences, and so we can conceive of an absolutely solitary self. But it is impossible to conceive of a self arising outside of social experience. When it has arisen we can think of a person in solitary confinement for the rest of his life, but who still has himself as a companion, and is able to think and to converse with himself as he had communicated with others. That process to which I have just referred, of responding to one's self as another responds to it, taking part in one's own conversation with others, being aware of what one is saying and using that awareness of what one is saying to determine what one is going to say thereafter—that is a process with which we are all familiar. We are continually following up our own address to other persons by an understanding of what we are saying, and using that understanding in the direction of our continued speech. We are finding out what we are going to say, what we are going to do, by saying and doing, and in the process we are continually controlling the process itself. In the conversation of gestures what we say calls out a certain response in another and that in turn changes our own action, so that we shift from what we started to do because of the reply the other makes. The conversation of gestures is the beginning of communication. The individual comes to carry on a conversation of gestures with himself. He says something, and that calls out a certain reply in himself which makes him change what he was going to say. One starts to say something, we will presume an unpleasant something, but when he starts to say it he realizes it is cruel. The effect on himself of what he is saying checks him; there is here a conversation of gestures between the individual and himself. We mean by significant speech that the action is one that affects the individual himself, and that the effect upon the individual himself is part of the intelligent carrying-out of the conversation with others. Now we, so to speak, amputate that social phase and dispense with it for the time being, so that one is talking to one's self as one would talk to another person.[2]

This process of abstraction cannot be carried on indefinitely. One inevitably seeks an audience, has to pour himself out to somebody. In reflective intelligence one thinks to act, and to act solely so that this action remains a part of a social process. Thinking becomes preparatory to social action. The very process of thinking is, of course, simply an inner conversation that goes on, but it is a conversation of gestures which in its completion implies the expression of that which one thinks to an audience. One separates the significance of what he is saying to the others from the actual speech and gets it ready before saying it. He thinks it out, and perhaps writes it in the form of a book; but it is still a part of social intercourse in which one is addressing other persons and at the same time addressing one's self, and in which one controls the address to other persons by the response made to one's own gesture. That the person should be responding to himself is necessary to the self, and it is this sort of social conduct which provides behaviour within which that self appears. I know of no other form of behaviour than the linguistic in which the individual is an object to himself, and, so far as I can see, the individual is not a self in the reflexive sense unless he is an object to himself. It is this fact that gives a critical importance to communication, since this is a type of behaviour in which the individual does so respond to himself.

We realize in everyday conduct and experience that an individual does not mean a great deal of what he is doing and saying. We frequently say that such an individual is not himself. We come away from an interview with a realization that we have left out important things, that there are parts of the self that did not get into what was said. What determines the amount of the self that gets into communication is the social experience itself. Of course, a good deal of the self does not need to get expression. We carry on a whole series of different relationships to different people. We are one thing to one man and another thing to another. There are parts of self which exist only for the self in relationship to itself. We divide ourselves up in all sorts of different selves with reference to our acquaintances. We discuss politics with one and religion with another. There are all sorts of different selves answering to all sorts of different social reactions. It is the social process itself that is responsible for the appearance of the self; it is not there as a self apart from this type of experience.

The peculiar character possessed by our human social environment belongs to it by virtue of the peculiar character of human social activity; and that character, as we have seen, is to be found in the process of communication, and more particularly in the triadic relation on which the existence of meaning is based: the relation of the gesture of one organism to the adjustive response made to it by another organism, in its indicative capacity as pointing to the completion or resultant of the act it initiates (the meaning of the gesture being thus the response of the second organism to it as such, or as a gesture). What, as it were, takes the gesture out of the social act and isolates it as such—what makes it something more than just an early phase of an individual act—is the response of another organism, or of other organisms, to it. Such a response is its meaning, or gives it its meaning. The social situation and process of behaviour are here presupposed by the acts of the individual organisms implicated therein. The gesture arises as a separable element in the social act, by virtue of the fact that it is selected out by the sensitivities of other organisms to it; it does not exist as a gesture merely in the experience of the single individual. The meaning of a gesture by one organism, to repeat, is found in the response of another organism to what would be the completion of the act of the first organism which that gesture initiates and indicates.

We sometimes speak as if a person could build up an entire argument in his mind, and then put it into words to convey it to someone else. Actually, our thinking always takes place by means of some sort of symbols. It is possible that one could have the meaning of 'chair' in his experience without there being a symbol, but we would not be thinking about it in that case. We may sit down in a chair without thinking about what we are doing, that is, the approach to the chair is presumably already aroused in our experience, so that the meaning is there. But if one is thinking about the chair he must have some sort of a symbol for it. It may be the form of the chair, it may be the attitude that somebody else takes in sitting down, but it is more apt to be some language symbol that arouses this response. In a thought process there has to be some sort of a symbol that can refer to this meaning, that is, tend to call out this response, and also serve this purpose for other persons as well. It would not be a thought process if that were not the case.

Our symbols are all universal. You cannot say anything that is absolutely particular; anything you say that has any meaning at all is universal. You are saying something that calls out a specific response in anybody else provided that the symbol exists for him in his experience as it does for you. There is the language of speech and the language of hands, and there may be the language of the expression of the countenance. One can register grief or joy and call out certain responses. There are primitive people who can carry on elaborate conversation just by expressions of the countenance. Even in these cases the person who communicates is affected by that expression just as he expects somebody else to be affected. Thinking always implies a symbol which will call out the same response in another that it calls out in the thinker. Such a symbol is a universal of discourse; it is universal in its character. We always assume that the symbol we use is one which will call out in the other person the same response, provided it is a part of his mechanism of conduct. A person who is saying something is saying to himself what he says to others; otherwise he does not know what he is talking about.

Among primitive people, as I have said, the necessity of distinguishing the self and the organism was recognized in what we term the 'double': the individual has a thing-like self that is affected by the individual as it affects other people and which is distinguished from the immediate organism in that it can leave the body and come back to it. This is the basis for the concept of the soul as a separate entity.

We find in children something that answers to this double, namely, the invisible, imaginary companions which a good many children produce in their own experience. They organize in this way the responses which they call out in other persons and call out also in themselves. Of course, this playing with an imaginary companion is only a peculiarly interesting phase of ordinary play. Play in this sense, especially the stage which precedes the organized games, is a play at something. A child plays at being a mother, at being a teacher, at being a policeman; that is, it is taking different rôles, as we say. We have something that suggests this in what we call the play of animals: a cat will play with her kittens, and dogs play with each other. Two dogs playing with each other will attack and defend, in a process which if carried through would amount to an actual fight. There is a combination of responses which checks the depth of the bite. But we do not have in such a situation the dogs taking a definite rôle in the sense that a child deliberately takes the rôle of another. This tendency on the part of the children is what we are working with in the kindergarten where the rôles which the children assume are made the basis for training. When a child does assume a rôle he has in himself the stimuli which call out that particular response or group of responses. He may, of course, run away when he is chased, as the dog does, or he may turn around and strike back just as the dog does in his play. But that is not the same as playing at something. Children get together to 'play Indian'. This means that the child has a certain set of stimuli which call out in itself the responses that they would call out in others, and which answer to an Indian. In the play period the child utilizes his own responses to these stimuli which he makes use of in building a self. The response which he has a tendency to make to these stimuli organizes them. He plays that he is, for instance, offering himself something, and he buys it; he gives a letter to himself and takes it away; he addresses himself as a parent, as a teacher; he arrests himself as a policeman. He has a set of stimuli which call out in himself the sort of responses they call out in others. He takes this group of responses and organizes them into a certain whole. Such is the simplest form of being another to one's self. It involves a temporal situation. The child says something in one character and responds in another character, and then his responding in another character is a stimulus to himself in the first character, and so the conversation goes on. A certain organized structure arises in him and in his other which replies to it, and these carry on the conversation of gestures between themselves.

If we contrast play with the situation in an organized game, we note the essential difference that the child who plays in a game must be ready to take the attitude of everyone else involved in that game, and that these different rôles must have a definite relationship to each other. Taking a very simple game such as hide-and-seek, everyone with the exception of the one who is hiding is a person who is hunting. A child does not require more than the person who is hunted and the one who is hunting. If a child is playing in the first sense he just goes on playing, but there is no basic organization gained. In that early stage he passed from one rôle to another just as a whim takes him. But in a game where a number of individuals are involved, then the child taking one rôle must be ready to take the rôle of everyone else. If he gets in a ball nine he must have the responses of each position involved in his own position. He must know what everyone else is going to do in order to carry out his own play. He has to take all of these rôles. They do not all have to be present in consciousness at the same time, but at some moments he has to have three or four individuals present in his own attitude, such as the one who is going to throw the ball, the one who is going to catch it, and so on. These responses must be, in some degree, present in his own make-up. In the game, then, there is a set of responses of such others so organized that the attitude of one calls out the appropriate attitudes of the other.

This organization is put in the form of the rules of the game. Children take a great interest in rules. They make rules on the spot in order to help themselves out of difficulties.

Part of the enjoyment of the game is to get these rules. Now, the rules are the set of responses which a particular attitude calls out. You can demand a certain response in others if you take a certain attitude. These responses are all in yourself as well. There you get an organized set of such responses as that to which I have referred, which is something more elaborate than the rôles found in play. Here there is just a set of responses that follow on each other indefinitely. At such a stage we speak of a child as not yet having a fully developed self. The child responds in a fairly intelligent fashion to the immediate stimuli that come to him, but they are not organized. He does not organize his life as we would like to have him do, namely, as a whole. There is just a set of responses to the type of play. The child reacts to a certain stimulus, and the reaction is in himself that is called out in others, but he is not a whole self. In his game he has to have an organization of these rôles; otherwise he cannot play the game. The game represents the passage in the life of the child from taking the rôle of others in play to the organized part that is essential to self-consciousness in the full sense of the term.

Play, the Game, and the Generalized Other

The fundamental difference between the game and play is that in the latter the child must have the attitude of all the others involved in that game. The attitudes of the other players which the participant assumes organize into a sort of unit, and it is that organization which controls the response of the individual. The illustration used was of a person playing baseball. Each one of his own acts is determined by his assumption of the action of the others who are playing the game. What he does is controlled by his being everyone else on that team, at least in so far as those attitudes affect his own particular response. We get then an 'other' which is an organization of the attitudes of these involved in the same process.

The organized community or social group which gives to the individual his unity of self may be called 'the generalized other'. The attitude of the generalized other is the attitude of the whole community. Thus, for example, in the case of such a social group as a ball team, the team is the generalized other in so far as it enters—as an organized process or social activity—into the experience of any one of the individual members of it.

If the given human individual is to develop a self in the fullest sense, it is not sufficient for him merely to take the attitudes of other human individuals towards himself and toward one another within the human social process, and to bring that social process as a whole into his individual experience merely in these terms: he must also, in the same way that he takes the attitudes of other individuals towards himself and toward one another, take their attitudes toward the various phases or aspects of the common social activity or set of social undertakings in which, as members of an organized society or social group, they are all engaged; and he must then, by generalizing these individual attitudes of that organized society or social group itself, as a whole, act toward different social projects which at any given time it is carrying out, or toward the various larger phases of the general social process which constitutes its life and of which these projects are specific manifestations. This getting of the broad activities of any given social whole or organized society as such within the experiential field of any one of the individuals involved or included in that whole is, in other words, the essential basis and prerequisite of the fullest development of that individual's self: only in so far as he takes the attitudes of the organized social group to which he belongs toward the organized, co-operative social activity or set of such activities in which that group as such is engaged, does he develop a complete self or possess the sort of complete self he has developed. And on the other hand, the complex co-operative processes and activities and institutional functionings of organized human society are also possible only in so far as every individual involved in them or belonging to that society can take the general attitudes of all other such individuals with reference to these processes and activities and institutional functionings, and to the organized social whole of experiential relations and interactions thereby constituted—and can direct his own behaviour accordingly.

It is in the form of the generalized other that the social process influences the behaviour of the individuals involved in it and carrying it on, that is, that the community exercises control over the conduct of its individual members; for it is in this form that the social process or community enters as a determining factor into the individual's thinking. In abstract thought the individual takes the attitude of the generalized other toward himself, without reference to its expression in any particular other individuals; and in concrete thought he takes that attitude in so far as it is expressed in the attitudes toward his behaviour of those other individuals with whom he is involved in the given social situation or act. But only by taking the attitude of the generalized other toward himself, in one or another of these ways, can he think at all; for only thus can thinking—or the internalized conversation of gestures which constitutes thinking—occur. And only through the taking by individuals of the attitude or attitudes of the generalized other toward themselves is the existence of a universe of discourse, as that system of common or social meanings which thinking presupposes as its context, rendered possible.

I have pointed out, then, that there are two general stages in the full development of the self. At the first of these stages, the individual's self is constituted simply by an organization of the particular attitudes of other individuals toward himself and toward one another in the specific social acts in which he participates with them. But at the second stage in the full development of the individual's self that self is constituted not only by an organization of these particular individual attitudes, but also by an organization of the social attitudes of the generalized other or the social group as a whole to which he belongs. These social or group attitudes are brought within the individual's field of direct experience, and are included as elements in the structure or constitution of his self, in the same way that the attitudes of particular other individuals are; and the individual arrives at them, or succeeds in taking them, by means of further organizing, and then generalizing, the attitudes of particular other individuals in terms of their organized social bearings and implications. So the self reaches its full development by organizing these individual attitudes of others into the organized social or group attitudes, and by thus becoming an individual reflection of the general systematic pattern of social or group behaviour in which it and the others are all involved—a pattern which enters as a whole into the individual's experience in terms of these organized group attitudes which, through the mechanism of his central nervous system, he takes toward himself, just as he takes the individual attitudes of others.

The game has a logic, so that such an organization of the self is rendered possible: there is a definite end to be obtained; the actions of the different individuals are all related to each other with reference to that end so that they do not conflict; one is not in conflict with himself in the attitude of another man on the team. If one has the attitude of the person throwing the ball he can also have the response of catching the ball. The two are related so that they further the purpose of the game itself. They are interrelated in a unitary, organic fashion. There is a definite unity, then, which is introduced into the organization of other selves when we reach such a stage as that of the game, as over against the situation of play where there is a simple succession of one rôle after another, a situation which is, of course, characteristic of the child's own personality. The child is one thing at a time and another at another, and what he is at one moment does not determine what he is at another. That is both the charm of childhood as well as its inadequacy. You cannot count on the child; you cannot assume that all the things he does are going to determine what he will do at any moment. He is not organized into a whole. The child has no definite character, no definite personality.

The game is then an illustration of the situation out of which an organized personality arises. In so far as the child does take the attitude of the other and allows that attitude of the other to determine the thing he is going to do with reference to a common end, he is becoming an organic member of society. He is taking over the morale of that society and is becoming an essential member of it. He belongs to it in so far as he does allow the attitude of the other that he takes to control his own immediate expression. What is involved here is some sort of organized process. That which is expressed in terms of the game is, of course, being continually expressed in the social life of the child, but this wider process goes beyond the immediate experience of the child himself. The importance of the game is that it lies entirely inside of the child's own experience, and the importance of our modern type of education is that it is brought as far as possible within this realm. The different attitudes that a child assumes are so organized that they exercise a definite control over his response, as the attitudes in a game control his own immediate response. In the game we get an organized other, a generalized other, which is found in the nature of the child itself, and finds its expression in the immediate experience of the child. And it is that organized activity in the child's own nature controlling the particular response which gives unity, and which builds up his own self.

Such is the process by which a personality arises. I have spoken of this as a process in which a child takes the rôle of the other, and said that it takes place essentially through the use of language. Language is predominantly based on the vocal gesture by means of which co-operative activities in a community are carried out. Language in its significant sense is that vocal gesture which tends to arouse in the individual the attitude which it arouses in others, and it is this perfecting of the self by the gesture which mediates the social activities that gives rise to the process of taking the rôle of the other. The latter phrase is a little unfortunate because it suggests an actor's attitude which is actually more sophisticated than that which is involved in our own experience. To this degree it does not correctly describe that which I have in mind. We see the process most definitely in a primitive form in those situations where the child's play takes different rôles. Here the very fact that he is ready to pay out money, for instance, arouses the attitude of the person who receives money; the very process is calling out to him the corresponding activities of the other person involved. The individual stimulates himself to the response which he is calling out in the other person, and then acts in some degree in response to that situation. In play the child does definitely act out the rôle which he himself has aroused in himself. It is that which gives, as I have said, a definite content in the individual which answers to the stimulus that affects him as it affects somebody else. The content of the other that enters into one personality is the response in the individual which his gesture calls out in the other.

We may illustrate our basic concept by a reference to the notion of property. If we say, 'This is my property, I shall control it,' that affirmation calls out a certain set of responses which must be the same in any community in which property exists. It involves an organized attitude with reference to property which is common to all the members of the community. One must have a definite attitude of control of his own property and respect for the property of others. Those attitudes (as organized sets of responses) must be there on the part of all, so that when one says such a thing he calls out in himself the response of the others. He is calling out the response of what I have called a generalized other. That which makes society possible is such common responses, such organized attitudes, with reference to what we term property, the cults of religion, the process of education, and the relations of the family. Of course, the wider the society the more definitely universal these objects must be. In any case there must be a definite set of responses, which we may speak of as abstract, and which can belong to a very large group. Property is in itself a very abstract concept. It is that which the individual himself can control and nobody else can control. The attitude is different from that of a dog toward a bone. A dog will fight any other dog trying to take the bone. The dog is not taking the attitude of the other dog. A man who says, 'This is my property,' is taking an attitude of the other person. The man is appealing to his rights because he is able to take the attitude which everybody else in the group has with reference to property, thus arousing in himself the attitude of others.

The 'I' is the response of the organism to the attitudes of the others; the 'me' is the organized set of attitudes of others which one himself assumes. The attitudes of the others constitute the organized 'me', and then one reacts toward that as an 'I'. I now wish to examine these concepts in greater detail.

There is neither 'I' nor 'me' in the conversation of gestures; the whole act is not yet carried out, but the preparation takes place in this field of gesture. Now, in so far as the individual arouses in himself the attitudes of the others, there arises an organized group of responses. And it is due to the individual's ability to take the attitudes of these others in so far as they can be organized that he gets self-consciousness. The taking of all of those organized sets of attitudes gives him his 'me'; that is the self he is aware of. He can throw the ball to some other member because of the demand made upon him from other members of the team. That is the self that immediately exists for him in his consciousness. He has their attitudes, knows what they want and what the consequence of any act of his will be, and he has assumed responsibility for the situation. Now, it is the presence of those organized sets of attitudes that constitutes that 'me' to which he as an 'I' is responding. But what that response will be he does not know and nobody else knows. Perhaps he will make a brilliant play or an error. The response to that situation as it appears in his immediate experience is uncertain, and it is that which constitutes the 'I'.

The 'I' is his action over against that social situation within his own conduct, and it gets into his experience only after he has carried out that act. Then he is aware of it. He had to do such a thing and he did it. He fulfils his duty and he may look with pride at the throw which he made. The 'me' arises to do that duty—that is the way in which it arises in his experience. He had in him all the attitudes of others, calling for a certain response; that was the 'me' of that situation, and his response is the 'I'.

The 'I', then, in this relation of the 'I' and the 'me', is something that is, so to speak, responding to a social situation which is within the experience of the individual. It is the answer which the individual makes to the attitude which others take toward him when he assumes an attitude toward them. Now, the attitudes he is taking toward them are present in his own experience, but his response to them will contain a novel element. The 'I' gives the sense of freedom, of initiative. The situation is there for us to act in a self-conscious fashion. We are aware of ourselves, and of what the situation is, but exactly how we will act never gets into experience until after the action takes place.

Such is the basis for the fact that the 'I' does not appear in the same sense in experience as does the 'me'. The 'me' represents a definite organization of the community there in our own attitudes, and calling for a response, but the response that takes place is something that just happens. There is no certainty in regard to it. There is a moral necessity but no mechanical necessity for the act. When it does take place then we find what has been done. The above account gives us, I think, the relative position of the 'I' and 'me' in the situation, and the grounds for the separation of the two in behaviour. The two are separated in the process but they belong together in the sense of being parts of a whole. They are separated and yet they belong together. The separation of the 'I' and the 'me' is not fictitious. They are not identical, for, as I have said, the 'I' is something that is never entirely calculable. The 'me' does call for a certain sort of an 'I' in so far as we meet the obligations that are given in conduct itself, but the 'I' is always something different from what the situation itself calls for. So there is always that distinction, if you like, between the 'I' and the 'me'. The 'I' both calls out the 'me' and responds to it. Taken together they constitute a personality as it appears in social experience. The self is essentially a social process going on with these two distinguishable phases. If it did not have these two phases there could not be conscious responsibility, and there would be nothing novel in experience.

NOTES

1. Man's behaviour is such in his social group that he is able to become an object to himself, a fact which constitutes him a more advanced product of evolutionary development than are the lower animals. Fundamentally it is this social fact—and not his alleged possession of a soul or mind with which he, as an individual, has been mysteriously and supernaturally endowed, and with which the lower animals have not been endowed—that differentiates him from them.

2. It is generally recognized that the specifically social expressions of intelligence, or the exercise

of what is often called 'social intelligence', depend upon the given individual's ability to take the rôles of, or 'put himself in the place of', the other individuals implicated with him in given social situations; and upon his consequent sensitivity to their attitudes toward himself and toward one another. These specifically social expressions of intelligence, of course, acquire unique significance in terms of our view that the whole nature of intelligence is social to the very core—that this putting of one's self in the places of others, this taking by one's self of their rôles or attitudes, is not merely one of the various aspects or expressions of intelligence or of intelligent behaviour, but is the very essence of its character. Spearman's 'X factor' in intelligence—the unknown factor which, according to him, intelligence contains—is simply (if our social theory of intelligence is correct) this ability of the intelligent individual to take the attitude of the other, or the attitudes of others, thus realizing the significations or grasping the meanings of the symbols or gestures in terms of which thinking proceeds; and thus being able to carry on with himself the internal conversation with these symbols or gestures which thinking involves.

PART 2

CONTEMPORARY
SOCIAL THEORISTS

*Yet with the shifting global balance of power away from the West, with more voices talk-
ing back to the West, there is a strong sense that modernity will not be universalized. This
is because modernity is seen as both a Western project and as the West's projection of its
values on to the world.*[1]

Contemporary society has often been characterized as basically ahistorical—that which
gets left behind needs to be abandoned and forgotten. On the contrary, there is renewed
discussion regarding our contemporary 'lack of memory' or 'social amnesia'. To move
into the twentieth century, as we have done, and now into the twenty-first century, we
perhaps have a greater obligation than ever before to reflect and renew our historical
understandings. In addition, it is important that we, particularly as people living in the
West, begin not only to recognize the context out of which our lives have emerged, but
to comprehend the global effects of European colonialism, particularly on those in the
now ex-colonies.

Contemporary society seems caught within the dialectic of monoculturalism and
multiculturalism—between one-dimensional realities (to use Marcuse's term) and the
tremendous diversities within world cultures. As we begin to explain our lives in terms
such as postmodernism, we need to see the historical roots of the modern. Anton
Allahar, in an article entitled 'Race and Racism: Strategies of Resistance', raises three significant issues regarding race and ethnic identities today:

> First, there is the large-scale international migration of peoples from more tradi-
> tional cultures and societies to the so-called more developed societies, where cul-
> ture is highly secularized, and where the values of liberalism, individualism and
> achievement have been constitutionally enshrined.
>
> The second source of conflict relates to the fact that constitutions *formally*
> embrace the ideas of social justice and equality, which implies that social, econom-
> ic and political opportunities are free and open to all individual citizens. But, in
> actuality, because those notions of freedom, equality and justice are ideological,
> confrontation and resistance are likely to result. . . .
>
> A third source of conflict concerns the international post-Cold War period,
> which began with the breaking down of the Berlin Wall and the dismantling of the
> Soviet Union. The removal of travel restrictions and the ensuing flood of refugees

from the former socialist bloc to the West have been accompanied by widespread ethno-national conflicts. Thus, in a world which sees 'ethnic groups as emerging transnational actors' . . . , ethno-racial identities are adding new dimensions to the older, pre-existing conflicts that are now so rife around the globe.[2]

Part II of this book pushes to the fore issues that may at first appear new, isolated, or disconnected from tradition as they attempt to explain and provide social analysis. Yet, feminist issues, issues of public versus private space, and issues regarding sexuality, for example, all emerge within the demands of the contemporary and theoretical. We continue to seek explanation. We continue to elaborate our tools of analysis. Allahar demands that we recognize the complexities of an ever-changing global geopolitics. The Eurocentric, patriarchal perspective excessively limits our ability to find explanatory power in contemporary theory—particularly in a post-September 11 world.

C. Wright Mills, in what has become a contemporary 'classic', conjoins the personal and the structural—what the modern feminists interpret as 'the personal is political'. Others here express this as the relationship between the public and the private domains/spheres as they commingle in people's everyday lives. The conceptualization of the public/private divide is clearly an emergent theme of contemporary interest to sociology.

As the work of each theorist in Part II appears less totalizing, or less oriented to grand theory, we begin the project facing us: weaving together meaning out of often contradictory explanations. Issues of power and sexuality (Foucault), role or impression management (Goffman), representations (Said), the differences between our work and our 'lifeworlds' (Habermas) all seem to lead to the overarching fragmentation of consciousness and identity explored by Featherstone in his discussion of postmodernism.

Yet, with bell hooks and her recognition of the 'intersection of race, gender and class', we begin to see the need to unite *macro* social analysis with *micro* experience within our everyday lives. The feminist theoretical perspective gains long needed credibility through its capacity to thread together these complex, multi-layered facets of experience and structure, its attempts at holistic interpretation.

At the same time that we are experiencing a deterioration of the traditional holds on the individual—aspects of people's everyday lives that give them continuity within the collectivity—thereby demanding more resilience from the individual, we are seeing the fragmentation of identities (ethnically, sexually, culturally). Ironically, as this moment 'consumes' us, and we it, we become 'branded' by transnational corporations and monoculturally configured within the institutions of society.

If sociology is to give us the power to explain our social relationships and make sense of our lives, we must witness the shift from theorists studied in Part I, with their criticisms and continuities, to the individualizing disjunctures emergent from theorists in Part II. Given these times of change and fundamental shift, both locally and globally, the theoretical insights and power in the selections presented here provide us with a solid starting point from which to depart in our attempt to understand the diversity of contemporary society.

Notes

1. Mike Featherstone, *Undoing Culture: Globalization, Postmodernism and Identity* (London: Sage, 1995), 10.
2. Anton Allahar, 'Race and Racism: Strategies of Resistance', in Vic Satzewich, ed., *Racism and Social Inequality in Canada* (Toronto: Thompson Educational Publishing, 1998), 336-7.

JESSIE BERNARD

1903–1996
UNITED STATES

Major Works

1942   *American Family Behavior*
1956   *Marriage and Family Among Negroes*
1957   *Remarriage: A Study of Marriage*
1964   *Academic Women*
1968   *The Sex Game: Communication Between the Sexes*
1971   *Women and Public Interest: An Essay on Policy and Protest*
1974   *The Future of Motherhood*
1975   *Women, Wives, Mothers—Values and Options*
1980   *The Female World*
1982   *The Future of Marriage*
1987   *The Female World in a Global Perspective*

> Women and other minority groups tend to be suspicious of emphasis on differences, for all too often it under-girds some version of the separate-but-equal form of discrimination. The 'you're-just-as-good-as-we-are-only-different' point of view is certainly valid. But it is always interpreted by patronizing men in their favour.[1]
>
> The difficulty of both the harsh and the tender versions of the male mystique is their unsuitability for life in the real world. Men become bored with having to protect the weaker vessel, and women become resentful at having to submit to the stronger male.[2]
>
> —*Jessie Bernard*

Bernard's sociology was originally grounded in the positivist approach: the scientific search for abstract laws of social life. In the process of her intellectual development—which she referred to as differing stages of *her* revolution—she moved to a more critical approach. Her move from positivism towards an understanding of how knowledge (and not just structure) is socially produced was influenced by the events of World War II that led her to question the role of science in bringing about social justice. She studied and wrote about women's lives from the 1940s on.

With her emphasis on the social specificity of knowledge and the need to study the lives of members of groups whose voices historically have been ignored, Bernard moved from examining women's lives within the traditional context of the sociology of the family to a position engendering feminist criticism.

In *The Future of Marriage* she challenges that institution, arguing that it is theoretically an egalitarian agreement between husband and wife, but in practice it places diametrically opposed obligations on men and women. Men, she argues, benefit greatly; they are allowed extensive power and privileges both in the wider society and in the home. Women are denied these privileges, and in the process develop a sense of dependence and helplessness. Dependence is perpetuated in the way the different genders are socialized. Men are not socialized to see domesticity as their destiny and have developed the freedom to traverse between the public and private spheres. Women, on the other hand, are socialized to see domesticity as their destiny and are rarely as free as men to traverse both spheres.

Bernard makes the point that we must be cognizant that realities are socially constructed and are therefore changeable, whether the reality is marriage, womanhood, or manhood. The impact of marriage on women continues to be the focus of much contemporary theorizing.

Notes

1. Jessie Bernard, *The Future of Marriage* (New York: Bantam Books, 1972), 159.
2. Ibid., 174.

WOMEN

The Mark of Eve

Despite universal recognition of differences among women, whatever their causes, women as everyone knows, are women.[1] Still, Ruth Useem, a sociologist, once commented on the inadequacy of the single mark she had to make on all documents asking for 'sex'. All she could do was check the F box. But she knew that this 'mark of Eve' told the reader very little about her. There were so many kinds of F: F_1, F_2 . . . F_n, and yet there was no way to let the reader know which one she was.[2]

Her comment was by no means trivial, facetious, or irrelevant to policy, for the 'mark of Eve' a woman makes in the F box ascribes a status to her that is quite independent of her qualities as an individual. Every other mark she makes on that document will be evaluated in terms of that mark. Assumptions will be made about her on the basis of it. Privileges, responsibilities, prerogatives, obligations will be assigned on the basis of it also.

Policy will rest on it. A great deal rides on that one mark, for it refers to the most funda-mental differentiation among human beings. But it leaves out differences among the Fs themselves, as important as the similarities. Yet, though there are few bodies of lore and literature more extensive than that on the nature of differences between men and women, there are few less extensive than those on the nature of differences among women them-selves.

The Visibility Gap

In the age of innocence, moving picture producers made it very clear to us at the very out-set of a picture who were the good guys and who the bad. The good guys wore white hats. In nineteenth-century melodramas the villain wore an identifying mustache so that we knew he was going to foreclose the mortgage unless the beautiful daughter capitulated to his advances. In Greek drama there were appropriate masks to inform us about the char-acters.

Despite our dependence on visual cues, however, there is always a visibility gap. The outer mark does not tell us all there is to know about the person inside. The same mark stamps a wide variety of people. Not all the farmers who bore the mark of Cain killed graz-ers and herders. A wide variety of men bore that mark. A wide variety of people inhabit the bodies of women (as also, of course, the bodies of men as well). For women are not interchangeable parts.

F_1, F_2, . . . F_n

Whatever the differences may be between M and F, and whatever the origin of these dif-ferences may be, they are matched and in some cases exceeded by differences among women themselves. A woman may in many ways be more like the average man than she is like another woman. A very considerable research literature undergirds the fact that there are extensible differences among women in such sociologically relevant variables as interests, values, and goals. These differences have to be taken into account when dealing with programs or policies involving women.

Two polar types turn up with singular consistency in the research literature on women, whether the point of view is sociological or psychological.[3] Alice Rossi assigned the terms 'pioneer' and 'housewife' to these types, using the term 'traditional' for those who fell in between (Rossi, 1965: 79–80). Another team of researchers called the polar types 'homemaking-oriented' and 'career-oriented' (Hoyt and Kennedy, 1958). Another researcher spoke of 'creative intellectual' when referring to a type that corresponded to pioneer or career-oriented (Drews, 1965). Eli Ginzberg and his associates found women they called 'supportive', who corresponded roughly to the housewife or home-oriented subjects in other studies, and 'influential' women who resembled the pioneer type (Ginzberg, 1966). The existence of such types can scarcely be challenged.

The exact numerical population size of these several types is not important, for it doubtless changes over time and is certainly changing today. In the recent past, however, one of the striking facts that emerged from the studies was the agreement they showed with respect to the incidence of the several types in different samples. At the high school senior level, 7 to 8 per cent of the 'creative intellectuals' had the drive to achieve the lifestyle they desired. Among college freshmen, 8 per cent fell into the career-oriented category. Among college graduates, 7 per cent were pioneers. Among women who had done graduate work, 10 per cent were living an influential lifestyle. At Cornell, 8 per cent of a sample of women in 1950 and 6 per cent of a sample in 1952 showed high career orientation (Goldsen, 1960: 136). At Vassar, however, also in the 1950s, two-thirds answered 'true' to the statement 'I would like a career' (Freedman, 1967: 136). In context, this answer was interpreted by Caroline Bird to mean 'career' in a secondary sense. Perhaps more indicative of a pioneer orientation was the answer to the statement 'I enjoy children', which elicited a negative in 8 per cent of the women. That the Vassar women were changing rapidly was suggested by Caroline Bird, who noted that the classes of 1964 and 1966 voted for 'career with as little time out for family as possible' and that there was even a notable rise in the number of girls who said they were pursuing a 'career period' (Bird, 1968: 184). The proportion in all the samples who fell into the housewife or homemaking or supportive category was consistently about a fifth or a fourth. It is interesting to compare this figure with the proportion, about 18 per cent, of college women who, a generation ago, were reported by Lewis M. Terman to be greatly interested in the domestic arts (Terman and Miles, 1936: 209–10).

It would require considerably more focused research to pinpoint with greater accuracy and precision the relative incidence of the several types and the reasons that explain these proportions. Equally important would be research to document trends in such incidence. My own reading of current trends is that one of the most drastic shake-ups in the social order today is the breaking up of old blocs and their re-forming into new configurations. Yesterday's data no longer reflect the current scene. In 1969 a national sample of youth showed 10 per cent of the young women to be radical reformers and 17.1 per cent moderate reformers (Yankelovich, 1969).

The characterization of the pioneer (or career-oriented or creative intellectual or influential) type varied with the interests of the researchers; but here, too, there was notable convergence. Among the high-school girls, the creative intellectuals tended to be more receptive than other girls to the new, to growth, and to change; they were less conventional and conforming. Among college students, those who fell into the pioneer or career-oriented category tended to show up in all the studies as different from other college women. The Kansas State career-oriented freshmen were higher on 'endurance' and 'achievement' than the homemaking-oriented women and lower on 'succorance' and 'heterosexuality'—in the sense of being interested in attracting young men, not as contrasted with homosexuality (Hoyt and Kennedy, 1968). Rossi's housewives characterized themselves as dependent; they showed strong nurturance toward the young; they were socially rather than occupationally competitive. In contrast, the pioneers were less dependent, less nurturant, more egalitarian; they valued the world of ideas more. They characterized themselves as dominant and occupationally competitive (the married less so than the single). Ginzberg's women with the influential lifestyle were characterized by a striving for autonomy; they found their major sources of gratification in the social significance of their work and the personal relations involved in it. In both the Rossi and the Ginzberg samples, the women in the pioneer or influential category were far more likely to be working (70 per cent in both samples) and less likely to be married; the reverse was true for the housewives and supportive women. At Cornell, it was found that the career-oriented women were more likely than the family-oriented women to be noncomformists with 'a certain irreverence for rules and conventions' (Freedman, 1967: 140). At Vassar, years of careful research yielded this picture of career-oriented students:

> Students who say 'true' to 'I would like a career' are somewhat more intellectual, unconventional, independent (perhaps rebellious), and flexible in thinking and out-look. They are also somewhat more alienated or isolated socially. [At Cornell, career women engaged in just as many extracurricular activities as other women and were just as likely to associate with men (Goldsen, 1960: 54).] It is interesting to observe that these differences are most pronounced [among seniors]. Results for the Ethnocentrism Scale . . . are in line with findings of other studies which demonstrate that attitudes toward the role and behaviour of women are likely to accord with atti-tudes toward members of outgroups or 'underprivileged' groups. Individuals, includ-ing women themselves, who hold somewhat stereotyped views of Negroes or for-eigners, for example, are likely to adhere to traditional or rather fixed notions of what is appropriate activity for women (Freedman, 1967: 140).

The explanations of such differences among women also vary according to the researchers' predilections. One team of psychologists is satisfied by a pattern of 'needs'. Career-oriented women, they believe, are motivated by one or more of four such needs: to establish one's worth through competitive behaviour or achievement, to know intellec-tually and understand ('intraception'), to accomplish concrete goals (endurance), and to avoid relations with men (heterosexuality). The homemaking women are motivated by needs of affection and acceptance (succorance) (Hoyt and Kennedy, 1958). But another psychologist is quite agnostic: 'Psychology has nothing to say about what women are real-ly like, what they need and what they want, essentially, because psychology does not know' (Weisstein, 1969: 78). Sociologists and social psychologists tend to look to social-ization variables to interpret the difference. Since career orientation may change with age and experience, it is hazardous to put too much credence in any analysis that makes it depend on personality variables, which are presumably quite stable. Such an approach, in any event, still leaves the genesis of the needs themselves to be explained.

Whatever the incidence and whatever the explanation, telescoping all these women into the single F box blots out a great deal of sociologically important diversity. In many situations F_1 may have more in common with M_1 than with any of the other Fs. Rank, for example, is more important than sex in many situations. A princess has more in common with a prince than with a domestic; a professional woman often has more in common with a colleague than with a cleaning woman; an heiress with an heir than with a woman receiving welfare payments. Sometimes F_1 and F_j have not only different but opposing points of view, each seeing the other as a threat either to a vested interest or to opportu-nity for achievement. The wife of a workingman may not agree with the woman worker on the principle of equal pay for equal work; she believes her husband should get more because he has to support his family. (Perhaps the only thing that all Fs have in common as yet is the concern that adequate gynecological, obstetrical, and pediatric services be widely available, and that public toilet facilities be supplied with emergency equipment.) It would, then, be more in line with the facts of life if, instead of compressing all women into the single F category, the diversity among them could be recognized by allowing for F_1, F_2, . . . F_n. Thus the woman who says she is content to devote her life to the traditional pattern of homemaking could be differentiated from the woman who is willing to settle for nothing less than the complete gamut—marriage, children, and a career. . . .

Sex

If both the layman and the scientist have underplayed the differences among women, they have tended to overplay the differences between females and males. A great deal of the work of running the world rests on making simple classificatory decisions. Into which category does X fall? Y? or Z? Which rules apply? Anything, therefore, that simplifies this process by predecision is welcomed by administrators and executives and copers in general. Sex is such a predecision-maker. F goes here, M there: so much easier than having to study each case individually to decide on its merits where it belongs, which rule to apply. It is such a simple, straightforward, ineffable, easily applied criterion that it has rarely been challenged.

But new research issuing from clinic and laboratory is beginning to shake our old naïveté about sex. We now know that, far from being a simple, straight-forward, genetically determined phenomenon, sex has at least three components—chromosomal, hormonal, anatomical—and conceivably more. Although for most people these three components are matched to produce a clear-cut male or female individual, such is not always the case. There can be mistakes. These 'errors of the body' have alerted us to some of the anomalies possible in the sphere of sexuality. When all goes normally, as it usually does, the M and F boxes fit very well to distinguish males and females. They can accommodate almost everyone. But things do not always go normally. Sometimes a genetic F is masculinized hormonally *in utero* with the result that anatomical anomalies confuse gender assignment at birth; or a genetic M is not masculinized *in utero*, making gender equivocal. Such errors are rare and turn up so infrequently that relatively little is yet known about them; they are so rare that, once they are recognized, we can disregard them in any analysis of large-scale sociological phenomena.[4] Their major relevance for our discussion here is the lesson they teach with respect to the relative contribution of biological, social, cultural, and sociological factors to gender.

With the exception of those who are victims of 'errors of the body' there is no overlap between male and female populations. They are categorically different. Still it is interesting to note that, different though the equipment at their disposal may be, they respond quite similarly to the same stimuli. Estrogens and androgens, for example, have the same effect on both sexes, making for greater or less sexual motivation, greater or less aggressiveness (Hamber and Lunde, 1966). This suggests that the two sexes also respond about the same way to other kinds of stimuli—psychological and social. What is important are the kinds of stimuli they are subjected to. Interesting also is the finding that creative personalities, whether housed in female or in male bodies, have similar personality characteristics.

Gender

Gender refers to the complex traits that determine whether one checks the M or the F box. It is, to be sure, inextricably related to sex, but 'the two realms, sex and gender, are not at all inevitably bound in anything like a one-to-one relationship, but each may go in its quite independent way' (Stoller, 1968: vii–ix). Sex is a biological fact; gender, though based on biology, is a social-cultural-sociological-psychological fact. Gender consists of gender identity and gender role (Stoller, 1968: 92): the first a social and psychological phenomenon; the second, a cultural and sociological and interactional one.

Gender identity begins in the hospital delivery room. As soon as an infant is born it is, on the basis of anatomical cues, assigned a gender which is well established by age two. The infant's life course is almost sealed by that act; for it is primarily this gender assignment, rather than anatomy, or even heredity, that, in Freud's terminology, is destiny. Almost every decision made by the outside world about this child is going to take this assignment into account. Every structured relationship will be defined in terms of it, and the child will accept it in most cases.

Gender Identity

Scarcely a woman alive would have any hesitation about marking the proper F or M box. A woman knows she is female. The whole matter of gender identity would probably never have occurred to a woman; it looks to her like a man-made problem manufactured by male psychoanalysts, illustrating the sexism that modern women are protesting against. This sexism of psychoanalysts is nowhere better portrayed than in their inability to understand how women could possibly have any sense of femaleness without something like a phallus to prove to themselves that they were women. An inverted phallus or vagina was invoked to solve the riddle. It has been a major contribution of recent gender research to show it does not take a vagina, notoriously lacking in sensitivity, to confer gender identity on females. Breasts and menstruation serve quite adequately to remind them that they are female, strange as it may seem to a breastless, nonmenstruating individual. To psychoanalysts, the muscle that daily (and, in youth, hourly) reminds males of their sex seemed the *sine qua non* of gender identity; a creature lacking it must be only a defective male. The results of this thinking showed up in therapy; 'It is possible that the analyst's view of a successful analysis may be skewed if he feels he has reached the core of a woman's femininity when he has been able to get her to share with equanimity his belief that she is really an inferior form of male' (Stoller, 1968: 63).

Actually a woman's gender identity is firm, even, in some cases, if her heredity or anatomy is not. In Table 1 for example, three women are discussed who would unhesitatingly mark the F box; they have female gender identity (numbers 2, 3, and 5). But both their heredities and their anatomies differ. One (number 3) has female heredity and external anatomy but no vagina. One (number 2) has female heredity but, as a result of masculinization *in utero*, male-appearing genitalia; female gender was assigned to her at birth and despite the anatomical anomaly she finds the F box acceptable. A third woman (number 5) has neuter heredity and anomalous anatomy; but, assigned female gender at birth, she, too, has no problem with the F box. Such women may be unhappy about their inadequate or flawed sexuality, but their gender identity is unimpaired; they feel like women and unequivocally check the F box. All are F even though either their heredity or their anatomy does not conform to F specifications.

Table 1: Deviances illustrating the equivocal relation of gender identity to heredity and anatomy

Genetic sex	Internal anatomy	External anatomy	Gender assignment	Gender identity
1. Female	Female	Equivocal	Male	Male
2. Female	Female	Equivocal	Female	Female
3. Female	Defective	Female	Female	Female
4. Female	Female	Female	Female	Male
5. Neuter (XO)	Defective	Female	Female	Female
6. Equivocal (XXY)	Female	Male	Male	Female
7. Male	Male	Equivocal	Female	Male
8. Male	Male	Equivocal	Male	Female

1. 'Money and the Hampsons . . . describe two children masculinized *in utero* by excessive adrenal androgens, both biologically normal females, genetically and in their internal sexual anatomy and physiology, but with masculinized external genitalia. The proper diagnosis having been made, one child was raised unequivocally as a female . . .; she turned out to be as feminine as other little girls' (p. 57).
2. 'The other, not recognized to be female, was raised without question as a male . . . and became an unremarkably masculine little boy' (p. 57).
3. 'The patient is a 17-year-old, feminine, attractive, intelligent girl who appeared anatomically completely normal at birth, but behind whose external genitalia there was no vagina or uterus. Her parents, having no doubts, raised her as a girl, and female and feminine is what she feels she is' (p. 56).
4. 'These people, living permanently as unremarkably masculine men, are biologically normal females and were so recognized as children . . . Among those I know one is an expert machine tool operator, another an engineering draftsman, another a research chemist. Their jobs are quiet, steady, and unspectacular; their work records as men are excellent. They are sociable, not recluses, and have friendships with both men and women. Neither their friends nor their colleagues at work know they are biologically female. They are not clinically psychotic' (pp. 194, 196).
5. '[She] is a person as biologically neuter as a human can be, chromosomally XO . . . And yet when she was first seen at age 18 . . . she was quite unremarkably feminine in her behaviour, dress, social and sexual desires, and fantasies, indistinguishable in these regards from other girls . . . Her gender identity is not based on some simple biologi-

cal given, such as endocrine state. It comes from the fact that she looked like a girl
. . . Given the anatomical prerequisites to the development of her femininity, it set in
motion the complicated process that results in gender identity' (p. 22).

6. '. . . born an apparently normal male, . . . the boy's body became feminized' (p. 77).

7. 'A child . . . at birth was found to be an apparently normal female and so was brought
   up as a girl for fourteen years . . . A physical examination [at adolescence] raised doubts
   shortly to be confirmed . . . The inquiry . . . revealed that although the external genitalia looked the same as those of a normal girl of her age, she was in fact a chromosomally normal male' (pp. 67, 69).

8. 'This patient . . . was male in anatomical appearance. However, as far back as memory
   goes, he was extremely feminine . . . Hospitalized as a result of hepatitis, he was discovered to be genetically and anatomically male' (p. 75).

Source: Data from Robert J. Stoller, *Sex and Gender, on the Development of Masculinity and Femininity*
(Science House, New York, 1968).

Such cases show the independence of gender identity from either heredity or anatomy.
They illustrate its social nature: 'those aspects of sexuality that are called gender are . . .
learned postnatally' (Stoller, 1968: xiii) primarily from the mother but also from the father,
siblings, and friends.

Cases number 1 and 2 also illustrate the social nature of gender identity or the acceptance of the gender assigned at birth. In both cases the infants were genetically females but
in both cases the external genitalia, according to which gender is assigned, had been masculinized *in utero* and were therefore anomalous. In the case of one of the children (number
2), the diagnosis of sex was correct and the child was assigned female gender and reared as
a female. In the other (number 1), the diagnosis was incorrect and the child was assigned
male gender and reared as a male. The first became as feminine as other little girls, the other
a masculine little boy. Same sex heredity, same prenatal 'error', but different gender assignment and hence different gender identity.

Gender is so thoroughly bred into the infant by the world around it and becomes so
much a part of its identity that even if the assignment is later discovered to be an error, it is
almost impossible to change. Despite the discovery that the individual is genetically a male,
he continues to have female gender identity.

All these findings warn us against taking the M and F boxes too much for granted.
Gender identity does not apparently always just come naturally. It has to be learned. And
there is no one-to-one relationship between it and sex.

The emphasis on the social and acquired nature of gender identity does not rule out a
biological component, for 'if the first main finding of [recent research] is that gender identity is primarily learned, the second is that there are biological forces that contribute to this'
(Stoller, 1968: xiii). Sometimes, for reasons not yet clear, gender assignment does not 'take',
as in cases 4, 6, 7, and 8. The resulting phenomena curb any dogmatism we may show with
respect to our knowledge of sex and gender. The nature of the biological component
involved in gender is still an open question. Beach calls it an unresolved issue (Beach, 1965:
565) and Stoller confesses that the evidence is equivocal, 'so we must leave this subject

without any sense of its having been settled' (Stoller, 1968: 85). For this reason as well as for the reason that sexual anomalies are so rare, the strictly biological factors in gender are given no further attention here. Although they teach us a great deal about the normal aspects of sex and gender, they cannot be invoked in sociological analyses. Further discussion would distort the picture by overemphasizing rare exceptions.

Although the etiological contribution of biological factors to gender identity may be equivocal and often irrelevant, the indirect or derivative contribution of biological factors cannot be denied. In the crucial years when both F and M are working out their mature identities, they are producing different reactions in one another. She produces an erection in him; another boy does not. His touch on her breasts thrills her; another girl's does not. She wants him to caress her; she does not want another girl to. Being reacted to by others as F is different from being reacted to by them as M. And the reaction to F is different from the reaction to M. She can receive him, he cannot receive her. It does not take a sophisticated analysis in terms of symbolic interactionism to see that the different effect each has *on* the other and the different reaction each has *to* the other will produce different conceptions of the self in both M and F. These differences are ultimately biological but, like the functional basis for differences (to be discussed later), in a derived rather than in a direct sense.

Gender Role

Along with gender assignment goes a constellation of traits suitable for characterizing the gender. When illustrating or demonstrating the gender identity of patients, Stoller gives such evidence of feminine gender identity as wanting babies and having a great interest in clothes, cooking, sewing, make-up, ornamentation, and the like (Stoller, 1968: 21-2). These are clearly not all the product of heredity nor of anatomy. They are traits that our society labels feminine.

Some of the specific contents or traits that constitute masculine or feminine gender may vary from place to place and time to time. In Iran, for example, some of the traits that we develop as parts of feminine gender are included in the pattern for masculine gender and vice versa:

> In Iran . . . men are expected to show their emotions . . . If they don't, Iranians suspect they are lacking a vital human trait and are not dependable. Iranian men read poetry; they are sensitive and have well-developed intuition and in many cases are not expected to be too logical. They are often seen embracing and holding hands. Women, on the other hand, are considered to be coldly practical. They exhibit many of the characteristics we associate with men in the United States. A very perceptive Foreign Service officer who had spent a number of years in Iran once observed, 'If you think of the emotional and intellectual sex roles reversed from ours, you will do much better out here.' . . . Fundamental beliefs like our concepts of masculinity and femininity are shown to vary widely from one culture to the next (Hall, 1963: 10).[5]

The specific contents of masculinity and femininity vary with time also; people worry over the 'masculinization of women' and the 'feminization of men'. The Victorian contents of feminine gender included weakness, helplessness, fragility, delicacy, and even ill health. Clark Vincent has pointed out how ill-fitting the traditional contents of gender roles are today for both F and M. On tradition-oriented tests, modern middle-class women tend to test low; middle-class men, on the other hand, 'tend to score high on femininity when items are included which formerly described the more dependent, intuitive, sensitive, "peacemaking" role of the female in a tradition-oriented society' (Vincent, 1966: 199).

Gender specifications vary not only with time and place but also with the researcher or scientist who reports them. One survey of the literature on the feminine character concluded that 'there is hardly any common basis to the different views. The difficulty is not only that there is disagreement on specific characteristics [of feminine gender] and their origin, but that even when there is agreement the emphasis is laid on absolutely different attributes' (Klein, 1946: 164).

The most widely recurrent traits attributed to women in western societies have been passivity, emotionality, lack of abstract interests, greater intensity of personal relationships, and an instinctive tenderness for babies (Klein, 1946: 164). The test of masculinity-femininity includes such items as passivity, disinclination for physical violence, sensitivity to personal slights and to interpersonal relations, lack of concern for abstractions, and a positive attitude toward culturally defined esthetic experience.

If femaleness and maleness are categorical, non-overlapping, the same cannot be said with respect to femininity and masculinity. Here the overlap can be considerable (Figure 1). Traits denominated as feminine show up in men, and those denominated as masculine show up in women.[6] Here the distinction between *typical* and *characteristic* is important. The typical is the average or the modal. And for many traits, where the overlap is great, the average woman and the average man may not be very different. But when women and men do differ, they differ in characteristic ways, women 'characteristically' in one direction, men in another. By and large, women tend to differ in the direction of passivity, nurturance, nonviolence, and men in the direction of aggression, dominance, and violence. The tendency of most societies is to pull women in one direction and men in the other, so that very often the distributions are skewed (Figure 2). For the convenience of managers and copers, it would be ideal if femininity and masculinity were as categorically clear-cut as femaleness and maleness; it would save them a great deal of trouble if all females were characteristically feminine and all males were characteristically masculine. But the fact is that they aren't. The important thing is not, therefore, whether or not 'women' are z-er than 'men', or 'men' v-er than 'women', but whether Mary is z-er than John, or John v-er than Mary.

Viola Klein has traced the conceptualization of sex differences through three stages, beginning with Aristotle's category of feminine traits which led him to conclude that femininity was a 'kind of natural defectiveness'. According to this conceptualization, women are underdeveloped beings with the external attributes of human beings but lacking individuality, intellectual ability, or character. A second stage granted that women were not inferior men but simply different, complementary, inverse. This point of view flourished at the end of the nineteenth and beginning of the twentieth centuries. The third, current, conceptualization sees personality traits as products of functional roles (Klein, 1946: 169-70).

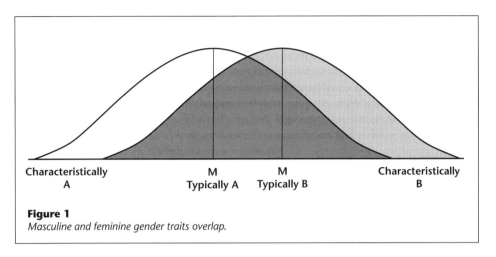

Figure 1
Masculine and feminine gender traits overlap.

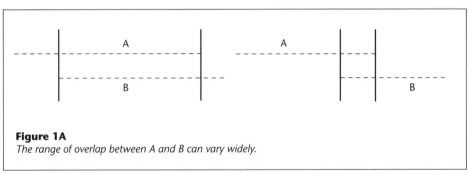

Figure 1A
The range of overlap between A and B can vary widely.

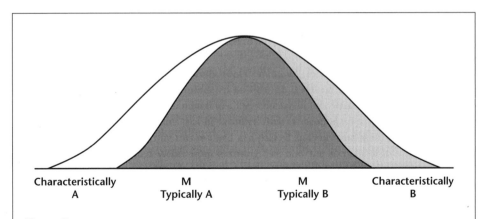

Figure 2
Skewed distribution of gender traits.
The socialization process has pulled A and B in different directions
so that the distributions are skewed in a desired direction.

Despite the enormous amount of ink that has been spilled in clearly specifying the nature of psychological gender differences, the conclusion seems to be that it is not so much *what* is defined as masculine or feminine as that such distinctions are made at all. It makes no difference whether pink is for girls and blue for boys, emotionality for girls and rationality for boys, or the other way round. What does make a difference is that a difference is made. It is not the explanations offered for the existence of differences (inherent, acquired, functional, structural) but the fact that there is something to explain. It is the bifurcation by sex that is the fundamental fact. The traits, functions, and work assigned to each part of the bifurcation are secondary; the bifurcation itself is what is primary.

Sex has inevitable structural concomitants and consequences. The structural components that operate differentially on the sexes are both horizontal and vertical; the world women live in tends to be different, and it is usually secondary to the world of men.

The Sphere of Women

Once an individual has been assigned a gender, he (or she) is thereafter relegated to the world or sphere designed for those with his (or her) gender. Even when the work of both women and men was in the home, they lived in different worlds: there was a sphere for men and a sphere for women. Even today there is a woman's world recognized by almost everyone and thoroughly exploited by the mass media. It has quite a different structure from the world of men.

These worlds can be described in terms of several dimensions or variables that those sociologists who follow Talcott Parsons have found useful in describing social systems. Five such dimensions have been encapsulated in terms of five pairs of variables. A community can, first of all, make one's position rest on what one *does* or on what one *is*; it can be the result of achievement or of ascription. Second, the expectations that parties in any relationship share may be specific or diffuse. Duties, obligations, and responsibilities may be defined specifically and contractually, or they may be left unspecified. If they are specified, each party knows precisely what is expected of him and of others; nothing more can be demanded than what is specified, and nothing less can be supplied. The accountant may not be asked to run the computer, the lawyer to run the elevator. If they are left diffuse, there is a rather amorphous, blurred set of expectations that leave precise limits undefined. A friend may be expected to lend money, arrange a date, or share a record collection. Third, a community can require that all relationships be governed by general universalistic principles, or it can permit them to be governed by particularistic personal loyalties and obligations tailored to the particular individuals involved. Fourth, it can permit behaviour to be oriented toward furthering one's own interests, or it can require that actions be oriented toward a larger group or the collectivity as a whole, regardless of individual wishes. Finally, the community can admit a wide range of relationships in which there is a minimum of affect or emotional gratification (in which relationships are neutral), or it can allow a wide range of relationships in which affectivity or emotional gratification plays a large part. It is clear that a society in which the first of each of these five pairs of variables prevails will be quite different from one in which the second of each does.

These dimensions or ways of patterning the variables have been used to describe communities or societies of different kinds. For example, ascription, diffuseness, particularism, collectivity-orientation, and affectivity have been used to describe preliterate societies. The first three pairs of dimensions have been used to characterize developing countries as contrasted with modern ones; the degree to which they approached achievement, specificity, and universalistic characteristics has been taken as a measure of modernization (Hoselitz, 1964).

It is not too fanciful to view the gender world or sphere in which women live as characterized, like a preliterate society, by ascription, diffuseness, particularism, collectivity-orientation, and affectivity. In effect, to view women as inhabiting an underdeveloped, if not a primitive, world.

The first step has been taken when feminine gender is ascribed to the female infant. A lifelong train of consequences then ensues. She is thereafter dealt with on the basis of what she is—a woman—rather than on what she does, on her (feminine) qualities rather than on her performance, just as reported for preliterate cultures.

Once this assignment and consequent ascription have been made, a woman is consigned to a world or 'sphere' in which her relationships are diffuse rather than specific or contractual. Even in a work situation where presumably relations are contractual and specific, the secretary has diffuse expectations to live up to, such as the variegated services expected of an 'office wife' or 'girl Friday'. The sphere of women is expected to be characterized by particularistic morality more than by universalistic morality, by intense personal loyalty more than by principles. Women are to protect their children even when the children are delinquents or criminals, to do everything they can for those near and dear to them rather than be blindly just or impartial. On the job, women, as part of their supportive function, are expected to be more loyal to their employers than are men. One reads from time to time that men have reported wrongdoing on the part of their employers; one rarely reads that women have. The 'developed' country that men inhabit almost forces them to undercut one another to get ahead. In the women's sphere, women are expected to be oriented toward the larger group or the collectivity and to make sacrifices for it. We know that in marriage it is wives who make more of the adjustments; it is taken for granted that mothers make more sacrifices for their children; it is expectable that if necessary, the daughter rather than the son will sacrifice marriage to take care of elderly parents. Yet the pursuit of self-interest is almost a virtue in the world men inhabit.

In using this form of 'pattern-variable' it is essential to make perfectly clear that the personal characteristics of the individuals involved are not the focus of attention; it is rather the shared expectations built into the situation. A social system leads to certain kinds of behaviour on the part of its members regardless of their personal qualities or traits. We tend thereafter to attribute to the individuals the qualities expected in them by the system. For example, Freud tells us that the superego of women 'is never as inexorable, as impersonal, as independent of its emotional origins as we require it to be in men [affectivity]. Character-traits which critics of every epoch have brought up against women—that they show less sense of justice than men . . . that they are more often influenced in their judgements by their feelings of affection or hostility [particularism]—all these would be amply accounted for by the modification in the formation of their super-ego' (Freud, 1925: 257–8). In terms of the pattern-variable frame of reference, Freud is saying that in women's world affectivity rather than affective neutrality is the expectation, and particularistic rather than universalistic morality. The expectation of this particular pattern in the world of women imposes it on them.

Spock offers specific examples of how such expectations are realized in the modal personality types of men and women. Women, he tells us, become indignant when legal logic results in an unfair decision. 'Her husband says, "Don't you see that the law *has* to take this position, even if it occasionally causes injustice?"' (Spock, 1970). The feminine modal personality type does not. That is not the logic of her (particularistic) world. Her perch is in a particularistic world, his in a universalistic one. They do not see the same things.

There are those who bemoan the passing of the ascriptive, diffusely defined, particularistic, collectivity-oriented, and affective pattern, who believe that a great loss was suffered when it gave way to an achievement-oriented, contractual, specifically defined, universalistic, and affectively neutral pattern. This judgement may have some validity. Still, so long as half the population inhabits a world patterned one way and the other half another world, the first is at a disadvantage. . . .

NOTES

1. There is, interestingly, less consensus with respect to the term *lady*. In Victorian times a lady was a special kind of person, refined, circumspect, noble, virtuous, sexless, well behaved, and well mannered. Both the term and the concept went out of fashion in the twentieth century. Modern women did not want to be ladies; to be called 'ladylike' came to be something to be resented. It has been with some surprise, therefore, that I have noted a return to the use of this term, even by fellow social scientists in research conferences. They speak of research subjects as 'ladies', as though at a loss of what else to call women.

2. In my book, *The Sex Game*, I used the concept of subsexes as a ploy to emphasize the importance of such intrasex differences among both women and men.

3. It is important always to note the date of any research on women. The era of the feminine mystique, from the end of the war through the 1950s, exerted a powerful influence on what women thought and felt.

4. Female anomalies are especially rare, being only one-third to one-eighth as common as male anomalies (Stoller, 1968: 197).

5. Margaret Mead also made a great deal of the cultural contents of gender, which she labelled *temperament* (Mead, 1925).

6. In a sample of 604 men and 696 women in the general population, Terman found both men and women in the range of scores on masculinity-femininity from -80 to +60; but above 60 there were no women and below -99 there were no men (Terman, 1936: 72).

REFERENCES

Adler, Alfred. 1924. *The Practice and Theory of Individual Psychology*. London: Kegan Paul

Beach, Frank. 1965. 'Retrospect and Prospect' in *Sex and Behavior*. New York: Wiley

Bernard, Jessie. 1945. 'Observation and Generalization in Cultural Anthropology', *American Journal of Sociology* 50: 284–91

——, 1968. *The Sex Game*. Englewood Cliffs, N.J.: Prentice-Hall

Bird, Caroline. 1968. *Born Female: The High Cost of Keeping Women Down*. New York: McKay

Drews, Elizabeth Munroe. 1965. 'Counseling for Self-Actualization in Gifted Girls and Young Women', *Journal of Counseling Psychology* 12 (Summer): 167ff.

Eells, John S., Jr. 1964. 'Women in Honors Programs: Winthrop College' in Philip I. Mitterling, ed., *Needed Research on Able Women in Honors Programs, College, and Society*. New York: Columbia University Press

Freedman, Mervin. 1966. *The College Experience*. San Francisco: Jossey-Bass

Freud, Sigmund. 1961. 'Some Psychological Consequences of the Anatomical Distinction between the Sexes', *Collected Works*, Standard edition, Vol. 19. London: Hogarth Press. This paper was originally published in 1925

Ginzberg, Eli, *et al.* 1967. *Life Styles of Educated Women*. New York: Columbia University Press

Goldsen, Rose K., *et al.* 1960. *What College Students Think*. New York: Van Nostrand

Hacker, Helen. 1951. 'Women as a Minority Group', *Social Forces* 30 (Sept.): 60–6

Hall, Edward T. 1962. *The Silent Language*. Greenwich: Premier Books

Hamberg, David A., and Donald T. Lunde. 1965. 'Sex Hormones in the Development of Sex Differences in Human Behavior' in Eleanor Maccoby, ed., *The Development of Sex Differences*. Stanford, Calif.: Stanford University Press, Ch. 1.

Hoselitz, Bert F. 1963. 'Social Stratification and Economic Development', *International Social Science Journal* 16, 2; also 'Social Structure and Economic Growth', *Economia Internationale* 6 (Aug. 1953)

Hoyt, Donald P., and Carroll E. Kennedy. 1958. 'Interest and Personality Correlates of Career-Motivated and Homemaking-Motivated College Women', *Journal of Counseling Psychology* 5 (Spring): 44–9

Klein, Viola. 1946. *The Feminine Character*. New York: International Universities Press

Mead, Margaret. 1935. *Sex and Temperance in Three Primitive Societies*. New York: Morrow

Riesman, David. 1964. 'Introduction', in Jessie Bernard, *Academic Women*. University Park: Pennsylvania State University Press

Rossi, Alice. 1965. 'Who Wants Women in the Scientific Professions?' in Jacqueline A. Mattfeld and Carol G. Van Aken, eds, *Women and the Scientific Professions*. Cambridge: MIT Press

Spock, Benjamin. 1969. 'Decent and Indecent', *McCall*, 1970. This citation from *Washington Post*, 5 Feb.

Stoller, Robert J. 1968. *Sex and Gender*. New York: Science House

Terman, Lewis M., and C.C. Miles. 1936. *Sex and Personality: Studies in Masculinity and Femininity*. New York: McGraw-Hill

Vaerting, Mathilde, and Mathias Vaerting. 1923. *The Dominant Sex, A Study in the Sociology of Sex Differences*. London: Allen and Unwin

Vincent, Clark. 1966. 'Implications of Change in Male-Female Role Expectations for Interpreting M-F Scores', *Journal of Marriage and the Family* 28 (May): 196–9

Weisstein, Naomi. 1969 'Kinder, Kuche, Kirche as Scientific Law: Psychology Constructs the Female', *Motive* 19 (March-April): 78–85

Yankelovich, Daniel. 1969. *Generations Apart*. Columbia Broadcasting Company

C. WRIGHT MILLS

1916–1962
UNITED STATES

Major Works

1946   *From Max Weber: Essays in Sociology* (with H.H. Gerth)
1948   *The New Men of Power*
1950   *The Puerto Rican Journey*
1951   *White Collar: The American Middle Classes*
1953   *Character and Social Structure*
1956   *The Power Elite*
1958   *The Causes of World War Three*
1959   *The Sociological Imagination*
1960   *Listen, Yankee: The Revolution in Cuba*
1962   *The Marxists*

> The sociological imagination enables us to grasp history and biography and the relations between the two within society. That is its task and its promise. To recognize this task and this promise is the mark of the classic social analyst.[1]
>
> I have tried to be objective, but I do not claim to be detached.[2]
>
> —C. Wright Mills

For several decades American sociology stressed that society remained stable through shared values and norms. The premise was so strongly dominant that Marxist theory was totally undermined. It was C. Wright Mills whose critical approach challenged this dominance, arguing that functionalist ideology supported the status quo by serving the interest of a few. Mills's challenge to the status quo was later to prove detrimental to his intellectual career because his forthright approach alienated his colleagues.

Although Mills worked closely with Hans Gerth and produced works of theoretical importance, his more radical works are better known. His earlier radical critiques of American sociology and American society are reflected in *White Collar* (1951) and *The Power Elite* (1956), both of which exposed the reality of domination in the United States by an elite class that included business, politics, and the military. After World War II, Mills became interested in the struggles of the Third World, and his ideas on the subject culminated in *Listen, Yankee: The*

Revolution in Cuba (1960) and *The Marxists* (1962). The perspectives in these texts furthered Mills's marginalization in sociology, and speaking from the margins he launched even fiercer attacks on the discipline.

Mills elaborates his notion of the sociological imagination in his 1959 book of that title. This imagination, he argues, is a particular way of understanding our social surroundings. The 'promise' of sociology to newcomers to the discipline is to locate them within a specific mode of thinking, one from which, when attained, there is no turning back. Mills's classic distinction between private troubles of milieu and public issues of social structure forces us to see ourselves not just as isolated individuals but as beings moulded by the wider social structures in a particular time and space. This perspective has been a major contribution to the study of society, encouraging the individual to delve beneath the surface of situations that have become so ritualized that they are taken for granted.

Mills died in 1962 in his mid-forties. Although his ideas met with great resistance, the contribution of a radical critique of the discipline, especially within the context of American society, can be attributed to him.

Notes

1. C. Wright Mills, *The Sociological Imagination* (New York: Oxford University Press, 1959), 6.
2. C. Wright Mills, *The Marxists* (New York: Dell, 1962), 10.

THE PROMISE OF SOCIOLOGY

The sociological imagination enables its possessor to understand the larger historical scene in terms of its meaning for the inner life and the external career of a variety of individuals. It enables him to take into account how individuals, in the welter of their daily experience, often become falsely conscious of their social positions. Within the welter, the framework of modern society is sought, and within that framework the psychologies of a variety of men and women are formulated. By such means the personal uneasiness of individuals is focused upon explicit troubles and the indifference of publics is transformed into involvement with public issues.

The first fruit of this imagination—and the first lesson of the social science that embodies it—is the idea that the individual can understand his own experience and gauge his own fate only by locating himself within his period, that he can know his own chances in life only by becoming aware of those of all individuals in his circumstances. In many ways it is a terrible lesson; in many ways a magnificent one. We do not know the limits of man's capacities for supreme effort or willing degradation, for agony or glee, for pleasurable brutality or the sweetness of reason. But in our time we have come to know that the limits of 'human nature' are frighteningly broad. We have come to know that every individual lives, from one generation to the next, in some society; that he lives out a biography, and that he lives it out within some historical sequence. By the fact of his living he contributes, however minutely, to the shaping of this society and to the course of its history, even as he is made by society and by its historical push and shove.

The sociological imagination enables us to grasp history and biography and the relations between the two within society. That is its task and its promise. To recognize this task and this promise is the mark of the classic social analyst. It is characteristic of Herbert Spencer—turgid, polysyllabic, comprehensive; of E.A. Ross—graceful, muckraking, upright; of Auguste Comte and Emile Durkheim; of the intricate and subtle Karl Mannheim. It is the quality of all that is intellectually excellent in Karl Marx; it is the clue to Thorstein Veblen's brilliant and ironic insight, to Joseph Schumpeter's many-sided constructions of reality; it is the basis of the psychological sweep of W.E.H. Lecky no less than of the profundity and clarity of Max Weber. And it is the signal of what is best in contemporary studies of man and society.

No social study that does not come back to the problems of biography, of history and of their intersections within a society has completed its intellectual journey. Whatever the specific problems of the classic social analysts, however limited or however broad the features of social reality they have examined, those who have been imaginatively aware of the promise of their work have consistently asked three sorts of questions:

(1) What is the structure of this particular society as a whole? What are its essential components, and how are they related to one another? How does it differ from other varieties of social order? Within it, what is the meaning of any particular feature for its continuance and for its change?

(2) Where does this society stand in human history? What are the mechanics by which it is changing? What is its place within and its meaning for the development of humanity as a whole? How does any particular feature we are examining affect, and how is it affected by, the historical period in which it moves? And this period—what are its essential features? How does it differ from other periods? What are its characteristic ways of history-making?

(3) What varieties of men and women now prevail in this society and in this period? And what varieties are coming to prevail? In what ways are they selected and formed, liberated and repressed, made sensitive and blunted? What kinds of 'human nature' are revealed in the conduct and character we observe in this society in this period? And what is the meaning for 'human nature' of each and every feature of the society we are examining?

Whether the point of interest is a great power state or a minor literary mood, a family, a prison, a creed—these are the kinds of questions the best social analysts have asked. They are the intellectual pivots of classic studies of man in society—and they are the questions inevitably raised by any mind possessing the sociological imagination. For that imagination is the capacity to shift from one perspective to another—from the political to the psychological; from examination of a single family to comparative assessment of the national budgets of the world; from the theological school to the military establishment; from considerations of an oil industry to studies of contemporary poetry. It is the capacity to range from the most impersonal and remote transformations to the most intimate features of the human self—and to see the relations between the two. Back of its use there is always the urge to know the social and historical meaning of the individual in the society and in the period in which he has his quality and his being.

That, in brief, is why it is by means of the sociological imagination that men now hope to grasp what is going on in the world, and to understand what is happening in themselves as minute points of the intersections of biography and history within society. In large part, contemporary man's self-conscious view of himself as at least an outsider, if not a permanent stranger, rests upon an absorbed realization of social relativity and of the transformative power of history. The sociological imagination is the most fruitful form of this self-consciousness. By its use men whose mentalities have swept only a series of limited orbits often come to feel as if suddenly awakened in a house with which they had only supposed themselves to be familiar. Correctly or incorrectly, they often come to feel that they can now provide themselves with adequate summations, cohesive assessments, comprehensive orientations. Older decisions that once appeared sound now seem to them products of a mind unaccountably dense. Their capacity for astonishment is made lively again. They acquire a new way of thinking, they experience a transvaluation of values; in a word, by their reflection and by their sensibility, they realize the cultural meaning of the social sciences.

Perhaps the most fruitful distinction with which the sociological imagination works is between 'the personal troubles of milieu' and 'the public issues of social structure'. This distinction is an essential tool of the sociological imagination and a feature of all classic work in social science.

Troubles occur within the character of the individual and within the range of his immediate relations with others; they have to do with his self and with those limited areas of social life of which he is directly and personally aware. Accordingly, the statement and the resolution of troubles properly lie within the individual as a biographical entity and within the scope of his immediate milieu—the social setting that is directly open to his personal experience and to some extent his willful activity. A trouble is a private matter: values cherished by an individual are felt by him to be threatened.

Issues have to do with matters that transcend these local environments of the individual and the range of his inner life. They have to do with the organization of many such milieux into the institutions of an historical society as a whole, with the ways in which various milieux overlap and interpenetrate to form the larger structure of social and historical life. An issue is a public matter: some value cherished by publics is felt to be threatened. Often there is a debate about what that value really is and about what it is that really threatens it. This debate is often without focus if only because it is the very nature of an issue, unlike even widespread trouble, that it cannot very well be defined in terms of the immediate and everyday environments of ordinary men. An issue, in fact, often involves a crisis in institutional arrangements, and often too it involves what Marxists call 'contradictions' or 'antagonisms'.

In these terms consider unemployment. When, in a city of 100,000, only one man is unemployed, that is his personal trouble, and for its relief we properly look to the character of the man, his skills, and his immediate opportunities. But when in a nation of 50 million employees, 15 million men are unemployed, that is an issue, and we may not hope to find its solution within the range of opportunities open to any one individual. The very structure of opportunities has collapsed. Both the correct statement of the problem and the range of possible solutions require us to consider the economic and political institutions of the society, and not merely the personal situation and character of a scatter of individuals.

Consider war. The personal problem of war, when it occurs, may be how to survive it or how to die in it with honour; how to make money out of it; how to climb into the higher safety of the military apparatus; or how to contribute to the war's termination. In short, according to one's values, to find a set of milieux and within it to survive the war or make one's death in it meaningful. But the structural issues of war have to do with its causes; with what types of men it throws up into command; with its effects upon economic and political, family and religious institutions, with the unorganized irresponsibility of a world of nation-states.

Consider marriage. Inside a marriage a man and a woman may experience personal troubles, but when the divorce rate during the first four years of marriage is 250 out of every 1,000 attempts, this is an indication of a structural issue having to do with the institutions of marriage and the family and other institutions that bear upon them.

Or consider the metropolis—the horrible, beautiful, ugly, magnificent sprawl of the great city. For many upper-class people, the personal solution to 'the problem of the city' is to have an apartment with private garage under it in the heart of the city, and forty miles out, a house by Henry Hill, garden by Garrett Eckbo, on a hundred acres of private land. In these two controlled environments—with a small staff at each end and a private helicopter connection—most people could solve many of the problems of personal milieux caused by the facts of the city. But all this, however splendid, does not solve the public issues that the structural fact of the city poses. What should be done with this wonderful monstrosity? Break it all up into scattered units, combining residence and work? Refurbish it as it stands? Or, after evacuation, dynamite it and build new cities according to new plans in new places? What should those plans be? And who is to decide and to accomplish whatever choice is made? These are structural issues; to confront them and to solve them requires us to consider political and economic issues that affect innumerable milieux.

In so far as an economy is so arranged that slumps occur, the problem of unemployment becomes incapable of personal solution. In so far as war is inherent in the nation-state system and in the uneven industrialization of the world, the ordinary individual in his restricted milieu will be powerless—with or without psychiatric aid—to solve the troubles this system or lack of system imposed upon him. In so far as the family as an institution turns women into darling little slaves and men into their chief providers and unweaned dependents, the problem of a satisfactory marriage remains incapable of purely private solution. In so far as the overdeveloped megalopolis and the overdeveloped automobile are built-in features of the overdeveloped society, the issues of urban living will not be solved by personal ingenuity and private wealth.

What we experience in various and specific milieux, I have noted, is often caused by structural changes. Accordingly, to understand the changes of many personal milieux we are required to look beyond them. And the number and variety of such structural changes increase as the institutions within which we live become more embracing and more intricately connected with one another. To be aware of the idea of social structure and to use it with sensibility is to be capable of tracing such linkages among a great variety of milieux. To be able to do that is to possess the sociological imagination.

What are the major issues for publics and the key troubles of private individuals in our time? To formulate issues and troubles, we must ask what values are cherished yet threatened, and what values are cherished and supported, by the characterizing trends of our period. In the case both of threat and of support we must ask what salient contradictions of structure may be involved.

When people cherish some set of values and do not feel any threat to them, they experience *well-being*. When they cherish values but *do* feel them to be threatened, they experience a crisis—either as a personal trouble or as a public issue. And if all their values seem involved, they feel the total threat of panic.

But suppose people are neither aware of any cherished values nor experience any threat? That is the experience of *indifference*, which, if it seems to involve all their values, becomes apathy. Suppose, finally, they are unaware of any cherished values, but still are very much aware of a threat. That is the experience of *uneasiness*, of anxiety, which, if it is total enough, becomes a deadly unspecified malaise.

Ours is a time of uneasiness and indifference—not yet formulated in such ways as to permit the work of reason and the play of sensibility. Instead of troubles—defined in terms of values and threats—there is often the misery of vague uneasiness; instead of explicit issues there is often merely the beat feeling that all is somehow not right. Neither the values threatened nor whatever threatens them has been stated; in short, they have not been carried to the point of decision. Much less have they been formulated as problems of social science.

In the thirties there was little doubt—except among certain deluded business circles—that there was an economic issue which was also a pack of personal troubles. In these arguments about 'the crisis of capitalism', the formulations of Marx and the many unacknowledged re-formulations of his work probably set the leading terms of the issue, and some men came to understand their personal troubles in these terms. The values threatened were plain to see and cherished by all; the structural contradictions that threatened them also seemed plain. Both were widely and deeply experienced. It was a political age.

But the values threatened in the era after World War Two are often neither widely acknowledged as values nor widely felt to be threatened. Much private uneasiness goes unformulated; much public malaise and many decisions of enormous structural relevance never become public issues. For those who accept such inherited values as reason and freedom, it is the uneasiness itself that is the trouble; it is the indifference itself that is the issue. And it is this condition, of uneasiness and indifference, that is the signal feature of our period.

All this is so striking that it is often interpreted by observers as a shift in the very kinds of problems that need now to be formulated. We are frequently told that the problems of our decade, or even the crises of our period, have shifted from the external realm of economics and now have to do with the quality of individual life—in fact with the question of whether there is soon going to be anything that can properly be called individual life. Not child labour but comic books, not poverty but mass leisure, are at the centre of concern. Many great public issues as well as many private troubles are described in terms of 'the psychiatric'—often, it seems, in a pathetic attempt to avoid the large issues and problems of modern society. Often this statement seems to rest upon a provincial narrowing of interest to the Western societies, or even to the United States—thus ignoring two-thirds of mankind; often, too, it arbitrarily divorces the individual life from the larger institutions within which that life is enacted, and which on occasion bear upon it more grievously than do the intimate environments of childhood.

Problems of leisure, for example, cannot even be stated without considering problems of work. Family troubles over comic books cannot be formulated as problems without considering the plight of the contemporary family in its new relations with the new institutions of the social structure. Neither leisure nor its debilitating uses can be understood as problems without recognition of the extent to which malaise and indifference now form the social and personal climate of contemporary American society. In this climate, no problems of 'the private life' can be stated and solved without recognition of the crisis of ambition that is part of the very career of men at work in the incorporated economy.

It is true, as psychoanalysts continually point out, that people do often have 'the increasing sense of being moved by obscure forces within themselves which they are unable to define'. But it is *not* true, as Ernest Jones asserted, that 'man's chief enemy and danger is his own unruly nature and the dark forces pent up within him.' On the contrary: 'Man's chief danger' today lies in the unruly forces of contemporary society itself, with its alienating methods of production, its enveloping techniques of political domination, its international anarchy—in a word, its pervasive transformations of the very 'nature' of man and the conditions and aims of his life.

It is now the social scientist's foremost political and intellectual task—for here the two coincide—to make clear the elements of contemporary uneasiness and indifference. It is the central demand made upon him by other cultural workmen—by physical scientists and artists, by the intellectual community in general. It is because of this task and these demands, I believe, that the social sciences are becoming the common denominator of our cultural period, and the sociological imagination our most needed quality of mind.

ERVING GOFFMAN

1922–1982
CANADA

Major Works

1959   *The Presentation of Self in Everyday Life*
1961   *Asylums*
1963   *Behavior in Public Places*
1967   *Interaction Ritual*
1974   *Frame Analysis*
1979   *Gender Advertisements*

All the world is not a stage—certainly the theatre isn't entirely. (Whether you organize a theatre or an aircraft factory, you need to find places for cars to park or coats to be checked, and these had better be real places, which, incidentally, had better carry real insurance against theft.)[1]

The perspective employed in this report is that of the theatrical performance, the principles derived are dramaturgical ones. I shall consider the way in which the individual in ordinary work situations presents himself and his inactivity to others, the ways in which he guides and controls the impression they form of him, and the kinds of things he may and may not do while sustaining his performance before them.[2]

—*Erving Goffman*

The dramaturgical sociology of Erving Goffman offers some important understandings of both social interaction and the social structure. Asking the question, 'What is going on here?' can equally address the structural dimensions of or the persons participating in the situation. Goffman works and reworks Thomas and Znaniecki's phrase, 'the definition of the situation'—that people give definition to situations as well as take definition from them.

In *The Presentation of Self in Everyday Life*, Goffman elaborates the importance of the performance in social relationships. People not only take on a role (one that may be structurally established for them) but they also perform within their own definition of the role, much as an actor would. In our interactions with others we take 'lines of action', which have a particular intent and give a particular impression. As 'actors' in everyday life we come to perform in ways that in appearance and manner suggest impression management.

The concept of 'performance team' extends the analysis to work situations and other zones of human interaction. The team is a group of people who work together or co-operate to bring off a particular routine or set of intended activities. Goffman notes the complexities of team loyalties, definitions of 'audience', and discrepant or 'abnormal' behaviour. Most importantly, he explores regions of behaviour, or what he calls frontstage and backstage behaviour. Frontstage behaviour takes place before an audience or in a social context where the team is 'in role'. For example, a salesperson in a bicycle shop meets the public with behaviours governed by the context, the socio-cultural demands of appearance and manner, and most probably the employer's expectations. Those who work in the repair area (backstage) of the shop 'let their hair down' and salespeople may find that they do likewise as they cross from frontstage to backstage. This line is well known by servers: the performance is mandatory, the tips the rewards.

> Given the values of a particular society, it is apparent that the backstage character of certain places is built into them in a material way, and that relative to adjacent areas these places are inescapably back regions.[3]

Goffman notes that the 'decorator's art often does this for us' in walls of unfinished concrete, or the ill-painted areas of kitchens. It is interesting to note his use of the term 'material'. Micro-analysis is always *in* a structural dimension; indeed, it elaborates the definitions of structure by sustaining or maintaining certain aspects of situations.

Goffman's contribution has extended the study of interactional contexts for sociology, but in many ways he defies placement in a particular school of thought. Some have emphasized his 'confidence-game' analysis or the 'con' dimension of the drama and thus have argued that our impression management or our hidden behaviours are the substance of human interaction and, indeed, human life. But Goffman's work has also been considered to be derivative of Durkheim's thought.[4] His work on such topics as interaction ritual, stigma, and behaviour in public places recognizes the pre-eminence of society over the individual as well as the fundamental importance of social structure. For example, *Asylums*, his study of total institutions, gives us powerful insight into the personal, interactional, and structural complex that makes up contemporary society and its institutions.

Notes

1. Erving Goffman, *Frame Analysis* (Boston: Northeastern University Press, 1975), 1.
2. Erving Goffman, *The Presentation of Self in Everyday Life* (New York: Doubleday, 1959), xi.

3. Ibid., 124.

4. See Randall Collins, *Three Sociological Traditions: Selected Readings* (New York: Oxford University Press, 1985).

THE PRESENTATION OF SELF

Introduction

When an individual enters the presence of others, they commonly seek to acquire information about him or to bring into play information about him already possessed. They will be interested in his general socio-economic status, his conception of self, his attitude toward them, his competence, his trustworthiness, etc. Although some of this information seems to be sought almost as an end in itself, there are usually quite practical reasons for acquiring it. Information about the individual helps to define the situation, enabling others to know in advance what he will expect of them and what they may expect of him. Informed in these ways, the others will know how best to act in order to call forth a desired response from him.

For those present, many sources of information become accessible and many carriers (or 'sign-vehicles') become available for conveying this information. If acquainted with the individual, observers can glean clues from his conduct and appearance which allow them to apply their previous experience with individuals roughly similar to the one before them or, more importantly, to apply untested stereotypes to him. They can also assume from past experience that only individuals of a particular kind are likely to be found in a given social setting. They can rely on what the individual says about himself or on documentary evidence he provides as to who and what he is. If they know, or know of, the individual by virtue of experience prior to the interaction, they can rely on assumptions as to the persistence and generality of psychological traits as a means of predicting his present and future behaviour.

However, during the period in which the individual is in the immediate presence of the others, few events may occur which directly provide the other with the conclusive information they will need if they are to direct wisely their own activity. Many crucial facts lie beyond the time and place of interaction or are concealed within it. For example, the 'true' or 'real' attitudes, beliefs, and emotions of the individual can be ascertained only indirectly, through his avowals or through what appears to be involuntary expressive behaviour. Similarly, if the individual offers the others a product or service, they will often find that during the interaction there will be no time and place immediately available for eating the pudding that the proof can be found in. They will be forced to accept some events as conventional or natural signs of something not directly available to the senses. In Ichheiser's terms,[1] the individual will have to act so that he intentionally or unintentionally *expresses* himself, and the others will in turn have to be *impressed* in some way by him.

The expressiveness of the individual (and therefore his capacity to give impressions) appears to involve two radically different kinds of sign activity: the expression that he *gives*, and the expression that he *gives off*. The first involves verbal symbols or their substitutes which he uses admittedly and solely to convey the information that he and the others are known to attach to these symbols. This is communication in the traditional and narrow sense. The second involves a wide range of action that others can treat as symptomatic of the actor, the expectation being that the action was performed for reasons other than the information conveyed in this way. As we shall have to see, this distinction has an only initial validity. The individual does of course intentionally convey misinformation by means of both of these types of communication, the first involving deceit, the second feigning.

Taking communication in both its narrow and broad sense, one finds that when the individual is in the immediate presence of others, his activity will have a promissory character. The others are likely to find that they must accept the individual on faith, offering him a just return while he is present before them in exchange for something whose true value will not be established until after he has left their presence. (Of course, the others also live by inference in their dealings with the psychical world, but it is only in the world of social interaction that the objects about which they make inferences will purposely facilitate and hinder this inferential process.) The security that they justifiably feel in making inferences about the individual will vary, of course, depending on such factors as the amount of information they already possess about him, but no amount of such past evidence can entirely obviate the necessity of acting on the basis of inferences. As William I. Thomas suggested:

> It is also highly important for us to realize that we do not as a matter of fact lead our lives, make our decisions, and reach our goals in everyday life either statistically or scientifically. We live by inference. I am, let us say, your guest. You do not know, you cannot determine scientifically, that I will not steal your money or your spoons. But inferentially I will not, and inferentially you have me as a guest.[2]

Let us now turn from the others to the point of view of the individual who presents himself before them. He may wish them to think highly of him, or to think he thinks highly of them, or to perceive how in fact he feels toward them, or to obtain no clear-cut impression; he may wish to ensure sufficient harmony so that the interaction can be sustained, or to defraud, get rid of, confuse, mislead, antagonize, or insult them. Regardless of the particular objective which the individual has in mind and of his motive for having this objective, it will be in his interests to control the conduct of the others, especially their responsive treatment of him.[3] This control is achieved largely by influencing the definition of the situation which the others come to formulate, and he can influence this definition by expressing himself in such a way as to give them the kind of impression that will lead them to act voluntarily in accordance with his own plan. Thus, when an individual appears in the presence of others, there will usually be some reason for him to mobilize his activity so that it will convey an impression to others which it is in his interests to convey. Since a girl's dormitory mates will glean evidence of her popularity from the calls she receives on the phone, we can suspect that some girls will arrange for calls to be made, and Willard Waller's finding can be anticipated:

> It has been reported by many observers that a girl who is called to the telephone in the dormitories will often allow herself to be called several times, in order to give all the other girls ample opportunity to hear her paged.[4]

Of the two kinds of communication—expressions given and expressions given off—this report will be primarily concerned with the latter, with the more theatrical and contextual kind, the non-verbal, presumably unintentional kind, whether this communication be purposely engineered or not. As an example of what we must try to examine, I would like to cite at length a novelistic incident in which Preedy, a vacationing Englishman, makes his first appearance on the beach of his summer hotel in Spain:

> But in any case he took care to avoid catching anyone's eye. First of all, he had to make it clear to those potential companions of his holiday that they were of no concern to him whatsoever. He stared through them, round them, over them—eyes lost in space. The beach might have been empty. If by chance a ball was thrown his way, he looked surprised; then let a smile of amusement lighten his face (Kindly Preedy), looked around dazed to see that there were people on the beach, tossed it back with a smile to himself and not a smile at the people, and then resumed careless his nonchalant survey of space.
>
> But it was time to institute a little parade, the parade of the Ideal Preedy. By devious handlings he gave any who wanted to look a chance to see the title of his book— a Spanish translation of Homer, classic thus, but not daring, cosmopolitan too—and then gathered together his beach-wrap and bag into a neat and sand-resistant pile (Methodical and Sensible Preedy), rose slowly to stretch at ease his huge frame (Big-Cat Preedy), and tossed aside his sandals (Carefree Preedy, after all).
>
> The marriage of Preedy and the sea! There were alternative rituals. The first involved the stroll that turns into a run and a dive straight into the water, thereafter smoothing into a strong splashless crawl towards the horizon. But of course not really to the horizon. Quite suddenly he would turn on his back and thrash great white splashes with his legs, somehow thus showing that he could have swum further had he wanted to, and then would stand up a quarter out of water for all to see who it was.
>
> The alternative course was simpler, it avoided the cold-water shock and it avoided the risk of appearing too high-spirited. The point was to appear to be so used to the sea, the Mediterranean, and this particular beach, that one might as well be in the sea as out of it. It involved a slow stroll down and into the edge of the water—not even noticing his toes were wet, land and water all the same to him!—with his eyes up to the sky gravely surveying portents, invisible to others of the weather (Local Fisherman Preedy).[5]

The novelist means us to see that Preedy is improperly concerned with the extensive impressions he feels his sheer bodily action is giving off to those around him. We can malign Preedy further by assuming he has acted merely in order to give a particular impression, that this is a false impression, and that the others present receive either no impression at all, or, worse still, the impression that Preedy is affectedly trying to cause them to receive this particular impression. But the important point for us here is that the kind of impression Preedy thinks he is making is in fact the kind of impression that others correctly and incorrectly glean from someone in their midst.

I have said that when an individual appears before others his actions will influence the definition of the situation which they come to have. Sometimes the individual will act in a thoroughly calculating manner, expressing himself in a given way solely in order to give the kind of impression to others that is likely to evoke from them a specific response he is concerned to obtain. Sometimes the individual will be calculating in his activity but be relatively unaware that this is the case. Sometimes he will intentionally and consciously express himself in a particular way, but chiefly because the tradition of his group or social status requires this kind of expression and not because of any particular response (other than vague acceptance or approval) that is likely to be evoked from those impressed by the expression. Sometimes the traditions of an individual's role will lead him to give a well-designed impression of a particular kind and yet he may be neither consciously nor unconsciously disposed to create such an impression. The others, in their turn, may be suitably impressed by the individual's efforts to convey something, or may misunderstand the situation and come to conclusions that are warranted neither by the individual's intent nor by the facts. In any case, in so far as the others act *as if* the individual had conveyed a particular impression, we may take a functional or pragmatic view and say that the individual has 'effectively' projected a given definition of the situation and 'effectively' fostered the understanding that a given state of affairs obtains.

There is one aspect of the others' response that bears special comment here. Knowing that the individual is likely to present himself in a light that is favourable to him, the others may divide what they witness into two parts; a part that is relatively easy for the individual to manipulate at will, being chiefly his verbal assertions, and a part in regard to which he seems to have little concern or control, being chiefly derived from the expressions he gives off. The others may then use what are considered to be the ungovernable aspects of his expressive behaviour as a check upon the validity of what is conveyed by the governable aspects. In this a fundamental asymmetry is demonstrated in the communication process, the individual presumably being aware of only one stream of his communication, the witnesses of this stream and one another. For example, in Shetland Isle one crofter's wife, in serving native dishes to a visitor from the mainland of Britain, would listen with a polite smile to his polite claims of liking what he was eating; at the same time she would take note of the rapidity with which the visitor lifted his fork or spoon to his mouth, the eagerness with which he passed food into his mouth, and the gusto expressed in chewing the food, using these signs as a check on the stated feelings of the eater. The same woman, in order to discover what one acquaintance (A) 'actually' thought of another acquaintance (B), would wait until B was in the presence of A but engaged in conversation with still another person (C). She would then covertly examine the facial expression of A as he regarded B in conversation with C. Not being in conversation with B, and not being directly observed by him, A would sometimes relax usual constraints and tactful deceptions, and freely express what he was 'actually' feeling about B. This Shetlander, in short, would observe the unobserved observer.

Now given the fact that others are likely to check up on the more controllable aspects of behaviour by means of the less controllable, one can expect that sometimes the individual will try to exploit this very possibility, guiding the impression he makes through behaviour felt to be reliably informing.[6] For example, in gaining admission to a tight social circle, the participant observer may not only wear an accepting look while listening to an informant, but may also be careful to wear the same look when observing the informant talking to others; observers of the observer will then not as easily discover where he actually stands. A specific illustration may be cited from Shetland Isle. When a neighbour dropped in to have a cup of tea, he would ordinarily wear at least a hint of an expectant warm smile as he passed through the door into the cottage. Since lack of physical obstructions outside the cottage and lack of light within it usually made it possible to observe the visitor unobserved as he approached the house, islanders sometimes took pleasure in watching the visitor drop whatever expression he was manifesting and replace it with a sociable one just before reaching the door. However, some visitors, in appreciating that this examination was occurring, would blindly adopt a social face a long distance from the house, thus ensuring the projection of a constant image.

This kind of control upon the part of the individual reinstates the symmetry of the communication process, and sets the stage for a kind of information game—a potentially infinite cycle of concealment, discovery, false revelation, and rediscovery. It should be added that since the others are likely to be relatively unsuspicious of the presumably unguided aspect of the individual's conduct, he can gain much by controlling it. The others of course may sense that the individual is manipulating the presumably spontaneous aspects of his behaviour, and seek in this very act of manipulation some shading of conduct that the individual has not managed to control. This again provides a check upon the individual's behaviour, this time his presumably uncalculated behaviour, thus re-establishing the asymmetry of the communication process. Here I would like only to add the suggestion that the arts of piercing an individual's effort at calculated unintentionality seem better developed than our capacity to manipulate our own behaviour, so that regardless of how many steps have occurred in the information game, the witness is likely to have the advantage over the actor, and the initial asymmetry of the communication process is likely to be retained.

When we allow that the individual projects a definition of the situation when he appears before others, we must also see that the others, however passive their role may seem to be, will themselves effectively project a definition of the situation by virtue of their response to the individual and by virtue of any lines of action they initiate to him. Ordinarily the definitions of the situation projected by the several different participants are sufficiently attuned to one another so that open contradiction will not occur. I do not mean that there will be the kind of consensus that arises when each individual present candidly expresses what he really feels and honestly agrees with the expressed feelings of the others present. This kind of harmony is an optimistic ideal and in any case not necessary for the smooth working of society. Rather, each participant is expected to suppress his immediate heartfelt feelings, conveying a view of the situation which he feels the others will be able to find at least temporarily acceptable. The maintenance of this surface of agreement, this veneer of consensus, is facilitated by each participant concealing his own wants behind statements which assert values to which everyone present feels obliged to give lip service. Further, there is usually a kind of division of definitional labour. Each participant is allowed to establish the tentative official ruling regarding matters which are vital to him but not immediately important to others, e.g., the rationalizations and justifications by which he accounts for his past activity. In exchange for this courtesy he remains silent or non-committal on matters important to others but not immediately important to him. We have then a kind of interactional *modus vivendi*. Together the participants contribute to a single over-all definition of the situation which involves not so much a real agreement as to what exists but rather a real agreement as to whose claims concerning what issues will be temporarily honoured. Real agreement will also exist concerning the desirability of avoiding an open conflict of definitions of the situation.[7] I will refer to this level of agreement as a 'working consensus'. It is to be understood that the working consensus established in one interaction setting will be quite different in content from the working consensus established in a different type of setting. Thus, between two friends at lunch, a reciprocal show of affection, respect, and concern for the other is maintained. In service occupations, on the other hand, the specialist often maintains an image of disinterested involvement in the problem of the client, while the client responds with a show of respect for the competence and integrity of the specialist. Regardless of such differences in content, however, the general form of these working arrangements is the same.

In noting the tendency for a participant to accept the definitional claims made by the others present, we can appreciate the crucial importance of the information that the individual *initially* possesses or acquires concerning his fellow participants, for it is on the basis of this initial information that the individual starts to define the situation and starts to build up lines of responsive action. The individual's initial projection commits him to what he is proposing to be and requires him drop all pretences of being other things. As the interaction among the participants progresses, additions and modifications in this initial informational state will of course occur, but it is essential that these later developments be related without contradiction to, and even built up from, the initial position taken by the several participants. It would seem that an individual can more easily make a choice as to what line of treatment to demand from and extend to the others present at the beginning of an encounter than he can alter the line of treatment that is being pursued once the interaction is underway.

In everyday life, of course, there is a clear understanding that first impressions are important. Thus, the work adjustment of those in service occupations will often hinge upon a capacity to seize and hold the initiative in the service relation, a capacity that will require subtle aggressiveness on the part of the server when he is of lower socio-economic status than his client. W.F. Whyte suggests the waitress as an example:

> The first point that stands out is that the waitress who bears up under pressure does not simply respond to her customers. She acts with some skill to control their behaviour. The first question to ask when we look at the customer relationship is, 'Does the waitress get the jump on the customer, or does the customer get the jump on the

waitress?' The skilled waitress realizes the crucial nature of this question. . . .

    The skilled waitress tackles the customer with confidence and without hesitation. For example, she may find that a new customer has seated himself before she could clear off the dirty dishes and change the cloth. He is now leaning on the table studying the menu. She greets him, says, 'May I change the cover please?' and, without waiting for an answer, takes his menu away from him so that he moves back from the table, and she goes about her work. The relationship is handled politely but firmly, and there is never any question as to who is in charge.[8]

When the interaction that is initiated by 'first impressions' is itself merely the initial interaction in an extended series of interactions involving the same participants, we speak of 'getting off on the right foot' and feel that it is crucial that we do so. Thus, one learns that some teachers take the following view:

    You can't ever let them get the upper hand on you or you're through. So I start out tough. The first day I get a new class in, I let them know who's the boss. . . . You've got to start off tough, then you can ease up as you go along. If you start out easygoing, when you try to get tough, they'll just look at you and laugh.[9]

Similarly, attendants in mental institutions may feel that if the new patient is sharply put in his place the first day on the ward and made to see who is the boss, much future difficulty will be prevented.[10]

    Given the fact that the individual effectively projects a definition of the situation when he enters the presence of others, we can assume that events may occur within the interaction which contradict, discredit, or otherwise throw doubt upon this projection. When these disruptive events occur, the interaction itself may come to a confused and embarrassed halt. Some of the assumptions upon which the responses of the participants have been predicated become untenable, and the participants find themselves lodged in an interaction for which the situation has been wrongly defined and is now no longer defined. At such moments the individual whose presentation has been discredited may feel ashamed while the others present may feel hostile, and all the participants may come out to feel ill at ease, nonplussed, out of contenance, embarrassed, experiencing the kind of anomy that is generated when the minute social system face-to-face interaction breaks down.

    In stressing the fact that the initial definition of the situation projected by an individual tends to provide a plan for the co-operative activity that follows—in stressing this action point of view—we must not overlook the crucial fact that any projected definition of the situation also has a distinctive moral character. It is this moral character of projections that will chiefly concern us in this report. Society is organized on the principle that any individual who possesses certain social characteristics has a moral right to expect that others will value and treat him in an appropriate way. Connected with this principle is a second, namely that an individual who implicitly or explicitly signifies that he has certain social characteristics ought in fact to be what he claims he is. In consequence, when an individual projects a definition of the situation and thereby makes an implicit or explicit claim to be a person of a particular kind, he automatically exerts a moral demand upon the others, obliging them to value and treat him in the manner that persons of his kind have a right to expect. He also implicitly forgoes all claims to be things he does not appear to be[11] and hence forgoes the treatment that would be appropriate for such individuals. The others find, then, that the individual has informed them as to what is and as to what they *ought* to see as the 'is'.

One cannot judge the importance of definitional disruptions by the frequency with which they occur, for apparently they would occur more frequently were not constant precautions taken. We find that preventive practices are constantly employed to avoid these embarrassments and that corrective practices are constantly employed to compensate for discrediting occurrences that have not been successfully avoided. When the individual employs these strategies and tactics to protect his own projections, we may refer to them as 'defensive practices'; when a participant employs them to save the definition of the situation projected by another, we speak of 'protective practices' or 'tact'. Together, defensive and protective practices comprise the techniques employed to safeguard the impression fostered by an individual during his presence before others. It should be added that while we may be ready to see that no fostered impression would survive if defensive practices were not employed, we are less ready perhaps to see that few impressions could survive if those who received the impression did not exert tact in their reception of it.

In addition to the fact that precautions are taken to prevent disruption of projected definitions, we may also note that an intense interest in these disruptions comes to play a significant role in the social life of the group. Practical jokes and social games are played in which embarrassments which are to be taken unseriously are purposely engineered.[12] Fantasies are created in which devastating exposures occur. Anecdotes from the past—real, embroidered, or fictitious—are told and retold, detailing disruptions which occurred, almost occurred, or occurred and were admirably resolved. There seems to be no grouping which does not have a ready supply of these games, reveries, and cautionary tales, to be used as a source of humour, a catharsis for anxieties, and a sanction for inducing individuals to be modest in their claims and reasonable in their projected expectations. The individual may tell himself through dreams of getting into impossible positions. Families tell of the time a guest got his dates mixed and arrived when neither the house nor anyone in it was ready for him. Journalists tell of times when an all-too-meaningful misprint occurred, and the paper's assumption of objectivity or decorum was humorously discredited. Public servants tell of times a client ridiculously misunderstood form instructions, giving answers which implied an unanticipated and bizarre definition of the situation.[13] Seamen, whose home away from home is rigorously he-man, tell stories of coming back home and inadvertently asking mother to 'pass the fucking butter'.[14] Diplomats tell of the time a near-sighted queen asked a republican ambassador about the health of his king.[15]

To summarize then, I assume that when an individual appears before others he will have many motives for trying to control the impression they receive of the situation. This report is concerned with some of the common techniques that persons employ to sustain such impressions and with some of the common contingencies associated with the employment of these techniques. The specific content of any activity presented by the individual participant, or the role it plays in the interdependent activities of an on-going

social system, will not be at issue; I shall be concerned only with the participant's dramaturgical problems of presenting the activity before others. The issues dealt with by
stage-craft and stage management are sometimes trivial but they are quite general; they
seem to occur everywhere in social life, providing a clear-cut dimension for formal sociological analysis.

It will be convenient to end this introduction with some definitions that are implied
in what has gone before and required for what is to follow. For the purpose of this report,
interaction (that is, face-to-face intervention) may be roughly defined as the reciprocal
influence of individuals upon one another's actions when in one another's immediate
physical presence. An *interaction* may be defined as all the interaction which occurs
throughout any one occasion when a given set of individuals are in one another's continuous presence; the term 'an encounter' would do as well. A *performance* may be defined
as all the activity of a given participant on a given occasion which serves to influence in
any way any of the other participants. Taking a particular participant and his performance
as a basic point of reference, we may refer to those who contribute the other performances as the audience, observers, or co-participants. The pre-established pattern of action
which is unfolded during a performance and which may be presented or played through
on other occasions may be called a 'part' or 'routine'.[16] These situational terms can easily
be related to conventional structural ones. When an individual or performer plays the
same part to the same audience on different occasions, a social relationship is likely to
arise. Defining social role as the enactment of rights and duties attached to a given status,
we can say that a social role will involve one or more parts and that each of these different parts may be presented by the performer on a series of occasions to the same kinds of
audience or to an audience of the same persons.

The Arts of Impression Management

In this chapter I would like to bring together what has been said or implied about the
attributes that are required of a performer for the work of successfully staging a character.
Brief reference will therefore be made to some of the techniques of impression management in which these attitudes are expressed. In preparation it may be well to suggest, in
some cases for the second time, some of the principal types of performance disruptions,
for it is these disruptions which the techniques of impression management function to
avoid.

In the beginning of this report, in considering the general characteristics of performances, it was suggested that the performer must act with expressive responsibility, since
many minor, inadvertent acts happen to be well designed to convey impressions inappropriate at the time. These events were called 'unmeant gestures'. Ponsonby gives an illustration of how a director's attempt to avoid an unmeant gesture led to the occurrence of
another.

> One of the Attachés from the Legation was to carry the cushion on which the insignia
> were placed, and in order to prevent their falling off I stuck the pin at the back of the
> Star through the velvet cushion. The Attaché, however, was not content with this, but

secured the end of the pin by the catch to make doubly sure. The result was that when Prince Alexander, having made a suitable speech, tried to get hold of the Star, he found it firmly fixed to the cushion and spent some time in getting it loose. This rather spoilt the most impressive moment of this ceremony.[17]

It should be added that the individual held responsible for contributing an unmeant gesture may chiefly discredit his own performance by this, a teammate's performance, or the performance being staged by his audience.

When an outsider accidentally enters a region in which a performance is being given, or when a member of the audience inadvertently enters backstage, the intruder is likely to catch those present *flagrante delicto*. Through no one's intention, the persons present in the region may find that they have patently been witnessed in activity that is quite incompatible with the impression that they are, for wider social reasons, under obligation to maintain to the intruder. We deal here with what are sometimes called 'inopportune intrusions'.

The past life and current round of activity of a given performer typically contain at least a few facts which, if introduced during the performance, would discredit or at least weaken the claims about self that the performer was attempting to project as part of the definition of the situation. These facts may involve well-kept dark secrets or negatively valued characteristics that everyone can see but no one refers to. When such facts are introduced, embarrassment is the usual result. These facts can, of course, be brought to one's attention by unmeant gestures or inopportune intrusions. However, they are more frequently introduced by intentional verbal statements or non-verbal acts whose full significance is not appreciated by the individual who contributes them to the interaction. Following common usage, such disruptions of projections may be called 'faux pas'. Where a performer unthinkingly makes an intentional contribution which destroys his own team's image we may speak of 'gaffes' or 'boners'. Where a performer jeopardizes the image of self projected by the other team, we may speak of 'bricks' or the performer having 'put his foot in it'. Etiquette manuals provide classic warnings against such indiscretions:

> If there is any one in the company whom you do not know, be careful how you let off any epigrams or pleasant little sarcasms. You might be very witty upon halters to a man whose father had been hanged. The first requisite for a successful conversation is to know your company well.[18]

> In meeting a friend whom you have not seen for some time, and of the state and history of whose family you have not been recently or particularly informed, you should avoid making enquiries or allusions in respect to particular individuals of his family, until you have possessed yourself of knowledge respecting them. Some may be dead; others may have misbehaved, separated themselves, or fallen under some distressing calamity.[19]

Unmeant gestures, inopportune intrusions, and faux pas are sources of embarrassment and dissonance which are typically unintended by the person who is responsible for making them and which would be avoided were the individual to know in advance the consequences of his activity. However there are situations, often called 'scenes', in which an individual acts in such a way as to destroy or seriously threaten the polite appearance of consensus, and while he may not act simply in order to create such dissonance, he acts with the knowledge that this kind of dissonance is likely to result. The common-sense phrase, 'creating a scene', is apt because, in effect, a new scene is created by such disruptions. The previous and expected interplay between teams is suddenly forced aside and a new drama forcibly takes its place. Significantly, this new scene often involves a sudden reshuffling and reapportioning of the previous team members into two new teams.

Some scenes occur when teammates can no longer countenance each other's inept performance and blurt out immediate public criticism of the very individuals with whom they ought to be in dramaturgical co-operation. Such misconduct is often devastating to the performance which the disputants ought to be presenting; one effect of the quarrel is to provide the audience with a backstage view, and another is to leave them with the feeling that something is surely suspicious about a performance when those who know it best do not agree. Another type of scene occurs when the audience decides it can no longer play the game of polite interaction, or that it no longer wants to do so, and so confronts the performers with facts or expressive acts which each team knows will be unacceptable. This is what happens when an individual screws up his social courage and decides to 'have it out' with another or 'really tell him off'. Criminal trials have institutionalized this kind of open discord, as has the last chapter of murder mysteries, where an individual who has theretofore maintained a convincing pose of innocence is confronted in the presence of others with undeniable expressive evidence that his pose is only a pose. Another kind of scene occurs when the interaction between two persons becomes so loud, heated, or otherwise attention-getting, that nearby persons engaged in their own conversational interaction are forced to become witnesses or even to take sides and enter the fray. A final type of scene may be suggested. When a person acting as a one-man team commits himself in a serious way to a claim or request and leaves himself no way out should this be denied by the audience, he usually makes sure that his claim or request is the kind that is likely to be approved and granted by the audience. If his motivation is strong enough, however, an individual may find himself making a claim or an assumption which he knows the audience may well reject. He knowingly lowers his defences in their presence, throwing himself, as we say, on their mercy. By such an act the individual makes a plea to the audience to treat themselves as part of his team or to allow him to treat himself as part of their team. This sort of thing is embarrassing enough, but when unguarded request is refused to the individual's face, he suffers what is called humiliation.

I have considered some major forms of performance disruption—unmeant gestures, inopportune intrusions, faux pas, and scenes. These disruptions, in everyday terms, are often called 'incidents'. When an incident occurs, the reality sponsored by the performers is threatened. The persons present are likely to react by becoming flustered, ill at ease, embarrassed, nervous and the like. Quite literally, the participants may find themselves out of countenance. When these flusterings or symptoms of embarrassment become perceived, the reality that is supported by the performance is likely to be further jeopardized and weakened, for these signs of nervousness in most cases are an aspect of the individual who presents a character and not an aspect of the character he projects, thus forcing upon the audience an image of the man behind the mask.

In order to prevent the occurrence of incidents and the embarrassment consequent upon them, it will be necessary for all the participants in the interaction, as well as those who do not participate, to possess certain attributes and to express these attributes in practices employed for saving the show. These attributes and practices will be reviewed under three headings: the defensive measures used by performers to save their own show; the protective measures used by the audience and outsiders to assist the performers in saving the performers' show; and, finally, the measures the performers must take in order to make it possible for the audience and outsiders to employ protective measures on the performers' behalf.

Conclusion

The Framework

A social establishment is any place surrounded by fixed barriers to perception in which a particular kind of activity regularly takes place. I have suggested that any social establishment may be studied profitably from the point of view of impression management. Within the walls of a social establishment we find a team of performers who co-operate to present to an audience a given definition of the situation. This will include conception of own team and of audience and assumptions concerning the ethos that is to be maintained by rules of politeness and decorum. We often find a division into back region, where the performance of a routine is prepared, and front region, where the performance is presented. Access to these regions is controlled in order to prevent the audience from seeing backstage and to prevent outsiders from coming into a performance that is not addressed to them. Among members of the team we find that familiarity prevails, solidarity is likely to develop, and that secrets that could give the show away are shared and kept. A tacit agreement is maintained between performers and audience to act as if a given degree of opposition and of accord existed between them. Typically, but not always, agreement is stressed and opposition is underplayed. The resulting working consensus tends to be contradicted by the attitude toward the audience which the performers express in the absence of the audience and by carefully controlled communication out of character conveyed by the performers while the audience is present. We find that discrepant roles develop: some of the individuals who are apparently teammates, or audience, or outsiders acquire information about the performance and relations to the team which are not apparent and which complicate the problem of putting on a show. Sometimes disruptions occur through unmeant gestures, faux pas, and scenes, thus discrediting or contradicting the definition of the situation that is being maintained. The mythology of the team will dwell upon these disruptive events. We find that performers, audience, and outsiders all utilize techniques for saving the show, whether by avoiding likely disruptions or by correcting for unavoided ones, or making it possible for others to do so. To ensure that these techniques will be employed, the team will tend to select members who are loyal, disciplined, and circumspect, and to select an audience that is tactful.

These features and elements, then, comprise the framework I claim to be characteristic of such social interaction as it occurs in natural setting in our Anglo-American society. This framework is formal and abstract in the sense that it can be applied to any social establishment; it is not, however, merely a static classification. The framework bears upon dynamic issues created by the motivation to sustain a definition of the situation that has been projected before others.

The Analytical Context

This report has been chiefly concerned with social establishments as relatively closed systems. It has been assumed that the relation of one establishment to others is itself an intelligible area of study and ought to be treated analytically as part of a different order in fact—the order of institutional integration. It might be well here to try to place the perspective taken in this report in the context of other perspectives which seem to be the ones currently employed, implicitly or explicitly, in the study of social establishments as closed systems. Four such perspectives may be tentatively suggested.

An establishment may be viewed 'technically', in terms of its efficiency and inefficiency as an intentionally organized system of activity for the achievement of predefined objectives. An establishment may be viewed 'politically', in terms of the actions which each participant (or class of participants) can demand of other participants, the kinds of deprivations and indulgences which can be meted out in order to enforce these demands, and the kinds of social controls which guide this exercise of command and use of sanctions. An establishment may be viewed 'structurally', in terms of the horizontal and vertical status divisions and the kinds of social relations which relate these several groupings to one another. Finally, an establishment may be viewed 'culturally', in terms of the moral values which influence activity in the establishment—values pertaining to fashions, customs, and matters of taste, to politeness and decorum, to ultimate ends and normative restrictions on means, etc. It is to be noted that all the facts that can be discovered about an establishment are relevant to each of the four perspectives but that each perspective gives its own priority and order to these facts.

It seems to me that the dramaturgical approach may constitute a fifth perspective, to be added to the technical, political, structural, and cultural perspectives.[20] The dramaturgical perspective, like each of the other four, can be employed as the end-point of analysis, as a final way of ordering facts. This would lead us to describe the techniques of impression management employed in a given establishment, the principal problems of impression management in the establishment, and the identity and interrelationships of the several performance teams which operate in the establishment. But, as with the facts utilized in each of the other perspectives, the facts specifically pertaining to impression management also play a part in the matters that are a concern in all the other perspectives. It may be useful to illustrate this briefly.

The technical and dramaturgical perspectives intersect most clearly, perhaps, in regard to standards of work. Important for both perspectives is the fact that one set of individuals will be concerned with testing the unapparent characteristics and qualities of the work-accomplishments of another set of individuals, and this other set will be concerned with giving the impression that their work embodies these hidden attributes. The political and dramaturgical perspectives intersect clearly in regard to the capacities of one individual to direct the activity of another. For one thing, if an individual is to direct others, he will often find it useful to keep strategic secrets from them. Further, if one individual attempts to direct the activity of others by means of example, enlightenment, persuasion, exchange, manipulation, authority, threat, punishment, or coercion, it will be necessary, regardless of his power position, to convey effectively what he wants done, what he is prepared to do to get it done and what he will do if it is not done. Power of any kind must be clothed in effective means of displaying it, and will have different effects depending upon how it is dramatized. (Of course, the capacity to convey effectively a definition of the situation may be of little use if one is not in a position to give example, exchange, punishment, etc.) Thus the most objective form of naked power, i.e., physical coercion, is often neither objective nor naked but rather functions as a display for persuading the audience; it is often a means of communication, not merely a means of action. The structural and dramaturgical perspectives seem to intersect most clearly in regard to social distance. The image that one status grouping is able to maintain in the eyes of an audience of other status groupings will depend upon the performers' capacity to restrict communicative contact with the audience. The cultural and dramaturgical perspectives intersect most clearly in regard to the maintenance of moral standards. The cultural values of an establishment will determine in detail how the participants are to feel about many matters and at the same time establish a framework of appearances that must be maintained, whether or not there is feeling behind the appearances.

Personality-Interaction-Society

In recent years there have been elaborate attempts to bring into one framework the concepts and findings derived from three different areas of inquiry: the individual personality, social interaction, and society. I would like to suggest here a simple addition to those inter-disciplinary attempts.

When an individual appears before others, he knowingly and unwittingly projects a definition of the situation, of which a conception of himself is an important part. When an event occurs which is expressively incompatible with this fostered impression, significant consequences are simultaneously felt in three levels of social reality, each of which involves a different point of reference and a different order of fact.

First, the social interaction, treated here as a dialogue between two teams, may come to an embarrassed and confused halt; the situation may cease to be defined, previous positions may become no longer tenable, and participants may find themselves without a charted course of action. The participants typically sense a false note in the situation and come to feel awkward, flustered, and, literally, out of countenance. In other words, the minute social system created and sustained by orderly social interaction becomes disorganized. These are the consequences that the disruption has from the point of view of social interaction.

Secondly, in addition to these disorganizing consequences for action at the moment, performance disruptions may have consequences of a more far-reaching kind. Audiences tend to accept the self projected by the individual performer during any current performance as a responsible representation of his colleague-grouping, of his team, and of his social establishment. Audiences also accept the individual's particular performance as evidence of his capacity to perform the routine and even as evidence of his capacity to perform any routine. In a sense these larger social units—teams, establishments, etc.—become committed every time the individual performs his routine; with each performance the legitimacy of these units will tend to be tested anew and their permanent reputation put at stake. This kind of commitment is especially strong during some performances. Thus, when a surgeon and his nurse both turn from the operating table and the anesthetized patient accidentally rolls off the table to his death, not only is the operation disrupted in an embarrassing way, but the reputation of the doctor, as a doctor and as a man, and also the reputation of the hospital may be weakened. These are the consequences that disruptions may have from the point of view of social structure.

Finally, we often find that the individual may deeply involve his ego in his identification with a particular part, establishment, and group, and in his self-conception as someone who does not disrupt social interaction or let down the social units which depend upon that interaction. When a disruption occurs, then, we may find that the self-conceptions around which his personality has been built may become discredited. These are consequences that disruptions may have from the point of view of individual personality.

Performance disruptions, then, have consequences at three levels of abstraction: personality, interaction, and social structure. While the likelihood of disruption will vary widely from interaction to interaction, and while the social importance of likely disruptions will vary from interaction to interaction, still it seems that there is no interaction in which the participants do not take an appreciable chance of being slightly embarrassed or a slight chance of being deeply humiliated. Life may not be much of a gamble, but interaction is. Further, in so far as individuals make efforts to avoid disruptions or to correct for ones not avoided, these efforts, too, will have simultaneous consequences at the three levels. Here, then, we have one simple way of articulating three levels of abstraction and three perspectives from which social life has been studied.

NOTES

1. Gustav Ichheiser, 'Misunderstandings in Human Relations', Supplement to *The American Journal of Sociology* LV (September, 1949): 6-7.
2. Quoted in E.H. Volkhart, editor, *Social Behavior and Personality*, Contributions of W.I. Thomas to Theory and Social Research (New York: Social Science Research Council, 1951): 5.
3. Here I owe much to an unpublished paper by Tom Burns of the University of Edinburgh. He presents the argument that in all interaction a basic underlying theme is the desire of each participant to guide and control the responses made by the others present. A similar argument has been advanced by Jay Haley in a recent unpublished paper, but in regard to a special kind of control, that having to do with defining the nature of the relationship of those involved in the interaction.
4. Willard Waller, 'The Rating and Dating Complex', *American Sociological Review* II: 730.
5. William Sansom, *A Contest of Ladies* (London: Hogarth, 1956): 230-2.
6. The widely read and rather sound writings of Stephen Potter are concerned in part with signs that can be engineered to give a shrewd observer the apparently incidental cues he needs to discover virtues the gamesman does not in fact possess.
7. An interaction can be purposely set up as a time and place for voicing differences in opinion,

but in such cases participants must be careful to agree not to disagree on the proper tone of voice, vocabulary, and degree of seriousness in which all arguments are to be phrased, and upon the mutual respect which disagreeing participants must carefully continue to express toward one another. This debaters' or academic definition of the situation may also be invoked suddenly and judiciously as a way of translating a serious conflict of views into one that can be handled within a framework acceptable to all present.

8. W.F. Whyte, 'When Workers and Customers Meet', Ch. VII, *Industry and Society*, ed. W.E. Whyte (New York: McGraw-Hill, 1946), 132-3.

9. Teacher interview quoted by Howard S. Becker, 'Social Class Variations in the Teacher-Pupil Relationship', *Journal of Educational Sociology* XXV: 459.

10. Harold Taxel, 'Authority Structure in a Mental Hospital Ward' (Master's thesis, Department of Sociology, University of Chicago, 1953).

11. This role of the witness in limiting what it is the individual can be has been stressed by Existentialists, who see it as a basic threat to individual freedom. See Jean-Paul Sartre, *Being and Nothingness*, tr. Hazel E. Barnes (New York: Philosophical Library, 1956): 365ff.

12. Goffman, *The Presentation of Self*: 319-27.

13. Peter Blau, 'Dynamics of Bureaucracy', (PhD diss., Department of Sociology, Columbia University, forthcoming, University of Chicago Press): 127-9.

14. Walter M. Beattie, Jr, 'The Merchant Seaman' (Master's report, Department of Sociology, University of Chicago, 1950): 35.

15. Sir Frederick Ponsonby, *Recollections of Three Reigns* (New York: Dutton, 1952): 46.

16. For comments on the importance of distinguishing between a routine of interaction and any particular instance when this routine is played through, see John von Neumann and Oskar Morgenstern, *The Theory of Games and Economic Behavior*, 2nd ed. (Princeton: Princeton University Press, 1947): 49.

17. Ponsonby, *op. cit.*: 351.

18. *The Laws of Etiquette* (Philadelphia: Carey, Lee and Blanchard, 1836): 101.

19. *The Canons of Good Breeding*: 80.

20. Compare the position taken by Oswald Hall in regard to possible perspectives for the study of closed systems in his 'Methods and Techniques of Research in Human Relations' (April 1952), reported in E.C. Hughes *et al.*, *Cases on Field Work* (forthcoming).

MICHEL FOUCAULT

1926–1984
FRANCE

Major Works

1965   *The Archaeology of Knowledge*
1965   *Madness and Civilization: A History of Insanity in the Age of Reason*
1966   *The Order of Things: An Archaeology of the Human Sciences*
1975   *The Birth of the Clinic: An Archaeology of Medical Perception*
1979   *Discipline and Punish: The Birth of the Prison*
1980   *The History of Sexuality, vol. 1, An Introduction*
1985   *The History of Sexuality, vol. 2, The Use of Pleasure*
1986   *The History of Sexuality, vol. 3, The Care of Self*

My point is not that everything is bad, but that everything is dangerous.[1]

The omnipresence of power: not because it has the privilege of consolidating everything under its invincible unity, but because it is produced
from one moment to the next, at every point, or rather in every relation
from one point to another. Power is everywhere; not because it
embraces everything, but because it comes from everywhere . . . power
is not an institution, and not a structure; neither is it a certain strength
we are endowed with; it is the name that one attributes to a complex
strategical situation in a particular society.[2]

—*Michel Foucault*

The work of Michel Foucault has been characterized as 'post-structuralist' and
'postmodernist'. His roots may be found in Weber, Marx, and the phenomenol-
ogists such as Husserl, as well as Friedrich Nietzsche. In the end, his theoretical
position challenges so many categories and taken-for-granted notions within
society and sociology that he must be seen as a theoretical pluralist. In effect, he
was suspicious of the possibility of conceptualizing a grand theory.

Foucault has attempted to transcend theoretical positions such as Karl
Marx's economic determinism, which he saw as excessively deterministic. He
saw in society multiple sites of power and relations of power. Indeed, his work
demands that we come to new understandings of power, that we explore
power not only as a negative or repressive function, but also as a productive
function. He suggests that we must not only examine sites of power in society

but must also recognize sites of resistance. The mechanisms of social control in society need investigation, and as we become more aware of the varieties of sites and moments of control in our everyday lives, we must carefully and critically scrutinize them.

Foucault recognizes not only that social life is contained within social structures but also that interactions are governed within discourses. Jana Sawicki writes, 'Foucault defines discourse as a form of power that circulates in the social field and can attach to strategies of domination as well as to those of resistance.'[3] In other words, discourse is the domain of the power of language within particular disciplines or fields of experience—ways of talking and thinking about particular topics. It orders not only topics but structure. Foucault suggests that our discourses profoundly affect the power dynamics within social experience.

In his studies of sexuality, for example, Foucault explores the discourses that surround sex and sexuality both historically and in contemporary society. He argues that over the past hundred years the discourse of sexuality has been medicalized or institutionalized. That does not mean that we have repressed sexuality; in fact, he argues the opposite. The discourse on sexuality has not been one of repression, but one of incipient and progressive linking of forms of pleasure and power. Social control has been expanded and extended.

> The pleasure that comes of exercising a power that questions, monitors, watches, spies, searches out, palpates, brings to light; and on the other hand, the pleasure that kindles at having to evade this power, flee from it, fool it, or travesty it. The power that lets itself be invaded by the pleasure it is pursuing; and opposite it, power asserting itself in the pleasure of showing off, scandalizing or resisting. Capture and seduction, confrontation and mutual reinforcement: parents and children, adults and adolescents, educator and students, doctors and patients, the psychiatrist with his hysteric and his perverts, all have played this game continually since the nineteenth century. These attractions, these evasions, these circular incitements have traced around bodies and sexes, not boundaries not to be crossed, but *perpetual spirals of power and pleasure*.[4]

Foucault mentions both the modernization of the practice of medicine—especially gynecology, doctor-controlled birth, and so forth—and the confessional as sites where the discourse of sexuality has been developed, elaborated, and hence become a powerful dimension of social control. He speaks of the 'deployment' of sexuality to characterize this development. The linking of sexuality with personal identity is a fundamental part of the nineteenth- and twentieth-century institutionalization of the person and in effect precipitated the intervention of the state, the church, and the medical profession into the family. He sees the twentieth century as creating sexuality as 'the key to self-understanding and human liberation'.[5]

In part, Foucault is suggesting 'de-sexualization' of political struggles. For example, with regard to the feminist movement he writes:

> . . . what I want to make apparent is precisely that the object 'sexuality' is in reality an instrument formed a long while ago, and one which has constituted a centuries-long apparatus of subjection. The real strength of the women's liberation movements is not that of having laid claim to the specificity of their sexuality and the rights pertaining to it, but that they have actually departed from the discourse conducted within the apparatus of sexuality. These movements do indeed emerge in the nineteenth century as demands for sexual specificity. What has their outcome been? Ultimately, a veritable movement of de-sexualization. A displacement effected in relation to the sexual centring of the problem, formulating the demand for forms of culture, discourse, language, and so on, which are no longer part of that rigid assignation and pinning-down to their sex which they had initially in some sense been politically obliged to accept in order to make themselves heard. The creative and interesting element in the women's movements is precisely that.[6]

In using the term 'de-sexualization', Foucault notes that women have begun 'to look for new forms of community, co-existence, and pleasure'. They do not 'reduce everything to the order of sex'.[7] In other words, women have seen that their power is in transcending sex—demanding and cultivating their identities beyond the patriarchal confines of sex and sexuality.

Foucault's work focuses our understanding of society on the power and forms of knowledge that structure the social realities we live in. His exploration of the social control of our lives by the institutional structures of prison, schools, churches, hospitals, and psychiatric institutions demands that we reconsider when we attempt to look at and for power. He argues that 'discipline' has two meanings: an area of study or knowledge, and the concept of orderly conduct. The implications of this melding within a word of two dimensions of human experience are especially profound within the social sciences. The discipline of sociology can thus be viewed itself as a form of social control.

Foucault's contribution within the contemporary intellectual community has been profound. His work is complex, at times poetic, and always demanding.

Notes

1. Michel Foucault, 'Afterword', in Herbert Dreyfus and Paul Rabinow, *Michel Foucault: Beyond Structuralism and Hermeneutics*, 2nd edn (Chicago: University of Chicago Press, 1983), 232.
2. Michel Foucault, *The History of Sexuality*, vol. 1 (New York: Random House, 1978), 93.

3. Jana Sawicki, 'Identity Politics and Sexual Freedom: Foucault and Feminism', in Irene Diamond and Lee Quinby, eds, *Feminism and Foucault: Reflections on Resistance* (Boston: Northeastern University Press, 1988), 185.
4. Foucault, *The History of Sexuality*, vol. 1, 45.
5. Ibid., 182.
6. Michel Foucault, *Power/Knowledge: Selected Interviews and Other Writings 1972-1977*, ed. Colin Gordon (New York: Pantheon Books, 1980), 219–20.
7. Ibid., 220.

SEXUALITY

The Repressive Hypothesis

One day in 1867, a farm hand from the village of Lapcourt, who was somewhat simple-minded, employed here then there, depending on the season, living hand-to-mouth from a little charity or in exchange for the worst sort of labour, sleeping in barns and stables, was turned in to the authorities. At the border of a field, he had obtained a few caresses from a little girl, just as he had done before and seen done by the village urchins round about him; for, at the edge of the wood, or in a ditch by the road leading to Saint-Nicholas, they would play the familiar game called 'curdled milk'. So he was pointed out by the girl's parents to the mayor of the village, reported by the mayor to the gendarmes, led by the gendarmes to the judge, who indicted him and turned him over first to a doctor, then to two other experts who not only wrote their report but also had it published.[1] What is the significant thing about this story? The pettiness of it all; the fact that this everyday occurrence in the life of village sexuality, these inconsequential bucolic pleasures, could become, from a certain time, the object not only of a collective intolerance but of a judicial action, a medical intervention, a careful clinical examination, and an entire theoretical elaboration. The thing to note is that they went so far as to measure the brainpan, study the facial bone structure, and inspect for possible signs of degenerescence the anatomy of this personage who up to that moment had been an integral part of village life; that they made him talk; that they questioned him concerning his thoughts, inclinations, habits, sensations, and opinions. And then, acquitting him of any crime, they decided finally to make him into a pure object of medicine and knowledge—an object to be shut away till the end of his life in the hospital at Maréville, but also one to be made known to the world of learning through a detailed analysis. One can be fairly certain that during this same period the Lapcourt schoolmaster was instructing the little villagers to mind their language and not to talk about all these things aloud. But this was undoubtedly one of the conditions enabling the institutions of knowledge and power to overlay this everyday bit of theatre with their solemn discourse. So it was that our society—and it was doubtless the first time in history to take such measures—assembled around these timeless gestures, these barely furtive pleasures between simple-minded adults and alert children, a whole machinery for speechifying, analysing, and investigating.

Between the licentious Englishman, who earnestly recorded for his own purposes the singular episodes of his secret life, and his contemporary, this village halfwit who would give a few pennies to the little girls for favours the older ones refused him, there was without a doubt a profound connection: in any case, from one extreme to another, sex became something to say, and to say exhaustively in accordance with deployments that were varied, but all, in their own way, compelling. Whether in the form of a subtle confession in confidence or an authoritarian interrogation, sex—be it refined or rustic—had to be put into words. A great polymorphous injunction bound the Englishman and the poor Lorrainese peasant alike. As history would have it, the latter was named Jouy.[2]

Since the eighteenth century, sex has not ceased to provoke a kind of generalized discursive erethism. And these discourses on sex did not multiply apart from or against power, but in the very space and as the means of its exercise. Incitements to speak were orchestrated from all quarters, apparatuses everywhere for listening and recording, procedures for observing, questioning, and formulating. Sex was driven out of hiding and constrained to lead a discursive existence. From the singular imperialism that compels everyone to transform their sexuality into a perpetual discourse, to the manifold mechanisms which, in the areas of economy, pedagogy, medicine, and justice, incite, extract, distribute, and institutionalize the sexual discourse, an immense verbosity is what our civilization has required and organized. Surely no other type of society has ever accumulated—and in such a relatively short span of time—a similar quantity of discourses concerned with sex. It may well be that we talk about sex more than anything else; we set our minds to the task; we convince ourselves that we have never said enough on the subject, that, through inertia or submissiveness, we conceal from ourselves the blinding evidence, and that what is essential always eludes us, so that we must always start out once again in search of it. It is possible that where sex is concerned, the most long-winded, the most impatient of societies is our own.

But as this first overview shows, we are dealing less with *a* discourse on sex than with a multiplicity of discourses produced by a whole series of mechanisms operating in different institutions. The Middle Ages had organized around the theme of the flesh and the practice of penance a discourse that was markedly unitary. In the course of recent centuries this relative uniformity was broken apart, scattered, and multiplied in an explosion of distinct discursivities which took form in demography, biology, medicine, psychiatry, psychology, ethics, pedagogy, and political criticism. More precisely, the secure bond that held together the moral theology of concupiscence and the obligation of confession (equivalent to the theoretical discourse on sex and its first-person formulation) was, if not broken, at least loosened and diversified: between the objection of sex in rational discourses, and the movement by which each individual was set to the task of recounting his own sex, there has occurred, since the eighteenth century, a whole series of tensions, conflicts, efforts at adjustment, and attempts at retranscription. So it is not simply in terms of continual extension that we must speak of this discursive growth; it should be seen rather as a dispersion of centres from which discourses emanated, a diversification in their forms, and the complex deployment of the network connecting them. Rather than the uniform concern to hide sex, rather than the general prudishness of language, what distinguishes these last three centuries is the variety, the wide dispersion of devices that were invented for speaking about, for having it be spoken about, for inducing it to speak of itself, for listening, recording, transcribing, and redistributing what is said about it: around sex, a whole network of varying, specific, and coercive transpositions into discourse. Rather than a massive censorship, beginning with the verbal proprieties imposed by the Age of Reason, what was involved was a regulated and polymorphous incitement to discourse.

The objection will doubtless be raised that if so many stimulations and constraining mechanisms were necessary in order to speak of sex, this was because there reigned over everyone a certain fundamental prohibition; only definite necessities—economic pressures, political requirements—were able to lift this prohibition and open a few approaches to the discourse on sex, but these were limited and carefully coded; so much talk about sex, so many insistent devices contrived for causing it to be talked about—but under strict conditions: does this not prove that it was an object of secrecy, and more important, that there is still an attempt to keep it that way? But this often-stated theme, that sex is outside of discourse and that only the removing of an obstacle, the breaking of a secret, can clear the way leading to it, is precisely what needs to be examined. Does it partake of the injunction by which discourse is provoked? Is it not with the aim of inciting people to speak of sex that it is made to mirror, at the outer limit of every actual discourse, something akin to a secret whose discovery is imperative, a thing abusively reduced to silence, and at the same time difficult and necessary, dangerous and precious to divulge? We must not forget that by making sex into that which, above all else, had to be confessed, the Christian pastoral always presented it as the disquieting enigma: not a thing which stubbornly shows itself, but one which always hides, the insidious presence that speaks in a voice so muted and often disguised that one risks remaining deaf to it. Doubtless the secret does not reside in that basic reality in relation to which all the incitements to speak of sex are situated—whether they try to force the secret, or whether in some obscure way they reinforce it by the manner in which they speak of it. It is a question rather of a theme that forms part of the very mechanics of these incitements: a way of giving shape to the requirement to speak about the matter, a fable that is indispensable to the endlessly proliferating economy of the discourse on sex. What is peculiar to modern societies, in fact, is not that they consigned sex to a shadow existence, but that they dedicated themselves to speaking of it *ad infinitum*, while exploiting it as *the* secret.

. . .

Although not without delay and equivocation, the natural laws of matrimony and the immanent rules of sexuality began to be recorded on two separate registers. There emerged a world of perversion which partook of that of legal or moral infraction, yet was not simply a variety of the latter. An entire sub-race was born, different—despite certain kinship ties—from the libertines of the past. From the end of the eighteenth century to our own, they circulated through the pores of society; they were always hounded, but not always by laws; were often locked up, but not always in prisons; were sick perhaps, but scandalous, dangerous victims prey to a strange evil that also bore the name of vice and sometimes crime. They were children wise beyond their years, precocious little girls, ambiguous schoolboys, dubious servants and educators, cruel or maniacal husbands, solitary collectors, ramblers with bizarre impulses; they haunted the houses of correction, the penal colonies, the tribunals, and the asylums; they carried their infamy to the doctors and their sickness to the judges. This was the numberless family of perverts who were on friendly terms with delinquents and akin to madmen. In the course of the century they successively bore the stamp of 'moral folly', 'genital neurosis', 'aberration of the genetic instinct', 'degenerescence', or 'physical imbalance'.

What does the appearance of all these peripheral sexualities signify? Is the fact that they could appear in broad daylight a sign that the code had become more lax? Or does the fact that they were given so much attention testify to a stricter regime and to its concern to bring them under close supervision? In terms of repression, things are unclear. There was permissiveness, if one bears in mind that the severity of the codes relating to sexual offences diminished considerably in the nineteenth century and that law itself often deferred to medicine. But an additional ruse of severity, if one thinks of all the agencies of control and all the mechanisms of surveillance that were put into operation by pedagogy or therapeutics. It may be the case that the intervention of the Church in conjugal sexuality and its rejection of 'frauds' against procreation had lost much of their insistence over the previous two hundred years. But medicine made a forceful entry into the pleasures of the couple: it created an entire organic, functional, or mental pathology arising out of 'incomplete' sexual practices; it carefully classified all forms of related pleasures; it incorporated them into the notions of 'development' and instinctual 'disturbances'; and it undertook to manage them.

Perhaps the point to consider is not the level of indulgence or the quantity of repression but the form of power that was exercised. When this whole thicket of disparate sexualities was labelled, as if to disentangle them from one another, was the object to exclude them from reality? It appears, in fact, that the function of the power exerted in this instance was not that of interdiction, and that it involved four operations quite different from simple prohibition.

1. Take the ancient prohibitions of consanguine marriages (as numerous and complex as they were) or the condemnation of adultery, with its inevitable frequency of occurrence; or on the other hand, the recent controls through which, since the nineteenth century, the sexuality of children has been subordinated and their 'solitary habits' interfered with. It is clear that we are not dealing with one and the same power mechanism. Not only because in the one case it is a question of law and penality, and in the other, medicine and regimentation; but also because the tactics employed are not the same. On the surface, what appears in both cases is an effort at elimination that was always destined to fail and always constrained to begin again. But the prohibition of 'incests' attempted to reach its objective through an asymptotic decrease in the thing it condemned, whereas the control of infantile sexuality hoped to reach it through a simultaneous propagation of its own power and of the object on which it was brought to bear. It proceeded in accordance with a twofold increase extended indefinitely. Educators and doctors combatted children's onanism like an epidemic that needed to be eradicated.

What this actually entailed, through this whole secular campaign that mobilized the adult world around the sex of children, was using these tenuous pleasures as a prop, constituting them as secrets (that is, forcing them into hiding so as to make possible their discovery), tracing them back to their source, tracking them from their origins to their effects, searching out everything that might cause them or simply enable them to exist. Wherever there was a chance they might appear, devices of surveillance were installed; traps were laid for compelling admissions; inexhaustible and corrective discourses were imposed; parents and teachers were alerted, and left with the suspicion that all children were guilty; and with the fear of being themselves at fault if their suspicions were not sufficiently strong; they were kept in readiness on the face of this recurrent danger; their conduct was prescribed and their pedagogy recodified; an entire medico-sexual regime took hold of the family milieu. The child's 'vice' was not so much an enemy as a support; it may have been designated as the evil to be eliminated, but the extraordinary effort went into the task that was bound to fail leads one to suspect that what was demanded of it was to preserve, to proliferate to the limits of the visible and the invisible, rather than to disappear for good. Always relying on this support, power advanced, multiplied its relays and its effects, while its target expanded, subdivided, and branched out, penetrating further into reality at the same pace. In appearance, we are dealing with a barrier system; but in fact, all around the child, indefinite *lines of penetration* were disposed.

2. This new persecution of the peripheral sexualities entailed an *incorporation of perversions* and a new *specification of individuals*. As defined by the ancient civil or canonical codes, sodomy was a category of forbidden acts; their perpetrator was nothing more than the judicial subject of them. The nineteenth-century homosexual became a personage, a past, a case history, and a childhood, in addition to being a type of life, a life form, and a morphology, with an indiscreet anatomy and possibly a mysterious physiology. Nothing that went into his total composition was unaffected by his sexuality. It was everywhere present in him: at the root of all his actions because it was their insidious and indefinitely active principle; written immodestly on his face and body because it was a secret that always gave itself away. It was consubstantial with him, less as a habitual sin than as a singular nature. We must not forget that the psychological, psychiatric, medical category of homosexuality was constituted from the moment it was characterized—Westphal's famous article of 1870 on 'contrary sexual sensations' can stand as its date of birth[3]—less by a type of sexual relations than by a certain quality of sexual sensibility, a certain way of inverting the masculine and the feminine in oneself. Homosexuality appeared as one of the forms of sexuality when it was transposed from the practice of sodomy onto a kind of interior androgyny, a hermaphrodism of the soul. The sodomite had been a temporary aberration; the homosexual was now a species.

So too were all those minor perverts whom nineteenth-century psychiatrists entomologized by giving them strange baptismal names: there were Krafft-Ebing's zoophiles and zooerasts, Rohleder's auto-monosexualists; and later mixoscopophiles, gynecomasts, presbyophiles, sexoesthetic inverts, and dyspareunist women. These fine names for heresies referred to a nature that was overlooked by the law, but not so neglectful of itself that it did not go on producing more species, even where there was no order to fit them into. The machinery of power that focused in this whole alien strain did not aim to suppress it, but rather to give it an analytical, visible, and permanent reality; it was implanted in bodies, slipped in beneath modes of conduct, made into a principle of classification and intelligibility, established as a *raison d'être* and a natural order of disorder. Not the exclusion of these thousand aberrant sexualities, but the specification, the regional solidification of each one of them. The strategy behind this dissemination was to strew reality with them and incorporate them into the individual.

3. More than the old taboos, this form of power demanded constant, attentive, and curious presences for its exercise; it presupposed proximities; it proceeded through examination and insistent observation; it required an exchange of discourses, through questions that extorted admissions, and confidences that went beyond the questions that were asked. It implied a physical proximity and an interplay of intense sensation. The medicalization of the sexually peculiar was both the effect and the instrument of this. Imbedded in bodies, becoming deeply characteristic of individuals, the oddities of sex relied on a technology of health and pathology. And conversely, since sexuality was a medical and medicalizable object, one had to try to detect it—as a lesion, a dysfunction, or a symptom—in the depths of the organism, or on the surface of the skin, or among all the signs of behaviour. The power which thus took charge of sexuality set about contacting bodies, caressing them with its eyes, intensifying areas, electrifying surfaces, dramatizing troubled moments. It wrapped the sexual body in its embrace. There was undoubtedly an increase in effectiveness and an extension of the domain controlled; but also a sensualization of power and a gain of pleasure. This produced a twofold effect: an impetus was given to power through its very exercise; an emotion rewarded the overseeing control and carried it further; the intensity of the confession renewed the questioner's curiosity; the pleasure discovered fed back to the power that encircled it. But so many pressing questions singularized the pleasures felt by the one who had to reply. They were fixed by a gaze, isolated and animated by the attention they received. Power operated as a mechanism of attraction; it drew out those peculiarities over which it kept watch. Pleasure spread to the power that harried it; power anchored the pleasure it uncovered.

The medical examination, the psychiatric investigation, the pedagogical report, and family controls may have the over-all and apparent objective of saying no to all wayward or unproductive sexualities, but the fact is that they function as mechanisms with double impetus: pleasure and power. The pleasure that comes of exercising a power that questions, monitors, watches, spies, searches out, palpates, brings to light; and on the other hand, the pleasure that kindles at having to evade this power, flee from it, fool it, or travesty it. The power that lets itself be invaded by the pleasure it is pursuing; and opposite it, power asserting itself in the pleasure of showing off, scandalizing, or resisting. Capture and seduction, confrontation and mutual reinforcement: parents and children, adults and adolescents, educator and students, doctors and patients, the psychiatrist with his hysterics and his perverts, all have played this game continually since the nineteenth century. These attractions, these evasions, these circular incitements have traced around bodies and sexes, not boundaries not to be crossed, but *perpetual spirals of power and pleasure.*

4. Whence those *devices of sexual saturation* so characteristic of the space and the social rituals of the nineteenth century. People often say that modern society has attempt-

ed to reduce sexuality to the couple—the heterosexual and, insofar as possible, legitimate couple. There are equal grounds for saying that it has, if not created, at least outfitted and made to proliferate, groups with multiple elements and a circulating sexuality: a distribution of points and power, hierarchized and placed opposite to one another; 'pursued' pleasures, that is, both sought after and searched out; compartmental sexualities that are tolerated or encouraged; proximities that serve as surveillance procedures, and function as mechanisms of intensification; contacts that operate as inductors. This is the way things worked in the case of the family, or rather the household, with parents, children, and in some instances, servants. Was the nineteenth-century family really a monogamic and conjugal cell? Perhaps to a certain extent. But it was also a network of pleasures and powers linked together at multiple points and according to transformable relationships. The separation of grown-ups and children, the polarity established between the parents' bedroom and that of the children (it became routine in the course of the century when working-class housing construction was undertaken), the relative segregation of boys and girls, the strict instructions as to the care of nursing infants (maternal breast-feeding, hygiene), the attention focused on infantile sexuality, the supposed dangers of masturbation, the importance attached to puberty, the methods of surveillance suggested to parents, the exhortations, secrets, and fears, the presence—both valued and feared—of servants: all this made the family, even when brought down to its smallest dimensions, a complicated network, saturated with multiple, fragmentary, and mobile sexualities. To reduce them to the conjugal relationship, and then to project the latter, in the form of a forbidden desire, onto the children, cannot account for this apparatus which, in relation to these sexualities was less a principle of inhibition than an inciting and multiplying mechanism. Educational or psychiatric institutions, with their large populations, their hierarchies, their spatial arrangements, their surveillance systems, constituted, alongside the family, another way of distributing the interplay of powers and pleasures; but they too delineated areas of extreme sexual saturation, with privileged spaces or rituals such as the classroom, the dormitory, the visit, and the consultation. The forms of a nonconjugal, nonmonogamous sexuality were drawn there and established.

Nineteenth-century 'bourgeois' society—and it is doubtless still with us—was a society of blatant and fragmented perversion. And this was not by way of hypocrisy, for nothing was more manifest and more prolix, or more manifestly taken over by discourses and institutions. Not because, having tried to erect too rigid or too general a barrier against sexuality, society succeeded only by giving rise to a whole perverse outbreak and a long pathology of the sexual instinct. At issue, rather, is the type of power it brought to bear on the body and on sex. In point of fact, this power had neither the form of the law, nor the effects of the taboo. On the contrary, it acted by multiplication of singular sexualities. It did not set boundaries for sexuality; it extended the various forms of sexuality, pursuing them according to lines of indefinite penetration. It did not exclude sexuality, but included it in the body as a mode of specification of individuals. It did not seek to avoid it; it attracted its varieties by means of spirals in which pleasure and power reinforced one another. It did not set up a barrier; it provided places of maximum saturation. It produced and determined the sexual mosaic. Modern society is perverse, not in spite of its puritanism or as if from a backlash provoked by its hypocrisy; it is in actual fact, and directly, perverse.

In actual fact. The manifold sexualities—those which appear with the different ages (sexualities of the infant or the child), those which become fixated on particular tastes or practices (the sexuality of the invert, the gerontophile, the fetishist), those which, in a diffuse manner, invest relationships (the sexuality of doctor and patient, teacher and student, psychiatrist and mental patient), those which haunt spaces (the sexuality of the home, the school, the prison)—all form the correlate of exact procedures of power. We must not imagine that all these things that were formerly tolerated attracted notice and received a pejorative designation when the time came to give a regulative role to the one type of sexuality that was capable of reproducing labour power and the form of the family. These polymorphous conducts were actually extracted from people's bodies and from their pleasures; or rather, they were solidified in them; they were drawn out, revealed, isolated, intensified, incorporated, by multifarious power devices. The growth of perversions is not a moralizing theme that obsessed the scrupulous minds of the Victorians. It is the real product of the encroachment of a type of power on bodies and their pleasures. It is possible that the West has not been capable of inventing any new pleasures, and it has doubtless not discovered any original vices. But it has defined new rules for the game of powers and pleasures. The frozen countenance of the perversions is a fixture of this game.

Directly. This implantation of multiple perversions is not a mockery of sexuality taking revenge on a power that has thrust on it an excessively repressive law. Neither are we dealing with paradoxical forms of pleasure that turn back on power and invest it in the form of a 'pleasure to be endured'. The implantation of perversions is an instrument-effect: it is through the isolation, intensification, and consolidation of peripheral sexualities that the relations of power to sex and pleasure branched out and multiplied, measured the body, and penetrated modes of conduct. And accompanying this encroachment of powers, scattered sexualities rigidified, became stuck to an age, a place, a type of practice. A proliferation of sexualities through the extension of power; an optimization of the power to which each of these local sexualities gave a surface of intervention: this concatenation, particularly since the nineteenth century, has been ensured and related by the countless economic interests which, with the help of medicine, psychiatry, prostitution, and pornography, have tapped into both this analytical multiplication of pleasure and optimization of the power that controls it. Pleasure and power do not cancel or turn back against one another; they seek out, overlap, and reinforce one another. They are linked together by complex mechanisms and devices of excitation and incitement.

We must therefore abandon the hypothesis that modern industrial societies ushered in an age of increased sexual repression. We have not only witnessed a visible explosion of unorthodox sexualities; but—and this is the important point—a deployment quite different from the law, even if it is locally dependent on procedures of prohibition, has ensured, through a network of interconnecting mechanisms, the proliferation of specific pleasures and the multiplication of disparate sexualities. It is said that no society has been more prudish; never have the agencies of power taken such care to feign ignorance of the thing they prohibited, as if they were determined to have nothing to do with it. But it is the opposite that has become apparent, at least after a general review of the facts: never have their existed more centres of power; never more attention manifested and verbal-ized; never more circular contacts and linkages; never more sites where the intensity of pleasures and the persistency of power catch hold, only to spread elsewhere.

NOTES

1. H. Bonnet and J. Bulard, *Rapport médico-légal sur l'état mental de Ch.-J. Jouy*, 4 January 1868.
2. Jouy sounds like the past participle of *jouir*, the French verb meaning to enjoy, to delight in (something) but also to have an orgasm, to come. (Translator's note)
3. Carl Westphal, *Archiv für Neurologie*, 1870.

DOROTHY SMITH

1926–
BRITAIN

Major Works

1977   *Feminism and Marxism*
1987   *The Everyday World as Problematic: A Feminist Sociology*
1990   *The Conceptual Practices of Power: A Feminist Sociology of Knowledge*
1990   *Texts, Facts and Femininity: Exploring the Relations of Ruling*
1999   *Writing the Social: Critique, Theory, and Investigations*

> Being excluded, as women have been, from the making of ideology, of knowledge, and of culture means that our experience, our interests, our ways of knowing the world have not been represented in the organization of our ruling nor in the systematically developed knowledge that has entered into it.[1]

> Working with the concept of social relation does not deprive subjects of activity. Class is not understood as a secret power behind our backs, determining how we think, how we understand the world and how we act. Rather class is seen as a complex of social relations coordinating the activities of our everyday worlds with those of others with whom we are not directly connected.[2]
>
> —*Dorothy Smith*

Dorothy Smith's sociological analyses begin with a challenge to traditional sociological inquiry. She argues that the very nature of such inquiry systematically reinforces the exclusion of women from the major social institutions of our culture, structures for the most part dominated by men of the privileged class, those who produce and reproduce the dominant ideas of society in politics, economics, law, medicine.

Countering this dominant ideology, Smith locates her discourse from the standpoint of women's experience. She argues that, historically, the gathering and analysis of sociological data have systematically excluded women. She regards this 'exclusion as a conscious and often cruel practice'. The male point of view was assumed to be universal; it automatically followed that male research could express the female point of view. Males were assumed to have power and authority and were considered to be in the vanguard of culture. For Smith, such a way of seeing the world rendered the female sex invisible, so that it was not even worthwhile to study their work or their lives. The contributions made by women were, of course, unacknowledged. Her exploration of women's reality demonstrated that women were objectified in sociological research and devalued within the society. Her theorizing has concentrated on the development of a *feminist epistemology*. To analyze women's conditions from the *standpoint of women* validates their experiential reality.

Smith places her feminist sociology of knowledge within the framework of the *relations of ruling*, showing how power has been appropriated and maintained by men. She argues that women must recognize this reality and be aware that since we have conceded to this authority, we have the power to withdraw from it.

Notes

1. Dorothy Smith, *The Everyday World as Problematic: A Feminist Sociology* (Toronto: University of Toronto Press, 1987), 17-18.
2. Ibid., 135.

FEMINISM AND MARXISM—
A PLACE TO BEGIN, A WAY TO GO

I want to dissociate myself from any notion that what I'm doing here is a performance. This is partly because I'd like to treat it as part of a political work and partly because preparing for this has been, for me, a process of trying to work through some of the difficulties I've experienced as a Marxist feminist, both in relation to Marxists and in relation to feminists . . . and feminism. I needed to try and locate for myself, and hopefully for other feminists, a base in Marxism, which has been difficult to establish. This is what I'm doing here. It is a work in progress.

Therefore as an introduction, I want to talk about my personal experience in becoming a feminist. It has been for me an important basis for my own political commitment as a Marxist. Earlier in my life when I lived in England, when I was a young woman, I worked as a socialist. I've realized since then that I had no idea what that meant. I certainly had no understanding of Marxism. I had very little idea of what I was doing, and indeed I think that few people with whom I worked at that particular time had either. Since then I've done a great deal of work, thought a great deal and worked in various ways within the women's movement, and I feel that I have some better grounding for a political position, some better basis for working. This began for me with discovering what feminism meant. So that has been very personal for me as it is indeed for all women—the discovery of what oppression means. It is the discovery that many aspects of my life which I had seen privately—perhaps better, experienced privately as guilt, or as pathology, or that

I'd learned to view as aspects of my biological inferiority—that all these things could be seen as aspects of an objective organization of a society—as features that were external to me, as they were external to other women. This is the discovery that the inner experiences which also involved our exercise of oppression against ourselves were ones that had their location in the society outside and originated there. Insofar as we co-operated in our oppression, we co-operated as people who did not know what we were doing. We were convinced by our own belief in the defectiveness of womanhood. The experience of this change—the discovery of these as objective aspects of the society and the world—was also the discovery of sisterhood.

Sisterhood has become something that is decried increasingly both in the women's movement and elsewhere. Yet it is a very important basis for feminists, because it is in sisterhood that we discover the objectivity of our oppression. That discovery is made in the relation to other women, in our discussion with other women, in exploring with other women the dimensions of the oppression. For we discover oppression in learning to speak of it as such, not as something which is peculiar to yourself, not as something which is an inner weakness, nor as estrangement from yourself, but as something which is indeed imposed upon you by the society and which is experienced in common with others. Whatever else sisterhood means, it means this opportunity. But what it also means is the discovery of women as your own people . . . as my people . . . as the people I stand with . . . as the people whose part I take.

Being a Marxist has for me developed in large part, though not entirely, out of this experience of discovering feminism. It has come to stand for me as an emblematic moment in my life that when I moved here to the University of British Columbia I moved into an office vacated by Lionel Tiger. For many years I couldn't bring myself to read his book *Men in Groups* because I was afraid he might be right. Part of the work I've done in learning how to be a Marxist originated because I wanted to understand how the society could be put together so that the relations among men and women and between men and women could be fictionalized into Lionel Tiger's account of men in groups. I was very happy when I finally came to read Lionel Tiger's book because by that time I had the beginnings of an understanding of women's oppression under capitalism and because I saw that it was, among other things, a trivial and insignificant piece of work, and totally inadequate as any kind of account of either men's experience of contemporary capitalism or of women's. And if men like to dwell on their likeness to baboons, they are welcome to.

So becoming a Marxist has been an enterprise in trying to discover and trying to understand the objective social, economic and political relations which shape and determine women's oppression in this kind of society. What has shaped this experience of mine as a woman? What has shaped the experience of other women? What are the social and economical determinations of this? These questions led me almost imperceptibly into an attempt to work with a Marxist framework as a way of understanding how society is put together. This was not a wilful choice nor an accidental one. It was made on the basis of a sense that the kind of understanding Marx and Engels offered tells you something about how the determinations of your particular space could be seen as arising as aspects of a social and economic process, of social relations outside it. I think that Marxism is the only method of understanding the world which allows you to do this. That was my first reason, rather than its political relevance in other ways, for working to grasp Marxism.

But trying to become engaged politically in other ways on the 'left' and in relation to Marxists has been an extremely painful and difficult experience. What you generally find among Marxists is a rejection of feminism. It is exactly the same rejection we experience in almost every other encounter that we have outside the women's movement. How Marxists, whether Social Democrats or Marxist-Leninists, responded to us as feminists does not differ from how we are responded to by the ruling class—the 'upstairs' people. This difficulty is of course a very serious one if you have become committed as a Marxist because it does not enable you to locate your work with those who are basing their work on a similar analysis, a similar approach, a similar understanding. This has been a really serious difficulty for the women's movement in Canada and I assume the women's movement in the United States as well—although it might be worth recognizing that in Britain, for example, this kind of difficulty does not appear to exist in the same way. There the women's movement appears to be more deeply anchored in the various Marxist groups than it is almost anywhere else, as well as having substantial roots in the working class. So these difficulties seem not to be fundamental to the relationship between Marxism and feminism, but are presumably structured by historically special features of contemporary capitalism in North America as we know it.

I'd like now to try to define what I see as distinctive about a feminist position. I want to do this in a way that doesn't commit me to any particular feminist theory because it must be clear to you that I would reject many of the theoretical positions identified as feminist. Yet I want to say that I am a feminist and I want to say what I think that to be, in ways that don't commit me to a determinate political position underlying the ideological formulations. I see perhaps three things here. One is that a feminist takes the standpoint of women. That is, we begin from this place and it is the place where we are. This is something that is very distinctive about feminism as a place to begin from politically—that we begin with ourselves, with our sense of what we are, our own experience. The second thing is that we oppose women's oppression. That is, we struggle against the oppression of women. And the third thing is the recognition of sisterhood. That is something that I find difficult to describe. It is difficult if you make it merely a sentimental basis for relations among women because it doesn't work for very long. It doesn't work if you treat sisterhood as something that organizes a political basis across class, across time, because you can't unite with all women politically. It certainly doesn't make sense to Marxists, and it has proved in our experience of working in the women's movement not to make sense in practice. Nevertheless sisterhood is that understanding of your relation to other women which comes prior to taking up a political position. Before the women's movement we did not see ourselves as women politically at all. We did not organize or speak as women and for women. Sisterhood is that first moment of discovery on which everything else depends. It is the discovery that women's experience matters to us, that women are people we are concerned to work with as women and that is how we also work for ourselves as women. We did not have that before. When we worked politically or otherwise organized or were active outside the little domestic space into which we were meant to squash our lives, we were neutered, we did not act as women, we worked in relation to and in enterprises organized by men. We did not 'identify' as women. We did not have a sisterhood.

Sisterhood is the change from being an outsider in, say, reading books, seeing movies and images, or hearing tell of, what has happened in the past or is happening in the world to women in their struggles and suffering, to locating yourself on their side and in their position. Sisterhood means a different understanding of women as they have experienced slavery and struggled against it, as they have been persecuted for speaking as women and for working politically as women for women, as they have struggled for the survival of their children in many different ways, as they have been oppressed as women by imperialist wars and have fought as the women of Vietnam fought against US imperialism. Sisterhood is a relocation. You take up a different place in the world. It is one in which the character and form of the oppression and the oppressor begin to take shape. As it takes shape, it becomes clearer whose side you are on. There's a difference then in hearing women tell of their oppression when you are detached from that and do not understand how you are related to their experience, and acknowledging sisterhood and finding yourself on their side and opposed to what oppresses them. The experience of sisterhood is a very powerful experience—a very great change in our experience of the world. It forces us to grasp our identity with those who are also oppressed and also more savagely oppressed, not as an altruistic and disinterested concern but because the basis of their oppression is or was their sex and you share that with them.

This is the fundamental experience of being a feminist. It is a political moment simply because without first a basis in sisterhood we can't understand the divergences and differences among women or the things we share, nor see with whom we can work and with whom we are fundamentally in conflict. Far from sisterhood proving a basis of spurious agreement in the women's movement, the discovery of sisterhood and the first experimental efforts to unify politically on that basis alone was precisely the context in which we learned about our differences. We could not see these until we first saw women as those we had to learn these things from and with. Shifts in the women's movement came about in part as women from other spaces than those originating the movement began to be heard and to be listened to—housewives, for example, who refused to be despised, women who had children or wanted children and could not accept the negation of motherhood that was important in the early stages. Sisterhood forced women in the movement to be open to other women and their experience. Issues and analyses had to shift and deepen accordingly. The narrow original focus—such as seeing the key to women's oppression in the control of their bodies and thence making abortion-law reform the central objective of struggle—came to be seen as only one aspect of a more general and grosser oppression. As other women made themselves heard and became part of the circle of authoritative voices, new experience sought political voice. Political alignments changed. Modes of organizing changed. New forms were innovated, sometimes discarding, sometimes incorporating the old. We had to shift from the simple and rather magical thinking of our first struggles and to take up aspects of women's experience which hadn't counted for us before. We had no choice—though we often tried to work as if we had. (I think this is what we were doing when we trashed or were trashed.) Women had to be relevant to us, they *had* to matter, they *had* to be those whose experience counted for us. Once sisterhood was our basis, once we took the standpoint of women, once we were feminists, we had to deal with that. This then is what sisterhood means—not well or clearly defined, I realize, but described as I understand it as an actual experience, as *my* actual experience.

When we come to feminism in its varieties as a political theory, we run into difficulties of a different kind. One of the problems is exactly that we do begin from the personal inner understanding, from this personal experience which is distinctive to women's experience of oppression. We begin from the ways in which oppression is not just an external constraint but part of our personal lives, part of our inter-personal relations, part of our sexuality, part of how we relate to men as individuals as well as in institutional context. In feminism as a political theory, the problem is that the political formulations are transposed by a metaphorical procedure from these personal locations, to the world as a way to talk about it. These personal locations are the bounded, powerless, and domesticated position from which women begin and their political formulations as radical feminism preserve this structure. Our personal experience of oppression becomes the analogue of a political theory. We talk about patriarchy as a political relation by going directly from personal situations of oppression and direct personal relations with men to treating that as a political form. In this way we are prevented from seeing that patriarchy is and must be located in a political and economic process. The formulation of oppression as patriarchal simply skips over this because our experience as women skips over it. We talk about the domination of men and of how men oppress women, as if the personal experience of oppression could be seen as the general and dominant mode in which the society is organized. And then we talk about a golden age of matriarchy in compensation. It is a means of restoring to us some sense of our power—a power women are supposed to have had some two thousand years ago, who knows when? It is a magical way of giving ourselves a sense that we as women truly have the possibility of overcoming our oppression. What was once, can be again. We need only to dip into that deep source, to draw on it, to take up our power, to act and we shall overcome. But then we do not see that power cannot exist apart from actual individuals organizing and working concertedly and hence that the power oppressing us is an actual organization of the work and energies of actual people, both women and men and that our power to struggle depends also upon working together with others confronting the same bases of oppression. When we call on the magic of a distant matriarchy as a source of power we depend upon a mythology, a mythology rather than an analysis of actual relations, a mythology rather than an attempt to grasp the actual character of the social and economic relations of the society oppressing us now. We must grasp the oppression of women in *this* society, the oppression of women elsewhere in the world *today*. Our oppression is now and this is what concerns us now. It must not be seen as something that you could spread like butter over the bread of time by using the term 'patriarchy'; and treating it as something which has always been there ever since the departure of the golden time. We have to see what's happening to us as what's happening to us now. It's happening to us here. It's part of what's happening to other women—other people—elsewhere in the world. And here and now for sure is the only place to begin. So we have to start to try to see what in hell is going on now. Why is it happening to us as it does happen? This is the only way we can begin to know how to act, how to organize, how to work, how to struggle against oppression.

Women Are Losing Ground

Women are confronting a difficult time now. The women's movement is confronting a difficult time. So I wanted to say something at this point about the achievements of the women's movement. I want to say something about the work women have done here in British Columbia, the work that has been done moving outwards from women's understanding of their experience as oppression in this society to attempt to make issues and to make changes. These have been first very straightforwardly related to doing something about women's oppression. Many of you here in this room have been part of efforts to make changes, to change the abortion laws, to establish adequate child care for women of all classes in B.C., to struggle against the ways in which the professions have oppressed women by establishing a health collective, by working in relation to the law, both attempting to secure legal changes in marriage laws and also trying to make legal help available to women in a form which is not just a further means of oppression. Women have established organizations such as Transition House which provides a refuge for women who are beaten by their husbands. (Because Transition House exists, we have learned how much more of this type of support for women is needed.) Women have done immense organizational work, in establishing women's studies courses throughout the province, in setting up feminist publishing collectives publishing magazines and books and other feminist literature. Women have created feminist media in film and television. We have created political organization and political networks throughout the province. The organizing of unions for clerical and service workers which the established unions would never actively take up has been taken up by feminists. We have done an incredible amount of work in the last six years in this province as well as elsewhere in Canada. It has been an enormous and often exhausting effort. It has had many failures as well as successes. But the greatest gain has been what women have learned about themselves and their capacities to work politically and how to do that. We have learned a great deal about how to organize, how to work, how to work outside the establishment, outside the recognized institutions of the society. This kind of learning is very important and must be seen as a major gain by feminists. It is particularly important because it is hard to see other kinds of consolidated and lasting gain. It is hard to see how we have made gains in terms of the kinds of changes we aimed to bring about, at least as permanent and lasting changes in women's situation. We would like to see equality in pay. We would like to see equality of access of women to employment of all kinds. We would like to see the widespread introduction of child care. We would like to see repeal of anti-abortion laws. We would like to see changes in the matrimonial property laws. We would like to see many changes of this kind and we do not see them. But what women have done, what women's organizations have developed, and the progress we have made in doing this is something that has to be remembered because this is an achievement and this is the basis on which it is possible for us to go forward, to work. I want to put this before you as something that must be seen as a background to what I believe to be otherwise a gloomy picture, and that is that as times are hard in general, they are specially difficult for women and difficult for the women's movement. There is a crisis in capitalism and changes are taking place which, as you look at them, can be seen as women being put back into the places that we were trying to escape from. That 'we' is not just this group here, but women in general in this society.

When the media begin to lay the death penalty on the women's movement one can treat this as a sign-off, not of the women's movement but of media interest in the women's movement. The media are closing down on the women's movement. It is not news any more—in so far as it ever was. There is a pervasive change in the women's pages. I don't know whether you look at the kinds of dressmaking patterns that are presented but they've gone back from pant suits to being dress patterns again. The styles are changing, make-up is coming back, red painted fingernails, brilliantly painted lips, and the frontiers of the deodorant continue to advance. 'Feminine' styles of being a woman that the women's magazines had laid on us are coming back. The media have worked over the women's movement so that its revolutionary implications are transposed into a particular 'feminine' style—careerism, the new marriage, couples without children. What remains of the fundamental critique is the style of the new woman. And the women's movement is over. It's had its day. It was a fad. Sexist advertising can be slipped back in if it ever in fact disappeared. Now we can get down to the kind of society we had before.

We can see the kind of retreat that is taking place if we look at the unemployment figures among women. If you do so, you will find that the unemployment rates among women in this province have gone up and that they are substantially higher than rates among men. When you look at the welfare crunch you see also how that is placed on women, remembering that the majority of single-parent families are women and that the majority of single-parent families fall below the so-called 'poverty-line' in income. If you begin to think through the implications of the withdrawal of funds not only from child care, which has a clear and direct impact, but in general from services to the handicapped, to the old—to all those who depend directly on others for their subsistence and daily care—these are all things that tend to fall back on women's work in the home. Look at the implications of the decline in real wages in terms of what that means for women's work in the home. There women's work must take up the slack that is created by the depreciation of the value of wages and the irregularity and uncertainty of income from wages when rates of unemployment are high. At the same time as married women must often try to get work because the family needs her wage, the difficulties of doing so are increased, and the burdens of work in the home are increased. When money is short, women's work in the home substitutes for labour embodied in goods bought at the store. There is a very straightforward relation here. You put more time in. You do more darning. You do more mending. You make more of your own clothes. You do more processing of food if you can't afford to buy that labour embodied in commodities. All these things are happening.

In addition there are those things that directly affect the women's movement in terms of women's ability to put forward the position of women and their oppression so that others can understand it and organize in struggle against it. Funds supporting women's magazines and media ventures are drying up. Funds supporting the organization of women for equality in all areas are getting harder to find. Financing for women's health care, for rape relief, is increasingly difficult to find. Women's studies courses in community colleges and universities are under pressure because of budgetary cuts. It's hard to maintain women's studies in the University of British Columbia. Though Simon Fraser University will have a women's studies program by virtue of the lucky accident of having a woman president, nevertheless even there budgetary cuts are experienced. And in many community colleges the established courses are under continual pressure. In all these areas, many of the concrete gains that we made are in the process of being eroded. This is the situation we are confronted with. As for the successes of International Women's Year, it's nice to know that they've changed some of the nomenclature of government forms and documents.

A Peculiar Eclipsing:
Women's Exclusion from Man's Culture

I Texts, Talk, and Power: Women's Exclusion

The relations of ruling in our kind of society are mediated by texts, by words, numbers, and images on paper, in computers, or on TV and movie screens. Texts are the primary medium (though not the substance) of power. The work of administration, of management, of government is a communicative work. Organizational and political processes are forms of action co-ordinated textually and getting done in words. It is an ideologically structured mode of action—images, vocabularies, concepts, abstract terms of knowledge are integral to the practice of power, to getting things done. Further, the ways in which we think about ourselves and one another and about our society—our images of how we should look, our homes, our lives, even our inner worlds—are given shape and distributed by the specialized work of people in universities and schools, in television, radio and newspapers, in advertising agencies, in book publishing and other organizations forming the 'ideological apparatuses' of the society.[1]

Being excluded, as women have been, from the making of ideology, of knowledge, and of culture means that our experience, our interests, our ways of knowing the world have not been represented in the organization of our ruling nor in the systematically developed knowledge that has entered into it. We explore in this chapter the history of this exclusion as a conscious and often a cruel practice; we look at aspects of its contemporary reproduction in the way women are distributed in an educational system that both produces and disseminates knowledge, culture, and ideology; we examine how these larger structures construct an authority for the writing and speech of individual men, which in the ordinary settings of our lives gives weight and influence to men and re-creates the circles in which men attend to what men have to say and carry forward the interests and perspectives of men. But we have assented to this authority and can withdraw our assent. Indeed this is essential to the making of knowledge, culture, and ideology based on the experiences and relevances of women.

This way of organizing society began to develop in western Europe some four hundred or five hundred years ago. It is an integral aspect of the development of a capitalist mode of production. Women have been at work in its making as much as men, though their work has been of a different kind and location. But women have been largely excluded from the work of producing the forms of thought and the images and symbols in which thought is expressed and ordered. We can imagine women's exclusion organized by the formation of a circle among men who attend to and treat as significant only what men say. The circle of men whose writing and talk was significant to each other extends backward as far as our records reach. What men were doing was relevant to men, was written by men about men for men. Men listened and listened to what one another said.

This is how a tradition is formed. A way of thinking develops in this discourse through the medium of the written and printed word as well as in speech. It has questions, solutions, themes, styles, standards, ways of looking at the world. These are formed as the circle of those present builds on the work of the past. From these circles women have been excluded or admitted only by special licence granted to a woman as an individual and never as a representative of her sex. Throughout this period in which ideologies become of increasing importance, first as a mode of thinking, legitimating, and sanctioning a social order, and then as integral in the organization of society, women have been deprived of the means to participate in creating forms of thought relevant or adequate to express their own experience or to define and raise social consciousness about their situation and concerns. They have never controlled the material or social means to the making of a tradition among themselves or to acting as equals in the ongoing discourse of intellectuals. They have had no economic status independent of men. They have not had, until very recently, access to the educational skills necessary to develop, sustain, and participate in the making of common culture.

Women, have, of course, had access to and used the limited and largely domestic zone of women's magazines, television programs, women's novels, poetry, soap operas, and the like. But this is a limited zone. It follows the contours of their restricted role in the society. The universe of ideas, images, and themes—the symbolic modes that are the general currency of thought—have been either produced by men or controlled by them. In so far as women's work and experience have been entered into it, it has been on terms decided by men and because it has been approved by men.

This is why women have had no written history until very recently, no share in making religious thoughts, no political philosophy, no representation of society from their view, no poetic tradition, no tradition in art.

II Men's Standpoint Is Represented as Universal

It is important to recognize that in this kind of society most people do not participate in the making of culture. The forms of thought and images we use do not arise directly or spontaneously out of people's everyday lived relationships. Rather, they are the product of the work of specialists occupying influential positions in the ideological apparatus (the educational system, communications, etc.). Our culture does not arise spontaneously; it is 'manufactured'.

The ideological apparatuses are part of the larger relations of ruling the society, the relations that put it together, co-ordinate its work, manage its economic processes, generally keep it running, and regulate and control it. The making and dissemination of the forms of thought we make use of to think about ourselves and our society are part of the relations of ruling and hence originate in positions of power. These positions of power are occupied by men almost exclusively, which means that our forms of thought put together a view of the world from a place women do not occupy. The means women have had available to them to think, image, and make actionable their experience have been made for us and not by us. It means that our experience has not been represented in the making of our culture. There is a gap between where we are and the means we have to express and act. It means that the concerns, interests, and experiences forming 'our' culture are those of men in positions of dominance whose perspectives are built on the silence of women (and of others).

As a result the perspectives, concerns, interests of only one sex and one class are represented as general. Only one sex and class are directly and actively involved in producing, debating, and developing its ideas, in creating its art, in forming its medical and psychological conceptions, in framing its laws, its political principles, its educational values and objectives. Thus a one-sided standpoint comes to be seen as natural, obvious, and general, and a one-sided set of interests preoccupy intellectual and creative work. Simone de Beauvoir describes the effect for women in this way:

> A man never begins by presenting himself as an individual of a certain sex; it goes without saying that he is a man. The terms masculine and feminine are used symmetrically only as a matter of form, as on legal paper. In actuality the relation of the two sexes is not quite like that of two electrical poles, for man represents both the positive and the neutral, as is indicated by the common use of man to designate human beings in general; whereas woman represents only the negative, defined by limiting criteria, without reciprocity.[2]

Issues such as the use of male pronouns to represent the general are not trivial after all. They address exactly this relation.

Let us be clear that we are not talking about prejudice or sexism as a particular bias against women or a negative stereotype of women. We are talking about the consequences of women's exclusion from a full share in the making of what becomes treated as our culture. We are talking about the consequences of a silence, an absence, a nonpresence. What is there—spoken, sung, written, made emblematic in art—and treated as general, universal, unrelated to a particular position or a particular sex as its source and standpoint, is in fact partial, limited, located in a particular position, and permeated by special interests and concerns.

For example, I heard on the radio excerpts of a musical made from a book of women's and men's reminiscences of the depression years. But the musical as it was described and excerpted on the radio had the voices only of men. Hence only men's viewpoint and experience of that time were there for all or any of us to hear. Women's experience and viewpoint were altogether missing. Or again, a radio program concerning violence between husbands and wives spent most of the time discussing violence of wives against husbands, though violence of husbands against wives constitutes by far the most frequent and most serious form of violence between husbands and wives.

The biases of beginning from the experience of men enter in all kinds of ways into our thinking. Take for example the Freudian conception of sexuality. It is clearly based on the man's experience of his body and his sexuality. Hence we have a conception of sexuality based on male genital sexuality and of woman's body as deviating from this sexuality so that her psychosexual development must be thought of somehow as an attempt to do away with this fundamental defect. Her child, particularly her male child, is represented as a substitute for a missing penis. How extraordinary this is if we do not treat a man's body as normative. Think for a moment what it might be like to account for our psychosexual being using women's experience of our bodies and sexuality as a norm. How odd that would be if it were imposed upon men as normative. And how is it that we could not have an account that begins indeed from the actualities of our experience and recognizes the difference as just that, or perhaps indeed as complementary, rather than treating the sexuality of one's sex as deviant *vis-à-vis* that of the other?

The enormous literature on the relation of family socialization and educational attainment, in which the role of the mother takes on such a prominent part, can be seen also to have its distinctive biases. The treatment of mothering in this literature is in various ways evaluative, critical, or instructive with respect to the practices and relations conducive to educational attainment or to the psychosocial well-being of children.[3] Virtually the whole of this literature presupposes a one-way relation between school and family whereby family practices, organization and, in particular, mothering practices are seen as consequential for the child's behaviour at school. The phenomenon of school phobia as it is vulgarly described is one notorious example, whereby the protectiveness of the mother is understood as creating a dependence in the child and hence the child's fearfulness at school.[4] Or take the psychiatric literature on the family and mental illness in which the mother is continually the focus of an inescapable indictment.[5]

Who has thought to take up the issue of these relations from the standpoint of women? Might we not then have studies concerned with the consequences of the school and the educational process for how the child matures in the family and for the family itself? Where are those studies showing the disastrous consequences of the school for the families of immigrants, particularly non-English speaking immigrants? Where are the studies suggesting that mothers' protectiveness of children who are terrified of school arises as a natural response to what is perceived as a source of damage and harm to the child? Where are the studies telling us anything about the consequences for family organization of societal processes that 'subcontract' educational responsibilities for homework and so forth to the family and in particular to the mother? What effect does this odd role—lacking authority and over-burdened with responsibility for outcomes over which in fact she has little control—have on women? What are the implications of this role for family relations, particularly for relations between mothers and children?[6]

In the field of education research itself, our assumptions are those of a world seen from men's position in it. Turn to that classic of our times, Philippe Ariès's *Centuries of Childhood*.[7] Interrogate it seriously from the standpoint of women. Ask, should this book not be retitled *Centuries of the Childhood of Men*? Or take Christopher Jencks's influential book entitled *Inequality*.[8] Should this not be described as an examination of the educational system with respect to its implications for inequality among men?[9] The very terms in which inequality is conceived are based on men's occupations, men's typical patterns of career and advancement. Women's experience of work in this kind of society is located in standstill jobs lacking career structure and in a status system in which their position is derived from that of men. A work examining the educational system with respect to the inequality of women would be focused quite differently. It would, among other matters, be concerned with the educational system as systematically producing a differential of competence among women and men in almost every education dimension, including that of physical development. It would focus on inequality between the sexes as a systematically organized product of the educational process.

These examples only illustrate the outcomes of women's absence. We cannot inventory them fully. The problem is not a special, unfortunate, and accidental omission of this or that field, but a general organizational feature of our kind of society.

III The Brutal History of Women's Silencing

The exclusion of women from the making of our culture is not the product of a biological deficiency or a biological configuration of some kind. As we learn more of our women's history we discover that a powerful intellectual and artistic current moves like an underground stream through the history of the last few centuries. It appears sometimes merely as a missing potentiality, as in the stories of women mathematicians whose biographies show in almost every case the effect of a general deprivation of education. In almost every case they have discovered mathematics by accident—sharing a brother's lessons, the interest of a family friend, the paper covered with calculus used to paper a child's room—some special incident or relation that introduced them to the territory of their art.[10] Lacking such an accident, there was no provision, no systematic training, no opening of an intellectual universe. Or we find that the intellectual or artistic practice itself was appropriated by a man, as Caroline Herschel's major work in astronomy, done in association with her brother William Herschel, is treated as his. We learn of the subordination of genius to the discipline of service in the home and in relation to children, and of the fragmentary realization of extraordinary powers of mind and dedication, as in the lives of Charlotte and Emily Brontë, of Emily Dickinson, and in our time, of Tillie Olsen—among others, known and unknown.

We can see also the submerged folk tradition of a true art sustained and perpetuated by women when the emergence of a high art excluded them and surely excluded distinctively womanly materials. Thus the artists of quilting have used forms, materials, and practices quite different from those that, until recently, have been identified with 'art'. Though if you see the quilts and read the accounts, you are clearly in the presence of artists of high technical excellence and design quality who were not treated or recognized as artists until the women's movement. A quilt was made to be used. It was integrated into particularistic relations—the piece of her grandmother's dress, her daughter's pinafore—and was sometimes made by a group of women working together. The making itself and the friendships were built into the design, the collection of fabrics, the stitching. A quilt was not a piece of art, therefore, to be seen in isolation from its history and the social relations of its making. It was not made to be set in the high walls of a gallery or a museum. It was always a moment in the moving skein of family and tradition, raising suspicion against time and its powers of separation.

We have evidence now also of a submerged and repressed political and spiritual intelligentsia dating at least from that moment when in Europe the translation of the Bible into the vernacular made the authorities' book available to anyone who could read, among them women.[11] We have as yet fragmentary intuitions of an emerging female intelligentsia and the repressions to which they were subject; we hear for example of women such as Joan Boughton and her daughter Lady Yonge, who were burned at the stake in the late fifteenth century because they held fast to their right to direct interpretation of the Scriptures and to speak and express their own understanding of the Bible rather than on the authority of the clergy.[12] We can see a similar phenomenon in the reign of Henry VIII, when the Reformation enlivened the intellectual possibilities for women as well as for men, and women such as Sara Ann Askew were tortured and martyred for heresy. In the founding and organization of the Quaker sect, Margaret Fell (later to be Margaret Fox) played a leading and important role. Her influence was such that the Quaker sect was one of the few to grant a position of equality to women in religious matters. She herself, imprisoned many times for her beliefs, wrote in the seventeenth century a powerful pamphlet arguing the scriptural justification for the right of women to preach and teach.[13] Those however who actually took up such responsibility, as many women have in many forms, were not always received as leaders, as was Margaret Fell. In seventeenth-century North America, Ann Hutchinson was banished from the Massachusetts Bay Colony because she chose to preach and teach religion and claimed the right to do so as a woman.[14] The same struggle emerged again from its underground existence during the French Revolution when women were active in women's revolutionary organizations. Again it was repressed. The clubs were proscribed and at least two of their leaders, Olympes de Gouges and Manon Roland, were guillotined as an example to other women of what happens to those who step so far out of their place as to claim wisdom, learning, and political leadership.[15] Sojourner Truth's power of thought and rhetoric was heard against militant efforts to prevent her speaking in the conventions on women's rights in the mid-nineteenth-century United States.[16] The underground movement of women surfaced again in Mrs Packard's struggle against her Calvinist husband, who had committed her (as under the law of that time he could) to the Illinois Insane Asylum on grounds not only that she held religious opinions different from his, but that she insisted on her right to do so.[17] Closer to our own time, as women in the 1960s began actively to take up women's issue in the civil rights movement, they encountered ridicule, vilification, and an opposition from men that exhibited to them for the first time how they were despised.[18]

Let us be clear that what we are hearing in these brief biographical moments is the emergence into our view, into the view of history written largely by men and with men's concerns in mind, of a continuing and active struggle renewed continually in different times and places by women who often had no knowledge of their predecessors and sometimes not even of their contemporary sisterhood.

The repression of the continuing underground sources of intellectual power and assertion among women shows us the rough stuff. There is an actively enforced barrier that we were unaware of until we looked at these kinds of examples. But studies accumulate, telling us of our history and breaking the silence of our past, we can see that other forces were at work, more conventional, seemingly more rational, but no less powerful and effective in ensuring the silence of women.

For example, we now have well-documented history of midwives in both England and the United States, showing how over a period of two hundred years they were reduced to an ancillary role in childbirth, or eliminated altogether, in a struggle fought consciously and deliberately by the medical profession. It was a struggle concerned to eliminate the competition not only of women, but of a continuing native tradition of learning that was at odds with the technical apparatus and technical knowledge of the emerging profession of gynecology. In the suppression of that art or the bringing of English midwives into a subordinate relation to the medical profession, the traditions perpetuated by the older art have been lost (we cannot now of course evaluate their possible importance). Further direct access to women's own knowledge of their sexual and procreative functions was cut off.[19]

We now know also that women were systematically and consciously excluded from the growing profession of medicine in the United States, where their admission to medical school was restricted to a very small number. Those who were trained found that the kinds of jobs open to them were largely in public health or institutional medicine. Again we find an organizational process that by excluding women also excludes their knowledge, experience, interests, and perspectives and prevents their becoming part of the systematic knowledge and techniques of a profession. This process has of course been of fundamental significance in the formation of practice and knowledge in gynecology. Its current practices are distinctively marked by the silence of women in its making.[20]

These are some of the forms in which silencing and exclusion of women have been practised. Some have arisen inadvertently as a concomitant of women's location in the world; some have been a process of active repression or strong social disapproval of the exercise by women of a role of intellectual or political leadership; others have been the product of an organizational process. It is this last form of exclusion I shall focus on now, for in our society we see less of the rough stuff (though do not assume that it is not there) and more of a steady institutional process, equally effective and much less visible in its exclusionary force.

IV Contemporary Institutional Forms of Women's Exclusion: Women's Place in the Hierarchies of Education

The exclusion of women from participating in creating the culture of the society is in this day largely organized by the ordinary social processes of socialization, education, work, and communication. These perform a routine, generalized, and effective repression. The educational system is an important aspect of this repression. It trains people in skills they need to participate at various levels in the ideological structuring of the society (they must be able to read at least); it teaches them the ideas, the vocabularies, images, beliefs; it trains them to recognize and approve ideologically sanctioned forms of relations and how to identify authoritative ideological sources (what kinds of books, newspapers, etc. to credit, what to discredit; who are the authoritative writers or speakers and who are not). This repression is part of the system that distributes ideas and ensures the dissemination of new ideological forms as these are produced by the intelligentsia. It is also active itself in producing ideology, both in the forms of knowledge in the social sciences, psychology, and education, and in the forms of critical ideas and theories in philosophy and literature.

Prior to the late nineteenth century, women were almost completely denied access to any form of higher education beyond the skills of reading and writing. In one of the first major feminist works, *A Vindication of the Rights of Women*,[21] Mary Wollstonecraft places women's right to education at the centre of her argument. She is responding specifically to Rousseau's prescriptions for educating women, aimed at training them for dependency, for permanent childishness, and for permanent incapacity for the autonomous exercise of mind.[22] During the latter part of the nineteenth century, in both Europe and North America, opportunities for women in higher education were a major focus of women's struggle. Though women's participation in the educational process at all levels has increased in this century, this participation remains within marked boundaries. Among the most important of these boundaries, I would argue, is that which reserves to men control of the policy-making and decision-making apparatus in the educational system.

When we look at where women are in the educational system, our focus should go beyond issues of social justice. Equality of opportunity is only one aspect of the problem. I want rather to draw attention to the significance of the inequalities we find for how women are located in the processes of setting standards, producing social knowledge, acting as 'gatekeepers' over what is admitted into the system of distribution, innovating in thought or knowledge or values, and in other ways participating as authorities in the ideological work done in the educational process.

We can look at the statistics from two points of view—education itself has a status structure organizing its internal relations so far as sources of knowledge and academic standards are concerned. Though there are of course other socially significant aspects of schools and community colleges that are not related to the university, the university is important as a source of intellectual leadership *vis-à-vis* the rest of the educational system. Second, these differing levels of the educational system are related to the age structure of the educational process. Generally, more advanced training for older students has a higher status than education for younger and less advanced students. This status structure has little to do with the skills required or the social importance of the work itself and a great deal to do with control over the standards and substance of education.

Table 1: Percentage of Women at Different Levels of the Canadian Educational System, Various Years, 1969–73

Level	% Women	Years
Elementary teachers (ex. Quebec)	78%	1972–73
Secondary teachers (ex. Quebec)	37%	1972–73
Community College teaching staff (ex. Quebec)	19.5%	1970–71
University (all ranks)	15%	1969–70

Source: Canadian Teachers' Federation Status of Women, *The Declining Majority* (Ottawa: Canadian Teachers' Federation, 1978).

As we go up the Canadian educational hierarchy from elementary to secondary school to community college to university we find a lower proportion of women teachers at each step (see Table 1). At each level upward in the hierarchy of control and influence over the education process, the proportion of women declines. At the elementary level, women are the majority (although the proportion had declined to 74 per cent in 1975–76),[23] but at the secondary school level they are already a minority, and their share of the educational process is lowest at the university level.

Further, within each level, we find women markedly unrepresented in administrative positions of professional leadership. In elementary and secondary schools women's relative share of administrative positions is much lower than their share of teaching positions. At each next position upward in the hierarchy we generally see the same pattern of decline as we have seen in the overall educational structure (see Table 2). A similar pattern shows in the figures for community colleges (Table 3). Within the university the same pattern is repeated (Table 4).

Table 2   Percentage of Women in Positions in Canadian Elementary and Secondary Schools (ex. Quebec), 1972–73

Position	Elementary	Secondary
Teachers	78%	37%
Department head	42%	21%
Vice-principal	20%	7%
Principal	20%	4%

Source: See Table 1.

Table 3   Percentage of Women Educational Staff in Canadian Community Colleges by Position (ex. Quebec), 1970–71

Position	% Women
Teaching staff	19.5%
Academic administrative staff	11.9%

Source: Women's Bureau, *Women in the Labour Force: Facts and Figures*, 1973 (Ottawa: Labour Canada, 1974), table 7.

The inverse relation between status level and proportion of women is obvious at every level. Women are most heavily concentrated in the positions of lecturer and instructor, which are not part of the promotional system leading to professional rank (the so-called ladder positions) and are usually held on only a one-year contract. There is an appreciable drop even to the next level of junior positions, the assistant professors—the first step on the promotion ladder. Women form a very small proportion of full professors.[24]

It is important to keep in mind that we are looking at rather powerful structures of professional control. It is through this structure of ranks and the procedures by which

Table 4   Percentage of Women in Canadian Academic Positions, All Ranks, 1969–70

Position	% Women
Lecturers and instructors	31%
Assistant professors	14%
Associate professors	8%
Full professors	3%

Source: Jill McCalla Vickers and June Adam, *But Can You Type? Canadian Universities and the Status of Women* (Toronto: Clarke Irwin/Canadian Association of University Teachers, 1977).

people are advanced from one to another that the professions maintain control over the nature and quality of work that is done and the kinds of people who are admitted to its ranks and to influential positions within it. Two points are of special importance: first, the concentration of women in the relatively temporary nonladder positions. This concentration means that women are largely restricted to teaching, that their work is subject to continual review, and that reappointment is conditional upon conformity. The second point to note is the marked break in the proportion of women between tenured and nontenured positions.

The tenured faculty to a large extent controls who shall be admitted to its ranks and what shall be recognized as properly scholarly work. This minimal 'voting power' of women helps us understand why women in more senior positions in the university do not ordinarily represent women's perspectives. They are those who have passed through this very rigorous filter. They are those whose work and style of work and conduct have met the approval of judges who are usually men. And, in any case, they are very few.

In sum, the statistics show a highly inequitable distribution of women throughout the educational system. Though women are more than half of all teachers, they are very under-represented in the ranks of principals; there are very, very few women superintendents. In the educational bureaucracies, women appear almost exclusively in secretarial and clerical roles. In universities and community colleges, women are very markedly under-represented in the academic staff. They are clustered in the lower ranks with the greatest turnover and in a very limited range of subjects (think of who taught you and who taught what subjects). The officers of organizations representing educators are also predominantly men. We find in general that the closer positions come to policy-making or innovation in the ideological forms, the smaller the proportion of women. Power and authority in the educational process are the prerogatives of men.

V   The Authority of the Male Voice

Men have authority in the world of thought as members of a social category and not as individuals. Authority is a form of power that is a distinctive capacity to get things done in words. What is said or written merely means what the words mean, until and unless it is given force by the authority as individuals, not because they have as individuals special competencies or expertise, but because as men they appear as representative of the power and authority of the institutionalized structures that govern the society. Their authority as individuals in actual situations of action is generated by a social organization. They do not appear as themselves alone. They are those whose words count, both for each other and for those who are not members of this category. The circle I spoke of earlier is formed of those whose words count for one another. It excludes those whose words do not count, whose speakers have no authority.

We have by now and in various forms a good deal of evidence of the ways in which this social effect works. It is one Mary Ellman has described as a distinction between women and men in intellectual matters, which is both obvious and unnoticed. A man's body gives credibility to his utterance, whereas a woman's body takes it away from hers.[25] A study done by Philip Goldberg, which was concerned with finding out whether women were prejudiced against women, demonstrates this effect very clearly.[26] Here is Jo Freeman's description:

> He gave college girls sets of booklets containing six identical professional articles in traditional male, female and neutral fields. The articles were identical, but the names of the authors were not. For example, an article in one set would bear the name John T. McKay and in another set the same article would be authored by Joan T. McKay. Each booklet contained three articles by 'women' and three by 'men'. Questions at the end of each article asked the students to rate the articles on value, persuasiveness, and profundity; and the authors on writing style and competence. The male authors fared better in every field, even in such 'feminine' areas as Art History and Dietetics.[27]

There seems to be something like a plus factor that adds force and persuasiveness to what men say and a minus factor that depreciates and weakens what women say.

The way in which the sex of the speaker modifies the authority of the message has been observed in other ideological fields. Lucy Komisar points out that in advertising it is men who give instructions to women on how to do their housework. Men tell women why one detergent or soap powder or floor polish is better than another. The reason, according to a leading advertising agency executive, is that the male voice is the voice of authority.[28]

Phyllis Chesler's study of preferences among psychotherapists and their patients shows that the majority of women patients prefer male therapists and that the majority of male psychotherapists prefer women patients. The reasons women give for preferring male psychotherapists are that they generally feel more comfortable with them and that they have more respect for and confidence in a man's competence and authority. Chesler reports that both men and women in her sample said they trusted and respected men as people and as authorities more than they did women.[29]

A study done by L.S. Fidell on sex discrimination in university hiring practices in psychology shows the intersection of this effect with the educational system of controls described in the preceding section. She used an approach very similar to Goldberg's, constructing two sets of fictional descriptions of academic background and qualifications (including the PhD). Identical descriptions in one set had a woman's name attached and in the other a man's. The sets of descriptions were sent to chairpersons of all colleges and universities in the United States offering graduate degrees in psychology. They were asked to estimate the chance of the described individuals' getting an offer of a position and at what level, and so forth. Her findings supported the hypothesis of discrimination on the basis of sex. Men were likely to be suggested for higher levels of appointment. They received more regular academic positions of the kind leading to promotion and tenure, and only men were offered full professorships.[30] It seems as though the attribution of authority which increases the value of men's work constitutes something like a special title to the positions of control and influence and hence to full active membership in the intelligentsia.

It seems that women as a social category lack proper title to membership in the circle of those who count for one another in the making of ideological forms. To identify a woman novelist as a woman novelist is to place her in a special class outside that of novelists in general. Doris Lessing is described as one of the greatest women novelists of this century, rather than just one of the greatest novelists. Among the professional problems confronted by women writers, Tillie Olsen cites the following:

> Devaluation: Still in our century, women's books of great worth suffer the death of being unknown, or at best a peculiar eclipsing, far outnumbering the similar fate of the few such books by men. I think of Kate Chopin, Mary Austin, Dorothy Richardson, Henry Handel Richardson (Ultima Thule), Jean Rhys, Storm Jameson, Christina Stead, Elizabeth Madox Roberts (The Time of Man), Janet Lewis, May Sarton, Harriette Arnouw (The Dollmaker), Agnes Smedley (Daughter of Earth), Djuna Barnes (Nightwood), Kay Boyle—every one of whom is rewarding, and some with the stamp of enduring. Considering their stature, how comparatively unread, untaught are Glasgow, Glaspell, Bowen, Parker, Stein, Mansfield—even Cather and Porter.[31]

And she points out further how work by women is treated quite differently from that by men. She describes 'the injurious reaction to a book not for its quality or content, but on the basis of its having been written by a woman, with consequent misreading, mistreatment'.[32] These effects are not confined to literature written by women. They are rather special instances of a general social organization of relations among women and men when the medium is communicative. Men have title of entry to the circle of those who count for one another. Women do not. The minus factor attached to what women say, write, or image is another way of seeing how what they say, write, or image is not a 'natural' part of the discourse.

The examples so far given have been mainly of the written word. But the metaphor of a game points to our experience in actual everyday interactional settings.[33] We can and have observed these patterns ourselves, which serve to fill out our description of how male control over the topics and themes of discourse is maintained in actual situations of interactions. For example, F.I. Strodtbeck and R.D. Mann in their study of jury deliberations report that men talked considerably more than women. These differences, however, were more than quantitative. They also describe what seems to be a general pattern of interaction between women and men. Men's talk was more directed toward the group task while women reacted with agreement, passive acceptance, and understanding.[34] The pattern I have observed also involves women becoming virtually an audience, facilitating with support or comments, but not carrying the talk or directing remarks toward one another.

It is like a game in which there are more presences than players. Some are engaged in tossing a ball between them; the others are consigned to the roles of audience and supporter, who pick the ball up if it is dropped and pass it back to the players. They support, facilitate, encourage but their action does not become part of the play. In ordinary situations of meeting and working together we can find these same patterns. What women have to say may simply remain unsaid. Or it is treated as a byplay—not really integral to the game. If it comes into play at all it is because a male player has picked it up and brought it into play as his.

Characteristically, women talking with men use styles of talk that throw the control to others, as for example by interspersing their words with interjections that reassign the responsibility for its meaning to others, by saying 'you know' or failing to name objects or things or to complete sentences. Expectations of how much and for how long men and women should talk have an effect on how much and how long they are seen to talk. William Caudill describes a supervisor of nurses as an assertive person, willing to express her opinion in unequivocal terms. Yet his data show that in meetings she spoke less on the average than the hospital administrative and psychiatric personnel, including a resident described as 'passive and withdrawn'.[35]

Candace West has made a study of differences between single-sex and mixed-sex conversations which focuses upon men's and women's different rights to speak. She observed a variety of 'devices' used by men, apparently with women's consent, that serve to maintain male control of the topics of conversation. For example, men tended to complete women's sentences, to give minimal responses to topics initiated and carried by women, and to interrupt without being sanctioned. Her study describes how men control conversation through the use of interruption and by withdrawing active participation when women are developing their topics.[36]

In professional conversations we can also identify a collection of devices that may be used to restrict women's control of the development of topics. Among them are the devices used to recognize or enter what women have said into the discourse under male sanction. For example, a suggestion or point contributed by a woman may be ignored at its point of origin. When it is reintroduced at a later point by a man, it is then 'recognized' and becomes part of the topic. Or if it is recognized at the time, it is reattributed by the responder to another male (in the minutes of the meeting, it will appear as having been said by someone else). Or the next speaker after the woman may use a device such as, 'What Dorothy really means is . . .'. Or the woman's turn is followed by a pause, after which the topic is picked up at the previous speaker's turn as if she had not spoken.

Celia Gilbert makes a vivid symbolic presence of this circle and the practices that exclude women in her poem 'On Refusing Your Invitation to Come to Dinner'. The dinner table reflects (both metaphorically and actually) the unspoken presence of women. Gilbert looks back on it from the standpoint of one who has already learned another practice of her being. She writes:

> But I am forgetting the language,
> sitting has become difficult,
> and the speaking, intolerable,

to say, 'how interesting'
makes me weep.
I can no longer bear to hear
the men around the table laugh,
argue, agree,
then pause, politely
while we speak,
their breath held in, exhaled
when we've finished,
politely,
then turn to the real conversation,
the unspoken expectation of applause.[37]

The interpersonal order symbolizes and is the local expression of the circle of men across time and space whose discourse has excluded women. But it is also the actual practice of the circle. It is a practice we can and probably have experienced in our working and our personal lives. At the interpersonal level it is not a conspiracy among men that they impose on women. It is a complementary social process between women and men. Women are complicit in the social practices of their silence.

The practices extend to women's participation in art, music, literature, science, the health sciences, education. The figures showing us where women are in education represent an organization of social relations of a deeper level, extending throughout the educational structure and its articulation to the society it both serves and structures. In the education system at all levels and in all aspects, women have access and participate so that they may be present as subordinates, as marginal. Their training and education ensure that at every level of competence and leadership there will be a place for them that is inferior and subordinate to the positions of men.

VI Grasping Our Own Authority to Speak

It is important to recognize that the deprivation of authority and the ways in which women have been trained to practise the complement of male-controlled 'topic development'[38] have the effect of making it difficult for women to treat one another as relevant figures. We have difficulty asserting authority for ourselves. We have difficulty grasping authority for women's voices and for what we have to say. We are thus deprived of the essential basis for developing among ourselves the forms of thought and images that express the situations we share and make it possible to begin to work together. Women have taken for granted that our thinking is to be authorized by an external source of authority. Anya Bostock tells us that this is because we live in a world dominated intellectually by men. As a consequence women's opinions tend to conform to the approved standards, and these in the last analysis are men's. In consequence women's opinions are sharply separated from their lived experience. As they begin to develop their own opinions, they have to check them against their collective experience as women rather than merely their personal experience.[39] But it has not been easy for women to find their own voices convincing. It is hard for us to listen to each other. The voice of our own experience is equally defective.

Lack of authority, then, is lack of authority for ourselves and for other women. We have become familiar in the women's movement with the importance of women learning to relate to one another. We need also to learn how to treat what other women say as a source and basis for our own work and thinking. We need to learn to treat one another as the authoritative speakers of our experience and concerns.

It is only when as women we can treat one another, and ourselves, as those who count for one another that we can break out of our silence—to make ourselves heard; to protest against the violence done to women (and there is violence done); to organize politically for justice and equality in law; to work together to resist the unloading of economic crisis onto women; and, as educators, to advance, develop, and pass on to our children (our daughters *and* our sons) a knowledge of women's history and experience, of our poetry, our art, our political skills, and our confidence. This is the road to full and equal membership in our society for women.

The institutionalized practices of excluding women from the ideological work of society are the reason we have a history constructed largely from the perspective of men, and largely about men. This is why we have so few women poets and why the records of those who survived the hazards of attempting poetry are so imperfect.[40] This is why we know so little of women visionaries, thinkers, and political organizers.[41] This is why we have an anthropology that tells us about other societies from the perspective of men and hence has so distorted the cross-cultural record that it may now be impossible to learn what we might have known about how women lived in other forms of society. This is why we have a sociology that is written from the perspective of positions in a male-dominated ruling class and is set up in terms of the relevances of the institutional power structures that constitute those positions.[42] This is why in English literature there is a corner called 'women in literature' or 'women novelists' and an overall critical approach to literature that assumes it is written by men and perhaps even largely for men. This is why the assumptions of psychological research[43] and of educational research and philosophy take for granted male experience, orientation, and concerns and treat as normative masculine modes of being.

The ideological practices of our society provide women with forms of thought and knowledge that constrain us to treat ourselves as objects. We have learned to set aside as irrelevant, to deny, or to obliterate our own subjectivity and experience. We have learned to live inside a discourse that is not ours and that expresses and describes a landscape in which we are alienated and that preserves that alienation as integral to its practice. In a short story, Doris Lessing describes a girl growing up in Africa whose consciousness has been wholly formed within traditional British literary culture. Her landscape, her cosmology, her moral relations, her botany are those of the English novels and fairy tales. Her own landscape, its forms of life, her immediate everyday world do not fully penetrate and occupy her consciousness. They are not named.[44] Lessing's story is a paradigm of the situation of women in our society. Its general culture is not ours.[45]

Clearly the issue is more than bias. It is more than simply an omission of certain kinds of topics. It involves taking up the standpoint of women as an experience of being, of society, of social and personal process that must be given form and expression in the culture, whether as knowledge, as art, or as literature or political action. This is the work we see now in progress in many forms in the women's movement and beyond. When we speak of 'women's studies', we are identifying a broad range of work that develops and makes way for research, philosophic and theological thinking, poetry, literature, the study of art, history, sociology, law, and other fields giving expression to and building essential knowledge of this whole range of seeing the world from women's place in it. Women's studies identifies space in universities, colleges, and schools, making room for these developments and opening a conduit into the educational system for the astonishing work that is now being done by women in art, philosophy, poetry, scholarship, and political and social theory.

Notes

1. The concept of an 'ideological apparatus' is taken from Althusser's conception of 'ideological state apparatus'. Although I have not used it here with any theoretical rigour, I use it to identify in general the same social forms to which his conception of 'ideological state apparatuses' is applied. See Louis Althusser, 'Ideology and ideological state apparatuses', in *Lenin and Philosophy and Other Essays* (New York: Monthly Review Press, 1971): 127–86.
2. Simone de Beauvoir, *The Second Sex* (New York: Bantam Books, 1961): xv.
3. In much of this literature, women are not directly mentioned. It is the family that is represented as the operative social unit in a child's school achievement. But in practice it has been mothers who actually do the work of child raising, supervision of homework, management of school schedule, and the like in relation to children's schooling. The literature focusing on family and school achievement is largely concerned with what kinds of family organization and practices are most conducive to children's success in school. For example, see the studies in Maurice Craft, ed., *Family, Class and Education: A Reader* (London: Longmans, 1970).
4. J. Kahn and J. Nurstein, *Unwillingly to School* (London: Pergamon Press, 1964): 13–15.
5. Elinor King, 'How the psychiatric profession views women' in Dorothy E. Smith and Sara David, eds, *Women Look at Psychiatry* (Vancouver: Press Gang, 1975).
6. Though the feminist thinking and rethinking of 'the family' is substantial and various, there is still a curious absence of thinking and investigation that takes up women's work as mothers in relation to their children's schooling from the standpoint of women. The latter has been provided with broad theoretical shelter by AnnMarie Wolpe, 'Education and the sexual division of labour', in Annette Kuhn and AnnMarie Wolpe, eds, *Feminism and Materialism* (London: Routledge and Kegan Paul, 1978), but has yet to be established as integral to feminist thinking on mothering and family organization. Nancy Jackson has provided a valuable analysis of these relations at a general level in 'Stress on schools + stress on families = distress for children' (Canadian Teachers' Federation, Ottawa, 1982).
7. Philippe Ariès, *Centuries of Childhood* (Harmondsworth: Penguin, 1975).
8. Christopher Jencks with Marshall Smith, Henry Acland, Mary Jo Bane, David Cohen, Herbert Gintis, Barbara Heyns, and Stephen Michelson, *Inequality: A Reassessment of the Effect of Family and Schooling in America* (New York: Basic Books, 1972).
9. Curiously, although there is now a considerable literature showing how the educational system produced gender inequalities, this tends not to be conceived as a general property of the edu-

cational system, as is 'inequality' as Jencks conceives it or as the role of the educational system in producing inequalities of class. 'Inequality' in the educational context *means* class inequality. See for example the introduction to R.W. Connell, D.J. Ashenden, S. Kessler, and G.W. Dowsett, *Making the Difference: Schools, Families and Social Division* (Sydney: Allen and Unwin Australia, 1982), which is otherwise more successful than most in integrating gender into its description and analysis. Again, Marxist theories have been significant in remedying this deficiency. See Wolpe, 'Education and the sexual division of labour'; Michele Barrett, 'The educational system: Gender and class', in Michele Barrett, *Women's Oppression Today: Problems in Marxist-Feminist Analysis* (London: Virago, 1980); and Madeleine MacDonald, 'Schooling and the reproduction of class and gender relations' in Roger Dale, Geoff Esland, Ross Fergusson, and Madeleine MacDonald, eds, *Education and the State*, vol. 2, *Politics, Patriarchy and Practice* (Basingstoke, England: Falmer Press, 1981): 167–77.

10. See for example Lynn M. Osen, *Women in Mathematics* (Cambridge, Mass.: MIT Press, 1974).

11. These repressions have now, of course, been documented in many studies. Dale Spender's resurrection of the suppressed political thinking of women writing in the English language since the seventeenth century is a valuable introduction to this subterranean tradition: Dale Spender, *Women of Ideas and What Men Have Done to Them: From Aphra Behn to Adrienne Rich* (London: Routledge and Kegan Paul, 1982).

12. Sylvia L. Thrupp, *The Merchant Class of Mediaeval London, 1300–1500* (Ann Arbor: University of Michigan Press, 1962).

13. Margaret Fox, 'Women's speaking justified, proved, and allowed by the Scriptures, all such as speak by the spirit and power of the Lord Jesus' in *A Brief Collection of Remarkable Passages and Occurrences* (London: J. Sowle, 1710): 331–50.

14. Sheila Rowbotham, *Women, Resistance and Revolution* (Harmondsworth: Penguin, 1973).

15. Smache des Jacques, 'Women in the French Revolution: The thirteenth brumaire of Olympe de Gouges, with notes on French amazon battalions' in Ann Forfreedom, ed., *Women Out of History: A Herstory* (Culver City, Calif.: Peace Press, 1972): 131–40.

16. Angela Y. Davis, *Women, Race and Class* (New York: Random House, 1981): 60–4.

17. Thomas Szasz, ed., *The Age of Madness: The History of Involuntary Hospitalization Presented in Selected Texts* (Garden City, N.Y.: Doubleday/Anchor, 1973).

18. Juliet Mitchell, *Women's Estate* (Harmondsworth: Penguin, 1972).

19. Jean Donnison, *Midwives and Medical Men: A History of Inter-Professional Rivalries and Women's Rights* (London: Heinemann, 1977).

20. Mary Roth Walsh, *Doctors Wanted, No Women Need Apply: Sexual Barriers in the Medical Profession, 1835–1875* (New Haven: Yale University Press, 1977).

21. Mary Wollstonecraft, *A Vindication of the Rights of Women* (New York: W.W. Norton, 1967).

22. Jane Martin has given us a brilliant analysis of Rousseau's prescriptions for educating Sophie as Emile's proper mate. Jane Roland Martin, *Reclaiming a Conversation: The Ideal of the Educated Woman* (New Haven: Yale University Press, 1985).

23. With Jane Haddad and Yoko Ueda, I recently updated a study of the effects of declining enrolments for teachers in the public school system in Ontario, Canada. We found that in 1983–84, women were 13.2 per cent of principals and vice-principals in elementary schools, and 9.2 per cent of principals and vice-principals in secondary schools (Dorothy E. Smith, Jane Haddad, and Yoko Ueda, 'Teaching as an internally segregated profession: Women and men teachers in the

public schools of Ontario', typescript, Department of Sociology in Education, Ontario Institute for Studies in Education, January 1987). The larger figure for Canada in general in the early years is most probably due to the larger proportion of rural schools in other provinces. The Ontario records indicate a drop in the proportion of women principals when the smaller rural schools were amalgamated into larger units.

24. The contemporary figures cannot be intimately compared with the earlier ones because the bases are in some cases different. Though in general the overall patterns of male dominance persist, there do appear to be changes in the direction of greater equality, particularly among university academic staff. The situation of public school teachers, however, seems to have changed very little. Here is an update:

Note Table 1   Percentage of Women at Different Levels of the Canadian Educational System, Various Years, 1980–84

Level	% Women	Years
Elementary teachers	71.7%	(1980–81)
Secondary teachers (ex. Quebec)	33.8%	(1980–81)
Community College teaching staff (ex. Quebec)	30.5%	(1983–84)
University (all ranks)	16.3%	(1983–84)

Note Table 2   Percentage of Women in Positions in Canadian Elementary and Secondary Schools, 1980–81

Position	Elementary	Secondary
Teachers	71.7%	33.8%
Department head	33.5%	20.7%
Vice-principal	21.4%	7.6%
Principal	14.8%	3.9%

Source: Statistics Canada, *Educational Staff of Public Schools*, Cat. 81–202, Ottawa: Minister of Supply and Services, February 1982, table 1, 'Number of Educators by Teaching Level, Staff Position and Sex, 1980–81'.

Note Table 3   Percentage of Women Educational Staff in Canadian Community Colleges by Position, 1983–84

Position	% Women
Teaching staff	30.5%
Academic administrative staff	24.9%

Source: Statistics Canada, *Educational Staff of Community Colleges and Vocational Schools*, Cat. 81–241, Ottawa: Minister of Supply and Services, September 1985, table 1, 'Number of Full-time University Teachers by Rank, Sex and Region, Selected years, 1960–61 to 1983–84'.

Note Table 4   Percentage of Women in Canadian Academic Positions, All Ranks, 1983–84

Position	% Women
Nonladder positions	37%
Assistant professors	26.7%
Associate professors	14.3%
Full professors	5.3%

Source: Statistics Canada, *Teachers in Universities, 1983-84*, Cat. 81–254, Ottawa: Minister of Supply and Services, January 1986, table 2, 'Full-time staff by Province, Type of Institution, Staff Position and Sex, 1983–84'.

25. Mary Ellman, *Thinking about Women* (New York: Harcourt Brace Jovanovich, 1968).

26. Philip Goldberg, 'Are women prejudiced against women?' *Transaction*, April 1969: 28–30.

27. Jo Freeman, 'The social construction of the second sex' in Michele Hoffnung Garskoff, ed., *Roles Women Play: Readings towards Women's Liberation* (Belmont, Calif.: Brooks/Cole Publishing, 1971): 123–41.

28. Lucy Komisar, 'The image of women in advertising' in Vivian Gornick and Barbara Moran, eds, *Women in Sexist Society: Studies in Power and Powerlessness* (New York: Signet Books, 1972): 304–17.

29. Phyllis Chesler, 'Patient and patriarch: Women in the psychotherapeutic relationship' in Gornick and Moran, *Women in Sexist Society*: 362-92. Since her study, the situation has been radically transformed by the development of feminist therapeutic approaches. Editing a book on women and psychiatry and working with a feminist therapist in describing her experiments with a feminist strategy has given me some understanding. See Alison Griffith, 'Feminist counselling: A perspective', Rita MacDonald and Dorothy E. Smith, 'A feminist therapy session', and Sara J. David, 'Becoming a non-sexist therapist', in Dorothy E. Smith and Sara J. David, eds, *Women Look at Psychiatry* (Vancouver: Press Gang, 1975). Feminist therapy has made very considerable strides since those early days, but Miriam Greenspan's *A New Approach to Women and Therapy: Why Current Therapies Fail Women—And What Women and Therapists Can Do about It!* (New York: McGraw-Hill, 1983) indicates that there is still much to be done. Judith Antrobus's view is pessimistic.

The community of professional therapists committed to feminist therapy is extremely small. In the New York area virtually all therapists train at one of the psychoanalytic institutes after obtaining their advanced degrees. The institutes are conventional and traditional, and reflect a pervasive male bias. A few institutes offer a token course on the psychology of women or on psychotherapy with women. What impact will one course have alongside years of psychoanalytic training? Yet women as well as men flock to these institutes. When asked why, they say they need additional training or they need sources or referral later, or whatever. The point cannot be made often enough that most patients are women and most therapists are men who know little or nothing about the context of women's lives or the psychological development of women.

Judith Antrobus, 'In the final analysis', review of Hannah Lerman, *A Mote in Freud's Eye: From Psychoanalysis to the Psychology of Women, Women's Review of Books*, 4, 5 (February 1987).

30. L.S. Fidell, 'Empirical verification of sex discrimination in hiring practices in psychology', *American Psychologist* 2, 12 (1970): 1094–7.

31. Tillie Olsen, 'One out of twelve: Writers who are women in our century' in Tillie Olsen, *Silences* (New York: Delacorte Press/Seymour Lawrence, 1978): 40.

32. Ibid.

33. See Jessie Bernard, 'Talk, conversation, listening, silence' in *The Sex Game* (New York: Atheneum, 1972), chap. 6: 135–64, for a general characterization of these patterns.

34. F.I. Strodtbeck and R.D. Mann, 'Sex role differentiation in jury deliberations', *Sociometry* 19 (March 1956): 3–11.

35. William Caudill, *The Psychiatric Hospital as a Small Society* (Cambridge, Mass.: Harvard University Press, 1958): 249.

36. Candace West, 'Sexism and conversation: Everything you always wanted to know about Sachs (but were afraid to ask)', MA thesis, Department of Sociology, University of California, Santa Barbara, California. More recent work substantiating and further specifying the effects described here include Elizabeth Aries, 'Interaction patterns and themes of male, female, and mixed sex groups: Are traditional sex roles changing?' *Psychological Reports* 51 (1982): 127–34; Joseph Berger, Susan J. Rosenholtz, and Morris Zelditch, Jr, 'Status organizing processes' in Alex Inkeles *et al.*, eds, *Annual Review of Sociology* (Palo Alto, Calif.: Annual Revues, 1980), 6: 479–508; Mary Parlee Brown, 'Conversation politics', *Psychology Today*, May 1979: 48–56; John A. Courtright, Frank E. Millar, and L. Edna Rogers Millar, 'Domineeringness and dominance: Replication and expansion', *Communication Monographs* 46 (1979): 179–92; Starkey Duncan, Jr, and Donald W. Fiske, *Face-to-Face Interaction* (Hillsdale, N.J.: Lawrence Erlbaum Associates, 1977); Barbara Eakins and Gene Eakins, 'Verbal turn-taking and exchanges in faculty dialogue' in Betty Lou Dubois and Isabel Crouch, eds, *The Sociology of the Languages of American Women* (San Antonio, Tex.: Trinity University, 1976): 53–62; Carole Edelsky, 'Who's got the floor?' *Language in Society* 10 (1981): 383–421; Sheryle B. Eubanks, 'Sex-based language differences: A cultural reflection' in Reza Ordoubadian and Walburga von-Raffler Engel, eds, *Views on Langauge* (Murfreesboro, Tenn.: Inter-University Publishers, 1975): 109–20; Pamela M. Fishman, 'Conversational insecurity' in Howard Giles, W. Peter Robinson, and Philip M. Smith, eds, *Language: Social Psychological Perspectives* (New York: Pergamon Press, 1980): 127–32; Pamela M. Fishman, 'Interaction: the work women do', *Social Problems* 25 (1978): 397–406; Pamela M. Fishman, 'What do couples talk about when they're alone?' in Douglas Butturff and Edmund L. Epstein, eds, *Women's Language and Style* (Akron, Ohio, L&S Books, 1978): 11–22; Nancy Henley, *Body Politics: Power, Sex and Nonverbal Communication* (Englewood Cliffs, N.J.: Prentice-Hall, Spectrum, 1977); Susan Freeman Hoffman, 'Interruptions: Structure and tactics in dyadic conversations', paper given at the International Communication Association convention, Acapulco, Mexico, 1980; Janet L. Johnson, 'Questions and role responsibility in four professional meetings', *Anthropological Linguistics* 22 (1980): 66–76; Carol W. Kennedy, 'Patterns of verbal interruption among women and men in groups', paper given at Third Annual Conference on Communication, Language, and Gender, Lawrence, Kansas, 1980; Julie R. McMillan, A. Kay Clifton, Diane McGrath, and Wanda S. Gale, 'Women's language: Uncertainty or interpersonal sensitivity and emotionality?' *Sex Roles* 3 (1977): 545–59; Michael Natale, Elliot Entin, and

Joseph Jaff, 'Vocal interruptions in a dyadic communication as a function of speech and social anxiety', *Journal of Personality and Social Psychology* 37 (1979): 865–78; Mary Octigan and Sharon Niederman, 'Male dominance in conversations', *Frontiers* 4, 1 (1979): 50–4; Dale Spender, *Man Made Language* (London: Routledge and Kegan Paul, 1980); Marjorie Swacker, 'Women's verbal behaviour at learned and professional conferences' in Dubois and Crouch, *Sociology of the Language of American Women*: 155–60; Candace West, 'Against our will: Male interruption of females in cross-sex conversations' in Judith Orsanu, Miriam K. Slater, and Leonore Loeb Adler, eds, *Language, Sex and Gender* (New York: New York Academy of Sciences, 1979): 81–97; idem, 'When the doctor is a "lady": Power, status and gender in physician-patient dialogues' in Ann Stromberg, ed., *Women, Health and Medicine* (Palo Alto, Calif.: Mayfield, 1981); Candace West and Don Zimmerman, 'Sex roles, interruptions and silences in conversation' in Barrie Thorne and Nancy Henley, eds, *Language and Sex: Differences and Dominance* (Rowley, Mass.: Newbury House, 1975): 105–29; Frank N. Willis and Sharon J. Williams, 'Simultaneous talking in conversation and sex of speakers', *Perceptual and Motor Skills* 43 (1976): 1067–70.

37. Celia Gilbert, *Queen of Darkness* (New York: Viking Press, 1977).

38. West, *op. cit.*

39. Anya Bostock, talk on the British Broadcasting Corporation Third Programme, published in *The Listener*, August 1972.

40. Louise Bernikow, *The World Split Open: Four Centuries of Women Poets in England and America, 1552–1950* (New York: Vintage Books, 1974).

41. Rowbotham, *Women, Resistance and Revolution*.

42. Jessie Bernard, *Academic Women* (New York: New American Library, 1964).

43. Carolyn Woods Sherif, 'Bias in psychology' in Julia A. Sherman and Evelyn Torton Beck, *The Prism of Sex: Essays in the Sociology of Knowledge* (Madison: University of Wisconsin Press, 1979): 93–133.

44. Doris Lessing, 'The old chief Msh Langa' in *The Black Madonna* (St Albans, England: Granada Publishing, 1966).

45. This is a particular instance where I most powerfully feel the absence of nonwhite women. For of course the texts of the white women's movement have obliterated their subjectivity and experience in ways directly parallel with those described here and here attributed to a general women's experience with the totalitarianism of male texts.

JÜRGEN HABERMAS

1929–
GERMANY

Major Works

1970	*Toward a Rational Society*
1971	*Knowledge and Human Interest*
1973	*Theory and Practice*
1975	*Legitimation Crisis*
1979	*Communication and the Evolution of Society*
1984	*The Theory of Communicative Action*, vol. 1, *Reason and the Rationalization of Society*
1987	*The Theory of Communicative Action*, vol. 2, *Lifeworld and System: A Critique of Functional Reason*
1988	*Lectures on the Philosophical Discourse of Modernity*
1989	*The Structural Transformation of the Public Sphere*
1990	*Moral Consciousness and Communicative Action*
1998	*On the Pragmatics of Communication*
2001	*The Postnational Constellation: Political Essays*
2001	*The Liberating Power of Symbols: Philosophical Essays*

This concept of *communicative rationality* carries with it connotations based ultimately on the central experience of the unconstrained, unifying, consensus-bringing force of argumentative speech, in which different participants overcome their merely subjective views and, owing to the mutuality of rationally motivated conviction, assure themselves of both the unity of the objective world and the intersubjectivity of their lifeworld.[1]

The concept of knowledge-constitutive human interests already conjoins the two elements whose relation still has to be explained: knowledge and interest. From everyday experience we know that ideas serve often enough to furnish our actions with justifying motives in place of the real ones. What is called rationalization at this level is called ideology at the level of collective action. In both cases the manifest content of statements is falsified by consciousness' unreflected tie to interests, despite its illusion of autonomy.[2]

—Jürgen Habermas

The theoretical perspective known as 'Critical Theory', particularly that of the Frankfurt School of Social Research, had a long and varied tradition in the twentieth century. Its emergence out of the work of Marx within the sociological frame, occasionally melded with Freud's psychoanalytical theory, has given it a special place in theoretical discussion and what is often called 'emancipatory' political life and activism. The work of Jürgen Habermas continues much of this critical theoretical tradition and adds volumes to the body of sociological literature.

Habermas carries on and refines the work of the Frankfurt School in Germany, the real centre of critical theory. Not only does he add to this perspective, he traces the immense body of theory that makes up most of nineteenth- and twentieth-century sociology. His eclectic method freshly presented, reconstructed, and critiqued such theorists as Marx, Weber, Durkheim, Mead, Parsons, Lukacs, Horkheimer, and Adorno (the last three from the Frankfurt School). Habermas is a voluminous writer, often turgid, dense, and difficult. To attempt to capture here his thought, or even its historical development and progression, would be impossible. Within this introduction we hope to alert the reader to the major concepts he addresses and the main themes he sets in this particular excerpt.

In our present era, often described as postmodernist (a perspective for which Habermas had a formidable critique[3]), Habermas has been called 'the last great rationalist'.[4] Contemporary society is portrayed as fragmented and relativized by the postmodern. Habermas strives to sustain the power of the rational, reasoned perspective, advocating that we can move beyond the pessimism of Weber's 'rationalization of the world' to a new 'ideal' form of communicative competence and action utilizing a rational unity.

In the course of his work, Habermas examines and reiterates a number of central arguments and themes: he criticizes Weber's 'rationalization' thesis; he recognizes the shortcomings of Marx's presentation of the 'labour theory of value', given twentieth-century scientific and technological developments; he deals with the philosophical and sociological nature of knowledge and its relationship to 'interest'; he explores the 'legitimation crisis' within historical and contemporary understandings of capitalism; he outlines the transformations taking place within the public and private domains; and as noted, he attempts to explore the importance of communicative action within the various moments of our everyday lifeworlds. His analysis is extensive and often abstract (although he does mention at one point a National Football League team).

In the excerpt that follows, 'Technology and Science as "Ideology"', from *Toward a Rational Society* (1970), many of the themes that are developed in his later work are already emerging—these seeds are beginning to take root and grow. This is not to suggest that the immense complexity and trajectory of Habermas's work are easily or entirely revealed here. But, perhaps because this particular essay was written for Herbert Marcuse on his seventieth birthday in

1968, the writing seems somewhat more publicly available. Within this piece we re-encounter or encounter for the first time Marx, Weber, and Marcuse's *One-Dimensional Man.*

Habermas opens this work with Weber's conceptualization of 'rationalization'—means/end rationality ('instrumental' action)—and how this process has influenced every domain of human experience, including communicative rationality, a central concern of much of his work. Habermas sees two distinct worlds that have been subject to this incipient process of rationalization: the domain of *work* and the domain of *interaction.* He later expresses these domains as *the system world* and *lifeworld.* As Anthony Giddens explains, 'The evolution of human society proceeds in two separable but connected dimensions: the development of the forces of production (which can be thematised as instrumental knowledge, oriented to technical control), and the development of normative orders (which can be thematised as symbolic norms ordering communication).'[5]

For Habermas, the rationalization of these domains of human experience need not necessarily lead to greater domination and oppression—'rationality' has a liberating dimension as well as an oppressive dimension. Through more authenticity and sincerity within communicative actions, liberating tendencies might prevail. This leads him to questions of 'legitimacy' and the place of 'science and technology as ideology'. The development of bourgeois ideology, along with critical developments unifying science and technology, shift the manner in which legitimations are sustained within modern, capitalist societies. Legitimations are always present. Historical, traditional forms 'from above', he argues, are now being supplanted by materialist, productive forces 'from below'. As he writes, 'Today, domination perpetuates and extends itself not only through technology, but *as* technology.'[6] Science and technology, through their force as ideologies, generate a shift in forms of legitimation—from those of cultural tradition to those 'from below', the material forms created within purposive-rational action systems. The intertwining of these domains, recognized by Marcuse as political, means that technology, in particular, can no longer be seen as a 'neutral' phenomenon.

To reiterate, the domains of *work* and *interaction* become increasingly rationalized, bureaucratized, and indeed saturated by forms of action and communication that militate against sincere human encounters.

> Whether in city or country, it induces an urbanization of the *form* of life. That is, it generates subcultures that train the individual to be able to 'switch over' at any moment from an interaction context to purposive-rational action.[7]

Habermas also sees two other tendencies emerging in advanced capitalist countries: 'an increase in state intervention in order to secure the system's stability, and a growing interdependence of research and technology, which has turned the sciences into the leading productive force'.[8] With this increase in state intervention, the 'free market' ideology begins to disintegrate; indeed, it is replaced by a 'substitute' program, which is aimed at mitigating the dynamics of capitalism. Ironically (at least in Habermas's view), such increased intervention 'depoliticizes' the mass of the population. This moves him to ask the question related to the 'vital need for legitimation: how will the depoliticization of the masses be made plausible to them? Marcuse would be able to answer: by having technology and science *also* take on the role of an ideology.'[9]

Wrapped in all of this are central themes for Habermas: legitimation, domination, the rationalization of all human spheres of experience—the public and the private, the distortion of communication forms, adaptation of human beings to the technical, i.e., purposive-rational action or instrumentality. He inevitably calls for a 'decolonization' of the lifeworld.

Habermas ends this essay recognizing new zones of conflict within the public sphere. Because this piece was written in 1968, the place of student resistance is front and centre. Although he was critical of the dynamics emergent at that time (calling aspects of it 'left fascism'), his comments regarding forms of resistance and protest, as well as his extensive critique of the 'rationalization' of society and communicative competence within these social shifts and changes, seem equally useful today.

Notes

1. Jürgen Habermas, *The Theory of Communicative Action*, vol. 1, *Reason and the Rationalization of Society*, trans. Thomas McCarthy (Boston: Beacon Press, 1984), 10.
2. Jürgen Habermas, *Knowledge and Human Interest* (Boston: Beacon Press, 1971), 311.
3. See Jürgen Habermas, *Lectures on the Philosophical Discourse of Modernity*, trans. Frederick Lawrence (Cambridge, Mass.: MIT Press, 1988).
4. Habermas, *The Theory of Communicative Action*, vol. 1, vi. (Note: Thomas McCarthy's 'Translator's Introduction' is considered one of the most useful commentaries on Habermas's work.)
5. Anthony Giddens, *Profiles and Critiques in Social Theory* (Berkeley: University of California Press, 1982), 93.
6. Jürgen Habermas, *Toward a Rational Society: Student Protest, Science and Politics*, trans. Jeremy J. Shapiro (Boston: Beacon Press, 1970), 85.
7. Ibid., 98.
8. Ibid., 100.
9. Ibid., 104.

Technology and Science as 'Ideology'
Translated by Jeremy J. Shapiro

For Herbert Marcuse on his seventieth birthday, July 19, 1968

Max Weber introduced the concept of 'rationality' in order to define the form of capitalist economic activity, bourgeois private law, and bureaucratic authority. Rationalization means, first of all, the extension of the areas of society subject to the criteria of rational decision. Second, social labor is industrialized, with the result that criteria of instrumental action also penetrate into other areas of life (urbanization of the mode of life, technification of transport and communication). Both trends exemplify the type of purposive-rational action, which refers to either the organization of means or choice between alternatives. Planning can be regarded as purposive-rational action of the second order. It aims at the establishment, improvement, or expansion of systems of purposive-rational action themselves.

The progressive 'rationalization' of society is linked to the institutionalization of scientific and technical development. To the extent that technology and science permeate social institutions and thus transform them, old legitimations are destroyed. The secularization and 'disenchantment' of action-orienting worldviews, of cultural tradition as a whole, is the obverse of the growing rationality of social action.

Herbert Marcuse has taken these analyses as a point of departure in order to demonstrate that the formal concept of rationality—which Weber derived from the purposive-rational action of the capitalist entrepreneur, the industrial wage laborer, the abstract legal person, and the modern administrative official and based on the criteria of science as well as technology—has specific substantive implications. Marcuse is convinced that what Weber called 'rationalization' realizes not rationality as such but rather, in the name of rationality, a specific form of unacknowledged political domination. Because this sort of rationality extends to the correct choice among strategies, the appropriate application of technologies, and the efficient establishment of systems (with *presupposed* aims in *given* situations), it removes the total social framework of interests in which strategies are chosen, technologies applied, and systems established, from the scope of reflection and rational reconstruction. Moreover, this rationality extends only to relations of possible technical control and therefore requires a type of action that implies domination, whether of nature or of society. By virtue of its structure, purposive-rational action is the exercise of control. That is why, in accordance with this rationality, the 'rationalization' of the conditions of life is synonymous with the institutionalization of a form of domination whose political character becomes unrecognizable: the technical reason of a social system of purposive-rational action does not lose its political content. Marcuse's critique of Weber comes to the conclusion that

the very concept of technical reason is perhaps ideological. Not only the application of technology but technology itself is domination (of nature and men)—methodical, scientific, calculated, calculating control. Specific purposes and interests of domination are not foisted upon technology 'subsequently' and from the outside; they enter the very construction of the technical apparatus. Technology is always a historical-social project: in it is projected what a society and its ruling interests intend to do with men and things. Such a 'purpose' of domination is 'substantive' and to this extent belongs to the very form of technical reason.[1]

As early as 1956 Marcuse referred in a quite different context to the peculiar phenomenon that in industrially advanced capitalist societies domination tends to lose its exploitative and oppressive character and become 'rational', without political domination thereby disappearing: 'domination is dependent only on the capacity and drive to maintain and extend the apparatus as a whole.'[2] Domination is rational in that a system can be maintained which can allow itself to make the growth of the forces of production, coupled with scientific and technical progress, the basis of its legitimation although, at the same time, the level of the productive forces constitutes a potential in relation to which 'the renunciations and burdens placed on individuals seem more and more unnecessary and irrational.'[3] In Marcuse's judgment, the objectively superfluous repression can be recognized in the 'intensified subjection of individuals to the enormous apparatus of production and distribution, in the deprivatization of free time, in the almost indistinguishable fusion of constructive and destructive social labor.'[4] Paradoxically, however, this repression can disappear from the consciousness of the population because the legitimation of domination has assumed a new character: it refers to the 'constantly increasing productivity and domination of nature which keeps individuals . . . living in increasing comfort.'[5]

The institutionalized growth of the forces of production following from scientific and technical progress surpasses all historical proportions. From it the institutional framework draws its opportunity for legitimation. The thought that relations of production can be measured against the potential of developed productive forces is prevented because the existing relations of production present themselves as the technically necessary organizational form of a rationalized society. Here 'rationality', in Weber's sense, shows its Janus face. It is no longer only a critical standard for the developmental level of the forces of production in relation to which the objectively superfluous, repressive character of historically obsolete relations of production can be exposed. It is also an apologetic standard through which these same relations of production can be justified as a functional institutional framework. Indeed, in relation to its apologetic serviceability, 'rationality' is weakened as a critical standard and degraded to a corrective *within* the system: what can still be said is at best that society is 'poorly programmed'. At the stage of their scientific-technical development, then, the forces of production appear to enter a new constellation with the relations of production. Now they no longer function as the basis of a critique of prevailing legitimations in the interest of political enlightenment, but become instead the basis of legitimation. *This* is what Marcuse conceives of as world-historically new.

But if this is the case, must not the rationality embodied in systems of purposive-rational action be understood as specifically limited? Must not the rationality of science and technology, instead of being reducible to unvarying rules of logic and method have absorbed a substantive, historically derived, and therefore transitory a priori structure? Marcuse answers in the affirmative:

> The principles of modern science were a priori structured in such a way that they could serve as conceptual instruments for a universe of self-propelling, productive control; theoretical operationalism came to correspond to practical operationalism. The scientific method which led to the ever-more-effective domination of nature thus came to provide the pure concepts as well as the instrumentalities for the ever-more-effective domination of man by man through the domination of nature . . . Today, domination perpetuates and extends itself not only through technology but as technology, and the latter provides the great legitimation of the expanding political power, which absorbs all spheres of culture.
>
> In this universe, technology also provides the great rationalization of the unfreedom of man and demonstrates the 'technical' impossibility of being autonomous, of determining one's own life. For this unfreedom appears neither as irrational nor as political, but rather as submission to the technical apparatus which enlarges the comforts of life and increases the productivity of labor. Technological rationality thus protects rather than cancels the legitimacy of domination and the instrumentalist horizon of reason opens on a rationally totalitarian society.[6]

Weber's 'rationalization' is not only a long-term process of the transformation of social structures but simultaneously 'rationalization' in Freud's sense: the true motive, the perpetuation of objectively obsolete domination, is concealed through the invocation of purposive-rational imperatives. This invocation is possible only because the rationality of science and technology is immanently one of control: the rationality of domination.

Marcuse owes this concept, according to which modern science is a historical formation, equally to Husserl's treatise on the crisis of European science and Heidegger's destruction of Western metaphysics. From the materialist position Ernst Bloch has developed the viewpoint that the rationality of modern science is, in its roots, distorted by capitalism in such a way as to rob modern technology of the innocence of a pure productive force. But Marcuse is the first to make the 'political content of technical reason' the analytical point of departure for a theory of advanced capitalist society. Because he not only develops this viewpoint philosophically but also attempts to corroborate it through sociological analysis, the difficulties inherent in this conception become visible. I shall refer here to but one ambiguity contained in Marcuse's own conception.

If the phenomenon on which Marcuse bases his social analysis, i.e. the peculiar *fusion of technology and domination*, rationality and oppression, could not be interpreted otherwise than as a world 'project', as Marcuse says in the language of Sartre's phenomenology, contained in the material a priori of the logic of science and technology and determined by class interest and historical situation, then social emancipation could not be conceived without a complementary revolutionary transformation of science and technology themselves. In several passages Marcuse is tempted to pursue this idea of a New Science in connection with the promise, familiar in Jewish and Protestant mysticism, of the 'resurrection of fallen nature'. This theme, well-known for having penetrated into Schelling's (and Baader's) philosophy via Swabian Pietism, returns in Marx's *Paris Manuscripts*, today constitutes the central thought of Bloch's philosophy, and, in reflected forms, also directs the more secret hopes of Walter Benjamin, Max Horkheimer, and Theodor W. Adorno. It is also present in Marcuse's thought:

> The point which I am trying to make is that science, by virtue of its own method and concepts, has projected and promoted a universe in which the domination of nature has remained linked to the domination of man—a link which tends to be fatal to this universe as a whole. Nature, scientifically comprehended and mastered, reappears in the technical apparatus of production and destruction which sustains and improves the life of the individuals while subordinating them to the masters of the apparatus. Thus the rational hierarchy merges with the social one. If this is the case, then the change in the direction of progress, which might sever this fatal link, would also affect the very structure of science—the scientific project. Its hypotheses, without losing their rational character, would develop in an essentially different experimental context (that of a pacified world); consequently, science would arrive at essentially different concepts of nature and establish essentially different facts.[7]

In a logical fashion Marcuse envisages not only different modes of theory formation but a different scientific methodology in general. The transcendental framework within which nature would be made the object of a new experience would then no longer be the functional system of instrumental action. The viewpoint of possible technical control would be replaced by one of preserving, fostering, and releasing the potentialities of nature: 'there are two kinds of mastery: a repressive and a liberating one.'[8] To this view it must be objected that modern science can be interpreted as a historically unique project only if at least one alternative project is thinkable. And, in addition, an alternative New Science would have to include the definition of a New Technology. This is a sobering consideration because technology, if based at all on a project, can only be traced back to a 'project' of the human species *as a whole*, and not to one that could be historically surpassed.

Arnold Gehlen has pointed out in what seems to me conclusive fashion that there is an immanent connection between the technology known to us and the structure of purposive-rational action. If we comprehend the behavioral system of action regulated by its own results as the conjunction of rational decision and instrumental action, then we can reconstruct the history of technology from the point of view of the step-by-step objectivation of the elements of that very system. In any case technological development lends itself to being interpreted as though the human species had taken the elementary components of the behavioral system of purposive-rational action, which is primarily rooted in the human organism, and projected them one after another onto the plane of technical instruments, thereby unburdening itself of the corresponding functions.[9] At first the functions of the motor apparatus (hands and legs) were augmented and replaced, followed by energy production (of the human body), the functions of the sensory apparatus (eyes, ears, and skin), and finally by the functions of the governing center (the brain). Technological development thus follows a logic that corresponds to the structure of purposive-rational action regulated by its own results, which is in fact the structure of *work*. Realizing this, it is impossible to envisage how, as long as the organization of human nature does not change and as long therefore as we have to achieve self-preservation through social labor and with the aid of means that substitute for work, we could renounce technology, more particularly *our* technology, in favor of a qualitatively different one.

Marcuse has in mind an alternative *attitude* to nature, but it does not admit of the idea of a New Technology. Instead of treating nature as the object of possible technical control, we can encounter her as an opposing partner in a possible interaction. We can seek out a fraternal rather than an exploited nature. At the level of an as yet incomplete intersubjectivity we can impute subjectivity to animals and plants, even to minerals, and try to communicate with nature instead of merely processing her under conditions of severed communication. And the idea that a still enchained subjectivity of nature cannot be unbound until men's communication among themselves is free from domination has retained, to say the least, a singular attraction. Only if men could communicate without compulsion and each could recognize himself in the other, could mankind possibly recognize nature as another subject: not, as idealism would have it, as its Other, but as a subject of which mankind itself is the Other.

Be that as it may, the achievements of technology, which are indispensable as such, could surely not be substituted for by an awakened nature. The alternative to existing technology, the project of nature as opposing partner instead of object, refers to an alternative structure of action: to symbolic interaction in distinction to purposive-rational action. This means, however, that the two projects are projections of work and of language, i.e. projects of the human species as a whole, and not of an individual epoch, a specific class, or a surpassable situation. The idea of a New Science will not stand up to logical scrutiny any more than that of a New Technology, if indeed science is to retain the meaning of modern science inherently oriented to possible technical control. For this function, as for scientific-technical progress in general, there is no more 'humane' substitute.

Marcuse himself seems to doubt whether it is meaningful to relativize as a 'project' the rationality of science and technology. In many passages of *One-Dimensional Man*, revolutionizing technological rationality means only a transformation of the institutional framework which would leave untouched the forces of production as such. The structure of scientific-technical progress would be conserved, and only the governing values would be changed. New values would be translated into technically solvable tasks. The *direction* of this progress would be new, but the standard of rationality itself would remain unchanged:

> Technics, as a universe of instrumentalities, may increase the weakness as well as the power of man. At the present stage, he is perhaps more powerless over his own apparatus than he ever was before.[10]

This sentence reinstates the political innocence of the forces of production. Here Marcuse is only renewing the classical definition of the relationship between the productive forces and the production relations. But in so doing, he is as far from coming to grips with the new constellation at which he is aiming as he was with the assertion that the productive forces are thoroughly corrupted in their political implications. What is singular about the 'rationality' of science and technology is that it characterizes the growing potential of self-surpassing productive forces which continually threaten the institutional framework *and at the same time*, set the standard of legitimation for the production relations that restrict this potential. The dichotomy of this rationality cannot be adequately represented either by historicizing the concept nor by returning to the orthodox view: neither the model of the original sin of scientific-technical progress nor that of its innocence do it justice. The most sensible formulation of the matter in question seems to me to be the following:

> The technological a priori is a political a priori inasmuch as the transformation of nature involves that of man, and inasmuch as the 'man-made creations' issue from and reenter a societal ensemble. One may still insist that the machinery of the technological universe is 'as such' indifferent towards political ends—it can revolutionize or retard a society. An electronic computer can serve equally in capitalist or socialist administrations; a cyclotron can be an equally efficient tool for a war party or a peace party. . . . However, when technics becomes the universal form of material production, it circumscribes an entire culture; it projects a historical totality—a 'world'.[11]

The difficulty, which Marcuse has only obscured with the notion of the political content of technical reason, is to determine in a categorially precise manner the meaning of the expansion of the rational form of science and technology, i.e. the rationality embodied in systems of purposive-rational action, to the proportions of a life form, of the 'historical totality' of a life-world. This is the same process that Weber meant to designate and explain as the rationalization of society. I believe that neither Weber nor Marcuse has satisfactorily accounted for it. Therefore I should like to attempt to reformulate Weber's concept of rationalization in another frame of reference in order to discuss on this new basis Marcuse's critique of Weber, as well as his thesis of the double function of scientific-technical progress (as productive force and as ideology). I am proposing an interpretative scheme that, in the format of an essay, can be introduced but not seriously validated with regard to its utility. The historical generalizations thus serve only to clarify this scheme and are no substitute for its scientific substantiation.

By means of the concept of 'rationalization' Weber attempted to grasp the repercussions of scientific-technical progress on the institutional framework of societies engaged in 'modernization'. He shared this interest with the classical sociological tradition in general, whose pairs of polar concepts all revolve about the same problem: how to construct a conceptual model of the institutional change brought about by the extension of subsystems of purposive-rational action. Status and contract, *Gemeinschaft* and *Gesellschaft*, mechanical and organic solidarity, informal and formal groups, primary and secondary groups, culture and civilization, traditional and bureaucratic authority, sacral and secular associations, military and industrial society, status group and class—all of these pairs of concepts represent as many attempts to grasp the structural change of the institutional framework of a traditional society on the way to becoming a modern one. Even Parsons' catalog of possible alternatives of value-orientations belongs in the list of these attempts, although he would not admit it. Parsons claims that his list systematically represents the decisions between alternative value-orientations that must be made by the subject of any action whatsoever, regardless of the particular or historical context. But if one examines the list, one can scarcely overlook the historical situation of the inquiry on which it is based. The four pairs of alternative value-orientations,

> affectivity versus affective neutrality,
> particularism versus universalism,
> ascription versus achievement,
> diffuseness versus specificity,

which are supposed to take into account *all* possible fundamental decisions, are tailored to an analysis of *one* historical process. In fact they define the relative dimensions of the modification of dominant attitudes in the transition from traditional to modern society. Subsystems of purposive-rational action do indeed demand orientation to the postponement of gratification, universal norms, individual achievement and active mastery, and specific and analytic relationships, rather than to the opposite orientations.

In order to reformulate what Weber called 'rationalization', I should like to go beyond the subjective approach that Parsons shares with Weber and propose another categorial framework. I shall take as my starting point the fundamental distinction between *work* and *interaction*.[12]

By 'work' or *purposive-rational action* I understand either instrumental action or rational choice or their conjunction. Instrumental action is governed by *technical rules* based on empirical knowledge. In every case they imply conditional predictions about observable events, physical or social. These predictions can prove correct or incorrect. The conduct of rational choice is governed by *strategies* based on analytic knowledge. They imply deductions from preference rules (value systems) and decision procedures; these propositions are either correctly or incorrectly deduced. Purposive-rational action realizes defined goals under given condition. But while instrumental action organizes means that are appropriate or inappropriate according to criteria of an effective control of reality, strategic action depends only on the correct evaluation of possible alternative choices, which results from calculation supplemented by values and maxims.

By 'interaction', on the other hand, I understand *communicative action*, symbolic interaction. It is governed by binding *consensual norms*, which define reciprocal expectations about behavior and which must be understood and recognized by at least two acting subjects. Social norms are enforced through sanctions. Their meaning is objectified in ordinary language communication. While the validity of technical rules and strategies depends on that of empirically true or analytically correct propositions, the validity of social norms is grounded only in the intersubjectivity of the mutual understanding of intentions and secured by the general recognition of obligations. Violation of a rule has a different consequence according to type. *Incompetent* behavior, which violates valid technical rules or strategies, is condemned per se to failure through lack of success; the 'punishment' is built, so to speak, into its rebuff by reality. *Deviant* behavior, which violates consensual norms, provokes sanctions that are connected with the rules only externally, that is by convention. Learned rules of purposive-rational action supply us with *skills*, internalized norms with *personality structures*. Skills put us in a position to solve problems; motivations allow us to follow norms. The diagram below summarizes these definitions. They demand a more precise explanation, which I cannot give here. It is above all the bottom column which I am neglecting here, and it refers to the very problem for whose solution I am introducing the distinction between work and interaction.

	Institutional framework: symbolic interaction	**Systems of purposive-rational (instrumental and strategic) action**
action-orienting rules	social norms	technical rules
level of definition	intersubjectively shared ordinary language	context-free language
type of definition	reciprocal expectations about behavior	conditional predictions conditional imperatives
mechanisms of acquisition	role internalization	learning of skills and qualifications
function of action type	maintenance of institutions (conformity to norms on the basis of reciprocal enforcement)	problem-solving (goal attainment, defined in means-ends relations)
sanctions against violation of rules	punishment on the basis of conventional sanctions: failure against authority	inefficacy: failure in reality
'rationalization'	emancipation, individuation; extension of communication free of domination	growth of productive forces; extension of power of technical control

In terms of the two types of action we can distinguish between social systems according to whether purposive-rational action or interaction predominates. The institutional framework of a society consists of norms that guide symbolic interaction. But there are subsystems such as (to keep to Weber's examples) the economic system or the state apparatus, in which primarily sets of purposive-rational action are institutionalized. These contrast with subsystems such as family and kinship structures, which, although linked to a number of tasks and skills, are primarily based on moral rules of interaction. So I shall distinguish generally at the analytic level between (1) the *institutional framework* of a society or the sociocultural life-world and (2) the *subsystems of purposive-rational action* that are 'embedded' in it. Insofar as actions are determined by the institutional framework they are both guided and enforced by norms. Insofar as they are determined by subsystems of purposive-rational action, they conform to patterns of instrumental or strategic action. Of course, only institutionalization can guarantee that such action will in fact follow definite technical rules and expected strategies with adequate probability.

With the help of these distinctions we can reformulate Weber's concept of 'rationalization'.

The term 'traditional society' has come to denote all social systems that generally meet the criteria of civilizations. The latter represent a specific stage in the evolution of the human species. They differ in several traits from more primitive social forms: (1) A centralized ruling power (state organization of political power in contrast to tribal organization); (2) The division of society into socioeconomic classes (distribution to individuals of social obligations and rewards according to class membership and not according to kinship status); (3) The prevalence of a central worldview (myth, complex religion) to the end of legitimating political power (thus converting power into authority). Civilizations are established on the basis of a relatively developed technology and of division of labor in the social process of production, which make possible a surplus product, i.e. a quantity of goods exceeding that needed for the satisfaction of immediate and elementary needs. They owe their existence to the solution of the problem that first arises with the production of a surplus product, namely, how to distribute wealth and labor both unequally and yet legitimately according to criteria other than those generated by a kinship system.[13]

In our context it is relevant that despite considerable differences in their level of development, civilizations, based on an economy dependent on agriculture and craft production, have tolerated technical innovation and organizational improvement only within definite limits. One indicator of the traditional limits to the development of the forces of production is that until about three hundred years ago no major social system had produced more than the equivalent of a maximum of two hundred dollars per capita per annum. The stable pattern of a precapitalist mode of production, preindustrial technology, and premodern science makes possible a typical relation of the institutional framework to subsystems of purposive-rational action. For despite considerable progress, these subsystems, developing out of the system of social labor and its stock of accumulated technically exploitable knowledge, never reached that measure of extension after which their rationality would have become an open threat to the authority of the cultural traditions that legitimate political power. The expression 'traditional society' refers to the circumstance that the institutional framework is grounded in the unquestionable underpinning of legitimation constituted by mythical, religious or metaphysical interpretations of reality—cosmic as well as social—as a whole. 'Traditional' societies exist as long as the development of subsystems of purposive-rational action keep within the limits of the legitimating efficacy of cultural traditions.[14] This is the basis for the 'superiority' of the institutional framework, which does not preclude structural changes adapted to a potential surplus generated in the economic system but does preclude critically challenging the traditional form of legitimation. This immunity is a meaningful criterion for the delimitation of traditional societies from those which have crossed the threshold to modernization.

The 'superiority criterion', consequently, is applicable to all forms of class society

organized as a state in which principles of universally valid rationality (whether of technical or strategic means-ends relations) have not explicitly and successfully called into
question the cultural validity of intersubjectively shared traditions, which function as
legitimations of the political system. It is only since the capitalist mode of production has
equipped the economic system with a self-propelling mechanism that ensures long-term
continuous growth (despite crises) in the productivity of labor that the introduction of
new technologies and strategies, i.e. innovation as such, has been institutionalized. As
Marx and Schumpeter have proposed in their respective theories, the capitalist mode of
production can be comprehended as a mechanism that guarantees the *permanent* expansion of subsystems of purposive-rational action and thereby overturns the traditionalist
'superiority' of the institutional framework to the forces of production. Capitalism is the
first mode of production in world history to institutionalize self-sustaining economic
growth. It has generated an industrial system that could be freed from the institutional
framework of capitalism and connected to mechanisms other than that of the utilization
of capital in private form.

What characterizes the passage from traditional society to society commencing the
process of modernization is *not* that structural modification of the institutional framework
is necessitated under the pressure of relatively developed productive forces, for that is the
mechanism of the evolution of the species from the very beginning. What is new is a level
of development of the productive forces that makes permanent the extension of subsystems of purposive-rational action and thereby calls into question the traditional form of
the legitimation of power. The older mythic, religious, and metaphysical worldviews obey
the logic of interaction contexts. They answer the central questions of men's collective
existence and of individual life history. Their themes are justice and freedom, violence and
oppression, happiness and gratification, poverty, illness, and death. Their categories are
victory and defeat, love and hate, salvation and damnation. Their logic accords with the
grammar of systematically distorted communication and with the fateful causality of dissociated symbols and suppressed motives.[15] The rationality of language games, associated
with communicative action, is confronted at the threshold of the modern period with the
rationality of means-ends relations, associated with instrumental and strategic action. As
soon as this confrontation can arise, the end of traditional society is in sight: the traditional
form of legitimation breaks down.

Capitalism is defined by a mode of production that not only poses this problem but
also solves it. It provides a legitimation of domination which is no longer called down
from the lofty heights of cultural tradition but instead summoned up from the base of
social labor. The institution of the market, in which private property owners exchange
commodities—including the market on which propertyless private individuals exchange
their labor power as their only commodity—promises that exchange relations will be and
are just owing to equivalence. Even this bourgeois ideology of justice, by adopting the category of reciprocity, still employs a relation of communicative action as the basis of legitimation. But the principle of reciprocity is now the organizing principle of the sphere of
production and reproduction itself. Thus on the base of a market economy, political domination can be legitimated henceforth 'from below' rather than 'from above' (through invocation of cultural tradition).

If we suppose that the division of society into socio-economic classes derives from the differential distribution among social groups of the relevant means of production, and that this distribution itself is based on the institutionalization of relations of social force, then we may assume that in all civilizations this institutional framework has been identical with the system of political domination: traditional authority was political authority. Only with the emergence of the capitalist mode of production can the legitimation of the institutional framework be linked immediately with the system of social labor. Only then can the property order change from a *political relation* to a *production relation*, because it legitimates itself through the rationality of the market, the ideology of exchange society, and no longer through a legitimate power structure. It is now the political system which is justified in terms of the legitimate relations of production: this is the real meaning and function of rationalist natural law from Locke to Kant.[16] The institutional framework of society is only mediately political and immediately economic (the bourgeois constitutional state as 'superstructure').

The superiority of the capitalist mode of production to its predecessors has these two roots: the establishment of an economic mechanism that renders permanent the expansion of subsystems of purposive-rational action, and the creation of an economic legitimation by means of which the political system can be adapted to the new requisites of rationality brought about by these developing subsystems. It is this process of adaptation that Weber comprehends as 'rationalization'. Within it we can distinguish between two tendencies: rationalization 'from below' and rationalization 'from above'.

A permanent pressure for adaptation arises from below as soon as the new mode of production becomes fully operative through the institutionalization of a domestic market for goods and labor power and of the capitalist enterprise. In the system of social labor this institutionalization ensures cumulative progress in the forces of production and an ensuing horizontal extension of subsystems of purposive-rational action—at the cost of economic crises, to be sure. In this way traditional structures are increasingly subordinated to conditions of instrumental or strategic rationality: the organization of labor and of trade, the network of transportation, information, and communication, the institutions of private law, and, starting with financial administration, the state bureaucracy. Thus arises the substructure of a society under the compulsion of modernization. The latter eventually widens to take in all areas of life: the army, the school system, health services, and even the family. Whether in city or country, it induces an urbanization of the *form* of life. That is, it generates subcultures that train the individual to be able to 'switch over' at any moment from an interaction context to purposive-rational action.

This pressure for rationalization coming from below is met by a compulsion to rationalize coming from above. For, measured against the new standards of purposive rationality, the power-legitimating and action-orienting traditions—especially mythological interpretations and religious worldviews—lose their cogency. On this level of generalization, what Weber termed 'secularization' has two aspects. First, traditional worldviews and objectivations lose their power and validity *as* myth, *as* public religion, *as* customary ritual, *as* justifying metaphysics, *as* unquestionable tradition. Instead, they are reshaped into subjective belief systems and ethics which ensure the private cogency of modern value-orientations (the 'Protestant ethic'). Second, they are transformed into constructions that do both at once: criticize tradition and reorganize the released material of tradition according to the principles of formal law and the exchange of equivalents (rationalist natural law). Having become fragile, existing legitimations are replaced by new ones. The latter emerge from the critique of the dogmatism of traditional interpretations of the world and claim a scientific character. Yet they retain legitimating functions, thereby keeping actual power relations inaccessible to analysis and to public consciousness. It is in this way that ideologies in the restricted sense first came into being. They replace traditional legitimations of power by appearing in the mantle of modern science and by deriving their justification from the critique of ideology, Ideologies are coeval with the critique of ideology. In this sense there can be no prebourgeois 'ideologies'.

In this connection modern science assumes a singular function. In distinction from the philosophical sciences of the older sort, the empirical sciences have developed since Galileo's time within a methodological frame of reference that reflects the transcendental viewpoint of possible technical control. Hence the modern sciences produce knowledge which through its *form* (and not through the subjective intention of scientists) is technically exploitable knowledge, although the possible applications generally are realized afterwards. Science and technology were not interdependent until late into the nineteenth century. Until then modern science did not contribute to the acceleration of technical development nor, consequently, to the pressure toward rationalization from below. Rather, its contribution to the modernization process was indirect. Modern physics gave rise to a philosophical approach that interpreted nature and society according to a model borrowed from the natural sciences and induced, so to speak, the mechanistic worldview of the seventeenth century. The reconstruction of classical natural law was carried out in this framework. This modern natural law was the basis of the bourgeois revolutions of the seventeenth, eighteenth, and nineteenth centuries, through which the old legitimations of the power structure were finally destroyed.[17]

By the middle of the nineteenth century the capitalist mode of production had developed so fully in England and France that Marx was able to identify the locus of the institutional framework of society in the relations of production and at the same time criticize the legitimating basis constituted by the exchange of equivalents. He carried out the critique of bourgeois ideology in the form of *political economy*. His labor theory of value destroyed the semblance of freedom, by means of which the legal institution of the free labor contract had made unrecognizable the relationship of social force that underlay the wage-labor relationship. Marcuse's criticism of Weber is that the latter, disregarding this Marxian insight, upholds an abstract concept of rationalization, which not merely fails to express the specific class content of the adaptation of the institutional framework to the developing systems of purposive-rational action, but conceals it. Marcuse knows that the Marxian analysis can no longer be applied as it stands to advanced capitalist society, with which Weber was already confronted. But he wants to show through the example of Weber that the evolution of modern society in the framework of state-regulated capitalism cannot be conceptualized if liberal capitalism has not been analyzed adequately.

Since the last quarter of the nineteenth century two developmental tendencies have become noticeable in the most advanced capitalist countries: an increase in state intervention in order to secure the system's stability, and a growing interdependence of research and technology, which has turned the sciences into the leading productive force. Both tendencies have destroyed the particular constellation of institutional framework and subsystems of purposive-rational action which characterized liberal capitalism, thereby eliminating the conditions relevant for the application of political economy in the version correctly formulated by Marx for liberal capitalism. I believe that Marcuse's basic thesis, according to which technology and science today also take on the function of legitimating political power, is the key to analyzing the changed constellation.

The permanent regulation of the economic process by means of state intervention arose as a defense mechanism against the dysfunctional tendencies, which threaten the system, that capitalism generates when left to itself. Capitalism's actual development manifestly contradicted the capitalist idea of a bourgeois society, emancipated from domination, in which power is neutralized. The root ideology of just exchange, which Marx unmasked in theory, collapsed in practice. The form of capital utilization through private ownership could only be maintained by the governmental corrective of a social and economic policy that stabilized the business cycle. The institutional framework of society was repoliticized. It no longer coincides immediately with the relations of production, i.e. with an order of private law that secures capitalist economic activity and the corresponding general guarantees of order provided by the bourgeois state. But this means a change in the relation of the economy to the political system: politics is no longer *only* a phenomenon of the superstructure. If society no longer 'autonomously' perpetuates itself through self-regulation as a sphere preceding and lying at the basis of the state—and its ability to do so was the really novel feature of the capitalist mode of production—then society and the state are no longer in the relationship that Marxian theory had defined as that of base and superstructure. Then, however, a critical theory of society can no longer be constructed in the exclusive form of a critique of political economy. A point of view that methodically isolates the economic laws of motion of society can claim to grasp the overall structure of social life in its essential categories only as long as politics depends on the economic base. It becomes inapplicable when the 'base' has to be comprehended as in itself a function of governmental activity and political conflicts. According to Marx, the critique of political economy was the theory of bourgeois society only as *critique of ideology*. If, however, the ideology of just exchange disintegrates, then the power structure can no longer be criticized *immediately* at the level of the relations of production.

With the collapse of this ideology, political power requires a new legitimation. Now since the power indirectly exercised over the exchange process is itself operating under political control and state regulation, legitimation can no longer be derived from the unpolitical order constituted by the relations of production. To this extent the requirement for direct legitimation, which exists in precapitalist societies, reappears. On the other hand, the resuscitation of immediate political domination (in the traditional form of legitimation on the basis of cosmological worldviews) has become impossible. For traditions have already been disempowered. Moreover, in industrially developed societies the results of bourgeois emancipation from immediate political domination (civil and political rights and the mechanism of general elections) can be fully ignored only in periods of reaction. Formally democratic government in systems of state-regulated capitalism is subject to a need for legitimation which cannot be met by a return to a prebourgeois form. Hence the ideology of free exchange is replaced by a substitute program. The latter is oriented not to the social results of the institution of the market but to those of government action designed to compensate for the dysfunctions of free exchange. This policy combines the element of the bourgeois ideology of achievement (which, however, displaces assignment of status according to the standard of individual achievement from the market to the school system) with a guaranteed minimum level of welfare, which offers secure employment and a stable income. This substitute program obliges the political system to maintain stabilizing conditions for an economy that guards against risks to growth and guarantees social security and the chance for individual upward mobility. What is needed to this end is latitude for manipulation by state interventions that, at the cost of limiting the institutions of private law, secure the private form of capital utilization *and bind the masses' loyalty to this form.*

Insofar as government action is directed toward the economic system's stability and growth, politics now takes on a peculiarly negative character. For it is oriented toward the elimination of dysfunctions and the avoidance of risks that threaten the system: not, in other words, toward the *realization of practical goals* but toward the *solution of technical problems.* Claus Offe pointed this out in his paper at the 1968 Frankfurt Sociological Conference:

> In this structure of the relation of economy and the state, 'politics' degenerates into action that follows numerous and continually emerging 'avoidance imperatives': the mass of differentiated social-scientific information that flows into the political system allows both the early identification of risk zones and the treatment of actual dangers. What is new about this structure is . . . that the risks to stability built into the mechanism of private capital utilization in highly organized markets, risks that can be manipulated, prescribe preventive actions and measures that must be accepted as long as they are to accord with the existing legitimation resources (i.e., substitute program).[18]

Offe perceives that through these preventive action-orientations, government activity is restricted to administratively soluble technical problems, so that practical questions evaporate, so to speak. *Practical substance is eliminated.*

Old-style politics was forced, merely through its traditional form of legitimation, to define itself in relation to practical goals: the 'good life' was interpreted in a context defined by interaction relations. The same still held for the ideology of bourgeois society. The substitute program prevailing today, in contrast, is aimed exclusively at the functioning of a manipulated system. It eliminates practical questions and therewith precludes discussion about the adoption of standards; the latter could emerge only from a democratic decision-making process. The solution of technical problems is not dependent on public discussion. Rather, public discussions could render problematic the framework within which the tasks of government action present themselves as technical ones. Therefore the new politics of state interventionism requires a depoliticization of the mass of the population. To the extent that practical questions are eliminated, the public realm also loses its political function. At the same time, the institutional framework of society is still distinct from the systems of purposive-rational action themselves. Its organization continues to be a problem of *practice* linked to communication, not one of *technology*, no matter how scientifically guided. Hence, the bracketing out of practice associated with the new kind of politics is not automatic. The substitute program, which legitimates power today, leaves unfilled a vital need for legitimation: how will the depoliticization of the masses be made plausible to them? Marcuse would be able to answer: by having technology and science *also* take on the role of an ideology.

Since the end of the nineteenth century the other developmental tendency characteristic of advanced capitalism has become increasingly momentous: the scientization of technology. The institutional pressure to augment the productivity of labor through the introduction of new technology has always existed under capitalism. But innovations depended on sporadic inventions, which, while economically motivated, were still fortuitous in character. This changed as technical development entered into a feedback relation with the progress of the modern sciences. With the advent of large-scale industrial research, science, technology, and industrial utilization were fused into a system. Since then, industrial research has been linked up with research under government contract, which primarily promotes scientific and technical progress in the military sector. From there information flows back into the sectors of civilian production. Thus technology and science become a leading productive force, rendering inoperative the conditions for Marx's labor theory of value. It is no longer meaningful to calculate the amount of capital investment in research and development on the basis of the value of unskilled (simple) labor power, when scientific-technical progress has become an independent source of surplus value, in relation to which the only source of surplus value considered by Marx, namely the labor power of the immediate producers, plays an ever smaller role.[19]

As long as the productive forces were visibly linked to the rational decisions and instrumental action of men engaged in social production, they could be understood as the potential for a growing power of technical control and not be confused with the institutional framework in which they are embedded. However, with the institutionalization of scientific-technical progress, the potential of the productive forces has assumed a form owing to which men lose consciousness of the dualism of work and interaction.

It is true that social interests still determine the direction, functions, and pace of technical progress. But these interests define the social system so much as a whole that they coincide with the interest in maintaining the system. *As such* the private form of capital utilization and a distribution mechanism for social rewards that guarantees the loyalty of the masses are removed from discussion. The quasi-autonomous progress of science and technology then appears as an independent variable on which the most important single system variable, namely economic growth, depends. Thus arises a perspective in which the development of the social system *seems* to be determined by the logic of scientific-technical progress. The immanent law of this progress seems to produce objective exigencies, which must be obeyed by any politics oriented toward functional needs. But when this semblance has taken root effectively, then propaganda can refer to the role of technology and science in order to explain and legitimate why in modern societies the process of democratic decision-making about practical problems loses its function and 'must' be replaced by plebiscitary decisions about alternative sets of leaders of administrative personnel. This technocracy thesis has been worked out in several versions on the intellectual level.[20] What seems to me more important is that it can also become a background ideology that penetrates into the consciousness of the depoliticized mass of the population, where it can take on legitimating power.[21] It is a singular achievement of this ideology to detach society's self-understanding from the frame of reference of communicative action and from the concepts of symbolic interaction and replace it with a scientific model. Accordingly the culturally defined self-understanding of a social life-world is replaced by the self-reification of men under categories of purposive-rational action and adaptive behavior.

The model according to which the planned reconstruction of society is to proceed is taken from systems analysis. It is possible in principle to comprehend and analyze individual enterprises and organizations, even political or economic subsystems and social systems as a whole, according to the pattern of self-regulated systems. It makes a difference, of course, whether we use a cybernetic frame of reference for analytic purposes or *organize* a given social system in accordance with this pattern as a man-machine system. But the transferral of the analytic model to the level of social organization is implied by the very approach taken by systems analysis. Carrying out this intention of an instinct-like self-stabilization of social systems yields the peculiar perspective that the structure of one of the two types of action, namely the behavioral system of purposive-rational action, not only predominates over the institutional framework but gradually absorbs communicative action as such. If, with Arnold Gehlen, one were to see the inner logic of technical development as the step-by-step disconnection of the behavioral system of purposive-rational action from the human organism and its transferral to machines, then the technocratic intention could be understood as the last stage of this development. For the first time man can not only, as *homo faber*, completely objectify himself and confront the achievements that have taken on independent life in his products; he can in addition, as *homo fabricatus*, be integrated into his technical apparatus if the structure of purposive-rational action can be successfully reproduced on the level of social systems. According to this idea the institutional framework of society—which previously was rooted in a different type of action—would now, in a fundamental reversal, be *absorbed* by the subsystems of purposive-rational action, which were embedded in it.

Of course this technocratic intention has not been realized anywhere even in its beginnings. But it serves as an ideology for the new politics, which is adapted to technical problems and brackets out practical questions. Furthermore it does correspond to certain developmental tendencies that could lead to a creeping erosion of what we have called the institutional framework. The manifest domination of the authoritarian state gives way to the manipulative compulsions of technical-operational administration. The moral realization of a normative order is a function of communicative action oriented to shared cultural meaning and presupposing the internalization of values. It is increasingly supplanted by conditioned behavior, while large organizations as such are increasingly patterned after the structure of purposive-rational action. The industrially most advanced societies seem to approximate the model of behavioral control steered by external stimuli rather than guided by norms. Indirect control through fabricated stimuli has increased, especially in areas of putative subjective freedom (such as electoral, consumer, and leisure behavior). Sociopsychologically, the era is typified less by the authoritarian personality than by the destructuring of the superego. The increase in *adaptive behavior* is, however, only the obverse of the dissolution of the sphere of linguistically mediated interaction by the structure of purposive-rational action. This is paralleled subjectively by the disappearance of the difference between purposive-rational action and interaction from the consciousness not only of the sciences of man, but of men themselves. The concealment of this difference proves the ideological power of the technocratic consciousness.

In consequence of the two tendencies that have been discussed, capitalist society has changed to the point where two key categories of Marxian theory, namely class struggle and ideology, can no longer be employed as they stand.

It was on the basis of the capitalist mode of production that the struggle of social classes as such was first constituted, thereby creating an objective situation from which the class structure of traditional society, with its immediately political constitution, could be *recognized* in retrospect. State-regulated capitalism, which emerged from a reaction against the dangers to the system produced by open class antagonism, suspends class conflict. The system of advanced capitalism is so defined by a policy of securing the loyalty of the wage-earning masses through rewards, that is, by avoiding conflict, that the conflict still built into the structure of society in virtue of the private mode of capital utilization is the very area of conflict which has the greatest probability of remaining latent. It recedes behind others, which, while conditioned by the mode of production, can no longer assume the form of class conflicts. In the paper cited, Claus Offe has analyzed this paradoxical state of affairs, showing that open conflicts about social interests break out with greater probability the less their frustration has dangerous consequences for the system. The needs with the greatest conflict potential are those on the periphery of the area of state intervention. They are far from the central conflict being kept in a state of latency and therefore they are not seen as having priority among dangers to be warded off. Conflicts are set off by these needs to the extent that disproportionately scattered state interventions produce backward areas of development and corresponding disparity tensions:

> The disparity between areas of life grows above all in view of the differential state of development obtaining between the actually institutionalized and the possible level of technical and social progress. The disproportion between the most modern apparatuses for industrial and military purposes and, the stagnating organization of the transport, health, and educational systems is just as well known an example of this disparity between areas of life as is the contradiction between rational planning and regulation in taxation and finance policy and the unplanned, haphazard development of cities and regions. Such contradictions can no longer be designated accurately as antagonisms between classes, yet they can still be interpreted as results of the still dominant process of the private utilization of capital and of a specifically capitalist power structure. In this process the prevailing interests are those which, without being clearly localizable, are in a position, on the basis of the established mechanism of the capitalist economy, to react to disturbances of the conditions of their stability by producing risks relevant to the system as a whole.[22]

The interests bearing on the maintenance of the mode of production can no longer be 'clearly localized' in the social system as class interests. For the power structure, aimed as it is at avoiding dangers to the system, precisely excludes 'domination' (as immediate political or economically mediated social force) exercised in such a manner that one class subject *confronts* another as an identifiable group.

This means not that class antagonisms have been abolished but that they have become *latent*. Class distinctions persist in the form of subcultural traditions and corresponding differences not only in the standard of living and life style but also in political attitude. The social structure also makes it probable that the class of wage earners will be hit harder than other groups by social disparities. And finally, the generalized interest in perpetuating the system is still anchored today, on the level of immediate life chances, in a structure of privilege. The concept of an interest that has become *completely* independent of living subjects would cancel itself out. But with the deflection of dangers to the system in state-regulated capitalism, the political system has incorporated an interest—which transcends latent class boundaries—in preserving the compensatory distribution façade.

Furthermore, the displacement of the conflict zone from the class boundary to the underprivileged regions of life does not mean at all that serious conflict potential has been disposed of. As the extreme example of racial conflict in the United States shows, so many consequences of disparity can accumulate in certain areas and groups that explosions resembling civil war can occur. But unless they are connected with protest potential from other sectors of society no conflicts arising from such underprivilege can really overturn the system—they can only provoke it to sharp reactions incompatible with formal democracy. For underprivileged groups are not social classes, nor do they ever even potentially represent the mass of the population. Their *disfranchisement* and pauperization no longer coincide with *exploitation*, because the system does not live off their labor. They can represent at most a past phase of exploitation. But they cannot through the withdrawal of cooperation attain the demands that they legitimately put forward. That is why these demands retain an appellative character. In the case of long-term nonconsideration of their legitimate demands underprivileged groups can in extreme situations react with desperate destruction and self-destruction. But as long as no coalitions are made with privileged groups, such a civil war lacks the chance of revolutionary success that class struggle possesses.

With a series of restrictions this model seems applicable even to the relations between the industrially advanced nations and the formerly colonial areas of the Third World. Here, too, growing disparity leads to a form of underprivilege that in the future surely will be increasingly less comprehensible through categories of exploitation. Economic interests are replaced on this level, however, with immediately military ones.

Be that as it may, in advanced capitalist society deprived and privileged groups no longer confront each other as socioeconomic classes—and to some extent the boundaries of underprivilege are no longer even specific to groups and instead run across population categories. Thus the fundamental relation that existed in all traditional societies and that came to the fore under liberal capitalism is mediatized, namely the class antagonism between partners who stand in an institutionalized relationship of force, economic exploitation, and political oppression to one another, and in which communication is so distorted and restricted that the legitimations serving as an ideological veil cannot be called into question. Hegel's concept of the ethical totality of a living relationship which is sundered because one subject does not reciprocally satisfy the needs of the other is no longer an appropriate model for the mediatized class structure of organized, advanced capitalism. The suspended dialectic of the ethical generates the peculiar semblance of *posthistoire*. The reason is that relative growth of the productive forces no longer represents *eo ipso* a potential that points beyond the existing framework with emancipatory consequences, in view of which legitimations of an existing power structure become enfeebled. For the leading productive force—controlled scientific-technical progress itself—has now become the basis of legitimation. Yet this new form of legitimation has cast off the old shape of *ideology*.

Technocratic consciousness is, on the one hand, 'less ideological' than all previous ideologies. For it does not have the opaque force of a delusion that only transfigures the implementation of interests. On the other hand today's dominant, rather glassy background ideology, which makes a fetish of science, is more irresistible and farther-reaching than ideologies of the old type. For with the veiling of practical problems it not only justifies a *particular class's* interest in domination and represses *another class's* partial need for emancipation, but affects the human race's emancipatory interest as such.

Technocratic consciousness is not a rationalized, wish-fulfilling fantasy, not an 'illusion' in Freud's sense, in which a system of interaction is either represented or interpreted and grounded. Even bourgeois ideologies could be traced back to a basic pattern of just interactions, free of domination and mutually satisfactory. It was these ideologies which met the criteria of wish-fulfillment and substitute gratification; the communication on which they were based was so limited by repressions that the relation of force once institutionalized as the capital-labor relation could not even be called by name. But the technocratic consciousness is not based in the same way on the causality of dissociated symbols and unconscious motives, which generates both false consciousness and the power of reflection to which the critique of ideology is indebted. It is less vulnerable to reflection, because it is no longer *only* ideology. For it does not, in the manner of ideology, express a projection of the 'good life' (which even if not identifiable with a bad reality, can at least be brought into virtually satisfactory accord with it). Of course the new ideology, like the old, serves to impede making the foundations of society the object of thought and reflection. Previously, social force lay at the basis of the relation between capitalist and wage-laborers. Today the basis is provided by structural conditions which predefine the tasks of system maintenance: the private form of capital utilization and a political form of distributing social rewards that guarantees mass loyalty. However, the old and new ideology differ in two ways.

First, the capital-labor relation today, because of its linkage to a loyalty-ensuring political distribution mechanism, no longer engenders uncorrected exploitation and oppression. The process through which the persisting class antagonism has been made virtual presupposes that the repression on which the latter is based first came to consciousness in history and *only then* was stabilized in a modified form as a property of the system. Technocratic consciousness, therefore, cannot rest in the same way on collective repression as did earlier ideologies. Second, mass loyalty today is created only with the aid of rewards for *privatized needs*. The achievements in virtue of which the system justifies itself may not in principle be interpreted politically. The acceptable interpretation is immediately in terms of allocations of money and leisure time (neutral with regard to their use), and mediately in terms of the technocratic justification of the occlusion of practical questions. Hence the new ideology is distinguished from its predecessor in that it severs the criteria for justifying the organization of social life from any normative regulation of interaction, thus depoliticizing them. It anchors them instead in functions of a putative system of purposive-rational action.

Technocratic consciousness reflects not the sundering of an ethical situation but the repression of 'ethics' as such as a category of life. The common, positivist way of thinking renders inert the frame of reference of interaction in ordinary language, in which domination and ideology both arise under conditions of distorted communication and can be reflectively detected and broken down. The depoliticization of the mass of the population, which is legitimated through technocratic consciousness, is at the same time men's self-objectification in categories equally of both purposive-rational action and adaptive behavior. The reified models of the sciences migrate into the sociocultural life-world and gain objective power over the latter's self-understanding. The ideological nucleus of this consciousness is *the elimination of the distinction between the practical and the technical*. It reflects, but does not objectively account for, the new constellation of a disempowered institutional framework and systems of purposive-rational action that have taken on a life of their own.

The new ideology consequently violates an interest grounded in one of the two fundamental conditions of our cultural existence: in language, or more precisely, in the form of socialization and individuation determined by communication in ordinary language. This interest extends to the maintenance of intersubjectivity of mutual understanding as well as to the creation of communication without domination. Technocratic consciousness makes this practical interest disappear behind the interest in the expansion of our power of technical control. Thus the reflection that the new ideology calls for must penetrate beyond the level of particular historical class interests to disclose the fundamental interests of mankind as such, engaged in the process of self-constitution.[23]

If the relativization of the field of application of the concept of ideology and the theory of class be confirmed, then the category framework developed by Marx in the basic assumptions of historical materialism requires a new formulation. The model of forces of production and relations of production would have to be replaced by the more abstract one of work and interaction. The relations of production designate a level on which the institutional framework was anchored only during the phase of the development of liberal capitalism, and not either before or after. To be sure, the productive forces, in which the learning processes organized in the subsystems of purposive-rational action accumulate, have been from the very beginning the motive force of social evolution. But, they do not appear, as Marx supposed, *under all circumstances* to be a potential for liberation and to set off emancipatory movements—at least not once the continual growth of the productive forces has become dependent on scientific-technical progress that has *also* taken on functions of *legitimating political power*. I suspect that the frame of reference developed in terms of the analogous, but more general relation of institutional framework (interaction) and subsystems of purposive-rational action ('work' in the broad sense of instrumental and strategic action) is more suited to reconstructing the sociocultural phases of the history of mankind.

There are several indications that during the long initial phase until the end of the Mesolithic period, purposive-rational actions could only be motivated at all through ritual attachment to interactions. A profane realm of subsystems of purposive-rational action seems to have separated out from the institutional framework of symbolic interaction in the first settled cultures, based on the domestication of animals and cultivation of plants. But it was probably only in civilizations, that is under the conditions of a class society organized as a state that the differentiation of work and interaction went far enough for the subsystems to yield technically exploitable knowledge that could be stored and expanded relatively independently of mythical and religious interpretations of the world. At the same time social norms became separated from power-legitimating traditions, so that 'culture' attained a certain independence from 'institutions'. The threshold of the modern period would then be characterized by that process of rationalization which commenced with loss of the 'superiority' of the institutional framework to the subsystems of purposive-rational action. Traditional legitimations could now be criticized against the standards of rationality of means-ends relations. Concurrently, information from the area of technically exploitable knowledge infiltrated tradition and compelled a reconstruction of traditional world interpretations along the lines of scientific standards.

We have followed this process of 'rationalization from above' up to the point where technology and science themselves in the form of a common positivistic way of thinking, articulated as technocratic consciousness, began to take the role of a substitute ideology for the demolished bourgeois ideologies. This point was reached with the critique of bourgeois ideologies. It introduced ambiguity into the concept of rationalization. This ambiguity was deciphered by Horkheimer and Adorno as the dialectic of enlightenment, which has been refined by Marcuse as the thesis that technology and science themselves become ideological.

From the very beginning the pattern of human sociocultural development has been determined by a growing power of technical control over the external conditions of existence on the one hand, and a more or less passive adaptation of the institutional framework to the expanded subsystems of purposive-rational action on the other. Purposive-rational action represents the form of *active* adaptation, which distinguishes the collective *self*-preservation of societal subjects from the preservation of the species characteristic of other animals. We know how to bring the relevant conditions of life under control, that is, we know how to adapt the environment to our needs culturally rather than adapting ourselves to external nature. In contrast, changes of the institutional framework, to the extent that they are derived immediately or mediately from new technologies or improved strategies (in the areas of production, transportation, weaponry, etc.) have not taken the same form of active adaptation. In general such modifications follow the pattern of *passive* adaptation. They are not the result of planned purposive-rational action geared to its own consequences, but the product of fortuitous, undirected development. Yet it was impossible to become conscious of this disproportion between active and passive adaptation as long as the dynamics of capitalist development remained concealed by bourgeois ideologies. Only with the critique of bourgeois ideologies did this disproportion enter public consciousness.

The most impressive witness to this experience is still the *Communist Manifesto*. In rapturous words Marx eulogizes the revolutionary role of the bourgeoisie:

> The bourgeoisie cannot exist without constantly revolutionizing the instruments of production, and thereby the relations of production, and with them the whole relations of society.

In another passage he writes:

> The bourgeoisie, during its rule of scarce one hundred years, has created more massive and more colossal productive forces than have all preceding generations together. Subjection of nature's forces to man, machinery, application of chemistry to industry and agriculture, steam navigation, railways, electric telegraphs, clearing of whole continents for cultivation, canalization of rivers, whole populations conjured out of the ground . . .

Marx also perceives the reaction of this development back upon the institutional framework:

> All fixed, fast-frozen relations, with their train of ancient and venerable prejudices and opinions, are swept away, all new-formed ones become antiquated before they can ossify. All that is solid melts into air, all that is holy is profaned, and man is at last compelled to face with sober senses his real conditions of life and his relations with his kind.

It is with regard to the disproportion between the passive adaptation of the institutional framework and the 'active subjection of nature' that the assertion that men make their history, but not with will or consciousness, was formulated. It was the aim of Marx's critique to transform the secondary adaptation of the institutional framework as well into an active one, and to bring under control the structural change of society itself. This would overcome a fundamental condition of all previous history and complete the self-constitution of mankind: the end of prehistory. But this idea was ambiguous.

Marx, to be sure, viewed the problem of making history with will and consciousness as one of the *practical* mastery of previously ungoverned processes of social development. Others, however, have understood it as a *technical* problem. They want to bring society under control in the same way as nature by reconstructing it according to the pattern of self-regulated systems of purposive-rational action and adaptive behavior. This intention is to be found not only among technocrats of capitalist planning but also among those of bureaucratic socialism. Only the technocratic consciousness obscures the fact that this reconstruction could be achieved at no less a cost than closing off the only dimension that is essential, because it is susceptible to humanization, as a structure of interactions mediated by ordinary language. In the future the repertoire of control techniques will be considerably expanded. On Herman Kahn's list of the most probable technical innovations of the next thirty years I observe among the first fifty items a large number of techniques of behavioral and personality change:

30. new and possibly pervasive techniques for surveillance, monitoring and control of individuals and organizations;

33. new and more reliable 'educational' and propaganda techniques affecting human behavior—public and private;

34. practical use of direct electronic communication with and stimulation of the brain;

37. new and relatively effective counterinsurgency techniques;

39. new and more varied drugs for control of fatigue, relaxation, alertness, mood, personality, perceptions, and fantasies;

41. improved capability to 'change' sex;

42. other genetic control or influence over the basic constitution of an individual.[24]

A prediction of this sort is extremely controversial. Nevertheless, it points to an area of future possibilities of detaching human behavior from a normative system linked to the grammar of language-games and integrating it instead into self-regulated subsystems of the man-machine type by means of immediate physical or psychological control. Today the psychotechnic manipulation of behavior can already liquidate the old fashioned detour through norms that are internalized but capable of reflection. Behavioral control could be instituted at an even deeper level tomorrow through biotechnic intervention in the endocrine regulating system, not to mention the even greater consequences of intervening in the genetic transmission of inherited information. If this occurred, old regions of consciousness developed in ordinary-language communication would of necessity completely dry up. At this stage of human engineering, if the end of psychological manipulation could be spoken of in the same sense as the end of ideology is today, the spontaneous alienation derived from the uncontrolled lag of the institutional framework would be overcome. But the self-objectivation of man would have fulfilled itself in planned alienation—men would make their history with will, but without consciousness.

I am not asserting that this cybernetic dream of the instinct-like self-stabilization of societies is being fulfilled or that it is even realizable. I do think, however, that it follows through certain vague but basic assumptions of technocratic consciousness to their conclusion as a negative utopia and thus denotes an evolutionary trend that is taking shape under the slick domination of technology and science as ideology. Above all, it becomes clear against this background that *two concepts of rationalization* must be distinguished. At the level of subsystems of purposive-rational action, scientific-technical progress has already compelled the reorganization of social institutions and sectors, and necessitates it on an even larger scale than heretofore. But this process of the development of the productive forces can be a potential for liberation if and only if it does not replace rationalization on another level. *Rationalization at the level of the institutional framework* can occur only in the medium of symbolic interaction itself, that is, through *removing restrictions on communication*. Public, unrestricted discussion, free from domination, of the suitability and desirability of action-orienting principles and norms in the light of the sociocultural repercussions of developing subsystems of purposive-rational action—such communication at all levels of political and repoliticized decision-making processes is the only medium in which anything like 'rationalization' is possible.

In such a process of generalized reflection institutions would alter their specific composition, going beyond the limit of a mere change in legitimation. A rationalization of social norms would, in fact, be characterized by a decreasing degree of repressiveness (which at the level of personality structure should increase average tolerance of ambivalence in the face of role conflicts), a decreasing degree of rigidity (which should multiply the chances of an individually stable self-presentation in everyday interactions), and approximation to a type of behavioral control that would allow role distance and the flexible application of norms that, while well-internalized, would be accessible to reflection. Rationalization measured by changes in these three dimensions does not lead, as does the rationalization of purposive-rational subsystems, to an increase in technical control over objectified processes of nature and society. It does not lead per se to the better functioning of social systems, but would furnish the members of society with the opportunity for further emancipation and progressive individuation. The growth of productive forces is not the same as the intention of the 'good life'. It can at best serve it.

I do not even think that the model of a technologically possible surplus that cannot be used in full measure within a repressively maintained institutional framework (Marx speaks of 'fettered' forces of production) is appropriate to state-regulated capitalism. Today, better utilization of an unrealized potential leads to improvement of the economic-industrial apparatus, but no longer *eo ipso* to a transformation of the institutional framework with emancipatory consequences. The question is not whether we completely *utilize* an available or creatable potential, but whether we *choose* what we want for the purpose of the pacification and gratification of existence. But it must be immediately noted that we are only posing this question and cannot answer it in advance. For the solution demands precisely that unrestricted communication about the goals of life activity and conduct against which advanced capitalism, structurally dependent on a depoliticized public realm, puts up a strong resistance.

A new conflict zone, in place of the virtualized class antagonism and apart from the disparity conflicts at the margins of the system, can only emerge where advanced capitalist society has to immunize itself, by depoliticizing the masses of the population, against the questioning of its technocratic background ideology: in the public sphere administered through the mass media. For only here is it possible to buttress the concealment of the difference between progress in systems of purposive-rational action and emancipatory transformations of the institutional framework, between technical and practical problems. And it is necessary for the system to conceal this difference. Publicly administered definitions extend to *what* we want for our lives, but not to *how* we would like to live if we could find out, with regard to attainable potentials, how we *could* live.

Who will activate this conflict zone is hard to predict. Neither the old class antagonism nor the new type of underprivilege contains a protest potential whose origins make it tend toward the repoliticization of the desiccated public sphere. For the present, the only protest potential that gravitates toward the new conflict zone owing to identifiable interests is arising among certain groups of university, college, and high school students. Here we can make three observations:

1. Protesting students are a privileged group, which advances no interests that proceed immediately from its social situation or that could be satisfied in conformity with the system through an augmentation of social rewards. The first American studies of student activists conclude that they are predominantly not from upwardly mobile sections of the student body, but rather from sections with privileged status recruited from economically advantaged social strata.[25]

2. For plausible reasons the legitimations offered by the political system do not seem convincing to this group. The welfare-state substitute program for decrepit bourgeois ideologies presupposes a certain status and achievement orientation. According to the studies cited, student activists are less privatistically oriented to professional careers and future families than other students. Their academic achievements, which tend to be above average, and their social origins do not promote a horizon of expectations determined by anticipated exigencies of the labor market. Active students, who relatively frequently are in the social sciences and humanities, tend to be immune to technocratic consciousness because, although for varying motives, their primary experiences in their own intellectual work in neither case accord with the basic technocratic assumptions.

3. Among this group, conflict cannot break out because of the extent of the discipline and burdens imposed, but only because of their quality. Students are not fighting for a larger share of social rewards in the prevalent categories: income and leisure time. Instead, their protest is directed against the very category of reward itself. The few available data confirm the supposition that the protest of youth from bourgeois homes no longer coincides with the pattern of authority conflict typical of previous generations. Student activists tend to have parents who share their critical attitude. They have been brought up relatively frequently with more psychological understanding and according to more liberal educational principles than comparable inactive groups.[26] Their socialization seems to have been achieved in subcultures freed from immediate economic compulsion, in which the traditions of bourgeois morality and their petit-bourgeois derivatives have lost their function. This means that training for switching over to value-orientations of purposive-rational action no longer includes fetishizing this form of action. These educational techniques make possible experiences and favor orientations that clash with the conserved life form of an economy of poverty. What can take shape on this basis is a lack of understanding in principle for the reproduction of virtues and sacrifices that have become superfluous—a lack of understanding why despite the advanced stage of technological development the life of the individual is still determined by the dictates of professional careers, the ethics of status competition, and by values of possessive individualism and available substitute gratifications: why the institutionalized struggle for existence, the discipline of alienated labor, and the eradication of sensuality and aesthetic gratification are perpetuated. To this sensibility the structural elimination of practical problems from a depoliticized public realm must become unbearable. However, it will give rise to a political force only if this sensibility comes into contact with a problem that the system cannot

solve. For the future I see *one* such problem. The amount of social wealth produced by industrially advanced capitalism and the technical and organizational conditions under which this wealth is produced make it ever more difficult to link status assignment in an even subjectively convincing manner to the mechanism for the evaluation of individual achievement.[27] In the long run therefore, student protest could permanently destroy this crumbling achievement-ideology, and thus bring down the already fragile legitimating basis of advanced capitalism, which rests only on depoliticization.

NOTES

1. Herbert Marcuse, 'Industrialization and Capitalism in the Work of Max Weber', in *Negations: Essays in Critical Theory*, with translations from the German by Jeremy J. Shapiro (Boston, 1968), pp. 223 f.
2. Herbert Marcuse, 'Freedom and Freud's Theory of the Instincts', in *Five Lectures*, translations by Jeremy J. Shapiro and Shierry M. Weber (Boston, 1970), p. 16.
3. *Ibid.*, p. 3.
4. *Ibid.*
5. *Ibid.*
6. Herbert Marcuse, *One-Dimensional Man* (Boston, 1964).
7. *Ibid.*, pp. 166 f.
8. *Ibid.*, p. 236.
9. 'This law expresses an intratechnical occurrence, a process that man has not willed as a whole. Rather, it takes place, as it were, behind his back, instinctively extending through the entire history of human culture. Furthermore, in accordance with this law, technology cannot evolve beyond the stage of the greatest possible automation, for there are no further specifiable regions of human achievement that could be objectified.' Arnold Gehlen, 'Anthropologische Ansicht der Technik', in *Technik im technischen Zeitalter*, Hans Freyer *et al.*, eds. (Düsseldorf, 1965).
10. Marcuse, *One-Dimensional Man*, p. 235.
11. *Ibid.*, p. 154.
12. On the context of these concepts in the history of philosophy, see my contribution to the *Festschrift* for Karl Löwith: 'Arbeit und Interaktion: Bemerkungen zu Hegels Jenenser Realphilosophie', in *Natur und Geschichte. Karl Löwith zum 70. Geburtstag,* Hermann Braun and Manfred Riedel, eds. (Stuttgart, 1967). This essay is reprinted in *Technik und Wissenschaft als 'Ideologie'* (Frankfurt am Main, 1968) and will appear in English in *Theory and Practice*, to be published by Beacon Press.
13. Gerhard E. Lenski, *Power and Privilege: A Theory of Social Stratification* (New York, 1966).
14. See Peter L. Berger, *The Sacred Canopy* (New York, 1967).
15. See my study *Erkenntnis und Interesse* (Frankfurt am Main, 1968), to be published by Beacon Press as *Cognition and Human Interests*.
16. See Leo Strauss, *Natural Right and History* (Chicago, 1963); C.B. MacPherson, *The Political Theory of Possessive Individualism* (London, 1962); and Jürgen Habermas, 'Die klassische Lehre von der Politik in ihrem Verhältnis zur Sozialphilosophie', in *Theorie und Praxis*, 2d ed. (Neuwied, 1967), to appear in *Theory and Practice*.
17. See Jürgen Habermas, 'Naturrecht und Revolution,' in *Theorie und Praxis*.

18. Claus Offe, 'Politische Herrschaft und Klassenstrukturen', in Gisela Kress and Dieter Senghaas, eds., *Politikwissenschaft* (Frankfurt am Main, 1969). The quotation in the text is from the original manuscript, which differs in formulation from the published text.

19. The most recent explication of this is Eugen Löbl, *Geistige Arbeit—die wahre Quelle des Reichtums*, translated from the Czech by Leopold Grünwald (Vienna, 1968).

20. See Helmut Schelsky, *Der Mensch in der wissenschaftlichen Zivilisation* (Cologne-Opladen, 1961); Jacques Ellul, *The Technological Society* (New York, 1967); and Arnold Gehlen, 'Über kulturelle Kristallisationen', in *Studien zur Anthropologie und Soziologie* (Berlin, 1963), and 'Über kulturelle Evolution', in *Die Philosophie und die Frage nach dem Fortschritt*, M. Hahn and F. Wiedmann, eds. (Munich, 1964).

21. To my knowledge there are no empirical studies concerned specifically with the propagation of this background ideology. We are dependent on extrapolations from the findings of other investigations.

22. Offe, op. cit.

23. See my essay 'Erkenntnis und Interesse', in *Technik und Wissenschaft als 'Ideologie'*. It will appear in English as an appendix to *Cognition and Human Interests*.

24. Herman Kahn and Anthony J. Wiener, 'The Next Thirty-Three Years: A Framework for Speculation', in *Toward the Year 2000: Work in Progress*, Daniel Bell, ed. (Boston, 1969), pp. 80 f.

25. Seymour Martin Lipset and Philip G. Altbach, 'Student Politics and Higher Education in the U.S.A.', in *Student Politics*, Seymour Martin Lipset, ed. (New York, 1967); Richard W. Flacks, 'The Liberated Generation: An Exploration of the Roots of Student Protest', in *Journal of Social Issues*, 23:3, pp. 52–75; and Kenneth Keniston, 'The Sources of Student Dissent', *ibid.*, pp. 108 ff.

26. In Flacks' words, 'Activists are more radical than their parents; but activists' parents are decidedly more liberal than others of their status . . . . Activism is related to a complex of values, not ostensibly political, shared by both the students and their parents . . . . Activists' parents are more "permissive" than parents of non-activists.'

27. See Robert L. Heilbroner, *The Limits of American Capitalism* (New York, 1966).

EDWARD SAID

1935–
JERUSALEM

Major Works

. . . it bears repeating that no matter how apparently complete the dominance of an ideology or social system, there are always going to be parts of the social experience that it does not cover and control. From these parts very frequently comes opposition, both self-conscious and dialectical. This is not as complicated as it sounds. Opposition to a dominant structure arises out of a perceived, perhaps even militant awareness on the part of individuals and groups outside and inside it that, for example, certain of its policies are wrong.[1]

Every individual intellectual is born into a language, and for the most part spends the rest of his or her life in that language, which is the principal medium of intellectual activity.[2]

—*Edward Said*

Edward Said, literary critic, social theorist, aesthete, prolific writer, and political activist in the struggle for a Palestinian state is also a harsh critic of the Palestinian leadership and an even harsher critic of US foreign policy in the Middle East. His major study, *Orientalism*, published in 1978 and excerpted in this volume, is widely recognized as one of the founding texts of post-colonial studies. Orientalism, as Said explains:

> can thus be regarded as a manner of regularized (or Orientalized) writing, vision, and study, dominated by imperatives, perspectives, and ideological biases ostensibly suited to the Orient. The Orient is taught, researched, administered, and pronounced upon in certain discrete ways.[3]

The Orient is, then, a constructed entity built from a variety of assumptions from the viewpoint of Western scholars. Inherent in this construction is the notion of the Oriental as backward, helpless, and unimaginative. The Orient is seen as a monolith, ignoring the diverse cultures within the region. It is presented as different and strange, the embodiment of 'other' and inferior to the West. For Said, 'the Orient that appears in Orientalism . . . is a system of representations framed by a whole set of forces that brought the Orient into Western Learning, Western consciousness, and later Western empire.'[4]

Recurring themes in Said's works are those of the power relations between the dominant and the dominated, and the links between culture and imperialism. He found Michel Foucault's notion of a discourse as described by him in the *Archaeology of Knowledge* and in *Discipline and Punish* useful to identify Orientalism. Without this, he points out, it would not be possible to understand the systematic discipline deployed by Europeans in administering the Orient. For Said, 'The relationship between Occident and Orient is a relationship of power, of domination of varying degrees of a complex hegemony.'[5] Underpinning his study is the idea that these early representations of Orientalism are present in current portrayals of Arab cultures. His 1981 book, *Covering Islam*, continues the theme of representation, in this case focusing on how Western governments and the media have constructed, for the most part, stereotypical images of Islam and continue to portray the inhabitants of the Middle East as monolithic, violent, dangerous, and a threat to the West. The public's response in the aftermath of the 11 September 2001 attack on the United States clearly validates this point.

In an Afterword to the 1994 edition of *Orientalism*, which is both a response to his critics and a clarification of certain misunderstandings, Said distinguishes two broad theoretical currents, postmodernism and post-colonialism, pointing out that these 'emerged as related topics of engagement and investigation during the 1980's and in many instances, seemed to take account of such works as *Orientalism* as antecedents.'[6] He sees these as somewhat different approaches, although at times there is overlap. In postmodernism there is a tendency towards a more Eurocentric bias and disengagement with history, while for post-colonialism the history of domination and control is central. He has contributed to the theoretical debates within postmodernism through his analyses of postmodernist thinkers such as Derrida, Barthes, Foucault, and others. The impact of his work on post-colonial studies has been significant in that his analysis of Orientalism has helped in understanding how the characteristics of cultural groups may be built on assumptions and then dominated by the producers of these assumptions.

Said's examination of several Western literary classics in his 1993 *Culture and Imperialism* includes Conrad's *Heart of Darkness* and Austen's *Mansfield Park*. He demonstrates how novels, travel documents, and other cultural forms can conceal the realities of colonialism and imperialism through ideological maskings and the general unquestioning of facts of everyday life. Here he states:

> . . . cultural forms like the novel or the opera do not cause people to go out and imperialize—Carlyle did not drive Rhodes directly, and he certainly cannot be 'blamed' for the problems in today's southern Africa—but it is genuinely troubling to see how little Britain's great humanistic ideas, institutions and monuments, which we still celebrate as having the power ahistorically to command our approval, how little they stand in the way of the accelerating imperial process. We are entitled to ask how this body of humanistic ideas co-existed so comfortably with imperialism, and why—until the resistance to imperialism *in the imperial domain*, among Africans, Asians, Latin Americans developed—there was little significant opposition or deterrence to empire at home.[7]

He argues strongly for counterpoint in representations and seems to hold some optimism for the future in the sense that post-colonial writers, such as Aimé Césaire, Chinua Achebe, Salman Rushdie, and Ngũgĩ Wa Thiong'o, are revisiting the colonial experience and giving voice to the colonized through their prose and poetry.

In the 1993 Reith Lectures, also excerpted in this volume, Said articulates the political responsibilities of the intellectual. There should be a willingness to question and publicly speak about the power imbalances in society and double standards of governments when it comes to foreign and social policy issues. The intellectual should also be ready to confront issues around race, gender, and class.

Notes

1. Edward Said, *Culture and Imperialism* (New York: Alfred A. Knopf, 1993), 240.
2. Edward Said, *Representations of the Intellectual* (New York: Vintage Books, 1994), 27.
3. Edward Said, *Orientalism* (New York: Vintage Books, 1978), 202.
4. Ibid., 202–3.
5. Ibid., 5.
6. Edward Said, *Orientalism*, 2nd edn (New York: Vintage Books, 1994), 348.
7. Edward Said, *Culture and Imperialism*, 81-2.

REPRESENTATIONS OF THE INTELLECTUAL

Are intellectuals a very large or an extremely small and highly selective group of people? Two of the most famous twentieth-century descriptions of intellectuals are fundamentally opposed on that point. Antonio Gramsci, the Italian Marxist, activist, journalist and brilliant political philosopher who was imprisoned by Mussolini between 1926 and 1937, wrote in his *Prison Notebooks* that 'all men are intellectuals, one could therefore say: but not all men have in society the function of intellectuals.'[1] Gramsci's own career exemplifies the role he ascribed to the intellectual: a trained philologist, he was both an organizer of the Italian working-class movement and, in his own journalism, one of the most consciously reflective of social analysts, whose purpose was to build not just a social movement but an entire cultural formation associated with the movement.

Those who do perform the intellectual function in society, Gramsci tries to show, can be divided into two types: first, traditional intellectuals such as teachers, priests, and administrators, who continue to do the same thing from generation to generation; and second, organic intellectuals, whom Gramsci saw as directly connected to classes or enterprises that used intellectuals to organize interests, gain more power, get more control. Thus, Gramsci says about the organic intellectual, 'the capitalist entrepreneur creates alongside himself the industrial technician, the specialist in political economy, the organizers of a new culture, of a new legal system, etc.'[2] Today's advertising or public relations expert, who devises techniques for winning a detergent or airline company a larger share of the market, would be considered an organic intellectual according to Gramsci, someone who in a democratic society tries to gain the consent of potential customers, win approval, marshal consumer or voter opinion. Gramsci believed that organic intellectuals are actively involved in society, that is, they constantly struggle to change minds and expand markets; unlike teachers and priests, who seem more or less to remain in place, doing the same kind of work year in year out, organic intellectuals are always on the move, on the make.

At the other extreme there is Julien Benda's celebrated definition of intellectuals as a tiny band of super-gifted and morally endowed philosopher-kings who constitute the conscience of mankind. While it is true that Benda's treatise *La trahison des clercs*—The betrayal of the intellectuals—has lived in posterity more as a blistering attack on intellectuals who abandon their calling and compromise their principles than as a systematic analysis of intellectual life, he does in fact cite a small number of names and major characteristics of those whom he considered to be real intellectuals. Socrates and Jesus are frequently mentioned, as are more recent exemplars like Spinoza, Voltaire and Ernest Renan. Real intellectuals constitute a clerisy, very rare creatures indeed, since what they uphold are eternal standards of truth and justice that are precisely *not* of this world. Hence Benda's religious term for them—clerics—a distinction in status and performance that he always counterposes against the laity, those ordinary human beings who are interested in material advantage, personal advancement, and, if at all possible, a close relationship with secular powers. Real intellectuals, he says, are 'those whose activity is essentially not the pursuit of practical aims, all those who seek their joy in the practice of an art or a science or metaphysical speculation, in short in the possession of non-material advantages, and hence in a certain manner say: "My kingdom is not of this world."'[3]

Benda's examples, however, make it quite clear that he does not endorse the notion of totally disengaged, other worldly, ivory-towered thinkers, intensely private and devoted to abstruse, perhaps even occult subjects. Real intellectuals are never more themselves than when, moved by metaphysical passion and disinterested principles of justice and truth, they denounce corruption, defend the weak, defy imperfect or oppressive authority. 'Need I recall,' he says, 'how Fenelon and Massillon denounced certain wars of Louis XIV? How Voltaire condemned the destruction of the Palatinate? How Renan denounced the violences of Napoleon? Buckle, the intolerances of England toward the French Revolution? And, in our times, Nietzsche, the brutalities of Germany towards France?'[4] The trouble with today's lot according to Benda is that they have conceded their moral authority to what, in a prescient phrase, he calls 'the organization of collective passions' such as sectarianism, mass sentiment, nationalist belligerence, class interests. Benda was writing in 1927, well before the age of the mass media, but he sensed how important it was for governments to have as their servants those intellectuals who could be called on not to lead, but to consolidate the government's policy, to spew out propaganda against official enemies, euphemisms and, on a larger scale, whole systems of Orwellian Newspeak, which could disguise the truth of what was occurring in the name of institutional 'expediency' or 'national honor'.

The force of Benda's jeremiad against the betrayal of the intellectuals is not the subtlety of his argument, nor his quite impossible absolutism when it comes to his totally uncompromising view of the intellectual's mission. Real intellectuals, according to Benda's definition, are supposed to risk being burned at the stake, ostracized, or crucified. They are symbolic personages marked by their unyielding distance from practical concerns. As such therefore they cannot be many in number, nor routinely developed. They have to be thoroughgoing individuals with powerful personalities and, above all, they have to be in a state of almost permanent opposition to the status quo: for all these reasons Benda's intellectuals are inevitably a small, highly visible group of men—he never includes women—whose stentorian voices and indelicate imprecations are hurled at humankind from on high. Benda never suggests how it is that these men know the truth, or whether their blinding insights into eternal principles might, like those of Don Quixote, be little more than private fantasies.

But there is no doubt in my mind at least that the image of a real intellectual as generally conceived by Benda remains an attractive and compelling one. Many of his positive, as well as negative, examples are persuasive: Voltaire's public defense of the Calas family, for instance, or—at the opposite end—the appalling nationalism of French writers like Maurice Barrès, whom Benda credits with perpetuating a 'romanticism of harshness and contempt' in the name of French national honor.[5] Benda was spiritually shaped by the Dreyfus Affair and World War One, both of them rigorous tests for intellectuals, who could either choose to speak up courageously against an act of anti-Semitic military injustice and nationalist fervor, or sheepishly go along with the herd, refusing to defend the unfairly condemned Jewish officer Alfred Dreyfus, chanting jingoist slogans in order to stir up war fever against everything German. After World War Two Benda republished his book, this time adding a series of attacks against intellectuals who collaborated with the Nazis as well as against those who were uncritically enthusiastic about the Communists.[6] But deep in the combative rhetoric of Benda's basically very conservative work is to be found this figure of the intellectual as a being set apart, someone able to speak the truth to power, a crusty, eloquent, fantastically courageous and angry individual for whom no worldly power is too big and imposing to be criticized and pointedly taken to task.

Gramsci's social analysis of the intellectual as a person who fulfills a particular set of functions in the society is much closer to the reality than anything Benda gives us, particularly in the late twentieth century when so many new professions—broadcasters, academic professionals, computer analysts, sports and media lawyers, management consultants, policy experts, government advisers, authors of specialized market reports, and indeed the whole field of modern mass journalism itself—have vindicated Gramsci's vision.

Today, everyone who works in any field connected either with the production or distribution of knowledge is an intellectual in Gramsci's sense. In most industrialized Western societies the ratio between so-called knowledge industries and those having to do with actual physical production has increased steeply in favor of the knowledge industries. The American sociologist Alvin Gouldner said several years ago of intellectuals that they were the new class, and that intellectual managers had now pretty much replaced the old monied and propertied classes. Yet Gouldner also said that as part of their ascendancy intellectuals were no longer people who addressed a wide public; instead they had become members of what he called a culture of critical discourse.[7] Each intellectual, the book editor and the author, the military strategist and the international lawyer, speaks and deals in a language that has become specialized and usable by other members of the same field, specialized experts addressing other specialized experts in a *lingua franca* largely unintelligible to unspecialized people.

Similarly, the French philosopher Michel Foucault has said that the so-called universal intellectual (he probably had Jean-Paul Sartre in mind) has had his or her place taken by the 'specific' intellectual,[8] someone who works inside a discipline but who is able to use his expertise anyway. Here Foucault was thinking specifically of American physicist Robert Oppenheimer, who moved outside his specialist field when he was an organizer of the Los Alamos atomic bomb project in 1942–45 and later became a sort of commissar of scientific affairs in the U.S.

And the proliferation of intellectuals has extended even into the very large number of fields in which intellectuals—possibly following on Gramsci's pioneering suggestions in *The Prison Notebooks* which almost for the first time saw intellectuals, and not social classes, as pivotal to the workings of modern society—have become the object of study. Just put the words 'of' and 'and' next to the word 'intellectuals' and almost immediately an entire library of studies about intellectuals that is quite daunting in its range and minutely focused in its detail rises before our eyes. There are thousands of different histories and sociologies of intellectuals available, as well as endless accounts of intellectuals and nationalism, and power, and tradition, and revolution, and on and on. Each region of the world has produced its intellectuals and each of those formations is debated and argued over with fiery passion. There has been no major revolution in modern history without intellectuals; conversely there has been no major counterrevolutionary movement without intellectuals. Intellectuals have been the fathers and mothers of movements, and of course sons and daughters, even nephews and nieces.

There is a danger that the figure or image of the intellectual might disappear in a mass of details, and that the intellectual might become only another professional or a figure in a social trend. What I shall be arguing in these lectures takes for granted these late-twentieth-century realities originally suggested by Gramsci, but I also want to insist that the intellectual is an individual with a specific public role in society that cannot be reduced simply to being a faceless professional, a competent member of a class just going about her/his business. The central fact for me is, I think, that the intellectual is an individual endowed with a faculty for representing, embodying, articulating a message, a view, an attitude, philosophy or opinion to, as well as for, a public. And this role has an edge to it, and cannot be played without a sense of being someone whose place it is publicly to raise embarrassing questions, to confront orthodoxy and dogma (rather than to produce them), to be someone who cannot easily be co-opted by governments or corporations, and whose *raison d'être* is to represent all those people and issues that are routinely forgotten or swept under the rug. The intellectual does so on the basis of universal principles: that all human beings are entitled to expect decent standards of behaviour concerning freedom and justice from worldly powers or nations, and that deliberate or inadvertent violations of these standards need to be testified and fought against courageously.

Let me put this in personal terms: as an intellectual I present my concerns before an audience or constituency, but this is not just a matter of how I articulate them, but also of what I myself, as someone who is trying to advance the cause of freedom and justice, also represent. I say or write these things because after much reflection they are what I believe; and I also want to persuade others of this view. There is therefore this quite complicated mix between the private and the public worlds, my own history, values, writings and positions as they derive from my experiences, on the one hand, and, on the other hand, how these enter into the social world where people debate and make decisions about war and freedom and justice. There is no such thing as a private intellectual, since the moment you set down words and then publish them you have entered the public world. Nor is there *only* a public intellectual, someone who exists just as a figurehead or spokesperson or symbol of a cause, movement, or position. There is always the personal inflection and the private sensibility, and those give meaning to what is being said or written. Least of all should an intellectual be there to make his/her audiences feel good: the whole point is to be embarrassing, contrary, even unpleasant.

So in the end it is the intellectual as a representative figure that matters—someone who visibly represents a standpoint of some kind, and someone who makes articulate representations to his or her public despite all sorts of barriers. My argument is that intellectuals are individuals with a vocation for the art of representing, whether that is talking, writing, teaching, appearing on television. And that vocation is important to the extent that it is publicly recognizable and involves both commitment and risk, boldness and vulnerability; when I read Jean-Paul Sartre or Bertrand Russell it is their specific, individual voice and presence that makes an impression on me over and above their arguments because they are speaking out for their beliefs. They cannot be mistaken for an anonymous functionary or careful bureaucrat.

In the outpouring of studies about intellectuals there has been far too much defining of the intellectual, and not enough stock taken of the image, the signature, the actual intervention and performance, all of which taken together constitute the very lifeblood of every real intellectual. Isaiah Berlin has said of nineteenth-century Russian writers that, partly under the influence of German romanticism, their audiences were 'made conscious that he was on a public stage, testifying.'[9] Something of that quality still adheres to the public role of the modern intellectual as I see it. That is why when we remember an intellectual like Sartre we recall the personal mannerisms, the sense of an important personal stake, the sheer effort, risk, will to say things about colonialism, or about commitment, or about social conflict that infuriated his opponents and galvanized his friends and perhaps even embarrassed him retrospectively. When we read about Sartre's involvement with Simone de Beauvoir, his dispute with Camus, his remarkable association with Jean Genet, we situate him (the word is Sartre's) in his circumstances; in these circumstances, and to some extent because of them, Sartre was Sartre, the same person who also opposed France in Algeria and Vietnam. Far from disabling or disqualifying him as an intellectual, these complications give texture and tension to what he said, expose him as a fallible human being, not a dreary and moralistic preacher.

It is in modern public life seen as a novel or drama and not as a business or as the raw material for a sociological monograph that we can most readily see and understand how it is that intellectuals are representative, not just of some subterranean or large social movement, but of a quite peculiar, even abrasive style of life and social performance that is uniquely theirs. And where better to find that role first described than in certain unusual nineteenth- and early-twentieth-century novels—Turgenev's *Fathers and Sons*, Flaubert's *Sentimental Education*, Joyce's *A Portrait of the Artist as a Young Man*—in which the representation of social reality is profoundly influenced, even decisively changed by the sudden appearance of a new actor, the modern young intellectual.

Turgenev's portrait of provincial Russia in the 1860s is idyllic and uneventful: young men of property inherit their habits of life from their parents, they marry and have children, and life more or less moves on. This is the case until an anarchic and yet highly concentrated figure, Bazarov, erupts into their lives. The first thing we notice about him is that he has severed his ties with his own parents, and seems less a son than a sort of self-produced character, challenging routine, assailing mediocrity and clichés, asserting new scientific and unsentimental values that appear to be rational and progressive. Turgenev said that he refused to dip Bazarov in syrup; he was meant to be 'coarse, heart-less, ruthlessly dry and brusque'. Bazarov makes fun of the Kirsanov family; when the middle-aged father plays Schubert, Bazarov laughs loudly at him. Bazarov propounds the ideas of German materialist science: nature for him is not a temple, it is a workshop. When he falls in love with Anna Sergeyevna she is attracted to him, but also terrified: to her, his untrammeled, often anarchical intellectual energy suggests chaos. Being with him, she says at one point, is like teetering at the edge of an abyss.

The beauty and pathos of the novel is that Turgenev suggests, and portrays, the incompatibility between a Russia governed by families, the continuities of love and filial affection, the old natural way of doing things, and at the same time, the nihilistically dis-ruptive force of a Bazarov, whose history, unlike that of every other character in the novel, seems to be impossible to narrate. He appears, he challenges, and just as abruptly, he dies, infected by a sick peasant whom he had been treating. What we remember of Bazarov is the sheer unremitting force of his quest and deeply confrontational intellect; and although Turgenev claimed to have believed he was his most sympathetic character, even he was mystified and to some extent stopped by Bazarov's heedless intellectual force, as well as by his readers' quite bewilderingly turbulent reactions. Some readers thought that Bazarov was an attack on youth; others praised the character as a true hero; still oth-ers thought him dangerous. Whatever we may feel about him as a person, *Fathers and Sons* cannot accommodate Bazarov as a character in the narrative; whereas his friends the Kirsanov family, and even his pathetic old parents, go on with their lives, his peremp-toriness and defiance as an intellectual lift him out of the story, unsuited to it and some-how not fit for domestication.

This is even more explicitly the case with Joyce's young Stephen Dedalus, whose entire early career is a seesaw between the blandishments of institutions like the church, the profession of teaching, Irish nationalism, and his slowly emerging and stubborn self-hood as an intellectual whose motto is the Luciferian *non serviam*. Seamus Deane makes an excellent observation about Joyce's *Portrait of the Artist*: it is, he says, 'the first novel in the English language in which a passion for thinking is fully presented.'[10] Neither the pro-tagonists of Dickens, nor Thackeray, nor Austen, nor Hardy, nor even George Eliot are young men and women whose major concern is the life of the mind in society, whereas for young Dedalus 'thinking is a mode of experiencing the world.' Deane is quite correct in saying that before Dedalus the intellectual vocation had only 'grotesque embodiments' in English fiction. Yet in part because Stephen is a young provincial, the product of a colonial environment, he must develop a resistant intellectual consciousness before he can become an artist.

By the end of the novel he is no less critical and withdrawn from family and Fenians than he is from any ideological scheme whose effect would be to reduce his individuali-ty and his often very unpleasant personality. Like Turgenev, Joyce pointedly enacts the incompatibility between the young intellectual and the sequential flow of human life.

What begins as a conventional story of a young man growing up in a family, then moving on to school and university, decomposes into a series of elliptical jottings from Stephen's notebook. The intellectual will not adjust to domesticity or to humdrum routine. In the novel's most famous speech Stephen expresses what is in effect the intellectual's creed of freedom, although the melodramatic overstatement in Stephen's declaration is Joyce's way of undercutting the young man's pomposity: 'I will tell you what I will do and what I will not do. I will not serve that in which I no longer believe whether it call itself my home, my fatherland or my church: and I will try to express myself in some mode of life or art as freely as I can and as wholly as I can, using for my defence the only arms I allow myself to use—silence, exile, and cunning.'

Yet not even in *Ulysses* do we see Stephen as more than an obstinate and contrary young man. What is most striking in his credo is his affirmation of intellectual freedom. This is a major issue in the intellectual's performance since being a curmudgeon and a thoroughgoing wet blanket are hardly enough as goals. The purpose of the intellectual's activity is to advance human freedom and knowledge. This is still true, I believe, despite the often repeated charge that 'grand narratives of emancipation and enlightenment', as the contemporary French philosopher Lyotard calls such heroic ambitions associated with the previous 'modern' age, are pronounced as no longer having any currency in the era of postmodernism. According to this view grand narratives have been replaced by local situations and language games; postmodern intellectuals now prize competence, not universal values like truth or freedom. I've always thought that Lyotard and his followers are admitting their own lazy incapacities, perhaps even indifference, rather than giving a correct assessment of what remains for the intellectual a truly vast array of opportunities despite postmodernism. For in fact governments still manifestly oppress people, grave miscarriages of justice still occur, the co-optation and inclusion of intellectuals by power can still effectively quieten their voices, and the deviation of intellectuals from their vocation is still very often the case.

In *The Sentimental Education* Flaubert expresses more disappointment with, and therefore a more merciless critique of, intellectuals than anyone. Set in the Parisian upheaval of 1848 to 1851, a period described by the famous British historian Lewis Namier as the revolution of the intellectuals, Flaubert's novel is a wide-ranging panorama of bohemian and political life in 'the capital of the nineteenth century'. At its center stand the two young provincials, Frédéric Moreau and Charles Deslauriers, whose exploits as young men-about-town express Flaubert's rage at their inability to maintain a steady course as intellectuals. Much of Flaubert's scorn for them comes from what is perhaps his exaggerated expectation of what they should have been. The result is the most brilliant representation of the intellectual adrift. The two young men start out as potential legal scholars, critics, historians, essayists, philosophers, and social theorists with public welfare as their goal. Moreau ends up 'with his intellectual ambitions . . . dwindled. Years went by and he endured the idleness of his mind and the inertia of his heart.' Deslauriers becomes 'director of colonization in Algeria, secretary to a pasha, manager of a newspaper, and an advertising agent; . . . at present he was employed as solicitor to an industrial company.'

The failures of 1848 are for Flaubert the failures of his generation. Prophetically, the fates of Moreau and Deslauriers are portrayed as the result of their own lack of focused will and also as the toll exacted by modern society, with its endless distractions, its whirl of pleasures, and, above all, the emergence of journalism, advertising, instant celebrity, and a sphere of constant circulation, in which all ideas are marketable, all values transmutable, all professions reduced to the pursuit of easy money and quick success. The novel's major scenes are therefore organized symbolically around horse races, dances at cafés and bordellos, riots, processions, parades, and public meetings, in which Moreau tries ceaselessly to achieve love and intellectual fulfillment, but is continually deflected from doing so.

But Bazarov, Dedalus, and Moreau are extremes of course, but they do serve the purpose, which is something panoramic realistic novels of the nineteenth century can do uniquely well, of showing us intellectuals in action, beset with numerous difficulties and temptations, either maintaining or betraying their calling, not as a fixed task to be learned once and for all from a how-to-do-it manual but as a concrete experience constantly threatened by modern life itself. The intellectual's representations, his or her articulations of a cause or idea to society, are not meant primarily to fortify ego or celebrate status. Nor are they principally intended for service within powerful bureaucracies and with generous employers. Intellectual representations are the *activity itself*, dependent on a kind of consciousness that is skeptical, engaged, unremittingly devoted to rational investigation and moral judgment; and this puts the individual on record and on the line. Knowing how to use language well and knowing when to intervene in language are two essential features of intellectual action.

But what does the intellectual represent today? One of the best and most honest answers to this question was given, I think, by the American sociologist C. Wright Mills, a fiercely independent intellectual with an impassioned social vision and a remarkable capacity for communicating his ideas in a straightforward and compelling prose. He wrote in 1944 that independent intellectuals were faced either with a kind of despondent sense of powerlessness at their marginality, or with the choice of joining the ranks of institutions, corporations or governments as members of a relatively small group of insiders who made important decisions irresponsibly and on their own. To become the 'hired' agent of an information industry is no solution either, since to achieve a relationship with audiences like Tom Paine's with his would therefore be impossible. In sum 'the means of effective communication', which is the intellectual's currency, is thus being expropriated, leaving the independent thinker with one major task. Here is how Mills puts it:

> The independent artist and intellectual are among the few remaining personalities equipped to resist and to fight the stereotyping and consequent death of genuinely living things. Fresh perception now involves the capacity to continually unmask and to smash the stereotypes of vision and intellect with which modern communications [i.e. modern systems of representation] swamp us. These worlds of mass-art and mass-thought are increasingly geared to the demands of politics. That is why it is in politics that intellectual solidarity and effort must be centered. If the thinker does not relate himself to the value of truth in political struggle, he cannot responsibly cope with the whole of live experience.[11]

This passage deserves reading and rereading, so full of important signposts and emphases is it. Politics is everywhere; there can be no escape into the realms of pure art and thought or, for that matter, into the realm of disinterested objectivity or transcendental theory. Intellectuals are *of* their time, herded along by the mass politics of representations embodied by the information or media industry, capable of resisting those only by disputing the images, official narratives, justifications of power circulated by an increasingly powerful media—and not only media but whole trends of thought that maintain the status quo, keep things within an acceptable and sanctioned perspective on actuality—by providing what Mills calls unmaskings or alternative versions in which to the best of one's ability the intellectual tries to tell the truth.

This is far from an easy task: the intellectual always stands between loneliness and alignment. How difficult it was during the recent Gulf War against Iraq to remind citizens that the U.S. was not an innocent or disinterested power (the invasions of Vietnam and Panama were conveniently forgotten by policy-makers), nor was it appointed by anyone except itself as the world's policeman. But this was, I believe, the intellectuals' task at the time, to unearth the forgotten, to make connections that were denied, to cite alternative courses of action that could have avoided war and its attendant goal of human destruction.

C. Wright Mills's main point is the opposition between the mass and the individual. There is an inherent discrepancy between the powers of large organizations, from governments to corporations, and the relative weakness not just of individuals but of human beings considered to have subaltern status, minorities, small peoples and states, inferior or lesser cultures and races. There is no question in my mind that the intellectual belongs on the same side with the weak and unrepresented. Robin Hood, some are likely to say. Yet it's not that simple a role, and therefore cannot be easily dismissed as just so much romantic idealism. At bottom, the intellectual, in my sense of the word, is neither a pacifier nor a consensus-builder, but someone whose whole being is staked on a critical sense, a sense of being unwilling to accept easy formulas, or ready-made clichés, or the smooth, ever-so-accommodating confirmations of what the powerful or conventional have to say, and what they do. Not just passively unwillingly, but actively willing to say so in public.

This is not always a matter of being a critic of government policy, but rather of thinking of the intellectual vocation as maintaining a state of constant alertness, of a perpetual willingness not to let half-truths or received ideas steer one along. That this involves a steady realism, an almost athletic rational energy, and a complicated struggle to balance the problems of one's own selfhood against the demands of publishing and speaking out in the public sphere is what makes it an everlasting effort, constitutively unfinished and necessarily imperfect. Yet its invigorations and complexities, for me at least, make one the richer for it, even though it doesn't make one particularly popular.

NOTES

1. Antonio Gramsci, *The Prison Notebooks: Selections*, trans. Quintin Hoare and Geoffrey Nowell-Smith (New York: International Publishers, 1971), p. 9.
2. Ibid., p. 4.

3. Julien Benda, *The Treason of the Intellectuals*, trans. Richard Aldington (1928; rprt. New York: Norton, 1969), p. 43.

4. Ibid., p. 52.

5. In 1762 a Protestant merchant, Jean Calas of Toulouse, was judged, then executed for the alleged murder of his son, about to convert to Catholicism. The evidence was flimsy, yet what produced the speedy verdict was the widespread belief that Protestants were fanatics who simply did away with any other Protestant who wanted to convert. Voltaire led a successful public campaign to rehabilitate the Calas family's reputation (yet we now know that he too manufactured his own evidence). Maurice Barrès was a prominent opponent of Alfred Dreyfus. A proto-fascist and anti-intellectual late-nineteenth- and early-twentieth-century French novelist, he advocated a notion of the political unconscious, in which whole races and nations carried ideas and tendencies collectively.

6. *La Trahison* was republished by Bernard Grasset in 1946.

7. Alvin W. Gouldner, *The Future of Intellectuals and the Rise of the New Class* (New York: Seabury Press, 1979), pp. 28–43.

8. Michel Foucault, *Power/Knowledge: Selected Interviews and Other Writings 1972–1977*, ed. Colin Gordon (New York: Pantheon, 1980), pp. 127–28.

9. Isaiah Berlin, *Russian Thinkers*, ed. Henry Hardy and Aileen Kelly (New York: Viking Press, 1978), p. 129.

10. Seamus Deane, *Celtic Revivals: Essays in Modern Irish Literature 1880–1980* (London: Faber & Faber, 1985), pp. 75–76.

11. C. Wright Mills, *Power, Politics, and People: The Collected Essays of C. Wright Mills*, ed. Irving Louis Horowitz (New York: Ballantine, 1963), p. 299.

ORIENTALISM NOW

> On les apercevait tenant leurs idoles entre leurs bras comme de grands enfants paralytiques.
>
> —Gustave Flaubert, *La Tentation de Saint Antoine*

> The conquest of the earth, which mostly means the taking it away from those who have a different complexion or slightly flatter noses than ourselves, is not a pretty thing when you look into it too much. What redeems it is the idea only. An idea at the back of it; not a sentimental pretence but an idea; and an unselfish belief in the idea— something you can set up, and bow down before, and offer a sacrifice to ....
>
> —Joseph Conrad, *Heart of Darkness*

Latent and Manifest Orientalism

In Chapter One, I tried to indicate the scope of thought and action covered by the word *Orientalism*, using as privileged types the British and French experiences of and with the

Near Orient, Islam, and the Arabs. In those experiences I discerned an intimate, perhaps even the most intimate, and rich relationship between Occident and Orient. Those experiences were part of a much wider European or Western relationship with the Orient, but what seems to have influenced Orientalism most was a fairly constant sense of confrontation felt by Westerners dealing with the East. The boundary notion of East and West, the varying degrees of projected inferiority and strength, the range of work done, the kinds of characteristic features ascribed to the Orient: all these testify to a willed imaginative and geographic division made between East and West, and lived through during many centuries. In Chapter Two my focus narrowed a good deal. I was interested in the earliest phases of what I call modern Orientalism, which began during the latter part of the eighteenth century and the early years of the nineteenth. Since I did not intend my study to become a narrative chronicle of the development of Oriental studies in the modern West, I proposed instead an account of the rise, development, and institutions of Orientalism as they were formed against a background of intellectual, cultural, and political history until about 1870 or 1880. Although my interest in Orientalism there included a decently ample variety of scholars and imaginative writers, I cannot claim by any means to have presented more than a portrait of the typical structures (and their ideological tendencies) constituting the field, its associations with other fields, and the work of some of its most influential scholars. My principal operating assumptions were—and continue to be—that fields of learning, as much as the works of even the most eccentric artist, are constrained and acted upon by society, by cultural traditions, by worldly circumstance, and by stabilizing influences like schools, libraries, and governments; moreover, that both learned and imaginative writing are never free, but are limited in their imagery, assumptions, and intentions; and finally, that the advances made by a 'science' like Orientalism in its academic form are less objectively true than we often like to think. In short, my study hitherto has tried to describe the *economy* that makes Orientalism a coherent subject matter, even while allowing that as an idea, concept, or image the word *Orient* has a considerable and interesting cultural resonance in the West.

I realize that such assumptions are not without their controversial side. Most of us assume in a general way that learning and scholarship move forward; they get better, we feel, as time passes and as more information is accumulated, methods are refined, and later generations of scholars improve upon earlier ones. In addition, we entertain a mythology of creation, in which it is believed that artistic genius, an original talent, or a powerful intellect can leap beyond the confines of its own time and place in order to put before the world a new work. It would be pointless to deny that such ideas as these carry some truth. Nevertheless the possibilities for work present in the culture to a great and original mind are never unlimited, just as it is also true that a great talent has a very healthy respect for what others have done before it and for what the field already contains. The work of predecessors, the institutional life of a scholarly field, the collective nature of any learned enterprise: these, to say nothing of economic and social circumstances, tend to diminish the effects of the individual scholar's production. A field like Orientalism has a cumulative and corporate identity, one that is particularly strong given its associations with traditional learning (the classics, the Bible, philology), public institutions (governments, trading companies, geographical societies, universities), and generically determined writing (travel books, books of exploration, fantasy, exotic description). The result for Orientalism has been a sort of consensus: certain things, certain types of statement, certain types of work have seemed for the Orientalist correct. He has built his work and research upon them, and they in turn have pressed hard upon new writers and scholars. Orientalism can thus be regarded as a manner of regularized (or Orientalized) writing, vision, and study, dominated by imperatives, perspectives, and ideological biases ostensibly suited to the Orient. The Orient is taught, researched, administered, and pronounced upon in certain discrete ways.

The Orient that appears in Orientalism, then, is a system of representations framed by a whole set of forces that brought the Orient into Western learning, Western consciousness, and later, Western empire. If this definition of Orientalism seems more political than not, that is simply because I think Orientalism was itself a product of certain political forces and activities. Orientalism is a school of interpretation whose material happens to be the Orient, its civilizations, peoples, and localities. Its objective discoveries—the work of innumerable devoted scholars who edited texts and translated them, codified grammars, wrote dictionaries, reconstructed dead epochs, produced positivistically verifiable learning—are and always have been conditioned by the fact that its truths, like any truths delivered by language, are embodied in language, and what is the truth of language, Nietzsche once said, but

> a mobile army of metaphors, metonyms, and anthropomorphisms—in short, a sum of human relations, which have been enhanced, transposed, and embellished poetically and rhetorically, and which after long use seem firm, canonical, and obligatory to a people: truths are illusions about which one has forgotten that this is what they are.[1]

Perhaps such a view as Nietzsche's will strike us as too nihilistic, but at least it will draw attention to the fact that so far as it existed in the West's awareness, the Orient was a word which later accrued to it a wide field of meanings, associations, and connotations, and that these did not necessarily refer to the real Orient but to the field surrounding the word.

Thus Orientalism is not only a positive doctrine about the Orient that exists at any one time in the West; it is also an influential academic tradition (when one refers to an academic specialist who is called an Orientalist), as well as an area of concern defined by travelers, commercial enterprises, governments, military expeditions, readers of novels and accounts of exotic adventure, natural historians, and pilgrims to whom the Orient is a specific kind of knowledge about specific places, peoples, and civilizations. For the Orient idioms became frequent, and these idioms took firm hold in European discourse. Beneath the idioms there was a layer of doctrine about the Orient; this doctrine was fashioned out of the experiences of many Europeans, all of them converging upon such essential aspects of the Orient as the Oriental character, Oriental despotism, Oriental sensuality, and the like. For any European during the nineteenth century—and I think one can say this almost without qualification—Orientalism was such a system of truths, truths in Nietzsche's sense of the word. It is therefore correct that every European, in what he could say about the Orient, was consequently a racist, an imperialist, and almost totally ethnocentric. Some of the immediate sting will be taken out of these labels if we recall additionally that human societies, at least the more advanced cultures, have rarely offered the individual anything but imperialism, racism, and ethnocentrism for dealing with 'other' cultures. So Orientalism aided and was aided by general cultural pressures that tended to make more rigid the sense of difference between the European and Asiatic parts of the world. My contention is that Orientalism is fundamentally a political doctrine willed over the Orient because the Orient was weaker than the West, which elided the Orient's difference with its weakness.

This proposition was introduced early in Chapter One, and nearly everything in the pages that followed was intended in part as a corroboration of it. The very presence of a 'field' such as Orientalism, with no corresponding equivalent in the Orient itself, suggests the relative strength of Orient and Occident. A vast number of pages on the Orient exist, and they of course signify a degree and quantity of interaction with the Orient that are quite formidable; but the crucial index of Western strength is that there is no possibility of comparing the movement of Westerners eastwards (since the end of the eighteenth century) with the movement of Easterners westwards. Leaving aside the fact that Western armies, consular corps, merchants, and scientific and archaeological expeditions were always going East, the number of travelers from the Islamic East to Europe between 1800 and 1900 is minuscule when compared with the number in the other direction.[2] Moreover, the Eastern travelers in the West were there to learn from and to gape at an advanced culture; the purposes of the Western travelers in the Orient were, as we have seen, of quite a different order. In addition, it has been estimated that around 60,000 books dealing with the Near Orient were written between 1800 and 1950; there is no remotely comparable figure for Oriental books about the West. As a cultural apparatus Orientalism is all aggression, activity, judgment, will-to-truth, and knowledge. The Orient existed for the West, or so it seemed to countless Orientalists, whose attitude to what they worked on was either paternalistic or candidly condescending—unless, of course, they were antiquarians, in which case the 'classical' Orient was a credit to them and not to the lamentable modern Orient. And then, beefing up the Western scholars' work, there were numerous agencies and institutions with no parallels in Oriental society.

Such an imbalance between East and West is obviously a function of changing historical patterns. During its political and military heyday from the eighth century to the sixteenth, Islam dominated both East and West. Then the center of power shifted westwards, and now in the late twentieth century it seems to be directing itself back towards the East again. My account of nineteenth-century Orientalism in Chapter Two stopped at a particularly charged period in the latter part of the century, when the often dilatory, abstract, and projective aspects of Orientalism were about to take on a new sense of worldly mission in the service of formal colonialism. It is this project and this moment that I want now to describe, especially since it will furnish us with some important background for the twentieth-century crises of Orientalism and the resurgence of political and cultural strength in the East.

On several occasions I have alluded to the connections between Orientalism as a body of ideas, beliefs, clichés, or learning about the East, and other schools of thought at large in the culture. Now one of the important developments in nineteenth-century Orientalism was the distillation of essential ideas about the Orient—its sensuality, its tendency to despotism, its aberrant mentality, its habits of inaccuracy, its backwardness—into a separate and unchallenged coherence; thus for a writer to use the word *Oriental* was a reference for the reader sufficient to identify a specific body of information about the Orient. This information seemed to be morally neutral and objectively valid; it seemed to have an epistemological status equal to that of historical chronology or geographical location. In its most basic form, then, Oriental material could not really be violated by anyone's discoveries, nor did it seem ever to be revaluated completely. Instead, the work of various nineteenth-century scholars and of imaginative writers made this essential body of knowledge more clear, more detailed, more substantial—and more distinct from 'Occidentalism'. Yet Orientalist ideas could enter into alliance with general philosophical theories (such as those about the history of mankind and civilization) and diffuse world-hypotheses, as philosophers sometimes call them; and in many ways the professional contributors to Oriental knowledge were anxious to couch their formulations and ideas, their scholarly work, their considered contemporary observations, in language and terminology whose cultural validity derived from other sciences and systems of thought.

The distinction I am making is really between an almost unconscious (and certainly an untouchable) positivity, which I shall call *latent* Orientalism, and the various stated views about Oriental society, languages, literatures, history, sociology, and so forth, which I shall call *manifest* Orientalism. Whatever change occurs in knowledge of the Orient is found almost exclusively in manifest Orientalism; the unanimity, stability, and durability of latent Orientalism are more or less constant. In the nineteenth-century writers I analyzed in Chapter Two, the differences in their ideas about the Orient can be characterized as exclusively manifest differences, differences in form and personal style, rarely in basic content. Every one of them kept intact the separateness of the Orient, its eccentricity, its backwardness, its silent indifference, its feminine penetrability, its supine malleability; this is why every writer on the Orient, from Renan to Marx (ideologically speaking), or from the most rigorous scholars (Lane and Sacy) to the most powerful imaginations (Flaubert and Nerval), saw the Orient as a locale requiring Western attention, reconstruction, even redemption. The Orient existed as a place isolated from the mainstream of European progress in the sciences, arts, and commerce. Thus whatever good or bad values were imputed to the Orient appeared to be functions of some highly specialized Western interest in the Orient. This was the situation from about the 1870s on through the early part of the twentieth century—but let me give some examples that illustrate what I mean.

Theses of Oriental backwardness, degeneracy, and inequality with the West most easily associated themselves early in the nineteenth century with ideas about the biological bases of racial inequality. Thus the racial classifications found in Cuvier's *Le Règne animal*, Gobineau's *Essai sur l'inégalité des races humaines*, and Robert Knox's *The Races of Man* found a willing partner in latent Orientalism. To these ideas was added second-order Darwinism, which seemed to accentuate the scientific validity of the division of races into advanced and backward, or European-Aryan and Oriental-African. Thus the whole question of imperialism, as it was debated in the late nineteenth century by pro-imperialists and anti-imperialists alike, carried forward the binary typology of advanced and backward (or subject) races, cultures, and societies. John Westlake's *Chapters on the Principles of*

International Law (1894) argues, for example, that regions of the earth designated as 'uncivilized' (a word carrying the freight of Orientalist assumptions, among others) ought to be annexed or occupied by advanced powers. Similarly, the ideas of such writers as Carl Peters, Leopold de Saussure, and Charles Temple draw on the advanced/backward binarism[3] so centrally advocated in late nineteenth-century Orientalism.

Along with all other peoples variously designated as backward, degenerate, uncivilized, and retarded, the Orientals were viewed in a framework constructed out of biological determinism and moral-political admonishment. The Oriental was linked thus to elements in Western society (delinquents, the insane, women, the poor) having in common an identity best described as lamentably alien. Orientals were rarely seen or looked at; they were seen through, analyzed not as citizens, or even people, but as problems to be solved or confined or—as the colonial powers openly coveted their territory—taken over. The point is that the very designation of something as Oriental involved an already pronounced evaluative judgment, and in the case of the peoples inhabiting the decayed Ottoman Empire, an implicit program of action. Since the Oriental was a member of a subject race, he had to be subjected: it was that simple. The *locus classicus* for such judgment and action is to be found in Gustave Le Bon's *Les Lois psychologiques de l'évolution des peuples* (1894).

But there were other uses for latent Orientalism. If that group of ideas allowed one to separate Orientals from advanced, civilizing powers, and if the 'classical' Orient served to justify both the Orientalist and his disregard of modern Orientals, latent Orientalism also encouraged a peculiarly (not to say invidiously) male conception of the world. I have already referred to this in passing during my discussion of Renan. The Oriental male was considered in isolation from the total community in which he lived and which many Orientalists, following Lane, have viewed with something resembling contempt and fear. Orientalism itself, furthermore, was an exclusively male province; like so many professional guilds during the modern period, it viewed itself and its subject matter with sexist blinders. This is especially evident in the writing of travelers and novelists: women are usually the creatures of a male power-fantasy. They express unlimited sensuality, they are more or less stupid, and above all they are willing. Flaubert's Kuchuk Hanem is the prototype of such caricatures, which were common enough in pornographic novels (e.g., Pierre Louÿs's *Aphrodite*) whose novelty draws on the Orient for their interest. Moreover the male conception of the world, in its effect upon the practicing Orientalist, tends to be static, frozen, fixed eternally. The very possibility of development, transformation, human movement—in the deepest sense of the word—is denied the Orient and the Oriental. As a known and ultimately an immobilized or unproductive quality, they come to be identified with a bad sort of eternality: hence, when the Orient is being approved, such phrases as 'the wisdom of the East'.

Transferred from an implicit social evaluation to a grandly cultural one, this static male Orientalism took on a variety of forms in the late nineteenth century, especially when Islam was being discussed. General cultural historians as respected as Leopold von Ranke and Jacob Burckhardt assailed Islam as if they were dealing not so much with an anthropomorphic abstraction as with a religio-political culture about which deep generalizations were possible and warranted: in his *Weltgeschichte* (1881–1888) Ranke spoke of Islam as defeated by the Germanic-Romanic peoples, and in his 'Historische Fragmente' (unpublished notes, 1893) Burckhardt spoke of Islam as wretched, bare, and trivial.[4] Such intellectual operations were carried out with considerably more flair and enthusiasm by Oswald Spengler, whose ideas about a Magian personality (typified by the Muslim Oriental) infuse *Der Untergang des Abendlandes* (1918–1922) and the 'morphology' of cultures it advocates.

What these widely diffused notions of the Orient depended on was the almost total absence in contemporary Western culture of the Orient as a genuinely felt and experienced force. For a number of evident reasons the Orient was always in the position both of outsider and of incorporated weak partner for the West. To the extent that Western scholars were aware of contemporary Orientals or Oriental movements of thought and culture, these were perceived either as silent shadows to be animated by the Orientalist, brought into reality by him, or as a kind of cultural and intellectual proletariat useful for the Orientalist's grander interpretative activity, necessary for his performance as superior judge, learned man, powerful cultural will. I mean to say that in discussions of the Orient, the Orient is all absence, whereas one feels the Orientalist and what he says as presence; yet we must not forget that the Orientalist's presence is enabled by the Orient's effective absence. This fact of substitution and displacement, as we must call it, clearly places on the Orientalist himself a certain pressure to reduce the Orient in his work, even after he has devoted a good deal of time to elucidating and exposing it. How else can one explain major scholarly production of the type we associate with Julius Wellhausen and Theodor Nöldeke and, overriding it, those bare, sweeping statements that almost totally denigrate their chosen subject matter? Thus Nöldeke could declare in 1887 that the sum total of his work as an Orientalist was to confirm his 'low opinion' of the Eastern peoples.[5] And like Carl Becker, Nöldeke was a philhellenist, who showed his love of Greece curiously by displaying a positive dislike of the Orient, which after all was what he studied as a scholar.

A very valuable and intelligent study of Orientalism—Jacques Waardenburg's *L'Islam dans le miroir de l'Occident*—examines five important experts as makers of an image of Islam. Waardenburg's mirror-image metaphor for late-nineteenth- and early-twentieth-century Orientalism is apt. In the work of each of his eminent Orientalists there is a highly tendentious—in four cases out of the five, even hostile—vision of Islam, as if each man saw Islam as a reflection of his own chosen weakness. Each scholar was profoundly learned, and the style of his contribution was unique. The five Orientalists among them exemplify what was best and strongest in the tradition during the period roughly from the 1880s to the interwar years. Yet Ignaz Goldziher's appreciation of Islam's tolerance towards other religions was undercut by his dislike of Mohammed's anthropomorphisms and Islam's too-exterior theology and jurisprudence; Duncan Black Macdonald's interest in Islamic piety and orthodoxy was vitiated by his perception of what he considered Islam's heretical Christianity; Carl Becker's understanding of Islamic civilization made him see it as a sadly undeveloped one; C. Snouck Hurgronje's highly refined studies of Islamic mysticism (which he considered the essential part of Islam) led him to a harsh judgment of its crippling limitations; and Louis Massignon's extraordinary identification with Muslim theology, mystical passion, and poetic art kept him curiously unforgiving to Islam for what he regarded as its unregenerate revolt against the idea of incarnation. The manifest differences in their methods emerge as less important than their Orientalist consensus on Islam: latent inferiority.[6]

Waardenburg's study has the additional virtue of showing how these five scholars shared a common intellectual and methodological tradition whose unity was truly international. Ever since the first Orientalist congress in 1873, scholars in the field have known each other's work and felt each other's presence very directly. What Waardenburg does not stress enough is that most of the late-nineteenth-century Orientalists were bound to each other politically as well. Snouck Hurgronje went directly from his studies of Islam to being an adviser to the Dutch government on handling its Muslim Indonesian colonies; Macdonald and Massignon were widely sought after as experts on Islamic matters by colonial administrators from North Africa to Pakistan; and, as Waardenburg says (all too briefly) at one point, all five scholars shaped a coherent vision of Islam that had a wide influence on government circles throughout the Western world.[7] What we must add to Waardenburg's observation is that these scholars were completing, bringing to an ultimate concrete refinement, the tendency since the sixteenth and seventeenth centuries to treat the Orient not only as a vague literary problem but—according to Masson-Oursel—as 'un ferme propos d'assimiler adéquatement la valeur des langues pour pénétrer les moeurs et les pensées, pour forcer même des secrets de l'histoire.'[8]

I spoke earlier of incorporation and assimilation of the Orient, as these activities were practiced by writers as different from each other as Dante and d'Herbelot. Clearly there is a difference between those efforts and what, by the end of the nineteenth century, had become a truly formidable European cultural, political, and material enterprise. The nineteenth-century colonial 'scramble for Africa' was by no means limited to Africa, of course. Neither was the penetration of the Orient entirely a sudden, dramatic afterthought following years of scholarly study of Asia. What we must reckon with is a long and slow process of appropriation by which Europe, or the European awareness of the Orient, transformed itself from being textual and contemplative into being administrative, economic, and even military. The fundamental change was a spatial and geographical one, or rather it was a change in the quality of geographical and spatial apprehension so far as the Orient was concerned. The centuries-old designation of geographical space to the east of Europe as 'Oriental' was partly political, partly doctrinal, and partly imaginative; it implied no necessary connection between actual experience of the Orient and knowledge of what is Oriental, and certainly Dante and d'Herbelot made no claims about their Oriental ideas except that they were corroborated by a long *learned* (and not existential) tradition. But when Lane, Renan, Burton, and the many hundreds of nineteenth-century European travelers and scholars discuss the Orient, we can immediately note a far more intimate and even proprietary attitude towards the Orient and things Oriental. In the classical and often temporally remote form in which it was reconstructed by the Orientalist, in the precisely actual form in which the modern Orient was lived in, studied, or imagined, the *geographical space* of the Orient was penetrated, worked over, taken hold of. The cumulative effect of decades of so sovereign a Western handling turned the Orient from alien into colonial space. What was important in the latter nineteenth century was not *whether* the West had penetrated and possessed the Orient, but rather *how* the British and French felt that they had done it.

The British writer on the Orient, and even more so the British colonial administrator, was dealing with territory about which there could be no doubt that English power was truly in the ascendant, even if the natives were on the face of it attracted to France and French modes of thought. So far as the actual space of the Orient was concerned, however, England was really there, France was not, except as a flighty temptress of the Oriental yokels. There is no better indication of this qualitative difference in spatial attitudes than to look at what Lord Cromer had to say on the subject, one that was especially dear to his heart:

> The reasons why French civilisation presents a special degree of attraction to Asiatics and Levantines are plain. It is, as a matter of fact, more attractive than the civilisations of England and Germany, and, moreover, it is more easy of imitation. Compare the undemonstrative, shy Englishman, with his social exclusiveness and insular habits, with the vivacious and cosmopolitan Frenchman, who does not know what the word shyness means, and who in ten minutes is apparently on terms of intimate friendship with any casual acquaintance he may chance to make. The semi-educated Oriental does not recognise that the former has, at all events, the merit of sincerity, whilst the latter is often merely acting a part. He looks coldly on the Englishman, and rushes into the arms of the Frenchman.

The sexual innuendoes develop more or less naturally thereafter. The Frenchman is all smiles, wit, grace, and fashion; the Englishman is plodding, industrious, Baconian, precise. Cromer's case is of course based on British solidity as opposed to a French seductiveness without any real presence in Egyptian reality.

> Can it be any matter for surprise [Cromer continues] that the Egyptian, with his light intellectual ballast, fails to see that some fallacy often lies at the bottom of the Frenchman's reasoning, or that he prefers the rather superficial brilliancy of the Frenchman to the plodding, unattractive industry of the Englishman or the German? Look, again, at the theoretical perfection of French administrative systems, at their elaborate detail, and at the provision which is apparently made to meet every possible contingency which may arise. Compare these features with the Englishman's practical systems, which lay down rules as to a few main points, and leave a mass of detail to individual discretion. The half-educated Egyptian naturally prefers the Frenchman's system, for it is to all outward appearance more perfect and more easy of application. He fails, moreover, to see that the Englishman desires to elaborate a system which will suit the facts with which he has to deal, whereas the main objection to applying French administrative procedures to Egypt is that the facts have but too often to conform to the ready-made system.

Since there is a real British presence in Egypt, and since that presence—according to Cromer—is there not so much to train the Egyptian's mind as to 'form his character', it follows therefore that the ephemeral attractions of the French are those of a pretty damsel with 'somewhat artificial charms', whereas those of the British belong to 'a sober, elderly matron of perhaps somewhat greater moral worth, but of less pleasing outward appearance.'[9]

Underlying Cromer's contrast between the solid British nanny and the French coquette is the sheer privilege of British emplacement in the Orient. 'The facts with which he [the Englishman] has to deal' are altogether more complex and interesting, by virtue of their possession by England, than anything the mercurial French could point to. Two years after the publication of his *Modern Egypt* (1908), Cromer expatiated philosophically in *Ancient and Modern Imperialism*. Compared with Roman imperialism, with its frankly assimilationist, exploitative, and repressive policies, British imperialism seemed to Cromer to be preferable, if somewhat more wishy-washy. On certain points, however, the British were clear enough, even if 'after a rather dim, slipshod, but characteristically Anglo-Saxon fashion', their Empire seemed undecided between 'one of two bases—an extensive military occupation or the principle of nationality [for subject races].' But this indecision was academic finally, for in practice Cromer and Britain itself had opted against 'the principle of nationality'. And then there were other things to be noted. One point was that the Empire was not going to be given up. Another was that intermarriage between natives and English men and women was undesirable. Third—and most important, I think—Cromer conceived of British imperial presence in the Eastern colonies as having had a lasting, not to say cataclysmic, effect on the minds and societies of the East. His metaphor for expressing this effect is almost theological, so powerful in Cromer's mind was the idea of Western penetration of Oriental expanses. 'The country', he says, 'over which the breath of the West, heavily charged with scientific thought, has once passed, and has, in passing, left an enduring mark, can never be the same as it was before.'[10]

In such respects as these, nonetheless, Cromer's was far from an original intelligence. What he saw and how he expressed it were common currency among his colleagues both in the imperial Establishment and in the intellectual community. This consensus is notably true in the case of Cromer's viceregal colleagues, Curzon, Swettenham, and Lugard. Lord Curzon in particular always spoke the imperial lingua franca, and more obtrusively even than Cromer he delineated the relationship between Britain and the Orient in terms of possession, in terms of a large geographical space wholly owned by an efficient colonial master. For him, he said on one occasion, the Empire was not an 'object of ambition' but 'first and foremost, a great historical and political and sociological fact.' In 1909 he reminded delegates to the Imperial Press Conference meeting at Oxford that 'we train here and we send out to you your governors and administrators and judges, your teachers and preachers and lawyers.' And this almost pedagogical view of empire had, for Curzon, a specific setting in Asia, which as he once put it, made 'one pause and think'.

> I sometimes like to picture to myself this great Imperial fabric as a huge structure like some Tennysonian 'Palace of Art', of which the foundations are in this country, where they have been laid and must be maintained by British hands, but of which the Colonies are the pillars, and high above all floats the vastness of an Asiatic dome.[11]

With such a Tennysonian Palace of Art in mind, Curzon and Cromer were enthusiastic members together of a departmental committee formed in 1909 to press for the creation of a school of Oriental studies. Aside from remarking wistfully that had he known the vernacular he would have been helped during his 'famine tours' in India, Curzon argued for Oriental studies as part of the British responsibility to the Orient. On September 27, 1909, he told the House of Lords that

> our familiarity, not merely with the languages of the people of the East but with their customs, their feelings, their traditions, their history and religion, our capacity to understand what may be called the genius of the East, is the sole basis upon which we are likely to be able to maintain in the future the position we have won, and no step that can be taken to strengthen that position can be considered undeserving of the attention of His Majesty's Government or of a debate in the House of Lords.

At a Mansion House conference on the subject five years later, Curzon finally dotted the i's. Oriental studies were no intellectual luxury; they were, he said,

> a great Imperial obligation. In my view the creation of a school [of Oriental studies— later to become the London University School of Oriental and African Studies] like this in London is part of the necessary furniture of Empire. Those of us who, in one way or another, have spent a number of years in the East, who regard that as the happiest portion of our lives, and who think that the work that we did there, be it great or small, was the highest responsibility that can be placed upon the shoulders of Englishmen, feel that there is a gap in our national equipment which ought emphatically to be filled, and that those in the City of London who, by financial support or by any other form of active and practical assistance, take their part in filling that gap, will be rendering a patriotic duty to the Empire and promoting the cause and goodwill among mankind.[12]

To a very great extent Curzon's ideas about Oriental studies derive logically from a good century of British utilitarian administration of and philosophy about the Eastern colonies. The influence of Bentham and the Mills on British rule in the Orient (and India particularly) was considerable, and was effective in doing away with too much regulation and innovation; instead, as Eric Stokes has convincingly shown, utilitarianism combined with the legacies of liberalism and evangelicalism as philosophies of British rule in the East stressed the rational importance of a strong executive armed with various legal and penal codes, a system of doctrines on such matters as frontiers and land rents, and everywhere an irreducible supervisory imperial authority.[13] The cornerstone of the whole system was a constantly refined knowledge of the Orient, so that as traditional societies hastened forward and became modern commercial societies, there would be no loss of paternal British control, and no loss of revenue either. However, when Curzon referred somewhat inelegantly to Oriental studies as 'the necessary furniture of Empire', he was putting into a static image the transactions by which Englishmen and natives conducted their business and kept their places. From the days of Sir William Jones the Orient had been both what Britain ruled and what Britain knew about it: the coincidence between geography, knowledge, and power, with Britain always in the master's place, was complete. To have said, as Curzon once did, that 'the East is a University in which the scholar never takes his degree' was another way of saying that the East required one's presence there more or less forever.[14]

But then there were the other European powers, France and Russia among them, that made the British presence always a (perhaps marginally) threatened one. Curzon was certainly aware that all the major Western powers felt towards the world as Britain did. The transformation of geography from 'dull and pedantic'—Curzon's phrase for what had now dropped out of geography as an academic subject—into 'the most cosmopolitan of all sciences' argued *exactly* that new Western and widespread predilection. Not for nothing did Curzon in 1912 tell the Geographical Society, of which he was president, that

> an absolute revolution has occurred, not merely in the manner and methods of teaching geography, but in the estimation in which it is held by public opinion. Nowadays we regard geographical knowledge as an essential part of knowledge in general. By the aid of geography, and in no other way, do we understand the action of great natural forces, the distribution of population, the growth of commerce, the expansion of frontiers, the development of States, the splendid achievements of human energy in its various manifestations.
>
> We recognize geography as the handmaid of history. . . . Geography, too, is a sister science to economics and politics; and to any of us who have attempted to study geography it is known that the moment you diverge from the geographical field you find yourself crossing the frontiers of geology, zoology, ethnology, chemistry, physics, and almost all the kindred sciences. Therefore we are justified in saying that geography is one of the first and foremost of the sciences: that it is part of the equipment that is necessary for a proper conception of citizenship, and is an indispensable adjunct to the production of a public man.[15]

Geography was essentially the material underpinning for knowledge about the Orient. All the latent and unchanging characteristics of the Orient stood upon, were rooted in, its geography. Thus on the one hand the geographical Orient nourished its inhabitants, guaranteed their characteristics, and defined their specificity; on the other hand, the geographical Orient solicited the West's attention, even as—by one of those paradoxes revealed so frequently by organized knowledge—East was East and West was West. The cosmopolitanism of geography was, in Curzon's mind, its universal importance to the whole of the West, whose relationship to the rest of the world was one of frank covetousness. Yet geographical appetite could also take on the moral neutrality of an epistemological impulse to find out, to settle upon, to uncover—as when in *Heart of Darkness* Marlow confesses to having a passion for maps.

> I would look for hours at South America, or Africa, or Australia, and lose myself in all the glories of exploration. At that time there were many blank spaces on the earth, and when I saw one that looked particularly inviting on a map (but they all look that) I would put my finger on it and say, When I grow up I will go there.[16]

Seventy years or so before Marlow said this, it did not trouble Lamartine that what on a map was a blank space was inhabited by natives; nor, theoretically, had there been any reservation in the mind of Emer de Vattel, the Swiss-Prussian authority on international law, when in 1758 he invited European states to take possession of territory inhabited only by mere wandering tribes.[17] The important thing was to dignify simple conquest with an idea, to turn the appetite for more geographical space into a theory about the special relationship between geography on the one hand and civilized or uncivilized peoples on the other. But to these rationalizations there was also a distinctively French contribution.

By the end of the nineteenth century, political and intellectual circumstances coincided sufficiently in France to make geography, and geographical speculation (in both senses of that word), an attractive national pastime. The general climate of opinion in Europe was propitious; certainly the successes of British imperialism spoke loudly enough for themselves. However, Britain always seemed to France and to French thinkers on the subject to block even a relatively successful French imperial role in the Orient. Before the Franco-Prussian War there was a good deal of wishful political thinking about the Orient, and it was not confined to poets and novelists. Here, for instance, is Saint-Marc Girardin writing in the *Revue des Deux Mondes* on March 15, 1862:

> La France a beaucoup à faire en Orient, parce que l'Orient attend beaucoup d'elle. Il lui demande même plus qu'elle ne peut faire; il lui remettrait volontiers le soin entier de son avenir, ce qui serait pour la France et pour l'Orient un grand danger: pour la France, parce que, disposée a prendre en mains la cause des populations souffrantes, elle se charge le plus souvent de plus d'obligations qu'elle n'en peut remplir; pour l'Orient, parce que tout peuple qui attend sa destinée de l'étranger n'a jamais qu'une condition précaire et qu'il n'y a de salut pour les nations que celui qu'elles se font elles-mêmes.[18]

Of such views as this Disraeli would doubtless have said, as he often did, that France had only 'sentimental interests' in Syria (which is the 'Orient' of which Girardin was writing). The fiction of 'populations souffrantes' had of course been used by Napoleon when he appealed to the Egyptians on their behalf against the Turks and for Islam. During the thirties, forties, fifties, and sixties the suffering populations of the Orient were limited to the Christian minorities in Syria. And there was no record of 'l'Orient' appealing to France for its salvation. It would have been altogether more truthful to say that Britain stood in France's way in the Orient, for even if France genuinely felt a sense of obligation to the Orient (and there were some Frenchmen who did), there was very little France could do to get between Britain and the huge land mass it commanded from India to the Mediterranean.

Among the most remarkable consequences of the War of 1870 in France were a tremendous efflorescence of geographical societies and a powerfully renewed demand for territorial acquisition. At the end of 1871 the Société de géographie de Paris declared itself no longer confined to 'scientific speculation'. It urged the citizenry not to 'forget that our former preponderance was contested from the day we ceased to compete . . . in the conquests of civilization over barbarism.' Guillaume Depping, a leader of what has come to be called the geographical movement, asserted in 1881 that during the 1870 war 'it was the schoolmaster who triumphed', meaning that the real triumphs were those of Prussian scientific geography over French strategic sloppiness. The government's *Journal officiel*

sponsored issue after issue centered on the virtues (and profits) of geographical exploration and colonial adventure; a citizen could learn in one issue from de Lesseps of 'the
opportunities in Africa' and from Garnier of 'the exploration of the Blue River'. Scientific
geography soon gave way to 'commercial geography', as the connection between national
pride in scientific and civilizational achievement and the fairly rudimentary profit motive
was urged, to be channeled into support for colonial acquisition. In the words of one
enthusiast, 'The geographical societies are formed to break the fatal charm that holds us
enchained to our shores.' In aid of this liberating quest all sorts of schemes were spun out,
including the enlisting of Jules Verne—whose unbelievable success, as it was called, ostensibly displayed the scientific mind at a very high peak of ratiocination—to head 'a round-
the-world campaign of scientific exploration', and a plan for creating a vast new sea just
south of the North African coast, as well as a project for 'binding' Algeria to Senegal by
railroad—'a ribbon of steel', as the projectors called it.[19]

Much of the expansionist fervor in France during the last third of the nineteenth century was generated out of an explicit wish to compensate for the Prussian victory in 1870-
1871 and, no less important, the desire to match British imperial achievements. So powerful was the latter desire, and out of so long a tradition of Anglo-French rivalry in the
Orient did it derive, that France seemed literally haunted by Britain, anxious in all things
connected with the Orient to catch up with and emulate the British. When in the late
1870s, the Société académique indo-chinoise reformulated its goals, it found it important
to 'bring Indochina into the domain of Orientalism'. Why? In order to turn Cochin China
into a 'French India'. The absence of substantial colonial holdings was blamed by military
men for that combination of military and commercial weakness in the war with Prussia, to
say nothing of long-standing and pronounced colonial inferiority compared with Britain.
The 'power of expansion of the Western races', argued a leading geographer, La Roncière
Le Noury, 'its superior causes, its elements, its influences on human destinies, will be a
beautiful study for future historians.' Yet only if the white races indulged their taste for voy-
aging—a mark of their intellectual supremacy—could colonial expansion occur.[20]

From such theses as this came the commonly held view of the Orient as a geographical space to be cultivated, harvested, and guarded. The images of agricultural care for and
those of frank sexual attention to the Orient proliferated accordingly. Here is a typical effu-
sion by Gabriel Charmes, writing in 1880:

> On that day when we shall be no longer in the Orient, and when other great
> European powers will be there, all will be at an end for our commerce in the
> Mediterranean, for our future in Asia, for the traffic of our southern ports. *One of the
> most fruitful sources of our national wealth will be dried up.* (Emphasis added)

Another thinker, Leroy-Beaulieu, elaborated this philosophy still further:

> A society colonizes, when itself having reached a high degree of maturity and of
> strength, it procreates, it protects, it places in good conditions of development, and
> it brings to virility a new society to which it has given birth. Colonization is one of
> the most complex and delicate phenomena of social physiology.

This equation of self-reproduction with colonization led Leroy-Beaulieu to the somewhat sinister idea that whatever is lively in a modern society is 'magnified by this pouring out of its exuberant activity on the outside.' Therefore, he said,

> Colonization is the expansive force of a people; it is its power of reproduction; it is its enlargement and its multiplication through space; it is the subjection of the universe or a vast part of it to that people's language, customs, ideas, and laws.[21]

The point here is that the space of weaker or underdeveloped regions like the Orient was viewed as something inviting French interest, penetration, insemination—in short, colonization. Geographical conceptions, literally and figuratively, did away with the discrete entities held in by borders and frontiers. No less than entrepreneurial visionaries like de Lesseps, whose plan was to liberate the Orient and the Occident from their geographical bonds, French scholars, administrators, geographers, and commercial agents poured out their exuberant activity onto the fairly supine, feminine Orient. There were the geographical societies, whose number and membership outdid those of all Europe by a factor of two; there were such powerful organizations as the Comité de l'Asie française and the Comité d'Orient; there were the learned societies, chief among them the Société asiatique, with its organization and membership firmly embedded in the universities, the institutes, and the government. Each in its own way made French interests in the Orient more real, more substantial. Almost an entire century of what now seemed passive study of the Orient had had to end, as France faced up to its transnational responsibilities during the last two decades of the nineteenth century.

In the only part of the Orient where British and French interests literally overlapped, the territory of the now hopelessly ill Ottoman Empire, the two antagonists managed their conflict with an almost perfect and characteristic consistency. Britain was *in* Egypt and Mesopotamia; through a series of quasi-fictional treaties with local (and powerless) chiefs it controlled the Red Sea, the Persian Gulf, and the Suez Canal, as well as most of the intervening land mass between the Mediterranean and India. France, on the other hand, seemed fated to hover over the Orient, descending once in a while to carry out schemes that repeated de Lesseps's success with the canal; for the most part these schemes were railroad projects, such as the one planned across more or less British territory, the Syrian-Mesopotamian line. In addition France saw itself as the protector of Christian minorities—Maronites, Chaldeans, Nestorians. Yet together, Britain and France were agreed in principle on the necessity, when the time came, for the partition of Asiatic Turkey. Both before and during World War I secret diplomacy was bent on carving up the Near Orient first into spheres of influence, then into mandated (or occupied) territories. In France, much of the expansionist sentiment formed during the heyday of the geographical movement focused itself on plans to partition Asiatic Turkey, so much so that in Paris in 1914 'a spectacular press campaign was launched' to this end.[22] In England numerous committees were empowered to study and recommend policy on the best ways of dividing up the Orient. Out of such commissions as the Bunsen Committee would come the joint Anglo-French teams of which the most famous was the one headed by Mark Sykes and Georges Picot. Equitable division of geographical space was the rule of these plans, which were deliberate attempts also at calming Anglo-French rivalry. For, as Sykes put it in a memorandum,

> it was clear . . . that an Arab rising was sooner or later to take place, and that the French and ourselves ought to be on better terms if the rising was not to be a curse instead of a blessing. . . .[23]

The animosities remained. And to them was added the irritant provided by the Wilsonian program for national self-determination, which, as Sykes himself was to note, seemed to invalidate the whole skeleton of colonial and partitionary schemes arrived at jointly between the Powers. It would be out of place here to discuss the entire labyrinthine and deeply controversial history of the Near Orient in the early twentieth century, as its fate was being decided between the Powers, the native dynasties, the various nationalist parties and movements, the Zionists. What matters more immediately is the peculiar epistemological framework through which the Orient was seen, and out of which the Powers acted. For despite their differences, the British and the French saw the Orient as a geographical—and cultural, political, demographic, sociological, and historical—entity over whose destiny they believed themselves to have traditional entitlement. The Orient to them was no sudden discovery, no mere historical accident, but an area to the east of Europe whose principal worth was uniformly defined in terms of Europe, more particularly in terms specifically claiming for Europe—European science, scholarship, understanding, and administration—the credit for having made the Orient what it was now. And this had been the achievement—inadvertent or not is beside the point—of modern Orientalism.

There were two principal methods by which Orientalism delivered the Orient to the West in the early twentieth century. One was by means of the disseminative capacities of modern learning, its diffusive apparatus in the learned professions, the universities, the professional societies, the explorational and geographical organizations, the publishing industry. All these, as we have seen, built upon the prestigious authority of the pioneering scholars, travelers, and poets, whose cumulative vision had shaped a quintessential Orient; the doctrinal—or doxological—manifestation of such an Orient is what I have been calling here latent Orientalism. So far as anyone wishing to make a statement of any consequence about the Orient was concerned, latent Orientalism supplied him with an enunciative capacity that could be used, or rather mobilized, and turned into sensible discourse for the concrete occasion at hand. Thus when Balfour spoke about the Oriental to the House of Commons in 1910, he must surely have had in mind those enunciative capacities in the current and acceptably rational language of his time, by which something called an 'Oriental' could be named and talked about without danger of too much obscurity. But like all enunciative capacities and the discourses they enable, latent Orientalism was profoundly conservative—dedicated, that is, to its self-preservation. Transmitted from one generation to another, it was a part of the culture, as much a language about a part of reality as geometry or physics. Orientalism staked its existence, not upon its openness, its receptivity to the Orient, but rather on its internal, repetitive consistency about its constitutive will-to-power over the Orient. In such a way Orientalism was able to survive revolutions, world wars, and the literal dismemberment of empires.

The second method by which Orientalism delivered the Orient to the West was the result of an important convergence. For decades the Orientalists had spoken about the Orient, they had translated texts, they had explained civilizations, religions, dynasties, cultures, mentalities—as academic objects, screened off from Europe by virtue of their inimitable foreignness. The Orientalist was an expert, like Renan or Lane, whose job in society was to interpret the Orient for his compatriots. The relation between Orientalist and Orient was essentially hermeneutical: standing before a distant, barely intelligible civilization or cultural monument, the Orientalist scholar reduced the obscurity by translating, sympathetically portraying, inwardly grasping the hard-to-reach object. Yet the Orientalist remained outside the Orient, which, however much it was made to appear intelligible, remained beyond the Occident. This cultural, temporal, and geographical distance was expressed in metaphors of depth, secrecy, and sexual promise: phrases like 'the veils of an Eastern bride' or 'the inscrutable Orient' passed into the common language.

Yet the distance between Orient and Occident was, almost paradoxically, in the process of being reduced throughout the nineteenth century. As the commercial, political, and other existential encounters between East and West increased (in ways we have been discussing all along), a tension developed between the dogmas of latent Orientalism, with its support in studies of the 'classical' Orient, and the descriptions of a present, modern, manifest Orient articulated by travelers, pilgrims, statesmen, and the like. At some moment impossible to determine precisely, the tension caused a convergence of the two types of Orientalism. Probably—and this is only a speculation—the convergence occurred when Orientalists, beginning with Sacy, undertook to advise governments on what the modern Orient was all about. Here the role of the specially trained and equipped expert took on an added dimension: the Orientalist could be regarded as the special agent of Western power as it attempted policy vis-à-vis the Orient. Every learned (and not so learned) European traveler in the Orient felt himself to be a representative Westerner who had gotten beneath the films of obscurity. This is obviously true of Burton, Lane, Doughty, Flaubert, and the other major figures I have been discussing.

The discoveries of Westerners about the manifest and modern Orient acquired a pressing urgency as Western territorial acquisition in the Orient increased. Thus what the scholarly Orientalist defined as the 'essential' Orient was sometimes contradicted, but in many cases was confirmed, when the Orient became an actual administrative obligation. Certainly Cromer's theories about the Oriental—theories acquired from the traditional Orientalist archive—were vindicated plentifully as he ruled millions of Orientals in actual fact. This was no less true of the French experience in Syria, North Africa, and elsewhere in the French colonies, such as they were. But at no time did the convergence between latent Orientalist doctrine and manifest Orientalist experience occur more dramatically than when, as a result of World War I, Asiatic Turkey was being surveyed by Britain and France for its dismemberment. There, laid out on an operating table for surgery, was the Sick Man of Europe, revealed in all his weakness, characteristics, and topographical outline.

The Orientalist, with his special knowledge, played an inestimably important part in this surgery. Already there had been intimations of his crucial role as a kind of secret agent *inside* the Orient when the British scholar Edward Henry Palmer was sent to the Sinai in 1882 to gauge anti-British sentiment and its possible enlistment on behalf of the Arabic revolt. Palmer was killed in the process, but he was only the most unsuccessful of the many who performed similar services for the Empire, now a serious and exacting business entrusted in part to the regional 'expert'. Not for nothing was another Orientalist, D.G. Hogarth, author of the famous account of the exploration of Arabia aptly titled *The Penetration of Arabia* (1904),[24] made the head of the Arab Bureau in Cairo during World War I. And neither was it by accident that men and women like Gertrude Bell, T.E. Lawrence, and St. John Philby, Oriental experts all, posted to the Orient as agents of empire, friends of the Orient, formulators of policy alternatives because of their intimate and expert knowledge of the Orient and of Orientals. They formed a band—as Lawrence called it once—bound together by contradictory notions and personal similarities: great individuality, sympathy and intuitive identification with the Orient, a jealously preserved sense of personal mission in the Orient, cultivated eccentricity, a final disapproval of the Orient. For them all the Orient was their direct, peculiar experience of it. In them Orientalism and an effective praxis for handling the Orient received their final European form, before the Empire disappeared and passed its legacy to other candidates for the role of dominant power.

Such individualists as these were not academics. We shall soon see that they were the beneficiaries of the academic study of the Orient, without in any sense belonging to the official and professional company of Orientalist scholars. Their role, however, was not to scant academic Orientalism, nor to subvert it, but rather to make it effective. In their genealogy were people like Lane and Burton, as much for their encyclopedic autodidacticism as for the accurate, the quasi-scholarly knowledge of the Orient they had obviously deployed when dealing with or writing about Orientals. For the curricular study of the Orient they substituted a sort of elaboration of latent Orientalism, which was easily available to them in the imperial culture of their epoch. Their scholarly frame of reference, such as it was, was fashioned by people like William Muir, Anthony Bevan, D.S. Margoliouth, Charles Lyall, E.G. Browne, R.A. Nicholson, Guy Le Strange, E.D. Ross, and Thomas Arnold, who also followed directly in the line of descent from Lane. Their imaginative perspectives were provided principally by their illustrious contemporary Rudyard Kipling, who had sung so memorably of holding 'dominion over palm and pine'.

The difference between Britain and France in such matters was perfectly consistent with the history of each nation in the Orient: the British were there; the French lamented the loss of India and the intervening territories. By the end of the century, Syria had become the main focus of French activity, but even there it was a matter of common consensus that the French could not match the British either in quality of personnel or in degree of political influence. The Anglo-French competition over the Ottoman spoils was felt even on the field of battle in the Hejaz, in Syria, in Mesopotamia—but in all these places, as astute men like Edmond Bremond noted, the French Orientalists and local experts were outclassed in brilliance and tactical maneuvering by their British counterparts.[25] Except for an occasional genius like Louis Massignon, there were no French Lawrences or Sykeses or Bells. But there were determined imperialists like Étienne Flandin and Franklin-Bouillon. Lecturing to the Paris Alliance française in 1913, the Comte de

Cressaty, a vociferous imperialist, proclaimed Syria as France's own Orient, the site of French political, moral, and economic interests—interests, he added, that had to be defended during this 'âge des envahissants impérialistes'; and yet Cressaty noted that even with French commercial and industrial firms in the Orient, with by far the largest number of native students enrolled in French schools, France was invariably being pushed around in the Orient, threatened not only by Britain but by Austria, Germany, and Russia. If France was to continue to prevent 'le retour de l'Islam', it had better take hold of the Orient: this was an argument proposed by Cressaty and seconded by Senator Paul Doumer.[26] These views were repeated on numerous occasions, and indeed France did well by itself in North Africa and in Syria after World War I, but the special, concrete management of emerging Oriental populations and theoretically independent territories with which the British always credited themselves was something the French felt had eluded them. Ultimately, perhaps, the difference one always feels between modern British and modern French Orientalism is a stylistic one; the import of the generalizations about Orient and Orientals, the sense of distinction preserved between Orient and Occident, the desirability of Occidental dominance over the Orient—all these are the same in both traditions. For of the many elements making up what we customarily call 'expertise', style, which is the result of specific worldly circumstances being molded by tradition, institutions, will, and intelligence into formal articulation, is one of the most manifest. It is to this determinant, to this perceptible and modernized refinement in early-twentieth-century Orientalism in Britain and France, that we must now turn.

NOTES

1. Friedrich Nietzsche, 'On Truth and Lie in an Extra-Moral Sense', in *The Portable Nietzsche*, ed. and trans. Walter Kaufmann (New York: Viking Press, 1954), pp. 46–7.

2. The number of Arab travelers to the West is estimated and considered by Ibrahim Abu-Lughod in *Arab Rediscovery of Europe: A Study in Cultural Encounters* (Princeton, N.J.: Princeton University Press, 1963), pp. 75–6 and passim.

3. See Philip D. Curtin, ed., *Imperialism: The Documentary History of Western Civilization* (New York: Walker & Co., 1972), pp. 73–105.

4. See Johann W. Fück, 'Islam as an Historical Problem in European Historiography since 1800', in *Historians of the Middle East*, ed. Bernard Lewis and P. M. Holt (London: Oxford University Press, 1962), p. 307.

5. Ibid., p. 309.

6. See Jacques Waardenburg, *L'Islam dans le miroir de l'Occident* (The Hague: Mouton & Co., 1963).

7. Ibid., p. 311.

8. P. Masson-Oursel, 'La Connaissance scientifique de l'Asie en France depuis 1900 et les variétés de l'Orientalisme', *Revue Philosophique* 143, nos. 7–9 (July-September 1953): 345.

9. Evelyn Baring, Lord Cromer, *Modern Egypt* (New York: Macmillan. Co., 1908), 2: 237–8.

10. Evelyn Baring, Lord Cromer, *Ancient and Modern Imperialism* (London: John Murray, 1910), pp. 118, 120.

11. George Nathaniel Curzon, *Subjects of the Day: Being a Selection of Speeches and Writings* (London: George Allen & Unwin, 1915), pp. 4–5, 10, 28.

12. Ibid., pp. 184, 191–2. For the history of the school, see C.H. Phillips, *The School of Oriental and African Studies, University of London, 1917–1967: An Introduction* (London: Design for Print, 1967).

13. Eric Stokes, *The English Utilitarians and India* (Oxford: Clarendon Press, 1959).

14. Cited in Michael Edwardes, *High Noon of Empire: India Under Curzon* (London: Eyre & Spottiswoode, 1965), pp. 38–9.

15. Curzon, *Subjects of the Day*, pp. 155–6.

16. Joseph Conrad, *Heart of Darkness*, in *Youth and Two Other Stories* (Garden City, N.Y.: Doubleday, Page, 1925), p. 52.

17. For an illustrative extract from de Vattel's work see Curtin, ed., *Imperialism*, pp. 42–5.

18. Cited by M. de Caix, *La Syrie* in Gabriel Hanotaux, *Histoire des colonies françaises*, 6 vols. (Paris: Société de l'histoire nationale, 1929–33), 3: 481.

19. These details are to be found in Vernon McKay, 'Colonialism in the French Geographical Movement,' *Geographical Review* 33, no. 2 (April 1943): 214–32.

20. Agnes Murphy, *The Ideology of French Imperialism, 1817-1881* (Washington: Catholic University of America Press, 1948), pp. 46, 54, 36, 45.

21. Ibid., pp. 189, 110, 136.

22. Jukka Nevakivi, *Britain, France, and the Arab Middle East, 1914–1920* (London: Athlone Press, 1969), p. 13.

23. Ibid., p. 24.

24. D.G. Hogarth, *The Penetration of Arabia: A Record of the Development of Western Knowledge Concerning The Arabian Peninsula* (New York: Frederick A. Stokes, 1904). There is a good recent book on the same subject: Robin Bidwell, *Travellers in Arabia* (London: Paul Hamlyn, 1976).

25. Edmond Bremond, *Le Hedjaz dans la guerre mondiale* (Paris: Payor, 1931), pp. 242 ff.

26. Le Comte de Cressaty, *Les Intérêts de la France en Syrie* (Paris: Floury, 1913).

CATHARINE A. MACKINNON

1946–
UNITED STATES

Major Works

1979   *Sexual Harassment of Working Women: A Case of Sex Discrimination*
1987   *Feminism Unmodified: Discourses on Life and Law*
1988   *Pornography and Civil Rights: A New Day for Women's Equality* (with Andrea Dworkin)
1989   *Toward a Feminist Theory of the State*
2001   *Sex Equality*

> The feminist theory of knowledge begins with the point of view of all women on social life. It takes as its point of departure the criticism that the male point of view of social life has constructed both social life and knowledge about it. In other words the feminist theory of knowledge is inextricable from the feminist critique of male power because the male point of view has forced itself upon the world, and does force itself upon the world, as its way of knowing.[1]

> From a feminist perspective, women have no more special relation to nature 'naturally' than men do; their relation to nature, like men's, is a social product.[2]
>
> —*Catharine MacKinnon*

Catharine MacKinnon, feminist theorist and legal scholar, focuses her concerns on sexual politics and the law. In her work on women and the law she argues convincingly that a great part of women's oppression is embedded in the law and reinforced by the dominance of patriarchal structures within society. Although the law reflects only an aspect of this domination, it will nevertheless have to address any significant change in women's condition.

Her analyses uncover the dynamics of gender, which she sees as an imposed hierarchical system placing women in a subordinate position. She is critical of Engels's analysis of the subordination of women. Her chapter on 'A Feminist Critique of Marx and Engels' takes Engels to task for not really explaining the origins of women's subordination. She states that he clearly pointed out that the situation needed explanation, but in his exposition he totally abandoned efforts to do so:

Even when Engels grants that women engage in production—not just socially necessary labour—he cannot manage to conclude that they derive social power from it. To the extent that women have power, it comes from their role as mothers and is exercised in the home. Men are workers, even when the women engage in production and men are recognizable parents. Men derived neither power nor social position from paternity, they derive these from their role in production. . . . a split between home and work is defined in terms of a split between male and female dominated spheres, and social power for women is reckoned not by relation to production but by sex.[3]

In the case of Marx, she argues that his treatment of gender is only 'in passing', which she says is 'his first failing and best defence'. She writes that his preoccupation with class divisions obscures a necessary analysis of gender, and he takes as his point of departure the traditional notion that women's position in the economy coincides with their nature. 'In spite of his brief insights into women's condition, he did not systematically see that he shared what he considered natural, and his considering it as natural, with the bourgeois society he otherwise criticized.'[4]

Overall, MacKinnon's major work challenges male hegemony, particularly with respect to the legal system. It is within that system that she sees women's oppression as most institutionalized. It is also within the legal system that she sees much hope for positive changes to women's material life. This is possible as long as women hold fast to their political demands and do not allow their positions to be compromised by the existing male power structure.

Notes

1. Catharine MacKinnon, *Feminism Unmodified: Discourses on Life and Law* (Cambridge, Mass.: Harvard University Press, 1987), 50.
2. Catharine MacKinnon, *Toward a Feminist Theory of the State* (Cambridge, Mass.: Harvard University Press, 1989), 15.
3. Catharine MacKinnon, 'A Feminist Critique of Marx and Engels', ibid., 27.
4. Ibid., 19.

A FEMINIST CRITIQUE OF MARX AND ENGELS

We often romanticize what we have first despised.
—Wendell Berry, *The Gift of a Good Land*

To Marx, women were defined by nature, not by society. To him, sex was within that 'material substratum' that was not subject to social analysis, making his explicit references to women or to sex largely peripheral or parenthetical.[1] With issues of sex, unlike with class, Marx did not see that the line between the social and the pre-social is a line society draws. Marx ridiculed treating value and class as if they were natural givens. He bitingly criticized theories that treated class as if it arose spontaneously and operated mechanistically yet harmoniously in accord with natural laws. He identified such theories as justifications for an unjust status quo. Yet this is exactly the way he treated gender. Even when women produced commodities as waged labour, Marx wrote about them primarily as mothers, housekeepers, and members of the weaker sex. His work shares with liberal theory the view that women naturally belong where they are socially placed.

Engels, by contrast, considered women's status a social phenomenon that needed explanation. He just failed to explain it. Expanding upon Marx's few suggestive comments, Engels tried to explain women's subordination within a theory of the historical development of the family in the context of class relations. Beneath Engels' veneer of dialectical dynamism lies a static, positivistic materialism that reifies woman socially to such an extent that her status might as well have been considered naturally determined. Marx and Engels each take for granted crucial features of relations between the sexes: Marx because woman is nature and nature is given, and Engels because woman is the family and he is largely uncritical of woman's work and sexual role within it.

Marx's theories of the division of labour and the social relations of production under capitalism were at the core of his theory of social life, as his views of women were not. In this context, Marx offered the analysis that differences 'in the sexual act' were the original division of labour. 'With (the increase of needs, productivity, population) there develops the division of labour, which was originally nothing but the division of labour in the sexual act, then that division of labour which develops spontaneously or "naturally" by virtue of natural predisposition (e.g., physical strength), needs, accidents, etc. etc.'[2] The reproductive difference of function between women and men apparently constitutes a division of labour. It is unclear whether this 'original' division then extends itself to become other divisions, or whether this 'original' division is a primary or cardinal example that other divisions then replicate or parallel or pattern themselves after. Marx accounts for neither the view that gender difference of function in reproduction is more 'original' than other differences of function that do not fall along gender lines; nor the view that reproduction is a species of labour; nor the appropriateness or necessity of the extension or duplication of this division throughout society. But then the gender division is not his subject; it is merely the 'origin' of his real subject, the class division.

Still one wonders why other differences of function do not constitute or underlie a division of labour, but sex does. When discussing the division of labour under capitalism, Marx sees the question of which individual gets which task, or becomes a member of which class, as originally an accident that then becomes historically fixed: an 'accidental repartition gets repeated, develops advantages of its own, and gradually ossifies into a systematic division of labour'.[3] Not so gender. Which sex gets which task is first a matter of biology and remains so throughout economic changes. Discussing woman's work in the home, Marx states: 'The distribution of the work within the family, and the regulation of the labour-time of the several members, depend as well upon the differences of age and sex as upon natural conditions. . . . Within a family . . . there springs up naturally a division of labour, caused by differences of sex and age, a division that is consequently based on a purely physical foundation.' Women are assigned housework by nature. Marx then abandons sex to discuss relations between tribes, for which 'the physiological division of labour (sex and age) is the starting-point'.[4]

Because women's role was naturally defined, Marx's view of the relationship of nature to labour is instructive. Nature's produce is 'spontaneous'. Society produces through the human activity of work: 'material wealth that is not the spontaneous product of Nature, must invariably owe (its) existence to a special productive activity, exercised with definite aim, an activity that appropriates particular nature-given materials to particular human wants.'[5] Appropriating materials of nature with intent to modify them to satisfy human wants, is a creative and purposive, as well as adaptive, activity. Nature produces of itself; work transforms the world.

Nature's forms change naturally or not at all. Labour's organization is social and is therefore subject to human intervention. 'If we take away the useful labour expended upon them, a material substratum is always left, which is furnished by Nature without the help of man. The latter can work only as Nature does, that is by changing the form of matter. Nay more, in this work of changing the form he (man) is constantly helped by natural forces. We see, then, that labour is not the only source of material wealth, of use-values produced by labour. As William Petty puts it, labour is its father and the earth its mother.'[6] Mother/woman is, is nature; father/man works, is social. The creative, active, transformative process of work is identified with the male, while the female is identified with the matter to be worked upon and transformed. Neither human reproduction nor housework features the intentionality and control of appropriating and modifying naturally given materials which characterize the labour process in socialist thought. Actually, factory work under capitalism possesses a few of these characteristics, yet it is considered for that reason alienated rather than spontaneous and natural.

To the extent that man's relation to nature is given by nature, relations between the sexes will also be defined by nature. To the extent that man's relation to nature has, for Marx, a social aspect—and it does—his relation to woman will have a social aspect. This may be the meaning of Marx's statement ' The production of life, both of one's own labour and of fresh life in procreation, now appears as a double relationship.'[7] From a feminist perspective, women have no more special relation to nature 'naturally' than men do; their relation to nature, like men's, is a social product. Man's relation to nature is probably equally profound and determinative of his being, but he is not socially limited to it. Men's supposed superior strength does not confine them to being beasts of burden. Men also reproduce; women also labour. If one applied Marx's approach to class to the problem of sex, one might try to understand the connection between a physical fact—say, male physical strength or female maternity—and the social relations that give that fact a limiting and lived meaning. One might try to identify the material interest of those who gain by such an arrangement, rather than abandoning the task of social explanation on the level of physiological observation, as Marx does with sex.

Marx thought that capitalism distorted the family by bringing women into social production under capitalist conditions. This development was both detrimental and historically progressive, much like the impact of capitalism on other aspects of social relations. The destructive impact of capitalism upon the family was deplored largely in terms of its impact on woman's performance of her sex role. The introduction of machinery permitted the enrolment of 'every member of the workman's family, without distinction of age or sex', so the working man who had previously sold his own labour power 'now sells his wife and child' in addition. They do not even sell themselves; he sells them. To Marx, this arrangement resulted in the 'physical deterioration . . . of the woman' and usurped 'the place not only of the children's play but also of free labour at home within moderate limits for support of the family'.[8] Perhaps dinner was not ready on time. This theorist, so sensitive to the contribution of labour to the creation of value and to its expropriation for the benefit of others, could see the work women do in the home only as free labour, when the only sense in which it is free is that it is unpaid.

When the cotton crisis turned women out of factory jobs, Marx found partial consolation in the fact that 'women now had sufficient leisure to give their infants the breast. . . . They had time to learn to cook. Unfortunately, the acquisition of this art occurred at a time when they had nothing to cook. But from this we see how capital . . . has usurped the labour necessary in the home of the family. This crisis was also utilized to teach sewing. . . .' Even women who do the same work men do are understood in terms of the cooking and sewing they should be doing at home—and, but for the excesses of capitalism, they would be doing. Marx further attributes the high death rate of children, 'apart from local causes, principally . . . to the employment of the mothers away from their homes. . . . [There] arises an unnatural estrangement between mother and child . . . the mothers become to a grievous extent denaturalized toward their offspring.'[9] The harm capitalism does to male workers is not measured by its distortion of their family relationships or the denaturing of men to their children, but women's employment itself means working women's children are neglected. Apparently, under the standard against which Marx compares capitalist distortions, the wife stays home, cooking and sewing and nursing children, while the husband goes off to work. When men work, they become workers, Marx's human beings. When women work, they remain wives and mothers, inadequate ones.[10]

Although he usually abjures moral critique as a bourgeois fetish, Marx displays moral sensitivities on women's work. Abhorring the 'moral degradation caused by capitalistic exploitation of women and children', Marx observes: 'Before the labour of women and children under 10 years of age was forbidden in mines, capitalists considered employment of naked women and girls, often in company with men, so far sanctioned by their moral code, and especially by their ledgers, that it was only after the passing of the Act that they had recourse to machinery.'[11] It is unclear how nudity is profitable. When men are exploited, it is problem of exploitation; when women are exploited, it is a problem of morality.[12]

Marx did not see the buying and selling of women for sexual use as natural, as liberal theorists tend to do, nor did he reject it as immoral, like the conservatives. In his early work, Marx criticized the man of money for whom even 'the species-relationship itself, the relationship of man to woman, etc., become an object of commerce! Woman is bartered.'[13] He does not inquire why it is woman who is bartered, nor mention by or to whom. He criticizes 'crude and thoughtless communism' for merely transforming private possession of women into collective possession of women, 'in which a woman becomes a piece of communal and common property'.[14] The woman thus 'passes from marriage to general prostitution'. He terms the exploitation of women in prostitution as 'only a specific expression of the general prostitution of the labourer'. The capitalist is analagous to the pimp. Although the analysis is fragmentary and largely metaphorical, prostitution is social exploitation, not merely morally condemned. Marx does not inquire why it is overwhelmingly women who are prostitutes, given that men also marry and are exploited as workers. In his later work with Engels, Marx observed that the bourgeoisie are hypocritical in deploring prostitution because 'bourgeois marriage is in reality a system of wives in common'. He is clear that the abolition of the present system of production 'must bring with it the abolition of the community of women springing from that system, i.e., of prostitution both public and private'.[15] He does not say why prostitution, which has adapted to every changed economic structure, must necessarily end with the abolition of capitalism.

One of Marx's most widely assimilated views of women has been that the working woman is a liability to the working class because women are more exploitable. To Marx, women's employment contributes to undermining the power of the working man to resist the hegemony of capitalism. 'By the excessive addition of women and children to the ranks of workers, machinery at last breaks down the resistance which the male operatives of the manufacturing period continued to oppose to the despotism of capital.' Mechanization and consequent attempts to prolong the working day are resisted by that 'repellant yet elastic natural barrier, man'. This resistance is undermined by 'the more pliant and docile character of the women and children employed on [machine work]'.[16] Women are more exploitable than men, not just more exploited, their character a cause rather than a result of their material condition. Women are exceptions to every rule of social analysis Marx developed for the analysis of human beings in society. They are defined in terms of their biology, with children as incompletely adult, in need of special protection, not real workers even when they work.[17] The woman who works outside the home is a class enemy by nature. The possibility that working-class women are specially exploited by capital—and with proper support and organization might be able to hold out for higher wages, better conditions, and fight mechanization—is absent. Men who work for lower wages are a special kind of organizing problem. Woman's exploitability makes her a liability to the working class unless she stays home.

Marx did find progressive potential in women working outside the home, as he did in much of capitalism. 'However terrible and disgusting the dissolution, under the capitalist system, of the old family ties may appear, nevertheless, modern industry, by assigning as it does an important part in the process of production, outside the domestic sphere, to women, to young persons, and to children of both sexes, creates a new economic foundation for a higher form of the family and the relations between the sexes.' He also found it obvious that 'the fact of the collective working group being composed of individuals of both sexes and all ages must necessarily, under suitable conditions, become a source of human development . . . [although in its capitalist form] that fact is a pestiferous source of corruption and slavery.'[18] Sex in marriage was another thing, however: 'the sanctification of the sexual instinct through exclusivity, the checking of instinct by laws, the moral beauty which makes nature's commandment ideas in the form of an emotional bond— [this is] the spiritual essence of marriage.'[19] Yet Marx perceived that under capitalism relations within the family 'remain unattached, in theory, because they are the practical basis on which the bourgeoisie has erected its domination, and because in their bourgeois form they are the conditions which make the bourgeois a bourgeois'.[20] In spite of his brief insights into women's condition, he did not systematically see that he shared what he considered natural, and his considering it *as* natural, with the bourgeois society he otherwise criticized.

Whatever one can say about Marx's treatment of women, his first failing and best defence are that the problems of women concerned him only in passing. Friedrich Engels can be neither so accused or excused. His *Origin of the Family, Private Property, and the State* is the seminal marxist attempt to understand and explain women's subordination. The work has been widely criticized, mostly for its data, but its approach has been influential. Often through Lenin, who adopted many of its essentials, the approach and direction of Engels' reasoning, if not all of its specifics, have become orthodox marxism on 'the woman question'.

To Engels, women are oppressed as a group through the specific form of the family in class society. In pre-class sexually egalitarian social orders, labour was divided by sex. Not until the rise of private property, and with it class society, did that division become hierarchical. Anthropological evidence is used to demonstrate this argument. Under capitalism, women divide into 'the bourgeois family' and 'the proletarian family', as 'personal life' reflections of capitalism's productive relations. Women's economic dependence is a critical nexus between exploitative class relations and the nuclear family structure. Women are not socially subordinate because of biological dependence, but because of the place to which class society regulates their reproductive capacity. Engels applies this analysis to housework and childcare, women's traditional work, and to monogamy and prostitution, issues of women's sexuality. Socialism would end women's oppression by integrating them into the workforce, transforming their isolated 'private' work in the home into 'public' social production. By eliminating the public/private split incident to the divisions between classes under capitalism, socialism provides the essential conditions for women's emancipation.[21]

Engels thus grants that women are specially oppressed, that they are second-class citizens compared with men, that this occurs structurally in the family, antedates the current economic order, and needs to be changed. Engels attempts to set women's subjection within a totality of necessary but changeable social relations—as necessary and changeable as class society. His work holds out the promise that women's situation has been grasped within a theory of social transformation that would also revolutionize class relations. He suggests, at least, that women's equality, including their entry into the wage labour force on an equal basis with men, would do more to change capitalist society than simply advance women as a group within it.

Engels' work has had a continuing impact on contemporary theorists.[22] Adaptations and extensions of his themes are often qualified by ritual disclaimers of his data while appropriating his 'insights'[23] or 'socio-historical approach',[24] or claiming to reach his 'conclusions . . . by a different route'.[25] Engels' views are often most accurately reflected when he is not quoted.[26] Zaretsky, for example, begins his analysis of the relation between socialism and feminism with: 'To talk about ending male supremacy takes us right back to the dawn of history—the creation of the family and class society.' He argues that the personal is 'a realm cut off from society' under capitalism, developed in response to the socialization of commodity production, where woman is oppressed because she is isolated.[27] Socialism is the solution. Many contemporary Marxists also share a tendency, in which Engels and liberal theory are indistinguishable, to interpret the division between work and life under capitalism in terms of coincident divisions between market and home, public and private, male and female spheres. While Engels' account is not universally accepted by Marxists, despite, or perhaps because of, the fact that he is widely misinterpreted—a fate his account deserves—his general approach to women's situation is sufficiently accepted among Marxists and socialist-feminists as not even to be mentioned by name or footnoted.[28] Or, one often suspects, read.

Engels legitimates women's interests within class analysis by subordinating those interests to his version of class analysis. His attempt to explain women's situation fails less because of his sexism than because of the nature of his materialism; rather, the positivism—more specifically the objectivism—of his materialism requires his sexism. He not only does, but must, assume male dominance at the very points at which it is to be explained. His account works only if essential features of male ascendancy are given; it moves from one epoch to another only if sex-divided control of tasks, and the qualities of male and female sexuality under male dominance, are presupposed. His positivism makes the inaccuracy of his data fatal. He describes what he thinks, attributes it to what he sees, and then ascribes coherence and necessary dynamism to it. In his theory, if something exists, it is necessary that it exist; this does not explain why one thing exists instead of something else. What becomes of such a theory if the facts turn out not to exist, or—as with sex equality—never to have existed? Perhaps this is why Engels must believe that women were once supreme, despite data and suggestions to the contrary, for eventual equality of the sexes to be historically imaginable. He is dependent for explanation on a teleology of what is; he must explain what is in terms of what is, not in terms of what is not. Sex equality, unfortunately, is not.

According to Engels, women's status is produced through social forces that give rise to 'the origin of the family, private property, and the state'. He assumes that answering the question 'How did it happen that women were first subordinated to men?' is the same as addressing the question 'Why are women oppressed and how can we change it?' He equates the temporally first with the persistently fundamental. For Engels, capitalism presents the most highly evolved form both of women's subjection and of economic class antagonism; that subjection must therefore be understood in its capitalist form if it is to be changed. But women's oppression, he also finds, predates capitalism; it arises with the first class society. Engels does not situate history within the present so as to tell whether or not fighting capitalism is fighting all of woman's subordination.

In his double sense, women 'originally' became 'degraded, enthralled, the slave of man's lust, a mere instrument for breeding children' when and because female monogamy was required to guarantee paternity for the inheritance of private property. The same exclusive appropriation of surplus product in the form of private property divided society into antagonistic classes, first into pre-capitalist forms (slave, feudal, mercantile) and later into the capitalist form, as commodity production became generalized. These developments increasingly required a state to contain the social conflict between classes for the advantage of the ruling classes. Thus the rise of private property, class divisions, women's oppression, and the state 'coincided with' and required each other, linking the exploitation of man by man in production and social control through the instrument of the state with the subordination of woman to man in monogamy and household drudgery.[29]

Before these four 'coincident' developments inaugurated 'civilization', Engels argued, labour was divided by sex within the clan, often with women in domestic roles, but woman's social power was equal to or greater than man's. In pairing marriage, the family form which preceded monogamy, woman was supreme in the household, and lineage was reckoned according to 'mother right'. With the rise of private property, the unity of the clan dissolved into antagonistic classes and isolated family units. As production shifted out of the household, leaving women behind in it, and more private wealth accumulated in men's hands, lineage came to be traced by 'father right', marking what Engels called 'the world historical defeat of the female sex'.[30] The socialization of housework and the full entry of women into production is necessary to end women's isolation in the family and her subordination to men within it. Woman's liberation will therefore come with the end of the private property ownership and class relations that caused her oppression.

Engels summarizes his view in an often quoted and as often misread paragraph:

> Monogamous marriage comes on the scene as the subjugation of one sex by the other; it announced a struggle between the sexes unknown throughout the whole previous pre-historic period. The first division of labour is that between man and woman for the propagation of children . . . the first class opposition that appears in history coincides with that of the female sex by the male. Monogamous marriage was a great historical step forward; nevertheless, together with slavery and private wealth it opens the period that has lasted until today in which every step forward is also relatively a step backward, in which prosperity and development for some is won through the misery and frustration of others. It is the cellular form of civilized society in which the nature of the oppositions and contradictions fully active in that society can be already studied.[31]

Of this analysis, Wilhelm Reich wrote that 'Engels . . . correctly surmised the nature of the relationships . . . the origin of class divisions was to be found in the antithesis between man and woman.'[32] Kate Millett concludes that Engels views 'sexual dominance (as) the keystone to the total structure of human injustice'.[33] Both interpretations share a one-sided social causality with Engels, yet both read Engels' causality precisely backward. Engels does not think that a division of labour, on the basis of sex or anything else, is inherently exploitative. The first division of labour, he says, was by sex for the propagation of children. The first class opposition, on the other hand, was presumably between slaves and slave owners. The *antagonism* between women and men—not the division of labour between women and men—arose with economic classes. In Engels' view, classes and sexual antagonism 'coincided' in that they developed at the same time, but they did not coincide in the sense of falling along the same lines.

Women were not a class for Engels. He cannot be taken to mean, as he often is, that 'this first class division among women and men forms the basis for the exploitation of the working class', nor did he think that the oppression of workers 'is an extension of the oppression of women'.[34] To Engels, sex divides labour, not relations to the means of production. His widely-quoted spectacular references to woman as man's 'slave' ('who only differs from the ordinary courtesan in that she does not let her body on piecework as a wage worker, but sells it once and for all into slavery') and to the man in the family as 'the bourgeois [while] the wife represents the proletariat',[35] though highly suggestive, are essentially metaphors. To argue that women are a class renders capitalism one form of patriarchal society, rather than one form of (economic) class society, in which the patriarchal family is the appropriate family structure. Basing class relations on gender relations would make the fundamental motive force of history a struggle or dialectic between the sexes. This is an argument, but it is not Engels'.[36] In his work, family forms support and respond to changes in economic organization, not to a sex-based historical dialectic. Changes in family forms changing productive structure would be contrary to all that Engels takes historical materialism to be about.[37]

In Engels' history of gender, the transition from group marriage to pairing marriage places woman in the household with one man within a communal setting marked by matrilineal descent. The transition from pairing marriage to monogamy eliminates the communal context and the woman's right to descent, leaving her in the modern nuclear household. Because dialectical materialism claims special competency in explaining social change, the inadequacy of Engels' treatment of these dynamic moments is particularly telling.

Pairing marriage first arose, according to Engels, in the transition from barbarism to savagery, at a time when slavery and private property existed but were not generalized. Class society had not emerged. Although women and men laboured in separate spheres, no distinction existed between the public world of men's work and the private world of women's household service. The community was still a large collective household within which both sexes worked to produce goods primarily for use. Pairing marriage was primarily distinguished from the previous communal form in that one man lived with one woman. Men could be polygamous or unfaithful, but infidelity by women was severely punished. Either party could dissolve the marriage bond; children were considered members of the mother's family ('mother right'). Why and how did this form of marital relationship arise to replace group marriage?

> The more the traditional sexual relations lost the naïve, primitive character of forest
> life [sometimes translated 'jungle character'] owing to the development of economi-

cal conditions with consequent undermining of the old communism and the growing density of population, the more oppressive and humiliating [sometimes translated 'degrading'] must the women have felt them to be; and the greater their longing
for the right to chastity, of temporary or permanent marriage with one man only, as
a way of release [sometimes translated 'deliverance']. This advance could not in any
case have originated from the man, if only because it has never occurred to them,
even to this day, to renounce the pleasures of actual group marriage.[38]

Engels seems to think that the existence of more people in a smaller space—higher
density—of itself generates greater demand for sexual intercourse per woman. The basis
for his view that women preferred marriage to one man is unclear. It seems to assume that
the present reality that women largely have intercourse at men's will rather than their own
was present at the 'origin' of this system. Pairing marriage arose because the women,
besieged by sexual demands, wanted it. Could not increased population density as well
support less intercourse, producing less crowding, or the continuance of extended groups,
since people were living so close together anyway? Engels assumes, rather than explains,
that a system of restricting women to one man but not restricting men to one woman is
an improvement over a system of equal lack of restraint on both. He assumes rather than
explains that sexual intercourse with diverse partners is imposed by and desired by men,
imposed upon and unwanted by women.[39] Male lust is not explained. Under what conditions would women 'long for chastity'? The more Marxist approach, methodologically,
would be to inquire into the conditions that would create a person who experienced this
desire or found such a social rule necessary or advantageous. The fact that men remained
able to have many wives or to be unfaithful while women's fidelity was demanded makes
one wonder what women gained from the rearrangement. Since 'mother right' had supposedly given them supremacy in the clan household, women at this point presumably
need not have accepted a situation they did not want.

To assert that frequent and varied sexual intercourse necessarily appeared degrading
and oppressive to women fails to explain the 'origins' of a society in which it is so.
Consequence is presented as cause. The explanation for the social change is: virtuous
women wanted husbands. (Unvirtuous women, presumably, were having intercourse with
the unfaithful husbands.) Men are ready at all times for 'the pleasures of actual group marriage'. Here we have the sexed men, the virgins and the whores, characters in the basic
pornographic script set before the dawn of history.

Engels goes on: 'Just as the wives whom it had formerly been so easy to obtain had
now acquired an exchange value and were bought, so also with labour power, particularly since the herds had definitely become family possessions . . . according to the social
custom of the time, the man was also the owner of the new source of subsistence, the cattle, and later of the new instruments of labour, the slaves.'[40] Engels connects things and
social meanings, relations between things and relations between people, with extraordinary offhandedness. How did wives come to be 'obtained', much less sold? Women were
sold because herds were family possessions? What can the power of 'mother right' have
been if the wife was purchased by the husband? Labour power came to be sold 'just as'
women were sold? How did these divisions come to be 'the social custom of the time'?

What made herds considered wealth in the first place? Why did not women own or tend herds? Why were not husbands bought and sold? Could it really be that slavery arose because 'The family did not multiply so rapidly as the cattle. More people were needed to look after them; for this purpose use could be made of the enemies captured in war, who could also be bred just as easily as the cattle themselves.'[41] Because cattle reproduce more efficiently than people, slavery rose?

In contrast with this approach to explaining the social status of a non-class group, Marx asked: 'What is a Negro slave? A man of the black race. The one explanation is as good as the other. A Negro is a Negro. He only becomes a slave in certain relations. A cotton spinning jenny is a machine for spinning cotton. It becomes capital only in certain relations. Torn from these relationships it is no more capital than gold in itself is money or sugar is the price of sugar.'[42] Yet even Marx was apparently convinced that what makes a domesticated woman is not social relations, but being a person of the female sex. Engels proceeds as if one can explain the creation of the social relations of slavery by pointing to the existence of the need for the work the slaves performed.

Engels also notes that 'the exclusive recognition of the female parent, owing to the impossibility of recognizing the male parent with certainty, means that the women—the mothers—are held in high respect.'[43] Out of a context that grants specific social meaning to descent and maternity, there is no basis to believe that social respect is a necessary correlate of the only possible system of tracing descent. Mothers' recognizability need not make them respected. As a prior matter, it is most unclear why women, a biologically defined group are 'in the house' at all, or, rather, why the men are not there with them. Engels says, 'According to the division of labour within the family at that time, it was the man's part to obtain food and the instruments of labour necessary for the purpose. He therefore also owned the instruments of labour, and in the event of husband and wife separating, he took them with him, just as she retained her household goods.'[44] To Engels, this state of affairs does not require explanation. Woman's place in the household is an extension of the division of labour between the sexes—originally non-exploitative and 'for purposes of procreation only'. How did it become housework? This question is addressed at most by: 'The division of labour between the two sexes is determined by quite other causes than by the position of women in society. Among peoples where the women have to work far harder than we think suitable, there is often much more real respect for women than among our Europeans.' Engels does not specify the 'quite other causes' that determine this division of labour between the sexes. It does not seem to have occurred to him that the social division of labour might influence the social position of the people who fill the roles, as well as the reverse. He reassures us that the hard-working woman of barbaric times 'was regarded among her people as a real lady . . . was also a lady in character'.[45] Just in case anyone is worried that socialism, by having women do real work, would make women unladylike.

No other division of labour in Engels' account divides work along the same lines as another human characteristic in the way sex does. Other than the division between the sexes, divisions of labour separate 'men' in production. Each advance in the division of labour fully supersedes the previous historical one.[46] 'The division of labour slowly insinuates itself into this process of production. It undermines the collectivity of production and appropriation, elevates appropriation by individuals into the general rule, and thus creates exchange between individuals . . . Gradually commodity production becomes the dominating form.'[47] It would seem that when work is divided between women and men (as it continues to be under capitalism without being superseded) Engels feels no need to explain it, but sees it as justified by unspecified 'quite other causes'. But when work is divided between men and men in production, particularly in class society, it lies at the root of the exploitation of one class by another.[48]

Even when Engels grants that women engage in production—not just socially necessary labour—he cannot manage to conclude that they derive social power from it. To the extent women have power, it comes from their role as mothers and is exercised in the home. Men are workers, even when women engage in production and men are recognizable parents.[49] Men derive neither power not social position from paternity; they derive these from their role in production. Engels' analysis of pairing marriage precisely tracks liberal theory. A split between home and work is defined in terms of a split between male- and female-dominated spheres, and social power for women is reckoned not by relation to production but by sex.

Engels' purpose is to explain how male dominance occurred. Yet it is present before it is supposed to have happened. The picture of pairing marriage that emerges looks like nothing so much as class society under male supremacy: women are 'obtained' or sold as wives, they labour in the house; men own and control the dominant means of subsistence, women are sexually possessed. This arrangement does not describe the exceptions to the general rule later to emerge full-blown in class society, but the general conditions of women's life in this period. Although antagonism between women and men is not supposed to have begun until civilization, the relations described here do not look especially harmonious, unless one thinks of them as somehow suitable. One is left wondering how female monogamy, 'father right', and other oppressive features of class society could make women's lives substantively worse and sexual relations newly antagonistic.

With the generalization of private property and class relations, the communal family was replaced by the modern nuclear family. The nuclear family is characterized by monogamy 'for women only' for the sole purpose of 'mak[ing] the man supreme in the family and to propagate, as the future heirs to his wealth, children indisputably his own'. Only the husband can dissolve the marriage bond. Female monogamy is accompanied by male adultery, hetaerism, and prostitution: 'the step from pairing marriage to monogamy can be put down to the credit of the men, and historically the essence of this was to make the position of the women worse and the infidelities of the men easier.'[50] The initial stimulus for monogamous marriage came when (and because) improved labour productivity increased social wealth. Considerable wealth could concentrate in the hands of one man. To guarantee that the man's children would inherit his wealth, 'father right' had to replace 'mother right', a change that Marx said 'in general . . . seems to be the most natural transition'.[51] In Engels' words, 'Thus on the one hand, in proportion as wealth increased it made the man's position in the family more important than the woman's and on the other hand created an impulse to exploit this strengthened position in order to overthrow, in favour of his children, the traditional order of inheritance.'[52]

Thus female monogamy arose from the concentration of wealth in the hands of one 'man' and from the need to bequeath this wealth to his children.[53] Again many connections between material objects and their social meanings are simply presupposed. Engels assumes that an increase in wealth stimulates private appropriation of that wealth; that private wealth is male-owned; that an increase in male-owned private wealth creates a need for its inheritance; and that an increase in wealth by husbands has an effect on relations with their wives in the family. He also assumes that the mother's power in the home both can and must be overthrown in order to guarantee that inheritance will pass to his children, even though under pairing marriage paternity was traceable because female fidelity was demanded. And that descent systems automatically correlate with power.

Why would an increase in the produced numbers of any object above immediate need constitute of itself an increase in wealth, in the sense of having the social consequences wealth has for the individual owner?[54] If increased productivity created surplus wealth, why was it not communally owned? The existence of more things does not dictate the form of social relations their organization will take. Must one assume that people inherently desire to have private possessions? If so, the prospect for socialism under any but subsistence conditions seems dim indeed. Why did not women acquire wealth for themselves? Why was the wealth acquired by men not considered owned by the paired unit? Just because man did the labour of tending herds, why did that mean he owned them? Surely a division of labour does not automatically produce a corresponding division of ownership.

Why does having private property imply a belief that it is important that someone, specifically one's 'own' children, acquire it on one's death? A discussion of the social meaning of private property is needed to attach property ownership to fathers through marriage and to children as heirs. Possessiveness of objects, parental possessiveness of other children ('his children'), possessiveness of spouses for each other, all require grounding in the meaning of social relations. If, for example, private property ownership reflects positively on personality in a given culture, and if death culturally means the end of personality, one might want to pass on property to someone with whom one identifies. Inheritance becomes a defence against death by perpetuation of self through the mediation of property ownership, to which end monogamous marriage is (at least for men) a means. Whatever the account, one is needed. Engels proceeds as if the need to bequeath (or own) property is a physical quality of the objects themselves.[55]

Why does an increase in social wealth give men power over women in the household? Even presuming that wealth is male-owned, why is it relationally significant between the sexes? Under pairing marriage, women worked in the house, where they were supreme as well as socially coequal. Passing property on to children did not require that 'mother right' be overthrown; wealth could pass through the mother, whose maternity is seldom in question. What changed under monogamy was the importance for social power of production outside the home. The reason for that shift in social meaning and its effect for gender relations within the home remains unexplained.

When the home was the centre of productive activity, the fact that women laboured in the home had ensured female supremacy there. When the home was superseded by the marketplace as a productive centre, the fact that women laboured in the home ensured male supremacy. This may describe the status of women once commodity production takes over social production, and women are excluded from it. But it explains neither that exclusion on the basis of sex or its consequences for social power. How did the conception of domestic labour change from 'productive' to 'unproductive' with the rise of classes? At this point, not the rise of commodity production, women were to have lost power. Apparently, the move to clan society, private property, and monogamy devalued housework, that is, women. As women's work was devalued in society, women were deprived of power within the home. Would it have mattered for women's power whether their work produced a surplus to be accumulated as private wealth if the work were seen as essential production? Engels discusses the change as if work in the home were already trivialized as a result of being given the low value of women. The work itself changed little. Yet once the father had gained increased power through increased wealth in the society,

> Mother right . . . had to be overthrown and overthrown it was. This was by no means so difficult as it looks to us today. For this revolution—one of the most decisive ever experienced by mankind—could take place without disturbing one of the living members of a gens. All could remain what they were. The simple decree [sometimes translated 'decision'] sufficed that in the future the offspring of the male members should remain within the gens, but that those of the female should be excluded by being transferred to the gens of their father.[56]

Class power produced gender power. Marxists do not usually allow a 'simple decision' to overturn historically based power relations. Seemingly men made this decision. Why did the women, who were supposedly supreme in the family at this time, accept it?

The answer appears to be that when the division of labour between men outside the family changed, the domestic relation inside the family changed.[57] The division of labour within the family before the rise of social classes gave man the important property (such as herds). When the division of labour outside the family became a class relation based upon private property ownership, the domestic relation necessarily changed from female to male supremacy. Leaving aside the questions of why and in what sense men could have 'owned' property in the family before private property became the dominant mode of ownership, or why the women were all at home, the essence of the argument seems to be that the power of some men to dominate other men in production gave all men power over all women in the home. Engels explains the distribution of power between men and women in the family as a function of the position of the family unit in social production, which in turn expresses men's relations with men.

From the proposition that class power is the source of male dominance, it follows that only those men who possess class power can oppress women in the family. Engels divides his examination of women under capitalism into an exploration of 'the bourgeois family' and 'the proletarian family', making clear that the class position of the family unit within which the woman is subordinated defines his understanding of her subordination. Since working-class men command no increased wealth, probably own little private property, and are exploited by the few (men) who do, they lack Engels' prerequisite for male supremacy. The proletarian family lacks property, 'for the preservation and inheritance of which monogamy and male supremacy were established; hence there is no incentive to make this male supremacy effective.' Further, 'now that large scale industry has taken the (proletarian) wife out of the home into the labour market and into the factory, and made her often the breadwinner of the family, no basis for any kind of male supremacy is left in the proletarian household, except perhaps for something of the brutality toward women that has spread since the introduction of monogamy.'[58]

Proletarian and bourgeois women differ in the structure of their sexual relations with their husbands. Proletarians experience 'sex love'; the bourgeoisie has monogamy. Sex love 'assumes that the person loved returns the love; to this extent the woman is an equal footing with the man.' Sex love is intense, possessive, and long-lasting. Its morality asks of a relationship: 'Did it spring from love and reciprocated love or not?'[59] Individual marriage is the social form that corresponds to sex love, 'as sexual love is by its nature exclusive—although at present this exclusiveness is fully realized only in the woman'. Sex love is possible only in proletarian relationships. It 'becomes and can only become the real rule among the oppressed classes, which means today among the proletariat . . . the eternal attendants of monogamy, hetaerism and adultery, play only an almost vanishing part.'[60] In its relationships, the proletariat, the revolutionary class, prefigures the post-revolutionary society.[61]

The proletarian woman is not, then, oppressed as a woman. She is not dominated by a male in the family. She does not live in monogamy. She is neither socially isolated nor economically dependent, because she takes part in social production, as all women will under socialism. She is not jointly or doubly oppressed. Proletarian women are oppressed when, in working outside the home, they come into contact with capital as workers, a condition they share with working-class men.

The differences between proletarian sexual relationships of sex love and bourgeois sexual relationships of monogamy are highly vaunted but obscure. Sex love in its origins, and even upon its abolition, is merged with monogamy. Individual marriage is the social form of both. Removal of the economic basis for monogamy, and consequent equalization of the sexes, will not free women to experience sex love, but will make men 'really' monogamous: 'If now the economic considerations also disappear which made women put up with the habitual infidelity of their husbands—concern for their own means of existence and still more for their children's future—then, according to all previous experience, the equality of women thereby achieved will tend infinitely to make men really monogamous than to make women polyandrous.'[62] The distinction between sex love and monogamy in Engels' analysis serves to distinguish proletarian women's situation from that of bourgeois women in order to idealize the proletariat. Women of both classes are the exclusive possessions of men. Under socialism, the position of all women changes because private housekeeping is removed into social industry. 'The supremacy of the man in marriage is the simple consequence of his economic supremacy, and with the abolition of the latter will disappear of itself.'[63] At most this explains why women must tolerate male supremacy; it does not explain why men want it. A clearer example of one-sided causality between material relations and social relations would be hard to find.

Putting housekeeping into social industry 'removes all the anxiety about "consequences" which today is the most essential social—moral as well as economic—factor that prevents a girl from giving herself completely to the man she loves'. Knowing that communism will enable men more wholly to own women sexually because women will 'give [themselves] completely'—the major barrier to this being housework, which one infers is a euphemism for child care—does not make one particularly look forward to Engels' millennium. He asks whether communism will not 'suffice to bring about the gradual growth of unconstrained sexual intercourse and with it a more tolerant public opinion in regard to a maiden's honour and a woman's shame?'[64] How unrestrained sexual intercourse went from being the reason women sought deliverance from group marriage under barbarism to that deliverance itself under communism, not to mention the transformation of the meaning of intercourse for women from transformation in property relations, is entirely unexplained, but must be what is meant by vulgar materialism.

Sex love occurs only in proletarian relations, so proletarian women are not oppressed as women; monogamy occurs only in the ruling classes, so only bourgeois women are oppressed as women. Can it be that the entire exploration of the origins of women's oppression produces an explanation that excludes the majority of women? Only those women who benefit from class exploitation—that is, women of the ruling classes—are subordinated to men, and only to ruling-class men. It appears to come to this: women who are oppressed by their class position are not oppressed as women by men, but by capital, while only women who benefit from their class position, bourgeois women, are oppressed as women, and only by means of their class. But how would ruling-class men oppress ruling-class women, since class differential is the basis of sex oppression? And since working-class men cannot oppress ruling-class women, bourgeois women cannot be victims of male dominance either. Once working-class men are disqualified from engaging in male dominance, the oppression of women exists, but there is no account of who is oppressed by it, far less of who is doing it.

Engels explains sexism as a kind of inverse of class oppression, which correlates with no known data; it is consistent with one persistent view on the left that feminism is 'bourgeois'. It also substantiates a feminist view that much Marxist theory, in interpreting gender through class, convolutes simple realities to comprehend gender derivatively if at all. A theory that exempts a favoured male group from the problem of male dominance necessarily evades confronting male power over women as a distinctive form of power, interrelated with the class structure but neither derivative from nor a side-effect of it.[65]

Engels fails to grasp the impact across classes of women's relationship to the class division itself. He does notice that the tension between women's family duties and public production cuts across classes: 'if she carries out her duties in the private service to her family, she remains excluded from public production and unable to earn; and if she wants to take part in public production and earn independently, she cannot carry out family duties. And the wife's position in the factory is the position of women in all branches of business, right up to medicine and the law.'[66] Engels does not develop his implicit awareness that the relationship of women to class, while often direct and long-lasting, can also be attenuated or crosscut because it is vicarious as well.

From a feminist perspective, a woman's class position, whether or not she works for wages, is as much or more set through her relation first to her father, then to her husband. It changes through changes in these relations, such as marriage, divorce, or aging. It is more open to change, both up and down, than is a man's in similar material circumstances. Through relations with men, women have considerable class mobility, down as well as up. A favourable marriage can rocket a woman into the ruling class, while her own skills, training, work experience, wage scales, and attitudes, were she on her own, would command few requisites for economic independence or mobility. Divorce or aging can devalue a woman economically as her connections or attractiveness to men declines. Women's relation to men's relation to production fixes a woman's class in a way that cuts across the class position of the work she herself does. If she does exclusively housework, her class position is determined by her husband's work outside the home—in spite of the fact that housework is increasingly similar across classes and, when paid, is considered working-class work. This is not to suggest that women's relation to class is less potent than men's because it is vicarious, but to point out that women's relation to class is mediated through their relations with men.

Engels presupposes throughout, as liberal theorists do, that the distinction between the realm inside the family and the realm outside the family is a distinction between public and private.[67] 'Private' means 'inside the family'. 'Public' means the rest of the world. That is, the family is considered to be a truly private space, private for everyone in it— and not just because there is an ideological function served by regarding it so. In analysing women as a group in terms of their role in the family, and men in terms of their role in social production, Engels precludes seeing social relations, inside as well as outside the family, in terms of a sex-based social division. Are women really treated very differently by male employers in the marketplace from the way they are treated by husbands at home? in the work they do? in the personal and sexual services they perform? in the hierarchy between them? To consider the home 'private' is to privatize women's oppression and to render women's status a question of domestic relations to be analysed as a derivative of the public sphere rather than setting the family within a totality characterized by a sexual division of power which divides both home and marketplace.

Engels' private/public distinction parallels and reinforces Marx's nature/history distinction by defining women's issues in terms of one side of a descriptive dualism in which women's status is the least subject to direct social change. For Marx, woman's natural role is mirrored in her role as worker; for Engels, woman's natural role is mirrored in her role in the family. To identify women's oppression with the private and the natural, on the left no less than in capitalist society itself, works to subordinate the problem of women's status to the male and dominant spheres and to hide that relegation behind the appearance of addressing it.

The key dynamic assumption in Engels' analysis of woman's situation, that without which Engels' history does not move, is (in a word) sexism. The values, division of labour, and power of male supremacy are presumed at each crucial juncture. The account otherwise collapses into a parade of facts. The subject to be explained—the development of male supremacy—is effectively presumed. As an account of the 'origins' of that development, the analysis dissolves into a mythic restatement divided into ascending periods of an essentially static state of woman's subordination, within which one can see growing inequalities but cannot figure out how they started or why they keep getting worse. If the intent was to give 'the woman question' a place in Marxist theory, it did: woman's place.

Engels' method made this inevitable. His approach to social explanation is rigidly causal, unidirectional, and one-sided. Material conditions alone create social relations; consciousness and materiality do not interact. Thought contemplates things. Objects appear and relate to each other out there, back then. The discourse is mythic in quality, passive in voice. 'There arose' certain things; then something 'came over' something; this 'was bound to bring' that. Theory, for Engels, is far from a dialogue between observer and observed. He does not worry about his own historicity. He totally fails to grasp the subject side of the subject/object relation as socially dynamic.[68] And he takes history as a fixed object within a teleology in which what came before necessarily led to what came after. This is to fail to take the *object* side of the subject/object relation as socially dynamic. One must understand that society could be other than it is in order to explain it, far less to change it. Perhaps one must even understand that society could be other than it is in order to understand why it necessarily is as it is. Engels' empiricism can imagine only the reality he finds, and therefore he can find only the reality he imagines.

NOTES

1. This chapter does not address the ways in which Marx's theories of social life are, are not, or can be made applicable to women's experience or useful for women's liberation. It addresses what Marx and Engels explicitly said about women, women's status, and women's condition. This book treats the work of Marx as a whole, rather than dividing him into 'old' and 'young', but with the understanding that his work, like that of most people, did develop and change over time.

2. Karl Marx, *The German Ideology* (New York: International Publishers, 1972): 51. August Bebel, in his influential volume *Women under Socialism*, included sexuality in nature: 'The satisfaction of the sexual instinct is as much a private concern as the satisfaction of any other natural instinct'; Lise Vogel, 'The Earthly Family', *Radical America* 7 (July-October 1973): 4–5.

3. Karl Marx, *Capital*, 3 vols (New York: International Publishers, 1967), I: 337 (hereafter cited as *Capital*).

4. *Capital*, I: 351, 352.

5. *Capital*, I: 42; see also I: 177–8.

6. *Capital*, I: 43.

7. Marx, *German Ideology*: 50.

8. *Capital*, I: 395, 397, 395.

9. *Capital*, I: 395, 398.

10. No distinction exists between these views of Marx and those of contemporary 'pro-family' conservatives.

11. *Capital*, I: 399, 393–4.

12. Marx here appears to approve female protective laws, which have often seemed helpful but also detrimental in protecting women out of jobs they needed and wanted while failing to protect all workers from conditions that harmed them all.

13. Karl Marx, *On the Jewish Question*, in *Karl Marx: Selected Writings*, ed. David McLellan (Oxford: Oxford University Press, 1977): 60.

14. Karl Marx, *Economic and Philosophic Manuscripts of 1844*, ibid.: 87.

15. Karl Marx and Friedrich Engels, *The Communist Manifesto*, in *Selected Works*, ed. V. Adoratsky,

vol. I (New York: International Publishers, 1936): 224–5.

16. *Capital*, I: 402, 403.

17. In his discussion drawn from a parliamentary report on the employment of women as colliers in mines, Marx makes these points through quotations from interviews in which male miners find mining 'degrading to the sex', injurious to women's ability to care for children, to their dress ('rather a man's dress . . . it drowns all sense of decency'), and to their own and their husbands' morality. Marx's only comment in his own voice is that the apparent concern of the questioners for these women is a cloak for their financial self-interest; *Capital*, I: 499–500. Actually, what the male miners say supports women's exclusion from this work—a viewpoint inconsistent with the motive of material interest Marx attributes to them. For example, they are asked, 'Your feeling upon the whole subject is that the better class of colliers who desire to raise themselves and humanize themselves, instead of deriving help from the women, are pulled down by them?' 'Yes . . .'; *Capital*, I: 489–90. One can only conclude that Marx is able to understand the concern of the bourgeois questioner as inimical to his own, so attributes it to material interest even when it conflicts with material interest. In fact, the exclusion of women from these jobs, whatever else it may reflect of humanitarianism, is in the material interest of male workers, converging with a denial of material self-interest by the bourgeois employer through an affirmation of his sexism.

18. *Capital*, I: 489–90, 377. This is attributed to the fact that under capitalism 'the labourer exists for the process of production, and not the process of production for the labourer' (377).

19. Karl Marx, 'Chapitre de marriage', quoted in Juliet Mitchell, 'Women: The Longest Revolution', in *From Feminism to Liberation*, ed. Edith Hoshino Altbach (London: Schenkman, 1971): 107 n.9.

20. Marx, *The German Ideology* (Moscow: Progress Publishers, 1976): 194. See also Marx in *Marx: Selected Writings*, ed. McLellan: 'The bourgeoisie has torn away from the family its sentimental veil, and has reduced the family relation to a mere money relation' (224); and 'On what foundation is the present family, the bourgeois family, based? On capital, on private gain. In its completely developed form this family exists only among the bourgeoisie. But this state of things finds its complement in the practical absence of the family among the proletarians, and in public prostitution' (234).

21. *Origin*.

22. A diverse discussion that both illustrates and criticizes this impact is provided by Janet Sayers, Mary Evens, and Nanneke Redclift, eds, *Engels Revisited: New Feminist Essays* (London: Tavistock, 1987). The essay by Moira Maconachie, 'Engels, Sexual Divisions, and the Family' (98–112), criticizes Engels' naturalism.

23. Juliet Mitchell, *Woman's Estate* (New York: Random House, 1971); Gayle Rubin, 'The Traffic in Women: Notes on the "Political Economy" of Sex' in *Toward an Anthropology of Women*, ed. Rayna R. Reiter (New York: Monthly Review Press, 1975): 164.

24. Branka Magas, 'Sex Politics: Class Politics', *New Left Review* 80 (March-April 1971): 69.

25. Karen Sachs, 'Engels Revisited: Women, the Organization of Production, and Private Private Property', in *Woman, Culture, and Society*, ed. Michelle Z. Rosaldo and Louise Lamphere (Stanford University Press, 1974), uses this approach.

26. Lenin, for example, says: 'Notwithstanding all the liberating laws that have been passed, woman continues to be a domestic slave, because petty housework crushes, strangles, stultifies and degrades her, chains her to the kitchen and to the nursery, and wastes her labor on barbarously

unproductive, petty, nerve-racking stultifying and crushing drudgery. The real emancipation of women, real communism, will begin only when a mass struggle (led by the proletariat which is in power) is started against this petty domestic economy, or rather when it is transformed on a mass scale into large-scale socialist economy'; V.I. Lenin, 'Woman and Society' in *The Woman Question: Selections from the Writings of Marx, Engels, Lenin, and Stalin* (New York: International Publishers, 1951): 56.

27. Eli Zaretsky, 'Socialism and Feminism III: Socialist Politics and the Family', *Socialist Revolution* 4 (January-March 1974): 85, 91, 96.

28. Examples of the unannotated use of a very common misinterpretation of Engels include Richard Edwards, Michael Reich, and Thomas Weiskopf, *The Capitalist System: A Radical Analysis of American Society* (Englewood Cliffs, N.J.: Prentice-Hall, 1972): 325. 'Male supremacy was probably the first form of oppression of one group in society by another; men were dominant over women in most precapitalist societies.' The general theme of primitive sexual egalitarianism disrupted by the rise of private property is accepted by Evelyn Reed, *Woman's Evolution: From Matriarchal Clan to Patriarchal Family* (New York: Pathfinder Press, 1975); Eleanor Leacock, Introduction to *Origin*; and Heidi I. Hartmann, 'Capitalism, Patriarchy, and Job Segregation by Sex', *Signs: Journal of Women in Culture and Society* I (Spring 1976): 137. It is interesting that the influence of Engels' theoretical approach seems quite independent of the data by Morgan on which it was purportedly based, data which have been rather widely discredited.

29. *Origin*: 129.

30. *Origin*: 120.

31. *Origin*: 129.

32. William Reich, *Sex-Pol: Essays, 1929–1934* (New York: Random House, 1972): 182.

33. Kate Millett, *Sexual Politics* (Garden City, N.Y.: Doubleday, 1970): 120.

34. Susan Williams, *Lesbianism: A Socialist Feminist Perspective*, Radical Women Position Paper (Mimeograph, Seattle, April 1973): 3.

35. *Origin*: 137, 134.

36. If this relation is understood as causal and not correlational, it could just as well mean that sex contradictions cause class contradictions. So Shulamith Firestone can refer to Engels when she argues that 'beneath economics, reality is psychosexual', and proposes an analysis of the 'psychosexual roots of class'; *The Dialectic of Sex: The Case for Feminist Revolution* (New York: Bantam Books, 1970): 5, 11. Charlotte Bunch elaborates this argument as follows: 'Class distinctions are an outgrowth of male domination as such, and not only divide women along economic lines but also serve to destroy vestiges of women's previous matriarchal strength'; Charlotte Bunch and Nancy Myron, eds, *Class and Feminism* (Baltimore: Diana Press, 1974): 8.

37. In a characteristic formulation, Engels writes that historical materialism is 'that view of the course of history which seeks the ultimate cause and the great moving power of all important historical events in the economic development of society, in the changes in the modes of production and exchange, in the consequent division of society into distinct classes, and in the struggles of these classes against one another'; Friedrich Engels, *Socialism: Utopian and Scientific*, trans. E. Aveling (New York: International Publishers, 1935): 16.

38. *Origin*: 117.

39. The burden of maternity cannot be the answer, because a woman can as readily be kept pregnant by one man as by many.

40. *Origin*: 118–19.

41. *Origin*: 118.

42. Karl Marx, *Wage-Labor and Capital* (New York: International Publishers, 1971): 28.

43. *Origin*: 113.

44. *Origin*: 119.

45. *Origin*: 113–14.

46. *Origin*: 172, 218, 222, 224–5.

47. *Origin*: 223.

48. This difference in treating the division of labour could be accounted for under capitalism by the tacit assumption that women's housework is not properly 'production' because its dominant form is not commodities. But at the time of pairing marriage, housework was properly social production, yet the division of labour between women and men was somehow both nonexploitative and justifiable.

49. For pairing marriage places 'by the side of the natural mother of the child . . . its natural and attested father with a better warrant of paternity, probably, than that of many a "father" today'; *Origin*: 129.

50. *Origin*: 128, 144.

51. Notes by Marx, quoted in *Origin*: 128.

52. *Origin*: 119.

53. Paraphrase of *Origin*: 138.

54. This ceases to be a problem with the introduction and generalization of money, as sheer exchange value can then be accumulated and commanded.

55. Without knowing the connection between the material relations and their imputed social meanings, one could equally well argue, 'didn't the lust for property begin with man's lust to own "his" children by owning their mother?' Barbara Deming, in Barbara Deming and Arthur Kinoy, *Women and Revolution: A Dialogue* (New York: National Interim Committee for a Mass Party of the People, April 1975): 32.

56. *Origin*: 119–20.

57. Engels is clear, however, that he does not know 'how and when this revolution took place'; *Origin*: 120.

58. *Origin*: 135. Since it costs money to enforce laws, legal requirements have little effect on workers' interpersonal relations; 'here quite other personal and social conditions decide'; ibid.

59. *Origin*: 140. 'Only now (in Roman times) were the conditions realized in which through monogamy—within it, parallel to it, or in opposition to it—the greatest moral advance we owe to it could have been achieved: modern individual sex love, which had hitherto been unknown to the entire world'; ibid.: 140.

60. *Origin*: 135.

61. This position contrasts with the views of both Lenin and Trotsky, who thought that as the underclass, the proletariat would often contain society's most oppressive relations. See, e.g., Leon Trotsky, *Problems of Everyday Life and Other Writings on Culture and Science*, eds G.R. Fidler *et al.* (New York: Pathfinder Press, 1973): 78–87.

62. *Origin*: 144–5. When private wealth disappears, will monogamy disappear? . . . 'far from disappearing, it will, on the contrary, begin to be realized completely'; ibid.: 139.

63. *Origin*: 139.

64. *Origin*: 139.
65. Some theorists on the left have tried to revive this failed account by arguing that both proletarian women and men are oppressed by the ruling class through imposed sex roles. Male workers' brutality toward their wives compensates for their powerlessness as workers. Why women are not brutal to men to compensate for their powerlessness as workers is never explained. It also follows that ruling-class men, who also learn sex roles, must both be oppressed by them and receive the benefits of them. This seems, in a feminist view, to be an attempt to define favored male groups out of the problem, evading the more straightforward and elegant feminist explanation: male power over women is a distinctive form of power that interrelates with the class structure but is neither derivative from nor a side effect of it. In this view, men oppress women to the extent that they can because it is in their interest and to their advantage to do so.
66. *Origin*: 137.
67. 'With the patriarchal family and still more with the single monogamous family, a change came. Household management lost its public character. It no longer concerned society. It became a private service; the wife became the head servant, excluded from all participation in social production. Not until the coming of modern large-scale industry was the road to social production opened to her again—and then only to the proletarian wife'; *Origin*: 137.
68. This is what Lukács means by his criticism of 'contemplative materialism': 'Dialectics, [Engels] argues, is a continuous process of transition from one definition into the other. In consequence, a one-sided and rigid causality must be replaced by interaction. But he does not even mention the most vital interaction, namely the dialectical relation between subject and object in the historical process, let alone give it the prominence it deserves. Yet without this factor dialectics ceases to be revolutionary despite attempts (illusory in the last analysis) to retain "fluid" concepts. For it implies a failure to recognize that in all metaphysics the object remains untouched and unaltered so that thought remains contemplative and fails to become practical; while for the dialectical method the central problem is to change reality. If this central function of the theory is disregarded, the virtues of forming "fluid" concepts become altogether problematic: a purely "scientific" matter. The theory might then be accepted or rejected in accordance with the prevailing state of science without any modification at all to one's basic attitudes, to the question of whether or not reality can be changed.' George Lukács, *History and Class Consciousness: Studies in Marxist Dialectics*, Rodney Livingstone (Cambridge, Mass.: MIT Press, 1971): 3–4.

MIKE FEATHERSTONE

1946–
BRITAIN

Major Works

1991   *Consumer Culture and Postmodernism*
1995   *Undoing Culture: Globalization, Postmodernism and Identity*
1995   *Global Modernities*
1996   (ed. with Roger Burrows) *Cyberspace/Cyberbodies/Cyberpunk*
1999   *Love and Eroticism*
1999   (ed.) *Body Modification*

The problems we encounter in everyday practice because culture fails to provide us with a single taken-for-granted recipe for action introduce difficulties, mistakes, and complexity. Culture which once seemed invisible, as it was habitually inculcated into people over time and became sedimented into well-worn social routines, now surfaces as a problem. Taken-for-granted tacit knowledge about what to do, how to respond to particular groups of people and what judgement of taste to make, now becomes more problematic. Within consumer culture newspapers, magazines, television and radio all offer advice on how to cope with a range of new situations, risks and opportunities—yet this only adds to rather than reduces complexity.[1]

The international and trans-societal processes which are taking place in the late twentieth century are speeding up the process of globalization. This term refers to the sense of global compression in which the world is increasingly regarded as 'one place' and it becomes much more difficult for nation-states to opt out of, or avoid the consequences of being drawn together into a progressively tighter figuration through the increasing volume and rapidity of the flows of money, goods, people, information, technology and images. Part of the problem of conceptualization which is highlighted by postmodernism may well have something to do with the attempts to comprehend this resultant rise in global complexity.[2]

—*Mike Featherstone*

As we attempt to engage a new century (engage in the mechanical sense of using the clutch in an automobile and also in some much wider ethereal sense), the three terms in the subtitle of Mike Featherstone's book, *Undoing Culture: Globalization, Postmodernism and Identity*, seem so central to our lives, regardless how abstract or distant they appear to be. Globalization, postmodernism, and identity call us to comprehend the early theorists of sociology, and call forth new understandings, within the reality now called the 'post-September 11' world.

Featherstone's work explores a wide-ranging number of themes and although the centrality of globalization, postmodernism, and identity within contemporary analysis is crucial, our emphasis here is on his work on postmodernism. 'Postmodernism' as a term can create a good deal of variability in people's thoughts, orientations, and understandings. Featherstone chooses to explore a 'sociology of postmodernism' rather than a 'postmodernist sociology', meaning that sociological analysis can be brought to bear on the study of this complex theme rather than seeing postmodernism as a central vein of the sociological frame itself (see Featherstone's *Consumer Culture and Postmodernism*). An important understanding that emerges is the decentring of the concept of 'society' and a centring of the concept of 'culture'. What are the places of the production, reproduction, and most importantly, the consumption of culture and cultural productions within modern/postmodern societies?

Postmodernism with all its complexities of definition and understanding emerges within art, architecture, literature, popular culture, and a myriad of other cultural phenomena in such diverse ways that we need to rethink many of our taken-for-granted perceptions of our everyday lives. Let's begin with Featherstone's definition of postmodernism:

> The main features associated with postmodernism can be briefly summarized. *First*, a movement away from the universalistic ambitions of master-narratives where the emphasis is upon totality, system and unity towards an emphasis upon local knowledge, fragmentation, syncretism, 'otherness' and 'difference'. *Second*, a dissolution of symbolic hierarchies, which entail canonical judgements of taste and value, towards a popular collapse of the distinction between high and popular culture. *Third*, a tendency towards the aestheticization of everyday life which gained momentum both from efforts within the arts to collapse the boundary between art and life (pop art, Dada, surrealism, and so on) and the alleged movement towards a simulational consumer culture in which an endlessly reduplicated hallucinatory veil of images effaces the distinction between appearance and reality. *Fourth*, a decentring of the subject, whose sense of identity and biographical continuity give way to fragmentation and superficial play with images, sensations and 'multiphrenic intensities'. . . .

> . . . It refers to a breakdown of individual's sense of identity through the bombardment of fragmented signs and images which erode all continuity between past, present and future. . . .
>
> In opposition to the notion that life is a meaningful project, here we have the view that the individual's primary mode of orientation is an aesthetic one.[3]

The complexity of these definitional perspectives leads us to a historical imagination that traces the traditional and the modern into the postmodern. Of fundamental importance historically is the place of the individual and, indeed, whether the individual is the centre, or the site, of control. The Enlightenment shifted the emphasis from traditional forms of religious authority to place 'Reason' as the generator of knowledge and understanding. The locus of control became the individual, the individual in control and 'capable' of controlling the forces of nature through science, of controlling the social through reason, planning, and eventually, management. Order seemed possible; the process of ordering became sanctified. Weber's 'rationalization of the world' came to be seen as part of a systematic progression towards an end—one that became monolithic in expression—'McDonaldized' in experience. 'Progress' united with the ultimate faith in Reason, characterized most explicitly by 'science', became the master narrative, the 'overarching symbolic universe' (to use the phraseology of Berger and Luckmann[4]).

But, as Featherstone argues, if we carefully study modernity, we recognize and perceive *modernities*.[5] So, the latter part of the twentieth century and the entry into this new century disclose the dynamic dialectic of monoculturalism and diversity—the ordered propensity of the modern to the multiplicity of the postmodern.

But let us return to Featherstone's definition: 'fragmentation', 'decentring', 'otherness', 'difference', 'collapse of canonical master narratives'—all of these demand that we search for new forms of authority, new measures, new values to guide our daily lives, as our lives become commodified and saturated with images and symbols perpetrated by an ever-expanding form of corporate capitalism.

Featherstone's perception of contemporary postmodern life moves to this globalized nature of our everyday lives and how the West's place in exporting images, cultural productions, and structures has begun to meet with some resistance, at the same time as we begin the *internal* recognition of the postmodern within Western experience. For example, he notices how in such cities as Los Angeles the new class divisions and structures of difference make us aware that modern perspectives and postmodern perspectives are melding within current realities. And he points out how, internationally, the recognition of difference and post-colonial realities has begun to change:

> . . . with more voices talking back to the West, there is a strong sense that modernity will not be universalized. This is because modernity is seen as both a Western project and as the West's projection of its values on to the world.[6]

Careful reading of Featherstone demands we recognize the work of Marx, Weber, Foucault, hooks, Habermas, and Said. The place of the West (read US) within world geopolitics is more than ever contested and complex. Postmodernism and post-colonialism become theoretical domains that begin to shape our possible understanding in new and exciting ways. Featherstone's contribution to this furthering of our analysis and understanding is most insightful.

Notes

1. Mike Featherstone, *Undoing Culture* (London: Sage, 1995), 5.
2. Ibid., 81–2.
3. Ibid., 43–4.
4. Peter Berger and Thomas Luckmann, *The Social Construction of Reality* (New York: Anchor Books, 1967).
5. Note that Max Weber added an 's' to the term, 'capitalism', which allows us to think and rethink masses of material otherwise taken for granted. Addition of an 's' to 'feminism' is a good example of this.
6. Featherstone, *Undoing Culture*, 10.

GLOBALIZING CULTURAL COMPLEXITY

> Things fall apart; the centre cannot hold.
> —W.B. Yeats, 'The Second Coming'

> Those who write, travel.
> The art of being there is to go there.
> —Joseph de Maistre

Undoing Cultural Unities

The above quotation from Yeats has been used numerous times, both directly and indirectly, to highlight the current sense of cultural fragmentation and dislocation. It is assumed that culture has become decentred, that there is an absence of coherence and unity; culture can no longer provide an adequate account of the world with which to construct or order our lives. The lines which directly precede the above quotation at the start of Yeats's poem run: 'Turning and turning in the widening gyre/The falcon cannot hear the falconer'. This inability to find the way home, to return to the lost point of coherence and order, was of course a well-worked theme in the events surrounding the end of the First World War and its immediate aftermath, the time when Yeats wrote the poem.

Our current sense of cultural fragmentation which is indicated in titles of books such as *Off Center* (Miyoshi, 1991), *Dislocating Masculinity* (Cornwall and Lindisfarne, 1994), *Relocating Cultural Studies* (Blurtdell et al., 1993), *Border Dialogues* (Chambers, 1990), *Disrupted Borders* (Gupta, 1993), *The Nation and its Fragments* (Chatterjee, 1993), *Decentring Leisure* (Rojek, 1995), then is not new. Indeed people have long been *Undoing Culture*, to add the title of this book to the rapidly growing list. Yet what is noticeable is that late twentieth-century analysts of culture rarely seek to examine other potentially parallel phases of history, such as the time in which Yeats wrote 'The Second Coming' just after the First World War, a phase in which there was a marked sense of cultural relativism and crisis, as the writings of Spengler, Scheler, Weber and others demonstrate. If we wanted to cast further afield the culture of the baroque in the seventeenth century which fascinated Walter Benjamin (1977) and others (Buci-Glucksmann, 1994; Maravall, 1986) also comes to mind. Yet ours would not be the first generation to be accused of harbouring 'men [or today we should say people] without memories', to play off Adorno's phrase.

It can be argued that the sense that there is a cultural crisis, that we need a 'diagnosis of our times', has long been the meat and drink of cultural specialists (artists, intellectuals and various types of cultural intermediaries). In effect they have a professional interest in undoing and reworking the knots of culture. This is not to suggest that cultural specialists are arbitrarily, or capriciously, inventing cultural crises. They are clearly responding to perceptions and images of events happening in the world. Yet it is the relationship between their immediate world, the conditions of intellectual and cultural production and consumption within which they work, and this larger world 'out there' which needs investigation. Noticeable in the post-war era have been the specific shifts within intellectual practices which occurred as tightly controlled establishments, able to monopolize the supply of intellectual goods, gave way to a phase of demonopolization, which has provided a range of opportunities for outsider groups.

This was one of the arguments of my previous book, *Consumer Culture and Postmodernism* (1991a), that postmodernism should not merely be understood as an epochal shift, or new stage of capitalism. Rather, attention should be given to the mediations between the economy and culture by focusing on the activities of cultural specialists and intermediaries and the expanding audiences (the post-war baby boom generation) for a new range of cultural goods. *Contra* some strands of postmodern theory which proclaim the triumph of culture and along with it the end of the social, it argued that we have not so readily moved towards a stage in the development of social life which has broken down completely the power balances and interdependencies which bind together groups of people. At the same time it must be conceded that concepts such as 'the social' and 'society' are no longer able to deliver the theoretical benefits they once promised. As we shall see in some of the later chapters in the book, the process of globalization has been helping to undermine the alleged integrity and unity of nation-state societies. Yet we should be aware of assuming that this is the whole story, because the notion of 'society' has long been as much a projected image of what social life should be like as a reality. It glossed many social processes which were never domesticated, regulated and integrated. One of these processes, the shifting role of travel and mobility in constructing images of social life, is the subject of the final chapter.

A central aim of this book is to explore some of the processes which are alleged to have uncoupled culture from the social and some of the ways in which this particular image itself has been formed. It has, therefore, been argued that culture has gained a more significant role within social life and that today everything is cultural (e.g. Baudrillard, 1993). In effect culture is now beyond the social and has become released from its traditional determinisms in economic life, social class, gender, ethnicity and region. In terms of our reference to the decentring of culture, this could be taken to be a counter-argument: in effect culture has not been decentred, rather, it has become recentred. Certainly, if we take into account the rise in significance accorded to the study of culture within academic life this could well be the case. Culture, long on the periphery of the social science field, has now been moved towards the centre. To take an example: my book *Consumer Culture and Postmodernism* (Featherstone, 1991a) was reviewed by the *British Journal of Industrial Relations* in the early 1990s. For a book on culture and theory to be reviewed by an industrial relations journal would hardly have seemed possible in the 1970s. Today a number of new journals have appeared in the fields of business, management and organizational studies which address many of the theoretical and cultural issues which were taken on board in *Theory, Culture & Society* and other places in the early 1980s. It can be argued that this is part of a wider tendency within academic life which has seen the weakening of the divisions between subject areas alongside a much stronger approval for inter- and trans-disciplinary studies. From this perspective, then, the more general decentring and fragmentation of culture has been accompanied by a re-centring of culture within academic life.

An aim, then, of this book, is to investigate the processes both inside and outside the academy and wider field of cultural producers, which form our sense of culture as something unified or fragmented. In one sense we are all cultural producers in that we engage in practices which not only reproduce the cultural repertoires we are provided with and need as we move through social life, but are to some extent able to modify and shape them as they are passed down the unbroken chain of generations which constitutes human life. Yet the extent to which we can all participate in cultural production and consumption clearly varies historically and between societies. It also varies between groups within societies, as almost all societies and social entities possess groups of specialists who engage in the production and dissemination of culture (priests, artists, intellectuals, educators, teachers, academics, cultural intermediaries, etc.). This power potential they possess through their ability to produce and mobilize culture is, of course, not unimpeded, but is itself dependent upon the interdependencies and power balances these groups enjoy with other, usually more powerful, groups such as economic and military specialists. It is possible, then, that our overall sense of the value, meaning and potential unity or crisis-ridden nature of a culture will depend not only on the conditions of social life we find ourselves in, but on the conditions of those who specialize in cultural production as well. Under certain circumstances the power potential of certain groups of cultural specialists may increase to the extent that particular cultural forms gain greatly in autonomy and prestige. This is the subject of Chapter 2, which explores the processes that lead to the formation and autonomization of the cultural sphere. [This and subsequent references are to later chapters in Featherstone's Undoing Culture.] The relatively autonomous cultural sphere which developed alongside the public sphere (Habermas, 1989) since the eighteenth century, was accompanied by a rise in the prestige of artists and intellectuals, to the extent that for some groups in the middle classes art became a heroic way of life, which was seen as more important than life itself.

This subject is taken up in Chapters 3 and 4, which address the ways in which the ordered heroic life has been formed as part of the processes which led to the autonomization of the culture sphere. Max Weber's respect for the sense of unity generated by the ordered life of the Puritan is well known, as is his assumption that it is impossible to reproduce this in modern times. For Weber the artistic, intellectual or erotic lives are necessarily incomplete and lack fundamental coherence, something which became the fate of the individual in modernity. Yet the topic is given an intriguing twist when we consider those accounts of Weber's life which sought to present it as a form of heroic stoicism, perhaps the only viable 'noble' response to the meaninglessness generated by the rationalization of life and the confusion resulting from the clashing of incompatible values in the modern world. Against the possibility of striving for an ordered life we have to place the sacrifice and isolation demanded by this masculine form of heroic self-formation. This theme is taken up in the next chapter, in which everyday life, the world of sociability, maintenance and women is contrasted against the masculine heroic ideal. Yet this ideal, which became such a powerful force in the arts and intellectual life in the late nineteenth century, has since been weakened with the deformation of the cultural sphere and the rise of consumer culture. This should not be taken as merely entailing a tragic loss, but as allowing new forms of identity development to take place amongst previously excluded outsider groups.

It is assumed, then, that in the twentieth century the process of the formation and autonomization of the cultural sphere has given way to deformation. One of the strands associated with postmodernism in the late twentieth century has been that we are witnessing the 'end of art', and the end of the artist as a heroic figure concerned to carve out a distinctive form of life. The extension of consumer culture particularly through the mass production and proliferation of commodity-signs and images is seen to have spelled the end of a separate cultural sphere.

Yeats's 'Second Coming' can again be used to illustrate this process. While the poem has regularly been taught in schools and universities as part of the specialist canon of high culture, it has recently been popularized and packaged for a mass audience. The poem has been used as lyrics for a song recorded by Joni Mitchell on a recent CD. W.B. Yeats might well have approved this popularization of the poem and its capacity to reach wider audiences, yet the problem is complicated because the binary opposition high culture/mass culture no longer seems appropriate. Joni Mitchell writes for intermediate audiences which cannot easily be designated as belonging to popular culture or mass culture — not that they are high culture either. This, then, is an example of a 'cross-over', where previously sealed-off cultural forms more easily flow over what were once strictly policed boundaries, to produce unusual combinations and syncretisms.

This question of the difficulty of categorizing culture which flows across boundaries is a central issue in Chapters 5, 6 and 7. It can be argued that the intensification of the flow of cultural goods and images within consumer culture makes it more difficult to read culture, to attribute a fixed meaning and relationship between a cultural sign or image and the social attributes of the person who uses or consumes the item. As is argued in Chapter 2, on the autonomization of the cultural sphere, there is the assumption, derived from anthropological studies of tightly bounded societies, that the logic of the system of cultural classification is somehow homologous to the distinctions, differences and divisions between social groups who unconsciously use culture as relatively fixed markers in status games. Yet it can be argued that the difficulty in controlling the flow of new goods, images and information, which is generated by the modernist and market impulses within consumer societies, leads to problems of misreading the signs. The problems we encounter in everyday practice because culture fails to provide us with a single taken-for-granted recipe for action introduces difficulties, mistakes and complexity. Culture which once seemed invisible, as it was habitually inculcated into people over time and became sedimented into well-worn social routines, now surfaces as a problem. Taken-for-granted tacit knowledge about what to do, how to respond to particular groups of people and what judgement of taste to make, now becomes more problematic. Within consumer culture newspapers, magazines, television and the radio all offer advice on how to cope with a range of new situations, risks and opportunities—yet this only adds to rather than reduces complexity.

While some would see this as essentially a postmodern problem, we should be aware that Simmel (1968), writing around the turn of the century, identified this as a characteristic feature of modernity, or perhaps we should say 'the modern condition': the difficulties of coping with, and meaningfully assimilating, the overproduction of objective culture. Nearly a century later what we refer to as postmodernism can be associated with a further tightening and intensification of this process. As will be argued in Chapters 6, 7 and 8, the global dimension plays a crucially important part in our attempt to understand this process. It is not sufficient to regard the intensification of the flows of commodities, money, images, information and technology as globalizing the postmodern by exporting its cultural forms and complexity problematic from the Western centres to the rest of the world. This is to assume a neat sequence of social change based upon West European experience via its assumed master concepts of tradition, modernity and post-modernity, largely propelled by economic changes.

It is also important to examine the ways in which globalization has produced both the modern and the postmodern, in the sense that the power struggles between nation-states, blocs and other collectivities gradually became globalized as more and more parts of the world were drawn into the competing figuration of interdependencies and power balances. As is argued in the final chapter, there is an important spatial and relational dimension to modernity which is lost when we conceive it as coming out of one particular time and place with all others necessarily condemned to traverse the same route. Hence it is possible now to see the beginnings of differential reactions to modernity, through the production of a series of different cultural frames, of which the rise in the power potential of non-Western nation-states (in particular the rise of East Asia) is making us in the

West increasingly aware. It might, then, be advisable to speak of global modernities, with the emphasis given to the plural forms.

Global Modernities and Cultural Complexity

The process of globalization suggests simultaneously two images of culture. The first image entails the extension outwards of a particular culture to its limit, the globe. Heterogeneous cultures become incorporated and integrated into a dominant culture which eventually covers the whole world. The second image points to the compression of cultures. Things formerly held apart are now brought into contact and juxtaposition. Cultures pile on top of each other in heaps without obvious organizing principles. There is too much culture to handle and organize into coherent belief systems, means of orientation and practical knowledge. The first image suggests a process of conquest and unification of the global space. The world becomes a singular domesticated space, a place where everyone becomes assimilated into a common culture. In one version this dream of a secular ecumene (Tenbruck, 1990) as the endpoint of historical development, represents a global culture as the culture of the nation-state writ large. Few today would adhere to this faith in the unfolding of a historical logic to deliver us into a world state with an integrated culture. While there are processes of cultural integration, homogenization and unification at work, it is clear that they are by no means uncontested.

It may well be better to consider a global culture in the first sense to be a form, a space or field, made possible through improved means of communication in which different cultures meet and clash. This points directly towards the second aspect of the globalization of culture and at the same time suggests greater cultural movement and complexity. Yet once the spiral of relativization of culture through increased contact, juxtaposition and clashing has begun, many questions start to surface about long-held formulations of culture in the social sciences and the humanities. We need to consider the question of the perception of complexity: which groups of people represent cultures as more complex and why? What does this assertion of complexity suggest about our image of cultures as more simple and integrated in the past? How were such images possible and sustainable? How far does this point towards the need to develop a new set of cultural concepts with which to reconceptualize the role of culture in social life?

For those who like to detect the play of logics in the historical process, globalization could be seen as entailing a social integration process which runs from tribal groups to nation-state societies, superstate blocs and eventually a world state-society. While many would hesitate to go so far as to see the emergence of a world state-society based upon the global monopolization of violence and taxation, we already find references to a 'global society' (Giddens, 1994: 96-7), suggesting that various modes of global integration and forms of organization are well under way. Such an emergent global society is clearly far from being comparable to the conventional sociological notion of society which is grounded in the nation-state, and as in the case of the influential Durkheimian tradition, emphasizes normative integration and common cultural values.

If there is an emergent global society, the impetus would seem to be coming from technological developments and the economy (and it is important to conceive both in relation to social and cultural frameworks and the activities of specific groups of people and other collective agents such as nation-states, which further these developments in terms of their potential as forms of empowerment). Technological developments such as means of transportation (motor cars, railways and aeroplanes) enable the binding together of larger expanses of time-space not only on an intra-societal level, but increasingly on an inter-societal and global level. The same can be said for the mass media (radio, terrestrial and satellite TV) and new communications technology (telephones, fax, and the emergent computer network, the 'internet'). Unlike the first set of devices, which have generally been designed for monological, or one-way communication, the latter range of devices have a dialogical and interactive capacity which enables distant others across the world to pursue us and make demands on us to hit deadlines, as we strive to manage wider networks with more intense information interchanges. The development of weaponry also provides a further dramatic means of binding people together in conflict over vast areas of time and space.

In a similar way global integration can be conceived as being furthered through the expansion of economic activity to the extent that common forms of industrial production, commodities, market behaviour, trade and consumption also become generalized around the world. The expansion of the modern world system can be conceived in this way, which points to the ways in which particular nation-states and groups within nation-states have sought to expand markets and production systems (Wallerstein, 1974, 1980). To take the parallel case of global consumption, it is clear that certain retailing forms of business, techniques, sites and modes of marketing have rapidly proliferated around the world.

One noticeable example is the tremendous success of fast-food franchises such as McDonald's. George Ritzer (1993) has analysed this process which he refers to as 'McDonaldization', namely 'the process by which the principles of the fast-food restaurant are coming to dominate more and more sectors of American society as well as of the rest of the world'. Ritzer argues that we are witnessing the McDonaldization of society and the world—something which is to be found not only in food but in car maintenance, education, child care, supermarkets, video rental outlets, cinemas, theme parks and sex. It is part of a massive bureaucratization of everyday life which leads to a progressive standardization, and this, as we shall see, cannot easily be integrated into definitions of the postmodern.

There is a further aspect to McDonaldization which Ritzer does not go into: it not only entails economic (in the form of time/money) 'efficiency' gains through standardization of the product and delivery, but also represents a cultural message. The burger is not only consumed physically as material substance, but is consumed culturally as an image and an icon of a particular way of life. Even though McDonald's do not go in for elaborate imagistic advertising, the burger is clearly American and it stands for the American way of life. It is a product from a superior global centre, which has long represented itself as *the* centre. For those on the periphery it offers the possibility of the psychological benefits of identifying with the powerful. Along with the Marlboro Man, Coca-Cola, Hollywood, Sesame Street, rock music and American football insignia, McDonald's is one of a series of icons of the American way of life. They have become associated with transposable themes which are central to consumer culture, such as youth, fitness, beauty, luxury, romance, freedom.

American dreams have become intertwined with those of the good life. The extent to which these images and artefacts are exported around the world has been seen by some to point to the global homogenization of culture in which tradition gives way to American mass consumer culture. In this model of cultural imperialism (Mattelart, 1979; Schiller, 1976) the weight of economic power possessed by US corporations backed by the world's most powerful nation-state is sufficient to provide points of entry into national markets around the globe. In effect culture follows the economy.

This is well documented by travel writers who venture to the world's far-flung and wild places only to discover that the paraphernalia of American culture has got there first. Hence Pico Ayer in his *Video Nights in Kathmandu* subtitled *Reports from the Not-So-Far East*, remarks how he found that 'Everywhere, in fact, dreams of pleasure and profit were stamped "Made in America"' (1989: 23-4). The book's back-cover blurb says: 'Mohawk haircuts in Bali. In Gungzhou—in the new China—a Buffeteria serving dishes called "Yes, Sir Cheese My Baby," and "Ike and Tuna Turner."' Noticeable here too is the fact that the language of global mass consumer culture is English.

Yet even if one believes that cultures flow like water and easily dissolve the differences they encounter, there is a problem with the assumption that the United States is the centre from which everything flows out towards the periphery. This may have been relatively true up until the 1970s, but it is hard to sustain today. The United States still dominates the culture and information industries which transmit globally, but there is a growing sense of multipolarity and the emergence of competing centres. Certainly Japan and East Asia are of growing global significance, currently largely in terms of the flow of consumer goods and finance rather than images and information. The celebration of Japanese national identity, or *Nihonjinron*, has been muted or directed inwards in the post-war era, but this may not always be the case. Japanese consumer goods do not seek to sell on the back of a Japanese way of life. Indeed it can be argued that if the term Japanization of the world means anything it is in terms of a market strategy built around the notion of *dochaku*, or glocalism. The term refers to a global strategy which does not seek to impose a standard product or image, but instead is tailored to the demands of the local market. This has become a popular strategy for multinationals in other parts of the world who seek to join the rhetoric of localism.

In addition to global processes of Americanization and Japanization, or Westernization and Orientalization, it is possible also to speak of 'the Brazilianization' of the world: the dual processes of zoning and cultural syncretism. A number of commentators have pointed to the emergence of 'dual cities' (Mollenkopf and Castells, 1991) which provide new juxtapositions of the new rich and the new poor. In his analysis of the development of Los Angeles, Mike Davis (1992: 20) draws attention to the way in which it is a highly segregated zoned city with its fortified core and middle- and upper-class apartment complexes in close proximity, yet separated and protected from contact with lower- and underclass ethnic ghettos and the zones of crime and disorder. Despite being an 'informational city' (Castells, 1994), Davis argues, Los Angeles more closely approximates the urban sprawl described in William Gibson's science fiction novels: a trajectory which means that it has begun to resemble São Paulo more than postmodern Tokyo-Yokohama. This form of Brazilianization based on the model of fortified zoned, divided, dangerous cities (see Banck, 1994 for a discussion of the invasions of the exclusive beach culture by *favela* people), provides an interesting alternative to the *Carmen Miranda* or samba/beach culture image of Brazil (see Enloe, 1989 for a discussion of the globalization of *Carmen Miranda*).

The ease with which people can slip in and out of ethnic identities has been remarked on by a number of commentators (Abu-Lughod, 1991). In contrast to the assimilation, or melting pot, models which worked off strong insider/outsider divisions in which identity was seen as fixed, today there is a greater acknowledgement that people can live happily with multiple identities. Hence both the evaluative stance and the terminology for those people who move around the world as migrants and are caught between culture shifts. Here we think of groups such as third-generation Brazilian Japanese living in São Paulo, who go to Japan to seek employment as migrant workers—the so-called 'Nickeys'. It is no longer adequate to seek to understand such groups through categories such as 'the marginal man', or 'halfies'. Rather, their situation is given a positive impetus in the use of the term 'doubles'.

What this suggests is that an important part of the processes which are leading to intensified globalization has to be understood in terms of the movement of people around the world. More people are living between cultures, or on the borderlines, and European and other nation-states, which formerly sought to construct a strong exclusive sense of national identity, more recently have had to deal with the fact that they are multicultural societies as 'the rest' have returned to the West in the post-1945 era.

In this context we should endeavour to draw lessons from postcolonial theory, which shares a number of the assumptions found in the postmodern critique of identity. From the point of view of postmodernism, modernity has been seen as entailing a quest to impose notions of unity and universality on thought and the world. In effect its mission is to impose order on disorder, to tame the frontier. Yet with the shifting global balance of power away from the West, with more voices talking back to the West, there is a strong sense that modernity will not be universalized. This is because modernity is seen as both a Western project and as the West's projection of its values on to the world. In effect modernity has allowed Europeans to project *their* civilization, history and knowledge as civilization, history and knowledge in general.

Instead of the confident sense that one is able to construct theory and map the world from the secure place of the centre, which is usually seen as higher and more advanced in symbolic and actual terms, postmodernism and postcolonialism present theory as mobile, or as constructed from an eccentric site, somewhere on the boundary. The movement of people from the global boundaries to the centre is coupled with a displacement of theory to the boundary, with a weakening of its authority. There is a lowering of theory's capacity to speak for people in general, to a greater acknowledgement of the limited and local nature of its assertions.

The very notion that we can undertake a comparative analysis based upon homogeneous national cultures, consensual traditions or 'organic' ethnic communities is being challenged and redefined. As Homi Bhabha (1994: 5) argues

> there is overwhelming evidence of a more transnational and translational sense of the hybridity of imagined communities. Contemporary Sri Lankan theatre represents the deadly conflict between the Tamils and the Sinhalese through allegorical references to

state brutality in South Africa and Latin America; the Anglo-Celtic canon of Australian literature and cinema is being rewritten from the perspective of Aboriginal political and cultural imperatives; the South African novels of Richard Rive, Bessie Head, Nadine Gordimer, John Coetzee are documents of a society divided by apartheid that enjoin the international intellectual community to mediate on the unequal, asymmetric worlds that exist elsewhere; Salman Rushdie writes the fabulist historiography of postindependence India and Pakistan in *Midnight's Children* and *Shame*, only to remind us in *The Satanic Verses* that the truest eye may now belong to the migrant's double vision; Toni Morrison's *Beloved* revives the past of slavery and its murderous rituals of possession and self-possession, in order to project a contemporary fable of a woman's history that is at the same time the narrative of an affective, historic memory of an emergent public sphere of men and women alike.

This conscious mixing of traditions and crossing of boundaries highlights the ways in which the rest, now so obviously visible in the West, have always been a part of the West. This destroys the unitary clean and coherent images of modernity that have been projected out of the Western centres. Postcoloniality, as Bhabha (1994: 6) remarks, points to the hybrid and syncretic perspectives of those who were confined to the borders, half inside and half outside of modernity. This for Bhabha suggests a postcolonial *contra-modernity*, visible not only in the South but in the North, not only in the countryside but in the world cities.

This position resonates with Paul Gilroy's (1993: 36) depiction of black culture and music as a distinctive counterculture of modernity in its refusal of 'the modern occidental separation of ethics and aesthetics, culture and politics'. For Gilroy, discussions of modernity rarely mention slavery and the African diaspora; nor, we might add, does colonialism manage to enter the largely intra-societally inspired sociological accounts of modernity of eminent theorists such as Giddens and Habermas. It is not only that modernity is coupled with barbarism through the degradation of shipping African slaves across the Atlantic. It is not that the figure of Columbus does not appear alongside the standard pairing of Luther and Copernicus as key figures of modernity, or that Las Casas's (1992) accounts of the genocide in Latin America are rarely spoken of alongside Auschwitz, which they dwarf. Nor that accounts of slavery are somehow confined to black history and not the intellectual history of the West as a whole. Or that slavery is often viewed sociologically as a part of a plantation economy regarded as a premodern residue fundamentally incompatible with capitalism and modern rationality.

All these factors should be grounds for rethinking the category; yet it is the fact that blacks are both inside and outside the development of Western culture within modernity which is the biggest problem. Gilroy (1993: 54) argues that slavery is the premise of modernity, something which exposes the foundational ethnocentricism of the Enlightenment project with its idea of universality, fixity of meaning and coherence of the subject. The problem is that it has produced members of society who are living denials of the validity of the project, whose existence within society, or capacity to be seen as persons or citizens was long denied. Yet black people are both Americans and black, or Europeans and black, and participate in a culture and set of collective memories which cannot be integrated with or limited to the cultures of the nation-states in which they reside. Their culture is African and

Western and their identity lived through a form of 'double consciousness', formed from experiences which are both inside and outside the West, inside and outside modernity.

This clearly demands a concept of culture which can account for such displacements, which have been at the heart of the formation of modernity and which postcolonial theory will increasingly bring to the surface. It demands a conception of culture which not only discovers increasing complexity in the current phase of globalization, but also looks at previous phases of globalization and its relationship to modernity. Here we can think of the need to investigate the ways in which particular European notions of culture were generated within modernity which presented its culture as unified and integrated, which neglected the spatial relationships to the rest of the world that developed with colonialism, in effect the dark side of modernity that made this sense of unity possible.

Sociology has long taken as its subject matter society, a notion which, as is argued in Chapter 8, was developed at a particular point in the late nineteenth century when nations were preoccupied with integration as part of a nation-state formation process. It can also be argued that the focus on intra-societal mechanisms of integration was perceived as especially relevant at a point in time when nation-states were increasingly drawn into a tighter competing figuration, which encouraged the strong assertion of national identity. Today the level of global interdependencies and conflict across and through the boundaries of the nation-state make the heritage of this artificial division of labour harder to justify.

Postmodernism and postcolonialism have pointed to the problem of cultural complexity and the increasing salience of culture in social life through the greater production, mixing and syncretism of cultures which were formerly held separate and firmly attached to social relationships. The radical implications of postmodernism and postcolonial theory are to question the very idea of the social, the unity of modernity and the metanarratives of the Western Enlightenment tradition with its belief in universalism and progress. This suggests a spatial relativization of the West in a world which ceases to be its own projection or mirror image (c.f. Said on Orientalism). Works such as Said's (1978) emerged from the fact that: (a) more people are crossing boundaries and have multiple affiliations which question taken-for-granted stereotypes; and (b) there has been a shift in the global balance of power away from the West to the extent that it cannot now avoid listening to the 'other', or assume that the latter is at an earlier stage of development.

The Western self-image and that of the passive other, are under increasing contestation, so it is not surprising that one of the forces associated with postmodernism has been postcolonialism (Spivak, Trin T. Minh-ha, Bhabha, Gilroy, Hall, *et al.*). The changing global circumstance as a result of the process of globalization has provoked a particular Western reaction to this situation in the form of postmodernism, which has engaged in a far-reaching questioning of its own tradition, albeit generally conceived in *internal* terms and not addressed to the spatial relations of the West to the rest of the world.

It is no longer possible to conceive global processes in terms of the dominance of a single centre over the peripheries. Rather there are a number of competing centres which are bringing about shifts in the global balance of power between nation-states and blocs and forging new sets of interdependencies. This is not to suggest a condition of equality between participants but a process which is seeing more players admitted to the game who are demanding access to means of communication and the right to be heard. The expansion and speed of forms of communication means that it is more difficult for governments to police and control the volume of information and image flows that cross their frontiers.

Our image of culture has become more complex. This leads to a number of important questions about the image of culture we have long operated with in the social sciences. This image may have presented an over-simplified view of a culture as something integrated, unified, settled and static; something relatively well-behaved which performed the task of oiling the wheels of social life in an ordered society. If this image is now seen as inadequate to capture the current phase of globalization with its nation-state deformation processes, how did it arise and become so influential? If it was associated with the construction of national cultures alongside state formation, was it always more of an ideal, an intention rather than an actuality? Something which suppressed the various levels of complexity and difference already inherent within modern societies?

Rather than the emergence of a unified global culture there is a strong tendency for the process of globalization to provide a stage for global differences not only to open up a 'world showcase of cultures' in which the examples of the distant exotic are brought directly into the home, but to provide a field for a more discordant clashing of cultures. While cultural integration processes are taking place on a global level the situation is becoming increasingly pluralistic, or polytheistic, a world with many competing gods, along the lines Weber (1948b) discusses in his 'Science as a vocation' essay. This has been referred to as the global babble. It has meant that 'the rest are increasingly speaking back to the West' and along with the relative decline of Western power it has required that the West has increasingly been forced to listen. It is no longer as easy for Western nations to maintain the superiority of adopting a 'civilizational mission' towards the rest of the world, in which the others are depicted as occupying the lower rungs of a symbolic hierarchy, which they are gradually being educated to climb up to follow their betters. Rather, this modernist image, at the heart of modernization theory, is being disputed and challenged. As we shall see, the term 'postmodernism' can be understood as pointing to this process of cultural fragmentation and collapse of symbolic hierarchies which, I would argue, gains much of its impetus from the awareness of a shift in the value of the symbolic power and cultural capital of the West, rather than a move to a new stage of history, 'postmodernity,' itself premised upon a developmental model of tradition and modernity constructed from Western experience. This, then, is one important sense in which postmodernism points to the decentring of culture and the introduction of cultural complexity.

The process of globalization, then, does not seem to be producing cultural uniformity; rather it makes us aware of new levels of diversity. If there is a global culture it would be better to conceive of it not as a common culture, but as a field in which differences, power struggles and cultural prestige contests are played out. Something akin to an underlying form which permits the recognition and playing out of differences along the lines of Durkheim's non-contractual aspects of contract, or Simmel's analysis of the taken-for-granted common ground underpinning social conflict. Hence globalization makes us aware of the sheer volume, diversity and many-sidedness of culture. Syncretisms and hybridizations are more the rule than the exception—which makes us raise the question of the origins and maintenance of the particular image of culture we have long operated with in the social sciences, to which we will now turn.

REFERENCES

Abu-Lughod, J. 1991. 'Going beyond the global babble', in A.D. King, ed., *Culture, Globalization and the World-system*. London: Macmillan.

Banck, G.A. 1994. 'Mass consumption and urban contest in Brazil: some reflections on lifestyle and class', *Bulletin of Latin American Research* 13, 1: 45-60.

Baudrillard, J. 1993. *Symbolic Exchange and Death*. London: Sage.

Benjamin, W. 1977. *The Origin of German Tragic Drama*. London: New Left Books.

Bhabha, H.K. 1994. *The Location of Culture*. London: Routledge.

Blundell, V., J. Shepherd, and I. Taylor, eds. 1993. *Relocating Cultural Studies*. London: Routledge.

Buci-Glucksmann, C. 1994. *Baroque Reason*. London: Sage.

Castells, M. 1994. 'European cities, the informational society and the global economy', *New Left Review* 204: 19-32.

Chambers, I. 1990. *Border Dialogues: Journeys in Postmodernity*. London: Routledge.

Chatterjee, P. 1993. *The Nation and its Fragments*. Princeton University Press.

Cornwall, A. and N. Lindisfarne, eds. 1994. *Dislocating Masculinity*. London: Routledge.

Davis, M. 1992. 'Beyond *Blade Runner*: urban control and the ecology of fear'. Westfield, NJ: Open Magazine Pamphlet Series.

Enloe, C. 1989. *Bananas, Beaches and Bases: Feminism and International Politics*. Berkeley: California University Press.

Featherstone, M. 1991. *Consumer Culture and Postmodernism*. London: Sage.

Giddens, A. 1994. 'Living in a post-traditional society', in U. Beck, A. Giddens, and S. Lash, eds, *Reflexive Modernization*. Cambridge: Polity.

Gilroy, P. 1993. *The Black Atlantic*. London: Verso.

Gupta, S. ed. 1993. *Disrupted Borders*. London: Rivers Oram Press.

Habermas, J. 1989. *The Structural Transformation of the Public Sphere*. Cambridge: Polity.

Las Casas, B. de. 1992. *A Short Account of the Destruction of the Indies*. Harmondsworth: Penguin.

Maravall, J.A. 1986. *Culture of the Baroque*. Manchester: Manchester University Press.

Mattelart, A. 1979. *Multinational Corporations and the Control of Culture*. Brighton: Harvester.

Miyoshi, M. 1991. *Off Center: Power and Culture Relations between Japan and the United States*. Cambridge: Harvard University Press.

Mollenkopf, J. and M. Castells, eds. 1991. *Dual City: Restructuring New York*. New York: Russell Sage Foundation.

Ritzer, G. 1993. *The McDonaldization of Society*. London: Sage.

Rojek, C. 1995. *Decentring Leisure*. London: Sage.

Said, E.W. 1978. *Orientalism*. Harmondsworth: Penguin.

Schiller, H.I. 1976. *Communications and Cultural Domination*. New York: Sharpe.

Simmel, G. 1968. 'On the concept of the tragedy of culture', in *The Conflict in Modern Culture and Other Essays*. New York: Teachers College Press.

Tenbruck, F. 1990. 'The dream of a secular ecumene: the meaning and politics of development', in M. Featherstone, ed., *Global Culture*. London: Sage.

Wallerstein, I. 1974. *The Modern World-System I*. London: Academic Press.

———. 1980. *The Modern World-System II*. London: Adademic Press.

Weber, Max. 1948. 'Science as a vocation', in H.H. Berth and C.W. Mills, eds, *From Max Weber*. London: Routledge.

BELL HOOKS

1952–
UNITED STATES

Major Works

1981   *Ain't I a Woman: Black Women and Feminism*
1984   *Feminist Theory: From Margin to Center*
1988   *Talking Back: Thinking Feminist, Thinking Black*
1990   *Yearning: Race, Gender and Cultural Politics*
1991   *Breaking Bread: Insurgent Black Intellectual Life*
1992   *Black Looks: Race and Representation*
2000   *Feminism is for Everybody: Passionate Politics*

> All theory as I see it emerges in the realm of abstraction, even that which emerges from the most concrete of everyday experiences. My goal as a feminist thinker and theorist is to take that abstraction and articulate it in a language that renders it accessible—not less complex or rigorous— but simply more accessible.[1]

> Feminism is a struggle to end sexist oppression. Therefore, it is neces- sarily a struggle to eradicate the ideology of domination that permeates western culture on various levels as well as a commitment to re-organ- izing society so that the self-development of people can take precedence over imperialism, economic expansion, and material desires.[2]
>
> —*bell hooks*

bell hooks is a leading African-American feminist theorist and cultural critic. She believes that theory, in order to be useful, ought to evolve from the lived expe- riences of its subjects, and so aims to make the processes of her social analyses available to the literate masses in an accessible language. She finds it problem- atic that most of the theorizing taking place in the academy is so dominated by jargon that it renders itself irrelevant. She argues that the theory proliferating within the academy reflects dominant, white, patriarchal structures and is sexist at its core. The dominant theories marginalize those who are perceived as 'other' and have created an environment in which individuals internalize these notions to the point that their reality is felt immutable.

In *Feminist Theory: From Margin to Center*, hooks challenges the reader to deconstruct the notion of the centre as powerful and the margin as powerless, and to begin to see the margin as a potential power base. She remarks that globally more people occupy the margins than the centre.

hooks's approach forces us to develop the processes of critical consciousness and to articulate it in our everyday concerns. She defies the academic status quo claim that theory should be objective and removed from activism. Her works endorse Paulo Freire's position that education should be liberating.

Although hooks's theorizing is informed by the experiences of women of African descent in the United States, her work includes a diversity of other oppressed groups. As an activist-theorist, her goal is to eradicate the oppressive forces so destructive within the culture. The discourse, she argues, should engender the intersection of race and class at all levels. She is committed to an inclusive feminist theory, one possible only if the voices that have been silenced by marginalization are allowed to be heard.

Although hooks is critical of the academy, she continues to be an integral part of it while maintaining her intellectual honesty.

Notes

1. bell hooks, *Talking Back: Thinking Feminist, Thinking Black* (Toronto: Between the Lines, 1988), 39.
2. bell hooks, *Feminist Theory: From Margin to Center* (Boston: South End Press, 1984), 24.

THE SIGNIFICANCE OF FEMINISM

Contemporary feminist movement in the United States called attention to the exploitation and oppression of women globally. This was a major contribution to feminist struggle. In their eagerness to highlight sexist injustice, women focused almost exclusively on the ideology and practice of male domination. Unfortunately, this made it appear that feminism was more a declaration of war between the sexes than a political struggle to end sexist oppression, a struggle that would imply change on the part of women and men. Underlying much white women's liberationist rhetoric was the implication that men had nothing to gain by feminist movement, that its success would make them losers. Militant white women were particularly eager to make feminist movement privilege women over men. Their anger, hostility, and rage were so intense that they were unable to resist turning the movement into a public forum for their attacks. Although they sometimes considered themselves 'radical feminists', their responses were reactionary. Fundamentally, they argued *that all men are the enemies of all women* and proposed as solutions to this problem a utopian woman nation, separatist communities, and even the subjugation or extermination of all men. Their anger may have been a catalyst for individual liberatory resistance and change. It may have encouraged bonding with other women to raise consciousness. It did not strengthen public understanding of the significance of authentic feminist movement.

Sexist discrimination, exploitation, and oppression have created the war between the sexes. Traditionally the battle-ground has been the home. In recent years, the battle ensues in any sphere, public or private, inhabited by women and men, girls and boys. The significance of feminist movement (when it is not co-opted by opportunistic, reactionary forces) is that it offers a new ideological meeting ground for the sexes, a space for criticism, struggle, and transformation. Feminist movement can end the war between the sexes. It can transform relationships so that the alienation, competition, and dehumanization that characterize human interaction can be replaced with feelings of intimacy, mutuality, and camaraderie.

Ironically, these positive implications of feminist movement were often ignored by liberal organizers and participants. Since vocal bourgeois white women were insisting that women repudiate the role of servant to others, they were not interested in convincing men or even other women that feminist movement was important for everyone. Narcissistically, they focused solely on the primacy of feminism in their lives, universalizing their own experiences. Building a mass-based women's movement was never the central issue on their agenda. After many organizations were established, leaders expressed a desire for greater participant diversity; they wanted women to join who were not white, materially privileged, middle-class, or college-educated. It was never deemed necessary for feminist activists to explain to masses of women the significance of feminist movement. Believing their emphasis on social equality was a universal concern they assumed the idea would carry its own appeal. Strategically the failure to emphasize the necessity for mass-based movement, grassroots organizing, and sharing with everyone the positive significance of feminist movement helped marginalize feminism by making it appear relevant only to those women who joined organizations.

Recent critiques of feminist movement highlight these failures without stressing the need for revision in strategy and focus. Although the theory and praxis of contemporary feminism with all its flaws and inadequacies has become well established, even institutionalized, we must try and change its direction if we are to build a feminist movement that is truly a struggle to end sexist oppression. In the interest of such a struggle we must, at the onset of our analysis, call attention to the positive, transformative impact the eradication of sexist oppression could have on all our lives.

Many contemporary feminist activists argue that eradicating sexist oppression is important because it is the primary contradiction, the basis of all other oppressions. Racism as well as class structure is perceived as stemming from sexism. Implicit in this line of analysis is the assumption that the eradication of sexism, 'the oldest oppression', 'the primary contradiction', is necessary before attention can be focused on racism or classism. Suggesting a hierarchy of oppression exists, with sexism in first place, evokes a sense of competing concerns that is unnecessary. While we know that sex role divisions existed in the earliest civilizations, not enough is known about these societies to conclusively document the assertion that women were exploited or oppressed. The earliest civilizations discovered so far have been in archaic black Africa where presumably there was no race problem and no class society as we know it today. The sexism, racism, and classism that exist in the West may resemble systems of domination globally but they are forms of oppression which have been primarily informed by Western philosophy. They can be best understood within a Western context, not via an evolutionary model of human development. Within our society, all forms of oppression are supported by traditional Western thinking. The primary contradiction in Western cultural thought is the belief that the superior should control the inferior. In *The Cultural Basis of Racism and Group Oppression*, the authors argue that Western religious and philosophical thought is the ideological basis of all forms of oppression in the United States.

Sexist oppression is of primary importance not because it is the basis of all other oppression, but because it is the practice of domination most people experience, whether their role be that of discriminator or discriminated against, exploiter or exploited. It is the practice of domination most people are socialized to accept before they even know that other forms of group oppression exist. This does not mean that eradicating sexist oppression would eliminate other forms of oppression. Since all forms of oppression are linked in our society because they are supported by similar institutional and social structures, one system cannot be eradicated while the others remain intact. Challenging sexist oppression is a crucial step in the struggle to eliminate all forms of oppression.

Unlike other forms of oppression, most people witness and/or experience the practice of sexist domination in family settings. We tend to witness and/or experience racism or classism as we encounter the larger society, the world outside the home. In his essay, 'Dualist Culture and Beyond', philosopher John Hodge stresses that the family in our society, both traditionally and legally, 'reflects the Dualist values of hierarchy and coercive authoritarian control' which are exemplified in the parent-child, husband-wife relationships:

> It is in this form of the family where most children first learn the meaning and practice of hierarchical, authoritarian rule. Here is where they learn to accept group oppression against themselves as non-adults, and where they learn to accept male supremacy and the group oppression of women. Here is where they learn that it is the male's role to work in the community and control the economic life of the family and to mete out the physical and financial punishments and rewards, and the female's role to provide the emotional warmth associated with motherhood while under the economic rule of the male. Here is where the relationship of superordination-subordination, of superior-inferior, or master-slave is first learned and accepted as 'natural'.[1]

Even in families where no male is present, children may learn to value dominating, authoritative rule via their relationship to mothers and other adults, as well as strict adherence to sexist-defined role patterns.

In most societies, family is an important kinship structure, a common ground for people who are linked by blood ties, heredity, or emotive bonds; an environment of care and affirmation, especially for the very young and the very old who may be unable to care for themselves; a space for communal sharing of resources. In our society, sexist oppression perverts and distorts the positive function of family. Family exists as a space wherein we are socialized from birth to accept and support forms of oppression. In his discussion of the cultural basis of domination, John Hodge emphasizes the role of the family:

> The traditional Western family, with its authoritarian male rule and its authoritarian adult rule, is the major training ground which initially conditions us to accept group oppression as the natural order.[2]

Even as we are loved and cared for in families, we are simultaneously taught that this love is not as important as having power to dominate others. Power struggles, coercive authoritarian rule, and brutal assertion of domination shapes family life so that it is often the setting of intense suffering and pain. Naturally, individuals flee the family. Naturally, the family disintegrates.

Contemporary feminist analyses of family often implied that successful feminist movement would either begin with or lead to the abolition of family. This suggestion was terribly threatening to many women, especially non-white women.[3] While there are white women activists who may experience family primarily as an oppressive institution (it may be the social structure wherein they have experienced grave abuse and exploitation), many black women find the family the least oppressive institution. Despite sexism in the context of family, we may experience dignity, self-worth, and a humanization that is not experienced in the outside world wherein we confront all forms of oppression. We know from our lived experiences that families are not just households composed of husband, wife, and children or even blood relations; we also know that destructive patterns generated by belief in sexism abound in varied family structures. We wish to affirm the primacy of family life because we know that family ties are the only sustained support system for exploited and oppressed peoples. We wish to rid family life of the abusive dimensions created by sexist oppression without devaluing it.

Devaluation of family life in feminist discussion often reflects the class nature of the movement. Individuals from privileged classes rely on a number of institutional and social structures to affirm and protect their interests. The bourgeois woman can repudiate family without believing that by so doing she relinquishes the possibility of relationship, care, protection. If all else fails, she can buy care. Since many bourgeois women active in feminist movement were raised in the modern nuclear household, they were particularly subjected to the perversion of family life created by sexist oppressions; they may have had material privilege and no experience of abiding family love and care. Their devaluation of family life alienated many women from feminist movement. Ironically, feminism is the one radical political movement that focuses on transforming family relationships. Feminist movement to end sexist oppression affirms family life by its insistence that the purpose of family structure is not to reinforce patterns of domination in the interest of the state. By challenging Western philosophical beliefs that impress on our consciousness a concept of family life that is essentially destructive, feminism would liberate family so that it could be an affirming, positive kinship structure with no oppressive dimensions based on sex differentiation, sexual preference, etc.

Politically, the white supremacist, patriarchal state relies on the family to indoctrinate its members with values supportive of hierarchical control and coercive authority. Therefore, the state has a vested interest in projecting the notion that feminist movement will destroy family life. Introducing a collection of essays, *Re-thinking the Family: Some Feminist Questions*, sociologist Barrie Thorne makes the point that feminist critique of family life has been seized upon by New Right groups in their political campaigns:

> Of all the issues raised by feminists, those that bear on the family—among them, demands for abortion rights, and for legitimating an array of household and sexual arrangements, and challenges to men's authority, and women's economic dependence and exclusive responsibility for nurturing—have been the most controversial.[4]

Feminist positions on the family that devalue its importance have been easily co-opted to serve the interests of the state. People are concerned that families are breaking down, that positive dimensions of family life are overshadowed by the aggression, humiliation, abuse, and violence that characterizes the interaction of family members. They must not be convinced that anti-feminism is the way to improve family life. Feminist activists need to affirm the importance of family as a kinship structure that can sustain and nourish people; to graphically address links between sexist oppression and family disintegration; and to give examples, both actual and visionary, of the way family life is and can be when unjust authoritarian rule is replaced with an ethic of communalism, shared responsibility, and mutuality. The movement to end sexist oppression is the only social change movement that will strengthen and sustain family life in all households.

Within the present family structure, individuals learn to accept sexist oppression as 'natural' and are primed to support other forms of oppression including heterosexist domination. According to Hodge:

> The domination usually present within the family—of children by adults, and of female by male—are forms of group oppression which are easily translated into the 'rightful' group oppression of other people defined by 'race' (racism), by nationality (colonialism), by 'religion', or by 'other means'.[5]

Significantly, struggle to end sexist oppression that focuses on destroying the cultural basis for such domination strengthens other liberation struggles. Individuals who fight for the eradication of sexism without supporting struggles to end racism or classism undermine their own efforts. Individuals who fight for the eradication of racism or classism while supporting sexist oppression are helping to maintain the cultural basis of all forms of group oppression. While they may initiate successful reforms, their efforts will not lead to revolutionary change. Their ambivalent relationship to oppression in general is a contradiction that must be resolved or they will daily undermine their own radical work.

Unfortunately, it is not merely the politically naïve who demonstrate a lack of awareness that forms of oppression are inter-related. Often brilliant political thinkers have had such blind spots. Men like Franz Fanon, Albert Memmi, Paulo Freire, and Aime Cesaire, whose works teach us much about the nature of colonization, racism, classism, and revolutionary struggle, often ignore issues of sexist oppression in their own writing. They speak against oppression but then define liberation in terms that suggest it is only oppressed 'men' who need freedom. Franz Fanon's important work, *Black Skin, White Masks*, draws a portrait of oppression in the first chapter that equates the colonizer with white men and the colonized with black men. Towards the end of the book, Fanon writes of the struggle to overcome alienation:

> The problem considered here is one of time. Those Negroes and white men will be disalienated who refuse to let themselves be sealed away in the materialized Tower of the Past. For many other Negroes, in other ways, disalienation will come into being through their refusal to accept the present definitive.
>
> I am a man, and what I have to recapture is the whole past of the world. I am not responsible solely for the revolt in Santo Domingo.
>
> Every time a man has contributed to the victory of dignity of the spirit, every time a man has said no in an attempt to subjugate his fellows, I have felt solidarity with his act.[6]

In Paulo Freire's book, *Pedagogy of the Oppressed*, a text which has helped many of us to develop political consciousness, there is a tendency to speak of people's liberation as male liberation:

> Liberation is thus a childbirth, and a painful one. The man who emerges is a new man, viable only as the oppressor-oppressed contradiction is superseded by the humanization of all men. Or to put it another way, the solution of this contradiction is borne in the labor which brings into the world this new man: no longer oppressor, no longer oppressed, but man in the process of achieving freedom.[7]

The sexist language in these translated texts does not prevent feminist activists from identifying with or learning from the message content. It diminishes without negating the value of the works. It also does support and perpetuate sexist oppression.

Support of sexist oppression in much political writing concerned with revolutionary struggle as well as in the actions of men who advocate revolutionary politics undermines all liberation struggles. In many countries wherein people are engaged in liberation struggle, subordination of women by men is abandoned as the crisis situation compels men to accept and acknowledge women as comrades in struggle, e.g., Cuba, Angola, Nicaragua. Often when the crisis period has passed, old sexist patterns emerge, antagonism develops, and political solidarity is weakened. It would strengthen and affirm the praxis of any liberation struggle if a commitment to eradicating sexist oppression was a foundation principle shaping all political work. Feminist movement should be of primary significance for all groups and individuals who desire an end to oppression. Many women who would like to participate fully in liberation struggles (the fight against imperialism, racism, classism), are drained of their energies because they are continually confronting and coping with sexist discrimination, exploitation, and oppression. In the interest of continued struggle, solidarity, and sincere commitment to eradicating all forms of domination, sexist oppression cannot continue to be ignored and dismissed by radical political activists.

An important stage in the development of political consciousness is reached when individuals recognize the need to struggle against all forms of oppression. The fight against sexist oppression is of grave political significance—it is not for women only. Feminist movement is vital both in its power to liberate us from the terrible bonds of sexist oppression and in its potential to radicalize and renew other liberation struggles.

Black Women: Shaping Feminist Theory

Feminism in the United States has never emerged from the women who are most victimized by sexist oppression; women who are daily beaten down, mentally, physically, and spiritually—women who are powerless to change their condition in life. They are a silent majority. A mark of their victimization is that they accept their lot in life without visible question, without organized protest, without collective anger or rage. Betty Friedan's *The Feminine Mystique* is still heralded as having paved the way for contemporary feminist movement—it was written as if these women did not exist. Friedan's famous phrase 'the problem that has no name', often quoted to describe the condition of women in this society, actually referred to the plight of a select group of college-educated, middle-, and upper-class, married white women—housewives bored with leisure, with the home, with children, with buying products, who wanted more out of life. Friedan concludes her first chapter by stating: 'We can no longer ignore that voice within women that says: "I want something more than my husband and my children and my house".' That 'more' she defined as careers. She did not discuss who would be called in to take care of the children and maintain the home if more women like herself were freed from their house labour and given equal access with white men to the professions. She did not speak of the needs of women without men, without children, without homes. She ignored the existence of all non-white women and poor white women. She did not tell readers whether it was more fulfilling to be a maid, a babysitter, a factory worker, a clerk, or a prostitute, than to be a leisure-class housewife.[8]

She made her plight and the plight of white women like herself synonymous with a condition affecting all American women. In so doing, she deflected attention away from her classism, her racism, her sexist attitudes towards the masses of American women. In the context of her book, Friedan makes clear that the women she saw as victimized by sexism were college-educated, white women who were compelled by sexist conditioning to remain in the home. She contends:

> It is urgent to understand how the very condition of being a housewife can create a sense of emptiness, non-existence, nothingness in women. There are aspects of the housewife role that make it almost impossible for a woman of adult intelligence to retain a sense of human identity, the firm core of self or 'I' without which a human being, man or woman, is not truly alive. For women of ability, in America today, I am convinced that there is something about the housewife state itself that is dangerous.[9]

Specific problems and dilemmas of leisure class white housewives were real concerns that merited consideration and change but they were not the pressing political concerns of masses of women. Masses of women were concerned about economic survival, ethnic and racial discrimination, etc. When Friedan wrote *The Feminine Mystique*, more than one third of all women were in the work force. Although many women longed to be housewives, only women with leisure time and money could actually shape their identities on the model of the feminine mystique. They were women who, in Friedan's words, were 'told by the most advanced thinkers of our time to go back and live their lives as if they were Noras, restricted to the doll's house by Victorian prejudices'.[10]

From her early writing, it appears that Friedan never wondered whether or not the plight of the college-educated, white housewives was an adequate reference point by which to gauge the impact of sexism or sexist oppression on the lives of women in American society. Nor did she move beyond her own life experience to acquire an expanded perspective on the lives of women in the United States. I say this not to discredit her work. It remains a useful discussion of the impact of sexist discrimination on a select group of women. Examined from a different perspective, it can also be seen as a case study of narcissism, insensitivity, sentimentality, and self-indulgence which reaches its peak when Friedan, in a chapter titled 'Progressive Dehumanization', makes a comparison between the psychological effects of isolation on white housewives and the impact of confinement on the self-concept of prisoners in Nazi concentration camps.[11]

Friedan was a principal shaper of contemporary feminist thought. Significantly, the one-dimensional perspective on women's reality presented in her book became a marked feature of the contemporary feminist movement. Like Friedan before them, white women who dominate feminist discourse today rarely question whether or not their perspective on women's reality is true to the lived experience of women as a collective group. Nor are they aware of the extent to which their perspectives reflect race and class biases, although there has been a greater awareness of biases in recent years. Racism abounds in the writings of white feminists, reinforcing white supremacy and negating the possibility that women will bond politically across ethnic and racial boundaries. Past feminist refusal to draw attention to and attack racial hierarchies suppressed the link between race and class. Yet class structure in American society has been shaped by the racial politic of white supremacy; it is only by analysing racism and its function in capitalist society that a thorough understanding of class relationships can emerge. Class struggle is inextricably bound to the struggle to end racism. Urging women to explore the full implication of class in an early essay, 'The Last Straw', Rita Mae Brown explained:

> Class is much more than Marx's definition of relationship to the means of production. Class involves your behavior, your basic assumptions about life. Your experience (determined by your class) validates those assumptions, how you are taught to behave, what you expect from yourself and from others, your concept of a future, how you understand problems and solve them, how you think, feel, act. It is these behavioral patterns that middle class women resist recognizing although they may be perfectly willing to accept class in Marxist terms, a neat trick that helps them avoid

really dealing with class behavior and changing that behavior in themselves. It is these behavioral patterns which must be recognized, understood, and changed.[12]

White women who dominate feminist discourse, who for the most part make and articulate feminist theory, have little or no understanding of white supremacy as a racial politic, of the psychological impact of class, of their political status within a racist, sexist, capitalist state.

It is this lack of awareness that, for example, leads Lea Fritz to write in *Dreamers and Dealers*, a discussion of the current women's movement published in 1979:

> Women's suffering under sexist tyranny is a common bond among all women, transcending the particulars of the different forms that tyranny takes. Suffering cannot be measured and compared quantitatively. Is the enforced idleness and vacuity of a 'rich' woman, which leads her to madness and/or suicide, greater or less than the suffering of a poor woman who barely survives on welfare but retains somehow her spirit? There is no way to measure such difference, but should these two women survey each other without the screen of patriarchal class, they may find a commonality in the fact that they are both oppressed, both miserable.[13]

Fritz's statement is another example of wishful thinking, as well as the conscious mystification of social divisions between women, that has characterized much feminist expression. While it is evident that many women suffer from sexist tyranny, there is little indication that this forges 'a common bond among all women'. There is much evidence substantiating the reality that race and class identity creates differences in quality of life, social status, and lifestyle that takes precedence over the common experience women share— differences which are rarely transcended. The motives of materially privileged, educated, white women with a variety of career and lifestyle options available to them must be questioned when they insist that 'suffering cannot be measured'. Fritz is by no means the first white feminist to make this statement. It is a statement that I have never heard a poor woman of any race make. Although there is much I would take issue with in Benjamin Barber's critique of the women's movement, *Liberating Feminism,* I agree with his assertion:

> Suffering is not necessarily a fixed and universal experience that can be measured by a single rod: it is related to situations, needs, and aspirations. But there must be some historical and political parameters for the use of the term so that political priorities can be established and different forms and degrees of suffering can be given the most attention.[14]

A central tenet of modern feminist thought has been the assertion that 'all women are oppressed'. This assertion implies that women share a common lot, that factors like class, race, religion, sexual preference, etc. do not create a diversity of experience that determines the extent to which sexism will be an oppressive force in the lives of individual women. Sexism as a system of domination is institutionalized but it has never determined in an absolute way the fate of all women in this society. Being oppressed means the *absence of choices.* It is the primary point of contact between the oppressed and the oppressor. Many women in this society do have choices (as inadequate as they are), therefore exploitation and discrimination are words that more accurately describe the lot of women collectively in the United States. Many women do not join organized resistance against sexism precisely because sexism has not meant an absolute lack of choices. They may know they are discriminated against on the basis of sex, but they do not equate this with oppression. Under capitalism, patriarchy is structured so that sexism restricts women's behaviour in some realms even as freedom from limitations is allowed in other spheres. The absence of extreme restrictions leads many women to ignore the areas in which they are exploited or discriminated against; it may even lead them to imagine that no women are oppressed.

There are oppressed women in the United States, and it is both appropriate and necessary that we speak against such oppression. French feminist Christine Delphy makes the point in her essay, 'For a Materialist Feminism', that the use of the term oppression is important because it places feminist struggle in a radical political framework:

> The rebirth of feminism coincided with the use of the term 'oppression'. The ruling ideology, i.e. common sense, daily speech, does not speak about oppression but about a 'feminine condition'. It refers back to a naturalist explanation: to a constraint of nature, exterior reality out of reach and not modifiable by human action. The term 'oppression', on the contrary, refers back to a choice, an explanation, a situation that is political. 'Oppression' and 'social oppression' are therefore synonyms or rather social oppression is a redundance: the notion of a political origin, i.e. social, is an integral part of the concept of oppression.[15]

However, feminist emphasis on 'common oppression' in the United States was less a strategy for politicization than an appropriation by conservative and liberal women of a radical political vocabulary that masked the extent to which they shaped the movement so that it addressed and promoted their class interests.

Although the impulse towards unity and empathy that informed the notion of common oppression was directed at building solidarity, slogans like 'organize around your own oppression' provided the excuse many privileged women needed to ignore the differences between their social status and the status of masses of women. It was a mark of race and class privilege, as well as the expression of freedom from the many constraints sexism places on working-class women, that middle-class white women were able to make their interests the primary focus of feminist movement and employ a rhetoric of commonality that made their condition synonymous with 'oppression'. Who was there to demand a change in vocabulary? What other group of women in the United States had the same access to universities, publishing houses, mass media, money? Had middle-class black women begun a movement in which they had labelled themselves 'oppressed', no one would have taken them seriously. Had they established public forums and given speeches about their 'oppression', they would have been criticized and attacked from all sides. This was not the case with white bourgeois feminists for they could appeal to a large audience of women, like themselves, who were eager to change their lot in life. Their isolation from women of other class and race groups provided no immediate comparative base by which to test their assumptions of common oppression.

Initially, radical participants in women's movement demanded that women penetrate the isolation and create a space for contact. Anthologies like *Liberation Now*, *Women's Liberation: Blueprint for the Future*, *Class and Feminism*, *Radical Feminism*, and *Sisterhood is Powerful*, all published in the early 1970s, contain articles that attempted to address a wide audience of women, an audience that was not exclusively white, middle-class, college-educated, and adult (many have articles on teenagers). Sookie Stambler articulated this radical spirit in her introduction to *Women's Liberation: Blueprint for the Future*:

> Movement women have always been turned off by the media's necessity to create celebrities and superstars. This goes against our basic philosophy. We cannot relate to women in our ranks towering over us with prestige and fame. We are not struggling for the benefit of the one woman or for one group of women. We are dealing with issues that concern all women.[16]

These sentiments, shared by many feminists early in the movement, were not sustained. As more and more women acquired prestige, fame or money from feminist writings or from gains from feminist movement for equality in the work-force, individual opportunism undermined appeals for collective struggle. Women who were not opposed to patriarchy, capitalism, classism, or racism labelled themselves 'feminist'. Their expectations were varied. Privileged women wanted social equality with men of their class; some women wanted equal pay for equal work; others wanted an alternative lifestyle. Many of these legitimate concerns were easily co-opted by the ruling capitalist patriarchy. French feminist Antoinette Fouque states:

> The actions proposed by the feminist groups are spectacular, provoking. But provocation only brings to light a certain number of social contradictions. It does not reveal radical contradictions within society. The feminists claim that they do not seek equality with men, but their practice proves the contrary to be true. Feminists are a bourgeois avant-garde that maintains, in an inverted form, the dominant values. Inversion does not facilitate the passage to another kind of structure. Reformism suits everyone! Bourgeois order, capitalism, phallocentrism are ready to integrate as many feminists as will be necessary. Since these women are becoming men, in the end it will only mean a few more men. The difference between the sexes is not whether one does or doesn't have a penis, it is whether or not one is an integral part of a phallic masculine economy.[17]

Feminists in the United States are aware of the contradictions. Carol Ehrlich makes the point in her essay, 'The Unhappy Marriage of Marxism and Feminism: Can It Be Saved?' that 'feminism seems more and more to have taken on a blind, safe, nonrevolutionary outlook' as 'feminist radicalism loses ground to bourgeois feminism', stressing that 'we cannot let this continue':

Women need to know (and are increasingly prevented from finding out) that feminism is not about dressing for success, or becoming a corporate executive, or gaining elective office; it is not being able to share a two-career marriage and take skiing vacations and spend huge amounts of time with your husband and two lively children because you have a domestic worker who makes all this possible for you, but who hasn't the time or money to do it for herself; it is not opening a Women's Bank, or spending a weekend in an expensive workshop that guarantees to teach you how to become assertive (but not aggressive); it is most emphatically not about becoming a police detective or CIA agent or marine corps general.

But if these distorted images of feminism have more reality than ours do, it is partly our own fault. We have not worked as hard as we should have at providing clear and meaningful alternative analyses which relate to people's lives, and at providing active, accessible groups in which to work.[18]

It is no accident that feminist struggle has been so easily co-opted to serve the interests of conservative and liberal feminists since feminism in the United States has so far been a bourgeois ideology. Zillah Eisenstein discusses the liberal roots of North American feminism in *The Radical Future of Liberal Feminism*, explaining in the introduction:

One of the major contributions to be found in this study is the role of the ideology of liberal individualism in the construction of feminist theory. Today's feminists either do not discuss a theory of individuality or they unself-consciously adopt the competitive, atomistic ideology of liberal individualism. There is much confusion on this issue in the feminist theory we discuss here. Until a conscious differentiation is made between a theory of individuality that recognizes the importance of the individual within the social collectivity and the ideology of individualism that assumes a competitive view of the individual, there will not be a full accounting of what a feminist theory of liberation must look like in our Western society.[19]

The ideology of 'competitive, atomistic liberal individualism' has permeated feminist thought to such an extent that it undermines the potential radicalism of feminist struggle. The ursurpation of feminism by bourgeois women to support their class interests has been to a very grave extent justified by feminist theory as it has so far been conceived. (For example, the ideology of 'common oppression'.) Any movement to resist the co-optation of feminist struggle must begin by introducing a different feminist perspective—a new theory—one that is not informed by the ideology of liberal individualism.

The exclusionary practices of women who dominate feminist discourse have made it practically impossible for new and varied theories to emerge. Feminism has its party line and women who feel a need for different strategy, a different foundation, often find themselves ostracized and silenced. Criticisms of or alternatives to established feminist ideas are not encouraged, e.g. recent controversies about expanding feminist discussions of sexuality. Yet groups of women who feel excluded from feminist discourse and praxis can make a place for themselves only if they first create, via critiques, an awareness of the factors that alienate them. Many individual white women found in the women's movement a liberatory solution to personal dilemmas. Having directly benefited from the movement, they are less inclined to criticize it or to engage in rigorous examination of its structure than those who feel it has not had a revolutionary impact on their lives or the lives of masses of women in our society. Non-white women who feel affirmed within the current structure of feminist movement (even though they may form autonomous groups) seem to also feel that their definitions of the party line, whether on the issue of black feminism or on other issues, is the only legitimate discourse. Rather than encourage a diversity of voices, critical dialogue, and controversy, they, like some white women, seek to stifle dissent. As activists and writers whose work is widely known, they act as if they are best able to judge whether other women's voices should be heard. Susan Griffin warns against this overall tendency towards dogmatism in her essay, 'The Way of All Ideology':

> . . . when a theory is transformed into an ideology, it begins to destroy the self and self-knowledge. Originally born of feeling, it pretends to float above and around feeling. Above sensation. It organizes experience according to itself, without touching experience. By virtue of being itself, it is supposed to know. To invoke the name of this ideology is to confer truthfulness. No one can tell it anything new. Experience ceases to surprise it, inform it, transform it. It is annoyed by any detail which does not fit into its world view. Begun as a cry against the denial of truth, now it denies any truth which does not fit into its scheme. Begun as a way to restore one's sense of reality, now it attempts to discipline real people, to remake natural beings after its own image. All that it fails to explain it records as its enemy. Begun as a theory of liberation, it is threatened by new theories of liberation; it builds a prison for the mind.[20]

We resist hegemonic dominance of feminist thought by insisting that it is a theory in the making, that we must necessarily criticize, question, re-examine, and explore new possibilities. My persistent critique has been informed by my status as a member of an oppressed group, experience of sexist exploitation and discrimination, and the sense that prevailing feminist analysis has not been the force shaping my feminist consciousness. This is true for many women. There are white women who had never considered resisting male dominance until the feminist movement created an awareness that they could and should. My awareness of feminist struggle was stimulated by social circumstances. Growing up in a Southern, black, father-dominated, working-class household, I experienced (as did my mother, my sisters, and my brother) varying degrees of patriarchal tyranny and it made me angry—it made us all angry. Anger led me to question the politics of male dominance and enabled me to resist sexist socialization. Frequently, white feminists act as if black women did not know sexist oppression existed until they voiced feminist sentiment. They believe they are providing black women with 'the' analysis and 'the' program for liberation. They do not understand, cannot even imagine, that black women, as well as other groups of women who live daily in oppressive situations, often acquire an awareness of patriarchal politics from their lived experience, just as they develop strategies of resistance (even though they may not resist on a sustained or organized basis).

These black women observed white feminist focus on male tyranny and women's oppression as if it were a 'new' revelation and felt such a focus had little impact on their

lives. To them it was just another indication of the privileged living conditions of middle-
and upper-class white women that they would need a theory to inform them that they
were 'oppressed'. The implication being that people who are truly oppressed know it even
though they may not be engaged in organized resistance or are unable to articulate in written form the nature of their oppression. These black women saw nothing liberatory in
party-line analyses of women's oppression. Neither the fact that black women have not
organized collectively in huge numbers around the issues of 'feminism' (many of us do not
know or use the term) nor the fact that we have not had access to the machinery of power
that would allow us to share our analyses or theories about gender with the American
public negate its presence in our lives or place us in a position of dependency in relationship to those white and non-white feminists who address a larger audience.

The understanding I had by age thirteen of patriarchal politics created in me expectations of the feminist movement that were quite different from those of young, middle-
class, white women. When I entered my first women's studies class at Stanford University
in the early 1970s, white women were revelling in the joy of being together—to them it
was an important, momentous occasion. I had not known a life where women had not
been together, where women had not helped, protected, and loved one another deeply. I
had not known white women who were ignorant of the impact of race and class on their
social status and consciousness (Southern white women often have a more realistic perspective on racism and classism than white women in other areas of the United States). I
did not feel sympathetic to white peers who maintained that I could not expect them to
have knowledge of or understand the life experiences of black women. Despite my background (living in racially segregated communities) I know about the lives of white
women, and certainly no white women lived in our neighbourhood, attended our schools,
or worked in our homes.

When I participated in feminist groups, I found that white women adopted a condescending attitude towards me and other non-white participants. The condescension they
directed at black women was one of the means they employed to remind us that the
women's movement was 'theirs'—that we were able to participate because they allowed it,
even encouraged it; after all, we were needed to legitimate the process. They did not see
us as equals. They did not treat us as equals. And though they expected us to provide first-
hand accounts of black experience, they felt it was their role to decide if these experiences
were authentic. Frequently, college-educated black women (even those from poor and
working-class backgrounds) were dismissed as mere imitators. Our presence in movement
activities did not count, as white women were convinced that 'real' blackness meant
speaking the patois of poor black people, being uneducated, street-wise, and a variety of
other stereotypes. If we dared to criticize the movement or to assume responsibility for
reshaping feminist ideas and introducing new ideas, our voices were tuned out, dismissed,
silenced. We could be heard only if our statements echoed the sentiments of the dominant
discourse.

Attempts by white feminists to silence black women are rarely written about. All too
often they have taken place in conference rooms, classrooms, or the privacy of cozy living
room settings, where one lone black woman faces the racist hostility of a group of white
women. From the time the women's liberation movement began, individual black women

went to groups. Many never returned after a first meeting. Anita Cornwall is correct in 'Three for the Price of One: Notes from a Gay Black Feminist', when she states, '. . . sadly enough, fear of encountering racism seems to be one of the main reasons that so many black womyn refuse to join the women's movement.'[21] Recent focus on the issue of racism has generated discourse but has had little impact on the behaviour of white feminists towards black women. Often the white women who are busy publishing papers and books on 'unlearning racism' remain patronizing and condescending when they relate to black women. This is not surprising given that frequently their discourse is aimed solely in the direction of a white audience and the focus solely on changing attitudes rather than addressing racism in a historical and political context. They make us the 'objects' of their privileged discourse on race. As 'objects', we remain unequals, inferiors. Even though they may be sincerely concerned about racism, their methodology suggests they are not yet free of the type of paternalism endemic to white supremacist ideology. Some of these women place themselves in the position of 'authorities' who must mediate communication between racist white women (naturally they see themselves as having come to terms with their racism) and angry black women who they believe are incapable of rational discourse. Of course, the system of racism, classism, and educational élitism remain intact if they are to maintain their authoritative positions.

In 1981, I enrolled in a graduate class on feminist theory where we were given a course reading list that had writings by white women and men, one black man, but no material by or about black, Native American Indian, Hispanic, or Asian women. When I criticized this oversight, white women directed an anger and hostility at me that was so intense I found it difficult to attend the class. When I suggested that the purpose of this collective anger was to create an atmosphere in which it would be psychologically unbearable for me to speak in class discussions or even attend class, I was told that they were not angry. *I* was the one who was angry. Weeks after class ended, I received an open letter from one white female acknowledging her anger and expressing regret for her attacks. She wrote:

> I didn't know you. You were black. In class after a while I noticed myself, that I would always be the one to respond to whatever you said. And usually it was to contradict. Not that the argument was always about racism by any means. But I think the hidden logic was that if I could prove you wrong about one thing, then you might not be right about anything at all.

And in another paragraph:

> I said in class one day that there were some people less entrapped than others by Plato's picture of the world. I said I thought we, after fifteen years of education, courtesy of the ruling class, might be more entrapped than others who had not received a start in life so close to the heart of the monster. My classmate, once a close friend, sister, colleague, has not spoken to me since then. I think the possibility that we were not the best spokespeople for all women made her fear for her self-worth and for her PhD.

Often in situations where white feminists aggressively attacked individual black women, they saw themselves as the ones who were under attack, who were the victims. During a heated discussion with another white female student in a racially mixed women's group I had organized, I was told that she had heard how I had 'wiped out' people in the feminist theory class, that she was afraid of being 'wiped out' too. I reminded her that I was one person speaking to a large group of angry, aggressive people; I was hardly dominating the situation. It was I who left the class in tears, not any of the people I had supposedly 'wiped out'.

Racist stereotypes of the strong, superhuman black women are operative myths in the minds of many white women, allowing them to ignore the extent to which black women are likely to be victimized in this society and the role white women may play in the maintenance and perpetuation of that victimization. In Lillian Hellman's autobiographical work *Pentimento*, she writes, 'All my life, beginning at birth, I have taken orders from black women, wanting them and resenting them, being superstitious the few times I disobeyed.' The black women Hellman describes worked in her household as family servants and their status was never that of an equal. Even as a child, she was always in the dominant position as they questioned, advised, or guided her; they were free to exercise these rights because she or another white authority figure allowed it. Hellman places power in the hands of these black women rather than acknowledge her own power over them; hence she mystifies the true nature of their relationship. By projecting onto black women a mythical power and strength, white women both promote a false image of themselves as powerless, passive victims and deflect attention away from their aggressiveness, their power (however limited in a white supremacist, male-dominated state), their willingness to dominate and control others. These unacknowledged aspects of the social status of many white women prevent them from transcending racism and limit the scope of their understanding of women's overall social status in the United States.

Privileged feminists have largely been unable to speak to, with, and for diverse groups of women because they either do not understand fully the inter-relatedness of sex, race, and class oppression or refuse to take this inter-relatedness seriously. Feminist analyses of woman's lot tend to focus exclusively on gender and do not provide a solid foundation on which to construct feminist theory. They reflect the dominant tendency in Western patriarchal minds to mystify woman's reality by insisting that gender is the sole determinant of woman's fate. Certainly it has been easier for women who do not experience race or class oppression to focus exclusively on gender. Although socialist feminists focus on class and gender, they tend to dismiss race or they make a point of acknowledging that race is important and then proceed to offer an analysis in which race is not considered.

As a group, black women are in an unusual position in this society, for not only are we collectively at the bottom of the occupational ladder, but our overall social status is lower than that of any other group. Occupying such a position, we bear the brunt of sexist, racist, and classist oppression. At the same time, we are the group that has not been socialized to assume the role of exploiter/oppressor in that we are allowed no institutionalized 'other' that we can exploit or oppress. (Children do not represent an institutionalized other even though they may be oppressed by parents.) White women and black men have it both ways. They can act as oppressor or be oppressed. Black men may be victimized by racism, but sexism allows them to act as exploiters and oppressors of women. White women may be victimized by sexism, but racism enables them to act as exploiters and oppressors of black people. Both groups have led liberation movements that favour their interests and support the continued oppression of other groups. Black male sexism has undermined struggles to eradicate racism just as white female racism undermines feminist struggle. As long as these two groups or any group defines liberation as gaining social equality with ruling class white men, they have a vested interest in the continued exploitation and oppression of others.

Black women with no institutionalized 'other' that we may discriminate against, exploit, or oppress often have a lived experience that directly challenges the prevailing classist, sexist, racist social structure and its concomitant ideology. This lived experience may shape our consciousness in such a way that our world view differs from those who have a degree of privilege (however relative within the existing system). It is essential for continued feminist struggle that black women recognize the special vantage point our marginality gives us and make use of this perspective to criticize the dominant racist, classist, sexist hegemony as well as to envision and create a counter-hegemony. I am suggesting that we have a central role to play in the making of feminist theory and a contribution to offer that is unique and valuable. The formation of a liberatory feminist theory and praxis is a collective responsibility, one that must be shared. Though I criticize aspects of feminist movement as we have known it so far, a critique which is sometimes harsh and unrelenting, I do so not in an attempt to diminish feminist struggle but to enrich, to share in the work of making a liberatory ideology and a liberatory movement.

NOTES

1. John Hodge, 'Dualist Culture and Beyond' in J. Hodge *et al.*, *The Cultural Basis of Racism and Group Oppression* (Two Riders, 1975): 233.
2. Ibid.
3. In their essay, 'Challenging Imperial Feminism', *Feminist Review* (Autumn 1984) Valerie Amos and Pratibha Parmar examine the way in which EuroAmerican feminist discussions of family are ethnocentric and alienate black women from feminist movement.
4. Barrie Thorne, 'Feminist Rethinking of the Family: An Overview' in *Re-Thinking the Family: Some Feminist Questions*, eds B. Thorne and M. Yalom (New York: Longman, 1981): 1.
5. Hodge, *op. cit.*
6. Frantz Fanon, *Black Skin, White Masks*, tr. Charles L. Markman (Grove, 1988): 226.
7. Paulo Freire, *Pedagogy of the Oppressed*, tr. Myra B. Ramos (Continuum, 1970): 33. In a discussion with Freire on this issue, he supported wholeheartedly this criticism of his work and urged me to share this with readers.
8. Although *The Feminine Mystique* has been criticized and even attacked from various fronts I call attention to it again because certain biased premises about the nature of woman's social status put forth initially in this context continue to shape the tenor and direction of feminist movement.
9. Betty Friedan, *The Feminist Mystique* (New York: Norton, 1963): 15.
10. Ibid.: 32.

11. Betty Friedan, 'Progressive Dehumanization', 305.

12. Rita Mae Brown, 'The Last Straw' in *Class and Feminism*: 15.

13. Leah Fritz, *Dreamers and Dealers*: 51.

14. Benjamin Barber, *Liberating Feminism*: 30.

15. Christine Delphy, 'For a Materialist Feminism', 211. A fuller discussion of Christine Delphy's perspective may be found in the collected essays of her work *Close to Home: A Materialist Analysis of Women's Oppression*, tr. and ed. Diane Leonard (Boston: University of Massachusetts Press, 1984).

16. Sookie Stambler, *Women's Liberation: Blueprint for The Future*: 9.

17. Antoinette Fouque, 'Warnings' in *New French Feminisms: An Anthology*, eds Elaine Marks and Isabelle De Courtivron (Schocken, 1981): 117–18.

18. Carol Ehrlich, 'The Unhappy Marriage of Marxism and Feminism: Can It Be Saved?': 130.

19. Zillah Eisenstein, *The Radical Future of Liberal Feminism* (Boston: Northeastern University, 1981).

20. Susan Griffin, 'The Way of All Ideology', *Signs* (Spring 1982): 648.

21. Anita Cornwell, 'Three for the Price of One: Notes from a Gay Black Feminist' in *Lavender Culture*: 471.

FEMINISM:
A MOVEMENT TO END SEXIST OPPRESSION

A central problem within feminist discourse has been our inability to either arrive at a consensus of opinion about what feminism is or accept definition(s) that could serve as points of unification. Without agreed upon definition(s), we lack a sound foundation on which to construct theory or engage in overall meaningful praxis. Expressing her frustrations with the absence of clear definitions in a recent essay, 'Towards A Revolutionary Ethics', Carmen Vasquez comments:

> We can't even agree on what a 'Feminist' is, never mind what she would believe in and how she defines the principles that constitute honor among us. In key with the American capitalist obsession for individualism and anything goes so long as it gets you what you want. Feminism in America has come to mean anything you like, honey. There are as many definitions of Feminism as there are feminists, some of my sisters say, with a chuckle. I don't think it's funny.[1]

It is not funny. It indicates a growing disinterest in feminism as a radical political movement. It is a despairing gesture expressive of the belief that solidarity between women is not possible. It is a sign that the political naïveté which has traditionally characterized woman's lot in male-dominated culture abounds.

Most people in the United States think of feminism or the more commonly used term 'women's lib' as a movement that aims to make women the social equals of men. This broad definition, popularized by the media and mainstream segments of the movement, raised problematic questions. Since men are not equals in white supremacist, capitalist, patriarchal class structure, which men do women want to be equal to? Do women share a common vision of what equality means? Implicit in this simplistic definition of women's liberation is a dismissal of race and class as factors that, in conjunction with sexism, determine the extent to which an individual will be discriminated against, exploited, or oppressed. Bourgeois white women interested in women's rights issues have been satisfied with simple definitions for obvious reasons. Rhetorically placing themselves in the same social category as oppressed women, they were not anxious to call attention to race and class privilege.

Women in lower class and poor groups, particularly those who are non-white, would not have defined women's liberation as women gaining social equality with men since they are continually reminded in their everyday lives that all women do not share a common social status. While they are aware that sexism enables men in their respective groups to have privileges denied them, they are more likely to see exaggerated expressions of male chauvinism among their peers as stemming from the male's sense of himself as powerless and ineffectual in relation to ruling male groups, rather than an expression of an overall privileged social status. From the very onset of the women's liberation movement, these women were suspicious of feminism precisely because they recognized the limitations inherent in its definition. They recognized the possibility that feminism defined as social equality with men might easily become a movement that would primarily affect the social standing of white women in middle- and upper-class groups while affecting only in a very marginal way the social status of working-class and poor women.

Not all the women who were at the forefront of organized women's movement shaping definitions were content with making women's liberation synonymous with women gaining social equality with men. On the opening pages of *Woman Power: The Movement for Women's Liberation*, Cellestine Ware, a black woman active in the movement, wrote under the heading 'Goals':

> Radical feminism is working for the eradication of domination and elitism in all human relationships. This would make self-determination the ultimate good and require the downfall of society as we know it today.[2]

Individual radical feminists like Charlotte Bunch based their analyses on an informed understanding of the politics of domination and a recognition of the inter-connections between various systems of domination even as they focused primarily on sexism. Their perspectives were not valued by those organizers and participants in women's movement who were more interested in social reforms. The anonymous authors of a pamphlet on feminist issues published in 1976, *Women and the New World*, make the point that many women active in women's liberation movement were far more comfortable with the notion of feminism as a reform that would help women attain social equality with men of their class than feminism defined as a radical movement that would eradicate domination and transform society.

> Whatever the organization, the location or the ethnic composition of the group, all the women's liberation organizations had one thing in common: they all came togeth-

er based on a biological and sociological fact rather than on a body of ideas. Women came together in the women's liberation movement on the basis that we were women and all women are subject to male domination. We saw all women as being our allies and all men as being the oppressor. We never questioned the extent to which American women accept the same materialistic and individualistic values as American men. We did not stop to think that American women are just as reluctant as American men to struggle for a new society based on new values of mutual respect, cooperation and social responsibility.[3]

It is now evident that many women active in feminist movement were interested in reform as an end in itself, not as a stage in the progression towards revolutionary transformation. Even though Zillah Eisenstein can optimistically point to the potential radicalism of liberal women who work for social reform in *The Radical Future of Liberal Feminism*, the process by which this radicalism will surface is unclear. Eisenstein offers as an example of the radical implications of liberal feminist programs the demands made at the government-sponsored Houston conference on women's rights issues which took place in 1978:

> The Houston report demands as a human right a full voice and role for women in determining the destiny of our world, our nation, our families, and our individual lives. It specifically calls for (1) the elimination of violence in the home and the development of shelters for battered women, (2) support for women's business, (3) a solution to child abuse, (4) federally funded nonsexist child care, (5) a policy of full employment so that all women who wish and are able to work may do so, (6) the protection of homemakers so that marriage is a partnership, (7) an end to the sexist portrayal of women in the media, (8) establishment of reproductive freedom and the end to involuntary sterilization, (9) a remedy to the double discrimination against minority women, (10) a revision of criminal codes dealing with rape, (11) elimination of discrimination on the basis of sexual preference, (12) the establishment of nonsexist education, and (13) an examination of all welfare reform proposals for their specific impact on women.[4]

The positive impact of liberal reforms on women's lives should not lead to the assumption that they eradicate systems of domination. Nowhere in these demands is there an emphasis on eradicating the politic of domination, yet it would need to be abolished if any of these demands were to be met. The lack of any emphasis on domination is consistent with the liberal feminist belief that women can achieve equality with men of their class without challenging and changing the cultural basis of group oppression. It is this belief that negates the likelihood that the potential radicalism of liberal feminism will ever be realized. Writing as early as 1967, Brazilian scholar Heleith Saffioti emphasized that bourgeois feminism has always been 'fundamentally and unconsciously a feminism of the ruling class', that:

> Whatever revolutionary content there is in petty-bourgeois feminist praxis, it has been put there by the efforts of the middle strata, especially the less well off, to move

up socially. To do this, however, they sought merely to expand the existing social structures, and never went so far as to challenge the status quo. Thus, while petty-bourgeois feminism may always have aimed at established social equality between the sexes, the consciousness it represented has remained utopian in its desire for and struggle to bring about a partial transformation of society; this it believed could be done without disturbing the foundations on which it rested. . . . In this sense, petty-bourgeois feminism is not feminism at all; indeed it has helped to consolidate class society by giving camouflage to its internal contradictions.[5]

Radical dimensions of liberal women's social protest will continue to serve as an ideological support system providing the necessary critical and analytical impetus for the maintenance of a liberalism that aims to grant women greater equality of opportunity within the present white supremacist capitalist, patriarchal state. Such liberal women's rights activism in its essence diminishes feminist struggle. Philosopher Mihailo Markovic discusses the limitations of liberalism in his essay, 'Women's Liberation and Human Emancipation':

Another basic characteristic of liberalism which constitutes a formidable obstacle to an oppressed society group's emancipation is its conception of human nature. If self-ishness, aggressiveness, the drive to conquer and dominate, really are among defining human traits, as every liberal philosopher since Locke tries to convince us, the oppression in civil society—i.e. in the social sphere not regulated by the state—is a fact of life and the basic civil relationship between a man and a woman will always remain a battlefield. Woman, being less aggressive, is then either the less human of the two and doomed to subjugation, or else she must get more power-hungry herself and try to dominate man. Liberation for both is not feasible.[6]

Although liberal perspectives on feminism include reforms that would have radical implications for society, these are the reforms which will be resisted precisely because they would set the stage for revolutionary transformation were they implemented. It is evident that society is more responsive to those 'feminist' demands that are not threatening, that may even help maintain the status quo. Jeanne Gross gives an example of this co-optation of feminist strategy in her essay 'Feminist Ethics from a Marxist Perspective', published in 1977:

If we as women want change in all aspects of our lives, we must recognize that capitalism is uniquely capable of co-opting piecemeal change . . . Capitalism is capable of taking our visionary changes and using them against us. For example, many married women, recognizing their oppression in the family, have divorced. They are thrown, with no preparation or protection, into the labor market. For many women this has meant taking their places at the row of typewriters. Corporations are now recognizing the capacity for exploitation in divorced women. The turnover in such jobs is incredibly high. 'If she complains, she can be replaced.'[7]

Particularly as regards work, many liberal feminist reforms simply reinforced capitalist, materialist values (illustrating the flexibility of capitalism) without truly liberating women economically.

Liberal women have not been alone in drawing upon the dynamism of feminism to further their interests. The great majority of women who have benefited in any way from feminist-generated social reforms do not want to be seen as advocates of feminism. Conferences on issues of relevance to women, that would never have been organized or funded had there not been a feminist movement, take place all over the United States and the participants do not want to be seen as advocates of feminism. They are either reluctant to make a public commitment to feminist movement or sneer at the term. Individual African-American, Native American Indian, Asian-American, and Hispanic American women find themselves isolated if they support feminist movement. Even women who may achieve fame and notoriety (as well as increased economic income) in response to attention given their work by large numbers of women who support feminism may deflect attention away from their engagement with feminist movement. They may even go so far as to create other terms that express their concern with women's issues so as to avoid using the term feminist. The creation of new terms that have no relationship to organized political activity tends to provide women who may already be reluctant to explore feminism with ready excuses to explain their reluctance to participate. This illustrates an uncritical acceptance of distorted definitions of feminism rather than a demand for redefinition. They may support specific issues while divorcing themselves from what they assume is feminist movement.

In a recent article in a San Francisco newspaper, 'Sisters—Under the Skin', columnist Bob Greene commented on the aversion many women apparently have to the term feminism. Greene finds it curious that many women 'who obviously believe in everything that proud feminists believe in dismiss the term "feminist" as something unpleasant; something with which they do not wish to be associated'. Even though such women often acknowledge that they have benefited from feminist-generated reform measures which have improved the social status of specific groups of women, they do not wish to be seen as participants in feminist movement:

> There is no getting around it. After all this time, the term 'feminist' makes many bright, ambitious, intelligent women embarrassed and uncomfortable. They simply don't want to be associated with it.
>
> It's as if it has an unpleasant connotation that they want no connection with. Chances are if you were to present them with every mainstream feminist belief, they would go along with the beliefs to the letter—and even if they consider themselves feminists, they hasten to say no.[8]

Many women are reluctant to advocate feminism because they are uncertain about the meaning of the term. Other women from exploited and oppressed ethnic groups dismiss the term because they do not wish to be perceived as supporting a racist movement; feminism is often equated with white women's rights effort. Large numbers of women see feminism as synonymous with lesbianism; their homophobia leads them to reject association with any group identified as pro-lesbian. Some women fear the word 'feminism' because they shun identification with any political movement, especially one perceived as radical. Of course there are women who do not wish to be associated with women's rights movement in any form so they reject and oppose feminist movement. Most women are more familiar with negative perspectives on 'women's lib' than the positive significations of feminism. It is this term's positive political significance and power that we must now struggle to recover and maintain.

Currently feminism seems to be a term without any clear significance. The 'anything goes' approach to the definition of the word has rendered it practically meaningless. What is meant by 'anything goes' is usually that any woman who wants social equality with men regardless of her political perspective (she can be a conservative right-winger or a nationalist communist) can label herself feminist. Most attempts at defining feminism reflect the class nature of the movement. Definitions are usually liberal in origin and focus on the individual woman's right to freedom and self-determination. In Barbara Berg's *The Remembered Gate: Origins of American Feminism*, she defines feminism as a 'broad movement embracing numerous phases of woman's emancipation'. However, her emphasis is on women gaining greater individual freedom. Expanding on the above definition, Berg adds:

> It is the freedom to decide her own destiny; freedom from sex-determined role; freedom from society's oppressive restrictions; freedom to express her thoughts fully and to convert them freely into action. Feminism demands the acceptance of woman's right to individual conscience and judgement. It postulates that woman's essential worth stems from her common humanity and does not depend on the other relationships in her life.[9]

This definition of feminism is almost apolitical in tone; yet it is the type of definition many liberal women find appealing. It evokes a very romantic notion of personal freedom which is more acceptable than a definition that emphasizes radical political action.

Many feminist radicals now know that neither a feminism that focuses on woman as an autonomous human being worthy of personal freedom nor one that focuses on the attainment of equality of opportunity with men can rid society of sexism and male domination. Feminism is a struggle to end sexist oppression. Therefore, it is necessarily a struggle to eradicate the ideology of domination that permeates Western culture on various levels as well as a commitment to reorganizing society so that the self-development of people can take precedence over imperialism, economic expansion, and material desires. Defined in this way, it is unlikely that women would join feminist movement simply because we are biologically the same. A commitment to feminism so defined would demand that each individual participant acquire a critical political consciousness based on ideas and beliefs.

All too often the slogan 'the personal is political' (which was first used to stress that woman's everyday reality is informed and shaped by politics and is necessarily political) became a means of encouraging women to think that the experience of discrimination, exploitation, or oppression automatically corresponded with an understanding of the ideological and institutional apparatus shaping one's social status. As a consequence, many women who had not fully examined their situation never developed a sophisticated understanding of their political reality and its relationship to that of women as a collective group. They were encouraged to focus on giving voice to personal experience. Like revolutionaries working to change the lot of colonized people globally, it is necessary for feminist activists to stress that the ability to see and describe one's own reality is a significant step in the long process of self recovery; but it is only a beginning. When women internalized the idea that describing their own woe was synonymous with developing a critical political consciousness, the progress of feminist movement was stalled. Starting from such incomplete perspectives, it is not surprising that theories and strategies were developed that were collectively inadequate and misguided. To correct this inadequacy in past analysis, we must now encourage women to develop a keen, comprehensive understanding of women's political reality. Broader perspectives can only emerge as we examine both the personal that is political, the politics of society as a whole, and global revolutionary politics.

Feminism defined in political terms that stress collective as well as individual experience challenges women to enter a new domain—to leave behind the apolitical stance sexism decrees is our lot and develop political consciousness. Women know from our everyday lives that many of us rarely discuss politics. Even when women talked about sexist politics in the heyday of contemporary feminism, rather than allow this engagement with serious political matters to lead to complex, in-depth analysis of women's social status, we insisted that men were 'the enemy', the cause of all our problems. As a consequence, we examined almost exclusively women's relationship to male supremacy and the ideology of sexism. The focus on 'man as enemy' created, as Marlene Dixon emphasizes in her essay, 'The Rise and Demise of Women's Liberation: A Class Analysis', a 'politics of psychological oppression' which evoked world views which 'pit individual against individual and mystify the social basis of exploitation'.[10] By repudiating the popular notion that the focus of feminist movement should be social equality of the sexes and emphasizing eradicating the cultural basis of group oppression, our own analysis would require an exploration of all aspects of women's political reality. This would mean that race and class oppression would be recognized as feminist issues with as much relevance as sexism.

When feminism is defined in such a way that it calls attention to the diversity of women's social and political reality, it centralizes the experiences of all women, especially the women whose social conditions have been least written about, studied, or changed by political movements. When we cease to focus on the simplistic stance 'men are the enemy', we are compelled to examine systems of domination and our role in their maintenance and perpetuation. Lack of adequate definition made it easy for bourgeois women, whether liberal or radical in perspective, to maintain their dominance over the leadership of the movement and its direction. This hegemony continues to exist in most feminist organizations. Exploited and oppressed groups of women are usually encouraged by those in power to feel that their situation is hopeless, that they can do nothing to break the pattern of domination. Given such socialization, these women have often felt that our only response to white, bourgeois, hegemonic dominance of feminist movement is to trash, reject, or dismiss feminism. This reaction is in no way threatening to the women who wish to maintain control over the direction of feminist theory and praxis. They prefer us to be silent, passively accepting their ideas. They prefer us speaking against 'them' rather than developing our own ideas about feminist movement.

Feminism is the struggle to end sexist oppression. Its aim is not to benefit solely any specific group of women, any particular race or class of women. It does not privilege women over men. It has the power to transform in a meaningful way all our lives. Most importantly, feminism is neither a lifestyle nor a ready-made identity or role one can step into. Diverting energy from feminist movement that aims to change society, many women concentrate on the development of a counter-culture, a woman-centred world wherein participants have little contact with men. Such attempts do not indicate a respect or concern for the vast majority of women who are unable to integrate their cultural expressions with the visions offered by alternative women-centred communities. In *Beyond God the Father*, Mary Daly urged women to give up 'the securities offered by the patriarchal system' and create new space that would be woman-centred. Responding to Daly, Jeanne Gross pointed to the contradictions that arise when the focus of feminist movement is on the construction of new space:

> Creating a 'counterworld' places an incredible amount of pressure on the women who attempt to embark on such a project. The pressure comes from the belief that the only true resources for such an endeavour are ourselves. The past which is totally patriarchal is viewed as irredeemable. . . .
>
> If we go about creating an alternative culture without remaining in dialogue with others (and the historical circumstances that give rise to their identity) we have no reality check for our goals. We run the very real risk that the dominant ideology of the culture is re-duplicated in the feminist movement through cultural imperialism.[11]

Equating feminist struggle with living in a counter-cultural, woman-centred world erected barriers that closed the movement off from most women. Despite sexist discrimination, exploitation, or oppression, many women feel their lives as they live them are important and valuable. Naturally the suggestion that those lives could be simply left or abandoned for an alternative 'feminist' lifestyle met with resistance. Feeling their life experiences devalued, deemed solely negative and worthless, many women responded by vehemently attacking feminism. By rejecting the notion of an alternative feminist 'lifestyle' that can emerge only when women create a subculture (whether it is living space or even space like women's studies that at many campuses has become exclusive) and insisting that feminist struggle can begin wherever an individual woman is, we create a movement that focuses on our collective experience, a movement that is continually mass-based.

Over the past six years, many separatist-oriented communities have been formed by women so that the focus has shifted from the development of woman-centred space towards an emphasis on identity. Once woman-centred space exists, it can be maintained only if women remain convinced that it is the only place where they can be self-realized and free. After assuming a 'feminist' identity, women often seek to live the 'feminist' lifestyle. These women do not see that it undermines feminist movement to project the assumption that 'feminist' is but another pre-packaged role women can now select as they search for identity. The willingness to see feminism as a lifestyle choice rather than a political commitment reflects the class nature of the movement. It is not surprising that the vast majority of women who equate feminism with alternative lifestyle are from middle-class backgrounds, unmarried, college-educated, often students who are without many of the social and economic responsibilities that working-class and poor women who are labourers, parents, homemakers, and wives confront daily. Sometimes lesbians have sought to equate feminism with lifestyle but for significantly different reasons. Given the prejudice and discrimination against lesbian women in our society, alternative communities that are woman-centred are one means of creating positive, affirming environments. Despite positive reasons for developing woman-centred space, (which does not need to be equated with a 'feminist' lifestyle) like pleasure, support, and resource-sharing, emphasis on creating a counter-culture has alienated women from feminist movement, for such space can be in churches, kitchen, etc.

Longing for community, connection, a sense of shared purpose, many women found support networks in feminist organization. Satisfied in a personal way by new relationships generated in what was called a 'safe', 'supportive' context wherein discussion focused on feminist ideology, they did not question whether masses of women shared the same need for community. Certainly many black women as well as women from other ethnic groups do not feel an absence of community among women in their lives despite exploitation and oppression. The focus on feminism as a way to develop shared identity and community has little appeal to women who experience community, who seek ways to end exploitation and oppression in the context of their lives. While they may develop an interest in a feminist politic that works to eradicate sexist oppression, they will probably never feel as intense a need for a 'feminist' identity and lifestyle.

Often emphasis on identity and lifestyle is appealing because it creates a false sense that one is engaged in praxis. However, praxis within any political movement that aims to have a radical transformative impact on society cannot be solely focused on creating spaces wherein would-be-radicals experience safety and support. Feminist movement to end sexist oppression actively engages participants in revolutionary struggle. Struggle is rarely safe or pleasurable.

Focusing on feminism as political commitment, we resist the emphasis on individual identity and lifestyle. (This should not be confused with the very real need to unite theory and practice.) Such resistance engages us in revolutionary praxis. The ethics of Western society informed by imperialism and capitalism are personal rather than social. They teach us that the individual good is more important than the collective good and consequently that individual change is of greater significance than collective change. This particular form of cultural imperialism has been reproduced in feminist movement in the form of individual women equating the fact that their lives have been changed in a meaningful way by feminism 'as is' with a policy of no change need occur in the theory and praxis even if it has little or no impact on society as a whole, or on masses of women.

To emphasize that engagement with feminist struggle as political commitment we could avoid using the phrase 'I am a feminist' (a linguistic structure designed to refer to some personal aspect of identity and self-definition) and could state 'I advocate feminism'. Because there has been undue emphasis placed on feminism as an identity or lifestyle, people usually resort to stereotyped perspectives on feminism. Deflecting attention away from stereotypes is necessary if we are to revise our strategy and direction. I have found that saying 'I am a feminist' usually means I am plugged into preconceived notions of identity, role, or behaviour. When I say 'I advocate feminism' the response is usually 'what is feminism?' A phrase like 'I advocate' does not imply the kind of absolutism that is suggested by 'I am'. It does not engage us in the either/or dualistic thinking that is the central ideological component of all systems of domination in Western society. It implies that a choice has been made, that commitment to feminism is an act of will. It does not suggest that by committing oneself to feminism, the possibility of supporting other political movements is negated.

As a black woman interested in feminist movement, I am often asked whether being black is more important than being a woman; whether feminist struggle to end sexist oppression is more important than the struggle to end racism and vice versa. All such questions are rooted in competitive either/or thinking, the belief that the self is formed in opposition to an other. Therefore one is a feminist because you are not something else. Most people are socialized to think in terms of opposition rather than compatibility. Rather than see anti-racist work as totally compatible with working to end sexist oppression, they are often seen as two movements competing for first place. When asked 'Are you a feminist?' it appears that an affirmative answer is translated to mean that one is concerned with no political issues other than feminism. When one is black, an affirmative response is likely to be heard as a devaluation of struggle to end racism. Given the fear of being misunderstood, it has been difficult for black women and women in exploited and oppressed ethnic groups to give expression to their interest in feminist concerns. They have been wary of saying 'I am a feminist'. The shift in expression from 'I am a feminist' to 'I advocate feminism' could serve as a useful strategy for eliminating the focus on identity and lifestyle. It could serve as a way women who are concerned about feminism as well as other political movements could express their support while avoiding linguistic structures that give primacy to one particular group. It would also encourage greater exploration in feminist theory.

The shift in definition away from notions of social equality towards an emphasis on ending sexist oppression leads to a shift in attitudes in regard to the development of theory. Given the class nature of feminist movement so far, as well as racial hierarchies, developing theory (the guiding set of beliefs and principles that become the basis for action) has been a task particularly subject to the hegemonic dominance of white academic women. This has led many women outside the privileged race/class group to see the focus on developing theory, even the very use of the term, as a concern that functions only to reinforce the power of the élite group. Such reactions reinforce the sexist/racist/classist notion that developing theory is the domain of the white intellectual. Privileged white women active in feminist movement, whether liberal or radical in perspective, encourage black women to contribute 'experiential' work, personal life stories. Personal experiences are important to feminist movement but they cannot take the place of theory. Charlotte Bunch explains the special significance of theory in her essay, 'Feminism and Education: Not By Degrees':

> Theory enables us to see immediate needs in terms of long-range goals and an over-all perspective on the world. It thus gives us a framework for evaluating various strategies in both the long and the short run and for seeing the types of changes that they are likely to produce. Theory is not just a body of facts or a set of personal opinions. It involves explanations and hypotheses that are based on available knowledge and experience. It is also dependent on conjecture and insight about how to interpret those facts and experiences and their significance.[12]

Since bourgeois white women had defined feminism in such a way as to make it appear that it had no real significance for black women, they could then conclude that black women need not contribute to developing theory. We were to provide the colourful life stories to document and validate the prevailing set of theoretical assumptions.[13] Focus on social equality with men as a definition of feminism led to an emphasis on discrimination, male attitudes, and legalistic reforms. Feminism as a movement to end sexist oppression directs our attention to systems of domination and the inter-relatedness of sex, race, and class oppression. Therefore, it compels us to centralize the experiences and the social predicaments of women who bear the brunt of sexist oppression as a way to understand the collective social status of women in the United States. Defining feminism as a movement to end sexist oppression is crucial for the development of theory because it is a starting point indicating the direction of exploration and analysis.

The foundation of future feminist struggle must be solidly based on a recognition of the need to eradicate the underlying cultural basis and causes of sexism and other forms of group oppression. Without challenging and changing these philosophical structures, no feminist reforms will have a long-range impact. Consequently, it is now necessary for advocates of feminism to collectively acknowledge that our struggle cannot be defined as a movement to gain social equality with men; that terms like 'liberal feminist' and 'bourgeois feminist' represent contradictions that must be resolved so that feminism will not be continually co-opted to serve the opportunistic ends of special interest groups.

NOTES

1. Carmen Vasquez, 'Towards a Revolutionary Ethics': 11.
2. Cellestine Ware, *Woman Power*: 3.
3. *Women and the New World* (1976): 33.
4. Zillah Eisenstein, *The Radical Future of Liberal Feminism*: 232.
5. Heleith Saffioti, *Women in Class Society*, tr. Michael Vale (New York: Monthly Review Press, 1980): 223.
6. Mihailo Markovic, 'Women's Liberation and Human Emancipation': 145–67.
7. Jeanne Gross, 'Feminist Ethics from a Marxist Perspective' (1977): 52–6.
8. Bob Greene, 'Sisters—Under the Skin': 3.
9. Barbara Berg, *The Remembered Gate: Origins of American Feminism—The Woman and The City*

1800–1860 (New York: Oxford University Press, 1980).

10. Marlene Dixon, 'The Rise and Demise of Woman's Liberation: A Class Analysis': 61.

11. Jeanne Gross, *op. cit*: 54.

12. Charlotte Bunch, 'Feminism and Education: Not By Degrees' in *Passionate Politics and Essays 1968–1986* (New York: St Martin's Press, 1987): 7–18.

13. An interesting discussion of black women's responses to feminist movement may be found in the essay 'Challenging Imperial Feminism', Valerie Amos and Pratibha Parmar, *Feminist Review* (Autumn 1984).

GLOSSARY

Aestheticization (of everyday life)
Term used by Featherstone to emphasize the saturation and continued enhancement of the social world with images, logos, artistic expressions, expressions on clothing, etc. 'turning life into a work of art'. The term 'aesthetics' refers to domains of beauty and artistic expression.

Alienated labour
The notion of one's work being removed from one's self. Work becomes mechanized and routinized, undermining one's creative ability.

Alienation
A feeling of disconnectedness from one's self, one's work, one's community. For Marx, this term is used in reference to the ills of capitalism.

Altruistic suicide
One of Durkheim's four types of suicide, altruistic suicide is characterized by excessive integration of the individual into the structures of society.

Androcentrism
A perspective that is centred on male norms and is a dominant view in our society. Situations are viewed from the standpoint of men.

Anomic suicide
One of Durkheim's four types of suicide, anomic suicide is characterized by lack of social regulation or rapid social or economic shifts within society.

Anomie
Emile Durkheim's term, most easily understood as boundlessness or normlessness, the breakdown of society's normative structures; the elements that 'hold' society together are considered to be losing power and effect. The term is used more specifically in his *The Division of Labour in Society*, with regard to anomic division of labour in work situations, and in *Suicide*, with regard to anomic suicide.

Backstage behaviour
Erving Goffman's term 'backstage behaviour' recognizes the behind-the-scenes interactions that take place away from the public view, actions that may consolidate team performance and differentiate backstage from frontstage behaviour.

Bourgeoisie
Class of modern capitalists; owners of the means of social production and employers of wage labourers who produce goods for profits for the capitalists.

Bureaucracy
The formal structural arrangements of a complex organization. Max Weber's description of bureaucratic organization is exemplified by rational-legal forms of authority; logical, abstract rules for performance; written information and records; separation of public from private spheres of control, etc.

Calvinism
The Protestantism advanced by John Calvin during the sixteenth-century Reformation; characterized by the concept of predestination, asceticism, and worldly vocation or calling.

Capitalism
A mode of production whereby capital is privately owned by a small elite. Under this system, the majority of people do not have direct access to the means of producing for themselves. They survive by selling their labour to the capitalists.

Causality
The concept that one act leads directly to or determines subsequent events or actions. Causal connections between events are often considered proof that systematic explanations of the social world are possible.

Causal pluralism
Multiple causes for social and historical phenomena; Weber's position developed to count-

er the determinism he imputed to Marx.

Charismatic authority

One of Max Weber's three kinds of authority; authority located in or given to a special or 'gifted' person. Examples of this type of authority are Mao Tse-tung, Adolf Hitler, and various religious figures.

Class consciousness

The awareness of individual members of a class of belonging to that particular class and the recognition that their interests correspond to the interests of others in that class.

Class struggle

The conflict that develops between those who own the means of production (capitalists or bourgeoisie) and those who do not (proletariat). Marx saw this struggle as necessary in bringing about change in social relations.

Colonialism

The conquest and control (direct or indirect) of one society over another. It represents a stage in the history of imperialism, i.e., the globalization of the capitalist mode of production from the sixteenth century through to its current neo-colonial stage.

Communicative competence

Originally coined by Dell Hymes (1966) in an essay entitled 'On Communicative Competence' to recognize the need of social theorists to explore and examine the skills and knowledge that actors in communication with one another need to have in order to communicate adequately. These skills and knowledge are for the most part tacit and taken for granted. For Habermas, the term explores 'an ideal speech situation', one from which 'consensus-bringing' understandings of truth and justice may emerge.

Conscience collective

Emile Durkheim's term, translated as both 'collective consciousness' and 'collective conscience'. As a body of sentiments or beliefs common to all members of society, the two translations have important distinct qualities: collective consciousness assumes some common internal awareness or state; collective conscience suggests more the external moral regulation of consciousness.

Consciousness

The internal state of human awareness; a part of the self that imagines and interprets as well as chooses a person's relationship with social reality. Although some behaviourists deny the existence of consciousness (i.e., humans respond only to external stimuli rather than choose their interactional relationships with the outside stimuli), the concept has been elaborated and given depth by such social behaviourists as George Herbert Mead.

Constraint

The power of social forces external to the individual that influence his/her social relationships. Durkheim suggests that 'social facts' are both exterior to the individual and have the power to constrain the actions and behaviours of individuals.

'Corporations'

Professional bodies or professional associations; Durkheim sees this group's place in modern society as the site of continuity, consensus-building, and moral stability.

Definition of the situation

The recognition that as individuals we are born into an already defined social world, but that our lives in effect give definition to it as well; links macro and micro moments in sociological considerations. 'Preliminary to any self-determined act of behaviour there is always a stage of examination and deliberation which we may call *the definition of the situation*' (William I. Thomas, *The Unadjusted Girl* [Boston: Little, Brown, 1923], 41).

Depoliticize

To remove from public political discussion, to attempt to 'neutralize' something that is overtly political in nature. Often this process means taking something out of a contested domain and making it appear to be neutral, hiding or obscuring its political dimensions. Medicalization is an example of this: that which had a history of being within the contested community is relocated within the domain of experts, in this case physicians and other health-care professionals.

De-sexualization

In Foucault's use of the term, the process of

moving away from or transcending the 'sexual specificity' that has been assigned to women. This 'assignation' limits the personhood of women, women being 'more than' their sexual objectification. Not to be confused with 'neutering' as done to animals or with the sterilization of social deviants and mental patients that was promoted by eugenicists during the first half of the twentieth century.

Determinism

The concept that human behaviour is controlled by forces independent of choice or will. The term also has wider importance related to causality (the power of events, actions, etc. to influence, condition, and cause other events and actions) in the study of Marx's work, the source of ongoing debate as to whether the Marxian position is based in a strict economic determinism, i.e., that the economic life of society determines the ideological realities of a society.

Dialectical materialism

Using the dialectical method (i.e., the movement from thesis to antithesis to synthesis) in understanding the organization of the productive process.

Dialectical method

Applying dialectical thinking to a particular problem; examining the situation, analyzing the contradictions, and looking for a way to resolve the contradictions.

Dialectics

Dialectics involves conflicting positions, a two-way interactive relationship rather than a one-way determinism. Georg Friedrich Hegel argued that history is the history of conflicting ideas, i.e., a thesis is forwarded, an antithesis conflicts with it, resulting in a new synthesis, which becomes a new thesis, and so on. The dialectical method of Marx suggested that the basis of historical movement is located in the contradictions of the material world.

Differentiation

Herbert Spencer's term refers to specialization in social forms, that is, the realization of the complexity that develops with increasing division of labour.

Discipline

In the work of Michel Foucault, this term has two very distinct but interrelated meanings: first, the academic discipline of sociology (for example, a recognition of the scientific requirements and academic exigencies to fulfill a research task within the social sciences); second, an act of control, either social or personal, relating to various mechanisms and arrangements in society. For Durkheim, this term is seen as crucial to the development of a moral society and as the basic element of authentic education.

Discourse

A logical articulation of social reality. In essence, how we make sense of our social world through language.

Discourses

Both the specific form of language (for example, jargon) used within a particular language community, and also the systematic arrangements or forms of communication fundamental to the structure of such a language context.

Division of labour

Perhaps the most primal division of labour is sexual: i.e., that women and men have specific or differing responsibilities in relationship to society. More generally, 'division of labour' refers to the specialization and differentiation of tasks within communities or societies. In Marx, this describes an exploitative situation in terms of how work is organized in capitalist society.

Domestic labour

The situation whereby women reproduce labour power for capitalist society by taking care of the home and socializing the children.

Dominant ideas

The ideas of the powerful class that pervade the society.

Domination

The situation whereby one group in society exerts an inordinate amount of power over others. One translation of Max Weber's term *herrschaft*, rather than the term 'authority'. On the surface, domination and authority have very different meanings, domination being the exercise of power regardless of consent, while authority is considered the legitimate power located within a role or position. When the relationship between power and consent is explored, the two terms begin to have greater utility for understanding bureaucratic structures.

Dramaturgics

The rubric characterizing Erving Goffman's sociological framework. He uses the principles of the theatre—role, performance, frontstage, backstage—to make sense of social interactions in society.

Economic determinism

The notion that the system of production causes or determines all aspects of social life.

Egoistic suicide

One of Durkheim's four types of suicide, egoistic suicide is characterized by lack of integration of the individual into the society.

Empirical observation

A general scientific term arising from philosophical 'empiricism': social observation assuming that the data are available to the senses or experience, i.e., can be quantified and measured either directly or indirectly, as opposed to being abstractly or logically reasoned. From a positivist position, empirical work avoids making claims concerning first and final causes; it looks at what is observable and describes causal relationships within situations.

Enlightenment

The shift/change/questioning that transformed Western European cultural, intellectual, and scientific life at the end of the eighteenth century. The transformation shifted the world view from traditional, religious formations as the basis of authority to the new formations based in rational, reasoned, scientific foundations for thought and argument.

Epistemology

A set of assumptions about the nature of knowledge and how we acquire that knowledge.

Essentialism

Derived from 'essence', in its general sense essentialism refers to the intrinsic properties of a phenomenon. The term can carry nega-

tive connotations when, for example, an 'unchanging nature' among certain groups (e.g., women, Africans, Asians, etc.) is stressed to the exclusion of everything else.

Exteriority

In Durkheim's methodology, social facts are both exterior to and have power over the individual (i.e., constraint). Exteriority demands that social facts must transcend individual manifestations; they must be of sociological, not merely psychological, consequence.

False consciousness

The condition of some members of the working class who fail to understand their own class interests. In effect, they tend to support a system of production that is not in their own best interest.

Family wage

In reality, this is men's income. Implied in this concept is the notion that the 'male breadwinner' is the only or most important economic contributor to the family.

Fatalistic suicide

One of Durkheim's four types of suicide, fatalistic suicide is characterized by excessive regulation of the individual by the social structures.

Feminism

A movement towards greater equal rights for women, with a focus on putting mechanisms in place to ensure that these rights are maintained. First-wave feminism, which sought enfranchisement for women and pursued various social issues from a moral point of view, is frequently placed between the mid-nineteenth century and the early twentieth century. Second-wave feminism is often identified with the women's liberation movement in the late 1960s in North America, Britain, and Germany. Currently, feminism is manifested in a number of different forms.

Feminist epistemology

Acquiring knowledge from the standpoint of women, that is, being cognizant of the socio-historical context from which individuals emerge and exist.

Feminist theory

A theoretical approach that takes as its starting

point the experiences of women in challenging analyses of society.

Forces of production

The resources and technology necessary for the modes of production.

Frontstage behaviour

Erving Goffman's term; those actions or roles that are undertaken in public performance, i.e., before some 'audience'.

Game stage

George Herbert Mead's term, referring to the development of the 'generalized other'. Stage of the socialization process in which the individual begins to recognize the roles played by other members of a community.

Gender

A social grouping of characteristics that apply to males and females. These characteristics are culturally constructed.

Generalized other

George Herbert Mead's term for the common, shared values of the community to which a child is socialized. The 'significant others' are those people immediate to the child, i.e., his/her parents most usually. The 'generalized other' refers to the wider community and its part in the primary socialization of individuals.

Globalization

The significant shift in the later half of the twentieth century to world economies, world ideologies, world cultural/consumer realities that dominate and envelop the national/regional/local worlds, i.e., interdependent, interlocked trans-global economies. The globalized world of transnational corporations (TNCs) transcends the power of nation-states and transforms the social/political/economic realities that people experience in their everyday lives and communities.

Hegemony

The ideological domination of the ruling class (or nation) over the subordinate classes (or nations). This is accomplished and maintained as the dominant ideas are presented as the only reasonable ones, particularly in ideological institutions such as the media and the educational system. Alternative ideas are usu-

ally not considered. Antonio Gramsci termed this 'ideological hegemony'.

Heterogeneity

Diversity and difference within communities or groups. Spencer refers to the greater differentiation that characterizes increasing division of labour in societies as precipitating heterogeneity in social organization.

Heterosexism

The sexual and social relationships between men and women. There is a common assumption that this form of relationship is the 'norm' in our society.

Historical materialism

The notion that the ways by which people meet their basic needs represent the foundation of social organization. In essence, the analysis of social life should begin with an investigation of the modes of production and the social relations that develop from this mode.

Homogeneity

Refers to communities or groups that are similar or alike in kind. Spencer sees the movement to communities or societies of greater differentiation, i.e., greater heterogeneity, as resulting from increasing division of labour, and consequently there is a movement away from people living in traditional, homogeneous groups.

The I and the Me

Mead's terms for different aspects of the self. The I is the spontaneous, idiosyncratic aspect of the self immediate to a given situation. The Me is the historical self, that part of the self upon which one can reflect.

Ideal type

An analytical construct of utility to the social scientist for purposes of comparison. It is in no way 'ideal' or idyllic; its intent is as a measuring rod for comparative purposes in the study of social processes or social structures. For example, Weber describes the ideal type of bureaucratic structure and behaviour in his work. No specific bureaucracy replicates this ideal typical description, but it allows the social observer a point of departure for exploration of differences among various bureaucracies.

Ideology

A belief system that explains and justifies how society works; any ideas that help us to make sense of our everyday world, although such ideas can obscure certain contradictions in society, such as social inequality, and can help to maintain the status quo.

Imperialism

The situation whereby one state forcibly imposes its sovereignty over another for the purpose of economic exploitation.

Impression management

Human beings' management of their 'face-work' or interaction with each other. Goffman suggests that we are constantly managing our impressions or what we 'give off' in social settings.

Inner-worldly asceticism

Self-denial—a kind of moral governance of the self. It demands denial of physical pleasures and personal discipline; from Weber's work on the Protestant ethic.

Integration

The necessary interdependence of parts to make an organic whole. In Spencer's work this integration would demand a central co-ordinating agency, i.e., the state.

Iron cage

Max Weber's term describing the possible negative consequences for individuals of modern bureaucratic structures and organizations. The rationalized procedures that characterize bureaucratic arrangements become an 'iron cage' surrounding and denying the creative, spontaneous individual.

Labour theory of value

In Marxist theory, the notion that the average labour time that goes into producing a commodity, with a given level of technology, determines the exchange value of that commodity.

Latent Orientalism

For Said, it is an almost unconscious certainty of what the Orient is. The Orient is perceived as separate, backward, and different. It is judged in relation to the West and is always the 'other'.

Law of Three Stages

Auguste Comte's exploration of the evolution-

ary movement within modern society suggested that society would shift from the theological stage to the metaphysical stage to the positive or scientific stage.

Legitimation

For forms of authority to create and maintain credibility in society, Max Weber described the need for justifications of such power relationships in order that they are acceptable to the public. Legitimation can also be a subtle form of social control, acting in lieu of force to control ideas, actions, and power relationships. Karl Marx saw ideologies as playing a central role in the legitimation of power relationships, for example, that religions placate populations or justify various forms of oppression.

Liberal feminism

One of the main theoretical approaches that argues for individual freedom for women.

Lines of action

The actions of human beings in given social interactions, often prefigured, intentional, or almost habitual in character. From the point of view of social observers, within certain contexts the individual's lines of action are possible and often predictable as well.

Looking-glass self

Charles Horton Cooley's definition of self—that we acquire our self in part by the reactions of others, that other people's judgements of our actions or appearance, as well as our imagined perception of their judgement, has profound impact on how we view ourselves.

Lumpenproletariat

In Marxist theory, unemployed workers who form a reserve army of labourers. They can be employed as cheap labour power by the capitalists whenever additional labour is required.

Manifest Orientalism

The various stated views about Oriental society, languages, literatures, history, sociology etc.

Marginality

Traditionally the term referred to those who were part insider, part outsider of a social group. In its contemporary usage, the term is somewhat synonymous with 'other' and refers to those excluded politically, economically, socially, and from intellectual discussions and who are located on the margins of society.

Marginalization

The process whereby individuals find themselves at the fringes of society, whether political, social, or economic.

Marxism

Ideas and practice based on the ideas of Karl Marx, who argued that capitalists exploit their workers in the interests of profit. He believed that the contradictions inherent in capitalism would eventually lead to a final takeover of the society by the exploited workers.

Marxist feminism

This feminist approach analyzes women's oppression in material life in relation to women's position in the modes of production.

Mechanical solidarity

Durkheim's term for societies based on likenesses, i.e., shared or common values, with little division of labour or social differentiation.

Medicalization

The appropriation of more and more areas of social life by the medical community; generally, a form of social control that increasingly puts the power in the hands of the 'experts'. Social problems, natural physiological changes related to the human life cycle, and individual physical and emotional problems caused by larger societal dysfunctions, which once were outside the domain of professional or institutionalized services, come under the control of the medical profession.

Milieu

One's immediate social setting or environment—one's surroundings.

Modes of production

How a society organizes its goods and services and how these goods and services are distributed.

Morality of conviction

In Weber's work, the domains of social life governed by instrumental means, i.e., the logical, rational aspects of practical everyday life experiences.

Orient

As expressed by Said, the Orient signifies a system of representations within a framework of political forces that brought the Orient into 'Western learning, Western consciousness and Western Empire'. Constructed by and in the interest of the West, the image projected is one of inferiority and strangeness, 'other'.

Orientalism

The academic study of the Orient founded on the notion of Western superiority. It is the subject of Edward Said's 1978 book, *Orientalism*. He argues that eighteenth-century Western writers have constructed an essentialized image of the Oriental as weak and strange and that this imagery continues to be significant in Western thought.

Organicism

The view that society's structure is similar to that of a biological organism, e.g., Spencer's view of society as being differentiated much like a biological organism with different but interdependent parts or organs.

Other

A term commonly used in post-colonial and cultural studies; in its most general sense 'the other' refers to a person or group (object) defined as different 'culturally, racially etc.' in relation to a subject that represents the standard point of reference.

Organic solidarity

Durkheim describes societies characterized by organic solidarity as being based in differences and diversity, with greater interdependence of the parts due to the greater division of labour. Modern societies exemplify organic solidarity.

Patriarchy

A system where power is exercised through the males. This power is reflected in society's political, social, and economic structures.

Performance

Goffman's term (also, 'team performance') for the actions of individuals in social settings. He suggests that work groups often form common performance patterns when meeting their 'public'.

Personal troubles

A term coined by C. Wright Mills to refer to the private matters of individuals.

Petite bourgeoisie

Members of this class own and control their own means of production, work at their own business, and hire none or very few wage workers. They have a tendency to fall within the category of the proletariat, although in many cases they become small capitalists.

Play stage

George Herbert Mead's term; an early process in socialization of the child, in which the child 'takes the role of the other', i.e., of the significant other, often in make-believe or imagined situations. In other words, the children perceive a situation through the eyes and actions of their immediate others, such as parents or family.

Politicize

To give political meaning to or to recognize the publicly contested nature of a particular event or idea. Also, to move an experience or idea from private to public domain, thereby laying it open to public debate.

Positive science

The final, highest form in Auguste Comte's Law of Three Stages, the realization of positive science, i.e., the scientific mode of positivism.

Positivism

The scientific approach (using the methods of the physical sciences) that attempts to explain those dimensions of reality that are observable, measurable, and available to human 'objective' scrutiny. Positivism abandons attempts to deal with first or final causes. It suggests that dimensions of reality not accessible to empirical observation are beyond the ken of science.

Post-colonial theory

Analysis of the global effects of European colonialism through an examination of the political, social, and economic realities of the previously colonized societies. The writings of the ex-colonized are central in these analyses. Said's *Orientalism* is a significant post-colonial work, as is Franz Fanon's *The Wretched of the Earth* (1963).

Postmodernism

A term for contemporary social reality that emerged from art and architecture to herald the transcendence of established 'modern' forms, then extended to forms of authority, legitimacy, rationality, etc. in a more general social sense. Related to post-structuralism, postmodernism characterizes a society that is fragmented, with a multiplicity of identities and subjective realities, in which the canon of science and other forms of legitimacy and authority are open to question.

Power

'The possibility of imposing one's own will upon the behaviour of other persons' (Weber, 1922: 942). It is assumed that one has the resources available to carry out such actions.

Praxis

Praxis (in the theory-practice dialectic usually understood as practice) assumes a complex of reflexive action that is united intimately with the theoretical or conceptual formations that drive it. As Paulo Freire notes, it is the complex of 'word/thought/action' as a unity.

Predestination

A central dimension of the doctrine of Calvinism; the tenet that a mighty, unknowable God has decided whether the individual will be saved or damned prior to existence on this earth.

Primary group

The basic unit of community or neighbourhood; those people one encounters on a face-to-face basis.

Primitive communism

A mode of production dominated by hunting and gathering. There is no private property.

Profane

The world of the ordinary; the utilitarian, instrumental domains of everyday life. Durkheim's sociology of religion considers the duality of the sacred and the profane as universal.

Proletariat

Wage labourers who are 'forced' to sell their labour to survive because they do not own the means of production.

Public issues

A term coined by C. Wright Mills to refer to the social forces that affect individuals within the society.

Public/Private Divide

The emergent and complex separation of the public and private domains of human experience. Specifically, men tend to be over-represented in the public sphere and women in the private sphere.

Radical feminism

The position that women are oppressed in society as a result of their gender being relegated as subordinate to men. This perspective focuses on the roots of male domination and supports the idea that all forms of oppression are a reflection of male dominance.

Rationalization

'Rationalization' characterized the twentieth century's developing, means-ends, instrumental forms of action and organization. Habermas and a number of others took this term from Weber's work and extended its meaning and intensity within sociological analysis.

Rational-legal authority

Weber's term for the form of authority most common within modern, bureaucratized society; authority based less in the individual than in his/her position or role within an organization. The underlying notion is that this form of authority is based in reasoned, logical, rational arrangements.

Reification

The ability of human beings to forget the human origins of institutions, roles, and other aspects of life. It has been referred to as 'thing-izing'—an extreme form of objectification, i.e., the taking on of objective status of human creations. To reify is to separate from ourselves aspects of our own creation. De-reification assumes a renewal of understanding of the human origins of many of our modern institutional experiences.

Relations of production

The social relationships that people enter into within the modes of production.

Repoliticize

The process of returning an action or term to the public/political arena. An action or term that had previously been politicized, then depoliticized, now regains a place in the public domain (see *Politicize* and *Depoliticize*).

Representation

The process of putting forward an image or presentation of a particular phenomenon. This process has been called into question as to whether there can be a true representation of reality and the role power plays, especially pertaining to questions regarding race, gender, and class.

Repression

The pushing down into the subconscious of those aspects of one's life that are too problematic to deal with. Sigmund Freud's work informed us of this dimension of human experience. Michel Foucault's work on sexuality uses the term and challenges the level of repression that is taken for granted by modern society.

Repressive law

Durkheim argues that repressive law or penal law is characteristic of societies that exhibit mechanical solidarity. These laws are considered of religious origin and punish violations of the shared or generally agreed-upon social norms.

Reproduction of labour power

The biological and social processes involved in reproducing individuals for participation in the modes of production.

Restitutive law

Durkheim's work argues that restitutive or contractual law is characteristic of societies exhibiting organic solidarity. Rather than punishment, restitutive law demands restoration of relationships within a community on a contractual basis.

Routinization of Charisma

Charismatic authority, i.e. authority based on the personal qualities of the leader, eventually needs to be routinized. This involves stabilizing the relationships of authority by adopting rational-legal forms of authority or in some cases moving to traditional forms. The problem of succession, as well as times of crisis and instability within societies, can demand that charismatic authority be supplanted by other forms.

Sacred

An idea or material reality (object or animal) set apart by the community and imbued with social power and force not inherent in the object, but added to it by the social community. Durkheim considered this aspect of religious life to be universal, that all societies had both the sacred and the profane.

Self-reflexivity

The ability to reflect upon one's self, i.e., make an object of oneself. George Herbert Mead suggests that the ability to reflect upon our own utterances, for example, is in part what makes us truly human. It is also fundamental to the development of critical consciousness.

Sexism

Discriminatory behaviour, usually negative, towards individuals of one sex.

Significant other

Those who are close, immediate to a child while he or she is going through the processes of primary socialization. In most cases, these are parents or immediate family, people whose opinions are seen to be of great importance.

Sites of resistance

Sites or domains within institutions, organizations, or social life that can provide an effective context for change. For critical social change, it is crucial to begin building forms of resistance to dominant ideologies and social realities.

Social action

The focal point of sociological investigation—that we must look to the experiences and perceptions of the actors within a particular social context. Weber identifies four major kinds of social action: rational action towards a goal, rational action towards a value, affective action, and traditional action.

Social class

Within Marxist theory 'class' is defined as being one's location in relation to the modes of production, so that in broad terms there are those who own (the capitalists or bourgeoisie) and those who do not (the proletariat), but with some other classes in between (the petite bourgeoisie) or at the bottom (lumpenproletariat). Weber expanded on Marx's definition to include

social status and the influence of that status.

Social Darwinism

Herbert Spencer's transposition of the biological theories of natural selection to a theory of society. Notions such as 'survival of the fittest', competition, and competitive advantage for those who are stronger are part of this orientation to social life. It must be noted that what is stronger or more capable is not a given or 'natural' dimension within society, but is socially constructed.

Social dynamics

In Comte's work this term refers to the process of social change within society. See also *Social Statics*.

Social facts

The centrepiece of Durkheim's methodological concerns, social facts are exterior to the individual in society and act in some way to constrain him or her. Durkheim also argued that social facts must be considered as 'things', i.e., as objects of social investigation.

Social physics

The term that Comte intended to use to describe his science of society had been used by someone else, so he coined the term 'sociology'. The first term informs us of the central methodological emphasis that Comte brought to the study of society.

Social solidarity

Emile Durkheim's main concern was to explore what holds society together, i.e., social cohesion. He identified two forms of solidarity: mechanical and organic.

Social statics

In Comte's work this term refers to the process of social order or the status quo. See also *Social dynamics*.

Socialization

The general theory of the development or genesis of the self in society. Socialization is the induction of the neophyte into a society that is already underway. The works of both George Herbert Mead and Charles Horton Cooley are, essentially, theories of socialization.

Sociological imagination

The ability to understand the inner dynamic of society and through a process of critical consciousness locate oneself within this dynamic; a concept discussed by C. Wright Mills in a book of the same title.

State

Powerful institutions and organizations related to and including the wide range of civil government and its administration by non-elected officials.

Sui generis

Emile Durkheim used this term to describe society: that society takes on a life of its own, that it is a whole greater than the sum of its parts.

Survival of the fittest

Often accredited to Charles Darwin and his theory of evolution, this term's origin is with Herbert Spencer. Within the social world (Darwin, of course, argued within the biological world) Spencer suggested that competition for advantage, adaptation, or survival of the most adequate would be a basic tenet of society. See *Social Darwinism*.

Symbolic interactionism

Term coined by Herbert Blumer, the American sociologist, to characterize the work of George Herbert Mead and Charles Horton Cooley: the micro-theoretical perspective of these theorists, i.e., their theories of social interaction, based in the symbolic dimensions (language and gesture) of human experience and action.

Syncreticism

The unification of opposing positions. Rather than focusing on the conflict in situations, syncreticism focuses on potential unities that may emerge.

Taking the role of the other

The process in socialization of taking on the roles and values from those 'significant others' who are immediate to early childhood experience. In effect, the child 'sees' the world through the other's frame of reference.

Theodicy

A term used by Weber in his work on the sociology of religion with particular reference to religious formations that explain why people experience pain and suffering.

Total institutions

Erving Goffman's term for prisons and asylums as distinguished from other social institutions. Total institutions resocialize people in a place where individuals 'together lead an enclosed, formally administered round of life' (Goffman, 1961: xiii). Michel Foucault's work, *Discipline and Punish*, takes up this aspect of social control.

Totemism

The social creation of sacred objects from the ordinary elements, usually animal or plant, of a people's everyday life. Totems are socially invested with meaning and therefore take on sacred power or force within society.

Traditional authority

One of Weber's three kinds of authority, along with charismatic authority and rational-legal authority; characterized by the custom of passing on of authority within tribal groups, or the habitual forms of authority typified by family relationships and the power allocated within them.

Value-neutrality

Also called a value-free perspective; Weber advocated passion in one's choice of research but, once chosen, research demands objective, detached observation.

Verstehen

German term meaning understanding or meaning. Weber suggested that in studies of social action, the researcher must take account of the actor's experience of the situation, i.e., that the meaning is both given to a situation and taken from it by the actor himself or herself—thus, the development of the interpretive perspective in sociology.

Vocation

Literally, 'a calling'. Max Weber uses the term in *The Protestant Ethic and the Spirit of Capitalism* to indicate that the worldly work of individuals is believed to be a calling by God—a calling to work for the glory of God here, in this world, in order to reach salvation.

FURTHER READINGS

Abdo, N. *Sociological Thought: Beyond Eurocentric Theory*. Toronto: Canadian Scholars' Press, 1996.

Abrahamson, M. *Sociological Theory: An Introduction to Concepts, Issues, and Research*, 2nd edn. Englewood Cliffs, NJ: Prentice-Hall, 1990.

Agger, B. *Critical Social Theories: An Introduction*. Boulder, Colo.: Westview Press, 1998.

Alessandrini, A., ed. *Franz Fanon*. London: Routledge, 1999.

Anderson, P. *The Origins of Postmodernity*. New York: Verso, 1998.

Andreski, S., ed. *Max Weber on Capitalism, Bureaucracy and Religion: A Selection of Texts*. London: George Allen and Unwin, 1983.

Arneil, B. *Politics and Feminism*. Oxford: Basil Blackwell, 1999.

Aron, R. *Main Currents in Sociological Thought*, 2 vols. New York: Doubleday, 1967.

Ashcroft, B., G. Griffiths, H. Tiffin, eds. *The Post-Colonial Studies Reader*. London: Routledge, 1995.

_____, _____, _____. *The Empire Writes Back: Theory and Practice in Post-Colonial Literatures*. London: Routledge, 1989.

Baran, P., and P. Sweezy. *Monopoly Capital: An Essay on the American Economic and Social Order*. New York: Monthly Review Press, 1966.

Barrett, M., and A. Phillips, eds. *Destabilizing Theory: Contemporary Feminist Debates*. Stanford, Calif.: Stanford University Press, 1993.

Bauman, Z. *Postmodern Ethics*. Oxford: Basil Blackwell, 1993.

Beauvoir, S. de. *The Second Sex*. New York: Alfred A. Knopf, 1952.

Bendix, R. *Max Weber: An Intellectual Portrait*. London: Methuen, 1959.

Berger, P. *Invitation to Sociology*. New York: Doubleday, 1963.

_____ and T. Luckmann. *The Social Construction of Reality*. Garden City, NY: Anchor, 1967.

Berlin, I. *Karl Marx*. London: Oxford University Press, 1963.

Bernard, J. *The Female World from a Global Perspective*. Bloomington: Indiana University Press, 1987.

_____. *The Future of Marriage*, 2nd edn. New Haven: Yale University Press, 1982.

_____. *The Female World*. New York: Free Press, 1981.

_____. *Women, Wives, Mothers: Values and Options*. Chicago: Aldine-Atherton, 1975.

_____. *The Future of Motherhood*. New York: Penguin Books, 1974.

_____. *Women and the Public Interest: An Essay on Policy and Protest*. Chicago: Aldine-Atherton, 1971.

_____. *The Sex Game: Communication Between the Sexes*. Englewood Cliffs, NJ: Prentice-Hall, 1968.

_____. *Academic Women*. New York: New American Library, 1964.

Best, S., and D. Kellner. *Postmodern Theory: Critical Interrogations*. New York: Guilford Press, 1991.

bhabha, h. *The Location of Culture*. London: Routledge, 1994.

Bobo, J., ed. *Black Feminist Cultural Criticism*. Oxford: Basil Blackwell, 2001.

Bottomore, T. *The Frankfurt School*. Chichester, UK: Ellis Horwood, 1984.

Bourdieu, P. *Practical Reason*. Stanford, Calif.: Stanford University Press, 1998.

_____ and J.C. Passeron. *Reproduction in Education, Society and Culture*. London: Sage, 1990.

Braaten, J. *Habermas's Critical Theory of Society*. Albany: State University of New York Press, 1991.

Braverman, H. *Labour and Monopoly Capital: The*

Degradation of Work in the Twentieth Century. New York: Monthly Review Press, 1974.

Campbell, M., and A. Manicom. *Knowledge, Experience, and Ruling Relations: Studies in the Social Organization of Knowledge.* Toronto: University of Toronto Press, 1995.

Césaire, A. *Discourse on Colonialism.* New York: Monthly Review Press, 1972.

Charon, J. *Symbolic Interactionism: An Introduction, an Interpretation, an Integration,* 6th edn. Englewood Cliffs, NJ: Prentice-Hall, 1998.

Collins, R. *Theoretical Sociology.* New York: Harcourt Brace Jovanovich, 1988.

_____, ed. *Three Sociological Traditions: Selected Readings.* New York: Oxford University Press, 1985.

_____ and M. Makowsky. *The Discovery of Society.* New York: McGraw-Hill, 1993.

Comte, A. *Systeme de Politique Positive,* 4th edn, 4 vols. Paris: Gres, 1912.

_____. *Cours de Philosophie Positive,* trans. Harriet Martineau. London: Bell, 1896.

Cooley, C.H. *Social Process.* Carbondale: Southern Illinois University Press, 1966.

_____. *Human Nature and the Social Order.* New York: Schocken, 1964.

_____. *Social Organization.* New York: Schocken, 1962.

_____. *Sociological Theory and Social Research.* New York: Holt, Rinehart and Winston, 1930.

_____. *Life and the Student.* New York: Alfred A. Knopf, 1927.

Coser, L. *The Pleasures of Sociology.* New York: New American Library, 1980.

_____. *Masters of Sociological Thought.* New York: Harcourt Brace Jovanovich, 1971.

_____ and B. Rosenberg, eds. *Sociological Theory: A Book of Readings.* Prospect Heights, Ill.: Waveland Press, 1989.

Cuzzort, R.P., and E.W. Kind. *Twentieth Century Social Thought.* Chicago: Holt, Rinehart and Winston, 1989.

Delphy, C. *Close to Home: A Materialist Analysis of Women's Oppression.* London: Hutchinson, 1984.

Dreyfus, H.L., and P. Rabinow. *Michel Foucault: Beyond Structuralism and Hermeneutics.* Chicago: University of Chicago Press, 1982.

During, S., ed. *The Cultural Studies Reader.* London: Routledge, 1993.

Durkheim, E. *Socialism,* ed. Alvin Gouldner. New York: Collier Books, 1958.

_____. *The Division of Labour in Society.* New York: Free Press, 1956.

_____. *Education and Sociology.* New York: Free Press, 1956.

_____. *The Elementary Forms of Religious Life.* New York: Free Press, 1954.

_____. *Suicide.* New York: Free Press, 1951.

_____. *The Rules of Sociological Method.* New York: Free Press, 1950.

Eagleton, T. *Ideology: An Introduction.* London: Verso, 1991.

_____. *The Illusions of Post-Modernism.* Oxford: Basil Blackwell, 1997.

Eichler, M. *The Double Standard: A Feminist Critique of Feminist Social Science.* London: Croom Helm, 1980.

Eisenstein, Z. *The Color of Gender: Reimaging Democracy.* Berkeley: University of California Press, 1994.

Eldridge, J. *C. Wright Mills.* London: E. Horwood, 1983.

Engels, F. *Socialism: Utopian and Scientific.* New York: International Publishers, 1975.

_____. *The Origin of the Family, Private Property and the State.* New York: International Publishers, 1970.

_____. *The Condition of the Working Class in England.* St Albans, UK: Panther Books, 1969.

_____. *Completion of Vol. II of Capital from Marx's Sketchy Notes.* Moscow: Progress Publishers, 1967.

_____. *Completion of Vol. III of Capital: The Process of Capitalist Production as a Whole.* New York: International Publishers, 1967.

_____. *Anti-Dühring.* Moscow: Foreign Languages Publishing House, 1947.

Fanon, F. *A Dying Colonialism.* New York: Grove Press, 1965.

_____. *The Wretched of the Earth.* New York: Grove Press, 1963.

Farganis, J. *Readings in Social Theory: The Classics*

to Post-Modernism, 3rd edn. Toronto: McGraw-Hill, 2000.

Featherstone, M., ed. Body Modification. London: Sage, 2000.

_____. Love and Eroticism. London: Sage, 1999.

_____. Undoing Culture: Globalization, Postmodernism and Identity. London: Sage, 1995.

_____, ed. Cultural Theory and Cultural Change. London: Sage, 1992.

_____. Consumer Culture and Postmodernism. London: Sage, 1990.

_____. Global Culture: Nationalism, Globalization and Modernity. London: Sage, 1990.

_____ and R. Burrows, eds. Cyberspace/Cyberbodies/Cyberpunk. London: Sage, 1995.

_____ with D. Frisby, eds. Simmel on Culture: Selected Writings. London: Sage, 1997.

_____ and M. Hepworth. Surviving Middle Age. Oxford: Basil Blackwell, 1982.

_____, _____, and B.S. Turner, eds. The Body: Social Process and Cultural Theory. London: Sage, 1991.

_____ and S. Lash, eds. Spaces of Culture: City, Nation, World. London: Sage, 1999.

_____, _____, and R. Robertson, eds. Global Modernities. London: Sage, 1995.

Ferguson, K. The Feminist Case Against Bureaucracy. Philadelphia: Temple University Press, 1984.

Ferguson, R. et al., eds. Out There: Marginalization and Contemporary Cultures. Cambridge, Mass.: MIT Press, 1990.

Firestone, S. The Dialectic of Sex. London: The Women's Press, 1971.

Foucault, M. The History of Sexuality, vol. 3, The Care of Self. New York: Vintage, 1986.

_____. The History of Sexuality, vol. 2, The Use of Pleasure. New York: Vintage, 1985.

_____. The History of Sexuality, vol. 1, An Introduction. New York: Vintage, 1980.

_____. Discipline and Punish: The Birth of the Prison. New York: Vintage, 1979.

_____. The Birth of the Clinic: An Archaeology of the Medical Perception. New York: Vintage, 1975.

_____. The Archaeology of Knowledge and Discourse on Language. New York: Harper Colophon, 1969.

_____. The Order of Things: An Archaeology of the Human Sciences. New York: Vintage, 1966.

_____. Madness and Civilization: A History of Insanity in the Age of Reason. New York: Vintage, 1965.

Freire, P. The Pedagogy of the Oppressed. New York: Seabury Press, 1970.

Fromm, E. Marx's Concept of Man. New York: Frederick Ungar, 1961.

Garfinkel, H. Studies in Ethnomethodology. Englewood Cliffs, NJ: Prentice-Hall, 1967.

Gerth, H.H., and C.W. Mills. From Max Weber: Essays in Sociology. New York: Oxford University Press, 1946.

Gibson-Graham, J.K. The End of Capitalism (as we know it): A Feminist Critique of Political Economy. Oxford: Basil Blackwell, 1996.

Giddens, A. Beyond Left and Right: The Future of Radical Politics. Stanford, Calif.: Stanford University Press, 1994.

_____. Politics, Sociology and Social Theory: Encounters with Classical and Contemporary Social Thought. Stanford, Calif.: Stanford University Press, 1995.

_____. Social Theory and Modern Sociology. Stanford, Calif.: Stanford University Press, 1987.

_____. Profiles and Critiques in Social Theory. Berkeley: University of California Press, 1982.

_____. Sociology: A Brief but Critical Introduction. New York: Harcourt Brace Jovanovich, 1982

_____. Central Problems in Social Theory. London: Macmillan, 1979.

_____. Capitalism and Modern Social Theory. Cambridge: Cambridge University Press, 1971.

Goffman, E. Gender Advertisements. Cambridge, Mass.: Harvard University Press, 1979.

_____. Frame Analysis. New York: Harper and Row, 1974.

_____. Interaction Ritual. New York: Doubleday, 1967.

_____. Behaviour in Public Places. Glencoe, Ill.: Free Press, 1963.

_____. Stigma. Englewood Cliffs, NJ: Prentice-Hall, 1963.

_____. *Asylums*. New York: Doubleday, 1961.

_____. *The Presentation of Self in Everyday Life*. Garden City, NY: Anchor, 1959.

Gramsci, A. *Selections from the Prison Notebooks*. New York: International Publishers, 1971.

Grossburg, L., C. Nelson, and P. Treichler, eds. *Cultural Studies*. London: Routledge, 1992.

Habermas, J. *The Liberating Power of Symbols: Philosophical Essays*. Cambridge: Polity Press, 2001.

_____. *The Postnational Constellation: Political Essays*. Cambridge, Mass.: MIT Press, 2001.

_____. *The Inclusion of the Other: Studies in Political Theory*. Cambridge, Mass.: MIT Press, 1998.

_____. *On the Pragmatics of Communication*. Cambridge, Mass.: MIT Press, 1998.

_____. *Moral Consciousness and Communicative Action*. Cambridge, Mass.: MIT Press, 1990.

_____. *The Structural Transformation of the Public Sphere*. Cambridge, Mass.: MIT Press, 1989.

_____. *On Logic of the Social Sciences*. Cambridge, Mass.: MIT Press, 1988.

_____. *The Philosophical Discourse of Modernity: Twelve Lectures*. Cambridge, Mass.: MIT Press, 1987

_____. *The Theory of Communicative Action*, vol. 2, *Lifeworld and System: A Critique of Functionalist Reason*. Boston: Beacon Press, 1987.

_____. *The Theory of Communicative Action*, vol. 1, *Reason and the Rationalization of Society*. Boston: Beacon Press, 1984.

_____. *Communication and the Evolution of Society*. Boston: Beacon Press, 1979.

_____. *Legitimation Crisis*. Boston: Beacon Press, 1975.

_____. *Theory and Practice*. Boston: Beacon Press, 1973.

_____. *Knowledge and Human Interest*. Boston: Beacon Press, 1971.

_____. *Toward a Rational Society*. Boston: Beacon Press, 1970.

Hale, S. *Controversies in Sociology*, 2nd edn. Mississauga, Ont.: Copp Clark, 1995.

Hamilton, R., and M. Barrett, eds. *The Politics of Diversity: Feminism, Marxism and Nationalism*. Montreal: Book Centre, 1986.

Held, D. *Introduction to Critical Theory: Horkheimer to Habermas*. Berkeley: University of California Press, 1980.

Hill-Collins, P. *Black Feminist Thought*. Boston: Unwin Hyman, 1990.

Hofstadter, R. *Social Darwinism in American Thought*. New York: Braziller, 1959.

hooks, b. *Feminism is for Everybody: Passionate Politics*. Cambridge, Mass.: South End Press, 2000.

_____. *Reel to Real: Race, Sex and Class at the Movies*. London: Routledge, 1996.

_____. *Art on My Mind: Visual Politics*. New York: The New Press, 1995.

_____. *Killing Rage: Ending Racism*. New York: Henry Holt, 1995.

_____. *Outlaw Culture: Resisting Representations*. London: Routledge, 1994.

_____. *Teaching to Transgress: Education as the Practice of Freedom*. London: Routledge, 1994.

_____. *Black Looks: Race and Representation*. Toronto: Between the Lines, 1992.

_____, with C. West. *Breaking Bread: Insurgent Black Intellectual Life*. Toronto: Between the Lines, 1991.

_____. *Yearning: Race, Gender and Cultural Politics*. Toronto: Between the Lines, 1990.

_____. *Talking Back: Thinking Feminist, Thinking Black*. Toronto: Between the Lines, 1988.

_____. *Feminist Theory: From Margin to Center*. Boston: South End Press, 1984.

_____. *Ain't I a Woman: Black Women and Feminism*. Boston: South End Press, 1981.

Hutcheon, L. *The Politics of Post-Modernism*. London: Routledge, 1989.

Jameson, F., and M. Miyoshi, eds. *The Cultures of Globalization*. Durham, NC: Duke University Press, 1998.

Jay, M. *The Dialectical Imagination*. Boston: Little, Brown, 1973.

_____. *Marxism and Totality: The Adventures of a Concept from Lukacs to Habermas*. Berkeley: University of California Press, 1984.

Kandal, T.R. *The Woman Question in Classical Sociological Theory*. Miami: Florida International University Press, 1988.

Kane, A., ed. *Culture, Globalization and the World System: Contemporary Conditions for the Representation of Identity*. Minneapolis: University of Minnesota Press, 1997.

Kuhn, T. *The Structure of Scientific Revolutions*, 2nd edn. Chicago: University of Chicago Press, 1970.

Laclau, E. *Politics and Ideology in Marxist Theory*. London: New Left Books, 1977.

Lemert, C. *Social Theory: The Multicultural and Classical Readings*. Boulder, Colo.: Westview Press, 1993.

Lenzer, G., ed. *Auguste Comte and Positivism: The Essential Writings*. Magnolia, Mass.: Peter Smith, 1975.

Lenzer, G. *August Comte and Positivism: The Essential Writings*. New York: Harper & Row, 1975.

Lerner, G. *The Creation of Feminist Consciousness*. New York: Oxford University Press, 1993.

Lukes, Steven. *Emile Durkheim: His Life and Work*. London: Penguin, 1973.

Lyotard, J.F. *The Postmodern Condition*. Minneapolis: University of Minnesota Press, 1984.

McCarthy, T. *The Critical Theory of Jurgen Habermas*. Cambridge, Mass.: MIT Press, 1982.

McIntosh, I., ed. *Classical Sociological Theory*. New York: New York University Press, 1997.

MacKinnon, C. *Sex Equality*. Minneapolis: West Publishing, 2001.

_____. *Toward a Feminist Theory of the State*. Cambridge, Mass.: Harvard University Press, 1989.

_____. *Feminism Unmodified: Discourses on Life and Law*. Cambridge, Mass.: Harvard University Press, 1987.

_____. *Sexual Harassment of Working Women: A Case of Sex Discrimination*. New Haven: Yale University Press, 1979.

_____ and A. Dworkin. *Pornography and Civil Rights: A New Day for Women's Equality*. Minneapolis: Organizing Against Pornography, 1988.

McLellan, D. *Karl Marx: His Life and Thought*. London: Macmillan, 1973.

Mannheim, K. *Ideology and Utopia*. New York:

Harcourt Brace and World, 1936.

Martineau, H. *Selected Letters*, ed. Valerie Saunders. Oxford: Clarendon Press, 1990.

_____. *Society in America*. New York: Anchor, 1962.

_____. *The Positive Philosophy of Auguste Comte*, 2 vols. London: Kegan Paul, 1895.

_____. *An Autobiography*, 3 vols. London: Smith Elder, 1877.

_____. *History of the Thirty Years Peace*, rev. edn, 4 vols. London: Bell, 1877.

_____. *How to Observe Morals and Manners*. London: Knight, 1838.

_____. *Illustrations of Political Economy*, 9 vols. London: Charles Fox, 1834.

Marx, K. *Pre-Capitalist Economic Formations*. New York: International Publishers, 1977.

_____. *The Grundrisse: Foundations of the Critique of Political Economy*. New York: Vintage Books, 1973.

_____. *The Poverty of Philosophy*. New York: International Publishers, 1973.

_____. *Capital: Critical Analysis of Capitalist Production*, vol. 1. New York: International Publishers, 1967.

_____. *The Economic and Philosophical Manuscripts of 1844*. New York: International Publishers, 1964.

_____. *The Contribution to the Critique of Political Economy*. London: Lawrence and Wishart, 1962.

_____. *The 18th Brumaire of Louis Bonaparte*. New York: International Publishers, 1935.

_____ and Friedrich Engels. *The German Ideology*. New York: International Publishers, 1974.

_____ and _____. *The Communist Manifesto*. New York: Washington Square Press, 1972.

Mead, G.H. *Selected Writings*, ed. Andrew Reck. Indianapolis: Bobbs-Merrill, 1964.

_____. *The Philosophy of the Present*. La Salle, Ill.: Open Court, 1959.

_____. *The Philosophy of the Act*. Chicago: University of Chicago Press, 1938.

_____. *Movements of Thought in the Nineteenth Century*. Chicago: University of Chicago Press, 1936.

_____. *Mind, Self and Society*. Chicago: University of Chicago Press, 1934.

Memmi, A. *The Colonizer and the Colonized.* Boston: Beacon Press, 1965.

Meyers, D.T., ed. *Feminist Social Thought: A Reader.* London: Routledge, 1997.

Milliband, R. *The State in Capitalist Society.* New York: Basic Books, 1969.

Mills, C. Wright. *The Marxists.* New York: Dell, 1962.

_____. *Listen, Yankee: The Revolution in Cuba.* New York: McGraw-Hill, 1960.

_____. *The Sociological Imagination.* New York: Grove Press, 1959.

_____. *The Power Elite.* London: Oxford University Press, 1956.

_____. *White Collar: The American Middle Classes.* New York: Oxford University Press, 1951.

_____. *The New Men of Power.* New York: Harcourt Brace, 1945.

_____ and Hans Gerth. *Character and Social Structure.* New York: Harcourt Brace, 1953.

Natanson, M. *The Social Dynamics of George H. Mead.* The Hague: Martinus Nijhoff, 1973.

Nisbet, R.A. *Emile Durkheim.* Englewood Cliffs, NJ: Prentice-Hall, 1965.

Nkrumah, K. *Neo-Colonialism: The Last Stage of Imperialism.* London: Panaf Books, 1965.

O'Brien, M. *The Politics of Reproduction.* London: Routledge & Kegan Paul, 1981.

Olson, G, and L. Worsham, eds. *Race, Rhetoric and the Post-Colonial.* Albany: State University of New York Press, 1999.

Owen, D. *Sociology after Postmodernism.* London: Sage, 1997.

Parkin, F. *Max Weber.* London: Routledge, 1982.

Parsons, T., et al., eds. *Theories of Society.* New York: Free Press, 1961.

Pickering, M. *Auguste Comte: An Intellectual Biography*, vol. 1. Cambridge: Cambridge University Press, 1993.

Quayson, A. *Post-Colonialism: Theory, Practice or Process?* Oxford: Polity Press, 2000.

Ritzer, G. *Modern Sociological Theory,* 5th edn. Toronto: McGraw-Hill, 2000.

_____. *Postmodern Social Theory.* New York: McGraw-Hill, 1997.

_____. *The McDonaldization of Society,* rev. edn.

Thousand Oaks, Calif.: Pine Forge Press, 1996.

_____. *Sociological Beginnings: On the Origins of Key Ideas in Sociology.* New York: McGraw-Hill, 1994.

_____. *The McDonaldization of Society.* Thousand Oaks, Calif.: Pine Forge Press, 1993.

_____. *Classical Sociological Theory.* New York: McGraw-Hill, 1992.

_____. *Contemporary Sociological Theory,* 2nd edn. New York: Alfred A. Knopf, 1988.

_____. *Sociological Theory,* 2nd edn. New York: Alfred A. Knopf, 1988.

Rowbotham, S. *Women's Consciousness, Man's World.* Harmondsworth: Penguin.

Said, E. *Out of Place: A Memoir.* New York: Alfred A. Knopf, 1999.

_____. *Representations of the Intellectual: The 1993 Reith Lectures.* New York: Vintage Books, 1996.

_____. *The Politics of Dispossession.* New York: Vintage Books, 1995.

_____. *Orientalism,* 2nd edn (with Afterword). New York: Vintage Books, 1994.

_____, with David Barsamian. *The Pen and the Sword.* Toronto: Between the Lines, 1994.

_____. *Culture and Imperialism.* New York: Alfred A. Knopf, 1993.

_____. *The World, the Text and the Critic.* Cambridge, Mass.: Harvard University Press, 1983.

_____. *Covering Islam: How the Media and the Experts Determine How We See the Rest of the World.* New York: Pantheon Books, 1981.

_____. *The Question of Palestine.* New York, Vintage Books, 1979.

_____. *Beginnings: Intention and Method.* Baltimore: Johns Hopkins University Press, 1978.

_____. *Orientalism.* New York: Vintage Books, 1978.

Sayers, J., et al. *Engels Re-Visited.* London: Tavistock, 1987.

Schroeder, R. *Max Weber and the Sociology of Culture.* London: Sage, 1992.

Schroyer, T. *The Critique of Domination.* Boston: Beacon Press, 1973.

Schutz, A. *The Phenomenology of the Social World.* Evanston, Ill.: Northwestern University Press, 1932, 1967.

Seidman, S. *Contested Knowledge: Social Theory in the Postmodern Age.* Oxford: Basil Blackwell, 1994.

Slater, D. *Consumer Culture and Modernity.* Cambridge: Polity Press, 1997.

Smart, B. *Foucault: Marxism and Critique.* London: Routledge & Kegan Paul, 1983.

Smith, D. *Writing the Social: Critique, Theory, and Investigations.* Toronto: University of Toronto Press, 1999.

_____. *Text, Facts and Femininity: Exploring the Relations of Ruling.* London: Routledge, 1991.

_____. *The Conceptual Practices of Power: A Feminist Sociology of Knowledge.* Toronto: University of Toronto Press, 1990.

_____. *The Everyday World as Problematic: A Feminist Sociology.* Toronto: University of Toronto Press, 1987.

_____. *Feminism and Marxism.* Vancouver: New Star Books, 1977.

Smith, M.E.G., ed. *Early Modern Social Theory: Selected Interpretive Readings.* Toronto: Canadian Scholars' Press, 1998.

Spencer, H. *An Autobiography*, 2 vols. New York: Appleton, 1904.

_____. *The Principles of Biology.* London: Williams and Norgate, 1899.

_____. *The Principles of Sociology.* New York: Appleton, 1896.

_____. *The Study of Sociology.* New York: Appleton, 1891.

_____. *The Principles of Psychology.* London: Longman, Brown, Green, and Longmans, 1855.

_____. *Social Statics.* London: Chapman, 1851.

Strauss, A.L., ed. *The Social Psychology of George Herbert Mead.* Chicago: University of Chicago Press, 1956.

Sydie, R.A. *Natural Women, Cultured Men: A Feminist Perspective on Sociological Theory.* Toronto: Methuen, 1987.

Thiong'o, N.W. *Moving the Centre: The Struggle for Cultural Freedoms.* Portsmouth: Heine-mann, 1993.

_____. *Decolonising the Mind: The Politics of Language in African Literature.* Nairobi: Heinemann, 1991.

Thompson, E.P. *The Poverty of Theory.* London: Merlin Press, 1978.

Thompson, K. *Emile Durkheim.* London: Routledge, 1982.

Touraine, A. *Critique of Modernity.* Oxford: Basil Blackwell, 1995.

Tucker, R.C., ed. *The Marx-Engels Reader.* New York: Norton, 1970.

Turner, J.H. *The Structure of Sociological Theory*, 5th edn. Belmont, Calif.: Wadsworth, 1991.

Wallace, R.A., and A. Wolf. *Contemporary Sociological Theory.* Toronto: Prentice-Hall, 1999.

Weber, M. *Economy and Society.* Berkeley: University of California Press, 1978.

_____. *Max Weber: A Biography*, ed. and trans. Harry Zohn. New York: Wiley, 1975.

_____. *The Basic Concepts in Sociology.* New York: Citadel Press, 1964.

_____. *The Sociology of Religion.* Boston: Beacon Press, 1963.

_____. *The Protestant Ethic and the Spirit of Capitalism.* New York: Scribner's, 1958.

_____. *General Economic History.* Glencoe, Ill.: Free Press, 1950.

_____. *The Methodology of the Social Sciences.* Glencoe, Ill.: Free Press, 1949.

Weedon, C. *Feminism, Theory and the Politics of Difference.* Oxford: Basil Blackwell, 1999.

Wexler, P. *Critical Theory Now.* London: Falmer Press, 1991.

White, S.K. *The Recent Work of Jurgen Habermas: Reason, Justice and Modernity.* Cambridge: Cambridge University Press, 1988.

Williams, P., and L. Chrisman, eds. *Colonial Discourse and Post-Colonial Theory: A Reader.* New York: Columbia University Press, 1994.

Williams, R. *The Politics of Modernism: Against the New Conformists.* New York: Verso, 1994.

Worsley, P. *Marx and Marxism.* London: Routledge, 1982.

Zeitlin, I. *Ideology and the Development of Sociological Theory.* Englewoods Cliffs, NJ: Prentice-Hall, 1987.

ACKNOWLEDGEMENTS

JESSIE BERNARD. Excerpts from *Women and the Public Interest* by Jessie Bernard. Chicago: Aldine • Atherton, 1971. Reprinted by permission of the Estate of Jessie Bernard.

AUGUSTE COMTE. 'The Spirit of Positive Science' from *Auguste Comte and Positivism*, ed. Gertrud Lenzer. Copyright © 1975 by Gertrud Lenzer. Reprinted by permission of Georges Borchardt, Inc.

EMILE DURKHEIM. Reprinted and edited with the permission of The Free Press, a Division of Simon & Schuster Adult Publishing Group: 'The Division of Labour in Society', from *The Division of Labor in Society* by Emile Durkheim, translated by George Simpson, Copyright © 1933 by The Macmillan Company, copyright 1964 by The Free Press; 'Sociological method', from *The Rules of Sociological Method* by Emile Durkheim, translated by Sarah A. Solovan and George H. Mueller, edited by George E.G. Catlin, Copyright © 1938 by George E.G. Catlin, copyright renewed 1966 by Sarah A. Solovay, John H. Mueller, and George E.G. Catlin; 'Egoistic and Anomic Suicide', from *Suicide: A Study in Sociology* by Emile Durkheim, translated by John A. Spaulding and George Simpson, Copyright © 1951, copyright renewed 1979 by The Free Press. 'Religion as a Collective Force' from *The Elementary Forms of the New Religious Life*, Roy Wallis. London: Routledge & Kegan Paul, 1983. Reprinted with permission.

FRIEDRICH ENGELS. 'The Overthrow of the Mother-Right and Monogamous Marriage' from *Selected Works*, Karl Marx and Friedrich Engels, pp. 487–518. New York: International Publishers, 1968. Reprinted by permission of International Publishers Co. Inc.

MIKE FEATHERSTONE. 'Introduction: Globalizing Cultural Complexity' from *Undoing Culture: Globalization, Postmodernism and Identity* by Mike Featherstone. London: Sage Publications, 1995. Reprinted by permission of Sage Publishing Ltd.

MICHEL FOUCAULT. Excerpt from 'The Repressive Hypothesis' from *The History of Sexuality* by Michel Foucault. Copyright © Random House, Inc., New York, 1978. Originally published in French as *La Volonté du Savoir*. Copyright © Editions Gallimard 1976. Reprinted by permission of Georges Borchardt, Inc., for the Editions Gallimard.

ERVING GOFFMAN. Excerpts from *The Presentation of Self in Everyday Life* by Erving Goffman, copyright © 1959 by Erving Goffman. Used by permission of Doubleday, a division of Random House, Inc.

JÜRGEN HAABERMAS. 'Technology as "Ideology"' from *Toward a Rational Society* by Jürgen Habermas. Copyright © 1970 by Beacon Press. Reprinted by permission of Beacon Press, Boston.

BELL HOOKS. 'The Significance of Feminist Movement', 'Black Women: Shaping Feminist Theory', and 'Feminism: A Movement to End Sexist Oppression' from *Feminist Theory: From Martin to Center*. Boston: South End Press, 1984. Reprinted by permission of South End Press.

CATHARINE A. MACKINNON. 'A Feminist Critique of Marx and Engels' from *Toward a Feminist Theory of the State*. Cambridge, MA: Harvard University Press, 1989.

HARRIET MARTINEAU. Chapter IV: Morals of Politics from *Society in America* edited by Seymour Martin Lipset. Copyright © 1962 by Seymour Martin Lipset. Used by permission of Doubleday, a division of Random House, Inc.

KARL MARX. 'The Materialist Conception of History', Preface to *A Contribution to the Critique of Political Economy* (pp. 181–5), 'Theses on Feuerbach' (pp. 28–30), 'The Class Struggle', and 'Manifesto of the Communist

Party' (pp. 35–46), from *Selected Works*, Karl Marx and Friedrich Engels. New York: International Publishers, 1968. Reprinted by permission of International Publishers Co. Inc. 'Alienated Labor' from *Marx's Concept of Man*, Erich Fromm. Copyright © 1961. Reprinted by permission of The Continuum International Publishing Group. Excerpts from *The German Ideology*, Karl Marx and Friedrich Engels, edited by C.J. Arthur, pp. 39–48 and 64–8. New York: International Publishers, 1947. Reprinted by permission of International Publishers Co. Inc.

HERBERT MEAD. 'Thought as Internalized Conversation' from *Mind, Self, and Society* by George Herbert Mead, edited by Charles W. Morris. Chicago: The University of Chicago Press, 1934. Reprinted by permission of The University of Chicago Press.

C. WRIGHT MILLS. From *The Sociological Imagination* by C. Wright Mills, copyright © 2000 by Oxford University Press, Inc. Used by permission.

EDWARD SAID. Used by permission of Pantheon Books, a division of Random House, Inc.: 'Latent and Manifest Orientalism' from *Orientalism* by Edward W. Said, copyright © 1978 by Edward W. Said; 'Representations of the Intellectual' from *Representations of the Intellectual* by Edward W. Said, copyright © 1994 by Edward W. Said.

DOROTHY SMITH. 'Feminism and Marxism—A Place to Begin, A Way to Go' from *Feminism and Marxism*. Vancouver: New Star Books, 1977. 'A Peculiar Eclipsing: Women's Exclusion from Man's Culture' from *The Everyday World as Problematic: A Feminist Sociology*, pp. 17–43. Toronto: University of Toronto Press, 1987. Reprinted by permission of University of Toronto Press Inc.

MAX WEBER. Used by permission of Oxford University Press, Inc.: 'Class, Status, Party', 'Social Scientific Method', and 'Bureau-cracy,' from *From Max Weber: Essays in Sociology* by Max Weber, edited by H.H. Gerth and C. Wright Mills, translated by H.H. Gerth and C. Wright Mills, copyright 1946, 1958 by H.H. Gerth and C. Wright Mills. Reprinted and edited with the permission of The Free Press, a Division of Simon & Schuster Adult Publishing Group: 'The Definitions of Sociology and of Social Action' and 'Legitimate Domination', from *The Theory of Social and Economic Organization* by Max Weber, translated by A.M. Henderson and Talcott Parsons. Edited by Talcott Partons. Copyright © 1947, copyright renewed 1975 by Talcott Parsons. Reprinted by permission of Taylor & Francis Books Ltd: 'The Protestant Ethic and the Spirit of Capitalism'. From *The Protestant Ethic and the Spirit of Capitalism* by Max Weber, translated by Talcott Parsons. London: Allen & Unwin, 1958.

INDEX